# In Search of Jesus

# In Search of Jesus

## Insider and Outsider Images

Clinton Bennett

CONTINUUM
London and New York

**Continuum**

The Tower Building, 11 York Road, London SE1 7NX

370 Lexington Avenue, New York, NY 10017-6503

First published 2001

**British Library Cataloguing-in-Publication Data**
A catalogue record for this book is available from the British Library.

ISBN 0-8264-4915-8 (hardback)
    0-8264-4916-6 (paperback)

**Library of Congress Cataloging-in-Publication Data**
Bennett, Clinton
    In search of Jesus: insider and outsider images / Clinton Bennett.
        p.   cm.
    Includes bibliographical references and index.
    ISBN 0-8264-4915-8 — ISBN 0-8264-4916-6 (pbk.)
    1. Jesus Christ — Person and offices. 2. Christianity and other religions. I. Title.
    BT202.B365 2001
    232—dc21

                                                                00-046588

Typeset by CentraServe Ltd, Saffron Walden, Essex
Printed and bound in Great Britain by Biddles Ltd, Guildford and Kings Lynn

# Contents

# Acknowledgements

The idea behind this book dates from a conversation between Dr Paul Harwell, a United Methodist Minister from Georgia, and myself, which took place when he was in Oxford during March 1998. At the time, I was finishing the proof-reading of my *In Search of Muhammad* and thinking about the next project. The scope and focus of this book evolved and changed as I wrote it. However, I wish to acknowledge Dr Harwell's initial encouragement and enthusiasm for this 'search'. There are some single volumes surveying Jesus' images across various religions, as well as studies specific to particular religions' images of Jesus. What I attempt is therefore not entirely novel. None the less, I hope this detailed discussion of a wide range of Jesus' images does contain enough worthwhile analysis and interpretation to reward its readers. I have included quite a lot of information about the religions and cultures that have encountered Jesus, as well as on the relationship between perceptions of Jesus, Christian missions and colonial encounter. This may interest a wider audience, especially perhaps as I also draw on postcolonial and postmodern theory to elucidate my subject.

I started researching this text in the Bodleian Library of the University of Oxford and in the Learning Resource Centre of what is now the Westminster Institute of Education, Oxford. Following my move to Baylor University, Texas, in late 1998 I have used the library facilities on campus here, as well as visiting the Birmingham Central Library, England, where I accessed some of the early 'Jesus never existed' literature. I have made extensive use of electronic media. Internet material is referenced as accurately as possible, giving a copyright date or the date of a hard copy original whenever I could identify this. Sites belonging to institutions or to domain name owners are likely to be more permanent than those hosted by free providers. It is therefore possible that some addresses cited are no longer valid.

Two museum visits gave me valuable insight and data. The first was some while ago. In 1992 I learned for the first time of the Jews of Harlem from a powerful exhibition, 'Bridges and Boundaries: African Americans and American Jews', at the Jewish Museum, New York, 22 March – 19 July 1992. This contributed to my writing of Chapter 4, where I refer to some black responses to Jesus, especially those who rejected him as a Jesus for white people only. In January 2000, Birmingham Museum and Art Gallery held an exhibition of 'Images of Jesus', which made me more aware of Indian and African ways of 'seeing' Jesus.

Many friends and colleagues have given advice. Several have read and commented on various sections of this book. I especially want to thank Professor Charles Talbert for reading some of my chapters and for supporting this project from its inception. Professor Talbert edited the 1970 Fortress Press Lives of Jesus edition of Reimarus' *Fragments*, and is a distinguished and prolific scholar in this field. I am honoured to have had his invaluable counsel. Professor William Pitts and Dr Leo Percer also critiqued chapters, for which I am extremely grateful. Professor Marc Ellis deserves special thanks for many useful and insightful conversations. I explore his Jesus image in Chapter 5. Professor Dan McGee drew my attention to the need for a goal beyond liberation, which is now reflected in my concluding chapter. Dr McGee is my deacon at Seventh and James Baptist Church, Waco, where I am currently a member.

My student helper, Valerie Marie Aguero, assisted me with proof-reading and with bibliographical references. My graduate assistant, Laju Balani, helped me by constantly asking questions, by his willingness to engage in discussion about images of Jesus and by efficiently performing many tasks for me which would have delayed my finishing this one! In his own doctoral research, he will pursue in more detail some Buddhist understandings of Jesus, which I analyse in Chapter 6. It is always invidious to name names, because inevitably some get left off the list. However, one of my graduate students, Dan Reilly, an Arabist and Hebraist, drew my attention to a number of useful sources, including the work of Abraham Rihbany, and he well deserves mention in these acknowledgements. Other students and colleagues have also expressed interest in this project. I would like to express my gratitude to all of them. For commenting on the manuscript, I am also indebted to my long-time friend, Professor Martin Forward.

References in this book to the text of the Gospels and to other books of the Christian Bible are derived from the Greek text (see References, under *Η Καινη Διαθηκη*), with reference to the English texts of the Revised Standard and New International Versions. The renderings given are usually my own, although some may resemble the RSV or the NIV, since it is difficult not to replicate familiar translations. The RSV is copyright of the Division of Christian Education of the National Council of Churches of Christ, USA. For my rendering of Hebrew Bible passages, I was guided by Young (1939), as well as by the two English versions referred to above. Qur'an verses cited are again my own interpretation, based on the Arabic and English text of Yusuf 'Ali (1989). I have not used diacritical markings except for the ' and ' for the Arabic *ayn* and *hamza*. I have used accents and umlauts. If I have missed any accents, I did not do so deliberately.

I again want to thank Janet Joyce and her team at what is now the Continuum International Publishing Group for their diligence and hard work in getting everything ready for the printer. Thanks, too, Continuum, for supporting this project. This is now the third 'In Search of' book that I have written and Janet Joyce has been my editor for all of them.

I dedicated my last book to the memory of my father, Howard Bennett (1922–1997), whose love of travel stimulated my eagerness to study the religions and cultures of the world, and to my wife, Rekha Sarker Bennett. My keen interest in all things South Asian will be evident from the contents of this book. My wife, at least in part, is responsible for that! Our several visits to the Indian subcontinent contributed to this and to my previous book. In this dedication, I want to bring my wife and my mother, Joan Bennett, née Cooper, together. Both of them put up with neglect and with negligence, as my computer gets much more attention and time than they do.

Clinton Bennett<br>
Baylor University, Texas

This book is dedicated to
Rekha Sarker Bennett, BA (Dhaka), Dip.Ed
(Birmingham), MSc (Oxford Brookes),
and to Joan Bennett, née Cooper, SRN, SCM

# Introduction
# Why Another Jesus Book?

Any new book about Jesus has to justify its existence. (Tatum, 1982, back cover)

Recently, a colleague, eager to assist me in my research on Jesus, telephoned to say he had just seen seven new Jesus books in our university library's acquisitions room! Given the proliferation of texts about the quest, or search, for the real or for the historical Jesus, I begin this book with an attempt to justify why I want to add a book called *In Search of Jesus* to the many texts already available. Meier (1991) put it like this: 'There are enough Jesus books to last three lifetimes and a sinful Buddhist might well be condemned to spend his next three incarnations wading through them' (p. 3). Why, I have to ask, might anyone, sinner or saint, find it less than a penance to read my Jesus book? My answer is that, more so than most Jesus books, I will follow Jesus outside the doors of the church into the world beyond where, to cite Pelikan (1985), his 'universality-with-particularity' has become 'an issue not only for Christians, but for humanity' (p. 232). My main focus will be Jesus as he encounters new cultures, faiths and 'other teachers of the Way' (*ibid.*, p. 228). First, to introduce the methodology and the rationale of this book, I locate its origin within the context of my own recent writing and research.

## In Search of the Sacred

This is the third book I have written called 'In Search of'. I did not set out to write a series. However, my first book suggested the second, which in its turn suggested this one. The first book, *In Search of the Sacred* (1996a), discussed some of the ways in which scholars in two related but distinct disciplines – anthropology and religious studies – have defined, studied and interpreted the religious dimension of human life. Whether religious beliefs and practices are or are not eternally meaningful, linked as it were with a transcendent or infinite 'reality', people throughout the world continue to denote certain places, rituals, objects, practices and beliefs as 'sacred'. My interest was in what people regard as 'sacred' and why.

My own academic career has involved the study of religions; I have studied my own, Christian religion but primarily Islam, the religion of another community, the Muslims. As a Christian committed to my own worldview I have tried to understand the worldview of others. Almost from the start of my academic work I realized just how difficult it is to see as others see. The temptation to impose my ideas and prejudices on what I see is omnipresent. Thus, much of my work has wrestled with the 'outsider-insider' problem. This was the focus of my first 'In Search of' book. There is an increasing amount of literature on the 'insider-outsider' issue (for a recent discussion, see McCutcheon, 1999). What I attempted to do was to fill a perceived gap by offering an examination of how scholars actually study the 'sacred' within my two disciplines.

My thesis was that early Religious Studies' almost exclusive use of classical texts left it unconcerned with the contemporary voices of religious people, while anthropology's early neglect of written sources made the study of change and of cultural origins rather difficult. Thus, a Religious Studies portrait of a religion tended towards an abstract, classical ideal (bearing little relationship with the living tradition), while an anthropological account tended to divorce present practice from historical origins, leaving it somehow incomplete. When Religious Studies, borrowing from anthropology, started to take contemporary religious voices seriously, its agenda was enriched. Arguably, too, Religious Studies became more relevant to life in the real world. When, in its turn, anthropology began to borrow historical and literary study from the humanities, including Religious Studies (known in many contexts as the History of Religions), its ability to explore the full story that a people tell about themselves was extended. Both disciplines became less concerned with telling others who they are, more concerned with learning through dialogue; 'we' writing about 'you' yielded to 'us' talking with 'us' about 'ourselves'.

## In Search of Muhammad

As I discussed how scholars study religious phenomena, I used examples from a range of religious traditions. My concern was with the sacred generically. In my second 'In Search of' book, I decided to focus on a particular example of what a single tradition deems sacred. Since I am primarily an Islamicist and all scholars aspire to make a contribution within their specialism, Islam presented itself as my choice of a tradition. Next, for a variety of reasons, I chose Muhammad, the Holy Prophet of Islam, as my subject. Sacred places within Islam, or Islam's scripture, would have made equally interesting examples of what a tradition regards as 'sacred' but it seemed to me that Muhammad plays such a key role in Islam that, by focusing on him, I could also usefully discuss a range of other issues. Almost every question we want to pose of Islam can be answered by first enquiring what Muhammad said (or might have said) on the issue. Nor can any study of Muhammad fail to discuss the nature of the Qur'anic revelation or of how this text was communicated to Muhammad. Thus my book on Muhammad also had quite a lot to say about Islam's most sacred text and about its understanding of revelation. When Ayesha (one of Muhammad's wives) was once asked what Muhammad's life was like, she replied, 'read the Qur'an'. Muhammad and the text he received are so intimately related that it is impossible to study the Qur'an without simultaneously studying Muhammad's life.

*In Search of Muhammad* (1998) also discussed how our starting points, whether from inside or outside Islam, influence if not predetermine our evaluation of Muhammad, our reading of the 'texts' before us. Even when scholars agree about the reliability of the historical texts involved in Muhammad study, they may radically depart from each other in their understanding of Muhammad's religious experience. Did he really receive God's word? Did he believe that he did? Did he invent Islam himself? Did he suffer from some type of psychological disorder? Was his life a moral paradigm, or fatally flawed? Although I did discuss and evaluate the historical record, my aim was less to deal exhaustively with the texts than to explore what might be called 'responses' to Muhammad, asking, 'What did this or that writer think about Muhammad?' In researching the book, too, I tried to listen to contemporary voices as well as reading texts. I therefore drew on anthropological methodology as well as literary analyses. My aim was to practise what *In Search of the Sacred* had preached.

For myself, as a Christian committed to fostering better relations between Islam and Christianity, the Muhammad question will not go away: 'Who do I, as a Christian, think that he was?' Towards the end of the book, I tried to incorporate personal regard for Muhammad within my Christian worldview. While acknowledging the problematic of a Jesus–Muhammad comparison, I offered some comments suggesting that Jesus and Muhammad present us with complementary rather than rival claims. I suggested that 'aspects of Muhammad's *sunnah* (example)' that 'do not contradict, but are consonant with' God's self-revelation in Christ can be regarded as 'complementary', not rival, to Jesus' teaching (p. 238). In this section, then, I found myself writing about my own tradition, at least inasmuch as I wrestled with the challenge of Muhammad *vis-à-vis* my personal faith conviction.

## In search of Jesus?

It was this attempt to create a kind of discourse between these two exemplars that prompted the idea of writing a third 'In Search of' book. As I finished the Muhammad project and began to contemplate another, several colleagues suggested I might turn to a parallel examination of Jesus. Aware that one critic of my first 'In Search of' book had found it curious that my examples all came from outside my own tradition, I thought I might redress this neglect by turning to my own tradition's seminal personality. My critic wrote: 'The book is . . . engagingly personal: he does not hesitate to quote from his own books on Islam or to use illustrations from one of his own encounters with other religions (though not, interestingly, his own)' (Gellner, 1996, p. 46).

## A parallel search?

At first, I thought that I would treat Jesus more or less as I had treated Muhammad. I would begin with a description of the sources available to us, then explore how these sources have been evaluated by scholars inside and outside the tradition. I would then explore inside and outside responses to Jesus, including some contemporary personal voices. In fact, my Muhammad book paid more attention to 'outside' voices because, as I argue below, 'insiders' tend to tell more or less the same story. Therefore, the insider response does not invite a lengthy description. However, as I turned to my new search, I soon realized that a different approach would be needed. This was mainly because, while Muslim opinion about the value and reliability of the sources for Muhammad study, and also about Muhammad's character, achievements and significance, is fairly homogeneous, outsider opinion differs radically on both counts. Muslims broadly accept the *sirah* (biographical texts) as historically reliable, and believe that Muhammad was God's prophet to whom God revealed the text of the Qur'an, which is a divine, not a human, text. This contrasts starkly with non-Muslim opinion, which is much more sceptical about the historical reliability of the texts, and divided about whether Muhammad was in some sense a prophet. Many non-Muslims read Islam as totally Muhammad's construct.

On Jesus, however, Christians offer many more diverse opinions about the reliability of their texts than Muslims do about theirs, and disagree radically among themselves about who Jesus was, both in relation to God and in relation to the tradition, Christianity, that treasures his name. This makes it impossible to clearly distinguish insider from outsider opinion. Those Christians who are sceptical that we can know very much at all about the historical Jesus, who see Christianity as largely a post-Jesus construct, sound more like outsiders than insiders when compared with Muslims speaking of Muhammad. Ferdinand Christian Baur (1792–1860), founder of the Tübingen school of theological thought, and a Lutheran pastor, argued that what emerged in the third century as Catholic Christianity was the result of a Hegelian process, whereby two rival tendencies or antitheses were finally united in a synthesis that bore no real relationship to the Jesus of history.

Baur's Jesus has been described as a 'cypher, or near-abstraction'. For him, the events of Jesus' life, 'including the crucifixion, held no particular theological meaning' (Allen, 1998, pp. 148–9). The Cambridge anthropologist, James George Frazer (1854–1941), a lifelong Presbyterian, strongly suggested that the whole Jesus story was an amalgam of ancient sun, fertility and sacrificial myths such as those of Adonis, Osiris and Tammuz (see Frazer, 1994). No Muslim sees Islam even as Muhammad's construct, let alone as anybody else's. Some outsiders, for their part, do see Islam as Muhammad's construct, or as the construct of his peers (see Bennett (1998, p. 114) for a discussion of this issue). This is not to deny diversity of opinion within Islam; rather, it is to claim that the ground of disagreement among Muslims is narrower than that occupied by Christian scholars. No Muslim academic, for example, applies to the Qur'an the type of form, source and redaction criticism that Christian scholars apply to the Gospels. On Muhammad, it has been outsider scholars who have applied redaction, source and form criticism to the *sirah*. On Jesus, insiders themselves pioneered this critical apparatus.

When I turned to what outsiders have said about Muhammad, I found many more parallels with what insiders have said about Jesus. For example, outsider scholars of Muhammad have had problems with his sex life, his miracles (as recounted in the *sirah*) and with his religious experience. Inside scholars on Jesus have addressed the same issues: Jesus' miraculous birth, his miracles, his resurrection, his religious experience, his sex life or lack of one, have all attracted debate. Some treatments of the two birth narratives are in fact remarkably similar. I have to confess that I was somewhat taken aback to find what amounts to quite a substantial discussion about Jesus' sexuality in the Jesus literature (see Phipps, 1970, 1996; also Kazantikas, 1961; also the Mormons, who 'associate the Cana wedding with Jesus' own marriage' (Phipps, 1996, p. 63)). Some Christians have problems with Jesus' attitude towards sexual relations or with his lack of direct sexual experience.

The biography.com film, *The Unknown Jesus* (1999), presented by Jack Perkins, recently made a strong argument for a married Jesus. The film points out that Jewish custom required that men marry before the age of 20, and that one of a father's five duties towards his son was to find a wife for him. Yet a married Jesus seems to contradict the celibate Jesus of Christian history, if not of the traditional Gospel portrait of him, which actually does not say whether or not he was married. In contrast, no Muslim disputes that Muhammad enjoyed sexual relations, or that he was a married man, although there is debate about the number of women whom he married. Outsiders, of course, have criticized Muhammad's sexuality but that he was a sexually active man is beyond dispute. In my view, the kind of general consensus on Muhammad shared by Muslims fails to emerge in Christian discourse on Jesus.

A few more examples will strengthen my case. There is relatively little debate, even between insiders and outsiders, about which texts are to be taken seriously as material for Muhammad's biography. In contrast, there is a great deal of debate about which texts can be used to construct Jesus' life. Many accounts available to us were not included in the official canon of the Christian Church, yet some scholars believe they contain reliable and authentic data. Thus it is less easy to list the sources of Jesus study than it is those of Muhammad study. In addition, even given the divergence of opinion about the reliability of the Muhammad sources, what emerges by way of a biography is more or less accepted by insiders and outsiders alike, give or take divine and miraculous content. Even among outsiders, only a very few scholars challenge this consensus (pride of place goes to Patricia Crone; see Crone, 1987).

Almost all scholars accept that Muhammad was born in Makkah (in 570 CE), migrated to Madinah (in 622 CE), led his followers in a sequence of battles, defeated his enemies (in 630 CE) and died as master of an emerging world power (in 632 CE). The exact order of some of the battles is disputed but not the details of the incidents involved. Many of these dates, too, are widely accepted as factual (perhaps the most contested being 570 as a safe birth date). Where scholars' opinions differ is how they interpret these events and how they understand Muhammad's inner life. Even when scholars deny that Muhammad was a genuine prophet of God, and offer alternative explanations of his rise to power, they do not dispute that he *thought* he was a prophet, or at least *claimed* to be one.

## Will the real Jesus please stand up?

Turning to Jesus, major disagreements emerge about the dating and sequence of events, about when and where he was born. Many favour Nazareth over Bethlehem, even though faithful crowds still gather in the latter town on 25 December, itself chosen as the day to celebrate Jesus' birth as late as the fourth century, when it began to substitute for the feast of *Natalis Solis Invicti*. As well as marking the winter solstice, 25 December was the birthday of the popular Iranian dying and rising saviour god Mithras, and of the virgin-born Egyptian god Horus, which may well account for its choice. Clement of Alexandria (d. 215) had suggested 20 May. Some eastern churches celebrate Christmas on 6 January. On the other hand, Baigent *et al.* (1986) claim that Nazareth did not even exist 'in Biblical times' (p. 30).

Scholars debate whether Jesus ever visited Egypt, how many times he visited Jerusalem, which languages he spoke, who he thought he was, the events surrounding his birth, death and alleged resurrection. While most of the world thinks that Jesus was born in the year '0', Bible scholars debate whether 4, 5, 6 or even 7 BCE are the correct dates (see Sanders, 1993, p. 11). He may have died any time 'between 26 and 36 CE . . . The Gospels are also in conflict with regard to the day he died' (*ibid.*, p. 54). Some insiders (at least in their own estimation) reject what other Christians believe to be fundamental aspects of the Jesus tradition, such as his incarnate birth and resurrection from the dead – for example, members of the Jesus Seminar, many of whom remain Christian (see Funk *et al.*, 1993).

We know that Muhammad earned his living as a tradesman and merchant. In contrast, it is unclear whether Jesus ever actually worked for a wage; Matthew 13:55 calls him 'a carpenter's son', Mark 6:3 refers to him as 'the carpenter'. 'Stonemason' may be a better translation. In the film, *The Last Temptation of Christ*, Jesus made crosses for the Romans. We know that Muhammad smiled (see Muir, 1894, p. 509); there are no gospel references to Jesus smiling or laughing. Did Jesus like animals? From his treatment of pigs (Mark 5:13) we may perhaps assume that he did not, yet the Gospels are actually silent on this issue (see Chapter 5 for Islamic traditions on Jesus' attitude towards animals). We know from Muslim sources that Muhammad was very fond of cats and horses. Did Jesus have any siblings? Muslim sources tell us that Muhammad was an only child. The Gospels mention 'brothers and sisters' (see Mark 6:3); yet the Church's teaching that Mary was a perpetual virgin resulted in these siblings being called Jesus' cousins.

While there is a great deal of material available for scholars to flesh out Muhammad's life, it is estimated that the Gospels cover at most a three-week period. What did Jesus do or say during the rest of his life? Ur-Rahim (1977) comments, 'The record of how Jesus acted is almost non-existent' (p. 201). 'There is no record', he points out, 'of how Jesus walked, how he sat . . . kept himself clean . . . how he conducted his transactions in the marketplace' (p. 200). Rudolf Bultmann (1884–1976), the German New Testament scholar, and a practising Lutheran pastor and preacher, was infamous for his pessimism about our ability to construct anything resembling a biography of Jesus:

I do think indeed that we can know almost nothing concerning the life and personality of Jesus, since the early Christian sources show no interest in either . . . what has been written in the last hundred and fifty years on the life of Jesus, his personality and the development of his inner life, is fantastic and romantic. (Bultmann, 1958a, p. 8)

This has no parallel in Muslim discourse. It also seems to me that there is much more diversity of opinion about what Jesus thought about himself than there is about what Muhammad thought about himself. There is debate both from within and outside the tradition about whether Jesus regarded himself as Messiah, as Son of God, as Son of Man, as there is debate about what this title or designation means. There is debate about whether Jesus' mission was primarily political or spiritual, about whether he was mainly concerned with the historical moment in which he lived, or with eternity. Muhammad's religious claims are also subject to debate but nobody denies that his mission was *political*.

## Jesus of history, Christ of faith

While insiders and outsiders disagree about Muhammad's motives, sincerity or religious status, they more or less agree that the Muhammad of the sources is the Muhammad of history. Among academics at least, many Christians, for their part, believe that the real Jesus lies behind the sources which so reflect the convictions, agendas and concerns (life situation) of the early Church that only textual archaeology can uncover the real Jesus of history. As we shall see, this gives us the distinction between the *Jesus of history* and the *Christ of faith*; the first is the 'real Jesus' who once lived, walked and taught in Palestine, the second is Christian conviction about Jesus contained in the Church's later creeds and confessional statements.

How much of himself would the Jesus of history recognize in the Gospels, let alone in the later creeds and confessions, scholars ask? (see the 1998 Public Broadcasting Service series, *From Jesus to Christ*, directed by William Cran, for an excellent discussion). This is not to deny that many Christians see a remarkable resemblance between all three (the real Jesus, the Jesus of the Gospels and the Jesus of Church dogmatics) but by no means all Christians see this correspondence. For example, the Jesus Seminar members posit an almost total distinction; the Jesus of Christian faith and of the Gospels is 'a mythical figure, whose connection with the sage from Nazareth is limited to his suffering and death under Pontius Pilate' (Funk *et al.*, 1993, p. 7).

I discuss the Jesus Seminar further in following chapters. For some of the issues that make up what I call the agenda of Jesus study, see William M. Thompson's *The Jesus Debate: A Survey and Synthesis* (1985) and John Bowden's *Jesus: The Unanswered Questions* (1988). Dominic Crossan's popular little book, *Who Is Jesus?* (1996), was very usefully written as a question and answer dialogue between the author and his readers. His chapters include 'Son of God, Son of the Virgin Mary?' 'Did Jesus perform miracles?', 'Who executed Jesus and why?', and 'From Jesus to Christ?' W. Barnes Tatum's *In Quest of Jesus: A Guidebook*, written as a college text, gives us several pages of questions (original 1982; revised edn 1999, pp. 87–90). Here we find 'What did Jesus think about himself? Did he believe himself to be a Messiah? A prophet? A rabbi? If Messiah, what kind of Messiah? . . .' He continued: 'The questions asked in this chapter have been asked repeatedly throughout the extensive search for the historical Jesus.' The back cover of Douglas Groothuis' *Revealing the New Age Jesus* (1990) asks, 'Did Jesus study with Eastern holy men?', 'Are we all potential Christs?' and 'Did Jesus survive the crucifixion and go to India?'

## A new direction?

After securing the contract to write this book, my early reading revealed just how extensive and varied Jesus literature is, addressing both the historical reliability of the sources and whether what Christians believe about Jesus is or is not justified by what can be verified historically about him. This literature includes popular and non-specialist books, some excellent, some not so excellent, as well as academic texts, not to mention www.sites, films, videos and television series. These document the quest of the historical Jesus, and pose and explore the questions very thoroughly. As I read and reread many of these texts, returning to some which I had not read since my days as a theology undergraduate, I started to ask whether I could possibly add anything worthwhile.

Of course, much has also been written about the Islamic sources. However, there is very little by way of a popular treatment of the quest of the historical Muhammad, so inasmuch as my Muhammad book was intended for a general readership, it tried to fill that gap. Moreover, my Muhammad book had focused on how starting agendas and assumptions determine outcomes, which seemed to me to be, if not novel, at least under-explored in terms of Muhammad study. This can by no means be claimed of Jesus books. Ever since Albert Schweitzer's classic *Quest of the Historical Jesus* (first published in 1910), we have known that 'each epoch of theology [has] found its own thoughts in Jesus; that [this] was indeed the only way it could make him live'; and that 'it was not only each epoch that found its reflection in Jesus; each individual created Him in accordance with his own character.'

Schweitzer continued (in this much-cited passage):

There is no historical task which so reveals a man's true self as the writing of a Life of Jesus. No vital force comes into the figure unless a man breathes into it all the love of which he is capable. The stronger the love, or the stronger the hate, the more life-like is the figure which is produced. For hate as well as love can write a Life of Jesus . . . not so much hate of the Person of Jesus as of the supernatural nimbus with which it was so easy to surround him. (1998b, p. 4)

Schweitzer's book, which reviewed more than 200 texts on Jesus, launched a new genre of literature: histories of the quest of the historical Jesus. He has had many successors.

## A dazzling gallery of images

The multiplicity of images of Jesus is almost dazzling, as Meier (1991) put it:

From Jesus the violent revolutionary to Jesus the gay magician, from Jesus the apocalyptic fanatic to Jesus the wisdom teacher or Cynic philosopher unconcerned with eschatology, every conceivable scenario, every extreme theory imaginable, has long since been proposed, with opposite reactions canceling each other out and eager new writers repeating the mistakes of the past. (p. 3)

In other words, liberals look at the Gospels and discover a liberal Jesus, whose main concern was social justice and human liberation (see Borg, 1998), while Sanders (1993) reaches the opposite conclusion: 'it is unlikely that the main thrust of his career was social reform' (p. 188). Feminists see a feminist Jesus (see Fiorenza, 1994), while Marxists see a Marxist Jesus (see Machovec, 1976). Edwina Sandys has sculpted a 'statue of a female Jesus' called 'Christa', with 'arms outstretched as though crucified' (Fiorenza, 1994, p. 50). Sexual libertarians see a promiscuous Jesus (a search on the internet revealed numerous sites arguing this view of Jesus). In the 1960s, Anglican Bishop Hugh Montefiore became infamous for suggesting that Jesus may have been homosexual (see Wilson, 1985, p. 80).

Isabel Carter Hayward offers *A Lesbian Feminist Voice* in her *Speaking of Christ* (1989).

Those who believe that Jesus' message and mission were thoroughly eschatological see a Jesus who anticipated the imminent end of all human history (or the end of history as we know it). Weiss (1892) remains worth reading as the classic text on Jesus as eschatological prophet. Those who think that Jesus was unconcerned with eschatology, taught timeless truths and called for an existential decision see an existentialist Jesus (for example, the nineteenth-century liberals criticized by Weiss but also recent writers such as Borg, Crossan and the Jesus Seminar). Others see a black Jesus (for example, Cone, 1986). To complete Meier's list, we can add to the above the contributions of Brandon (1967) on Jesus as religious militant, Smith (1978) on Jesus as a sexually active magician, and Downing (1992) on Jesus as a Cynic sage. The world of film and stage gives us Jesus the 'superstar' and Jesus the 1960s hippie (*Jesus Christ, Superstar* and *Godspell*).

Good histories of Jesus scholarship are as concerned with the biographies of those who write Jesus books as they are with the biography of Jesus. Schweitzer's *Quest*, by entering into the psychology of his authors, helped to deconstruct constructions of Jesus. On Jesus, then, my ground of starting points determining outcomes is already well occupied. I soon realized that my Jesus book would need to identify another distinctive approach, or ground, if it was to have any claim to originality. Nor, as I suggested above, could I easily compare and contrast insider with outsider 'responses'. Put bluntly, no easy contrast exists. I would have to pursue a different agenda.

In fact, I had anticipated this early on in my research, describing my project as follows (on my website):

I am researching for a book about images of Jesus. I am interested in exploring who Jesus is for those people and communities who possess images of him, both inside and outside the Christian religion. What do Muslims believe about Jesus? Who is Jesus for Hindus (I have observed images of Jesus in Temples)? Who is Jesus for members of the Unitarian tradition? Who is Jesus for Rastafari? And so on. I would be interested to hear from anyone who would like to contribute their understanding of who Jesus is to my project. I am interested in contemporary perceptions (in the Jesus of faith) rather than in the quest of the historical Jesus. (www.clintonbennett.net)

## Jesus for all the world

As I read material on Jesus, I realized that Christians have no monopoly on him. Some Christians may like to think that their understanding of Jesus is the only correct one. Many Christians export their 'Jesus' to peoples of other cultures and religions, only to discover that once they have done so they have no control over people's response. In other words,

Buddhists, Hindus and others 'saw' the Jesus of the missionaries but viewed him through their own cultural lenses. Hindus and Buddhists actually use the same texts as Christians, the very Gospels given to them by the Christian missionaries, but they incorporate what they see within a very different worldview.

Jesus, it seems, exists as an 'idea' outside of the sources, outside of the community or tradition which regards him and the sources as its own. As my former colleague Sugirtharajah has written: 'Jesus . . . was now in the hands of people who did not accept him on conventional Christian terms nor perceive him through traditional Biblical categories' (1997, p. 154). Or, as the humanist Renan put it, 'Jesus cannot belong solely to those who call themselves his disciples. He is the common honor of all who share a common humanity' (1927, p. 65). Bowden asks, 'What is the relationship between the historical Jesus of Nazareth and representations of him as having been of another culture, color or race?' (1988, p. 101).

There is also a whole genre of what I call 'bloodline' literature, best-sellers all, in which Jesus did not die on the cross but continued to work towards his political goals. These titles include Christopher Knight and Robert Lomas' *The Hiram Key: Pharaohs, Freemasons and the Discovery of the Dead Sea Scrolls* (1997) and *The Second Messiah: Templars, The Turin Shroud and the Great Secret of Freemasonry* (1998). Gardner (1996) reveals for us *The Hidden Lineage of Jesus* (his subtitle), while Lynn Picknett and Clive Prince (1997) tell us that the Templars were the *Secret Guardians of the True Identity of Christ* (also their subtitle). In some texts, Jesus travels to India where he sat at the feet of Buddhist and Hindu divines (see Notovitch, 1984; Kersten, 1986). In others, he dies in Rome (see Thiering, 1992). Thiering gives us a married Jesus and is often cited in 'bloodline' literature whose Jesus, of course, fathered children.

Jesus, we are told, was an Essene (see Allegro (1984), but also earlier texts such as de Régla (1894) and Bahrdt (1786)). He learned his wisdom in Egypt (Nahor, 1905; also Smith, 1978). Or, he never actually existed but was a mythical deity associated with the consumption of a hallucinogenic mushroom, whose cult included secret sexual rituals (also Allegro, 1970). Or, Jesus was a manifestation of the same *chi* or life force that has incarnated itself in all the great religions (see Peter Longley's website, www.spiritualchallenge.com). The desire to link Jesus with 'other teachers of the Way' is by no means novel. Mani (*c.*216–276 CE), founder of Manichaeism, attributed the same mission to Jesus, Buddha and the Prophets (to release for us the 'light' which, stolen by Satan, remains hidden in our brains). Elmar R. Gruber and Holger Kersten tell us bluntly that 'Jesus was not a Christian. He was a Buddhist' (1995, p. x). Or, Jesus was a figment of St Paul's imagination (see Wells, 1975).

I am interested in the question, 'What lies behind these accounts?' A desire, perhaps, to discredit the 'official version', or to elevate a 'suppressed version'? I include here much of the material on Mary Magdalene. Haskins (1994) regards her work on Magdalene as one of retrieval, as an ally of female ordination. 'Mary Magdalen', she writes, the 'first preacher of good news', stands before us as a 'key that helps unlock the door to a new age of sexual equality and liberation' (p. 399). This is what Edward Said and others call 'writing back', a process in which the unheard or silenced voices, those written about by others, start to tell their own stories. Closely related to the Mary Magdalene material, which it draws on, is a whole genre of what I call 'neo-Gnostic' literature, such as Douglas Lockhart's *Jesus the Heretic* (1997). Lockhart tells us that: 'For far, far too long, ordinary human beings have been denied access to Christ's higher consciousness by a Christianity bound to the notion of a Christ so unimaginably elevated that he must forever remain out of reach' (p. 329). He also writes: 'By the time the process of sorting the various writings ended – probably as late as the year 200 – virtually all the feminine images of God had disappeared from orthodox Christian traditions' (p. 68). The 'bloodline' material posits an orthodox Christian conspiracy in which 'the eccentric and embellished teachings of Paul' adopted by the Imperial Roman authority were made to triumph over original Christianity, which then went underground as the Knights Templar, Rosicrucians and Freemasons (Gardner, 1996, p. 203).

## Alternative sources

Some writers use alternative materials to construct their images of Jesus, which serious scholars may discount. Interestingly, Muslims may be included in this category, since their primary source of information about Jesus is the Qur'an, not the Christian Gospels. For some, this raises the question: Are the Issa of the Qur'an and the Jesus of the Gospels the same? For their part, Muslims may claim that their source is the more authentic. Similarly, since Jesus was a Jew, Jews may claim that their reading of Jesus is a more authentic reading than a Christian's. Both Muslims and Jews may claim that Christians have a distorted picture of Jesus. Mormons, too, view their *Book of Mormon* as an authentic gospel that corrects the earlier versions. Many believe that Jesus had visited America as the Aztec god Quetzalcoatl, for whom Hernando Cortéz (1485–1547), the Spanish invader, was mistaken. Some alternative texts emerge in my discussion of Indian responses to Jesus.

Others use the *same* texts as do the most renowned Christian scholars, but apply *different* hermeneutical tools to analyse and interpret these texts. Thiering, for example, uses a 'code' to uncover the true meaning of the Gospel. Yet however bizarre these accounts may appear to be to someone who is committed to what we might call a conventional view of Jesus, the fact that they even exist suggests they meet some genuine human need, or respond to some genuine question about who Jesus was. As such, they are of interest. Why does Jesus continue to be the subject of so much debate and speculation, discussion and scholarship, serious, popular and exotic, even erotic? Incidentally, the much-heralded CBS mini-series, *Jesus*

(2000), directed by Lorenzo Minoli and starring Jeremy Sisto (who has Buddhist leanings), in my opinion missed a historic opportunity to benefit from the explosion of Jesus scholarship of recent times. This opportunity was not missed by such well-informed documentaries on Jesus as Tully (1996), Perkins (1999) and Jennings (2000). The mini-series confused the Johanine and synoptic chronology (see Chapter 1) and knew nothing of the Messianic secret (see Chapter 3). Jesus' miracles looked like magic.

## How, why, by whom?

What drives my exploration and analyses of all the images encountered is 'How, why, by whom were these images produced?', 'What human needs do they address?' and 'What does Jesus mean to those who possess this particular image of him?' I suggest that all images of Jesus which respond to his universal appeal represent interpretations that have validity, or authenticity, for those individuals or communities who possess them. In his chapter, 'The man who belongs to the world', Pelikan began to create discourse between Jesus and 'other teachers of the Way', and concludes his book with these words:

Jesus has thus become an issue not only for Christians . . . but also for humanity . . . there is much more in him than is dreamt of in the philosophy and Christology of the theologians. Within the church, but also far beyond its walls, his person and his message are, in the phrase of Augustine, a 'beauty ever ancient, ever new' and now he belongs to the world. (1985, p. 233)

Pelikan's book, *Jesus through the Centuries: His Place in the History of Culture*, identified eighteen images of Jesus portraying 'his place in the history of culture'. His interest, like mine, was not so much in the 'real Jesus' (although I will summarize efforts to identify the Jesus of history) but in 'ideas' of him, the 'effect' that 'he' has had on people's lives. Pelikan also asks, 'What was it that each age brought to its portrayal' of Jesus? (p. 2). In my opinion, Pelikan's text is one of the most important Jesus books yet written. The illustrated version (1997) adds colour and visual effect to his erudite and eloquent prose.

My book, like Charlotte Allen's *The Human Christ: The Search for the Historical Jesus* (1998), is not an:

Attempt to offer a theory of who the historical Jesus was, or whether he actually said or did those things attributed to him in the Gospels [but to explore] the way in which the image of Jesus has functioned as a vehicle for some of the best and worse ideas [she has, 'of Western civilization'; my canvas is broader]. (p. 5)

Allen, who is a freelance writer rather than a professional academic, has given us one of the best modern survey texts, even though I do not always agree with her comments.

I am in search of ideas, of interpretations, of Schweitzer's 'Spirit of Jesus' who comes to people across the centuries, the cultures and the worldviews which make his world so very different from our own that he seems alien and exotic. 'But the truth is,' Schweitzer continued:

It is not Jesus as historically known, but Jesus as spiritually arisen within men, who is significant for our time. Not the historical Jesus, but the spirit which goes forth from Him and in the spirits of men strives for new influence and rule, is that which overcomes the world. (1998b, p. 401)

This, finally, clarified my goal. I would begin much as I had begun with *In Search of Muhammad*, with a description and evaluation of the sources. Choosing scholars to represent different approaches, as I had done in my Muhammad book, I would identify factors that seem to have predetermined outcomes.

However, while my purpose in *Muhammad* had been to illustrate the contrast between insider and outsider voices, my aim here will be rather to convey something of the diversity of insider views. To prove my point that no real consensus exists among insiders I will highlight similarities between what insiders and outsiders have had to say. I shall then turn in much more detail to the Jesus beyond the Christian tradition, who has declared independence from that tradition. Jesus, it seems, perhaps more so than Muhammad, has been appropriated by others and made their own. Thus, instead of writing, at long last, as an insider about my own tradition, I find myself unclear about my status. When I wrote my book on Muhammad, I knew that I was writing as an outsider, as a Christian academic, albeit one aiming to listen to insider voices. Turning to what has been said about my own tradition's seminal and most sacred personality, I find as many alien *inside* voices as I find *outside* voices.

Perhaps I have struggled too much with the insider-outsider problem. Perhaps my task here is simply to listen to as many voices as I can – insider, outsider – and to enquire why these voices say what they say of Jesus. Others, of course, have written about how Jews, Muslims, Hindus and Buddhists perceive Jesus, and I unashamedly draw on their work in my analysis. While I am not at all confident that I have done anything in this book to improve on their work, I have aimed for distinctiveness in these areas:

(1) By analysing Jewish, Muslim, Hindu and Buddhist perceptions of Jesus in a single volume as well as a range of other responses to Jesus, such as neo-Gnostic, black and feminist. To explore these Jesus responses, I draw on conventional and unconventional sources, on electronic as well as printed media.

(2) By attempting this within the context of exploring how, whatever our faith commitments may or may not be, our personal agendas, environments and a priori assumptions influence our seeing of Jesus. A major concern of this book is an encounter between Jesus and the religions of the world. It is an examination of insider and outsider images of Jesus, and of their treatment of the textual

sources. The initial encounter often resulted from Christian missionary preaching, so this is also a missiological study. Nor can
encounter be separated from the story of Europe's encounter with
the other, or from the story of colonial expansion.

(3) Despite or perhaps because of all I have said about the difficulty of
sustaining my outsider and insider categories, I continue to work
with this distinction as an analytical tool. Identifying how writers
perceive themselves *vis-à-vis* traditional Christianity seemed to be
of some use as I attempted to shed light on their assumptions,
agendas and goals.

Anton Wessels (1990) perhaps comes closest to what I am attempting. He
analyses perceptions of Jesus in non-European cultures. However, he does
not compare insider-outsider images or offer a detailed discussion of
scholarship of the sources, which I do. His book, though, is an excellent
treatment of Jesus as seen through diverse cultural lenses.

A recent *Newsweek* article (27 March 2000) by Kenneth Woodward,
entitled 'The Other Jesus', published during Pope John Paul II's tour of
the Holy Land, presents Jewish, Muslim, Buddhist and Hindu images of
Jesus in popular form (and quotes scholars whose books I used during my
research). This is an excellent introduction to some of the issues and
themes involved in my search of Jesus. Woodward concludes: 'there are
lessons all believers can savor by observing Jesus in the mirrors' of others.
'That the image of a benign Jesus has universal appeal', he says, comes as
'no surprise'. On the other hand, neither should the fact that 'most of the
world cannot accept the Jesus of the cross' (p. 60). His article elicited high
praise from the General Secretary of the Reformed Church in America,
who commented that it 'provided more information about the understanding of other faiths than the hundreds of books, seminars and conferences
written and held on this subject' (Granberg-Michaelson, 2000). Perhaps
this is a good reason *not* to write this book!

## My personal voice

Notwithstanding the problem of identifying whether I am on the inside or
outside of my subject, I intend to make my personal voice heard. My
conviction that no theology can be meaningfully read without also reading
the theologian applies equally to myself. By honestly and openly laying my
own cards on the table, I hope that my readers will be able to discern when
my own preferences are influencing my handling of other people's material.
I may well enthuse when I agree, and censure when I disagree, but at least
my reasons will be public. I do not think it fair for readers to have to
engage in archaeology to find out where a writer's sympathies lie. Like
Charlotte Allen, 'I am certain that my own theological presuppositions
have colored my perceptions of the people I have surveyed, just as their

theological and ideological presuppositions have colored their presentations of Jesus' (1998b, p. 7).

Allow me to place several of my cards on the table. First, it should be clear that I am sceptical that any external creed can do justice to the 'faith that is within'. As Frances Young rightly states:

There are as many different responses to Jesus Christ as there are different fingerprints. . . . To reduce any living faith to a set of definitions and propositions one is bound to distort it. Attempts to produce creeds are inevitably divisive or compromising. Eusebius of Caesarea signed the creed of Nicaea for the sake of church unity, but he was clearly embarrassed about it. What we need is not new creeds, but a new openness which will allow manifold ways of responding and elucidating that response. (1977, p. 38)

Or, as my colleague Charles Talbert said to me when I began this research: 'The Church decided to include four gospels, not one, in the canon. This means that we too should not privilege a single view of Jesus.' Similarly, speaking on the series *From Jesus to Christ* (1998), Holland Lee Henrix of Union Theological Seminary, New York, said: 'In my own view, the earliest layer of evidence is still interpretation, so what we can know is only a range of interpretations that we first encounter in Jesus' traditions. And that is really a plurality of Jesuses' (episode *Jesus' Many Faces: What Can We Really Know About Jesus?*, pbs, 1998).

Second, I am more inclined than many contemporary Jesus scholars to see a high degree of resemblance between the Jesus who really was and the Jesus of the four Gospels. This places me closer to such recent writers as Luke Timothy Johnson and N. T. Wright than to the Jesus Seminar (although, as I shall show, I am very attracted to aspects of the work of Jesus Seminar members Marcus Borg and Dominic Crossan). Wright (1992) writes, 'if we keep our wits about us there is no reason why we should not be able to make a fair start at understanding the Jesus of the gospels as the Jesus of first-century Palestine' (p. 97). At the launch of what is widely called the 'new quest', Ernst Käsemann suggested that 'defeatism and skepticism' about reconstructing 'something like a life of Jesus' both failed to grasp 'the nature of the primitive Christian concern with the identity behind the exalted and the humiliated Lord', and overlooked 'pieces in the Synoptic tradition [the Gospels of Mark, Matthew and Luke] which the historian has to acknowledge as authentic if he wishes to remain a historian at all' (1964, p. 46).

Third, as a Christian, Jesus for me is alive and well, and continues to speak to me and to millions of my brothers and sisters in today's world. This means that, for me, the locus of revelation is the living Christ, not texts that purport to tell the story of his earthly life. Thus I believe it is not scripture or texts that determine who Jesus is but Jesus who determines my reading of the texts. Of course, this claim is of a religious nature and cannot be scientifically tested. However, it explains my sympathy with such theologians as Schweitzer, Bultmann and Tillich, for whom the authentication of Christian faith is not historical proof but existential experience. Schweitzer's historical Jesus always withdrew, tantalizingly, back into his own time, yet his spirit strove 'for new influence and rule' in 'the spirits of men' (1998b, p. 401). Christian faith, said Bultmann, challenged science, which thinks that it can control human destiny, because such faith invites us to put our trust absolutely in God, 'who is beyond the world and scientific thinking': 'Faith in this sense is both the demand of and the gift offered by preaching. Faith is the abandonment of man's own security and the readiness to find security only in the unseen beyond, in God' (1958b, p. 41). For Tillich, 'participation, not historical argument, guarantees the reality of the event upon which Christianity is based'. By 'participation' he means becoming what he calls 'the New Being', while for him 'faith' is 'the immediate . . . evidence of the New Being within' and 'no historical criticism can question the immediate awareness of those who find themselves transformed into the state of faith' (1957, p. 114).

Incidentally, it is not only devout Christians who speak of visions or dreams of Jesus or of encountering him, but people whose faith is less than certain or even non-existent. In a fascinating study, *Visions of Jesus* (1997), Phillip H. Wiebe analyses thirty accounts of 'ordinary men and women' who believe that they have seen Jesus. Ernie Hollands saw Jesus while in prison, a frequent occurrence in his life. Maria Martinez saw Jesus as she crossed a busy intersection in Miami, Florida. In Chapters 5 and 6, we encounter Muslims and Hindus who have had visions of Jesus.

I draw much from the ideas of Edward Said, on postmodern and postcolonial theory, in my analyses of the quest for Jesus. For the latter, one of the best and most lucid texts is Homi Bhabha's *The Location of Culture* (1994). I am not especially convinced that meaning is always brought to, never derived from, a text, but I am persuaded that texts bear multiple interpretations and that conventional readings often represent particular interests over and against other interests, usually those of superiors over subordinates. I am also persuaded that most historical texts voice an elite, male version of events, and that archaeology and the recovery of silenced and sidelined voices can help to construct a fuller picture. Bhabha writes:

The 'right' to signify from the periphery of authorized power and privilege does not depend on the persistence of tradition; it is resourced by the power of tradition to be reinscribed through the conditions of contingency and contradictoriness that attend upon the lives of those who are 'in the minority'. (1994, p. 2)

Many of the Jesus responses represent a claiming of the right to reinterpret the texts, to argue for *ignored* or *contended readings* that speak to, for and *from out of* the particular viewpoint of black, feminist, environmental, or other specific sets of experiences. Liberation theology, feminist theology, challenge the prerogative of 'authorized power' to protect and preserve a 'received tradition' and do so from the bottom up. New Age Jesus images, the Jesus images of Jews, Hindus, Muslims, Buddhists, also challenge

Christianity's claim to any exclusive privilege to determine what is or is not an *authentic interpretation of Jesus*.

## Synopsis of my search

In Chapter 1, I describe the sources available to us for a reconstruction of Jesus' life. I raise some of the problematic issues that feature in subsequent discussion of the texts' reliability and historicity. In Chapter 2, I trace the development of the traditional Christian view of Jesus and the beginning of the breakdown of consensus that resulted in the quest of the historical Jesus. In Chapter 3, I discuss insider responses to the question, 'What do you think about Jesus?' I attempt to identify how different Christians have approached the texts, how their a priori agendas and concerns have predetermined, or at least influenced, outcomes. This is an ambitious chapter, which covers what others survey in entire books. While I follow a general chronological scheme I do not always introduce writers in chronological sequence; instead, I give priority to where their ideas fit the developing story.

I consulted and used primary texts to the greatest possible degree. Indeed, my aim is to allow each author to speak for him or herself. However, secondary texts by Schweitzer (1998b), Witherington (1995) and Allen (1998) proved useful in analysing and critiquing the material. Allen (1998) tells us that after Schweitzer finished each section he would return the texts to the library. Consequently, he did not create much by way of a conversation between his sources, and his book 'tends to read like a compilation of book reports' (p. 237). I have tried to avoid this criticism. As I wrote this book, I could not but be aware of how many scholars have reviewed the same material. Several television programmes were also dealing with many of the issues even as I worked on my project (for example, *The Unknown Jesus*, broadcast in December 1999; *66 AD: The Last Revolt*, broadcast in February 2000 and Peter Jennings' ABC documentary, *The Search for Jesus*, in June 2000).

Meier (1991) commented that books on Jesus often begin with a summary of the quest, and decided that there were enough good ones around for him to refrain from taking his readers on yet 'another stroll down quest-for-Jesus lane' (p. 35). My excuse for doing so is that the quest's story forms an essential part of my insider-outsider exploration. Of course, Christians have also written novels on Jesus and have produced plays and films about him, just as they have painted his image. Allen's book discusses quite a lot of this material, while Tatum (1997) looks at the first hundred years of *Jesus at the Movies*. The chapters 'Jesus as Moving Image' by John Thompson and 'Christ Imagery in Recent Film' by David Graham in *Images of Christ* (Porter *et al.*, 1997) also discuss celluloid Jesuses (Graham's subtitle is 'A Savior from Celluloid?').

I have not attempted a detailed survey or critique of this creative enterprise but deal mainly with academic texts. However, I did use multimedia in researching this book, so I incorporate some reflections on film and on stage, on works of art and fiction, as well as internet material, in this study. I also draw on literature to illustrate aspects of my search, including 'us' and 'them' encounters. Internet sites proved invaluable. Most of my citations from the Gnostic corpus are taken from material posted on the web (for example, at the Gnostic Society Virtual Library and the Non-Canonical Homepage of the Wesley Center, wesley.nnu.edu). For the Church Fathers, I used Calvin College's excellent Christian Classics Ethereal Library at www.ccel.org. For Josephus, I used William Whiston's translation, widely available electronically; for example, also at the Northwest Nazarene University, the Wesley Center for Applied Theology homepage (wesley.nnu.edu/josephus/).

In Chapter 4, I discuss outsider responses. I focus on what rationalists, free-thinkers, humanists, atheists and others (that is, scholars who do not regard themselves as Christians) have made of the Jesus material. I begin with initial encounter between the Jesus movement and pagan thought, then explore more recent outsider responses to Jesus, including theories that Jesus never existed, that he survived the crucifixion to found, not the Church which is based on a fraud, but an underground, secret society. Some writers began as Christians but ended up as free-thinkers. Of course, Christian thought did not develop in isolation from what such outsiders were saying. Indeed, outsider opinion has had a major impact on Christian apology.

In Chapter 5, I examine images of Jesus that emerged within Christianity's two sister or fellow Abrahamic faiths, Judaism and Islam. Both religions have their own, independent claims on Jesus. Jesus lived and died a Jew, while, according to the Qur'an, he was a prophet in the same revelatory tradition as Muhammad. Again, there was a great deal of useful internet material, as referenced in my text, although who knows how permanent some of this will prove to be? Next, in Chapter 6, I follow Jesus even further from his traditional ground (of Europe and the Middle East) to Asia, where, exported by missionaries, he encounters Hinduism and Buddhism and 'teachers of these ways'. As in my last two books, I combine some interpersonal research – that is, material from conversation and encounter – with textual criticism, which I weave into my text. In all the chapters dealing with outsider images I am interested in what happens to Christian views as a result of encountering others. How does encounter impact Christian attitudes towards the religious and cultural other?

Finally, in my conclusion, I ask, 'Can any sense be made of the dazzling gallery of Jesus images before us?' 'Can any single image be privileged above all others, used as a criterion of authenticity?' Confronted by Hindu and Buddhist 'images of Jesus', can even Christians claim any privileged hermeneutic? I give two responses. First, I believe that Christians benefit from a multiplicity of images of Jesus and that openness to what others elsewhere, facing different dilemmas, see in Jesus fruitfully challenges our often too comfortable if not domesticated 'Jesus'. This applies equally to 'responses' inside and outside of the Church. Second, I believe that without privileging a single response we can retrieve from the texts (there may be debate here about *which* texts) certain key elements of what Jesus taught and intended. I believe that we can identify the type of agenda of which Jesus would approve, and that, with caution, humility and prudence, this agenda may be used as the criterion of authenticity. Indeed, for all his pessimism, Bultmann may be close to identifying this yardstick when he writes:

He [Jesus] proclaimed also the will of God, which is God's demand, the demand for the good. Jesus demands truthfulness and purity, readiness to sacrifice and to love. He demands that the whole man be obedient to God, and he protests against the delusion that one's duty to God can be fulfilled by obeying certain external commandments. (1958b, pp. 17f.)

I believe all 'responses' to Jesus (and here I hint at my checklist) must be judged by their fruits, by their effect on people's lives; do they liberate or enslave, do they turn people away from self towards communal solidarity, or encourage love of self? Do they encourage the privileging of some above others? Do they challenge hierarchies, elitism and unjust exclusion?

To illustrate my point, I discuss black and feminist responses to Jesus in my concluding observations. While I admit that my checklist sounds quite conventional, at least for someone steeped in the social gospel tradition, I do not automatically exclude what might be thought of as the more 'bizarre' responses. Rather, I want to ask of these, 'What needs do they meet?' For example, the way in which the Church has silenced dissent (as the blood-line literature claims) may well have privileged the powerful over the vulnerable, which is un-Jesus-like. We may not buy the whole argument, but we might resolve to be better disciples today than were our forebears yesterday. The way in which dissident or alternative voices have been silenced may represent a valid challenge to a church whose wealth and power sometimes seem to be out of keeping with the simple, nomadic lifestyle of its founder.

## Writing about Jesus is a risky enterprise

In 1984, British television's Channel 4 broadcast a series called *Jesus: The Evidence*. Its presenter, Ian Wilson, comments how the series 'raised howls of protest', including calls for its banning. He believes this was because 'virtually for the first time on television it brought the world of New Testament criticism to the *real* layman's level' (1985, p. 155). In my opinion, the book version treats its subject fairly, and easily deserves the praise printed on its cover: 'a serious study devised with sincerity and integrity' (*Guardian*). Recently, the ABC journalist and correspondent Peter Jennings described the experience of filming his excellent and sensitive documentary, *The Search for Jesus* (2000) as 'nerve wracking'. While Jennings wanted to carry as many people with him as he could, he felt that he had to avoid certain issues – such as 'Was Jesus God's son?' – as lying beyond what, as a journalist, he could properly investigate. Jennings draws on his many years' experience of reporting from the Middle East in his film. Among other 'witnesses', Tom Wright, Paula Fredriksen and members of the Jesus Seminar share their views. Earlier, in 1996, the BBC's former South Asia correspondent Mark Tully had also set out to find Jesus. His series, *Lives of Jesus* (in which many of the same scholars appear), looked at Jesus within Hinduism, Judaism and Islam as well as at Christian images, although his treatment of the non-Christian Jesus was not as exhaustive as it might have been.

The publicity material for the biography.com video, *The Unknown Jesus* (1999), warned that 'Some may find *The Unknown Jesus* disturbing and even heretical, but this fearless BIOGRAPHY® probes the truth about the man that millions believe was the Son of God'. Michael Baigent, Robert Funk, Dominic Crossan, Christopher Knight, Robert Eisenmann and Holger Kersten (all cited in this book) appear in the video. Among other issues, it discusses Jesus' hidden years (his possible visits to India and Britain), links with the Essenes, whether he was married, whether he was a violent revolutionary or a pacifist reformer, his relationship with Judaism, and the circumstances surrounding his death and resurrection. While it does not follow Jesus into the world beyond the Church, the video offers an excellent presentation of the state of Jesus scholarship, not excluding its more controversial aspects.

Over the years, jobs have been lost, careers ruined, books banned and demonstrations held against the screening of films about Jesus. In 1990 five Roman Catholic extremists were gaoled for bombing Paris cinemas which had shown *The Last Temptation of Christ*, declared immoral by the Catholic Church. For evangelicals, says Haskins, 'Jerry Falwell . . . urged Christians to shun all MCA products' (1994, p. 366). In Argentina, a theatre staging the musical *Jesus Christ, Superstar* (lyrics by Tim Rice, 1970) was burned to the ground. In England, the last blasphemy case to be successfully prosecuted (in 1976) was against *Gay News* for publishing James Kirkup's poem, 'The Love That Dares to Speak His Name'. This is an explicit homoerotic fantasy featuring the crucified Jesus and his male lover (available at various websites, such as www.alsopreview.com/jklove.html).

Another homoerotic representation of Jesus, the play *Corpus Christi* by Terrence McNally (1998), resulted in a condemnation by the Muslim Shari'ah Court of the United Kingdom. Their *fatwa* (legal opinion) stated that 'whoever insults any messenger of God must be killed'. A spokesperson stated, 'In our religion, Jesus is a very important figure as a messenger chosen by God', and criticized the British Government for 'allowing the blasphemous production to be performed' (Pulford, 1999, p. 2). In the play, the Jesus-like figure, crucified as 'King of the Queers', is betrayed by his lover, Judas.

Schweitzer's autobiography tells us that he was troubled, when writing his *Quest*, 'by the painful consciousness that this new knowledge in the realm of history would mean unrest and difficulty for Christian piety' (1998a, pp. 53–4). Reimarus made sure that his work on Jesus remained secret until after his death: 'in order not to become a martyr of his convictions he suffered a martyrdom of another sort caused by his silence' (Talbert, 1970, p. 7). Schillebeeckx, author of *Jesus: An Experiment in Christology* (1979), had to defend his views before the Vatican Congregation for the Doctrine of the Faith on three occasions (1968, 1976 and 1981). Several members of the Jesus Seminar had to resign from the project 'as a consequence of institutional pressure'. One Fellow 'lost his academic post as a result of membership of the group' (Funk *et al.*, 1993, p. 35).

On the other hand, Crossan's *The Historical Jesus: The Life of a Mediterranean Jewish Peasant* (1991) topped the *Publishers Weekly* religious bestsellers' list. This highly technical text brought considerable public exposure for its author, who could not have been more surprised (see Crossan, 1996, p. xvi). His shorter, more popular version, *Jesus: A Revolutionary Biography* (1994), also stayed in the list's top ten for eight months. In later chapters, I relate how other authors have lost jobs, been censured, even sent to prison. Sometimes, the same book earned them a personal fortune. However, perhaps the greater risk for any Christian writing about Jesus is not other people's reactions, good or bad, but the inner challenge to their own faith in Jesus.

Let the search begin.

# 1   The Sources for Jesus' Life

It may prove disappointing to some, perhaps to many, to conclude that the canonical Gospels, particularly the synoptic Gospels, remain the only reliable sources for the historical Jesus. (Evans, 1997, p. 72)

## External sources

The sources for the study of Jesus are almost entirely products of the faith community, of the Christian Church, which cherished Jesus as its founder. To use the singular 'church' implies a monolithic body which has probably never existed ('churches' would be more accurate). However, at least in theory there is one church, just as in theory there is a single Muslim *ummah*, or community, so I use the singular when referring to the theoretically single and united Christian community. The insider nature of the Christian sources compares with those of other religious leaders. Buddha sources, for example, were all written by Buddhists, just as Muhammad sources were all written by Muslims. There are brief references to Jesus, or to Christus, in Josephus' *Antiquities* (written during the 90s CE) and in Tacitus' *Annals*.

Josephus (33–100 CE) was a Jewish commander during the revolt of 66 to 70 CE. He and his soldiers defended themselves from the Romans for six weeks in the almost impregnable fortress of Jotapata, until the summer of 67 when Josephus surrendered. He appears to have been the only survivor, and tells how many of his soldiers chose suicide instead of falling into Roman hands: 'when they saw that they could kill none of the Romans, they resolved to prevent being killed by the Romans, and got together in great numbers in the utmost parts of the city, and killed themselves' (*War*, Book 3, Chapter 7, p. 34). Predicting that Vespasian (see below), the Roman general in charge of suppressing the revolt, would become Emperor, Josephus was later retained by him to write an account of the war. Part of Josephus' motive was to show how revolt against Rome was misguided and futile. His text is very detailed. For example, all 28 high priests from Herod's time until the fall of Jerusalem are named (see my summary of Jewish history later in this chapter).

Archaeology, too, has confirmed much of what Josephus wrote about Jewish history, for example, his account of the fall of Masada. He also records the considerable impact, and popularity, of John the Baptist's preaching: 'many came in crowds about him, for they were greatly moved (or pleased) by hearing his words' (*Ant.* 18:5:2). The execution of James, brother of Jesus 'called the Christ' at Jerusalem is mentioned at *Ant.* 20:9:1. The longer paragraph on Jesus' death is at *Ant.* 18:3:3.

Josephus' references to Jesus, later known as the *Testimonium Flavinium*, have attracted criticism that they were actually added later, by Christian editors. Others think that Christians probably revised a less sympathetic passage to show Jesus in a better light; thus after Josephus' original 'Jesus . . . a wise man' they added 'if indeed one might call him a man' (Vermes, cited in Wilson, 1985, p. 53). They also added, 'He was the Messiah', which does not sound at all like the Jewish Josephus. The description of Jesus as a 'wise man' is 'untypical of any Christian writer but characteristic of Josephus' (*ibid.*). Morton Smith comments that since 'no Christian would have forged a reference to Jesus in this style, the text has generally been accepted as genuine' (1978, p. 44).

Sanders (1993) points out that had Christians inserted the Jesus reference, they would almost certainly have placed it 'adjacent to Josephus' account of John' instead of where it is found, namely two chapters earlier (p. 50). G. A. Wells, who does not believe that Jesus existed, reaches the opposite conclusion: 'it has been shown fairly conclusively to be wholly a Christian interpolation' (1975, p. 10). While Schweitzer believed that Jesus had existed, he also thought that the Josephus passage 'was undoubtedly interpolated by Christian writers' (1998a, p. 126). Whealey (1995, 1998) discusses the *Testimonium Flavinium* at length, as well as the history of its criticism, and concludes in favour of authenticity, suggesting that the original text read 'he was believed to be the Messiah', as in Jerome's version. She thinks it unlikely that Josephus' description of James as Christ's brother was of Christian origin, since Christians 'typically call James the Just' (1998, p. 4). Reference to Jesus as 'called the Christ (*Ant.* 20.200), although not derogatory, certainly implies some distance from the Christian affirmation that Jesus is the Christ' (*ibid.*). Whealey observes that the *Testimonium* is probably 'the most discussed passage in all ancient literature' (p. iv). She is more reluctant than others to second-guess 'what a first century Jew . . . might have said about Jesus' (1995, p. 264).

Tacitus tells us that followers of Christ, who had been 'executed during the reign of Tiberius on the orders of the procurator Pontius Pilate', were causing trouble, 'not only in Judea, the place where this evil originated, but also in Rome' (XV, 44, 3). His reference to Christus appears in the context of Nero's persecution of Christians, whom he blamed for the fire that destroyed much of Rome in July 64 CE. Tacitus says, however, that Christians were 'convicted not so much of the crime of arson as of hatred of the human race'. I return to this charge, and to the Great Fire, in Chapter 4. Tacitus was born about 55 CE, and wrote his historical work in the second century, by which time the 'totally illusory belief that Jesus was a historical figure might have grown up' (Wilson, 1985, p. 51). Neither Josephus nor Tacitus contributes anything to our knowledge of Jesus' biography (see Sanders, 1993, pp. 49–56, and Theissen, 1987, pp. 189–95). On the other hand, as Rivkin (1986) says, Josephus does 'provide a highly reliable framework of time, place, structure and circumstance that can be used as a filter for separating out the historical Jesus from the resurrected Christ of the Gospel stories' (p. 103). In other words, Josephus considerably aids any attempt to reconstruct the historical, political and religious context in which Jesus lived.

Theissen's *The Shadow of the Galilean* (1987), written in the form of a novel, uses Josephus to weave history into his narrative. He begins with a demonstration against Pilate's use of temple funds to build an aqueduct, taken directly from Josephus. He draws on Josephus' description of Jewish resistance groups, and on his description of the Essenes, to whom Josephus devotes almost a whole chapter (see below). Jesus does not actually appear in Theissen's narrative; others speak about him. Josephus says quite a lot about the various groups within first-century Judaism, including the Sadducees and the Pharisees (see *Ant.* 18:1:3f.). The Pharisees became the dominant group after Jesus' death, especially after the destruction of the Temple (70 CE) when their stress on study of the Torah, and their comparative flexibility, enabled the Rabbis to substitute for the priests, the Torah for the Temple. Thus, Judaism survived the loss of temple, a functioning priesthood and land. The Pharisees developed the oral Torah (which became the *Mishnah*) alongside the written Torah. The Pharisaic movement is sometimes characterized as democratic; it aimed to allow all Jews to be holy and pure. Their opponents, the Sadducees, were more aristocratic, including the high priestly families. They recognized only the Pentateuch, or the written Torah. According to Josephus, they also denied the doctrine of the resurrection from the dead. I return to these Second Temple Jewish movements later in this chapter.

Josephus describes how, under Roman rule, power was delegated to the high priest and his council of advisers, mainly aristocratic priests, the Sanhedrin (the death sentence remained in the hands of the Roman governor). It has been suggested that this 'theocratic'-style government was attractive to many Jews who preferred it to a monarchy; kings could be dictatorial. Many people did not want a military-type king either (Sanders, 1993, p. 242). There was discontent with Roman rule, however, and some Jews thought that the priesthood had compromised itself by collaborating with the occupiers. The Zealots wanted political independence: 'They have an inviolable attachment to liberty and say that God is to be their only Ruler and Lord' (*Ant.* 18:1:6). Advocating armed rebellion, they were involved in a number of insurrections.

Others thought that God would somehow 'save' his people, that is, by supernatural intervention. Some (Sanders, 1993, p. 32, says 'relatively few') expected a Davidic Messiah (a Messiah from King David's family) who would lead a successful revolt against Rome (the descendant of David referred to at Ezekiel 37:24 and Isaiah 9:7). Messianic claims were not unknown, and several would-be Messiahs lost their lives at Roman hands. Many may well have supported Judas the Galilean, one of the founders of the Zealots, because they thought he was the Messiah. Bar Kokhba, who led the last revolt against Rome (in 135 CE; see below), was 'hailed by the greatest rabbi of his age [Rabbi Akiba] as the Messiah' (Vermes, 1973, p. 123; see also Cohen, 1949, p. 349).

### Messianism and first-century Judaism

Not all who looked for, and predicted, supernatural intervention, however, saw themselves as Messiahs; Theudas and 'the Egyptian' were prophets (Josephus calls the Egyptian a 'false prophet: *War* 2:13:5). At Acts 21:38 Paul was mistaken for the Egyptian: 'Aren't you the Egyptian who started a revolt and led four thousand terrorists out into the desert some time ago?' (see also Acts 5:36). These men led resistance movements but believed that God would somehow signify his support and their impending victory. Theudas thought that the waters of the River Jordan would part for him as a sign of divine support. Both of these resistance leader-prophets were executed and their followers hunted down.

Some rebels claimed to be kings (see Saldarini, 1994, p. 21). Josephus also records that the Romans executed potential as well as actual trouble-makers. In his account of the feeding of the crowd John has the people wanting to make Jesus 'king by force' (6:15). Pilate (who, according to the Gospel, was governor when Jesus was executed) was especially harsh; he ordered mass executions and was eventually summoned to Rome to answer 'to the accusations of the Jews' who accused him of murder (*Ant.* 18:4:2). This makes Jesus' execution seem quite likely, although he probably posed no real threat to Rome or to the Jewish leadership (see my discussion of Sanders in Chapter 3). In fact, Josephus tells us that thousands of Jews were crucified in the first century, from 'two thousand' during Varus' regime to 'five hundred or more' every day by Titus in 70 CE (*War* 2:5:2; *War* 5:11:1). Others associated the Messiah less with revolt than with the beginning of a new era of human existence, an age of godliness, peace, justice and righteousness. There would be a new temple, and the twelve tribes would reassemble from the corners of the earth. Gentiles, too, would be included in this dispensation, or 'submit' to the Jews (see Isaiah 56:1–8, 60:3–7, 66:18–24).

Sanders comments that perhaps the majority of Jews simply wanted the end of Roman rule, 'with no expectation that God's ultimate, final kingdom would be established', and continues, 'we can not say that Jewish hopes were necessarily "Messianic", or even more generally eschatological' (1993, p. 30). Debate about exactly what Jews of Jesus' day thought about the Messiah will surface again and again in this study. Speaking of Jesus' time, Segal writes, 'We cannot assume that Judean Society had a fixed concept of Messiah at all. There was no job description, for which Jesus applied and received the job' (1994, p. 127). Segal points out that 'there is no future messiah in the Hebrew Bible at all', since passages applied by Christians to Jesus do not contain the word 'Messiah' (p. 129). Segal maintains that even within end-time scenarios, 'the messiah was not a necessary part of the drama' (p. 128). On the other hand, William Horbury (1998a) argues that Messianic beliefs were varied, complex and certainly widespread during Jesus' day. As this book shows, how Jews and others understood Messianism at the time of Jesus remains a matter of intense debate. Indeed, Jews continue to differ on the issue of Messianism to the present day.

Speaking of a later period, Johnson (1987) comments, 'There was such a variety of views about the Messiah in Judaism that it was almost impossible to be heretical on the subject' (p. 219; here, Johnson was drawing on the work of Hyam Maccoby: see Chapter 5). Much later still, Nahmanides (1194–1270) responded to Christian polemic by arguing that 'the doctrine of the Messiah was not of paramount importance for Jews' (*ibid.*). Schoeps (1977) argues that what became important for Jews was not the person of the Messiah but 'the earthly *kingdom* expected for the Messianic age' (p. 200). Others suggest that Jewish belief or beliefs about the Messiah were ambiguous, even incoherent: 'Jews did not profess a coherent and normative messianology' (Donahue, 1994, p. 104). Perhaps one can say that the Messiah would definitely be *distinct from God*.

## Jesus and the Zealots

Below, I mention speculation that Jesus may have had links with the Essenes, which emerges as a major theme in this book. Some scholars have also argued for a link between Jesus and the Zealots, although the consensus is that they did not exist as an organized group until 66–68 CE. However, S. G. F. Brandon (1907–71), professor at Manchester University, argued that Jesus may have had Zealot sympathies (based partly on the description of Simon as a Zealot at Luke 6:15). Brandon is often misquoted as having identified Jesus with the Zealots. What he actually argued was that his aims and theirs were similar. They wanted to restore absolute conformity to the Torah, and absolute loyalty to God, and 'were prepared to resort to violent action against the Romans' (1967, p. 47). Jesus wanted to make Israel ready for the coming of the Kingdom. However, the 'sacerdotal aristocracy who waxed fat . . . from their co-operation with Rome' stood in his way (p. 338). Yet he may have anticipated the use of violence to restore the Temple, corrupted by the greed of the priests. Brandon therefore thinks that the 'cleansing of the Temple' was a much more violent affair than implied by the Gospel accounts, 'involving violence and pillage' (p. 339).

Brandon surmises that Jesus' aim may have been to install a new high priest, just as the Zealots did when they took control of the Temple in 66 CE (p. 335). Brandon is unable to suggest what Jesus planned to do after the incident in the Temple but fails to rule out some type of violent insurrection. When the soldiers came to arrest him, Jesus resisted: 'it is certain that armed resistance was offered to the force sent to arrest him' (p. 342). When the situation proved hopeless, Jesus surrendered to avoid further bloodshed. The Gospel account, in which Jesus forbids resistance (and heals the soldier's ear), is back projection. Brandon claims that Jesus was indeed guilty of sedition, since an attack on the Temple was a direct challenge to Roman rule (p. 332). The Church later tried to deny any anti-Roman sentiment on Jesus' part by supplying him with words suggesting a neutral, even submissive, attitude towards Rome ('render to Caesar what is Caesar's': Mark 12:17). It also exonerated Pilate of any blame, deflecting this on to the Jews.

## Alternative sources

In my Introduction I referred to another genre of external sources, for example, various stories of Jesus in India, and to the Mormons' version of the Jesus story told in the *Book of Mormon*. I discuss these in later chapters. There are also legends of Jesus visiting England. According to ancient myth, in his youth (during the 'hidden years') Jesus had worked and travelled with Joseph of Arimathaea, with whom he spent some time at Glastonbury, then on a river island called Avalon. After the crucifixion, Joseph returned to Avalon, bringing the Christian faith with him but also the 'Holy Grail', the cup which Jesus had used at the Last Supper. Somehow, the Grail was lost: hence the many 'quests of the Holy Grail' in such stories as those of Arthur and Perceval. Later, the Knights Templar are said to have found and kept the Grail. William Blake (1757–1827) clearly had these legends in mind when he wrote:

> And did those feet in ancient times
> Walk upon England's mountains green?
> And was the Holy Lamb of God
> On England's pleasant pastures seen?
> (*Milton*, in Keynes, 1966, p. 480)

One of Blake's earliest etchings was *Joseph of Arimathaea* (1773). I return to Blake's view of Jesus in Chapter 4.

For many Christians, too, relics such as the crown of thorns, the true cross and the holy shroud represent irrefutable proof that the Jesus story is true. Jesus is said to have worn the crown, kept in Paris' Sainte-Chapelle (built in 1248), on the cross. Pieces of the true cross are venerated in various shrines, such as at Santa Croce in Gerusalemme, Rome. The shroud, believed to be Jesus' grave-cloth and preserved at Turin, Italy, has an image of a human body on its front and back which bears the traditional imprint of the stigmata. Many believe that this is the true likeness of the historical Jesus, proving that the crucifixion took place as portrayed in the Gospels.

As I also noted in my Introduction, the Qur'an represents what we might call an 'alternative source' for Jesus study, at least from an Islamic perspective. Both the Qur'an and Muslim traditions will be explored in Chapter 5. Some Jewish scholars also look to rabbinical sources as aids in reconstructing Christian origins. These are principally the Mishnah and the Talmud which, although not recorded until the end of the second and fourth centuries CE, draw on much older, verbal material. There are not many explicit references to Jesus. However, scholars read between the lines to identify material that may have been influenced by Christian polemic, or which may represent Jewish response to Christian polemic. Lauterbach's chapter 'Jesus in the Talmud' in *Jewish Expressions of Jesus* (Weiss-Rosmarin, 1977) is still an excellent overview.

It is commonly argued that while we learn about Jewish attitudes towards Christianity from the Talmud, it is of no help as a source of historical information: 'the scanty references to [Jesus] that are still to be found in the *Midrashim* are of such a nature that they do not at all prove his historicity, any more than the records of the New Testament' (Lauterbach, in Weiss-Rosmarin, 1977, p. 5). Lauterbach says that the Rabbis had no interest in Jesus' historicity, since 'To deny that he had lived would not have disproved the teachings ascribed to him'; thus, 'They could . . . believe that such a person had lived, and nevertheless dispute his greatness or reject and argue against his teachings' (*ibid.*, p. 6). Some Talmudic references seem to associate Jesus with two Rabbis, Joshua b Perahyah and Simon b Shetah, who lived about 130 years 'before the time in which the Jesus of the gospels is supposed to have lived' (*ibid.*, p. 9). One passage (*Babylonian Talmud, Sanhedrin* 107b) suggests that Jesus was a disgruntled student of Perahyah, 'who repulsed [him] with both hands' (Epstein, 1935, Vol. 2, p. 735). I explore the Talmud on Jesus in Chapter 5. A critical examination both of Muslim and Jewish (also Hindu) Jesus sources may very well determine that they lack historical value. They are late, they do not draw on firsthand accounts – that is, on eyewitness evidence – and they reflect particular theological agendas. On the other hand, they tell us what Muslims, Jews and Hindus *believe about Jesus*.

Christians, believing that Jesus can only be understood as part of God's dealings with the Hebrew, or Jewish people, see the Hebrew Bible (which they call the Old Testament) as second in importance only to the New Testament as a source of information on Jesus. The expression 'Hebrew Bible' is of comparatively recent origin. *Bible* is derived from the Latin *biblia*, for little library. Jews often prefer the term *Tanakh*, from *Torah* (Guidance), *Neviim* (Prophets) and *Ketuvim* (Writings), which are the three divisions of the Hebrew canon. From an early date, Christians found not only predictions of Jesus in the Hebrew Bible, but what Origen (185–254 CE) called 'types', that is, 'a figure that came before us in the fathers, but is fulfilled in us' (cited in Pelikan, 1985, p. 41). These 'types' are the Hebrew patriarchs and prophets, as well as incidents in their lives. To set the theological and historical context in which Christians locate Jesus, what follows is a summary of how Jesus is read into Jewish history as well as into Jewish scripture. As a Christian reading, this also hints at some of the differences between Jewish and Christian readings, to which I return in Chapter 5.

## Historical context

The history of the Jews (recorded in the books of the Hebrew Bible) goes back to Abraham (between 2000 and 1500 BCE), who, in obedience to God's command, left his home in the Chaldean mountains to travel to a 'Promised Land'. Abraham had lived among polytheists. His recognition of the one God may mark the beginning of biblical monotheism, although some argue that while Abraham gave exclusive allegiance to God, he did not actually deny the existence of other gods (see Goldberg and Raynor, 1989, p. 9). His story starts in Chapter 12 of Genesis. Chapters 1–12 deal with creation, with the origin of human life, with the dispersion of people and languages, and with the flood when God punished people's wickedness by causing a deluge. Chapter 3 is a significant text for Christians. They call the incident when Adam and Eve ate of the forbidden fruit the 'Fall', and believe that as a result of this all human beings are born sinful. Jews do not share this belief, which for Christians is central, necessitating the need of salvation that only God's grace can provide. Jesus becomes the Second Adam, the new father of the human race, restoring what Adam had lost. The flood story is also a 'type'. Here, the ship that sheltered and saved Noah's family represents Jesus (and subsequently the Church); those who shelter in Jesus are saved, while all others drown.

### The old covenant

From Chapter 12 onwards, Genesis focuses on one group of people, with whom God enters into a 'covenant' (marked by the circumcision of males). Abraham's children were to serve and worship God, 'testify to His One-ness' and obey God's commands. In return, God would teach and instruct them and 'give them . . . the strength and means (including a territorial base) to carry out their assignment' (Goldberg and Raynor, 1989, pp. 274–5). The purpose, though, of calling or choosing the one out of the many was the eventual establishment of God's kingly rule for the benefit of all people (see Genesis 12:3). For Christians, the patriarch Abraham is an example of the true believer, who trusted God so completely that he journeyed with him into the unknown. It was his faith, not his 'good works', that redeemed him. Isaac, Abraham's grandson, is renamed Israel and fathers twelve sons, whose own descendants become the twelve tribes of Israel.

One of the twelve, Joseph, after a series of misfortunes, is appointed viceroy of Egypt (possibly under the Hyksos rulers, 1690–1580). Later, during a famine, his brothers join him in Egypt, where they settle. After several generations, a king 'who did not know Joseph' enslaved their descendants, because their number and success posed a threat. This may have been Amosis, founder of the nineteenth dynasty. King Amenophis IV, who was also of this dynasty, declared that the sun god Aten was the sole deity; thus, 'less than a century before the probable dates of Moses and the Exodus, a religion of monotheistic character had emerged in Egypt' (*ibid.*, p. 11).

### The Exodus

God did not abandon his people to their bondage and suffering but raised up a leader for them called Moses. Moses was almost lost at birth, due to the King's command to kill all first-born Hebrew children (an early attempt at enforced population control, in this instance a subject people). However, with God's help and the assistance of his brother Aaron, Moses was able to lead his people out of Egypt into the wilderness area, possibly towards the Sinai Peninsula. They wandered for forty years, during which period God granted them the Torah (teaching), or *mitzvot* (commands). This included regulations on diet, marriage, commercial transactions, festivals, sacrifices, the office of a high priest (Aaron assumed this position), and the construction of a portable 'ark' to contain the Torah.

For Christians, Moses is a type or forerunner of Jesus: through Moses, God acted to redeem *Israel*; through Jesus he acted to redeem *all people*. As Moses received the Torah on Mount Sinai, 'so the heart of the New Law is given through God's chosen spokesperson on the Mount (Matthew 5, 6, 7)' (Kee and Young, 1960, p. 70). Christians point out that Matthew appears to have divided his Gospel into five sections, representing each of the Books of the Torah. As Moses' people were tempted in the wilderness, so was Jesus; however, they sinned while he did not. As Pharaoh ordered the slaying of infants when the first Moses was born, so Herod ordered a slaying when the second Moses was born.

The rescue of Israel from Egypt, or the Exodus, represents God's great act of redemption on behalf of His people. The people are now a nation, and re-enter the promised land under Moses' successor, Joshua. The Torah gives them much more detailed information about God's will, which is to be God's special, holy people in the midst of others (Leviticus 20:26). Fundamental to the Torah is a concern to demarcate the 'holy' from the 'profane'. Jews believe that the Torah was created before the world, and offered simultaneously to seventy nations in seventy languages, but they all refused except Israel (see Johnson, 1987, p. 179). The Torah is therefore their distinct badge of identity, worn as described at Deuteronomy 6:4–9. It is their 'bride'. It sustains and nourishes them. Far from its 613 *mitzvot* being thought of as a burden, its yoke is a joy to bear. Its commands, David would sing, 'are the theme of my songs' (Psalm 119:54).

So special is the relationship between Israel and the Torah in Jewish thought that it is peculiarly theirs; Gentiles are not to keep the Torah but the five Noachide commandments found in the account of the flood. The keeping of the seventh day as a holy day, as Shabbath, also symbolizes the special status of the Torah as Israel's unique responsibility. One story goes that after creation, Shabbath complained that while Sunday was partnered by Monday, Tuesday by Wednesday, Thursday by Friday, Saturday had no partner. God's response was, 'Your partner is the congregation of Israel.' I want to stress that Israel did not think that God was unconcerned about other nations; rather, she saw her own role – to be holy as God is holy – as eventually benefiting all people. Many years later, in medieval mystical Judaism, the belief developed that, by keeping the Torah, the Jewish people were combating evil and maintaining the harmony of the universe: 'The keeping of the *mitzvot* by the Jew, and the avoidance of sin, are seen . . . as of great cosmic consequence for the human and divine worlds' (Unterman, 1981, p. 101). Or, as Rabbi Simon the Just put it, 'Upon three things the world is based, upon the Torah, upon divine worship, and upon acts of benediction' (Cohen, 1949, p. 126).

### The tribes become a kingdom

After the Jews had resettled in the promised land, God raised up a series of charismatic leaders (known as judges) who enabled Israel to survive external threats and other crises. The tribes existed as a loose confederacy, with no permanent leadership. God was their king. However, during the reign of the last judge, Samuel, the Israelites demanded a king, complaining that they lacked secure leadership. They wanted to be like other nations (1 Samuel 8:5). God, who saw this as a rejection of His kingship, warned the people that a king would exploit them, recruit their sons for his army and take their daughters as his concubines. Then, when they insisted, God consented and Saul became the first king. His rule began well but soon degenerated, proving that God was right. Saul became embroiled in a fight with his own young champion and musician David, who emerged as a type of Christ.

Eventually succeeding Saul, David became the ideal king. Saul had substituted himself for God, but David was God's anointed servant (= Messiah). A shepherd in childhood, shepherd imagery is found in many of the beautiful psalms that are attributed to David. Jesus also made much use of shepherd imagery. For Christians, he is the shepherd of God's flock. David was not perfect, however (see 2 Samuel 11). He committed adultery, then arranged for the girl's husband to be sent into the front line of battle. As a result, David was refused permission to build God's Temple in his new capital of Jerusalem. Prior to this, sacrifices (as described in the Torah) had been offered at various high holy places, such as Bethel, Shechem and Shiloh. Instead, David's son, the wise Solomon, built the Temple. Under Solomon, the kingdom reached its zenith. He, too, is depicted as a good and righteous king. After Solomon's death, Israel's political fortunes entered a long period of gradual decline.

## A divided people

After Solomon's death (922 BCE) the kingdom was split into two, the northerly Israel and the southerly Judaea. The north was cut off from the Temple and both kingdoms faced internal unrest. Questions were raised about the legitimacy of the succession, while others wanted less centralization and more tribal autonomy, as in the pre-monarchy period. The considerable empire acquired by Solomon was soon lost. What remained were two 'rival states of second rate importance' (Bright, 1972, p. 225). During this period, some kings approximated the Davidic ideal, but most were preoccupied with their own agendas. Justice was neglected. The poor, for whom much of the Hebrew Bible expresses a special concern, were exploited. Pagan practices were even substituted for the Torah. God continued to plead with His people for true holiness through prophets, holy men whom God called and commissioned as His agents, but they often opposed and challenged the kings.

## The prophets

These prophets are also 'types' of Christ; for example, Elijah, who battled against the priests of the false god Baal on Mount Carmel (1 Kings 18) and opposed their patron, Queen Jezebel. Elijah encouraged the faithful to remain true to their calling, to be holy and pure. He fed and healed people and was eventually taken into heaven by God (2 Kings 2:1) as Enoch had been before him (see Genesis 5:24). Later, Jews began to believe that Elijah and Enoch would return before God was able to restore Israel to her path of righteousness. During this period, God is depicted as using other nations to discipline Israel's people, who took it for granted that God would protect them, even though they neglected his commands.

In the prophets Jeremiah, Amos and Micah especially, the link between justice and righteousness is explicit. Worship and sacrifices in the Temple are all worthless while wicked behaviour persists, negating any claim to holiness. Jeremiah warned that the Temple would itself fall unless justice was restored (Jeremiah 7:5). While the fatherless and widows were being oppressed, the Temple liturgy was a sham: 'Has this house, which bears my name, become a den of robbers'? (7:11). These are the very words Jesus used when he cleansed the Temple. At Matthew 16:14, Jesus was taken to be Jeremiah redivivus.

Amos put it like this:

I hate, I despise your religious feasts, I cannot stand your assemblies, even though you bring me burnt offerings and grain offerings, I will not accept them. Though you bring choice fellowship offerings, I will have no regard for them. Away with the noise of your songs. I will not listen to the music of your harps. But let justice roll down like a river and righteousness like a never-failing stream. (5:21–4)

Eventually, the North fell to Assyria (722/1 BCE). The North was depopulated. Its peoples, known later as the ten lost tribes, were dispersed. Various claims to be their descendants surface in this book. The Emmy Award-winning filmmaker Simcha Jacobovichi has made a fascinating documentary, *The Quest for the Lost Tribes* (1999). The South struggled on until 587 BCE, when Jerusalem fell to Babylon. The Temple was destroyed, and the Jews were sent into exile.

### The exile

Christians interpret this as the beginning of the end for the unique relationship between Israel and God. Israel's waywardness outweighed her devotion. Her external acts of worship were not accompanied by inner piety; nor could her endless sacrifices atone for her sins. One day, God would send a new Moses, a new David, a new Elijah, who would do away with the external paraphernalia of the law and sacrifices and substitute inner, spiritual, direct communion with God. Jeremiah spoke of this:

The time is coming when I will make a new covenant with the house of Israel and the house of Judah, it will not be like the old covenant, instead I will put my law in their minds and write it on their hearts. (Jeremiah 31:31–3)

Other passages, communicated through the prophets during the Babylonian exile, predict a day when Israel would be restored to her Davidic glory. Some passages suggest that this would involve a descendant of David, who would once again reign as the Lord's anointed (Messiah): 'He will raise a banner for the nations and gather the exiles of Israel' (Isaiah 11:12).

Some passages suggest that Israel would once more be a great nation. Others suggest that non-Jews would flock to Jerusalem, to join in the praise and service of the one true God (see Isaiah 60). Some passages seem to depict a restored Israel within the normal space-time continuum, while others suggest that this Israel will be on a transformed earth: 'Behold, I will create a new heaven and a new earth' and 'Jerusalem to be a delight' (Isaiah 65). Almost all passages associate this restored, renewed, transformed Israel, which will include gentiles, with an era of peace and justice. The broken relationship between humanity and God, and between humanity and nature (broken by the Fall) will be mended. Children will no longer die as infants, no one will build houses for others to live in, wolves and lambs will lie down together, babies will play with snakes without getting hurt and so on.

For Christians, this is what Jesus will accomplish when the final judgment takes place. He is the promised Messiah. However, Jews believed that this would all follow from a triumphant victory over Israel's enemies, possibly led by the Messiah. Christians point to other verses that suggest to them that the Messiah would first have to suffer in order to atone for humanity's sins (see Isaiah 53). The Temple sacrifices were insufficient; only the death of God's own, sinless son could bring about salvation (see my section on messianism earlier in this chapter (p. 26), and also my discussion of this in Chapters 3 and 5).

### The return

In 538 BCE, Cyrus, Emperor of Persia, who had conquered Babylon, gave permission for the exiles to return to Jerusalem to rebuild the Temple. During their period in exile, the Jews had actually thrived. Reflecting on their experiences, they interpreted their exile as punishment, just as Jeremiah had warned. They turned to a renewed study of the Torah, which, with the Temple in ruins, became central to their understanding of God's purposes. The *beit ha'knesset* (synagogue) emerged in Babylon as a place for Torah study and informal worship. In contrast, Jews who sought refuge in Egypt actually built themselves a temple at Elephanta. They appear to have become eclectic in their religious practices, worshipping other divine beings alongside YHWH (Hebrew letters for God). Scholars suggest that these may well have been regarded as 'hypostatizations of aspects of Yahweh' (Bright, 1972, p. 377). This is interesting when compared with later Christian belief in a trinity of three persons, or hypostases.

In Babylon, the 'suffering servant' passage (which Christians see as predicting the crucifixion) may have been a product of Jewish reflection on the experience of exile; Israel was suffering for her sins, yet this suffering was 'too deep to be explained simply as a punishment for sin' (*ibid.*, p. 359). Jeremiah now advised the exiles to plant vineyards and to work and to pray for the welfare of their cities (29:7). If the city prospered, they would prosper. This may represent the beginning of the idea that the Messiah might come once the right social conditions have been achieved.

After Cyrus' edict, the Temple was rebuilt under the scribe Ezra, with Nehemiah as governor (this is known as the Second Temple). A period of quasi independence followed: 'they formed a recognized community licensed to regulate internal affairs in accordance with the law of their God' (*ibid.*, p. 392). It seems the Torah, and its observance, was more vital now than the restored Temple. Many Jews, too, remained in Diaspora, and for them the Temple played no role in their religious life. Some may have hoped for much more, for the Messiah to come and revive Israel's greatness. Some thought in terms of a cosmic battle between good and evil. Some believed this would be at a place called Megiddo (see 2 Chronicles 35:22), the Armageddon of Revelation 16:16, but not before the lost tribes had all returned to Jerusalem.

Scholars see here the influence of Zoroastrian dualism (between the rival cosmic principles of good and evil). Many also think that belief in resurrection of the dead was borrowed from Zoroastrianism at about the same time. In Judaism, this became a debated dogma. Zerubbabel, who took the initiative in rebuilding the Temple, was from the House of David, and appears to have been hailed by the prophet Zechariah in messianic language (Zechariah 3:8). The people may well have believed that he was the Davidide who would rule over the restored kingdom, yet nothing materialized. Zerubbabel disappears, 'David's throne was not re-established and the age of promise did not dawn' (*ibid.*, p. 373).

## Alexander and the vision of a Hellenic world

In 333 BCE, Alexander the Great added Palestine to his empire. After his premature death in 323 BCE, his generals divided the empire among themselves. Palestine went to the Ptolemies, whose capital was in Egypt. The Seleucids, though, always regarded Palestine as theirs, and finally succeeded in annexing it in 198 BCE. During this period of Greek rule, city-colonies were built as part of a civilizing mission that had begun with Alexander, who had wanted to spread Greek culture, learning and philosophy. To help to eradicate racial differences, he 'arranged mass marriages between his troops and the native population' (Bright, 1972, p. 428). Some of these colonies, the cities of the Decapolis, were in the region of Galilee, where Jesus spent most of his life. Some Jews resisted Greek influence (the emerging Sadducees), while others developed an appetite for Greek culture, Greek sports and Greek philosophy. Some attempted to synthesize Greek and Hebrew thought, so much so that Bright speaks of 'an irreconcilable schism . . . within the Jewish community' (pp. 419–20).

The Jews of Egypt appear to have embraced cosmopolitanism with some enthusiasm, adopting Greek language and producing the Septuagint early in the third century BCE. Philo (30 BCE–45 CE) appears to have known no Hebrew. In his writing, he tried to explain biblical anthropomorphisms and other apparently problematical Bible passages, as well as Jewish rites, to Jews and Greeks alike. He used allegory a great deal, influencing Origen and other later Christian scholars. He also incorporated the 'logos' into his system; this was 'at once the creative power which orders the world and the intermediary through whom men know God. It was the logos who spoke to Moses at the burning bush, and who is represented in the Hebrew Bible as the high priest' (Cross and Livingstone, 1983, p. 1084). If we are looking for a source for John's prologue, or for Christian belief in Jesus as the logos through which the world was made, Philo may be a candidate.

## Maccabean revolt

When the Seleucid King, Antiochus IV, went so far as to abolish Jewish feast days and to install an altar to Zeus in the Temple, the resistance party rebelled. Led by Judas Maccabeus, a band of guerrilla fighters actually defeated the Greeks and won independence for Israel (169 BCE), the first time since 587 BCE. Judas' successors also managed to win back a considerable portion of Solomon's old empire. Perhaps God would soon intervene on behalf of His people. The regime set up by Judas, the Hasmoneans, was more Temple- than Torah-centred, probably in order to centralize political and religious power. They appointed their own high priests and later combined the offices of high priest and king. As they were not members of the traditional Zadokite family, this alienated some. The Essenes (see below) appear to have opposed the Hasmonean high priest (their wicked priest) and, under their teacher of righteousness, set up their own alternative Temple in the wilderness.

The Essenes opposed the assimilation of Greek culture. The Pharisees, who focused on the Torah, may also have disapproved of the Hasmoneans, although they did not rebel. In fact, their predecessors are thought to have given the Hasmoneans their victory, and for two brief periods they actually gained power, under John Hyrcanus (134–104 BCE) and Alexandra (76–67 BCE) (Saldarini, 1994, p. 31). The Hasmoneans also tried to eradicate alternative forms of Judaism which had developed due to the political disintegration of Solomon's kingdom, and during the long periods of living in exile, and they destroyed the Samaritans' Temple at Mount Gerizim. In the year 63 BCE the Roman general, Pompey, brought the Hasmonean kingdom within Roman jurisdiction, intervening in the dispute between Hyrcanus and Aristobulus for the Hasmonean throne. We can only speculate why, having gained autonomy, the Hasmoneans made no effort to place a member of David's family on the throne. Instead, they occupied this themselves.

## The Herodian project

In 37 BCE, the Hasmoneans lost power to Herod the Great, who seized control with Roman support, then ruled as a client king. It was during his reign that Jesus was born (probably in 4 BCE). Herod was ambitious. He killed all those who had any claim on his throne, including his own sons. As Allen (1998) says, 'the story in Matthew's gospel of his massacre of boy babies in Bethlehem . . . is in line with [his] bloodthirstiness and paranoia' (p. 19). He courted Roman favour and was a frequent visitor to Rome. He gathered money from what was now a wealthy Jewish community throughout the Roman world to rebuild the Second Temple, and to finance other building projects (libraries, baths, synagogues) and welfare initiatives (see *War* 5:5 for Josephus' detailed description of Herod's Temple).

Jews constituted some 10 per cent of the empire and Herod coveted recognition as leader of this whole community, which would considerably enhance his prestige. He also wanted to make Jerusalem more cosmopolitan, so he appointed Diaspora Jews to significant positions. They were much more open to Hellenization than were Palestinian Jews, whom Herod regarded as backward. They did not fit his picture of the ideal Jew, who would be second to no one as major contributors to culture, art and learning. He saw himself as a reformer, 'trying to drag an obstinate and conservative . . . people into the enlightened circle of the modern world' (Johnson, 1987, p. 112).

Herod lost direct control of Jerusalem, however, so the high priests were actually appointed by the Roman governor. They, and a council of aristocratic advisers, exercised delegated authority. Those who ran the Temple were all Sadducees, and 'focused solely on the Temple ritual and cared little about morality or the hereafter' (Allen, 1998, p. 32). While they opposed cultural assimilation, they collaborated with whoever was in power. This was the best strategy to keep the Temple intact.

The Pharisees, for their part, seem to have been concerned not only with keeping the *mitzvot* and with ritual purity but also with the moral demands of the Torah. They believed that the priestly purity laws *applied equally to all Jews*. They appear to have wanted to democratize Judaism by minimizing the distinction between priest and lay person and by focusing on the Torah, which was available to all Jews. As the Talmud says, 'The Torah is greater than the priesthood and than royalty' (Cohen, 1949, p. 130). Although represented in the Gospels as legalistic, and as overly concerned with outer appearances of piety, they actually taught that the spirit of the law was as important as the letter, and 'usually represented a position more sympathetic toward the people' (Kee and Young, 1960, p. 37). After the destruction of the Temple (see below), it was a form of Pharisaic Judaism, led by Johanan ben Zakkai, who believed that God was 'better served without the burden and corruption of the state' that produced rabbinical Judaism (Johnson, 1987, p. 149).

Palestine was no backwater. Galilee, where Jesus grew up, was a 'cultural crossroads' (Allen, 1998, p. 26). Indeed, historic happenings were going on in, or close to, where Jesus lived. Caesar and Antony both fell in love with the last Ptolemy, Cleopatra of Egypt, just south of Palestine; thus 'The ministry of Jesus . . . took place not on the sidelines . . . but on a great world stage where Pompey and Caesar, Antony and Cleopatra, and Augustus, Tiberius, and Caligula trod the boards at various times' (*ibid.*, p. 20). The early years of the first century CE were certainly turbulent for Jesus' native land. Intrigue between the Herod family and their rivals and opposition to Roman rule by an increasing number of Jews led to mass executions and general instability. Armed bands known as *sicarii* roamed the countryside, assassinating Roman collaborators with their short swords. Farmers, heavily taxed, were especially discontented. Jerusalem itself was placed under direct Roman rule from 6 CE until well after Jesus' crucifixion. Between 6 BCE and 66 CE, fourteen procurators, including Pontius Pilate, governed the capital. None were of very high calibre (the posting was not considered to be very prestigious) and they were 'often . . . guilty of inordinate cruelty in carrying out political policies' (Kee and Young, 1960, p. 30). This eventually fuelled the Zealots to rebel; only God should rule Israel. As I indicated above (in my section on Josephus, pp. 25–6), some Jews expected divine intervention. Might not Elijah, or Enoch, soon return as a sign that the final battle was near? There were several would-be Messiahs, among whose number Jews count Jesus. For Christians, Jesus is the real Messiah. Jesus certainly appears to have detested the Temple authorities, who grew fat and rich by collaborating with Rome. Jesus may well have had more reason to clash with the Sadducees (as Brandon suggested) than with the Pharisees, a point that Geiger raises (see Chapter 5).

The nature of Jesus' relationship with Second Temple Judaism emerges as a major issue in Chapter 3 of this book (and is of central concern in Chapter 5). He seems to have believed that if Israel repented, God would establish his reign of peace and justice. He may have believed that this would involve Israel regaining her former political prestige. Alternatively, as Christians would later claim, he saw himself as the one in whom God's purposes for Israel would be fulfilled. By dying and rising again for the sins and tribulations not only of Jews *but of all people*, he would become a living substitute for both Temple and the law. Through faith in his sacrificial death, those who believed in him would receive forgiveness of their sins and new, restored life. This would anticipate the promised new life in a restored Israel, which would follow when enough time had passed for the disciples to spread the message worldwide. Based on Matthew 24:14, many Christians believe that when every person alive has heard the Gospel preached, Jesus will return in glory as the one promised in so many Hebrew prophecies:

one like the son of man was there before me. . . . He was given authority, glory and sovereign power over all nations and men of every language worshipped him. His dominion is an everlasting dominion that will not pass away, and his kingdom is one that will never be destroyed. (Daniel 7:13–14)

Christians call Jesus 'Prophet, Priest and King'. As prophet, he is a second Elijah. As priest, he offered himself as an eternal sacrifice, tearing down for ever the curtain in the Temple between priest and people. As king, he is the son of David who one day will be enthroned as Cosmic Lord. Hebrews calls Jesus 'a priest forever of the order of Melchizedek' (7:17). Melchizedek is the rather mysterious king and priest of Salem whom Abraham encountered in Genesis. Described as 'without Father and without mother', Melchizedek (who, for Christians, is a type of Christ) blessed Abraham and 'brought out bread and wine' (Genesis 14:18). Abraham gave Melchizedek 'a tenth of everything' (Genesis 14:20). Yet Melchizedek was not from Abraham's clan, let alone a member of the not yet established Jewish priesthood. Muslim tradition, for its part, identifies Jesus as of *priestly descent*; Khan (1983) writes in a footnote to his edition of *Sahih-al-Bukhari* that 'Mary was presumably of a priestly family' (Vol. IV, p. 429).

## The second exile

About thirty years after Jesus' execution, the Jews rebelled against Rome. In 66 CE, the Zealots seized the Temple, killing the incumbent high priest as a Roman collaborator, and thousands of other collaborators as well. The revolt was precipitated when the Roman governor tried to appropriate the Temple's Golden Minora. Roman garrisons were ransacked throughout the country. Caesar responded by sending 60,000 soldiers, under a distinguished general, Vespasian, to crush the rebellion. After he returned to Rome to claim the throne following Nero's death, Vespasian left his son Titus in charge. In the conflict, Jerusalem was burned to the ground (70 CE). Josephus says that Titus did not actually intend to destroy the Temple; however, he also records the ferocity with which the Roman soldiers slaughtered Jewish men, women and children. The Temple treasure was taken to Rome in triumph, and the Temple, as Jesus seems to have predicted, was destroyed.

As a result of the failed revolt, an extra tax (*fiscus Judaicus*) was levied on all Jews in the Roman world. One stronghold, the hilltop fort at Masada, remained in Zealot hands. The Romans laid siege. As recounted by Josephus, all 960, men, women and children, entered a death pact rather than surrender (*War*, Book 7, Chapter 9). This account, though, is disputed. Perhaps it was a device to make the Jews look heroic, or to make amends for Josephus' own defection. In 132 CE, the Zealots made one final attempt to regain independence under Simon ben Kokhba, whom many believed was the Messiah, but they were defeated. The Romans then banned all Jews from living in Jerusalem.

Later, Christians interpreted this as a sign that, in rejecting Jesus as the Messiah, the Jews forfeited the right to be considered God's children. Instead, they are under divine punishment, destined to wander from place to place as refugees and émigrés, homeless, without a land, and, for much of the last two millennia, without rights or even citizenship. Christians sometimes went even further; as the slayers of Christ, the Jews were now the devil's own, no longer human but subhuman (see Chapter 5 for a more detailed account). The Christian story, which began with the first Adam, ends with the Second Adam, Jesus Christ, and bypasses the Jews. Jesus' words had come true: 'people had come from east and west to sit at table with Abraham and Isaac, while the Jews were in outer darkness, gnashing their teeth' (Matthew 8:11–12). The old covenant is cancelled, replaced by the new. These adopted sons of Abraham do not need to be circumcised, or to keep the 613 *mitzvot*. The A & E documentary, *66 AD: The Last Revolt* (2000), covers the events described in this section.

## The non-canonical gospels

The canonical gospels, which I describe below, were just four of many available to Christians up until the end of the second century; Luke commented that 'Many have undertaken to draw up an account of the things that have been fulfilled among us' (1:1). Clearly, much material was written to score theological points against others. Thus, while diversity of scripture may in part have resulted from:

accidental differences in cultural, social and linguistic milieu [it] also stemmed from, the co-existence of essentially different theological opinions and traditions about the significance of Jesus, some of which seem to be as old as Christianity itself – traditions about Jesus as miracle worker, wisdom incarnate, revealer, Messiah of Israel, prophet, emanation from another world. (Layton, 1987, p. xviii)

Different scriptures therefore represented 'competing . . . options or denominations open to ancient Christians everywhere' (*ibid.*, p. xxii). Many of the non-canonical gospels emerged from groups such as the Gnostics; *gnosis* means knowledge.

The Gnostics believed that salvation depends on knowledge, not on faith in Jesus' redeeming death; Jesus communicated this knowledge to those capable of handling it. This world, in their view, is evil, the creation of a demiurge; the good god is beyond, a god of depth and silence. For many Gnostics, Jesus was thus an emanation from outside this world. Through *gnosis* mediated by Jesus, human souls, which are really 'sparks of divine light entrapped by the evil creator in the material world', can return to their real home, the heavens. *Gnosis*, though, is only available to the elect. Jesus was not human, but only 'appeared' or 'seemed' to be real (see Funk *et al.*, 1993, pp. 500–1). His crucifixion was also viewed in some of the Gnostic texts as only apparent; or his real nature as Son of God did not suffer. Rather, Jesus was 'alien to suffering and death' (Layton, 1987, p. 111). One text, the *Second Treatise of the Great Seth*, appears to substitute someone else for Jesus, who was 'rejoicing in the heights over their error . . . laughing at their ignorance' (Pagels, 1979, p. 87). This is remarkably close to the Qur'anic version that 'they slew him not, nor crucified him but it appeared so to them' (Q 4:157). Many Muslims believe that Judas was actually crucified instead of Jesus.

Some Gnostic texts substitute Barabbas. As Pagels points out, different interpretations of Jesus' suffering and death influenced what attitude Christians adopted towards martyrdom (1979, p. 108). Some thought that martyrdom was almost essential for salvation. Others said that any idea that, by dying, Christians were being Christlike, sharing his passion, was absurd since Jesus, as the *Acts of John* put it, 'suffered none of the things which they say of me; even that suffering which [he] showed to you . . . that [is] a mystery' (*ibid.*, pp. 89–90). Some see links between the Gnostic movement and the medieval Cathari, who called themselves 'Perfecti'. They paid tribute to the Father-Mother God, renounced all property, held their services outdoors and taught that Jesus saved humanity not by his death but by his life. They rebelled against the Church's corruption, against its wealth and against the immoral lives of many priests. In their turn, they were accused of gross immorality. They were persecuted and eventually stamped out. Many accepted martyrdom.

## Jesus and Gnostic cosmology

The Gnostics also developed a complex cosmology. Thus, their world was one of 'fantastic symbols, beautifully intricate myths, weird heavenly denizens, and extraordinary poetry' (Layton, 1987, p. xviii). Material about Jesus was woven into this framework, much of which appears to be pure invention. Two episodes from the Jesus story especially stimulated the Gnostic imagination: the time Jesus supposedly spent in Egypt as a child, and his descent into Hades (asserted by the early Christian creeds). The former includes such well-known stories as Jesus meeting the two thieves, Duchamus and Titus, who were to be crucified alongside him, and predicting that Titus would precede him into Paradise; the idols in the capital crashing into pieces as Jesus entered the city; and Jesus causing a palm to lower its fruit so that Mary could eat (see Hoffmann, 1996, pp. 86, 87, 89).

In *The Infancy Gospel of Thomas* (James, 1924b), the boy Jesus creates sparrows from clay, which fly away chirping (11:3). Similar stories are found at Qur'an 5:110 and at 19:25, which has led non-Muslims to suppose that Muhammad had access to Christian apocryphal stories, if not to actual texts. In *The Infancy Gospel of Thomas*, Jesus also kills a boy who 'dashed against his shoulder' (4: 1), cursed a teacher who displeased him (14: 1) and revived a child who fell from a roof. When the child's parents blamed Jesus for this incident, he approached the boy and cried, ' "Zeno (for so was his name called), arise and tell me, did I cast thee down." Zeno arose, and said, "Ney, Lord, thou did not cast me down but raised me up" ' (11:1; see James, 1924a).

Meier (1991) suggests that:

The reason why authors of both apocryphal infancy gospels (like the *Infancy Gospel of Thomas*) and modern novels have gravitated to the so-called 'hidden years' of Jesus' life is that they can give free rein to their imagination (pious or impious) with no facts to restrain them. (p. 257)

## The Nag Hammadi Library

Much of this material does seem to be fantastic, although this is not true of all non-canonical material, for example, *The Gospel of Thomas*. Bernard Grenfell and Arthur Hunt first discovered fragments of this at Oxyrhynchus in Egypt in 1895 (now on display in the Ashmolean Museum, Oxford). This site has long been associated with Jesus' flight into Egypt. There are many legends, among Muslims as well as Christians, about his time there. In 1945 a complete manuscript was discovered, together with other Coptic texts (such as *The Gospel of Philip* and *Pistis Sophia*) in a jar inside a cave at Nag Hammadi, Upper Egypt (these texts are in Coptic). References in this literature to disputes between Peter and Mary Magdalene, as well as to a special relationship between Mary Magdalene and Jesus, may explain why this material was suppressed. Kimball (1997), whose own work focuses on Jesus' childhood, comments, 'many of those who deal with The Apocrypha today are still afraid of the potential condemnation of their own churches ... or of scholars from around Christendom' (p. 21).

The following passage from *The Gospel of Philip* is much cited by those who argue that Jesus enjoyed a sexual relationship with Mary: 'The companion of the Saviour is Mary Magdalene. But Christ loved her more than all the disciples and used to kiss her often on the mouth' (Isenberg, 1990, p. 5). The same passage has Jesus speaking very positively about marriage: 'Great is the mystery of marriage! For without it the world would not have existed. Now the existence of the world depends on man, and the existence of man on marriage' (*ibid.*, p. 5). Later, Jesus says, 'marriage in the world is a mystery for those who have taken a wife' (*ibid.*, p. 11).

This literature also appeals to feminist writers, since there is much material on God as being both male and female; for example:

In the *Gospel of Thomas* Jesus contrasts his earthly parents, Mary and Joseph with his divine Father – the Father of Truth – and his divine Mother, the Holy Spirit. . . . So, according to the Gospel of Philip, whoever becomes a Christian gains 'both father and mother' for the Spirit (*ruah*) is 'mother of many'. (Pagels, 1979, p. 62; see Patterson and Meyer (1994) translation)

Irenaeus (130–200 CE) describes for us a Gnostic baptismal rite:

Others lead them to the water, and baptize them with the utterance of these words over them, 'Into the name of the unknown Father of the universe – into truth, the mother of all things, into Him who descended on Jesus, into union, and redemption, and communion with the powers'. (Stevenson, 1963, p. 132)

In *The Acts of Thomas* (see James, 1924a), a prayer contains the following invocation: 'Come, Compassionate Mother, Come, companion of the male, Come, she that revealeth the hidden mysteries' (verse 27; original probably Syriac, *c.* fourth century).

Since God had created male and female in His image, some said this meant that both the masculine and the feminine exist within the Godness of God (Pagels, 1979, p. 59; Genesis 1:27). The Valentians (a Gnostic group) had women priests, 'perhaps even bishops' (*ibid.*, p. 72). Valentinus was a distinguished teacher and a highly respected leader among Alexandrian Christians who moved to Rome (*c.* 140) where he may have been a strong candidate for the papacy. He was later condemned for heresy. The *Pistis Sophia* seems close to his doctrine of divine emanations; men and women may reunite with the *pleroma* (the spiritual world) when they receive the gift of *gnosis* from Jesus, with whom the emanation Christ had united himself (perhaps at Jesus' conception or at his baptism).

However, only the elect will be saved. In some of the literature, Jesus teaches seven women as well as his male disciples. Pagels (1979) points out how Gnostic groups also took 'the principle of equality between men into the social and political structures of their communities' (p. 79). A positive attitude towards women was not universal among Gnostics, however. Some associated women with the world of darkness. One text, addressing men, says, 'Woe to you who love intimacy with womankind, and polluted intercourse with it' (*ibid.*). Wisdom is also called Divine Mother, who created the world from her suffering. She is also identified as the Holy Spirit. Strife and chaos followed when her male partner claimed sole pre-eminence: '"It is I who am God, there is no other apart from me." . . . And Life, the daughter of Wisdom cried out . . . "you are wrong, Saklas"' (*ibid.*, p. 70).

In the last verse of *Thomas* (114), Peter says to Jesus, 'Make Mary leave us, for females don't deserve life'. Jesus responds, 'I will guide her to make her male, so that she too may become a living spirit . . . every female who makes herself male will enter the kingdom androgynous the goal for both men and women' (*ibid.*, p. 67). Some Jewish commentators interpret Adam's original state as androgynous, until the rib was used to create Eve. Orthodox Christian theology stresses faith, not knowledge. However, there are references to 'knowledge' in the canonical gospels; for example, at Luke 7:35, 'But wisdom is justified of all her children.' Matthew (11:25) speaks about hidden wisdom being revealed to 'little children'. In John's Gospel Jesus says that to know him is to know God, and that he has made known everything he learned from the Father (John 14:7; 15:15). Fiorenza (1994) points out that *sophia* language belongs to the earliest layer of gospel material known as 'Q' (see below). It also appears in 1 Corinthians, where Jesus is the *sophia* and *dunamis* of God (the wisdom and power; 1:24). I return to Fiorenza in my concluding chapter.

The Thomas associated with *The Gospel of Thomas*, who is described as Judas Thomas, a twin brother of Jesus (see John 20:24), may or may not be the disciple who travelled to India. The idea of twinship is an important motif, and readers of the text also become Jesus' twins: 'Whoever comes to understand these books discovers, like Thomas, that Jesus is his "twin", his spiritual "other self"' (*ibid.*, p. 22). In *The Acts of Thomas*, the risen Jesus appears to Thomas and sells him into slavery so that he can be taken to India:

Now the Lord seeing him walking in the market-place at noon said unto him: Wouldest thou buy a carpenter? And he said to him: Yea. And the Lord said to him: I have a slave that is a carpenter and I desire to sell him. And so saying he showed him Thomas afar off, and agreed with him for three *litrae* of silver unstamped, and wrote a deed of sale, saying: I, Jesus, the son of Joseph the carpenter, acknowledge that I have sold my slave, Judas by name, unto thee Abbanes, a merchant of Gundaphorus, king of the Indians. (*Acts of Thomas*, verse 2; see James' (1924a) translation)

Thomas had expressed reluctance to go to India, saying that 'by reason of the weakness of the flesh he could not travel, and "I am a Hebrew man; how can I go amongst the Indians and preach the truth?"' (*ibid.*, verse 1). I return to *Thomas* in Chapter 6.

## The status of Thomas

Several eminent scholars afford authenticity to portions of *Thomas*; Sanders thinks that some of its sayings 'are worth consideration' (1993, p. 64). The Jesus Seminar treat it with considerable respect: 'scholars take [it] to represent a tradition quite independent of the other gospels'. Its contents represent 'what scientists call a "control group" for the analysis of sayings and parables that appear in the other gospels' (Funk *et al.*, 1993, p. 15), and 'Thomas [has] to be included in any primary collection of gospels' (p. xiii). In fact, in the Jesus Seminar's *The Five Gospels*, *Thomas* is their fifth gospel (alongside Matthew, Mark, Luke and John). The Jesus Seminar view *Thomas* as 'an entirely independent sayings gospel, parts of which may be as old as Q' with which there is 35 per cent agreement (*ibid.*, p. 474; for 'Q', see below). Helmut Koester of Harvard thinks that 'the Thomas collection might contain material older than the gospels' (cited by Pagels, 1979, p. xvii).

Indeed, there is considerable overlap between *Thomas* and the synoptics; the parable of the mustard seed, the saying about the log in one's eye, the parable of the man who held a banquet to which the guests did not come, are all found in *Thomas*. Like other Gnostic gospels, *Thomas* does not contain any biographical information about Jesus or give us anything resembling a chronology, nor does it give us birth or death narratives. This may derive from the purpose it initially served – as an *aide-mémoire* of sayings of Jesus. However, some writers suppose that it lacked a death narrative because its compiler knew that Jesus had died an old man (see e.g. Lockhart, 1997, p. 277). Certainly, it seems to have been the case that for this Christian tradition, the 'crucifixion' was not a central dogma; 'it powerfully suggests', says Tully (1996), 'that there were at least some communities who saw Jesus as a spiritual master rather than as a crucified and risen Lord' (p. 188). Elizabeth Clare Prophet (1984) refers to a significant second-century tradition that deals 'with an extended post-resurrection stay on earth' (p. 382). In Chapter 5, I cite similar Islamic traditions. Baigent *et al.* (1986) cite traditions that descendants not only of Jesus' brother James, but also 'possibly of Jesus himself' (the Desposyni), 'survived to become leaders of various Christian churches' (p. 100).

*Thomas* belongs to a strand of apocryphal material that appears to have preached a distinctive message; in this literature there is an immediacy about Jesus' missive:

To follow the living Jesus was to know and integrate oneself. The divine light, or kingdom of light, is not only a distinct realm and power with which the individual

Christian must reunite, but also a reality around and within every person and thing. (Layton, 1987, p. 360)

People are lost in a state of sleepfulness, they are drunk, in darkness, dead, ruled by malevolent authorities, 'Pharisees, Scribes, Babylonian children, tyrannical demons of the Labyrinth', but Jesus' words bring sobriety (*ibid.*, p. 376). They bring a 'recognition of one's true nature' which, 'leading to repose', also renders 'death . . . trivial'; thus:

Whoever finds the meaning of these sayings will not taste death. (Thomas: 1)

The kingdom is inside of you . . . When you become acquainted with yourself . . . you will understand that it is you who are children of the living father. (Thomas: 3)

The Kingdom of God is spread out upon the earth, and people don't see it. (Thomas: 113)

The Thomas literature shares something in common with Gnosticism, but its real roots lie in the genre of Jewish wisdom literature. It has much in common, too, with the canonical gospel of John, suspected by many early Christians of being a Gnostic text (and attributed to Cerinthus; Tatum, 1999, p. 29).

John also preaches immediate renewal, rebirth: 'This life is eternal, extending beyond biological death. But this life is also a present possibility' (Tatum, 1999, p. 74; see especially John 11:17–27). He uses language of 'light' and 'darkness', speaks about his disciples being no longer 'of this world' (John 17:14) and of Jesus as 'coming from' and 'returning to' somewhere 'above the world'. Due to dispute about ownership, it was some thirty years after the discovery of the Nag Hammadi texts before the wider academic community was able to study this material, and then, once the Coptic Museum had established ownership, it was reluctant to allow access. Pagels (1979) tells the whole story.

Director Rupert Wainright picked up on rumours of secrecy surrounding both the Nag Hammadi collection and the Dead Sea Scrolls (see below) in his brilliantly photographed and provocative film, *Stigmata* (1999). Although reviews have been mixed, I thought the film did a good job in translating on to the screen some of the criticisms expressed by legitimate scholars and others about how the Christian tradition may have departed from the original simplicity of Jesus' life and teaching. In the film, the Vatican tries to suppress the text of a 'lost gospel' (written in Aramaic) which they fear contains Jesus' own words. Based on *The Gospel of Thomas*, this proclaims that the kingdom of God is *in us and all around us*: 'split a piece of wood and I am there, Lift up the stone and you will find me' (Thomas 77). In other words, people do not need priests or churches to communicate with God, and Jesus would fail to recognize his legacy in the wealthy, powerful and celibate hierarchy of Rome.

The plot is a little far-fetched, involving a banned priest (excommunicated for his work on the lost gospel) who dies and takes possession of an unsuspecting, non-religious and (of course) very attractive young women called Frankie Paige (played by Patricia Arquette). Subsequently, Paige develops the stigmata. The link between the dead priest in Brazil and the girl in Pennsylvania is a crucifix, which Frankie's mother bought for her while visiting Rio. Andrew Kiernan, a devil's advocate (a priest who investigates claims of miraculous happenings, or of would-be saints), is sent to investigate these events. Kiernan ends up saving Frankie from the wicked cardinal, who resorts to killing her to prevent the text of the gospel from becoming public knowledge.

While some of the scenes are ghoulish, I thought the film dealt sensitively with the developing relationship between the girl and the priest. It might even have been more explicitly sexual than it actually was. One scene, just before the stigmata begins, in which Frankie is seen nude, shows, as one of my students put it, 'the difference between art and pornography' (she is filmed side-on while lying in her bath). I thought it worth describing the film in a little detail, since it does touch on several interesting issues: What is the status of Thomas? Did Jesus envisage a wealthy and powerful Church? Did he demand celibacy? Can one be spiritually whole and sexually active at the same time? Did he think people needed mediators between God and themselves? These are all issues that keep surfacing in this book.

### Other non-canonical texts

Other texts include the Egerton Gospel, five fragments of which have been discovered, also in Egypt. These manuscripts date from about 125 CE (a date as early as 94 CE has been suggested). In addition to some miracle stories, there is material 'closely related to the Gospel of John' (Funk *et al.*, 1993, p. 544). More controversially, Morton Smith (see Chapter 4) claims to have discovered a letter to Clement of Alexandria which, in order to refute a non-canonical text, cites certain passages from that text. Smith calls this *The Secret Gospel of Mark*. Among other material, this contains the story of an initiation rite in which the participants, including Jesus, were naked. This is a favourite with those who want to argue for a sexually active Jesus.

Muslims often say that the real gospel (which they believe was revealed to Jesus in a way similar to how the Qur'an was revealed to Muhammad) was lost or even destroyed. Many Muslims point to a book called *The Gospel of Barnabas* (not to be confused with the Epistle of Barnabas) as the authentic gospel. There was probably an early Gnostic text called *The Gospel of Barnabas*, which was destroyed along with many texts of this genre. However, in the medieval period a text bearing this name began to circulate, and gained immense popularity in the Muslim world. This is generally held to be a forgery (see Glassé, 1991, p. 65). Its Jesus story seems to be more compatible with the Qur'an's account than with accounts found in the canonical material. In *Barnabas*, Jesus did not die on the cross; instead 'Judas Iscariot miraculously takes his form and is crucified in his place', which reflects the popular Muslim view to which I referred above. 'The disciples steal the dead body of Judas, and Jesus reappears' (*ibid.*, p. 64). I return to *The Gospel of Barnabas* in Chapter 5.

Kamal Salibi (1998) argues that Waraqqah, Muhammad's uncle by marriage, possessed a gospel written in Aramaic, which was later lost. Salibi writes, 'but one can safely assume that the story it related about Jesus was not much different from the [one related in the] . . . text of the Koran' (p. 61). In Chapter 4 I discuss other versions of the Jesus story which posit that he somehow survived the crucifixion and continued to live until a natural death (one such account also emerges in Chapter 3). In the Qur'an, Jesus ascends to heaven. Disappointingly, perhaps, none of what I have described so far in this chapter helps us much with any reconstruction of Jesus' life. I have to agree with Evans (1997) that 'The various portraits of Jesus in this vast assortment of gospels are intriguing, but they add little reliable information beyond what can be recovered in the canonical gospels' (p. 72).

## The Dead Sea Scrolls

The discovery and translation of the Dead Sea Scrolls have attracted wide interest. The scrolls have stimulated much speculation, to which a wealth of literature, academic, popular and sensationalist, gives ample testimony. Geza Vermes (1997), in what is probably the definitive English edition of the complete Dead Sea library (a book of 648 pages), asks:

Why have they appealed so strongly to the imagination of the non-specialist? [and continues] I would say, the outstanding characteristic of our age appears to be a desire to reach back to the greatest attainable purity, to the basic truth free of jargon. (p. 24)

The scrolls were discovered by a shepherd boy in a cave at Qumran, near the Dead Sea, in either late 1946 or early 1947. Later, more caves, and ancient manuscripts, were also discovered. It quickly became apparent that this was the lost library of a community of Jewish ascetics, almost certainly Essenes, about whom something was already known from Josephus, as noted above. Many of the manuscripts were copies of books from the Hebrew Bible, others were commentaries on these, or material related to the life and expectations of the community, including *The Community Rule*, the *Temple Scrolls*, and *The Rule of War*, and some non-canonical Jewish texts. There is also a list of false prophets (*ibid.*, p. 590) and the mysterious *Copper Scroll* (*ibid.*, pp. 598–9) which appears to refer to buried treasure. Allegro thought this might be Zealot gold (cited in *ibid.*, p. 583). All this has added considerably to knowledge of a previously poorly documented period, that of the Second Temple.

The Essenes (perhaps from Aramaic *hase* meaning 'pious', but possibly from a root for 'healer', s*y*) emerged as a distinctive movement against the background of intrigue around the office of high priest especially, and of growing dissatisfaction with Israel's leadership generally, after the Hasmonean victory. The Qumran community probably flourished between '140–130 BCE and the first Jewish revolution, CE 68' (Vermes and Goodman, 1989, p. 14). Their founder was the teacher of righteousness, a priest. He may have been the expelled Zadokite high priest who opposed the high priest (the wicked priest) in Jerusalem and retreated with his followers into the desert to form a community of the pure. As the final remnant of the faithful, children of the new covenant (see Jeremiah 31:31f.), they awaited the final war between good and evil, the 'War of the Sons of Light against the Sons of Darkness'. The teacher was gifted with special insight: he was 'the Priest in whose heart God set understanding that he might interpret all the words of his servants and prophets' (Vermes, 1997, p. 71). The just are assured of 'eternal joy in life without end, a crown of glory and a garment of majesty in unending light' (*ibid.*, p. 89).

The Essenes saw themselves as God's chosen, although they 'concentrated more on the blessedness of the chosen than on the damnation of the non predestined' (*ibid.*, p. 74). They believed that only their interpretation of the scriptures was correct, and spent a great deal of time studying the Torah to trace prophecies and predictions. Finkel (1964) says that the teacher of righteousness was 'believed to have possessed full knowledge in unveiling the hidden words of the prophets and to do so he applied the "pesher" to disclose the hidden meaning' (p. 152). Barbara Thiering (see Chapter 4) claims to use 'pesher' to decode the Gospels. According to Finkel, pesher took a biblical text and applied it to 'personalities who played an important role' within the teacher's own time. For example, 'Where a lion and a lioness walked and the lion's whelp and none made them afraid' (Nahum 2:11) refers to rivalry between the Seleucids and other claimants to the throne for possession of Jerusalem. In other words, the 'lion' and the 'lioness' refer to living people (*ibid.*, p. 153). As we shall see, Thiering's use of pesher is somewhat different.

Worship in the Temple, under the rule of its wicked priests, was replaced by the true worship of the community, by prayers offered at exactly the same time as the Temple sacrifices, which replicated the heavenly worship of the 'angels in the celestial Temple' (Vermes, 1997, pp. 77f.). There was also a morning prayer directed towards the sun. This worship substituted for the Temple ritual until, in the new age, their own priests would serve in the restored or new Temple. The Essenes held property in common, except for lay members who continued to live in the towns. They may have been more widespread than scholars have supposed.

The Essenes were very strict in the observance of the law; members were organized into groups of ten, led by a priest, who had a Levi as deputy, but all, whether lay or priest, studied the scriptures and 'laymen . . . could become as expert as the priests' (Sanders, 1993, p. 46). They elected 'judges' to dispense justice within the community. They were also divided into twelve tribes, each with a *nasi* (prince) as their head. Officers retired after a set number of years, or at a designated age. Postulants, if accepted, underwent a year's initial training before they were allowed to join the community, which involved the transfer of all their personal property. Common meals and purificatory bathing were important rituals, and members dressed in white robes. They practised an ascetic, celibate lifestyle (the associate city members could marry). Meat and alcohol were prohibited. They believed that their arcane doctrines were revealed to initiates and that God determined human destiny.

## Essene eschatology

The scrolls have shed most light on the eschatological ferment that characterized the period. The Essenes were thoroughly apocalyptic; they awaited the end battle, in which not one but three Messiahs feature: the kingly son of David, the priestly Messiah and a prophet-Messiah (promised by Moses, Deut. 18:15f.; see Vermes, 1973, pp. 135f.). The prophet would be preceded by a forerunner (Christians ascribe this role to John the Baptist). There would be a final liturgy, and a feast over which the priest-Messiah presided. The king-Messiah would defer to his authority. The angel Michael actually seems to play a more pro-active role in the final battle, opposing a false Messiah (possible a false 'son of the Most high'; see Vermes, 1997, p. 85). However, it is God himself who breaks the deadlock between the forces of good and evil: 'God's intervention alone would bring about the destruction of evil.' The forces of good would consist of twelve battalions, representing the twelve tribes and anticipating the birth of a restored Israel.

The Essenes took part in the final insurrection against Rome, which they presumably equated with the 'end battle'. Their settlements were destroyed in about 68 CE, when many Essenes were tortured and executed: 'They refused to the last to acknowledge the emperor as their master and showed amazing courage . . . in enduring torture' (Theissen, 1987, p. 203, n. 6, citing Josephus). Some Essenes fought at Masada, where a scroll identical to one of the Qumran documents was discovered. Josephus mentions four Essenes by name. Two, Judas under Aristobulus I (104–103 BCE) and Mehahem under Herod the Great, are called prophets. Simon, who was a dream interpreter, was active during the time of Archelaeus the ethnarch (4 BCE–6 CE), while John was killed 'at the battle of Ascalon during the early stages of the rebellion' (Vermes and Goodman, 1989, p. 14). The community of the Therapeutae, who lived in the desert outside Alexandria, may have been an Egyptain offshoot of the Essenes. They were also renowned for their study and practice of healing (see Vermes and Goodman, 1989, p. 16).

## Jesus and the Essenes

There is no reference to Jesus in the scrolls. Sanders (1993) does not think that Jesus had any direct contact with the Essenes, and only refers to them in passing (see p. 46). The Jesus Seminar think that the scrolls 'do not help us directly with the Greek text of the gospels, since they were created prior to the appearance of Jesus' (Funk *et al.*, 1993, p. 9). As I show later in this book, others identify Jesus with the teacher of righteousness, or with the wicked priest, or draw parallels between his teaching and theirs. Jesus predicted that his disciples would judge the twelve tribes, who may have believed that they would co-rule the new Israel with him once the kingdom had come. Like the Essenes, Jesus looked to a restored Israel. Like the Essenes, he enjoyed common meals with his disciples and ordered an initiation rite involving water.

Jesus may have used scripture, as did the Essenes, to elucidate eschatological hopes, and to locate himself in God's plan (see Vermes, 1997, p. 22). Certainly, the way Christans see Jesus in the Hebrew Bible is similar to how the Essenes interpreted scripture (and, later, to how Muslims would use the Bible to identify predictions of Muhammad). Like the Essenes, Jesus allowed ordinary people to exercise priest-like authority, sending the twelve out to extend his own ministry (see Matthew 10). The early Christian community's 'rule' may have owed something to the Essenes (see Acts 2:44–5). Jesus healed; the Essenes were renowned healers.

On the other hand, Jesus, in keeping company with lepers, tax collectors and sinners, would have been defiled in Essene eyes. Jesus may (as Sanders and others argue) have had due respect for the law but he did not share the Essenes' literal interpretation of obedience. Jesus gave priority to the spirit, not to the letter, of the law. Hillel, to whose school many commentators suggest Jesus may have actually belonged, also taught this approach. De Jong wrote, 'Jesus was . . . a pupil of Hillel' (cited in Schweitzer, 1998b, p. 323; see also Johnson, 1987, p. 128). Jesus' language resembles the Essenes'; he condemned 'this evil generation', he spoke about 'light' defeating 'darkness', about a new age of righteousness.

Yet Jesus does not easily fit the Essenes' Messianic scenario. While Christians see Jesus as a priest, they always associate his messiahship with the kingly role, which in the Essene literature is passive and symbolic rather than pivotal (see Vermes, 1973, p. 153; Jesus was not of priestly descent). Jesus appears to have assumed that he would have a significant role in the Kingdom of God: 'God was king, but Jesus represented him and would represent him in the coming kingdom' (Sanders, 1993, p. 248). Nor did Jesus think there would be a final battle: 'Unlike the Dead Sea sectaries . . . Jesus did not think in terms of a military miracle . . . He seems to have expected the son of Man to descend and God's angels to separate the elect from the wicked' (*ibid.*, p. 185). Jesus' view of God's Kingdom appears to have been much more inclusive than that of the

Essenes' faithful remnant of the few; for Jesus sinners, gentiles, outcasts would be included. Unlike the Essenes, Jesus was no ascetic but appears to have enjoyed feasting and drinking wine. He may even have rejected the role of priests, so central to Qumran's hierarchy; he seems to have regarded the central authorities as hindering rather than aiding the extension of holiness to the general Jewish populace (see Johnson, 1987, p. 127).

Whether the scrolls do or do not help to shed light on the historical Jesus, they surface several times in this book. Some scholars think that Jesus may have adopted the idea that the Messiah would have to suffer in order for redemption to occur from the Essenes. Vermes disagrees. He deems it 'groundless' that the theory of 'a suffering Messiah can be found in the scrolls', as claimed by some (1997, p. 86; 1999, p. 206). He does not think that any evidence of belief in a suffering Messiah can be found before 135 CE (see Vermes, 1983, p. 149; Segal, 1994, p. 128). Vermes does refer to the 'so-called Resurrection fragment' in which 'the eschatological kingdom is characterised, with the help of Psalm cxlvi and Isaiah lxi, 1., by the liberation of captives, the curing of the blind . . . and the raising of the dead' (1997, p. 23) which Christians associate with Jesus. Like Jesus, the Essenes clearly did believe in the eternal life of the soul, which was not a common belief within Second Temple Judaism. Vermes thinks it unlikely that the Essenes thought in terms of a physical resurrection (Vermes and Goodman, 1989, p. 12).

Speculation about the relationship between Jesus and the Essenes dates from a long time before the scrolls were discovered. For example, Karl Friedrich Bahrdt (1741–92) wrote a book in which Jesus was raised by Essenes, studied Plato and Aristotle, performed no miracles but did survive the crucifixion to return to the Essene community, where he died in old age (see Schweitzer, 1998b, pp. 38–44). In Chapter 4, I discuss several books which argue that Jesus was an Essene. In Chapter 6 I discuss the theory that the Essenes were influenced by Buddhism (some writers argue that they were Buddhists). Delay in releasing some of the scrolls fuelled speculation about their significance for Jesus study. Tully writes about rumours that the Vatican 'is sitting on some scrolls which are particularly damaging to its version of the life and times of Jesus' (1996, p. 83; see also Wright, 1992, p. 19). This rumour clearly influenced the film *Stigmata* (1999) described above. In the film, Vatican guards closely monitor the translator's every move. Both translator and manuscript are locked up in what looks more like a bank vault than a library. As a Jesuit, the translator in the film had only received every third page; the rest had been sent to Dominican and Franciscan scholars.

The Jesus Seminar condemn 'The sequestering of portions of the Dead Sea Scrolls', and the 'scholarly arrogance and procrastination' surrounding the documents in question (Funk *et al.*, 1993, p. 9). Vermes (1997) refers to obstinate refusals to 'release the list of unpublished texts from Caves 4 and 11'. 'Outsiders', he says, were not only denied access, 'but were not even allowed to know exactly what they were not permitted to see!'

(p. 601). In his autobiography (1999), Vermes devotes a whole chapter to 'The Battle Over the Scrolls'. Here, he describes how politics affected the Team's work: 'the editor-in-chief, and several members of . . . his team, were . . . pro-Arab . . . and . . . resented the de facto succession of the Israel Department of Antiquities . . . to the corresponding Jordanian Department' (p. 189). Baigent and Leigh (1991) offer a more sensationalist story in *The Dead Seas Scrolls Deception*, arguing that the scrolls' real relevance for Jesus study has been deliberately obscured: 'Those responsible for developing the consensus view of Christianity have been able to exercise a monopoly over certain crucial sources, regulating the flow of information in a manner that enables its release to serve one's own purpose' (1991, p. xviii). Drawing on, among others, the work of John Allegro (see Chapter 4) they claim that the early Church *was* Qumran (p. 174).

## Christian sources: the creation of a canon

While Josephus and the Dead Sea Scrolls are enormously helpful in reconstructing the historical and religious context of Jesus' life, it is to insider, Christian, sources that most scholars turn for information about Jesus. By the end of the second century, there were many gospels (literally, good news) in circulation. The name chosen for this genre of literature suggests that it served a theological function; it proclaimed a message. The primary intent of the writers and compilers was to preach 'good news', not to give detailed biographical or historical information, although some scholars defend the biographical nature of the Gospels (see below, and also Chapter 3). However, even if biography was not their primary concern, this does not mean that they were uninterested in history, or that they did not take care to pass on their material accurately.

What is clear is that there were many competing interpretations of who Jesus was, and that everyone utilized scriptures to support their particular views. Thus, sayings attributed to Jesus were 'one of the most authoritative types of literature for early Christians' (Layton, 1987, p. 376). Further, in the centuries prior to Emperor Constantine's conversion, which led to Christianity becoming the official religion of the Roman state, there was nothing 'resembling one mainstream church or one central tradition: instead of a mainstream one finds many traditions' (*ibid.*, p. xvii).

After Christianity became the state religion its leaders, with imperial encouragement, decided that a single creed and an official list of scriptures were needed. Politically, if loyal citizens were also to be good Christians, criteria were needed to decide who did and did not qualify as a 'sound' (orthodox) Christian. The idea of a canon (yardstick) to regulate belief was part of this process of drawing a sharp line between orthodox (right, sound, acceptable) and heterodox (wrong, heretical) opinions. Since scriptures championed all these 'false opinions', it followed that some scriptures must be censured. Layton (1987) describes the 'canon' as a battle strategy against heresy.

Thus, from the end of the second century, the Gospels of Matthew, Mark, Luke and John were declared canonical; all others were considered 'heretical', including the many Gnostic gospels (discussed above). Many non-canonical texts were also destroyed. In 333 CE, Constantine ordered all the works of Arius (see Chapter 2) to be destroyed. As late as 450 CE Bishop Theodoret of Cyrrhus discovered and destroyed 200 heretical books that divorced Jesus from his Jewish heritage. Works of anti-Christian polemic, such as Porphyry, were also destroyed, and have survived 'only in fragments' (Morton Smith, 1978, pp. 1–2).

Like Pagels, Crossan and others I am not anxious to perpetuate the traditional division between 'canonical' (or catholic) and 'non-canonical' sources. Pagels says: '[it's] not right to talk about catholic and Gnostic Gospels. You're just projecting and continuing an old stereotype in which all the good catholic stuff is in the New Testament, all the bad other stuff out there is Gnostic' (1999, p. 40). However, for many centuries, insiders and outsiders both gave priority to the 'canonical' texts, so I devote considerable attention to these in this chapter. Sanders' opinion, that it is in 'the four canonical gospels that we must search for traces of the historical Jesus', seems to me to represent a broad scholarly consensus (1993, p. 65). I sometimes think this is the only issue on which Jesus scholars agree.

My aim in this chapter is to describe the sources, to deal with the texts themselves, rather than with *scholarship of the texts*. To provide background for my chapter on the quest of the historical Jesus, I discuss such problems as different chronological orders and apparent inconsistencies between the accounts, and I indicate how some scholars approach these concerns. In Chapter 3, my focus will be less on the texts themselves than on scholarship of them. However, there is overlap between these chapters, especially as I cannot resist including my own opinion on some of the questions involved. Hopefully, this will serve as an appetizer for my later chapter.

## Gospel languages

Obviously, the formation of the canon was itself controversial. Many expressed scepticism about the status of the books of Hebrews, Jude, 2 Peter, 2 and 3 John and Revelation, as well as about the Gospel of John. Some wanted to include the Epistle of Barnabas. From 367 CE, when the great Alexandrian theologian Athanasius (296–373 CE) listed the books that now form the Christian canon, its contents have been universally agreed. The Gospels were written in Greek (according to early tradition Matthew had originally used Hebrew [see Augustine cited in Schaff, 1991, pp. 78–80]). Jesus probably spoke Aramaic, although he may also have known Hebrew. Paul says that he heard the voice of the risen Jesus speaking to him 'in Hebrew' (Acts 26:14). Jesus may even have known Greek (see Funk *et al.*, 1993, pp. 27–8), given the proximity of several Hellenic cities. According to tradition, Jesus' mother was born in nearby Sepphoris (about an hour's walk from Nazareth). Some surmise that as a carpenter or stonemason, Jesus may well have laboured in his maternal grandparents' city. *The Infant Gospel of Thomas* has Jesus learning first Greek, then Hebrew (14:1). This also opens up the possibility, discussed in Chapter 3, that Jesus may have been aware of the teachings of the Cynics. Others suggest that he also had access to the teachings of Socrates, Plato and Aristotle.

A little Aramaic survives in the Gospels, such as *Talitha cu'mi* in Mark 5:41, *Eph'phatha* ('be opened') at Mark 7:34 and Jesus' characteristic way of addressing God as *Abba* (Father). The consensus is that Jesus had not known Greek, or very much Greek, which means that the accounts of his life were written in a language that their subject had not himself spoken. It can be argued, then, that cross-cultural translation is built into the very make-up of the tradition itself. Sanneh (1996) claims that:

Christians are unique in abandoning the original language of Jesus and instead adopting the Greek 'koine' and Latin in its 'vulgar' as the central media of the Church. . . . Thus it is that translation, and its attendant cross-cultural implications, come to be built into the historical make-up of Christianity. (p. 48)

The four Gospels vary in length (Mark is the shortest), but none are lengthy in comparison with the oldest biography of Muhammad, by Ibn Ishaq, which in English translation runs to 600 pages (Guillaume, 1955). This text, though, falls into the category of extra-scriptural material known as *hadith*, that is, accounts of Muhammad's deeds and words.

### Manuscript evidence

There is no shortage of ancient manuscripts in existence: 'No other piece of ancient literature has such an abundance of manuscript witnesses as does the New Testament' (*New International Version*, 1973, Preface). Thus, the *NIV* was able to make use of eclectic sources. About 270 vellum scripts of the canonical gospels date from between the fourth and twelve centuries. About eighty-eight papyrus fragments, such as the Hulleatt fragments, have been dated from between the second and fourth centuries. In comparison, there is just one ancient manuscript copy of Tacitus, and this appears to be from the twelfth century (see Wilson, 1985, p. 29). On the other hand, there are no extant original copies of any of the Gospels, which leads Robert Funk to question, 'Why, if God took such pains to preserve an inerrant text for posterity, did the spirit not provide for the preservation of original copies of the gospels' (Funk *et al.*, 1993, p. 6). Funk, founder of the Jesus Seminar (see Chapter 3), was reacting against the view that, as a result of divine inspiration, the text of the Christian canon is 'without error'.

## Translations

Sanneh's observation, cited above, about the translatability of the Gospel should not be taken to imply that Christians have always readily accepted the work of translators. Early renditions, known as the Old Latin versions, were made from Greek into Latin in North Africa and South Gaul. They differed 'greatly among themselves', yet came to enjoy considerable popularity (Cross and Livingstone, 1983, p. 996). Indeed, they became so popular that when Jerome produced his new translation in 384, it encountered a rather hostile reception. Other early translations were made into Coptic, Syriac and Ethiopic (the languages of ancient Christian communities in Egypt, Syria and Ethiopia). Eventually, the Vulgate (a later revision of Jerome's work) was declared to be the only true version; a papal bull of 1590 pronounced that its text was unalterable.

This privileging of a Latin text meant that the masses, who did not know Latin, were unable to have direct access to their scriptures. Priests, preaching in the vernacular, had to interpret the Gospel for them. When reformers attempted to produce vernacular texts in German and English, they faced persecution. The issue, says Funk, was 'whether the Bible was to be made accessible to the general population, or whether it was to become the private province of theological scholars and the clergy' (in Funk et al., 1993, p. xvii). William Tyndale (1494–1536), translator of the Bible into English, lost his job when he told his bishop that he *would* render the Bible into English and that when he had done so a ploughman would know the Bible better than the bishop did. Tyndale was brutally executed for his audacity in attempting to make the Bible available to anyone literate in English. Copies of his translations were burned.

After the English Reformation, the translation known as the Authorized, or King James, Version (1611), gradually gained the type of authority that the Vulgate had enjoyed (and continued to enjoy until the nineteenth century) among Catholics. Indeed, I know no few Christians for whom the King James Version *is* the Bible, and for whom more recent translations are scandalous. As Funk puts it, 'Many English speaking people are not even cognizant that the original languages of the Bible were Hebrew and Greek' (*ibid*). Similarly, in Bangladesh, the high Bengali translation derived from the efforts of the pioneer Baptist missionary, William Carey, remains for most Bangladeshi Christians *the* Bible, and more modern, 'common language' translations are looked on with suspicion. Yet it is also true that translations have had a powerful impact; they make Jesus real and relevant to the world in which the reader or hearer lives. Pelikan (1985) praises Luther's German translation:

The outcome was a depiction of Jesus marked by such freshness of language that Jesus became a sixteenth century contemporary. To hearers who cooed sentimentally over the infant Jesus and clucked over his poverty, 'If only I had been there!

How quick I would have been to help the Baby!' Luther retorted, 'Why don't you do it now? You have Christ in your neighbor.' (p. 161)

While, as noted above, translations have not always had a positive reception, their eventual acceptance and popularity testifies to Christianity's belief in the *translatability* of the Gospel into different languages and cultures. This contrasts with Islam. The Qur'an is only the Qur'an, God's eternal word, *when recited and heard in Arabic*. Renditions into other languages are technically 'interpretations', not translations. Muslims speak about the *untranslatability* of the Qur'an, which has no parallel in Christian discourse.

### Gospel origins

I now examine the process by which the Gospel texts as we have them were compiled. From the early days of Christianity through to the Enlightenment, the Bible was 'off-limits, too sacred for . . . secular scholarship' to question its divine authorship, or inspiration (Sanders, 1993, p. 5). The creation account, for example, was taken as literally true. It was generally accepted that the Gospels were, if not eyewitness accounts, at least factual and accurate records of the life of a man called Jesus. It was commonly accepted as fact that Jesus was born in Bethlehem, had grown up in Nazareth, began to preach at the age of 30, and spent three years teaching and performing miracles. He had also selected twelve disciples as members of his immediate circle, had challenged the legalistic notion of righteousness prevalent in his day, and had finally faced crucifixion in order to die a redemptive, sacrificial death for all humankind.

Three days after this undeserved and cruel crucifixion, he had surprised even his closest disciples by rising from the dead. This proved to them, as it has proved to many subsequent believers, that he was the Son of God and universal saviour. What began as a sect within Judaism quickly became an international religious movement. Internal inconsistencies within the Gospel narratives did cause some consternation, but few if any expressed much doubt that the above represented a factually true biographical sketch of Jesus' life. References to places that Jesus had visited, as well as to historical personages such as Herod, Pilate and Quirinius, the Governor of Syria, seemed to give the Gospels a historical, authentic ring. Inconsistencies (see below) for their part were rather like the minor variations that occur in different journalists' reports of the same event. In a classic text such as Augustine's *The Harmony of the Gospel*, differences were not viewed as a major flaw:

And however they may appear to have kept each of them a certain order of narration proper to himself, this certainly is not to be taken as if each individual writer chose to write in ignorance of what his predecessors had done. . . . But the fact is, that just as they received each of them the gift of inspiration, they abstained from alluding adding to their several labors any superfluous conjoint compositions. (Schaff, 1991, Vol. 6, p. 80)

Books that paralleled passages from the four Gospels, too, would have satisfied many that there was a great deal of agreement between them. For example, Edward Taylor (1642–1729) produced a four-volume *Harmony of the Gospels*, reproduced by Scholars' Facsimiles and Reprints as recently as 1983.

Since people believed in miracles, the supernatural aspects of the Gospels did not trouble them. Thus, Jesus *was greeted* by visiting dignitaries and by humble shepherds, *all guided by a star*, Jesus had *healed the sick and predicted his suffering and resurrection*. Christians believed that the gospel writers were divinely inspired in their task of writing. Therefore, their accounts were historically reliable (see 2 Timothy 3:16). Today, Christians who still hold this view are usually called 'fundamentalists'; fundamentalists believe in the inerrancy of scripture (that is, that there are no errors whatsoever in scripture). When scripture is referred to as 'infallible', the claim is being made that the four Gospels represent true, factual, historical accounts of Jesus' life. Some Christians believe in what they call their 'verbal, plenary inspiration'.

The term 'fundamentalist' derives from the World's Christian Fundamentalist Association, formed in the USA in 1919, and from a series of pamphlets, *The Fundamentals: A Testimony to the Truth* (1910–15). These set out the movement's core convictions: namely, the inerrancy of scripture, the divinity of Christ, the virgin birth, a substitutionary theory of the atonement (Jesus' death substituted for ours), and the physical resurrection and bodily return of Jesus (see my summary of traditional Christian understanding of Jesus in Chapter 2). Volume 1 began, 'It is well known that the last ten or twenty years have been marked by a determined assault upon the virgin birth' (Orr, 1910, Vol. 1, p. 7). Contributors to the journal were scathing in their rejection of what they called 'higher criticism'. James Grey (1910) wrote, 'The Bible as we now have it, in its various translations and revisions, when freed from all the errors and mistakes of the translators, copyists and printers, is the very word of God, and consequently wholly without error' (Vol. 3, p. 41).

There are many Christians (including myself) who do not regard themselves as 'fundamentalist' but who believe that the Gospels represent substantially reliable historical accounts of Jesus' life. Where I and others critique the fundamentalist position is that it effectively adds a fourth partner to the Godhead to become God, Son, Spirit and Gospel. In my view, for Christians, God's 'word' became flesh in Jesus, who is still God's living word. The gospel writings represent human attestation to that 'word', and, as such, may err, even though I do not personally think that the writers or compilers deliberately altered their material. Rather, I think that information, sayings, parables, stories of Jesus' death, were passed on from person to person with integrity and honesty, until this material was used by the gospel writers. This, too, was within an environment that had long treasured its oral Torah.

## The 'Q' hypothesis

From about the mid-nineteenth century, Christian scholarly consensus has accepted that the four canonical gospels made use of earlier material. Some material – stories or sayings of Jesus – was oral, some information was probably remembered by the gospel writers themselves, but it is thought that they also had access to written sources. What scholars debate is the extent to which this material was not only shaped by the life situation, struggles and aspirations of the early Christian community, but also *fabricated* by it. Some scholars view the latter as wilful deceit, others as the accidental result of commentary and interpretation becoming confused with what Jesus actually said. The very earliest Christian scriptures were probably collections of sayings of Jesus, and stories about him, grouped into topics, such as sayings about the Kingdom of God, or about 'the poor', the miracle stories or nativity tales (see Sanders, 1993, p. 59).

An early collection of such base-sayings is believed to lie behind the Gospels of Matthew and Luke. Scholars call this 'Quelle', usually shortened to 'Q'. Funk *et al.* (1993) comment that 'The general acceptance of the 'Q' hypothesis by scholars became another of the pillars of scholarly wisdom' (p. 13). Detective work can piece 'Q' together; Burton L. Mack offers a version in *The Lost Gospel: The Book of Q and Christian Origins* (1993). Although the 'Q' hypothesis is widely accepted, some stress that its existence is only hypothetical (see Johnson, 1996, p. 138).

A gospel of signs may lie behind John's Gospel (see Funk *et al.*, 1993, p. 545, and Fortna, 1970). This process parallels the later collections of Muhammad's acts and sayings, the *hadith*. The earliest collections of *hadith* had no particular order but were identified by the name of their collectors. Later, the sayings were grouped under topics. Until the canon was agreed towards the end of the second century, there were many collections of Jesus' sayings available to early Christians, and Christians were free to prefer some of these over others. Only later were they told which they had to prefer, or face excommunication.

The most primitive scriptures were 'Q'-type sayings and stories, with no attempt to construct anything like a time-line of Jesus' life. The non-canonical *Gospel of Thomas* may represent a very early example of a 'Q'-type text. As we have noted, it also has no chronology. Mack (1993) claims that the close relationship between *Thomas* and 'Q' 'proved the existence of the genre in early Christian circles' (p. 34). Thomas does contain 'sayings' that help us to identify material in the four canonical texts as 'authentic' but, as I have already established, it adds nothing to our knowledge of the details of Jesus' life.

## The preaching of the early Church

Several examples of what scholars call the *kerygma*, or early preaching of the Church about Jesus, are found in the New Testament Book of Acts;

for example, Peter's speech on the day of Pentecost. This begins with a passage from Joel, which Peter cites to claim that prophecy has been fulfilled in and through the life of Jesus, then proceeds:

Jesus of Nazareth was a man accredited by God with many miracles . . . with the help of wicked men, he was put to death by being nailed to the Cross. But God raised him . . . because it was impossible for death to . . . hold . . . him.

Next, there is an extended section on resurrection, with two passages attributed to King David (again linking Jesus with Israel's salvation history). Then comes the punch line: 'Therefore let all Israel repent and be baptized.' This speech does not give much detail about Jesus' life, but Peter may rightly have assumed that people already knew something about this; 'as you yourselves know,' he said.

Later, speaking to a Gentile (non-Jewish) audience, he supplied more detail, although he could apparently still take some prior knowledge for granted: 'You know what has happened throughout Galilee after the baptism that John preached – how God anointed Jesus of Nazareth with the Holy Spirit . . . how he went around doing good and healing' (Acts 10:37f.). Again, Peter continues with the resurrection story. This time he does not have to invite his hearers to repent, because the Spirit had already come upon them. 'Can anyone prevent these people from being baptized?' he asked. Some preachers may have added examples of Jesus' good deeds to flesh out the middle section. What I find interesting about these speeches is that they were messages *about Jesus* (about the significance of his life, death and resurrection) and not speeches *about what Jesus had said*.

Jesus' own words are conspicuous by their absence. These may have followed later, as part of post-baptismal instruction, when the pastors of the early Christian community may have used examples of Jesus' teaching to help to nurture the flock. Scholars suppose that since the first Christians expected Jesus' imminent return, little effort was made, initially, to write much down. As time passed, and the 'delay' in the return was accepted, some began to write down material in the form of the collections referred to above, the 'Q'-type sayings. Later still, surmises Sanders (1993), 'Some Christians decided that they might after all need connected accounts of Jesus' (p. 59). He thus describes a four-stage process: first, units of material used in preaching were collected; second, related material was formed into pericopes; third, proto-Gospels were written, such as 'Q', possibly also *Thomas*; fourth, Matthew, Mark, Luke and John emerged (p. 60).

## Chronology and geography

If the early 'sayings' collections neglect chronology and geographical context, how did the fuller scheme contained in the four Gospels emerge? In my view, it is possible to construct a simple, threefold scheme from the primitive *kerygma* cited above (the speeches in Acts):

First, Jesus appears, and is announced as one anointed by God, often with reference here to John the Baptist and to Hebrew scripture;

second, Jesus moves about preaching, healing, and doing good;

third, he is crucified, dies, and rises.

There are also some geographical references: Galilee is the location of Jesus' activities in the middle section (where he went about doing good); the third section moves the location to Jerusalem (Acts 10:39).

Sanders' last two stages involved attempting to piece material into some sort of chronological order, using the primitive threefold scheme as a framework. Scholars suggest, though, that much of what at first sight seems to be chronological in the Gospels, such as 'immediately' or 'that evening', are in fact narrative devices 'to give pace and drive to the account' (Sanders, 1993, p. 73). The actual context with which a saying, or act, had been associated may well have been forgotten. Sanders goes so far as to say that 'Jesus' words and deeds were pulled out of their original context (in his own career) and thrust into another context, the disciples' preaching and teaching' (p. 59). Funk *et al.* (1993) suggest that Jesus 'must have repeated many of his witticisms many times', so not surprisingly the disciples 'did not remember the particular occasion on which Jesus first uttered a saying' (p. 21). Thus, contexts were 'created': 'the evangelists frequently relocate sayings and parables or invent new narrative contexts for them' (*ibid.*, p. 19).

Many scholars, such as Bultmann and the Jesus Seminar Fellows, believe that the process of 'clustering and contexting' included adding interpretive commentary to the original sayings: 'The evangelists frequently expand sayings or parables, or provide them with an interpretive overlay or comment' (*ibid.*, p. 21). Typically, as I demonstrate in Chapter 3, scholars think that the commentaries on, or explanations of, Jesus' parables were added by *Christian writers*, derived from their own sermons (which they believed to be inspired). There is another parallel here with traditions about Muhammad; what interested the narrators was their universal significance, not their geographical specificity. In the *hadith* more often than not, no specific context is mentioned; we read, 'one day, a beggar came to Muhammad and . . .', but we do not know where or when this incident took place.

## Mark's Gospel

Most scholars accept that Mark's Gospel was the first attempt to flesh out this framework (although the early Church dated Matthew first). The Gospels were written anonymously. The traditional identity of their authors derives from the guesswork of the early Church Fathers; Sanders deems this 'second century academic/detective work quite shrewd' (1993, p. 65). Tradition says that Mark wrote at the request of Peter, and drew largely from Peter's memories. On three occasions, he reports incidents that were witnessed only by Peter, James and John (see Baxter, 1988, p. 25). This may explain why Mark has something of a firsthand feel; I well remember my New Testament Greek lecturer at Manchester, Dr Eric Hull, pointing out such details as Jesus' cushion in the stern of the boat (Mark 4:38), 'taking little children in the crook of his arm (9:36) . . . striding ahead of his disciples, a great lonely figure, wholly absorbed in his Passion, on the road to Jerusalem (10.32)' (Hunter, 1972, p. 43).

Mark's Gospel is usually dated from about 66–70 (see Theissen, 1987, p. 189; Hunter, 1972, p. 39). While some parables on the same topic (for example, about the Kingdom of God) (see Mark, Chapter 4) are grouped together out of geographical and chronological sequence, other material is given a specific location. This probably reflects common knowledge that Jesus had spent time in Capernaum (which features in all four Gospels), or around Caesarea Philippi, as well as having preached throughout Galilee. This suggests to me that while some material was divorced from its original context, some remained associated with geographical locations where Jesus was known to have spent time. Mark seems to follow the threefold scheme, and divides neatly into three sections:

(1) In a preliminary section, Jesus is announced by John, who baptizes him. Then Jesus begins to preach (1:1–14).
(2) He moves around Galilee (the travel section, which ends with the journey to Jerusalem) (1:14 – 11:1).
(3) The trial and crucifixion, which cover a shorter time-scale, but take up one-third of the Gospel (11:1 – 16:8).

All four Gospels focus on Jesus' active, public career and contain nothing resembling a detailed, year-on-year description of what Jesus did, whom he studied under, who he knew, where he went. This was not uncommon in biographical works of the period, however; Morton Smith (1978) comments, 'Like most ancient biographies the gospels . . . had nothing much to say about their heroes' childhood and adolescence except a story or two attesting precocious powers' (p. 96; see also p. 108). Talbert (1977) similarly argues that the Gospels belong to an ancient genre of hero biographies. This genre, says Talbert, 'is prose narration about a person's life, presenting supposedly historical facts which are selected to reveal the character or essence of the individual, often with the purpose of affecting the behavior of the reader' (p. 17). I return to the Gospels as bona fide biographies in Chapter 3.

## Matthew and Luke

This geographical scheme was utilized by the later Gospels of Luke and Matthew (Tatum, 1999, pp. 62, 67). The generally accepted sequence is that Mark's Gospel is the oldest, followed by Luke and Matthew at about the same time (between 70 and 80; see Hunter, 1972, pp. 50, 56). Both

Matthew and Luke used Mark and 'Q', as well as some additional material of their own (see Funk *et al.*, 1993, pp. 14–16). These three are known as the 'synoptics'; that is, they share a common synopsis, or summary. The chronology of all three is roughly identical: Jesus started preaching after John had baptized him, moving through Galilee; then, after a turning point in his ministry, he travelled to Jerusalem to confront the authorities. The three synoptics agree not only in their general outline but often in their detail as well. However, there are inconsistencies. Jesus' comparison of himself with a child (Mark 9:36f.; Matthew 18:1–7; Luke 9:46–50) is *late* in Mark's and Matthew's narratives but *early* in Luke's account (see Sanders, 1993, p. 61). In Mark and Luke, Jesus healed the leper *after* he had stayed in the house of Simon Peter; Matthew has him healing the leper, *then* going to Peter's house (see Matthew 8, Mark 1, Luke 4). Matthew has the Roman centurion whose servant Jesus heals encountering him *face to face*; Luke says they communicated via *intermediaries* (see Matthew 8, Luke 7; also Wilson, 1954, pp. 30–1). Matthew and Luke give genealogies; Luke traces Jesus' descent (not very convincingly) to Adam, Matthew to Abraham. Mark lacks nativity stories, and his account of the resurrection ends with the women saying 'nothing to anyone because they were afraid' (Mark 16:8).

Sometimes, Mark lacks the details provided by Matthew and Luke; he covers Jesus' temptation in a single sentence; Matthew uses up eleven verses, Luke thirteen. Matthew does not appear to have Joseph and Mary travelling in order to reach Bethlehem; Luke places them in Nazareth, so they had to travel to get there. Only Matthew has the flight to Egypt (widely dismissed as pure invention; see Chapter 3). As I show later, different details in the resurrection stories were much discussed in nine-teenth-century literature; for example, in John, Mary Magdalene arrives *alone* at the empty tomb, while in Matthew and Luke she is accompanied by several other women. In Matthew, the women appear to be witnesses of the rolling back of the stone, whereas in the other accounts the tomb is already empty. Luke gives us two 'men/angels' while Matthew has one. The original Mark (which ends at 16:8) has no account of the ascension (Mark 16:9–20 were added later).

However, comparison of the three does indicate substantial agreement. Matthew reproduces about 90 per cent of Mark, supplemented with additional material (often biblical references); Luke has more independent material but replicates about half of Mark. There is also material common to Matthew and Luke but which is not found in Mark, which leads scholars to suppose that these 200 or so verses derive from 'Q'. When either Luke or Matthew deviates from Mark, the other agrees with Mark (see the leper example cited above). Thus a great deal of material has double attestation (see Hunter, 1972, p. 29). Attestation by more than one source is widely used as an indication of authenticity, although (see Chapter 3) other criteria often take priority. Some discrepancies, too, do not seem to me to be all that significant. For example, all three agree that

Jesus healed a leper and did so at about the time he was staying at Peter's house; I can almost hear the disciples arguing the point: 'No, that was just before . . .'; 'No, I distinctly remember that our Master went to Peter's house after . . .'.

The discrepancy about the centurion is harder to resolve. Differences in the account of Jesus' trial, or trials (in Mark and Matthew a Jewish trial is followed by a Roman trial, while Luke adds a trial before Herod), may arise because these are not firsthand accounts. The disciples were not present (see Sanders, 1993, pp. 269f. and discussion in Chapter 3). Thus the gospel writers could not have derived this information from the apostles. Sometimes, what is obviously the same parable has a different meaning. For example, in Matthew the 'lost sheep' is a new Christian who has strayed from the faith and who ought to be coaxed back (see Matthew 18:12–14). In Luke, the lost sheep is someone who is unsaved. Thus, the parable encourages Christians to preach the gospel to those who have not yet accepted Jesus (see Luke 15:4–7). In *The Gospel of Thomas*, the lost sheep is described as 'the biggest', and when the shepherd finds him, he says, 'I love you more than the ninety-nine.' Here, the lost sheep is the one who possesses *gnosis*, the gem among stones (see James, 1924a, p. 107).

Minor errors do not necessarily discredit a whole narrative. Mark may not have had access to the nativity stories (he almost certainly did not have 'Q' in front of him). Further, if he was fleshing out the threefold scheme of the Church's *kerygma*, he (like the preachers) would begin with Jesus as God's anointed. John, too, after his prologue, which takes the reader right back to creation, launches into the beginning of Jesus' adult ministry. On the other hand, Luke may have had a special relationship with Mary (Jesus' mother), who 'treasured all these things in her heart' (Luke 2:51) and, for some reason of her own, she may only have spoken of these events at a much later date. Material on Jesus' bias towards the poor, outcasts, Samaritans and women features prominently in Luke. This seems to reflect his own preferred 'image' of Jesus as open to outsiders, including foreigners and the socially marginalized. Luke also wrote the first history of the early Church, the Acts of the Apostles, and apparently shared some of Paul's journeys (see the so-called 'we passages': Acts 16:9–18; 20:5–15; 21:1–18; 27:1–28:16).

Both narratives are self-consciously historical; Luke is anxious to locate his narrative in world affairs by referring to such people as Caesar Augustus, Quirinius (Luke 2:1–2), Felix (Acts 23, 24) and King Agrippa (Acts 25). His style is more polished than Mark's. He also speaks of having 'carefully investigated everything' and of attempting to render 'an orderly account' (Luke 1:3). His Gospel and Acts are dedicated to Theophilus, which suggests that he had a Gentile readership in mind. Luke is often described as a gospel for *Gentiles*, which also reminded them of Christianity's Jewish roots; Matthew is contrasted as a gospel for *Jews*, which reminds them that Christianity is also a faith for the entire world.

Matthew's eagerness to depict events in Jesus' life as fulfilling Hebrew prophecy attracts a great deal of comment in Chapter 3. At Matthew 2:23 he cites a text that no one can identify: 'So was fulfilled what was said through the prophet, "He will be called a Nazarene"', while at 21:7, he supplies two animals for Jesus' ride into Jerusalem when one would have sufficed. Geza Vermes appears to think that Matthew was a Greek; otherwise why would he not have understood 'the Hebrew parallelism of Zechariah (an ass = the young of a she-ass)' (1973, p. 145)?

## The fourth Gospel

John's Gospel is traditionally dated as the latest. It may not have drawn on the earlier Gospels, since it presents a quite different geographical and chronological scheme. In John, Jesus makes several trips to Jerusalem (2:13; 5:1; 7:10; 10:22), where he created the incident in the Temple *early*, not *late*, in his career. John does not describe Jesus' baptism, the Lord's Supper, the transfiguration or the ascension. In John, Jesus is crucified on the day *before* Passover. His public ministry lasts for three years, compared with one in the synoptics. The most striking difference is stylistic; he has no parables. Instead, his Jesus delivers long discourses, within which the distinctive 'I am' sayings are found (e.g. 6:35, 8:12, 11:25).

Sanders (1993) concludes that it is 'impossible to think that Jesus spent his short ministry teaching in two such completely different ways' (p. 70). In his view, John's subject was the *Jesus of faith*, the Jesus who, through the Holy Spirit, taught John directly: 'John's view of Jesus was strongly trans-historical; the boundaries of ordinary history were inadequate' (p. 71). 'Meditations on the person and work of Christ are,' says Sanders, 'presented in the first person.' Tatum (1999) agrees: 'the discourses of Jesus in John must be attributed to the creativity of the Gospel writer and his community' (p. 78). Strauss (see Chapter 3 below) argued that 'the discourses in John's gospel are mainly the free composition of the Evangelist' (cited in Hodgson, 1972, p. xxxix). Renan (1927) wrote that John 'puts into the mouth of Jesus discourses of which the tone, the style, the treatment, and the doctrines have nothing in common with . . . the synoptics' (p. 43).

Of the 'I am' sayings, the Jesus Seminar concluded that 'in virtually every case, the reader is being confronted with the language of the evangelists and not the language of Jesus'. In their view, the 'I am' sayings reflect a formula 'widely used in the Greco-Roman world' for 'speech attributed to one of the Gods. It is even possible,' they continue, 'that the author alludes to the famous self-revelation of God . . . in Exodus 3:14' (Funk *et al.*, 1993, p. 419). This would also explain why John is characterized by 'openness' about Jesus' identity: he is 'the son of the father', while the synoptics keep his identity a secret: 'and he told them to tell nobody who he was'. John's Gospel, then, was written as *a theological manual for insiders*. Clement dubbed John 'a spiritual gospel' (cited in Eusebius, Vol. VI, pp. xiv, 5–7). Augustine thought it the most sublime of the four. Others call it the gospel of love.

I am not altogether convinced, though, that an accomplished communicator who, on the one hand, could teach common people, fishermen and farmers, using analogies from their workaday world, could not, in a different context, deliver philosophical discourses. A comparison here may perhaps be made with the German theologian Karl Barth, whose *Church Dogmatics* (1936–77) gives us complex German sentences and sophisticated theological language, but whose *New Sermons from Basel Prison* (1967) are written in straightforward and easy-to-understand prose. Personally, I find the latter much easier to understand than the *Dogmatics*, which may be why my professor at Manchester, Richard Hanson, expected us to read them in German. Many of the parables were preached to large crowds (see e.g. Mark 3:20; 4:1), while in John the audience for at least some of the long discourses was the disciples; see John 13, 14, 15, 16, 17, which are all directed to the twelve.

Scholars point out that the style of Jesus' discourses in John resembles that of the prologue, which is clearly the writer's own introduction to the story. The implication is thus that the writer composed Jesus' discourses as well as the prologue. In my view, it is at least possible that the opposite is true: that the writer composed his prologue in the style of discourses that Jesus had actually delivered. On the other hand, Jesus' references to himself are more veiled in the synoptics, where there is hardly any use of the first person. For example, in Matthew, speaking about his own death, Jesus says, 'the Son of Man is going to suffer . . .' (17:12; I am assuming here that Jesus identified himself as the Son of Man, which many scholars reject). Only in John does Jesus say 'I'.

## The status of John

The difference between the 'synoptics' and John certainly troubled the early Church. Consequently, John was probably the last to be given canonical status. Irenaeus defended the choice of four with his famous, if illogical, reference to the four points of the compass:

But it is not possible that the Gospels can not be either more or fewer in number. . . . Since there are four zones of the world . . . and four principal winds . . . the Word . . . gave us the gospel, fourfold under four forms but bound together by one spirit. (Stevenson, 1963, p. 122)

However, as B. H. Streeter (1874–1937) demonstrated, there *is* some overlap between Luke and John; compare Luke 22:3 with John 13:2, and Luke 10:38–42 with John 11:1. John's different chronology may be *theologically* justified.

All the gospel writers have allowed their theology to shape their material: Luke's universal Christ Jesus has his ancestry traced back to Adam, Son of

God; Matthew's Jewish Jesus has his traced back to the father of the covenant, Abraham, via David. The synoptics all have a dramatic turning point when, perhaps convinced that he had to force some response in Jerusalem, Jesus begins the journey towards the capital (Mark 8; Matthew 16; Luke 9). They do not mention other visits. This does not necessarily mean that Jesus did not make any; rather, reference is omitted because these lay outside of the dramatic framework. John's framework did not need a dramatic turning point; being more open about Jesus' identity, he gradually unfolds the truth about the one who has come as light into the darkness.

Sanders dismisses John as a useful source for any historical Jesus study (1993, p. 65). The Jesus Seminar's second pillar of wisdom is that 'the synoptic gospels [are] much closer to the historical Jesus than the Fourth Gospel' (Funk *et al.*, 1993, p. 3). As Chapter 3 will show, they attribute nothing in John to the lips of Jesus (see *ibid.*, p. 10). On the other hand, John A. T. Robinson (1919–83) proposed that John may actually be the earliest of the four Gospels. Commenting that it is odd that the writers failed to gloat even just a little over the fulfilment of Jesus' prediction that the Temple would not remain standing, he believes that all four must pre-date 70 CE. He writes, 'I do not believe that there is anything in the language even of the Johanine prologue which demands a date later than the 60s' (Robinson, 1976, p. 284). If they were writing after 70 CE, surely the four would have had Jesus predicting the Temple's destruction by fire, not by dismantling.

Robinson even deems John's father–son language to be 'nearer to the original parabolic source of this . . . language and its Hebrew understanding . . . than any other part of the New Testament'. Schillebeeckx (1980) also concedes that 'more historical material can be derived from John' than he had allowed (in his *Jesus* (1979)). Joseph Ernest Renan (1823–92) thought that John's graphic description of the passion had about it the touch of eyewitness recollection, and suggested that John may have set out, at a later date, to correct vexing inaccuracies which he found in the earlier gospels. The discourses were 'not authentic. . . . But what about statements of fact?' he asked (Schweitzer, 1998b, p. 182; for Renan, see Chapter 4 of this book). Here, Sanders also thinks that John's account may represent the more probable sequence of events: 'the vaguer account of John seems better to correspond with the way things actually worked' (1985, p. 318).

## Buddhist influence?

In addition to speculation about Gnostic influence in John, scholars have also identified possible borrowing from Indian sources. For example, the scene in which Jesus walks on water resembles an incident in the Buddha's life. J. Duncan Derrett, in his recent article in the *Journal of the Royal Asiatic Society*, sees borrowings in the notion of Jesus leading people from 'darkness into light', which, he says, 'is an Upanishadic notion which the Buddha [also] accepted'. Derrett claims that 'few doubt that the starting story of Jesus' conversation with the Samaritan woman (John 4) has found a place as a tale of the Buddha's favourite disciple, Ananda's conversation with an untouchable woman found in the Divyavadana', and asks, 'How did the parallel arise?' (1999, pp. 279–80); Vivekananda (1963, Vol. 4, p. 418) draws attention to the same parallel). I visit discussion of other similarities between the parables of Jesus and the teaching of the Buddha in Chapter 6.

When similarities are discovered between different cultures, scholars will inevitably attempt to explain this phenomenon. One obvious explanation is that, at some point, contact occurred between these cultures. Pagels does not rule out Buddhist and Hindu influence on the Gnostic corpus. She cites the eminent Buddhologist Edward Conze (1904–79): 'Buddhists were in contact with Thomas Christians (that is, Christians who knew and used such writings as the Gospel of Thomas) in South India.' Pagels thinks it likely that Buddhist missionaries 'had been proselytizing in Alexandria' when Gnosticism was flourishing between 80 and 200 CE (1979, pp. xx–xxi). This possibility cannot be dismissed. Another, more theological explanation is the claim that the teachings of all true spiritual masters derive from the same source. This, of course, is a possibility that those who restrict religious truth to their own tradition will automatically reject. I discuss these possibilities again, in Chapter 6 and in my conclusion.

## What did Jesus look like?

I ended the equivalent chapter of my *In Search of Muhammad* with a detailed description of the Prophet's physical appearance. This is well documented in the Muhammad sources. In contrast, none of the Gospels tells us anything about what Jesus looked like. On the other hand, while Islam adopted a negative attitude towards the visual representation of the human image, especially of Muhammad's (although these do exist), Christians have long since painted and sculpted Jesus' image. Some Christian artists have tried to depict Jesus, and his background, as authentically first-century Jewish. Others have minimized anything Jewish, instead depicting Jesus as a child of their own time and as a product of their own culture. Sometimes Jesus looks like a European, while everyone else around him has a hooked nose and devilish features, since they are all bad Jews (see many of the images in the 1999 Biography.com video *The Unknown Jesus*, presented by Jack Perkins). Muslim descriptions of Jesus will be cited in Chapter 5.

A letter which claims to be from the Roman consul Publius Lentulus to Caesar Tiberius does describe Jesus. Thought to be a thirteenth-century forgery, this represents an idealized portrait of the perfect human individual:

There lives . . . a man of singular virtue whose name is Jesus Christ . . . his followers love and admire him and adore him. . . . He calls men back from the dead and heals all sorts of disease. He is a tall man, well shaped . . . his hair of a color that can hardly be matched, falling into graceful curls. . . . His forehead high, large and imposing; his cheeks without a spot or wrinkle, beautiful with a lovely red; his nose and mouth formed with an exquisite symmetry . . . his eyes bright, blue, clear and serene. Look innocent, dignified, manly and mature. In proportion of body most perfect, and captivating; his arms and hands delectable to behold. (Downloaded from http:/www.answers.org/Bible/Descripion.html)

There is some resemblance between this description and the image that appears on the Turin Shroud. Others, alluding to Isaiah 53:2, have speculated that Jesus' appearance may have been rather unremarkable, even unattractive: 'he had no form or comeliness that we should look at him, no beauty that we should desire him.'

People followed Jesus not because of his physical good looks but because they recognized a quality in him that transcended the physical. Celsus, the early anti-Christian polemicist (see Chapter 4), reported: 'They claim that Jesus' body was just like the next man's, or was little, ugly, and repugnant' (Hoffmann, 1987, p. 105). Chapter 2 establishes the traditional Christian image of Jesus. I argue that when Christians peruse the Gospels, they see Jesus through the lens of what they already believe to be true about him. For Christians, the Jesus of the Bible and the Christ of faith merge, and the Christ of faith *is* the Jesus of history.

# 2 Christians on Jesus: The Traditional View

> It is necessary . . . to begin with the caution that every later picture of Jesus is in fact not a picture based on an unretouched Gospel original, but a picture of what in the New Testament is already a picture. (Pelikan, 1985, p. 10)

In this and in my next chapter I turn in more detail to debate, within Christianity, about the authenticity and reliability of the gospel record and the development of a Christian image, or images, of Jesus. In Chapter 1, I described the sources available to us for any study of Jesus, of his life, teaching and significance. Although my aim was to be descriptive, in practice I found it impossible to avoid raising issues of gospel criticism, thus anticipating the subject matter of this chapter. Over the past four hundred years especially, gospel criticism has developed into a complex and sophisticated science. This science has three subdivisions: source, form and redaction criticism. Source criticism attempts to penetrate behind the gospel accounts as they appear in the New Testament to identify what 'sources' were available to the compilers. As outlined in Chapter 1, these 'sources' include 'Q', a signs gospel and a miracles gospel, as well as material peculiar to each writer (referred to as special Mark, special Matthew, special Luke). In describing gospel origins, I drew heavily on the work of source critics and at least implicitly endorsed their approach.

Form critics focus on how the material, such as the sayings of Jesus, was shaped or formed by the life situation of the early Church. The most radical form critics go so far as to say that much of the material in the Gospels was not merely shaped but invented by the early Christian community. This exactly parallels radical criticism of the materials available for Muhammad study, except that while radical form critics of the Muhammad material are all non-Muslim, radical form critics of the Jesus material include Christians in their number. Redaction criticism, writes Tatum, 'Can be defined as that discipline which seeks to discover the theology of each gospel writer and his situation by studying the ways he has edited his sources and composed his gospel' (1999, p. 49). Redaction criticism presupposes our ability to identify sources, as well as how their redactors handled this material. In this chapter, I start with the unfolding story of gospel criticism. My aim is to see how much of the gospel account different scholars, pursuing different approaches, actually accept, and what image of Jesus results from their work. My thesis is that how a scholar interprets the texts, and views Jesus, is predetermined by the assumptions that he or she brings to bear on their scrutiny of the gospel record.

It is now customary to divide the quest of the historical Jesus into four or five periods (see Tatum's chart, 1999, p. 109): pre-quest (pre-1778), old quest (1778–1906), no quest (1906–53), the new quest (post-1953) and the third, or renewed, quest (post-1985). Like most neat and tidy schemes, this one has its flaws. For example, there are some Christians today for whom the assumptions of the 'pre-quest' period still hold, while I shall identify scholars in the so-called 'no quest' period who continued to operate with the working assumptions of 'old questors'. However, for convenience I follow Tatum's chronological scheme.

## Pre-quest period: Christian belief about Jesus

This period begins with the origin of the Gospels themselves, as written records of the life of a first-century Jewish man called Jesus. The choice of Matthew, Mark, Luke and John from out of the many gospels available as the canonical four was, as already noted, dictated by what the majority party within the Church considered to be orthodox belief, or doctrine, about Jesus. During the first two centuries of Christian history, no official dogmas existed, since no universal authority or indeed mechanism existed to determine or to police right believing. By the time the canon was being finalized, this situation had changed. After Christianity became the official religion of the Roman state, replacing the pagan cultus, the state itself provided both the mechanism and the need for doctrinal conformity.

If a good citizen must also be a good Christian, some means of recognizing good Christians from bad Christians was needed by Church and state alike. It was thus the Roman emperors themselves who convened and chaired the early Christian councils (known as ecumenical councils) that met at Nicaea (325) and Chalcedon (451) to determine and promulgate official Christian doctrine. Controversy and debate needed to be replaced by a single creed. Almost all the issues on the table at both councils focused, in various ways, on the Church's understanding of Jesus. Exactly who was he? What was his relationship to God? What was his relationship to humanity? How were his death and resurrection to be understood? It is, however, important to note that for almost 300 years, until Nicaea, there were competing theologies about Jesus, not one, single, dominant creed.

## Jesus the Man-God

Early Christians referred to Jesus most typically as the Son of God. In the Gospels, the designation that Jesus himself appears to have preferred was the Son of Man. He uses this expression some ninety times. Critics surmise that the Church back-projected many of these passages, since they include verses in which Jesus predicts his own future. Others remark that had the Church invented the title, it is odd that it disappears from sight within the New Testament documents, where 'Son of God' is characteristically used of Jesus. I return to Jesus' titles several times in this book. However, at his baptism, a heavenly voice proclaimed that he was the 'Son of God' (in Luke, this voice speaks to the crowd; in Matthew and Mark, it is a private message for Jesus). During the temptation experience in the wilderness, Satan challenges him as the Son of God. In Mark 3 and Matthew 8 (and elsewhere), unclean spirits hail him as 'the Son of God'. At Caesarea Philippi, Peter confesses that he is 'the Christ, the Son of the living God', which, in the synoptic gospels, marks the dramatic turn towards Jerusalem. Throughout, Jesus refers to God as his 'Father'.

Assuming that these passages are not the creation of early Christians reading their theology back into the text (which is argued by many scholars, who reject the authenticity of all the passage cited above), Jesus did regard himself as God's Son. Later in this chapter, I will discuss how Jesus himself may have thought of his 'Sonship', but it appears that the early Church understood his Sonship in a literal sense. Jesus had had a human mother, Mary, but not a human father. God was his father. He had been conceived miraculously, while Mary was still a virgin. The idea that gods had human children was, of course, not unusual; the Greek gods produced children by human partners, for example, Hercules. In the Greek world, although Hercules was believed to have had the gift of strength, he was thought to be a mortal and not a god. Christians, however, appear at a very early stage to have added to the view that Jesus was God's son the conviction that Jesus was also God and had eternally existed. In other words, his life did not begin at his human birth; like God, his existence has no beginning and will have no end. Again, scholars argue that verses supporting this conviction were later inventions of the Church, and projected back into the Jesus story.

Perhaps most supportive of this theology, or Christology, is John's prologue, which many scholars view as the gospel writer's own theological gloss. Similarly, Jesus' references in John to his 'oneness' with the Father (John 14:10), and to 'returning to the Father' (John 16:28), can be dismissed as the gospel writer's own theological commentary. Indeed it is less easy to find verses in the synoptics to support the idea that Jesus' existence somehow pre-dated his human birth. What is clear, since this conviction is evident in St Paul's letters (which pre-date the Gospels), is that Christians decided at a very early date that Jesus had existed before his birth at Bethlehem (or Nazareth). In fact, several passages in Paul where this conviction appears may actually have been very early hymns which, sung by Christians, were incorporated by Paul into his text; for example, Colossians 1:15–19: 'He is the first born of all creation, for in him all things were created . . . in him all the fullness of God was pleased to dwell.' Another passage (often called a Christological hymn) in Philippians 2 adds the notion that Jesus' birth as a man had been a voluntary act: 'though he was in the form of God, he did not count equality with God a thing to be grasped, but emptied himself . . . being born in the likeness of man.'

It seems to me, in terms of both style and content, that these passages, and John's prologue, in which the eternal word through which God had created all things became flesh in Jesus, could easily have been derived from the same source. Lack of verses suggesting Jesus' pre-existence in the synoptics might well be considered odd, given that this conviction pre-dates their writing. Here, John actually seems to be closer to the thought world of the early Christian community than the synoptics. An explanation, offered in fact by theologians of the pre-quest period, is that each gospel writer had his own agenda. The synoptics appear more focused on the life and work of the man Jesus; John focuses on wider theological aspects of the Christ event (a term used to embrace the whole Jesus story).

It is largely in Paul, not in the Gospels, that we find the idea that Jesus was the second Adam, through whose perfect life, and sacrificial death on behalf of humanity, creation would be renewed: 'Then, as one man's trespass led to condemnation for all men, so one man's act of righteousness leads to acquittal and life for all men' (Romans 5:18). The Letter to the Hebrews develops further the concept of Jesus' death as a 'sacrifice': 'he entered once and for all into the Holy Place, taking not the blood of goats and calves but his own blood thus securing an eternal redemption' (Hebrews 9:12). Jesus, who had no sin, and who did not deserve death, died as a substitute for our human dying, bearing our sins on the cross (Hebrews 9:28). His resurrection then becomes the symbol of the 'new life' that is available to us all: 'so that as Christ was raised from the dead by the glory of the father we too might walk in newness of life' (Romans 6:4). The synoptics do reflect the conviction that Jesus had consciously carried out what he believed to be 'God's will'.

Thus, Jesus is depicted throughout as God's instrument, not as a free agent. He appears to accept his own suffering and death as inevitable – 'From that time Jesus began to show his disciples how he must go to Jerusalem and suffer many things' – although he also predicts his eventual victory, and his rising again after three days (Matthew 16:21). In addition, Jesus' life is regarded as a fulfilment of scripture, and of God's dealings with the Hebrew people. This is indicated in the text of the Gospels by such phases as 'This took place to fulfil what was spoken by the prophet' (Matthew 21:4). Paul of Tarsus, a Roman citizen, was an educated Hellenic Jew who also identified himself with the Pharisees. After persecuting Christians in the early chapters of Acts, he became a Christian, following a mystical encounter with the risen Christ, described in Acts 9. While Peter remained the chief apostle (based on Jesus' words at Matthew 16:18–19), Paul emerges as the new movement's intellectual leader. Acts suggests some tension between Peter, who was reluctant to abandon Jewish practices, and Paul, who wanted to encourage Gentiles to join the movement. The relationship between Paul and the Jewish Church emerges as a major theme in this book.

The text of the beautiful oratorio *The Messiah* (1741) by George Frederick Handel (1685–1759) is a good compendium of those Hebrew Bible verses that Christians apply to Jesus. Exactly how Jesus was fulfilling scripture is not always clear; what emerges is the impression that Jesus' coming was promised (for example, at Isaiah 7:14), and that he was in some sense the mediator of a new covenant spoken of in Jeremiah 31:31–3 (see Luke 22:20). Luke's birth narrative, which places great emphasis on Jesus' descent from David, clearly depicts him as the Messiah: 'to you is born this day in the City of David a Saviour, who is the Messiah, the Lord' (Luke 2:11). Throughout, there is a closer association between Jesus and the 'Spirit' (see John the Baptist's words at Luke 3:16) than there is between Jesus and the 'law' (the Mosaic law), thus linking Jesus with the promised 'new covenant' of Jeremiah 31:31–3 which would 'be written on . . . hearts'. Jesus appears to refer to this 'new covenant' at Luke 22:20, during the Last Supper: 'This cup which is poured out for you is the new covenant in my blood.' Ezekiel's references to a renewed Israel, too, seem to be not too far from the surface of the gospel narrative: 'I will put my spirit within you and you shall live' (Ezekiel 37:14). Jesus appears to have understood that his own work would somehow replace, or substitute for, the Jerusalem Temple; as Wright puts it, 'he saw himself as the place and means of doing, decisively and eschatologically, that for which the Temple had stood' (in Borg and Wright, 1999, p. 49). This is suggested by a verse such as Mark 14:58, where Jesus is reported to have said, 'I will destroy this temple that is made with hands, and in three days I will build another, not made with hands'. Jesus also said that 'mercy is better than sacrifice' (Matthew 12:7).

This sounds like a threat against the Temple building, but it actually represents a claim that Jesus' own body is the Temple, that he will die and rise again after three days. On the other hand, Mark 13:2 – 'there will not be any stones left standing one on another' – seems to predict the Temple's destruction. Jesus' calling of twelve disciples probably symbolized the twelve tribes of Israel; his followers were to be a new Israel. From a very early time, Christians have read the Jesus story through the hermeneutical lens of the 'suffering servant' in Isaiah 53: 'Surely he has borne our griefs and carried our sorrows . . . he was bruised for our iniquities.' Christians assume that Jesus self-consciously saw himself as the biblical suffering servant, probably combining this with the 'Son of Man' from Daniel 7 who, 'presented to the Ancient of Days', is given 'dominion and glory and kingdom' over 'all nations'.

Certainly, many passages referring to the Son of Man in the Gospels seem to have Daniel 7 in mind (see e.g. Matthew 24:29–31). In other words, Jesus knew that his death, which was inevitable, would have a vicarious significance for humanity and that he would thereafter receive vindication. This is suggested by the oft-repeated expression that Jesus (or the Son of Man) would 'enter glory' or be glorified. Christians would later say that the Son of God became the Son of Man, that is, perfectly human, or the servant of humanity, so that they could become children of God.

Again, it is in other Christian writing that the details of Jesus' relationship with the Mosaic law, with the Temple and with God's dealings with his chosen people are more fully articulated. Jesus is identified as the 'Messiah', for example, in Peter's famous turning-point confession at Caesarea Philippi, when he called Jesus 'the Christ' (Greek for the Messiah). Exactly how the gospel writers understood Jesus' messiahship is unclear, given the plurality of beliefs about the Messiah at the time. They probably saw the Messiah as the one through whom God would complete his purposes for the people of Israel. Scholars debate at length whether Jesus was, or was not, self-consciously aware of his own messianic status.

Wright (in Borg and Wright, 1999) maintains that Jesus 'believed himself to be Israel's Messiah' (p. 49), while Marcus Borg thinks 'that the inference that [Jesus] was the Messiah was most likely first made by the early Christian movement after Easter' (*ibid.*, p. 57). Bultmann thought that although Jesus did not claim the title, he was popularly regarded as the Messiah and that this resulted in his death as a 'Messianic pretender' (1958b, p. 28). Sanders, who also thinks that Jesus did not himself use the title 'Messiah', observes that this was none the less an appropriate title for the disciples to give Jesus, since it was 'one of the highest honorific titles that they could think of' (1993, p. 242). Disappointingly, the CBS's much heralded mini-series *Jesus* (May 2000) reflected none of this scholarly opinion on whether Jesus had or had not openly proclaimed himself to be the Messiah.

Perhaps all that can be said is that the disciples were convinced that Jesus was the Messiah, whether Jesus had or had not personally claimed the title. I actually find it surprising that we do not see more theological reflection about who Jesus was recorded in the gospel accounts. Did the early Church, through its writers, distinguish between two different tasks, that of recording the words and deeds of Jesus the man, of the historical Jesus who had lived and died, and that of reflecting theologically on his significance? The latter task was certainly Paul's as he wrestled to understand what God had accomplished in Jesus. If a later date is accepted for John, perhaps by then the earlier distinction between these two tasks had become blurred. However, Paul tells us several times that he was passing on what he had received, which suggests that speculation about Jesus' theological significance began at a very early stage in Christian history. For example, at 1 Corinthians 15 we have quite a detailed statement: 'that Christ died for our sins, that he was buried, that he rose again on the third day in accordance with the scriptures . . . and appeared to Cephas, then to the twelve.'

With reference to the title 'Messiah', it is less surprising to find no worked-out articulation of how this title was understood, either before or after Jesus' death, since it quickly ceased to be anything more than a title.

Some Jews had been expecting a Messiah, even though they had no single concept of who the Messiah was, but as Christianity spread into the Greek-Roman world it encountered many for whom any concept of a messiah carried little or no meaning. Marcion, who died as early as 160 CE, saw any relationship between Jesus and Judaism as so irrelevant that he rejected the Hebrew Bible; the God of Jesus was a God of Love, not the 'contradictory, fickle, capricious, ignorant, despotic, cruel' demiurge of the Jews that Jesus had come to overturn (Cross and Livingstone, 1983, p. 870). While much discussion was to follow on the meaning of Jesus' divine sonship, and on the nature of his 'humanity', little took place on his messiahship. The Greek word 'Christ' became rather like a modern family name: 'Jesus Christ' as in 'Clinton Bennett'.

## The Trinity

What the above does suggest is that the process of developing a more sophisticated understanding of who Jesus was began with the production of the New Testament literature itself. However, even Paul does not leave us with what would today be called a systematic theology. He does not take each critical issue in sequence and address it with the specific intent of resolving problems and inconsistencies. For example, some verses say that Jesus was 'born' (Colossians 1:15: 'He is the first born of all creation'), which seems to imply that there was a time when Jesus did not exist. If this is so, is he equal with God (as Philippians 2:6 implies) or is he somehow less powerful than God? The latter is also suggested by John 14:28: 'the Father is greater than I.' This was one of the issues that the ecumenical councils set out to resolve. Some Christians, such as Arius (250–336 CE), taught that Jesus was neither equal with God nor eternal, but 'created' by God at a point in time: 'The son, who is tempted, suffers and dies, however exalted he may be, is not to be equal to the immutable Father beyond pain and death: if he is other than the Father, he is inferior' (Chadwick, 1967, p. 124). Three possible views appear to have competed against each other for recognition as orthodox dogma: Arius' view that Jesus was human at the expense of his divinity; the view that Jesus was God at the expense of his humanity; and the view that Jesus was equal to God and human. During the first four centuries of Christian history, the Arians formed an influential group.

Sometimes, Arianism is identified as an early form of Unitarianism. For Unitarians, the Godhead is 'singular'; Jesus was a mouthpiece for God who enjoyed an intimate relationship with God, but any reader of this book can potentially enjoy the same relationship with God as Jesus did. The second view, which saw Jesus as wholly divine, was a common view among the Gnostics, for whom Jesus had only appeared to be human but was actually pure spirit. Creation was often regarded by the Gnostics as 'impure', and they wanted to distance God and God's spirit-messenger Jesus from things material.

At Nicaea, which officially promulgated the doctrine of the Trinity, the official teaching was that God and Jesus are co-equal and that Jesus was, at one and the same time, wholly God and wholly human. Arius was condemned, as were the Gnostics. There was much debate about whether Jesus was of the same (*homoousios*), or similar (*homoiousios*), 'substance' to God the Father, and here agreement proved impossible. Christians in the western part of the Roman Empire (which had Rome as its capital) opted for 'same' substance, those in the eastern half (which had Constantinople as its capital) opted for 'similar' substance. Obviously, this division reflected political rivalry between the two halves of the Empire.

Eventually, Christians in the West, who accepted the special authority of the Bishop of Rome, became known as Catholics (later still as Roman Catholics) while those in the East became known as Orthodox. There, the Bishop of Constantinople claimed to be only first among equals (*primus inter pares*) alongside his brother bishops in other ancient Christians sees. Gradually, other differences emerged. Priests in the West cannot marry, those in the East can (though bishops cannot). Distinctive liturgical styles developed in the two rival Churches. The final schism did not occur until 1054, when the two bishops mutually excommunicated each other.

There are also some differences less of dogma than of theological emphasis. For example, the western Church links atonement with the cross; the eastern Church links atonement more with the incarnation. By becoming human in Jesus, God sanctified human life: 'Jesus Christ, by uniting humankind and God in His own person, reopened for us humans the path to union with God' (Ware, 1993, p. 225). Timothy Ware says that 'Where Orthodoxy sees chiefly Christ the Victor, the late medieval and post-medieval west sees chiefly Christ the Victim' (*ibid.*, p. 229). The western Church emphasizes the idea of 'original sin' as articulated by Paul in Romans 5 and the consequent need for 'salvation' which God alone can grant.

Augustine of Hippo (354–430 CE) came very close to equating sin with sexual intercourse; as the psalmist said, 'in sin did my mother conceive me' (Psalm 51:5; see Augustine, 1991, p. xviii). It is often claimed that he thought male sperm transmitted 'original sin' (see Funk, 1996, p. 313). He certainly thought that sex transmits egotism and irrationality, which block us from God. Parrinder (1996) says that he 'virtually equated' original sin with sexual emotion, so that every act of coitus was intrinsically evil, and every child was conceived by the 'sin' of its parents (p. 222). This may be why the idea that no sperm was involved in Jesus' conception grew increasingly popular; it protects Jesus' human nature from inherited sin. Eventually, although not until 1854, Pope Pius IX declared Mary too to have been immaculately conceived (see Pelikan, 1985, p. 81).

The Orthodox East agrees that human wrongdoing raises a barrier between humanity and God but rejects the idea of original sin (Ware, 1993, p. 224), arguing instead that 'human beings after the fall still possessed free will and were still capable of good action' (p. 225). In

Chapter 5, when I discuss Jewish objections to the Christian view of salvation, I note that Orthodox understanding here may be closer to a Jewish view than to that of western Christianity. Orthodoxy also sees salvation as embracing the whole cosmos, not only individual people. As John 4:16 says, Jesus came to redeem the world. Pelikan puts it like this: 'As Savior of the Cosmos, the Logos had not snatched humanity out of the goodness of the created order, but had transformed the created order into a fit setting for a transformed humanity' (1985, p. 69). For the East, death results less from sin than from the transient nature of human life, which finds perfection in Christ.

The western and eastern Churches also developed different understandings of church–state relations. In the West, where the Roman Empire (divided by Constantine into east and west jurisdictions) collapsed in 476 CE, the Pope emerged as the supreme authority in both temporal and spiritual affairs. Since Peter had been appointed chief apostle by Jesus, his own successors (as bishops of Rome) became known as vicars of Christ, that is, Christ's representatives on earth. The triple tiara worn by popes signified their rule over three realms: the temporal, the spiritual and purgatory. No king could, *de jure* at least, succeed to or stay on the throne without the Pope's blessing. In the East, it was the Byzantine emperor himself who represented Christ, who, risen and ascended, is now exalted as king of kings. Just as:

God the Father as king of the universe had conferred authority on Jesus, to whom, as he said just before his ascension, 'all authority in heaven and earth has been given' (Matthew 28:18) . . . that authority was transmitted to the emperor, beginning with Constantine; for Christ the king had elected to exercise his sovereignty over the world through the emperor, to whom he had appeared in visions. The emperor was 'crowned by God' (*theostephes*), a belief reflected in the ceremony of coronation. (Pelikan, 1985, p. 54)

The doctrine of the Trinity became one of the most central dogmas of Catholic and Orthodox Christianity.

Trinity refers to the view that there are three persons within the Godhead (*tres Personae*): Father, Son and Spirit. The Spirit is identified both with references to God's Spirit in the Hebrew Bible (for example, Genesis 1:2) and with the Spirit that, promised by Jesus (see, for example, John 15:26; Luke 11:13), came upon the disciples at Pentecost (see Acts, Chapter 2). This spirit is believed to be the same spirit that had guided Jesus (for example, Luke 4:1, 14). This does not mean that there are three Gods, as Muslims often assert, but that within the one God there are, if you like, three personalities. However, each of these persons has what the theologians called an independent 'hypostasis', or existence (technically, an individuation). This formulation (One in Three, Three in One) was believed to leave God's unity (oneness) intact. The formulation states that the Father is ungenerated, that the Son is eternally generated (or begotten) by the Father, while the Spirit proceeds from the Father through the Son.

Later, at the Council of Toledo (589 CE), the western Church changed the wording of the above to read that the Spirit proceeds from the Father and from the Son. The eastern Church never accepted this change. This is known as the double procession and is usually referred to as the *filioque* clause. Each hypostasis is said to be co-eternal and co-equal. Another view, rejected as heresy by the council, was that the three persons of the Trinity were not permanent hypostases but 'temporary' ones or modes, through which God acted to perform distinct functions at different moments. Yet another view, not altogether absent in Arius' teaching, was that Jesus had 'acquired' divinity; he was only divine inasmuch as God's influence rested upon him. Arius had argued that Jesus was not by nature God, but 'His dignity as Son of God was bestowed on him because of his righteousness'. Augustine is well worth reading on the 'footprints of the Trinity'. Always introspective, trying to understand the depths of his own soul, he saw the Trinity as a key to human psychology. Addressing those who disputed the doctrine, he wrote:

I wish that human disputants would reflect upon the triad within their own selves. These three aspects of the self are very different from the Trinity, but I may make the observation that on this triad they could well exercise their minds and examine the problem, thereby becoming aware of how far and distant they are from it. The three aspects I mean are being, knowing and willing. For I am and I know and I will. Knowing and willing I am. I know that I am and I will. I will to be and to know. In these three, therefore, let him who is capable of so doing contemplate how inseparable in life they are: one life, one mind and one essence, yet ultimately there is distinction, for they are inseparable yet distinct. (1991, p. 279)

The image of God in man, Augustine argued, is itself triune. When God said, 'Let us make man in our image' (Genesis 1:26) God was consulting God's self within the mystery of the Trinity (see Pelikan, 1985, p. 90).

The doctrine of the Trinity represents systematic thinking about Jesus in relationship with God; few would argue that the doctrine exists in anything like its Nicene formulation within the writings of the New Testament. *A New Handbook of Christian Theology* says:

The concept is nowhere explicitly expressed in the scriptures, though such passages as Matthew 29:19 and II Corinthians 13:14 are suggestive. . . . The doctrine was thus formulated in the church as the community sought to explicate the meaning of the revelation in Jesus Christ. (Musser and Price, 1992, p. 500)

My own understanding of the origin of the doctrine locates it more in early Christian piety, or experience, than in intellectual speculation. The first Christians, all of whom were Jews, believed in the oneness of God expressed in the great Jewish confession, 'Hear, O Israel, the Lord our God is One' (Deuteronomy 6:4); yet they also believed that God had been uniquely present in Jesus. Furthermore, they believed that God was present in their lives through the activity of the Holy Spirit, which they also associated with Jesus. While these convictions need not have led them to conclude that Jesus was God, this *is* what they concluded. They also concluded that Jesus was wholly God and wholly man, which led to yet more debate about the relationship within the 'person of Jesus' between his 'human nature' and his 'divine nature'. Nestorius (d. 451) argued that there were two separate persons in Christ: one human and one divine. Nestorius was anxious to safeguard Jesus' humanity, which he feared was somehow being submerged by his divinity. He rejected the title *theotokos*, or 'Mother of God', which was now being used of Mary, Jesus' mother. Condemned by the Bishop of Rome in 430 CE, he and his followers formed a separate Church, which continues to this day. Later, under Islamic rule, the Nestorians flourished; their patriarch 'was for some centuries a considerable political figure' (Cross and Livingstone, 1983, p. 962).

Another group, known as the 'monophysites', argued that Jesus possessed a single 'nature', and that that nature was divine. Distinct Christian Churches also emerged under the 'monophysite' banner, including the Coptic Church in Egypt, the ancient Church of Ethiopia, the Armenians and the Syrian Jacobites. Again, some political posturing was involved here; the ancient centres of Alexandria and Antioch, where the Coptic and Syrian patriarchs sat, did not easily recognize the supremacy of Rome. Chalcedon (451 CE) declared monophysitism heretical, and asserted that the correct Christian view is that within the single person of Jesus there co-exist two natures, one human and one divine. The idea that Jesus' divine and human natures were 'confused' or rather mixed was also rejected; Jesus' two natures are 'united unconfusedly, unchangeably, indivisibly, inseparably' (*ibid.*, p. 263).

The Christian creeds are also a product of a cultural translation; the language used was Greek and has little if any equivalent in Hebrew. This process had begun in the New Testament itself, with its use of the Greek word *Christos* instead of 'Messiah'. Further, John probably chose to call Jesus the logos (instead of Hebrew *hokhmah* [wisdom], which he might have used) because of its philosophical meaning for Greek speakers. This enabled Greeks to understand something of Jesus' cosmic significance without needing to root him in the Hebrew tradition, which was alien to them. The Church's task now was to convince intellectuals schooled in Greek philosophy that Christianity was a serious contender for their consideration and commitment. I discuss some of the political issues involved in the process that took Christianity from the foot of a cross to the throne of Constantine, from persecuted minority to state religion, in Chapter 4.

Obviously, theological questions about the nature of Jesus' relationship with God were not the only issues debated by Christians. Also on their agendas were questions such as: Could a Christian acknowledge Christ as Lord and also serve the emperor? Should Christians even marry and raise families, since Jesus did not, nor did he even have much to say about domestic, married life. Should Christians have many possessions, since Jesus 'had nowhere to lay his head'? Can a Christian be wealthy and remain a Christian, since Jesus said that it is difficult for a rich person to enter the kingdom? Was it right for the Church to be the wealthiest and most powerful institution in the western world?

Often, the Church has seemed to support repressive regimes over and against the poor and oppressed. Could a Christian serve in the military? Jesus seems to have condemned violence: 'he who lives by the sword will die by the sword', 'forgive your enemies', 'turn the other cheek'. Can violence against unjust rulers ever be justified? Some of these issues are still firmly on the Christian agenda. What attitude should Christians adopt towards secular authorities? What legal relationship, if any, should exist between Church and state? Although he does not discuss all the questions involved, H. Richard Niebuhr's *Christ and Culture* (1951) remains a very useful exploration of different Christian responses to the problematic relationship between Christ and the contemporary cultures we inhabit. Another hotly debated issue was whether or not Jesus could be pictured visually. Some opposed the use of icons, others supported their use, since Jesus had borne God's very image in his own person.

## The pre-quest view of Jesus

During the period between the formulation of orthodox dogma and 1778 CE, few if any Christians doubted that what they believed about Jesus was totally compatible with what the gospel record said of him. This does not mean that Christians thought that every detail of their Christological beliefs could be found in the Gospels; rather, they believed that the dogmas they asserted of Jesus (or of the Christ), whom they called Lord, could be justified by a reading of the gospel record. The Jesus who had lived, and the Christ of their faith, were one and the same. Their conviction that the gospel writers enjoyed divine inspiration naturally tended to place the gospel text beyond critical scholarship. However, this does not mean that they always understood scripture literally. Ambrose (339–97 CE), his convert Augustine (354–430 CE), as well as Origen (185–254 CE), could all speak of allegory and metaphor and of layers of meaning within the text. Origen wrote, 'for just as man consists of body, soul and spirit, so in the same way does the scripture' (Stevenson, 1963, p. 22).

Origen taught that events described in the Bible were not only historical happenings but also could be experienced, at a mystical level, by the believer. The gospel writers each had their particular theological agendas, which could explain differences, for example, between Matthew's and Luke's Jesus genealogies. In other words, neither list was intended to be an accurate, historical lineage but served a specific theological function. Further, even if certain aspects or details of Christian dogma on Jesus could not be found explicitly in scripture, Christians could and did claim that the Holy Spirit had guided and inspired their deliberations. Thus, the victory of orthodoxy and the condemnation of rival opinions as heretical was not just the result of human debate but a divinely sanctioned act of determining what properly constituted Christian belief. It might be said that the Christ of faith was a valid interpretation of the Jesus of history but Christians of this period tended to see their Christological dogmas as 'true', not as interpretation.

From this early period (the first four centuries after Jesus' death), which saw the fixing of two canons – the scriptural and dogmatic – until the start of the old quest (1778), Christians saw no need to doubt that the Gospels were historically reliable accounts of the life of Jesus. In other words, when they read the Gospels, they saw the Jesus of Christian faith. Their image *of* Jesus was filtered through their beliefs *about* Jesus. Below, I summarize what I call the traditional view of Jesus. This represents a synthesis between the Jesus of the Gospels and the Christ of faith, which is exactly what Christians saw when they looked at the Gospel record. It also represents the orthodox view of Jesus throughout the 'no quest' period. Broadly, it is the view to which both the Catholic West and the Orthodox East subscribed. In essence, it is the view to which Protestants also subscribed towards the end of this period.

Protestantism, which 'began' in 1517 when Martin Luther (1483–1546) pinned his '95 Theses' (1957) to the door of Wittenberg Cathedral, was a movement against the Western Church's substitution of its own authority for 'faith' in Jesus Christ. Salvation had become a commodity, controlled, sold or given away by pope and priest. Luther's goal was direct, personal access to Jesus, to know nothing 'except Jesus Christ and him crucified' (1 Corinthians 2:2). 'Faith' was God's free gift, said Luther. If anything, Protestantism's confidence in the self-sufficiency of scripture, without priestly interpretation, strengthened rather than weakened the conviction that the Jesus of history and the Christ of faith were identical. (Of course, Protestantism did not really begin on a single day but was built on existing ideas and tendencies, as well as on the contributions of such pioneer reformers as Peter Valdes (d. 1218), John Wycliffe (1330–84) and John Huss (1372–1415). The Waldenses may well be the oldest Protestant denomination.)

What follows is, I believe, a portrait that still represents the truth about Jesus for many Catholics and conservative evangelical Christians, and which they see when they pick up a Gospel and read it. A statement, 'The Gift of Salvation', on 'what we mean by the Gospel', issued by a group of evangelicals and Roman Catholics has much in common with this portrait (see George, 1997; statement issued 7 October 1997). The biblical references supplied here are examples, and are not the only passages that could be cited as sources for the points in question.

## A traditional portrait of the pre-quest Jesus

The man Jesus was miraculously born to his mother, Mary, while she was visiting Bethlehem with her husband, Joseph. She had had no sexual contact with anyone (see Matthew 1:20, 25). As a descendant of David, Jesus was the promised Messiah of Israel, a fact that several people recognized right at the start (see Luke 2:26). King Herod (the client king patronized by the Romans) feared the birth of a would-be king of the family of David and plotted to kill the infant, but failed (see Matthew 2:16). Instead, Joseph sought refuge for his family in Egypt. Afterwards, Jesus was raised in the Galilean town of Nazareth (Matthew 2:23). His cousin John began to preach repentance and renewal and to announce the coming of one who would judge and restore Israel (Luke 3:7–9). People assumed that he meant the Messiah and asked John if he was not in fact the 'Christ' (Luke 3:15; John 3:28–30). Jesus, at about 30 years of age, appeared alongside John (known as the Baptist) and received John's blessing as the one 'greater than he'. A voice from heaven also proclaimed that Jesus was 'my beloved son', which was taken to be God's voice (Mark 1:9–11).

Jesus then underwent a period of mental and physical preparation for his public mission. Known as the 'temptation', this took place in the desert and involved a struggle between his conscience and the Devil, or Satan, who for Christians is the personification of evil and the arch opponent of God's plans for human salvation, peace and 'the final good'. Many Christians believe that the Devil is an actual 'person' or 'power', and that Jesus' temptation, during which Satan took him to the top of the Temple in Jerusalem and dared him to test God by jumping off, really happened exactly as described (see Matthew 4:1–11).

Jesus began to preach that God's kingdom (*basileia*) was soon to become a reality (Matthew 4:17). Here, *basileia* refers not primarily to a geographical territory but to God's reign, or to a quality of human living (see my conclusion (Chapter 7) for feminist insight on this term). Jesus invited people to prepare themselves for citizenship of God's kingdom by repenting their sins and developing an inner at-one-ness with God's will. He called on people to love each other, to care for the disadvantaged, even to forgive their enemies (Matthew 5:38–48). 'Sell your belongings,' he said, 'and give to the poor' (Luke 12:33). 'When you give a feast,' Jesus said, 'invite the poor, the crippled, the lame, the blind' (Luke 14:13), 'because the hungry and the peacemakers of *today* will be satisfied and blessed in my kingdom *tomorrow*' (Luke 6:21; Matthew 5:9).

In passing, while many Christians have vivid images of the Devil, the Bible has comparatively little to say about him. The account of the Fall in Genesis, for example, does not specifically mention him, but Christians assume that the serpent and the Devil are synonymous. Elsewhere, rather than fitting the popular Christian picture of the Devil as a sort of autonomous evil power pitted against God, the biblical Devil seems to be more of a servant of God (see Job 1:6–12, where the Devil presents himself before God and is given a task to perform). The idea that the Devil is locked in a cosmic battle with God may derive from Zoroastrianism, in which the good god, Ahura Mazda, assisted by his angels, opposes the evil Ahriman and his demons. According to Zoroastrian prophecy, Ahura Mazda will win, but meanwhile human deeds can also aid his victory; as one of Salman Rushdie's characters says, 'We Parsis are proud to believe in a forward-moving view of the cosmos. Our words and deeds are part, in their small way, of the battle in which Ahura Mazda will vanguish Ahriman' (1999, p. 137).

Characteristically, Jesus preached through parables, earthly stories of everyday life imbued with spiritual or heavenly meaning. He spoke about fishermen, farmers, widows searching for lost coins. His dominant theme was preparation for the life of the kingdom, in which there would be fairness and equity: 'As you wish that people would do to you, do so to them' (Luke 6:31). Life in the kingdom, he implied, would be marvellous beyond words; it would be like attending a banquet at which the guest list reverses all social expectations (Luke 14:15–24). Jesus appeared to claim an authority that superseded the Jewish law, saying, 'You have heard . . . but I say to you'. He performed miracles, mainly healing the sick and giving sight to the blind, but he also exorcised demons (see Luke 7:21) and on one or two occasions fed a huge crowd, turning a very small amount of food into enough for everyone (see Mark 6:37–44; 8:1–9). On another occasion, he calmed a storm (Luke 8:24). Once he walked on the waters of the lake (Matthew 14:25).

Christians see these 'nature miracles' as proof that Jesus was not only a man, but also God, who was and is the lord and master of creation. That same God had brought order out of chaos at the start of creation; Jesus is this God (reflected in the prologue of John; see John 1:1–4). Jesus talked about offering 'new birth' or 'new life', especially in John's Gospel (see John 3:7), but this is also implied in such accounts as the conversion of Zacchaeus, who, after receiving forgiveness from Jesus, makes restoration to others for the wrongs he had committed against them (Luke 19:8). The 'new beginning' motif also occurs in passages where Jesus invites people to become 'childlike'; 'whoever does not receive the kingdom of God like a child shall not enter it' (Mark 10:15).

Jesus called on twelve men to be his special companions, or disciples. The choice of twelve is taken to symbolize the restoration of Israel, which, like Ezekiel's valley of dry bones, is spiritually dead and in need of new life. Increasingly, Jesus seems to be offering a version of the Jewish religion that challenged some of the assumptions of the day, including notions of purity and impurity. He is criticized for practising open table fellowship, for dining with 'tax collectors and sinners' (Mark 2:16; Matthew 9:11; Luke 15:2). What defiles us, he said, 'comes from within' (Mark 7:20). Jesus' offer of renewal and of a new beginning was for all Jews (sometimes non-Jews also seem to be included; see Luke 13:28–9), which openly critiqued the social divisions and conventions of his day. The humble, he said, would be exalted, while the proud would be humbled (Luke 18:14).

He also seems to have critiqued an over-literal and legalistic reading of the Jewish law, and accused the religious leaders of adding too many extra rules. To prevent breaking a commandment they added additional ones, which would have to be broken first before the rule that was being protected could possibly be broken, but Jesus said that they, 'loaded men with burdens too hard to bear'. They liked outward signs of piety, he said, while lacking inner purity (see Luke 11). This appears to have brought him into conflict with the religious authorities, who would ask him trick questions.

The Gospels depict the religious leaders as coming to 'argue' with Jesus, or to 'test' or 'trap him' (see Mark 8:11; 10:2; 12:13). They criticized him for appearing to claim an authority greater than that of the Torah: 'Tell us by what authority you do these things' (Luke 20:2). They took especial exception to his forgiving people their sins, which only God could do (Luke 7:49; 5:21). Increasingly, Jesus speaks about being 'rejected', as had been the prophets of old, and about the need for him, like them, to suffer and even to die. He explicitly predicts that he will be 'delivered to the chief priests and the scribes', be condemned to death, die and rise again 'after three days' (Mark 10:33–4). Passages suggest that Jesus viewed his forthcoming death as one that would somehow atone for the people's sins, he would 'give his life as a ransom for many' (Mark 10:45). Jesus himself makes direct reference to traditions that require the Son of Man to 'suffer many things and be treated with contempt' (Mark 9:12) before 'restoration' could take place.

Here, Christians call to mind the vindication of the suffering servant in Isaiah 53, and Israel being 'cleansed of all her iniquities' in Ezekiel 36. In some passages, Jesus predicts the actual manner in which he will die: 'he will be delivered to the Gentiles to be mocked and scourged and crucified' (Matthew 20:19). Jesus himself is depicted as believing that his suffering and vindication will take place in order to 'fulfil scripture', that is, God's promises to the Hebrew people (see Luke 24:43–4). Beyond his death and resurrection, Jesus also predicts that the Son of Man (by which he appears to have meant himself) will, while the disciples are themselves still alive (Mark 13:30; Matthew 24:34), 'return in the clouds with great power and glory' (Mark 13:26). These passages appear to predict a dramatic return of Jesus, who, aided by angels, will gather the elect (Matthew 24:31) and judge between the nations (Matthew 25:32).

Christians associate this 'second coming' with a final judgment day, when God through Christ will call on all people to offer an account of their lives. Ezekiel's restored, purified Israel under a new David seems to be somewhere in the background of these passages, as does Isaiah's vision of an Israel that is made to rise above the nations, whose people and kings will now acknowledge her special status. 'Nations,' says Isaiah, 'will come to Israel's light, and Kings to her brightness.' Israel will be exalted, but as a light to the Gentiles (60:3), and an age of justice and peace will commence (see especially Isaiah 65:17–25). The words with which Jesus began his mission, in Luke, are from this section of Isaiah: 'The Spirit of the Lord is upon me, because the Lord has anointed me to bring good tidings to the afflicted, he has sent me to bind up the broken-hearted, to proclaim liberty to the captives' (Isaiah 61:1–2; Luke 4:18–19). Christians understand Jesus as the vehicle through whom God's purposes for all people will be brought to fruition. Thus, the promise that God made to Abraham when God first entered into a covenant with the Hebrews would finally be fulfilled: 'By you all the families of the earth will be blessed' (Genesis 12:3). In John especially, there are passages in which Jesus speaks of a 'Spirit' that will continue to inspire and comfort the disciples even after he is physically no longer with them (see John 15:26). Certain passages in the synoptics also appear to promise some continued spiritual reality: 'it is not you who speak, but the Spirit of your Father speaking through you' (Matthew 10:20); 'how much more will the heavenly Father give the Holy Spirit to those who ask him!' (Luke 11:13).

The Gospels speak of the scribes and Pharisees plotting to kill Jesus. The turning point in the synoptics is Peter's confession that Jesus is indeed the Messiah. Prior to this, Jesus had seemed reluctant to acknowledge any claim either to the title 'Messiah' or 'Son of God', commanding spirits to remain silent (Mark 1:25). Even after Peter's confession, Jesus charges the disciples 'to tell no one about him' (Mark 8:30). There is also reference to the popular conviction that before the final restoration of Israel, which was probably taken to be God's intervention against her enemies, and a reinstatement of her sovereign status, Elijah would return, promised at Malachi 4:5. Elijah, the great Hebrew prophet who had challenged the king's abuse of power, had not died (as noted in Chapter 1) but rose up into heaven: 'And Elijah went up by a whirlwind into heaven' (2 Kings 2:11). Some had taken John to be Elijah, while others clearly thought that Jesus was Elijah (Mark 6:15; Luke 9:8). Others asked, 'Can this be the Son of David?' (Matthew 12:23).

Immediately after Peter's confession, Jesus takes his three closest disciples to a mountain peak, where Moses and Elijah appear and engage in conversation with him. As this took place, Jesus seemed to glow with a supernatural glory. This incident is called the transfiguration. It represents the view, as John makes explicit, that Jesus had come to complete the Torah ('The Law was given through Moses, grace and truth came through Jesus Christ'; John 1:17) and to fulfil the expectation that 'Elijah must come first to restore all things' (Mark 9:12). Passages that appear to threaten, or to predict, the destruction of the Temple would have fuelled the authorities' fears that Jesus intended, somehow, to replace them as leaders of Israel. Not one stone will be left standing upon another, he said (Luke 21:6; Mark 13:2). Jesus also predicted that Jerusalem would be surrounded by armies, and 'trodden down by Gentiles' (Luke 21:24). These apparent threats to Jerusalem and to the Temple, combined with Jesus' condemnation of how the priests handled Temple affairs (Mark 11:15–17), introduces the Gospels' announcement that 'the chief priests and the scribes' began to 'seek a way to destroy' Jesus (Mark 11:18).

As the Gospels move towards their climax, Jesus rides ceremoniously into Jerusalem on a donkey and is greeted by a seemingly enthusiastic and supportive crowd, who shout, 'Hosanna to the Son of David!' (Matthew

21:9). The scene looks very much like a public disclosure of Jesus' identity as the Davidic Messiah; it gives the impression that he is about to claim kingly authority. Matthew has it that the religious leaders met at night to plan how they might 'arrest Jesus by stealth and then kill him' (26:4). Judas Iscariot, one of Jesus' disciples, supposedly on his own initiative, then went to the plotters and offered to betray Jesus to them in exchange for thirty pieces of silver. Luke says that Satan 'entered Judas' (22:3). Scholars continue to debate why Judas decided to change sides; perhaps he was disappointed that Jesus had not led a revolt against Rome. All Jesus' talk of the necessity of his suffering and death may have convinced Judas that he was backing a loser.

On the night that his arrest took place, Jesus shared a meal with his disciples. This included a traditional Jewish blessing of the wine and bread. It may have been a Passover meal (since all these events took place near Passover), or a Shabbath meal. However, Jesus introduced new words into the blessing and said that the bread and wine were 'his body', and that in the future the disciples should 'eat and drink in remembrance of him'. He called the wine cup the 'cup of the new covenant, which is poured out for many for the forgiveness of sins' (Matthew 26:26–8). All this seems to predict what was about to happen. Jesus appears to believe that the shedding of his blood will bring about forgiveness of human sins and the possibility of a new relationship between the people and God.

This last supper shared by Jesus with his disciples soon became a central part of Christian worship. Today, it is known as the Lord's Supper, as the Eucharist or as the Mass. It was followed by Jesus' arrest by religious officials as he meditated and prayed to his Father in the Garden of Gethsemane. The account of his subsequent trial varies across the four Gospels; in Matthew and Mark he is taken before the high priest, who accuses him of blasphemy for claiming to be 'The Christ, Son of the Living God' (Matthew 26:63). Witnesses were heard and formal court procedures appear to have been followed. Declaring that this merited death, the high priest passed Jesus on to the Roman governor Pilate (who alone had the authority to pronounce a death sentence).

Pilate hesitated to execute Jesus, perhaps on the grounds that he had not actually created any trouble for the Roman rulers. Matthew says that Pilate's wife intervened, calling him 'a righteous man'. Then Pilate remembered a custom that allowed him to release one prisoner at Passover, so he offered Jesus, or another prisoner, Barabbas, to the priests and the crowd outside. The crowd chose Barabbas and Jesus was sentenced to crucifixion. Pilate tried to deflect responsibility from himself. He poured water and washed his hands, saying, 'I am innocent of this man's blood. See to it yourselves.'

In Luke, there is a third trial when Pilate, hearing that Jesus was from Galilee, sends him before Herod. Herod merely mocks Jesus' so-called royal pretensions, dresses him up in 'gorgeous apparel' and sends him back to Pilate. Luke's Pilate is also reluctant to sentence Jesus, having found him not 'guilty of any of your charges laid against him'. Again, Pilate gives in to the crowd, which demands Jesus' crucifixion. In John, the hearing before the priests is apparently informal, and Jesus is taken first to Annas, a senior priest (former high priest, and father of five men who served in that office), then to Caiaphas, the current high priest. No witnesses are called. The proceedings are more like a hearing to prepare a case for presentation to the Roman governor. They then take Jesus to Pilate and formally charge him with treason. Here, the charge is that he claimed to be King of the Jews (John 18:33).

Jesus is crucified, after carrying his cross through the streets of Jerusalem. On either side, a miscreant is also hung on a cross. It is now the afternoon of what Christians believe was a Friday. Jesus is mocked by the crowd. Few, if any, of his disciples appear to have stayed to watch his humiliation, although in John's account his mother is present with a disciple (John 19:26). Jesus is given bitter wine (or vinegar) to drink while hanging on the cross; in John, a soldier pierces his side. In Mark, it is soldiers who mockingly dress Jesus in purple as they lead him away from Pilate's palace. Matthew especially gives many Hebrew Bible quotations from Psalm 22. When he dies, Jesus himself utters a verse from that Psalm: 'My God, My God, Why Have You Forsaken Me?' Later Christian legend fleshed out Jesus' final hours with the story of Veronica wiping his face with her head-cloth on the way to Calvary (the sixth station of the cross) and by naming the two thieves between whom he was crucified (Duchamus and Titus).

Jesus is taken from the cross. A rich Jew named Joseph of Arimathaea requests the body, so that he can place it in a cave which he had prepared as his own sepulchre. John describes Joseph as a secret disciple of Jesus (John 19:38). Aware of the rumour that Jesus would rise after three days, and assuming that the disciples would 'steal the body' (Matthew 27:64), the priests place a guard at the tomb. Next day, early in the morning, a group of women followers of Jesus go to the tomb – Matthew says simply 'to see Jesus', Mark and Luke that they were taking spices to embalm him. In John, Mary Magdalene goes alone (without spices). In later chapters, the idea that Jesus had 'secret' helpers surfaces several times, especially in conspiracy theories.

In all the Gospels, the stone is rolled away and there is no body in the tomb. Matthew's account, as I have already noted, suggests that the women may have actually witnessed this event. An angelic messenger announces that the one they seek has risen; they will find him in Galilee. In Matthew and Mark there is a single messenger. Luke has two. John has two but they appear later in his account, after Mary Magdalene had run to find Peter. There then follows a series of resurrection appearances of Jesus, except in the original Mark, which concludes with the discovery of the empty tomb (16:8). References to touching Jesus, and to his eating with them, serve to confirm that Jesus' resurrected 'self' was 'bodily'.

All (except Mark) conclude with Jesus making one final appearance at which he tells his disciples that they must wait in the city until the Spirit comes upon them, then proclaim to all nations what they had witnessed. In Matthew, he also tells the disciples to 'baptize those who believe'. This is the only gospel passage where the Trinitarian formula occurs: 'in the Name of the Father and of the Son and of the Holy Spirit' (Matthew 28:19). After this, Jesus seems to disappear, rising up into the heavens. Neither Matthew, Mark nor John actually describes the ascension (the added ending to Mark, 16:9–19, includes this). Luke gives a brief description in his Gospel, then more detail in his account of the early spread of Christianity, the Acts of the Apostles: 'And when he had said this, as they were looking on, he was lifted up, and a cloud took him out of their sight' (Acts 1:9). This concludes the gospel account but it is not, for Christians, the end of the story. Christians believe that Jesus will return. Initially, they believed that this would happen very soon, possibly within the lifetime of the first disciples.

As the disciples began to die, some concern was expressed that the 'second coming' had not yet taken place. In the Book of 1 Thessalonians, the belief is expressed that those who die before Christ's return will be bodily raised from the dead so that 'those who are alive will not precede those who have fallen asleep'. Here, too, the conviction is expressed that, as Jesus returns, all Christians will be taken up into the clouds to 'meet the Lord in the air' (4:17). The New Testament writings are full of the belief that just as Jesus had been physically raised from the dead, so will Christians be raised. Jesus' return, too, would be 'bodily'. Jesus did not say very much about the resurrection, although he did respond to trick questions from the Pharisees and Sadducees, who disagreed on this issue. However, at Luke 14:14 he spoke about the 'resurrection of the just'. In addition, passages such as Matthew 25, where he spoke of the Son of Man coming in glory to sit on his throne and of him judging the nations, may well imply a resurrection of the dead. Those found unjust are sent into 'eternal punishment'; those declared righteous receive 'eternal life'.

Clearly, the concept of the Son of Man (of Jesus) returning was closely associated with the idea of a final judgment, since this is what emerges in the Christian creed: 'He will come again in glory to judge the living and the dead . . . we look for the resurrection of the dead' (Nicene Creed). Some Christians believe that when Jesus begins his 'descent', they will be 'raised up' to meet him as the 'trumpet' sounds (Matthew 24:31). This is known as the 'rapture'. The lost will be left behind (Matthew 24:40). Some novels have been written about what happens to those who are left; see Tim Lahaye and Jerry Jenkins' *The Assassins (Left Behind)* (1999). In March 2000 this was number two on the *Publishers Weekly* bestselling fiction list for evangelical Christians. Many have set dates for Jesus' return, often based on interpretations of the Book of Revelation. Jonathan Edwards (1703–58) did much to popularize 2000 as the year of Jesus' return.

As 2000 approached, some Christians began to move to Jerusalem. Often, the figure of the Anti-Christ, an evil figure who will take control of the world before Jesus' return, features in end-time predictions, again based on Revelation. Hal Lindsey and C. C. Carlson's *The Late Great Planet Earth* (1970) saw sinister omens in the formation of what is now the European Union. The book sold twenty-eight million copies. I read the book at the time. I was then a very young Christian, having been baptized just a year earlier. However, Lindsey and Carlson's theories were so far-fetched that I found myself questioning such a literal understanding of the Bible. Other Christians point to Jesus' warning, also in Matthew 24, that no one knows the day or the hour of his return (verse 36). Others, as we shall see in my next chapter, interpret Jesus' coming as a perpetual encounter with human experience, summoning us to radical obedience of God every minute of our lives. One beautifully crafted response to an excellent article, 'The Way the World Ends' by Kenneth L. Woodward, in *Newsweek* (1999) from a Unitarian-Universalist minister, Joel Miller, expressed the following opinion:

The Apocalypse prophesied by the Book of Revelation has already come. It comes every day that a child is murdered. It comes every year that we wage war. It comes every moment we damage the environment for future generations. It comes every time we adults blame lost and broken teenagers for our nation's troubles, instead of working to create better communities for them to live in. (Miller, 1999)

To conclude this section, Christians during the pre-quest period believed, as do many Christians today, that all of the above is true, that the events described really happened, and that the Christ of Christian belief and the Jesus of the gospel record are one and the same. Every word supplied to Jesus (coloured red in some editions of the Gospels), and every act which he is said to have done, were said and done exactly as described. John's prologue and Matthew's Hebrew Bible quotations to show how Jesus' life was fulfilling scripture do not represent fallible human opinion but divinely inspired truth. Miracles during this pre-quest period continued to be associated with the great Christian saints, and so it did not seem improbable that Jesus had performed miracles as well.

## The quest begins

As we move into the period of intellectual history known as the Enlightenment, some people began to question whether all the details of the above account of Jesus' life could be credibly accepted as true. As people 'dared to know', the Enlightenment saw a new confidence in scientific reasoning and in natural laws that seemed, to some, to make belief in a God who intervened supernaturally in human affairs, unnecessary and redundant. As scholars began to subtract from the gospel narrative what they found difficult to accept, the Jesus who had lived and the Christ of Christian faith began to look like two different people. Of course, many who concluded that the Gospels could not be accepted as reliable, authentic, historical accounts of Jesus concluded that Christianity was false, and ceased to call themselves Christians. Their contributions belong to Chapter 4 of this book.

However, many scholars who found themselves rejecting passages of the Gospels as non-historical continued to identify with Christianity; what they tried to do was to somehow reconcile what they could affirm of the Jesus of history with their Christian dogma. In many instances, this process involved a reformulation of Christian belief in the light of the new, critical analyses of the gospel record. The first victim, in terms of what scholars felt needed to be subtracted from the gospel account, was miracles and any type of supernatural happening. Scottish philosopher David Hume (1711–76), in his famous essay on miracles, argued that they were contrary to the law of probability:

Probability rests on what may be called the majority vote of our past experience. . . . There is unanimous experience against miracles, otherwise it would not be a miracle. A miracle is therefore the most improbable of all events. (Lewis, 1947, p. 105)

Hume argued that since 'no testimony of any kind of miracle has ever amounted to a probability, much less a proof', no such testimony could 'act as the foundation of a system of religion' (Hume, 1963, pp. 222–3).

Much of what the Church taught about Jesus involved miracles, from Jesus' birth, through his healing work, to his rising from the grave and ascension into heaven. Jesus' own foreknowledge of his future also necessitated belief that he had enjoyed some supernatural abilities. One response to the rationalist critique of miracles, represented by Christian Wolff (1679–1754), was to argue that miracles were rare and even improbable, and that God normally operated within the laws of nature that He had Himself created, but that He could override nature when He wanted. Wolff wrote: 'God can perform miracles to whatever extent he wills. He can annul an order of nature whenever and as often as he wills, although in a well ordered world, miracles will be rare' (cited in Talbert, 1970, pp. 12–13). The Deists, however, concluded that once God had created the world, He no longer took any interest in creation. Instead, the world operated according to natural laws. The Deist worldview had no place for a God who became human in Jesus, or for Jesus' miracles and resurrection. A Deist had to view the supernatural elements of the Gospels as legendary, and appeal to the ethical teachings of Jesus if he appealed to Jesus at all.

## John Toland

John Toland (1670–1722) may have been the first scholar to suggest that the supernatural in the Gospels was a borrowing from paganism, while true Christianity was not at all mysterious. His book *Christianity Not Mysterious* (1696; facsimile edition, 1995) was burnt by order of Parliament. Toland contended that God revealed only truth and that truth corresponded with what reason could rationally deduce (1995, p. 25). He wrote: '*what is evidently repugnant to clear and distinct Ideas, or to our common Notions, is contrary to Reason* . . . therefore . . . the *Doctrines of the Gospel,* if it be the word of God, *cannot be so*' (*ibid.*; italics in original; I have substituted s's for f's). 'Reason,' he declared, 'is the only Foundation of all certitude . . . and there is nothing in the Gospel contrary to reason' (p. 6). Any miracle that defied a natural explanation is fictitious (p. 146).

Toland may be the first Christian (for Christian he considered himself to be) who strongly implied that whatever contravenes reason in the Gospels and in Christian dogma belongs to the category of myth (even though he did not use the word). He blamed the machinations of priests for the import of pagan ideas into an originally rational Christianity: 'our pretended Christians outdid all the *Mysteries* of the *Heathens*' by placing dogma 'above the Reach of all sense and Reason' (p. 169). The 'Craft and Ambition of the *Priests* and *Philosophers*' transformed Christianity into 'mere Paganism' (p. 163). Toland wanted to free Jesus from the encumbrance of the supernatural, and from dogma: 'I am neither of Paul, nor of Cephas, nor of Apollos, but of the Lord Jesus Christ' (p. xxvi).

Toland, who spent most of his life working for various patrons, writing their memoirs or editing their personal papers, received his MA from Edinburgh in 1690, then studied at Leyden, Holland. For some time, he was also a private tutor at Oxford. Clergy denounced him as an infidel from their pulpits. In his native Ireland, the Bishop of Cork declared 'that Toland was setting up for head of a new sect, and meant to rival Mahomet' (Stephen, 1938, p. 919). He managed to avoid arrest, which Parliament had also sanctioned (9 September 1697). In fact, Toland referred to *The Gospel of Barnabas,* which he believed presented a more original Jesus picture; that is, a Jesus who claimed to be only a prophet and teacher. He had access to an Italian manuscript while in Holland (Leirvik, 1999, p. 131). As I pointed out earlier, many Muslims take this to be the real gospel (and see Chapter 5).

### Thomas Chubb and Peter Annet

Thomas Chubb (1679–1747), in his book *The True Gospel of Jesus Christ Asserted* (1738), also suggested that the gospel accounts might not retell exactly what happened but did reflect the later dogmas of the Church. In Chubb's view, the disciples had 'altered the original gospel of Jesus' (1738, p. 16). Chubb began life as a tallow-chandler; later he earned a modest income from his writing. He was self-taught, and, says Stephen, was never able 'to surmount the disadvantages of his education' (1887, p. 298). However, Chubb established a considerable reputation, so much so that some of his admirers thought he might outshine John Locke. Although he rejected Jesus' divinity, he 'regarded the mission of Christ as divine, and calls himself a Christian' (*ibid.*).

London schoolteacher Peter Annet (1693–1769), described as 'one of the most aggressive deists that the eighteenth century produced' (Price,

1995, p. vii), writing in 1744, singled out the resurrection as especially problematic since, more so in his view than some other miracles, it contravened reason. He compared and contrasted the Gospel accounts of Jesus' resurrection to expose what he saw as contradictions in the biblical text (Annet, 1995, pp. 265–378, 'The Resurrection of Jesus Considered'). Like Toland, Annet thought that faith required only reason and nature to support it, not supernatural intervention: 'If truth and nature agree, natural powers alone are capable of discovering truth and the supernatural, or superior power, can only confound it' (*ibid.*, p. 316). Indeed, a God who gave miracles to some but not to all was morally degraded (*ibid.*, p. 317). Annet believed that Deism was humankind's natural religion: 'the true, original religion of Reason and Nature, such as was believed and practiced by Socrates' (Price, 1995, p. vii).

## Thomas Jefferson

The US President Thomas Jefferson (1743–1826) wrote a life of Jesus in which everything supernatural – angels, visions, the Christmas star, the resurrection, and much more – was subtracted from the story. His book went through many revisions, and titles; the 1975 bicentennial edition that I consulted is called *Thomas Jefferson's Life of Jesus*. Rejecting Jesus' divinity, Jefferson accepted his moral teaching. Although he remained an Episcopalian, he expressed Unitarian sympathies. His Jesus was a great ethical exemplar. According to Jefferson, Jesus was:

A man, of illegitimate birth, of a benevolent heart . . . enthusiastic mind, who set out without any pretensions of divinity, ended in believing them, and was punished capitally for sedition by being gibbeted according to Roman law. (Adams, 1983, p. 388)

Jefferson aimed to abstract what was authentically Jesus', 'the very words only of Jesus' (1975, p. 1). He is cited as saying that he wanted to separate Jesus' words from 'the rubbish in which they had been buried, and that these were as easy to recognize as diamonds in a dung hill' (*ibid.*).

Jefferson was a Deist. Like Toland, he was hugely confident of the human capacity to create the good life by the exercise of reason. This was his vision for the United States of America, which he enshrined in its Declaration of Independence. Ethical truths, he believed, were self-evident. They were also taught by Jesus, whose life, once the supernatural has been extracted, represents 'the most sublime and benevolent code of morals which has ever been offered to man' (1975, p. 1). Jefferson's Jesus, as Sanders (1993) points out, was 'very much like Jefferson' (p. 7).

## Joseph Priestley

Pelikan discusses Jefferson in his chapter on Jesus as 'The Teacher of Common Sense'. Here, he also includes Joseph Priestley (1733–1804), the scientist and Unitarian minister. In an 1803 pamphlet, Priestley compared Jesus with Socrates. Both were teachers yet neither wrote anything, both were accused of treason by their co-religionists and both were executed (Priestley, 1972b, Vol. 17, pp. 400–39). For Enlightenment thinkers, the presence of wisdom in Socrates as well as in Jesus pointed to 'a wisdom and moral power that must come from the God whom Jesus called Father. . . . And if the true God had spoken through Socrates, that meant that truth was universal' and not exclusive to the revelation of God's self through the Bible (Pelikan, 1985, p. 189).

Of course, as I shall show in Chapter 4, Christians had compared Jesus with Socrates from a very early period in the history of their movement. A more recent writer, the philosopher Bertrand Russell (1872–1970), how-ever, thought Socrates more virtuous than Jesus, whose belief in hell was a serious moral defect. He wrote: 'I cannot feel that either in the matter of wisdom or in the matter of virtue Christ stands quite as high as some other people known to history. I think I should put Buddha and Socrates above Him in those respects' (1957, p. 19). Russell, a defender of atheism, believed that the decay of 'dogmatic belief' could 'only do good' (p. 206). Priestley's own conclusion favoured Jesus:

The life of Socrates and Jesus have an obvious resemblance, as they both went about graciously doing good, according to their several abilities, situations and opportunities; but we see an infinite superiority with respect to Jesus, though he had no such advantage of education or instruction as Socrates had. (1972b, Vol. 17, pp. 432–4)

Priestley wrote numerous volumes about the history of Christianity, argu-ing throughout that the primitive Church had been Unitarian (see e.g. 1972c, Vol. 7, p. 3).

Deist and Enlightenment thinkers such as Priestley did much to draw up the agenda of Jesus studies for the next hundred years or so. Anyone wanting to argue in favour of the traditional harmony between the Jesus of history and the Christ of faith had to defend miracles, Jesus' foreknowledge of his own destiny and the resurrection. Christians, though, could easily dismiss the Deists as unbelievers. It was their lack of faith in a caring God that prevented them from accepting the truthfulness of supernatural acts. Christian scholarship still saw little need to jettison gospel passages or to rethink Christian dogma.

Russell's objection to the concept of hell merits some comment. Did Jesus believe in a physical hell? Many Christians have a literal view of hell as a real place where the wicked will be eternally punished. The President of the Southern Baptist Theological Seminary, R. Albert Mohler, for example, states, 'Scripture clearly speaks of hell as a physical place of fiery torment and warns us we should fear' (cited by Sheler, 2000, p. 45). The Bible, though, just as it does not have that much to say about the Devil, lacks detail on hell. The Hebrew Bible speaks only of *Sheol*, a shadowy realm where both the good and the wicked go after death. Jesus did speak about punishment and reward, and he did describe hell as a place of fiery torment. Sometimes he called hell *hades*, as at Matthew 16:18. He often called hell *gehenna*, as at Matthew 5:22. This was actually Jerusalem's rubbish dump. Clearly, Jesus was not saying that souls reside there for eternity. He was not saying that hell was *gehenna* but that eternal punishment would be something like being thrown onto the rubbish dump.

This leaves open the possibility that Jesus was using metaphor. Thus other Christians understand hell to be a state of permanent godlessness; Pope John Paul II has said, 'rather than a place, hell indicates the state of those who freely and definitively separate themselves from God' (Sheler, 2000). Christian notions of hell, like those of angels and of the Devil, may derive more from ancient Zoroastrian traditions than from scant biblical references. The Zoroastrian hell replicates its heaven; while heaven's inmates eat delicious food, hell's eat 'a noxious counterpart'. There is even an 'intermediate place' for those whose 'good actions exactly match their evil deeds' (Duchesne-Guillemin, 1973, p. 225).

## The old quest begins

Most scholars identify 1778 as the beginning of the 'old quest' for the historical Jesus. This was the year in which the first part of Hermann Samuel Reimarus' *Fragments* was posthumously published. In his lifetime, Reimarus (1694–1768) had been a renowned defender of traditional Christianity and a disciple of Christian Wolff, whose arguments he supported. In private, however, he rebelled against what he, like Annet, saw as absurd and irrational in the Gospels. In his *Fragments*, he called miracles 'as improbable as they are incredible' (Talbert, 1970, p. 230).

Properly speaking, Reimarus' work does not fall within the scope of this chapter. Since he placed himself outside traditional Christianity, he belongs to Chapter 4. Yet his work impacted so dramatically on Christian scholarship that the subsequent story of the quest of the historical Jesus cannot be told without reference to his seminal contribution. Indeed, although he was an outsider, his reputation was such that his ideas could not be dismissed as easily as could those of the infidel Deists. Schweitzer called the *Fragments* 'not only one of the greatest events in the history of criticism' but 'also a masterpiece of general literature . . . so seldom has there been a hate so eloquent, so lofty a scorn' (1998b, p. 15).

For Reimarus, the real Jesus was not identical with the traditional Christian image of Jesus I have described above. Although placing himself outside the boundary of Christianity, Reimarus offered his book about Jesus as a more authentic Jesus story than that revered by the Church. While he repudiated orthodox Christian faith, he viewed the real Jesus with respect and saw his task as one of recovery. He wanted to separate the real Jesus from what he saw as fabricated material within the gospel narrative. His strategy, however, was one of attack and ridicule of the traditional view of Jesus. In the process, he sliced away huge portions of material from the gospel accounts. I characterize his account of Jesus as a work of *deconstruction*. Schweitzer called it 'full of hate':

There is no historical task which so reveals a man's true self as the writing of a Life of Jesus. No vital force comes into the figure unless a man breathes into it all the hate or all the love of which he is capable. The stronger the love, or the stronger that hate, the more life-like is the figure that is produced. For hate as well as love can write a Life of Jesus, and the greatest of them are written with hate: that of Reimarus, the Wolfenbuttel Fragmentist . . . it was not so much hate of the Person of Jesus as of the supernatural nimbus with which it was so easy to surround Him. (Schweitzer, 1998b, p. 4)

Many of the issues raised by Reimarus remain on the agenda of Jesus studies. First, he stripped the Gospels of all supernatural trappings: virgin birth – indeed the whole of the nativity stories went, as did miracles, the transfiguration, any predictions of future events by Jesus, the resurrection and the ascension.

Reimarus also subtracted any material said to be in fulfilment of scripture, claiming that all such material was back-projected by the disciples: 'not a single sentence applied by Matthew and others to the history of Jesus was written in the sense ascribed to it' (Talbert, 1970, p. 236). His most radical criticism of Christianity as conceived by the disciples and as perpetuated by the Roman Church was that it transformed Jesus' mission from a purely political one into a spiritual enterprise. Jesus' aim and intent, said Reimarus, had had nothing to do with spiritual salvation or with citizenship of a heavenly kingdom but with liberating Israel from Roman rule. His aim had been to 'Build up a worldly kingdom and to deliver the Israelites from bondage' (*ibid.*, p. 150).

Reimarus argued that this would have been the goal of anyone who thought himself to be the Messiah, and that Jesus had campaigned to be recognized as such (p. 144). Apparent reluctance to claim the title was part of a deliberate strategy: 'I am inclined to think that [his] intention [was to make] them more eager to spread the news' (p. 144). An independent Israel, for Jesus as for all Jews, was a theological imperative, but apart from this belief, Jesus had no explicitly religious aspirations. Reimarus did accept the historicity of Jesus' triumphant entry into Jerusalem. Expecting the people to rally to his cause, he deliberately posed as Messiah king, 'as though he were the king of whom it is written, "Behold, your king is coming to you" [Zechariah 9:9; Matthew 21:5]' (p. 144).

Reimarus claimed that Jesus may have had some expectation of divine intervention. The cry of desolation from the cross – 'My God, My God, Why have you forsaken me' – was 'a confession which can hardly be otherwise interpreted than that God had not helped him to carry out his intentions' (p. 150). When his plans did not succeed, and soldiers came to arrest him instead, Jesus was taken by complete surprise. He can hardly have predicted that he would be delivered to the high priest and crucified, said Reimarus, because death played no part in his strategy. A Jesus who did not intend to die on the cross, as well as a Jesus who survived the cross, surfaces repeatedly in this survey. Nor had Reimarus' Jesus any intention of establishing a new religion, with new ceremonies or beliefs to replace Jewish ones. At the Passover, Jesus may have introduced new words into the ritual, believing that he would not share another meal with his followers until after the revolution. However, he did nothing that 'was to serve as an abrogation and nullification of . . . Jewish ceremonies, of the Jewish law or religion' (p. 120).

Put bluntly, Jesus was a Jew. Nor did he issue the so-called missionary commission to go into the whole world preaching the Gospel. This was one of many additions by the early Church to justify its very existence among the Gentiles. Indeed, the whole story of God becoming human in Jesus in order to fulfil Hebrew prophecy and to die and rise again to redeem all people was invented by the disciples after Jesus' totally unexpected and unwanted death. Having dreamed of sharing some of the post-revolutionary glory with Jesus, the disciples had no desire to return to a life of anonymity in Galilee. Instead, they invented the resurrection and the idea that Jesus was a spiritual saviour, stole the body and waited fifty days in order to proclaim more confidently 'that they had seen him . . . eaten with him' and that he had 'ascended into heaven that he might return in glory' (p. 250). After a detailed discussion of contradictions in the accounts of the resurrection, Reimarus remarked that 'witnesses who differ so greatly in their testimony would not be recognized in any secular court as valid or legal' (p. 176).

All gospel references to the 'Son of Man' or to the Messiah or to Jesus' suffering or to his return were supplied by the disciples. They found their inspiration in the 'suffering servant' passages of Isaiah, and in the conviction of a few Jews who 'believed in a twofold coming of the Messiah, who was first to appear suffering . . . and again in glory' (pp. 248–9). Later, the disciples had to devise a way of explaining why Jesus had not yet returned. At the time, however, they had to offer an imminent return, or Jesus would have appeared a complete failure:

If the apostles had said that it would be about seventeen, eighteen or several hundred years before Christ returned . . . in the clouds . . . and begin his kingdom, people would simply have laughed at them. (p. 215)

Reimarus suggests that the Gospels were written in accordance with the new doctrines formulated by the disciples, who wrote into them whatever served their purposes. The Messiah would have performed miracles, so these were supplied, the Messiah would be at least the equivalent of Elijah, so he too would feed the people and raise the dead. Nothing was easier than for them to invent as many miracles as they pleased (p. 233). The flight to Egypt was pure invention; eager to depict Jesus as a second Moses, the disciples had to introduce a slaying of infants and find a substitute for the basket in the bull rushes in order to save the infant Jesus. Reimarus wrote:

A thousand asserted miracles cannot clear up and set straight one single evident contradiction in the accounts of the resurrection now before my eyes. All the asserted piety and holiness of the apostles cannot convince me that Jesus visibly returned with great power and glory, and began his glorious kingdom upon earth before some of those who stood round him had tasted death. All the martyrs with the unheard-of torments they endured will not convince me that the passage, 'Out of Egypt I have called my son' (Matt 2:15; Hos 11:1), refers to Jesus; or that the sentence, 'He shall be called a Nazarene' (Matt 2:23) stands in the existing writings of the Old Testament. (p. 240)

What emerges from Reimarus is a picture of Jesus that differs fundamentally from the traditional Christian image and which, for many, broke the comfortable assumption that the Gospels were wholly reliable accounts of Jesus' life.

Although, as noted, Reimarus was not the first to claim that the disciples had back-projected their later beliefs into the texts, it was his *Fragments* that put this argument centre stage. Reimarus also attributed to the disciples conscious deceit; others accepted that they edited their sources but argued that their motives were sincere. Most controversial, perhaps, was Reimarus' view that *Jesus' goals had been political*. This would remain unpopular among Christians. In 1967, Brandon acknowledged in his often misrepresented *Jesus and the Zealots: A Study of Political Factors in Primitive Christianity* that his contentions would shock many readers for whom the incarnate Son of God could not have been involved in, or conditioned by, the political relations of Jews and Romans (p. xi).

Brandon, as noted in Chapter 1, did not think that Jesus' primary goal was political but he shared the Zealots' opposition to Roman rule. He may, said Brandon, have supported armed rebellion inasmuch as the Romans and their collaborators were a major impediment to a restored people, deserving of God's salvation (p. 338). Like Reimarus, Brandon does not believe that Jesus or the early Jewish Christians had any concern for Gentiles (pp. 169–70). The idea of evangelizing Gentiles was Paul's, part of his strategy to gain power and influence within the movement. Chapter 3 continues to track the story of the quest of the historical Jesus as launched by Reimarus, whose theories clamoured for a Christian response. Many of the issues he raised would simply not go away. They feature through to the end of my next chapter, indeed to the end of this book.

# 3 Christians on Jesus: The Quest for the Real Jesus

It was not only each epoch that found its reflection in Jesus, each individual created him in accord with his own character. (Schweitzer, 1998b, p. 4)

## The agenda

After Reimarus, the quest of the historical Jesus revolved around three questions raised by his thesis. First, what had been the nature of Jewish messianic expectations? Were Jews expecting anything like a spiritual saviour? Was the Son of Man a messianic figure? Reimarus put eschatology, Jesus' understanding of the 'End Times', firmly on the agenda. Speculation about whether Jesus expected an imminent return, about whether his mission was political or spiritual, about the nature of his understanding of God's kingdom, remains bread-and-butter material for Jesus studies. Those who argue in favour of continuity between what Jesus believed about himself and what the early Church believed tend to argue (against Reimarus) for a timeless, spiritual mission. Those who stress discontinuity argue that Jesus had expected a sudden, cataclysmic consummation. The nature of first-century Jewish, of Jesus' and of the early Church's eschatological thought remains hotly contested, as I noted in Chapter 1.

Second, did Jesus intend to found a new religion, and what was the relationship between his movement and contemporary Judaism? For all that Reimarus depicted Jesus as a Jew he had nothing positive to say about Judaism:

Reimarus managed to convey a profound contempt for Judaism, which he denigrated as distorted 'ceremoniousness'. Whereas the Pharisees were obsessed with legalism, he argued Jesus preached hope and immortality: 'Consequently his teaching had a considerable advantage not only over that of the Pharisees, but also over that of the Old Testament, where such essential principles of religion were not even considered and where there is mention only of earthly promises and rewards, all hope for man ending with his death.' (Allen, 1998 p. 116)

Even as scholars sought to relocate Jesus more firmly in the Judaism of his day, they continued to see him as a good Jew among mainly bad Jews. The

Christian attitude towards Judaism is a major topic in Chapter 5 of this book.

Third, Reimarus' work raised the theological question of whether faith in Christ is *dependent on* or *independent of* whatever historical research tells us about the life of the man Jesus. This was the very question that his editor and posthumous publisher Gotthold Ephraim Lessing (1729–81) tackled in his own writing. Lessing questioned whether Christian faith either stood or fell on its historic base, arguing that:

if no historical truth can be demonstrated, then nothing can be demonstrated by means of historical truths. That is; *the accidental truths of history can never become the proof of necessary truths or reason.* . . . That the Christ . . . declared himself to be the Son of God . . . I gladly believe. . . . But to jump from that historical truth to a quite different class of truth, and to demand of me that I should form all my metaphysical and moral ideas accordingly . . . is the broad, ugly ditch which I cannot get across. . . . If anyone can help me to cross it, let him do it. I beg him, I adjure him. (1956, pp. 53–5; emphasis added)

Revelation, for Lessing, was progressive, part of the divine education of the human race. Scripture did not drop out of heaven but represented human response to their experience of God. Authors may understand imperfectly and express their understanding even less perfectly. Scripture, like any human work, is 'subject to the normal amount of errors and discrepancies' (Talbert, 1970, p. 32). As the human race grew up, it could discard what was no longer educationally appropriate: 'every primer is only for a certain age. To delay the child, that has outgrown it, longer at it than it was intended, is harmful' (Lessing, 1956, p. 91). History, then, is inadequate as the ground of inner religious truth; religious truth may be 'suggested or occasioned but never legitimized by historical events' (Talbert, *op. cit.*). Religious truths are essentially innate, validated by their own authenticity.

For Lessing, there was a 'broad, ugly ditch' between historical events, and any moral ideas, or values, which apparently depended upon history for their authenticity. Morality must be independent of historical evidence, since even eyewitnesses do not understand exactly what they observe. Many would suggest that this was true of the resurrection; since the disciples did not understand what happened, they used metaphor and symbolism to express what they had experienced but which they could not properly describe. In this view, Hume's scepticism that human testimony could ever verify a miracle also applied to the resurrection. Perceptively, Lessing also drew a distinction between the religion of Jesus, and Christianity:

The religion of Christ is contained in the clearest and most lucid language . . . the Christian religion is so uncertain and ambiguous, that there is scarcely a single passage which, in all the history of the world, has been interpreted in the same way. (1956, p. 106)

## Philosophical contributions

The old quest (1778–1906) was concerned primarily with reconciling the results of critical biblical scholarship, often in response to incredulity with things supernatural, with the Christ of faith. Almost all contributors to the old quest believed they could uncover a historically reliable account of Jesus, even if this demanded the rethinking of Christian belief. Many accepted, with Reimarus, that over-enthusiasm had led the disciples to insert bogus material into the Gospels. However, few if any of those who continued to identify themselves as Christians wanted to impute to the disciples insincerity, or to depict Jesus' mission as purely political. Allen (1998) convincingly shows how those who responded to Reimarus tended to do so from either a Kantian or an Hegelian perspective, inspired respectively by Immanuel Kant (1724–1804) and Georg Wilhelm Friedrich Hegel (1770–1831). By dressing Jesus up in philosophical clothes, scholars thought they could rehabilitate him for their sceptical peers. Their strategy was to downplay anything supernatural and to emphasize moral aspects (see Allen, 1998, p. 142).

What emerged are often described as liberal lives of Jesus, since what their authors attempted to rescue from the Gospels was Jesus' ethic, as had Jefferson. Kant's ideas on Jesus are found in his *Religion Within the Limits of Reason Alone* (1960). For Kantians, Jesus is the perfect man, whose radical moral fortitude overcomes human sin. Jesus thus emerges as the 'embodiment of a universal idea of goodness, of humanity in its moral perfection' (Allen, 1998, p. 123). Jesus was not the Son of God in a literal but in a metaphorical sense. Kantians reject supernatural intervention. Jesus was not 'sent' in a physical sense of descending from heaven; he is 'eternal' inasmuch as he personifies eternal truth. Jesus' sacrificial death takes a back seat to the example of his life of service, and to his ethical teaching. This understanding of Jesus' 'sonship' appears within the work of both philosophical schools.

Hegelians tend to see Jesus as an important contributor to humanity's quest for moral and spiritual progress. He represents a high moment in the history of humanity's emerging self-consciousness. For Hegel, a 'thesis' leads to an 'antithesis' and finally to a 'synthesis' which resolves apparent contradictions and conflicts. The human struggle to realize the highest level of self-consciouness characteristically involves tension between man/woman as 'nature' and as 'spirit'. The ideal is a synthesis of nature and spirit in which alienation between the two is overcome. Hegel's view of Jesus is found in his unfinished and posthumously published essay 'The Spirit of Christianity and Its Fate' (1948). Jesus, said Hegel, was one in whom the absolute spirit existed in complete harmony with his finite spirit, thus reconciling estrangement between these two conflicting aspects of human existence. His was a 'spirit raised above morality' (*ibid.*, p. 212). 'He possessed' said Hegel, 'a spirit entirely his own. He visualized the world as it is and was to be.'

Jesus' kingdom, according to Hegel, is 'the living harmony of men, their fellowship with God; it is the development of the divine among men' (*ibid.*, p. 277). In telling the story of Jesus, the disciples were captive to their context. The only way in which they could highlight Jesus' significance was with miracles, the virgin birth and resurrection. All these dogmas affirm Jesus' moral worth, even his Kantian embodiment of the idea of goodness, but they must be understood by modern, rational people as only metaphorically true. Effectively, the Kantian and the Hegelian Jesus does not need to be understood in a particular historical moment, since neither Jesus' moral perfection nor his overcoming of radical estrangement owed anything to the circumstances surrounding his life, that is, to Second Temple Judaism.

## Heinrich Eberhard Gottlob Paulus (1761–1851)

Some Kantians tried to explain supernatural content in the Gospels (instead of subtracting it) by reworking the text from a rationalist perspective. The most famous example of this approach is the work of Heinrich Eberhard Gottlob Paulus, who ended his career as Professor of Exegesis and Church History at Heidelberg. This is also an early example of supposing a link between Jesus and the Essenes, who Josephus tells us were great healers (*War* 2:136). Paulus thought Jesus may have attended an Essene school. In order to carry out some of his actions, Jesus required help from Essenes. Paulus' reconstruction of the gospel account supplies additional characters who assisted Jesus with his healings and other activities. Bahrdt (1792) also had Jesus healing with the use of secret potions. Paulus assumed that miracles had been written into the Gospels because people at that time accepted supernatural happenings as real.

Since they had no other, more scientific, means of understanding what they saw, belief in the miraculous provided a ready explanation for events they could not otherwise comprehend. Thus, the 'Jewish love of miracles "caused everything to be ascribed immediately to the Deity, and secondary causes to be overlooked"' (Schweitzer, 1998b, p. 53). When Jesus did not use medicines, or psychology, as in the calming of the storm, what we have described in the Gospels is simply what the disciples *thought* they experienced: 'Immediately after taking Jesus into the boat they doubled a headland and drew clear of the storm area; they therefore supposed that He had calmed the sea by His command' (*ibid.*, p. 52).

The feeding of the crowd was, said Paulus, a miracle of generosity, not of multiplication; Jesus and his disciples set a good example by sharing their food, and others followed. The transfiguration was a mountain-top meeting between Jesus and two of his secret followers, during which his appearance was 'illuminated by the beams of the rising sun'. The spear thrust into Jesus' side while he hung on the cross, says Paulus, served as a phlebotomy, while an earthquake conveniently moved the stone. Jesus thus recovered. Mary Magdalene thought that he was a gardener because he had somehow replaced his grave-clothes with a gardener's. Once Jesus had found out from her where the disciples were, he went there and 'appeared unexpectedly among them'. Later, he stage-managed his ascension, since he knew that he was so weak and exhausted that he could not live much longer: 'He assembled his followers for the last time. . . . He lifted up his hands to bless them . . . He moved away. . . . A cloud interposes itself between them and Him, so that their eyes cannot follow Him' (*ibid.*, p. 55). Jesus crept away and died a natural death. Since no one knew where he died, 'they came to describe His departure as an Ascension'.

While Paulus rejected the supernatural, he did not subtract the events themselves from the gospel account, nor did he accuse the writers of deceit or fraud, only of belonging to a worldview different from his own. Paulus represents an early example of a scholar who resisted the temptation to subtract material from the Gospels, yet who also rejected many traditional beliefs about Jesus. This strategy, of rereading the text while leaving it intact, is one which we will encounter again, especially in Chapter 4. However, what was left of Jesus after Paulus had explained the miraculous away as non-miraculous? Basically, his Jesus was a Kantian Jesus; what was special about his Jesus was the 'purity and serene holiness of His character', which he described as 'genuinely human, and adapted to the imitation and emulation of mankind' (*ibid.*, p. 51). Unfortunately, Paulus' Kantian Jesus was lost sight of amidst his ingenious and sometimes far-fetched rationalist explanations of miracles and of other supernatural content. None the less, these attempts still have some currency, and even modern preachers may be heard repeating Paulus' theories, although they are often unaware of their source.

### Friedrich Ernst Daniel Schleiermacher (1768–1834)

A more sophisticated Kantian response to Reimarus came from the pen of the man often dubbed modern theology's father, F. E. D. Schleiermacher, Berlin's first Professor of Theology. He rarely refers directly to Reimarus but he does discuss most of the issues raised by the *Fragments* (see 1975, p. 445, for a reference to Reimarus). He cites Paulus several times (*ibid.*, pp. 27, 117–18, 120). Schleiermacher's lifelong task was the re-articulation of Christian dogmas in language that might convince his contemporaries, for whom rationality and the laws of physics were the only tools with which the world might be understood, and knowledge of its working obtained. Yet the rationalist and Kantian Schleiermacher was also open to what he called 'religious feeling', having been influenced from an early age by the Moravian pietists.

Religion, he argued, belonged properly to the domain of 'feelings'; it is more akin to art, to music and to poetry than to engineering or science, if not to philosophy. Today, we might say that religion is a 'right' and not a 'left' brain activity. Schleiermacher developed his system in his *Religion: Speeches to Its Cultured Despisers* (1958) and *The Christian Faith* (1928), as well as in a series of lectures on Jesus delivered between 1819 and 1834. These lectures were posthumously published as *Das Leben Jesu* in 1864, reconstructed from student notes (I cite from the 1975 English edition). Throughout, even when rejecting such cherished gospel stories as the nativity narratives, he is anxious not to 'disadvantage Christian faith' (1975, p. 59). I characterize his book as a *constructive* attempt to deal with the critical issues.

His Jesus is the Kantian ideal of human perfection (an archetype). By radical submission to the will of God, Jesus lived a life that was so permeated with a sense or consciousness of God that over the course of time the distinction between his humanity and 'divinity' blurred (1975, pp. 14–15, 102). This involved the development of Jesus' inner self. Although a Jesus who undergoes inner development is not how Christians have habitually understood him, Schleiermacher offers this as proof of Jesus' humanity: 'If true human development in Christ were not assumed, it would be impossible to assume that his life was truly human' (*ibid.*, p. 15). Jesus' birth was just like that of any other woman or man: 'it cannot be maintained that the narrative of the supernatural conception of Christ is a wholly historically founded statement' (*ibid.*, p. 59).

Schleiermacher thus rejected a pre-existent Christ (although the archetype had always existed) but he still wanted to distinguish Christ from all other men, because Christian faith itself (which he was defending) 'draws a distinction between Christ and all other men' (*ibid.*, p. 24). His strategy for holding on to a Jesus whose relationship with God could be understood in purely human terms, and a Christ who 'is the embodiment of the divine principle, of God's knowledge and goal of the human race', was to affirm that Jesus' sense of absolute dependence on God was quantitatively rather than qualitatively different from that which other people experience (Verheyden, 1975, p. liv). His Jesus 'acquired' sonship in a way that is to my mind not altogether different from Arius' Jesus. Had Arius' Christology won the ancient debate, the world may never have had a Schleiermacher.

Through sympathy, Jesus communicates to Christians the power of his own God-consciousness, and draws them into the company of regenerated people, the Church: 'The Church takes shape through the coming together of regenerated individuals to form a system of mutual inter-action and co-operation' (Schleiermacher, 1928, p. 532). Jesus did not expect either 'the end of human affairs or a personal return' but 'was convinced only of a continuous judgment that takes place in the course of the development of the kingdom itself' (1975, p. 335). Schleiermacher's preference for John's Gospel effectively bypassed the problem of Jesus' eschatology; John's Jesus neither speaks of an imminent return, nor says that much about his own future (see Allen, 1998, p. 141). Schweitzer judged Schleiermacher's 'one-sided preference for the Fourth Gospel . . . fatal to a sound historical view' (1998b, p. 66).

For Schleiermacher, the corporate moral life achieved by regenerated people, by lives of cooperation and fellowship, represents the 'Spirit'. He thus retained the Trinity yet more or less stripped it of metaphysical significance. On the other hand, his constructionalist approach to the Gospels enabled him to retain some material that others would jettison, even when this was not necessary for his own Christology. For example, he retains at least some of Jesus' healing miracles, which he saw as examples of the influence that spirit can exercise on matter: 'there are analogies which show that purely organic illnesses can be cured by spiritual powers . . . performed because of Christ's concern for human need' (1975, p. 202).

Such 'miracles' represent 'moral acts on the part of Christ' (*ibid.*, p. 205) flowing from his love for humanity. Similarly, he had no wish to jettison the resurrection but was too much the rationalist to accept the historicity of the traditional account. Instead, after a detailed discussion of the Gospels, he hints that Jesus' post-death appearances should be regarded 'as wholly normal in human terms' (*ibid.*, p. 466). In my view, Schleiermacher thought that, as Paulus had surmised, Jesus had somehow survived the crucifixion. On the ascension he resorts to mystification: 'So, then, something happened in this instance, but what the disciples saw could not have been all there was to know, and the rest is only a supplement' (*ibid.*, p. 472).

## A Jewish Jesus?

While preference for John did not become characteristic of the liberal response to Reimarus, rejection of imminent eschatology did. Schleiermacher, though, was no more sympathetic towards Judaism than Reimarus had been. Eager to sell Jesus to his rationalist and increasingly sceptical peers, he depicted a Jesus whose significance was 'sui generis, immune from the influences of the surrounding Jewish culture' (Heschel, 1998, p. 129). Schleiermacher's Jesus, says Heschel, 'no longer had to be viewed as a Jew, because what was essential about him, his religious consciousness, was not subject to historical analyses' (*ibid.*). In fact, in *Fifth Speech* Schleiermacher declared that 'Judaism is long since dead' (1958, p. 238). Few Germans at this time were interested in acknowledging any Christian indebtedness to Judaism; Christianity had replaced Judaism because it had failed (the Jews had failed God). It was bankrupt and redundant.

Years of stereotyping Judaism as an outmoded, legalistic fossil, bypassed in favour of the religion of grace, Christianity, and of Jews as Christ killers, were difficult to forget. Luther had used the term 'Pharisee' as a synonym for hypocrisy and legalism, and applied it to the Roman Catholics (see Heschel, 1998, p. 70). Jesus as an original genius, who might have been born a German but who happened to be Jewish, was a much more attractive idea. In this view, 'the founder of Christianity is at the same time the moral hero who makes a great advance in the history of culture' (Niebuhr, 1951, p. 89). What Schleiermacher's mediating theology tried to do was to reduce the gap between Christ and his own contemporary culture. Some might say that this succeeded and bore fruit in Hitler's National Christian Church, where Christ was recruited to validate claims of racial and cultural superiority. Perhaps the most extreme case of a Jesus created in the image of an age was the Aryan Jesus of Nazi Germany. I return to this anti-Jewish theme in Chapter 5.

## Ferdinand Christian Baur (1792–1860)

Another Hegelian response to the problem of reconciling the possible differences between the Jesus of history and the Christ of faith was that of Ferdinand Christian Baur and the Tübingen school of historical criticism. I alluded to Baur in my Introduction. Baur regarded classical, orthodox Christology as articulated by the creeds to be the result of a dialectic process whereby an original split between Peter's exclusive, Jewish form (*tendenzen*, or tendency) of Christianity and Paul's universal, Hellenic form eventually merged to counter the common enemy, Gnosticism. Baur's *Church History of the First Three Centuries* (1853) is peppered with the word 'antithesis'. In this two-volume work, he first traces the split between Paul and the Peter–James-led Jewish Church, then shows how these two rival tendencies came together 'by a process of smoothing down their differences, and finding the mean between their opposing principles' (1878, Vol. 1, p. 77). For example, Paul's teaching on salvation by faith, and Peter's and James' on salvation by works, came to co-exist alongside each other (*ibid.*, pp. 128, 140). Peter emerged as head of the Catholic Church, because Paul's Gentile Christianity needed a 'Jewish-Christian imprimatur' for the merger to succeed in the eyes of the Peter party (1879, Vol. 2, p. 37).

However, for Baur this was all part of a strategy to effect harmony and 'brotherly agreement between the two apostles Peter and Paul' (1878, Vol. 1, p. 181). Catholic Christianity expressed itself both in this 'fraternal unity' at Rome (1878, Vol. 1, p. 153) and in the Gospel of John. In John, we see 'Christianity . . . as a universal principle of salvation', and 'all those antitheses which threatened to detain it within the narrow limits of Jewish particularism' appear 'merged in the universalism of Christianity' (*ibid.*, p. 180). Yet behind Paul's tendency the figure of the historical Jesus was but a shadowy presence. Paul's theology derived from his spiritual vision, and required 'no history to elucidate it. Why should [Paul] go to eye witnesses . . . of Christ's life to ask what he was according to the flesh, when he has seen himself in the spirit?' (1878, Vol. 1, p. 50). Nor did Paul need the Hebrew Bible, since for him the 'contents of Christianity' were found 'immediately in itself, in the spiritual consciousness which is awakened by faith'. Thus, the Hebrew Bible 'has only a very secondary importance' (*ibid.*, p. 144).

## Michael Goulder

There is clear evidence of debate in Acts about whether Gentiles had to be circumcised and keep the dietary laws, as at least a bare minimum of the 613 *mitzvot* (see Acts 10 and 11). For Baur, these were rival theological interpretations of Jesus' life and what emerged as Christianity was a synthesis of various strands. The synthesis was a valid theology but should not be confused with an account of Jesus based purely on what might be said of the historical Jesus. Arguably, this separated Jesus from his original context, making him an abstraction that could be comfortably incorporated into German culture, made to bear German values. Michael Goulder, a professor at Birmingham University, has recently revisited Baur's hypothesis in his *St Paul versus St Peter: A Tale of Two Missions* (1995). His version has the Pauline tendency triumphing over the Jewish tendency rather than synthesizing with it to combat Gnosticism.

The Jewish group, says Goulder, saw Jesus as a man, born in the usual way, adopted by God as Messiah (*ibid.*, p. 110), while the Paulists introduced such notions as pre-existence, divine birth, and of grace supplanting the law. Paul's role will be a recurring topic in Chapter 4. The view that the original followers of Jesus regarded him as a man, not as 'God', and that the notion of a divine Jesus was borrowed from outside, is an idea that emerged in very early anti-Christian polemic. Some of the scholars discussed later in this chapter, including Bultmann and the Jesus Seminar, advocate similar theories.

## David Friedrich Strauss (1808–74)

David Friedrich Strauss was a student of Baur at Tübingen who, after graduating, went to Berlin to study with Hegel. Unfortunately, Hegel died very soon after Strauss reached Berlin, so the young scholar was only able to attend a few of his hero's lectures. Schleiermacher's treatment of Jesus had little appeal for Strauss, who began to develop an approach which he believed would do more justice to the material than either Reimarus' extreme scepticism or Paulus' and Schleiermacher's Kantian rationalism. By 1832 a lecturer on Hegelianism at Tübingen, Strauss' *Life of Jesus* was first published in 1836. It created a storm. Strauss lost his job and was never to occupy an academic post again. The book, though, sold extremely well and earned Strauss no mean income. A British Unitarian woman with an interest in German philosophy, George Eliot (1819–80), who was herself to become a famous novelist, was responsible for translating it into English (1846). The leading free-thinker John M. Robertson praised Eliot's own novels as 'rationalist propaganda' and described her work as 'especially significant' in the 'history of modern English freethought' (1957, p. 424).

Allen explains Strauss' success in England, in terms of sales at least, by reference to Victorian fascination for material progress and development

(Allen, 1998, p. 162). The book circulated widely. Eliot's biographer states that 'few books of the nineteenth century have had a profounder influence on religious thought in England' (Haight, 1968, p. 59). In 1854, Anglican missionary Karl Pfander (1803–66), who debated with Muslim scholars in North India, was astonished when his opponents, who had a copy of *The Life of Jesus* on the table, used Strauss' thesis to confirm the Qur'an's charge of *tahrif*, or the Christian corruption of the Gospel (see Chapter 5). Pfander's pietist education at Basel Seminary had ignored form criticism; he later accused Catholic missionaries of sabotaging his endeavours (for Pfander, see Bennett, 1996b).

Although Strauss published three amended versions and a *New Life* (1868), in which he responded to critical comment, critics 'hounded him until his death' (Funk *et al.*, 1993, p. 3), and the acclaim he so much coveted was never forthcoming. Increasingly bitter that academic appointments and recognition were denied him, he spent the rest of his life writing political and intellectual biographies; briefly, he was also a representative in the Württemberg provincial assembly. 'He was not', Schweitzer wrote, 'either the greatest or the deepest' of theologians, but he was the most absolutely sincere' (1998b, p. 68). 'To understand Strauss,' Schweitzer continued, 'one must first love him.' 'Disappointment and suffering', too, gave Strauss' 'life its consecration' (*ibid.*). When Strauss first wrote his *Life of Jesus*, he saw himself as defending Christianity from its critics and as developing an apology that could rescue from Jesus something worth emulating. Reimarus' failed Jesus and opportunistic, self-serving disciples hardly represent role models. It was through Strauss' 'Reimarus and his Apology for the Rational Worship of God' (1862, 1970) that Reimarus became commonly known as the author of the controversial *Fragments*. Thus it was Strauss who made Reimarus' 'name known among literature' (Schweitzer, 1998b, p. 14).

## The old faith and the new

By the end of his life, when he wrote *The Old Faith and the New* (1872, 1997), Strauss was so disillusioned with Christianity's ability to deal with the changes in belief demanded by biblical criticism that he abandoned Christian faith for a belief in an evolving cosmos (1997, Vol. 1, p. 168) in which humanity 'not only can and should know Nature, but rule both the external nature, as far as his own powers admit, and the natural within himself' (Vol. 2, p. 58). Instead of preaching the ideas behind its myths, the Church was clinging on to them, and together with all its trappings, ought to be dismantled (Vol. 1, p. 6). Its insistence on limiting love to those who believed in the atonement was narrow and exclusive. However, abandoning 'the form of religion in which [the] kernel ripened' did not mean that all the good that Christianity brought into the world must be discarded, just as 'what was accomplished by Greece and Rome' still enriched human civilization (*ibid.*, p. 98). Schweitzer suggested that it was misplaced loyalty to Darwin which led Strauss, 'instead of developing the idea of this deep inner freedom, and presenting his religion in the form in which he had experienced it', to end up advocating an 'impersonal way' (1998b, p. 76). However, Strauss may have simply returned to some of the ideas of his youth, when he had been attracted to the views of Jakob Boehme (1575–1624), who saw God's presence permeating all creation (see Allen, 1998, p. 150). I do not think it coincidence that the 1997 English edition of *The Old Faith and The New* was edited by G. A. Wells, a contemporary leading advocate of the non-existence of Jesus whose theory I discuss in Chapter 4.

## A proper understanding of things oriental

Strauss suggested that while Reimarus had possessed all the requisite linguistic skills to deal with his texts, he lacked 'a proper understanding of things oriental' (Strauss, 1970, p. 51). This made 'the visions of the prophet, the raptures of the apocalyptic' foreign to him (*ibid.*, p. 52). To depict an 'internal event' as if it had been 'external' was for him deceit. Therefore, Reimarus had accused the disciples of fraud and invention. Strauss' thesis was that a much more complex process of myth-making was actually at work and that this process differs from conscious fraud. To the first-century Palestinian, expressing inner truth as an external event was natural:

a closer investigation of the life of the human soul and of the developmental history of religion has taught us that a truth can be revealed to men at first in an unsuitable form; if you will, within the husk of a delusion, where it nonetheless may possess the value and effectiveness of truth. (*ibid.*, p. 53)

The modern theologian 'who preaches, for example, on the resurrection' might not believe in the reality of that event as a 'single, sensible fact' but may 'nevertheless hold to be true the representation of the process of spiritual life which the resurrection of Christ affords' (Strauss, 1972, p. 782). Such an 'idea' has 'its confirmation no longer in history but in philosophy' (*ibid.*, p. 781). This serves, Strauss said, as a working explanation of how religious myths are created.

Passages in the Gospels which express convictions about Jesus may be mythic, the 'product of an idea of his earliest followers' (*ibid.*, p. 86). Sometimes, 'a definite individual fact' may have been 'seized upon by religious enthusiasm, and twined around with mythical conceptions culled from the idea of the Christ' (*ibid.*, p. 87). Some of the criteria that Strauss developed became part of the tool-kit of form criticism: material contrary to 'known and universal laws which govern the course of events' (*ibid.*, p. 88) is mythic; material that too conveniently fits messianic expectations, and has something of the legendary in its telling, is mythic, such as the visit of the Magi (p. 89) and the transfiguration (pp. 535f.). Of the latter, Strauss wrote:

it might seem that after deducting the marvelous, the presence of two men might be retained as historical facts. But the legend was predisposed, by virtue of the current idea concerning the relation of these two prophets, to make any two men . . . into Moses and Elijah. (p. 91)

In each section of what was a very large book (the 1972 English edition has 812 pages), he considers possible 'natural' and 'supernatural' aspects, and explanations, of his subject matter. If the former are convincing, and the 'matter related . . . could have taken place in the manner described', the material is judged to be historical. If not, he proceeds to explore the supernatural aspects, not to discredit the whole account but to separate the historical from the mythical (see his 'Criteria', pp. 87–92).

Detailed chapters expose the mythical origins of the following, among other material:

*The genealogical material*: which he judges inaccurate and unconvincing historically. Rather, it expresses the theological conviction that Jesus was 'of Davidic descent' (p. 118).

*The nativity stories*: the star was taken from Numbers 24:17. The shepherds appear because Moses was beside his flock when God spoke to him, and God had taken David from his sheep to become shepherd of his people. In addition, ancient myth often 'ascribed divine apparitions to countrymen and shepherds' (p. 160).

*The baptism*: the dove and voice from heaven at the baptism are mythic.

*The forty days in the wilderness*: this is based on Moses' and the refugees' wilderness sojourn (p. 261).

*Cross*: Strauss thinks it unlikely that Jesus cried, 'My God, My God' from the cross, and therefore judges Reimarus' inference that this was an acknowledgement of failure unjustified conjecture.

### Subjective truth

Like Reimarus, Strauss does not accept the historicity of the resurrection (1972, pp. 737–9). On the other hand, he thinks that the real truth of what happened is obscured by legend. Probably, the disciples did not know where the body was, otherwise 'it is difficult to conceive how the disciples . . . could believe and declare that Jesus was risen, without refuting themselves, or meeting with refutation from their adversaries' (p. 743). When told, the story was embellished with 'all the pomp which the Jewish imagination furnished' (p. 744), but the disciples cannot be blamed for telling their mythic story 'in a form from which, after subtracting the miracles only theft remained' (Strauss, 1970, p. 48).

Nor can Jesus himself 'be held to account for this belief in his resurrection, except indirectly'. In fact, 'its existence proves what a strong and lasting impression he must have made on his disciples' (Strauss, 1997, Vol. 1, pp. 83–4). The disciples experienced something that convinced them that he was alive, and thus heard him 'in every impressive sound, or saw him in every striking appearance' (Strauss, 1972, p. 743). This was *subjectively*, not *empirically*, true for them. By elaborating the conception of the resurrection of their slain master, the disciples had rescued his work; moreover, 'it was their honest conviction that they had actually beheld and conversed with their risen Lord' (Strauss, 1997, Vol. 1, p. 82).

Historical evidence for the ascension is 'peculiarly weak' (Strauss, 1972, p. 752). Based in part on the ascent of Elijah, the tradition was 'gradually formed' to provide a fitting finale for Jesus' earthly life. 'If it was expected . . . that his future return from heaven would be a visible descent in the clouds, this would naturally suggest that his departure . . . should be represented as a visible ascent on a cloud' (p. 755). Miracles, said Strauss, were devices to underline theological claims about Jesus. The feeding of the crowds, while also representing Jesus as the equal of Moses who had fed his people in the wilderness, and of the prophets Elijah and Elisha, also expressed the truth that Jesus is able to meet all human needs. By the time of writing *The Old Faith and the New*, though, Strauss' tone had changed. Now, he sounds much more like Reimarus, and comes very close to impugning the motives of the disciples:

The Messiah was also the second Moses, and the chief of the prophets, and the events and actions of their lives must necessarily be repeated in [his life, so] he must have been tempted in the wilderness . . . he must have been transfigured on a mountain top, even as his prototype Moses had descended Mount Sinai with shining countenance. It was necessary that he should have raised from the dead, should have multiplied sufficient food, else he would have lagged behind Elijah and Elisha. His whole career had to be one unbroken chain of miracles of healing. (1997, Vol. 1, pp. 58–9)

Strauss also gives a detailed discussion of the chronology of Jesus' career and of the problem of dating this precisely. From the dates of Pilate's prefectship and of Tiberius' reign (see Luke 3:1) he calculates a public ministry of anywhere between two and seven years (p. 277).

Strauss' Jesus, like Reimarus', believed himself to be the Messiah. He expected to rule over a kingdom but Strauss was much more open to a 'spiritual' understanding of Jesus' 'kingdom'. His Jesus was not a revolutionary and always expected supernatural intervention:

Thus we conclude that the messianic hope of Jesus was not political, nor even merely earthly, for he referred to its fulfillment to supernatural means, and to a supermundane theatre (the regenerated earth); as little was it a purely spiritual hope, in the modern sense of the term, for it included important and unprecedented changes in the external conditions of things: but it was the national, theocratic hope, spiritualized and ennobled by his own peculiar moral and religious views. (1972, p. 296)

Jesus, said Strauss, probably did link his role with prophecies about sitting in judgment on the living and the dead (see *ibid.*, p. 556), none of which features in Reimarus' conception of Jesus' purely political role.

Jesus may have hoped that the kingdom would come while he was still alive, but came to believe that 'he could enter into his messianic glorification by death alone' (p. 656). Strauss thought that Jesus reached this conviction for himself, by comparing 'Old Testament narratives and prophecies' (p. 572). This reminds me of a scene in *The Last Temptation of Christ* which shows Jesus reading from Isaiah 53 and parting company from his friend Judas' Zealot ambitions by deciding instead that his path would be one of suffering and death. Jesus probably did predict that he would return in glory very soon after his death, since 'it was natural that he could not conceive a very long interval as destined to elapse between his first messianic coming in humiliation, and his second, in glory' (p. 596). Strauss therefore restores to Jesus some of the passages that Reimarus had deemed fictitious, although he also changed his mind several times on both the issue of the second coming and the nature of the kingdom (see Hodgson, 1972, p. xxxiii).

In his third edition of *The Life*, and in his more popular *A New Life of Jesus for the German People* (1879), Strauss 'eliminated eschatology' and, says Schweitzer, 'instead of the historical Jesus, portrayed the Jesus of liberal theology' (1998b, p. 95). Jesus had 'understood himself as Messiah in a strictly nonpolitical, non apocalyptic sense' (Hodgson, 1972, p. xl). In these two works, Strauss also drew on Schleiermacher's concept of 'god-consciousness' in which Jesus emerges as

the one in whose self-consciousness the unity of the divine and the human first appeared with sufficient energy to reduce to a disappearing minimum all hindrances of this unity . . . to this extent [he] remains unique and unequalled in world history. (1972, p. 802; see Schweitzer, 1998b, pp. 62–7, on Schleiermacher's *Das Leben Jesus*)

In the fourth edition of *The Life of Jesus*, Strauss rejected the view that Jesus had taught a 'perpetual coming' (p. 590). John's Gospel, with its more 'ambiguous medium between a real event and an ideal, a present and a future event', represents a later reworking of primitive belief in the *parousia* (coming) (p. 598; for a modern discussion of these passages, see Sanders, 1993, pp. 180–2).

Strauss argued that 'traces of a futuristic eschatology in John should be discounted as secondary interpretation' (Hiers and Holland, 1971, pp. 26–7). In this edition, he also rejected Schleiermacher's Christology; it satisfied neither science nor dogma, since it required a miracle to explain how Jesus, of all men, could have achieved so perfectly what others are denied: 'the supposition that this . . . ideal was manifested in a single historical individual, involves a violation of the law of nature' (1972, p. 771). Arguing that the 'ideal is never realized in a single appearance but only in a complete cycle' (p. 770), Strauss concluded that it would be mean for divinity to be limited to one single individual (see p. 779). His final position was that divinity is available to all:

is not the idea of the unity of the divine with all human natures a real one in a far higher sense, than when I single out one man as such a realization? Is not an incarnation of God from eternity, a truer one than an incarnation limited to a particular point of time? (p. 780)

Schleiermacher's mistake, said Strauss, in *The Christ of Faith and the Jesus of History: A Critique of Schleiermacher* (1977), was that his convictions about the Christ of faith prevented him from seeing the Jesus of history. His 'standpoint was more dogmatic than historical', which is why he used 'the name of Christ virtually throughout', which is in fact 'a title of office and status which includes the entire church conception of the person' (p. 36). Schleiermacher's a priori conviction that 'science and Christian faith cannot contradict each other' (p. 21) disqualified him as an objective student of the text.

The problem with Reimarus' Jesus, says Strauss, is that nobody would die for him, yet the disciples who, according to Reimarus, were guilty of fraud and deceit did die for their Lord. In Strauss' view, the disciples *believed* what they proclaimed, and could not therefore be accused of deceit (see Strauss, 1970, p. 51). More recently, the Jewish scholar Pinchas Lapide similarly asked, 'can swindlers let themselves be tortured and persecuted in the name of an illusion – up to joyful martyrdom?' As 'a faithful Jew', he continues, he 'cannot explain . . . a historical development which . . . has carried the central message of Israel into the world . . . as the result of blind happenstance, or human error' (1983, pp. 141–2; for Lapide, see below and Chapter 5). It was, says Strauss, *psychology* that enabled the disciples to solve the problem presented by Jesus' death, by seizing on the suffering servant – now vindicated motif, *'in which he was invisibly with them, even unto the end of the world'* (1972, p. 742). Thus, for him, a spiritual interpretation does not represent a complete reversal of what Jesus had taught, or demand a work of pure fiction, as it had done for Reimarus.

In the end, though, Strauss may have found that he had subtracted too much from the Gospels for them to be able to sustain any faith. Having cut the mythic out of the Gospels, Strauss left 'the reader with a skeletal outline of the life of a fanatical Jewish preacher who had mistakenly believed that he was the Messiah' (Allen, 1998, p. 153). His Jesus had not really died to atone for the sins of men, even though Jesus may have thought his death had expiatory significance. Optimistic about human nature, Strauss was not convinced that humanity needed a saviour.

The problem for Strauss was that Christians were holding on to the nativity story, Easter and the ascension, not as mythically reinterpreted by him but as 'actual occurrence' (1997, Vol. 1, p. 102). Baptism, the Eucharist, were now relics; 'nothing remaining now than the repulsive oriental metaphor of drinking the blood and eating the body of a man' (*ibid.*,

p. 105). If one no longer believes that Jesus was 'god' but a 'man, however excellent', why continue to pray to him? (*ibid.*, p. 5). Ministers were faced with either elevating 'people to their ideas', or adapting themselves 'to the conception of the community', or leaving 'the ministerial profession' (1972, p. 784). For Strauss, progress demanded that outmoded beliefs be abandoned.

This does not mean that Jesus has nothing to offer; he taught the unity of humankind, and a universal moral code, while Jesus' idea of unifying the divine and the human 'represented an admirable and exalted human idea' (Allen, 1998, p. 156). Yet this Hegelian idea 'had no connection with the deluded Jew who had died so long ago', just as Jesus' messianic hope 'bore no resemblance to the theological beliefs of Christians of any age' (*ibid.*, p. 153). Strauss' essentially Hegelian Jesus was a good idea abstracted from what could be retrieved as fact from the gospel accounts.

## Albrecht Ritschl (1822–89) and the liberal theology of the kingdom

Of the many nineteenth-century theologians who produced liberal lives of Jesus, or who advocated a liberal Jesus, Ritschl was one of the most influential. At the centre of his theology was a definition of 'true Christianity' and the idea of the kingdom in Jesus' preaching. For Ritschl, true Christianity was:

The monotheistic, completely spiritual and ethical religion, which, based on the life of its Author as Redeemer and as Founder of the Kingdom of God, consists in the freedom of the children of God, involves the impulse to conduct from the motive of love, which aims at the moral organization of mankind, and grounds blessedness on the relation of sonship to God, as well as on the Kingdom of God. (1902, p. 13)

The kingdom, as taught by Jesus, was 'the organization of humanity through action inspired by love' (p. 12). For Ritschl, the Christian can:

Exercise his calling to seek the kingdom of God if, motivated by love of neighbor, he carries on his work in the moral communities of family and economic, national and political life. Indeed, 'family, private property, personal independence and honor (obedience to authority)' are goods that are essential to moral health and the formation of character. Only by engaging in civic work for the sake of the common good, by faithfulness in one's social calling, is it possible to be true to the example of Christ. (Niebuhr, 1943, p. 97)

Reimarus' eschatology was conspicuous by its absence from Ritschl's thought.

Following Schleiermacher, the liberals justified their eschatology by referring to John's Gospel and to passages in the synoptics such as Luke 10:9: 'the kingdom of God is near you.' What emerges from their work is a Jesus who taught eternal moral truths and spiritual values, who called people to citizenship of an eternal kingdom, and 'died to give His work its final consecration' (Schweitzer, 1998b, p. 398). As with Baur and liberal theology in general, a danger here is that Jesus emerges as the bearer of contemporary social and cultural values and loses any ability to critique cultural assumptions.

H. Richard Niebuhr (1951) says that with Ritschl, 'The movement towards the identification of Christ with culture doubtless reached its climax' (p. 94). Here, by 'culture' Niebuhr means nineteenth-century German culture, not first-century Jewish. The work of building up the kingdom, says Niebuhr, becomes 'human': 'All references are to man and to man's work: the word "God" seems to be an intrusion, as perhaps those later Ritschlians realized, who substituted the phrase "brotherhood of man" for "kingdom of God"' (p. 99). God's and Christ's voice speaking through culture may override the biblical Jesus.

## The no quest and the challenge of thoroughgoing eschatology

Although the end of the 'old quest' is usually dated from 1906 with the publication of Schweitzer's *Quest*, there is good reason to identify its demise with the appearance of Johannes Weiss' *Jesus' Proclamation of the Kingdom of God* (1971). This book, said Schweitzer, 'seems to break a spell. It closes one epoch and begins another' (1998b, p. 239). Weiss (1863–1914), who was Professor of New Testament at Marburg from 1898 until his death, where he taught Bultmann, was Ritschl's son-in-law, yet he seems to have had an undermining of liberal theology in his sights. 'Jesus' activity,' said Weiss, 'is governed by the strong and unwavering feeling that the messianic time is imminent' (1971, p. 129). Reimarus had been correct to argue that Jesus expected to rule a kingdom, but wrong to assume that this would be on earth. Jesus' kingdom, argued Weiss, was a 'thoroughly transcendental and apocalyptic' kingdom (p. 129). Indeed, Jesus has 'nothing in common with this world; he stands with one foot already in the future world' (cited in Hiers and Holland, 1971, p. 9).

Jesus, said Weiss, became certain that he must 'cross death's threshold' so that, as the Son of Man, he could 'return upon the clouds as at the establishment of the Kingdom' (1971, p. 130). Thus, the kingdom is not 'an ethical relationship of love and trust for God and man', as argued by the liberals, but an 'event' (Hiers and Holland, 1971, p. 8). Indeed, Jesus has not taught anything about correct human behaviour, or ethics, for the here-and-now, which he had expected would end. In the kingdom, people would become angels and need no ethic. Weiss rejected the possibility that Jesus had believed the kingdom to be in some sense already present (1971, p. 74). Jesus' ethic was 'not the positive ideal of worldly morality, such as Ritschl and his followers were disposed to elaborate, but the diametric opposite' (Hiers and Holland, 1971, p. 10).

## Liberalism lives!

Weiss' detailed and scholarly work in Jewish eschatology seemed to act as a death-knell to the liberal Jesus. However, as I have pointed out, liberal Jesuses continued to appear. Two important examples here, both from North America, are *The Social Teachings of Jesus* (1897) by Shailer Mathews (1863–1941), a professor at Chicago, and *The Social Principles of Jesus* (1916) by Walter Rauschenbusch (1861–1918), who had studied under Ritschl. Both books advocated ethical praxis as central to Christian obedience, yet Weiss had denied that Jesus had taught any social ethics. As a Baptist, I am proud that Rauschenbusch, a Baptist pastor and professor, was a leading advocate of what became known as the 'social gospel'. Christianity for Rauschenbusch was not just a matter of believing in Jesus, or even of inner renewal, but necessitated social action on behalf of the poor and oppressed. Rauschenbusch even saw Jesus as a feminist: 'In every case in which the interests of women came before Jesus, he took her side. . . . The attitude of historic Christianity has been a mixture between his spirit and the spirit of the Patriarchal family' (1916, p. 91).

Rauschenbusch's book was co-published by the Women's Press. A champion of disarmament and of the cooperative movement (he advocated wealth redistribution), he also hated racism:

The man who intelligently realizes the Chinese and the Zulu as his brothers, with whom he must share the earth, is an ampler mind, other things being equal – than the man who can think only in terms of pale faces. (1916, p. 27)

Long after liberalism was deemed to be dead, Rauschenbusch advocated a liberal understanding of Jesus' kingdom of God, which is almost synonymous in his writing with the concept of the social gospel; the kingdom:

is a real thing, now in operation. It is within us, and among us, gaining ground in our intellectual life and in our social institutions. It overlaps and interpenetrates all existing organizations . . . the kingdom of God is always coming. (1916, pp. 196–7)

*The Social Principles of Jesus* was written as a study guide for college Sunday School classes. On page 78, he asks: 'Is the kingdom of God to be brought about by an act of God in the future or by the work of men in the present? Does the one exclude the other?' His own answer to the second question is a loud no: 'we are most durably saved by putting in hard work for the kingdom' (p. 75).

Mathews' concept of the kingdom was also social and sapiential: 'By the kingdom of God Jesus *meant an ideal social order in which the relation of men to God is that of sons and to each other, that of brothers*' (and sisters, I would add; Mathews, 1897, p. 54). In 1927, one of Mathews' colleagues at Chicago, Shirley Jackson Case (1872–1947), produced what Allen (1998) describes as the 'most sophisticated life of Jesus to emerge from the social gospel movement', *Jesus: A New Biography*. While Bultmann (see below) would soon dismiss attempts to probe Jesus' inner life, this is exactly what Case did. Case may be one of the earliest scholars to state that Jesus, who was a prophet and a reformer, did not consider himself to be the Messiah. He did not intend to found a movement but he did want to bring about God-centredness in the lives of his hearers. Reinhold Neibuhr (1892–1971), too, in *The Nature and Destiny of Man* (1943), suggested that although the kingdom cannot be built by human hands, women and men can strive to achieve 'proximate solutions' (Hiers and Holland, 1971, p. 25).

## A fictional Jesus

In North America also, Lewis Wallace (1827–1905), in his bestselling novel, *Ben Hur: A Tale of the Christ* (1880; 1998), offered what can best be described as a liberal Jesus. Actually, the novel was really the story of Ben Hur, Prince of Judah, but Wallace wove references to Jesus into the narrative, which begins with the three Magi. At first, Ben Hur hopes Jesus will overthrow the Romans, then realizes that Jesus' kingdom is a spiritual one (see 1998, p. 262). The Jesus of the novel (and of the various film versions) is a compassionate, healing, faith-inspiring Jesus, but above all he is a Jesus for all the world, a non-sectarian teacher who can transcend racial, religious and cultural divides.

Wallace's three wise men travel from Greece, Egypt and India to find the true God, who 'to redeem the race . . . must make Himself once more manifest; HE MUST COME IN PERSON' (1998, p. 30). This suggests that God had had previous manifestations. Wallace appears to have regarded Jesus as a teacher of eternal wisdom in whom people from any faith might find inspiration and meaning. 'Heaven may be won,' say the three Magi, 'not by the sword, not by human wisdom, but by Faith, Love, and Good Works' (p. 31). Perhaps more so than any text considered so far in this book, Wallace treated the Jewish identity of Jesus and of his hero, Ben Hur, with real sympathy and respect.

Ben Hur is depicted as a muscular hero (especially in the chariot race, pp. 336–50), who overcomes adversity and who, throughout all his adventures, remains proud of his Jewishness. Wallace partly wrote the book to defend theism against the criticisms of Robert G. Ingersoll (1833–99), although he really makes no theological claims about Jesus. Wallace said that he 'became a believer in God and Christ' while writing the book (1906, p. 937). In his later book, *The Prince of India: Why Constantinople Fell* (1893), he has his hero rejecting Christianity for placing Jesus between people and God. 'There can be no reform or refinement of faith,' said the Indian mystic, 'unless God be the exclusive subject; and so certainly it leads to the lopping off of all parasitical worships such as are given to Christ and Mahomet' (Vol 1, p. 60).

Wallace's Jesus was close to Jefferson's teacher of eternal wisdom, around whom people of all faiths might unite in the worship of the one God. Wallace has one of his characters saying to another, 'He means you to bring men together in His name. Titles may remain – Jew, Moslem, Christian, Buddhist – but there shall be an end of wars in religion – all mankind are to be brethren in Him' (1893, Vol. 1, p. 286). 'He had conceived the idea of a Universal Religion,' wrote Wallace (*ibid.*, p. 60). Jesus, whose face remains unseen in the film versions of *Ben Hur*, only appears fleetingly until the end of the book when he cures the hero's mother and sister of leprosy, and where the crucifixion story is powerfully and faithfully narrated. Ben Hur's story is intended to parallel Jesus'. On the basis that no one is worthy enough to play Jesus, his features are obscured. Wallace himself supervised the first stage adaptation (1899). Wallace cannot be said to have stressed the social aspects of Jesus' teaching, yet the universal appeal of his Christ does offer a liberal image.

## Borg and Crossan

The more recent Jesuses of Marcus Borg and Dominic Crossan represent social activist Jesuses. They argue that Jesus' idea of the kingdom was 'sapiential'. Jesus offered people an immediate, unbrokered relationship with God in the here-and-now:

He was neither broker nor mediator but, somewhat paradoxically, the announcer that neither should exist between humanity and divinity or between humanity and itself. Miracle and parable, healing and spiritual contact with God were calculated to force individuals into unmediated physical and spiritual contact with God. (Crossan, 1994, p. 422)

Jesus' open fellowship with people from all social positions, and his rejection of privileges, challenged the social, political, economic status quo in which a few controlled 'two-thirds of the annual production of wealth' (Borg, 1998, p. 11).

Borg's Jesus is a spirit-person who enjoys direct, unmediated fellowship with God. Crossan's is a revolutionary Jewish peasant who invited people into the unbrokered Kingdom of God. Instead of twelve disciples, Jesus headed a diverse group: some travelled with him, others gave house hospitality, others travelled alone, but all shared 'a miracle and a kingdom. . . . Here, I think, is the heart of the original Jesus movement, a shared egalitarianism of spiritual and material resources' (Crossan, 1994, p. 341). Jesus' 'open commensuality' provides us with the key to understand who Jesus was; by breaking purity taboos he redefines honour and shame in a way that challenges privilege and rank (see Crossan, 1991, pp. 261–4). The Kingdom of God is a call to revolutionize social systems, to combat inequity and injustice. Crossan looks at the twentieth-century Civil Rights movement in the USA as a more recent example of the Jesus movement fulfilling its true calling (1996, p. 72). Crossan, who, despite some of his controversial views, considers himself a Christian, is a former Catholic priest. After leaving the priesthood he continued teaching at the Catholic De Paul University.

Crossan's bestselling *The Historical Jesus: The Life of a Mediterranean Jewish Peasant* (1991) is a big book (507 pages). It makes much use of cross-cultural anthropology to illuminate such aspects of Jesus study as magic, healing, eating and social stratification. While I always find anthropology of interest, Witherington (1995) says that Crossan's application of modern anthropology to the Gospels is sometimes anachronistic and irrelevant (p. 85). I return to some of Crossan's views towards the end of this chapter. Borg, raised and educated in the Lutheran tradition, is Hundere Distinguished Professor of Religion at Oregon State University. He sets out his Christian convictions in *Me and Jesus: The Journey Home*, available at http://westarinstitute.org/Fellows/Borg/Borg_bio/borg_bio.html. Borg has described Crossan as 'the premier Jesus scholar in the world today' (1997, p. xii).

## A Marxist Jesus

There is also a good deal of overlap between Crossan's and Borg's Jesuses and the Jesuses of some neo-Marxist texts, such as Fernando Belo's *A Materialist Reading of the Gospel of Mark* (1981) and Milan Machovec's *A Marxist Looks at Jesus* (1976). Departing from Marxism's normal negative appraisal of religion as the elite's tool to oppress and exploit workers today with the promise of paradise tomorrow, these writers re-examine the Jesus of the Gospels and see in him the champion of the proletariat against the bourgeoisie, just as do Borg and Crossan. To some degree, they see through Christianity's historical manifestation to its far from elitist or powerful origins. In doing so, these outsiders come very close to some insiders' images of Jesus. They value Jesus for the difference he can make in the fields of social justice and political rights *today*.

Machovec's Jesus 'was concerned with man, with his future and his present, his victories and failures, his love and pain, his despair and unconquerable hope' (1976, p. 204). A 'Materialist Christianity', says Belo, would no longer be concerned with 'grace for souls but the power (*puissance*) of bodies' (1981, p. xiv). 'The good news of Jesus', he says, is the '*grill* that enables us . . . to judge the power that works in our bodies, the curse from which our bodies are shaking loose (namely, the grip of the capitalist codes), and the blessing toward which they are moving' (p. 297). Here, he sounds very much like Crossan complaining of Christianity's anti-body bias.

In his first chapter, entitled 'Jesus For Atheists?', Machovec expresses 'sympathy with Jesus and his conceptual world' but clearly states that he remains 'a disciple of Marx' and 'does not . . . consider himself to be a Christian' (1976, p. 37). He also speaks of 'the burden of prejudice that Marxists bring to the question of Jesus' (p. 19). Belo complains of the monopolizing of Jesus by 'churches, theological discourses and Universities' (1981, p. xiv). Of course, the supernatural is redacted from the Jesus story, attributed to pagan and other influences, such as 'Egyptian or

Babylonian myths on dying and rising divinities' (Machovec, 1976, p. 170). Like Christian proponents of liberation theology, to whom I turn next, Belo is not interested in the Jesus of history but in the significance, or power, of the Jesus narrative. 'I pay no attention at all to "the history of Jesus",' he says, 'I am profoundly interested in the "narrative of Jesus"' (1981, p. xiii).

## Liberation theology

Reimarus' insistence that Jesus' goal was political, not absent from any of the above contributors, also emerges in the whole genre of twentieth-century liberation theology, itself influenced by Marxist theory. For liberation theologians, life in the kingdom is a life of shared liberation praxis:

Spirituality and salvation are above all a way of life according to the Spirit of God as revealed in Jesus: that is, a loving, tender, caring, joyful, celebrating community of sisters and brothers living in justice and peace and sharing in common the gifts that God gives us through our cooperation, compassionate laboring with mother earth. For liberation theology, this utopian reign of God is both 'already among us' – in each of our Spirit-filled acts and relationships of love, solidarity and justice – and 'not quite here yet' insofar as it is always possible and necessary to go further. (Musser and Price, 1992, p. 292)

The term 'liberation theology' was pioneered by Gustavo Gutiérrez, a Peruvian Roman Catholic priest, who certainly thought that Jesus called on Christians to 'do something' in the here-and-now, on behalf of the poor, despite Weiss' debunking of the idea that Jesus' teaching had had any this-worldly focus (see Gutiérrez, 1973).

Liberation theology criticizes any Christian lifestyle that is not concerned with the oppressed and the powerless, advocating the preferential option for the poor. Jon Sobrino's *Jesus in Latin America* (1987) and *Jesus the Liberator* (1993) describe a Jesus who is to be found among the poor, listening to them, speaking to them, empowering them. This Jesus does not need to be taken into the slums; he is already there. 'The poor of this world,' writes Sobrino, ' – the Galilee of today – are where we encounter the historical Jesus' (1993, p. 273). This Jesus is very different from the Jesus who for too long in South America and elsewhere has seemed to be the possession of the rich and powerful. 'The poor,' writes Sobrino, 'are a sort of sacrament of the presence of Christ . . . their very condition, like that of Christ crucified, is the greatest possible challenge that can be offered to Christians' (*ibid.*, p. 21).

Endorsing an already but not quite here view of the Kingdom of God (*ibid.*, p. 108), Sobrino defines 'building the Kingdom' as 'walking towards God, till the principalities – the anti-kingdom – are overthrown and God is all in all: the definite Kingdom of God' (*ibid.*, p. 134). Sobrino's 'anti-kingdom' here sounds like what Rauschenbusch called the 'kingdom of evil'. Some Christians who advocate that working towards the goal of social equality and justice is the task to which Jesus calls us have advocated non-violent protest, such as Martin Luther King (1929–68) in the Civil Rights movement, and Bishop Helder Camara in the context of Latin America. The Baptist King, an admirer of Mahatma Gandhi, is another of my heroes. Once asked why he had not become a Marxist and why those who followed him accepted his philosophy of non-violence, King answered, 'Because of the overpowering force of the Spirit of Jesus' (Pelikan, 1985, p. 218). For Camara, violence always begets violence (see Camara, 1974). For Camillo Torres, who put aside priestly duties to join the revolutionary forces, violence was justified. S. G. F. Brandon's version of Jesus, described in Chapter 1, justifies the Christian use of force against injustice. Theologies of liberation, including feminist and black theology (see my Conclusion), are products of worshipping Christian communities who claim the right to interpret scripture for themselves from their own experience of powerlessness and marginality.

## The no quest's historical scepticism and thoroughgoing eschatology

Schweitzer and Bultmann, giants of the 'no quest' period, both accepted Weiss' view of Jesus' eschatology as definitive. Schweitzer's *Quest* analysed in excess of 200 works on Jesus, from Reimarus (Chapter 2), through to Wrede's *The Messianic Secret* (1971). William Wrede (1859–1906), a professor at Breslau, taught that Christianity was largely a product of Paul's speculative theology, which radically transformed Jesus' own teaching, a view already encountered in this chapter. *The Quest* surveyed popular and fictional lives as well as works of biblical scholarship. In Chapter 19, which discusses Wrede, Schweitzer also reviews his own 1901 work, *The Mystery of the Kingdom of God: The Secret of Jesus' Messiahship and the Passion* (1914). The German edition of *The Quest* was published in 1906, the English translation in 1910. Johns Hopkins University Press rendered a valuable service when it reprinted the English edition, with a new foreword by Delbert R. Hillers, in 1998. With all his faults, Schweitzer is another of my heroes. It was certainly due in part to his own missionary career that I volunteered for overseas Christian service, and was accepted during my penultimate year as a theology undergraduate and Baptist ordinand at Manchester University. Schweitzer wrote *The Quest* when he was aged only 31. He was already a professor at Strasbourg and a doctor of theology, philosophy and music. Rescuing little substantive from his own reconstruction of the life of Jesus, Schweitzer still found sufficient inspiration from a Jesus who was totally committed, even unto death, to God's cause to become a medical missionary in Africa.

Schweitzer resigned his academic posts and entered medical school, graduating with an MD in 1913. His thesis was later published as *The Psychiatric Study of Jesus*. In this work, Schweitzer refuted the view of several recent medical dissertations which 'showed, at least to the authors' satisfaction, that Jesus was mentally diseased' (1948 edn, Prefatory Note). Schweitzer attributed the origin of belief in Jesus as a psychotic to Strauss, and asked whether someone who lived within 'the world of ideas contained in . . . Jewish apocalyptic literature and who considered himself the "Son of Man" and the "Messiah" soon to appear in supernatural glory, is to be adjudged in some fashion as psychotic?' (*ibid.*, p. 27). Others point to Jesus' cursing fig trees as a sign of mental illness (Mark 11:12–14). At Mark 3:21, Jesus' own family appear to have thought him mad. In a fascinating study, Walter E. Bundy (1922) explored the possibility that Jesus suffered from epilepsy, paranoia and some form of fanaticism. Before reading this book I had not been aware that anyone had tried to explain Jesus' behaviour with reference to epilepsy, a common Christian theme in writing on Muhammad.

After gaining his MD, Schweitzer went to Africa. As Allen points out, he rather liked to dramatize the radical nature of his African sojourn, leaving behind the prestige and honour of his university career while:

the break with the past was never quite as dramatic as he liked to think. In fact, he returned to Europe for extended periods every few years to lecture, teach and hold organ concerts. . . . As he became increasingly famous (he won the Nobel Peace Prize in 1952) he hobnobbed with aristocracy and literati who came like pilgrims to Lambarene and regarded him as a saint. (Allen, 1998, p. 239)

Allen continues to describe Schweitzer as 'at best a mediocre physician' and says that his old-fashioned hospital became an embarrassment to the newly independent Gabon. His 'reverence for life' philosophy resulted in a ban on flushing toilets or even on using insecticides 'for fear of harming other creatures' (*ibid.*, p. 239). Of course, even if Schweitzer's life after *The Quest* was a failure, this does not detract from the quality of the book's scholarship, so criticism of the later Schweitzer may seem irrelevant to my purposes. However, for reasons which I will articulate below, I think it is important to rescue something from Schweitzer's own response to Jesus.

### *Verdict on Schweitzer: a bold effort to do, not merely to preach*

Gerald McKnight's critical *Verdict on Schweitzer* (1964) shares Allen's assessment of his medical skills but also depicts him as a racial bigot (p. 33) who thought Africans incapable of responsibility and who failed to put development on his agenda:

This is the crux of the criticism leveled at Dr Schweitzer, M.D., – that he is much less concerned with preventing the tribulations which ignorance and custom have stamped on backward Africans, than in healing them. (p. 222)

McKnight refers to Schweitzer's 'stubborn refusal to move with the times' (p. 45). Personally, I suspect that the services of a not-too-brilliant physician may be preferable to lack of any medical care. Unwillingness to interfere in customs could equally suggest a respect for their beliefs; I have heard Africans speaking positively about Schweitzer's tolerance of such African practices as allowing them to bring their families and animals to the hospital, which McKnight criticizes (pp. 33, 48). Schweitzer's bigotry, too (and here the evidence is, I think, compelling), was no worse than that of many missionaries and European officials during colonial times. Neither was he worse than many in failing to encourage leadership or development. While his use of the word 'primitive' to describe Africans clearly reflects the language of the time, as does his speculation about whether 'they were mere prisoners of tradition . . . or . . . capable of independent thought', he does appear to have developed a positive appreciation of Africans as 'far more interested in the elemental questions about the meaning of life and the nature of good and evil than I had supposed' (Allen, 1998, p. 141).

Nor was he different from the norm in returning to Europe at intervals; the missionary furlough is a long-established custom. Further, in *Out of My Life and Thought* (1998a) he was quite open about his ongoing relationship with Europe. McKnight tells us that Schweitzer 'placed second those who suffered from his thwarted career, or those who – like his dutiful wife, Helene – stumbled along in his path. He over-rode all personal feeling for others, as for himself' (1964, p. 245). As tragic as this description of Mrs Schweitzer is, the account reminds me of the story of William Carey's first wife, who had not wanted to go to India and once there suffered mental illness until she died. I am also reminded of Gandhi's wife, who did not take as readily as others to some of Gandhi's ideals (such as sweeping the toilet; see Chapter 6). Many passages in Schweitzer's *Out of My Life and Thought* (1998a), too, express concern for his wife's welfare (see e.g. pp. 160, 155, 207).

I admit that the idea of my hero as a racial bigot is unattractive but I still think that even with these failings, and his sense of self-pride, Schweitzer did do something splendid. It is not so much always being a success, or getting it right, that counts as the initial, existential decision and the bold response. Yes, he remained famous; but he did live less comfortably in Africa than in Europe and he did do something in response to his vision of Lazarus and Dives, which he relates in *On the Edge of the Primeval Forest* (1956). He went to Africa, he says, to help to remedy the imbalance in the world's resources, to atone for European exploitation. Even if he did not succeed in this mission, his life represents a bold effort *to do* and not merely *to preach*. It represents an example of someone who, in spite of himself, as I argue below, was inspired by Jesus' ethic. Even McKnight describes his own meeting with Schweitzer in almost reverential language:

The first meeting is unforgettable. . . . Nobody can meet Schweitzer without liking him, without responding to some instinctive respect and regard for this great individual. His power to disarm remains immense. (1964, p. 47)

## Schweitzer's Jesus

Schweitzer's Jesus does not differ overmuch from Weiss'. Jesus 'did not assume that the kingdom of God would be realized in this natural world' but 'expected this natural world would speedily come to an end and be superseded by a supernatural world in which all that is imperfect and evil would be overcome by the power of God' (Schweitzer, 1936, p. 4). Jesus' ethic was only for the very short period between his own death and the coming of the kingdom: 'a special ethic of the interval before the coming of the kingdom' (*Interimsethik*) (p. 354). At first, Schweitzer's Jesus may have thought that by sending out the disciples to proclaim the kingdom, perhaps to suffer for doing so, he would trigger the kingdom's birth (see Matthew 10:23). When they returned and the kingdom had not come, he realized he had miscalculated. He then decided that he was the one who had to suffer (see p. 388) and 'set out for Jerusalem solely in order to die there' (p. 391). Jesus found his inspiration in Isaiah (p. 390). Schweitzer is close here to Strauss. Jesus also thought that he was voluntarily taking upon himself others' suffering: 'tribulation for others is set aside, abolished, concentrated in Him alone' (p. 389). Later, Schweitzer retracted the view that Jesus ascribed any atoning significance to his death (1966, p. 128). He died in order to usher in the kingdom, not to expiate human sins.

When nothing happened (only God could establish the kingdom, Jesus could not fix the time) he assumed it had been postponed. He did not view this as failure. Rather, it meant that an obstacle had to be removed, so he 'seized upon the audacious and paradoxical idea – or the idea seized him – that his death' could remove the chief obstacle to the kingdom's coming, that is, sin. He would 'ransom' his life for others (Mark 10:45). Schweitzer's Jesus then rode into Jerusalem on a donkey because 'he desired that the Messianic prophesy in Zech. ix, 9 should be secretly fulfilled' (p. 394). Only his disciples knew his intentions. Jesus died, says Schweitzer, 'because two of his disciples betrayed his command of silence' (p. 396). The first betrayer was Peter; Schweitzer took Peter's confession at Caesarea Philippi as the turning point in Jesus' career. In revealing the secret made known to him at the transfiguration, Peter 'betrayed to the Twelve Jesus' consciouness of His messiahship'. This was meant to be kept a secret, to be revealed only when the kingdom arrived (p. 386; on p. 385 Schweitzer reverses the order of the transfiguration and Peter's confession).

Finally, Judas betrayed Jesus' secret to the chief priests (p. 397), which resulted in his arrest, trial and crucifixion, but God did not intervene, and the kingdom did not come. Jesus had got it wrong: 'Jesus cried aloud and expired' (p. 397). There may be a contradiction here; if Jesus had to die, how could Schweitzer maintain that it was betrayal of the messianic secret that caused his death? Would Jesus not have had to engineer his death by some means or other? Although his medical dissertation vindicated Jesus of insanity, a Jesus who believed he had to die still raises questions of a psychological nature, as Sanders (1985) says of Schweitzer (p. 333; see also p. 413 n. 38).

## An exotic Jesus

Schweitzer ends his own treatment of Jesus with the crucifixion. He does not discuss the resurrection, probably because he did not believe it to be historical. The book, though, continues with its famous summing up of the quest thus far of the historical Jesus, 'Results' (Chapter 20). It is here that Schweitzer expresses pessimism about our ability to know enough for sure about the real Jesus to say very much about him. The liberals, he says, thought they knew who Jesus was, but their Jesus, a reflection of their own ideas, had never lived: 'he is a figure designed by rationalism, endowed with life by liberalism, and clothed by modern theology in an historical garb' (p. 396). The liberals' progressive eschatology was derived from Kant, not from a study of first-century Judaism (pp. 251, 324). The problem is that as soon as we think we have understood Jesus, he slips away from us into his Jewish, eschatological past, into a worldview which we do not share and cannot properly comprehend. Jesus is exotic and alien:

He does not stay; He passes by our time and returns to His own. What surprised and dismayed the theology of the last forty years was that, despite all forced and arbitrary interpretations, it could not keep Him in our times, but had to let him go. (p. 399)

The eschatology first exposed by Reimarus proved so frightening because it seemed that nothing might be retrieved from Jesus' teachings 'for our time' (p. 402).

We must accept, said Schweitzer, that Jesus believed in the imminent end of the world and that, while he was wrong about this, his belief was typical of first-century Judaism. What, then, can be said of Jesus for today? What matters, he says, is not who Jesus was, or even what he believed about himself, but that a 'spiritual force' flows from him into our time. This spiritual force is real. Historical enquiry cannot destroy it: 'This fact can neither be shaken nor confirmed by any historical discovery' (p. 399). We then have his famous and oft-quoted concluding paragraph:

He comes to us as One unknown, without a name, as of old, by the lakeside, He came to those who knew Him not. He speaks to us the same word: 'Follow thou me!' and sets us to the tasks which He has to fulfil for our time. He commands. And to those who obey Him, whether they be wise or simple, He will reveal Himself in the toils, the conflicts, the sufferings which they shall pass through in His fellowship and, as an ineffable mystery, they shall learn in their own experience Who He is. (p. 403)

Few, if any, other theological classics end with such an emotive, haunting, beautiful affirmation of the reality of existential response to the Christ of faith, in whom, for all his historical scepticism, Schweitzer continued to 'trust'.

Existentially, Schweitzer rescued something from Jesus' life. For him, the example of Jesus' love in action, his willingness to die instead of the disciples, demanded imitating: 'he sensed that the ethics of Jesus had to become, for him . . . a way of life' (Marshall and Poling, 2000, p. 61). Schweitzer saw his 'reverence for life' ethic as a universal code. He looked to eastern religion with some sympathy: 'Let us rejoice in the Truth, where ever we find its lamp burning,' he said in his 1923 lectures to missionaries and to missionaries-in-training at the Selly Oak Colleges, Birmingham (1923, p. 63). However, he also told them that Christianity was the 'deepest expression of the religious mind' (p. 20). If they could show those of other faiths 'what it means to be apprehended by the living, ethical God, something of the truth of Jesus' would go out from them (pp. 92–3). Later, his mysticism, 'union with Infinite Being . . . with God as subjectively experienced' (Seaver, 1947, p. 332), took him close to Strauss' cosmic worldview, but he remained theistic, and an ordained minister, until he died. Preaching in Africa, too, he paid more attention both to the sayings and to the ethic of Jesus, and praised a Christianity that avoided dogma (Allen, 1998, p. 141). His ethic derived, in part, from Jesus; he wrote:

With its active ethic of love, and through its spirituality, the concept of the world that is based on respect for life is in essence related to Christianity and to all religions that profess the ethic of love. (Allen, 1998, p. 138)

Jesus, said Schweitzer, 'sets up the eternal ethic of active love' (1998a, p. 58). Freed from the need to expect an end to the physical world (at least in the immediate future), we Christians, said Schweitzer, are at 'liberty to let the religion of Jesus become a living force in our thought, as its purely spiritual and ethical nature demands' (*ibid.*, p. 60). The Kingdom of God is here and now (p. 57). Schweitzer spoke of his deep 'devotion to Christianity' but saw 'What has been presented as Christianity during these nineteen centuries' as 'merely a beginning, full of mistakes, not a full grown Christianity springing from the spirit of Jesus' (*ibid.*, pp. 241–2). Jesus' 'images' cannot become ours, rather we must 'transpose them into modern concepts of the world' (*ibid.*, p. 55).

## Historical scepticism

Historical scepticism, namely that not very much could be said for sure about the historical Jesus, resulted in the 'no-quest' period. During this phase, scholars continued to examine how the Gospels were formed, how belief about Jesus was back-projected on to Jesus' lips but few attempted a nineteenth-century style life of Jesus. There was stress, though, on what

Jesus had taught. It was commonly assumed that, even if many passages in the Gospels could not be regarded as historically reliable, the parables could be accepted as authentic. Despite Weiss' view that Jesus never taught a social ethic, much that is of social and moral value was still found in the Gospels. This no-quest period was dominated by Rudolf Karl Bultmann (1884–1976), who from 1921 until 1951 was professor at Marburg, where one of my own teachers, Percy Scott, completed his doctoral work. Dr Scott used to entertain us with stories of Bultmann and his family. In conservative theological circles, Bultmann's name is synonymous with scepticism, with an approach to the Gospels that leaves little in place to support the traditional Jesus, or Christ, of Christian faith. Personally, I find Bultmann's existentialism compelling, even though I do not fully share his historical scepticism.

Bultmann wrote a foreword to a 1939 edition of Weiss, and his own work may be interpreted as a conscious response to Weiss' eschatology. Weiss' 'new and authentic understanding of the New Testament', said Bultmann, both 'pushed' its ideas 'back into the past' and 'brought the strangeness of the New Testament startlingly to light . . . over and against a middle class conception of Christianity'. Bultmann wanted to make these strange ideas somehow meaningful for his own day (Bultmann, 1971, p. xii). Weiss himself was uncomfortable with the implications of his transcendental, futuristic eschatology for contemporary faith, and suggested at the end of his book that systematic theology needed to dwell on what was 'universally valid in Jesus' preaching' (1971, p. 135).

While the idea that the kingdom can be built by ethical correctness is 'unbiblical and un-Jewish', said Weiss, Jesus had also preached that men (and women) must 'perform the conditions required by God' (p. 132). Thus, women and men can enter into the 'religious and ethical fellowship of the children of God' (p. 135) by serving God with all their heart (p. 134), which is the condition of preparedness Jesus had required of his followers. This, said Weiss, is the 'universally valid' idea in Jesus' preaching 'which should form the kernel of systematic theology' (p. 135). 'The supreme ethical ideal is to serve God,' said Weiss, 'with surrender of the whole heart and to become free from this world. The highest proofs of this *freedom . . . are the love of one's enemies and the sacrifice of one's life for the sake of God*' (p. 134). There seems, after all, to be some hope for liberal Jesus theology.

## Demythologizing

My analysis of Bultmann is based mainly on the English versions of his books *Jesus Christ and Mythology* (1958b) and *Jesus and the Word* (1958a). Bultmann followed Strauss and Schweitzer in suggesting that Jesus and the disciples lived with a different worldview from ourselves, which Bultmann characterized as 'mythic'. His description of the mythical worldview of Jesus' time, which he contrasts with the modern scientific worldview, is probably the best I have seen (see 1958b, pp. 14f.). Bultmann then set out to remove 'myth' from the Gospels by the process known as 'demythologizing'. The mythic worldview believed that supernatural powers intervened in this world. It posited three realms – heaven, earth and hell – and associated these with 'up', 'here' and 'down'. 'Mythology,' said Bultmann, 'is a primitive science . . . it expresses a certain understanding of the universe . . . that the world and human life have their ground and their limits in a power which is beyond all that we can calculate or control' (1958b, pp. 18–19). God was 'in heaven' meant that God was 'beyond the world', hell was 'dark' because darkness 'is terrible to men' (*ibid.*, p. 20). Jesus' self-understanding, either as 'Messiah' or as 'king of blessedness', or as 'Son of Man who would come on the clouds of heaven' (*ibid.*, p. 16) was mythological.

Bultmann did not believe that Jesus saw himself as Messiah, a view that has become increasingly common among Jesus scholars (see 1958a, p. 9; also Jewish scholars discussed in Chapter 5). He did accept that people believed Jesus to be the Messiah and that 'However little we know of the life of Jesus . . . we [know] that he was finally crucified as a messianic agitator' (1958a, p. 28). Consequently, for Bultmann, all passages with any Messianic content must be the creation of the early Church. Passages accepted by earlier scholars, including Reimarus and Schweitzer, are therefore suspect. Bultmann did not think that Jesus had called himself 'Son of God' but attributed this title and theology to the later influence 'of ideas of divine men who claimed to be sons of a god, son-divinities worshipped in mystery religions, and the figure of the redeemer in the gnostic myth' (Marshall, 1976, p. 121; see also Bultmann, 1952, p. 130). Bultmann's view that traditional Christology represents a paganization of Christianity is remarkably similar to the ideas of Celsus, the early anti-Christian polemicist, whose work I describe in Chapter 4.

What the theologian has to do, says Bultmann, is to decode the meaning of the eschatological myth, and ask whether it still has any message for today. Bultmann insisted that the Gospel, the good news, is not itself 'myth', nor does it 'require mythical expression' (Morgan, 1989, p. 122). Demythologizing does not reject scripture, but 'the world-view of a past epoch' (1958b, p. 35); it denies that the Christian message is 'bound to an ancient world-view, which is obsolete' (p. 36). For Bultmann, the real intent of Jesus' preaching about the Kingdom of God was to challenge men and women to 'decide', for God, or for the world. Jesus' preaching still challenges the scientific worldview, that the human race can control its own destiny (1958b, pp. 39–40). Jesus' preaching 'calls [man] to God, who is beyond the world and beyond scientific thinking. . . . Faith in this sense is both the demand and the gift offered by preaching. Faith is the abandonment of man's own security and the readiness to find security only in the unseen beyond, in God' (*ibid.*, p. 41).

## Who was Jesus?

According to Bultmann, Jesus had indeed expected an eschatological drama, and inasmuch as this did not happen, he was wrong: 'The same world exists and history has continued. History has refuted mythology. For the conception of the kingdom of God is mythical, as is the conception of the eschatological drama' (1958b, p. 14). Yet Jesus had not been wholly mistaken, for his preaching suggests that although the event of the kingdom was 'future', its effect was 'immediate':

the kingdom of God is genuinely future, because it is not a metaphysical reality or condition, but the future action of God, which can be in no sense something given in the present. None the less this future determines man in his present, and exactly for that reason is . . . not merely something to come, 'somewhere', 'sometime' but destined for man and constraining him to decision. (1958a, p. 51; see also 1958b, p. 31)

Bultmann saw this eschatology as consistent with John's, in whose gospel demythologizing had already started (as it had in Paul's writing): 'For John, the resurrection of Jesus, Pentecost and the parousia . . . are one and the same event, and those who believe already have eternal life' (1958b, p. 33). Bultmann thus accepts what Strauss rejected, that is, the Johannine version. Jesus' words, across the centuries, still demand response; the kingdom of God 'signifies for man the ultimate Either-Or, which constrains him to decision' (*ibid.*, p. 41). Although Bultmann rarely refers to Schweitzer, he sometimes appears to be responding to him. For example, he rejects the idea that Jesus had taught only an 'interim-ethic'; instead, his sayings about the will of God call for 'complete surrender' (1958a, p. 129). The status of John's Gospel remains problematical for Jesus studies, as indicated in Chapter 1. Some scholars reject any theories based on John, others argue that while the synoptics' chronology is the more *historical*, John is a valid *theological* interpretation of Jesus' significance, which I believe was Bultmann's view. It is not necessary to argue that a theological conviction about Jesus corresponds *exactly* with what Jesus believed of himself, only that it is *consistent* with what can be said of Jesus with some confidence.

## Miracles and the resurrection

On miracles, Bultmann thought it beyond doubt that Jesus, like his contemporaries, believed in divine intervention; also, 'there can be no doubt that Jesus did the kind of deeds which were miracles to his mind and to the mind of his contemporaries' (1958a, p. 173). Jesus, though, had not spoken about his death or resurrection; any saving or atoning significance 'originated in the faith of the primitive church' (1958b, p. 213). For Bultmann, forgiveness derives not from the cross, or from the resurrection, or from Jesus' metaphysical, incarnate nature (*ibid.*, p. 215), but from his word: 'in the word, and not otherwise, does Jesus bring forgiveness' (*ibid.*, p. 219). For Bultmann, Jesus rises in believers' hearts as they respond to the word. As a Lutheran, he wanted to place the word, and preaching, centre stage. He fills in, I suggest, the gap that Schweitzer left between Jesus hanging dead on the cross and his words crossing the centuries to speak to people today.

Bultmann spent long hours talking to his friend, the existentialist philosopher Martin Heidegger, and his theology is properly defined as existential; in the moment of response to the word as preached, Jesus becomes a real 'event' for the hearer, who responds in faith. Thus, for Bultmann, it is the word that crosses Lessing's 'ditch' and authenticates faith in every age. Heidegger's existentialism, though, was more secular than Bultmann's, an affirmation of human *Dasein* (there-ness) despite death's inevitability (see Cross and Livingstone, 1983, p. 629). Bultmann's own existentialism may have more in common with Søren Kierkegaard's. Kierkegaard (1813–55), who influenced Heidegger, resolved how to bridge Lessing's broad, ugly ditch by positing a leap of existential faith. Human life, said Kierkegaard, is confronted by suffering, by anxiety and by estrangement from God. This estrangement cannot be overcome through reason, since absurdity – the claim that God became human and died as a human – lies at the heart of the Christian message. The truthfulness of this message can only be grasped by a leap of faith that itself involves what for Kierkegaard was the crucifixion of the intellect. Truth, he said, 'is subjective', known in 'passionate conviction, though it is absurd' (Cunliffe-Jones, 1970, p. 109).

Kierkegaard also thought that Christianity had turned the creeds into idols; he wanted direct experience of God. Taught in childhood that suffering for the truth was the essence of Christian faith, the older he grew, the more he identified himself with Jesus' sufferings. He felt himself to be a martyr, dying for this world, for temporality, understanding himself only in suffering. This is all rather melancholy, but it represents an example of how a scholar's psychological, inner, spiritual experience influenced his academic thinking. I find it interesting to compare the above with some passages in Schweitzer, who also speaks of how his childhood inability to explain suffering found no better solution in later life: 'I gradually came to the conclusion that all we can understand about the problem is that we must follow our own way as those who want to bring about deliverance,' he wrote (1998a, p. 243).

## Biographical pessimism: 'I calmly let the fire burn'

Bultmann thought that Jesus' personality and self-understanding lay beyond historical study, and said that this held no interest for him:

I calmly let the fire burn, for I see that what is consumed is only the fanciful portraits of Life-of-Jesus theology, and that means nothing other than 'Christ after the flesh'. But the 'Christ after the flesh' is no concern of ours. How things looked in the heart of Jesus I do not know and do not want to know. (1969, p. 132)

Commenting on the storm created by Bultmann's biographical scepticism, Paul Tillich argued that all the quest of the historical Jesus had produced was 'insight that there is no Jesus picture behind the biblical one which could be made scientifically probable' (1957, p. 102). What scholars can offer are 'probabilities about Jesus of a higher or lower degree' (p. 103). Like Bultmann, Tillich thought it impossible to penetrate Jesus' inner self, since 'our knowledge of the person . . . behind the gospels is fragmented and hypothetical' (p. 107). 'Our records,' said Tillich, 'do not have a psychological description of Jesus' development, piety or inner conflicts. They only show the presence of New Being in him under the condition of existence' (p. 124). The many lives of Jesus are more like novels than biography (p. 105).

Yet something at least of what Jesus' heart may have looked like can be reconstructed from what Bultmann says about Jesus:

characteristic of him are exorcisms, the breach of the Sabbath commandment, the abandonment of ritual purification, polemic against Jewish legalism, fellowship with outcasts such as publicans and harlots; it can also be seen that Jesus was not an ascetic like John, but gladly ate and drank a glass of wine. (Thompson, 1985, p. 99, citing a 1959 lecture)

Bultmann's Jesus also preached love and sacrifice:

he proclaimed also the will of God, which is God's demand for the good. Jesus demands truthfulness and purity, readiness to sacrifice and to love. He demands that the whole man be obedient to God, and protests against the delusion that one's duty to God can be fulfilled by obeying certain external commandments. (1958b, pp. 17–18)

There is more here in this Jesus of love, sacrifice and total obedience to the Father's will than one might think a biographical pessimist would concede. This minimalist portrait can, I suggest, withstand historical critical scrutiny. Hunter (1969) does Bultmann an injustice when he asks, 'what is the use of a *kerygma* in which the central figure is only a faceless event?' (p. 126). Bultmann, he implies, subtracts God, grace and the Holy Spirit from the Gospel, reducing it to 'a gospel of self-salvation in which Jesus becomes simply the opportunity for man to save himself by making the right decision' (p. 138). Bultmann rejected as 'unfounded and not worth refutation' the theory, discussed in my next chapter, that Jesus never existed (1958a, p. 13).

## Charles Harold Dodd (1884–1973) and realized eschatology revisited

Bultmann's eschatology is generally classed as a 'realized eschatology', a term popularized by British New Testament scholar C. H. Dodd. The consummation of the kingdom lies beyond history but the kingdom is already *in some sense* present through Christ's teaching, death, resurrection, and continues in the witness of the Church, the leaven in the dough of the world. Personally, I warm to this interpretation. I think that it does justice to the biblical material, to texts which speak of a future event, and to those that suggest a present reality (such as Luke 11:20; 17:21; Thomas 113), requiring that none are elevated or downgraded. I prefer to work with the texts of the Gospels as they are than to judge some texts (sympathetic to my case) authentic and others (awkward for my case) non-authentic.

The argument against the present-but-also-future solution is that Jesus regarded his ministry as preparation for, not as the start of, the kingdom (Weiss, 1971, p. 80). However, as noted, this view is shared by liberation theology as well as by such writers as Borg and Crossan, whose Jesuses also invite us to challenge unjust social, political and economic systems. They think that Christians have substituted belief in Jesus for experience of the kingdom. Here, they are close to Jewish critics, who also 'deny that Jesus taught his disciples to put their trust in him. His message was not, make me, or my words, the means of your religion' (Enelow, 1920, p. 27). Judaism does not accept the need for a mediator between humankind and God. Of course, in this view, gospel passages such as Matthew 10:32–3 ('everyone who acknowledges me, I will acknowledge before my Father . . .') and Luke 9:48 must be rejected as creations of the Church.

## The 'threat and warrant' passages

Borg's *Conflict, Holiness and Politics in the Teachings of Jesus* (1998) looks systematically at the 'threat and warrant' passages in the synoptics, which predict some disaster or punishment, and concludes that the majority of these point to the contingent possibility that if the people did not reform, the Temple and Jerusalem would be destroyed 'by an invading military force' (p. 237) rather than to the end of time. By the 'kingdom', Jesus meant the 'presence and power of God known through mystical experience' (p. 262). It is not a future event but an 'existential reality known in Jesus' subjectivity' (p. 263). Those who experience this, however, in a sense live 'the life of the end, that other consciousness and style of existence that flow from the sacred. They are the community of the new age' (p. 265). Borg sees the life of the new age as characterized by compassion, action for others and a concern for justice in the here-and-now: 'A vision of the afterlife that takes Jesus seriously would not be very much concerned with the afterlife' but with cultivating 'a relationship with the Spirit that transforms our lives in the present' (in Borg and Wright, 1999, pp. 245–54).

## Bultmann and the Jewishness of Jesus

Bultmann wanted to establish some continuity between Jesus' actual life and what Christians have subsequently believed about him. However, he rejected many elements of traditional Christian dogma, including incarnation, resurrection and Jesus' messiahship. He upheld the historicity (*dass*) of the crucifixion but this was hardly central to his theology. What Jesus *said*, and not his *intention to die*, explains Christian faith. In some respects, Bultmann seems to see Jesus as a first-century Jew; like Strauss (see Hodgson, 1972, p. xxxii), he saw Jesus' teaching style as reminiscent of the Rabbis':

Jesus actually lived as a Jewish Rabbi . . . he gathers around him a small circle of pupils . . . he disputes over questions of the law . . . like them, he takes his place as a teacher in the synagogue, he coins proverbs and parables. (Bultmann, 1958a, p. 58)

Sanders, however, censures Bultmann for assuming that Jesus was 'the only Jew to seize Judaism's positive potentialities', and for 'leaving the rest of Judaism . . . mired in legalism' (1985, p. 361; see also p. 28). Bultmann, Sanders suggests, had only a limited knowledge of 'late Judaism' (1985, p. 29); his eschatology, which turns Jesus' teaching into 'timeless truth', pulls Jesus 'out of [his] concrete historical setting', in which he would have expected an imminent end. Heschel (1998) says that Bultmann utilized all 'the old stereotypes to explain the faith of the disciples as a tremendous protest against contemporary Jewish legalism' (p. 232).

## Bultmann and a racist Germany

I very much appreciate how Charlotte Allen places her subjects in the context not only of intellectual history but also of their times, but I do not always warm to her opinions. She criticizes Bultmann for bad timing when, with Hitler entrenched in power, he boldly questioned Christian orthodoxy's suitability for the twentieth century, which 'deeply shocked his colleagues' (1998, p. 246). While Bultmann did join the Confessing Church, and disliked the regime's racist views, he warmed to Hitler's emphasis on hard work and 'respect for authority'. Unlike Barth, he did not leave Germany, nor did he lose his life as did Bonhoeffer, or even his job, as did Tillich for vocal opposition to Hitler. Removed from his post at Frankfurt in 1933 (all others removed at that time were Jews), Tillich broadcast his *Against the Third Reich* from his new home in the USA. Nazi persecution of Jews, he said, meant:

human misery, not only shame for all Germans . . . not only a curse that redounds on those who have hurled it . . . it means hostility against the spirit, against human dignity, and against God. . . . It is the question of our existence or nonexistence as Christians, and human beings. (1998, pp. 15–16)

Tillich's condemnation of the effort to exterminate the Jews (*ibid.*, p. 63) and of concentration camps was perhaps more robust than that of any other Christian writer. Certainly, we find no equivalent of this in Bultmann's writing, but even the Confessing Church was all but silent on the Jewish question.

Two responses. First, I still do not see anything in Bultmann that could be interpreted as sympathetic towards Hitler's goals; even his view of Judaism as outmoded does not justify the extermination of Jews. He may have wanted respect for authority, but he strenuously denied that humanity could control its own destiny. Second, Allen herself points out how almost all the *theological* liberals (Strauss, Bauer, Ritschl) were far from liberal *politically*. They all tended to support German nationalism. Strauss, she says, 'infuriated the pro-democracy majority' when he was serving in the Württemberg Assembly by supporting use of troops to quell riots (Allen, 1998, p. 170). Adolf von Harnack (1851–1930), Ritschl's pupil, 'was a fervent Prussian (and German) patriot' and 'believed in the sacred cause of the German military effort' (*ibid.*, p. 174). He advocated the abandonment of the Apostles' Creed and 'old fashioned supernaturalistic dogmas'. Bultmann's conservative politics and liberal theology seem to fit a pattern, and if Hitler wanted to conscript a theologian to lend legitimacy to his totalitarian regime, there was no shortage of candidates. Others will disagree with my verdict on Bultmann. Martin Forward, in responding to the text of this book, suggested that 'Bultmann can not so easily get off the hook of sympathy towards Hitler's goals' (2000, p. 1).

### The no-quest period (1892/1906–53)

The no-quest period abandoned any effort to construct chronological, biographical accounts of Jesus' life and concentrated instead on developing criteria for determining which passages, usually sayings of Jesus, were traceable to him, and which to the early Church. Typical of this period was the work of Norman Perrin (1920–76), a British scholar who completed his doctoral work at Göttingen, and then taught in the USA. He shared Bultmann's scepticism that we can know very much about the Jesus of history and thought that the Christ of traditional faith could not be justified from any reading of the New Testament. Instead, in the light of what scholarship uncovered of the historical Jesus, Christian theology was morally compelled to reformulate its dogmas. Joachim Jeremias, Perrin's teacher, thought that what was typical of Jesus was the Aramaic speech pattern which characterized his parables. Since we know that Jesus spoke Aramaic, said Jeremias, Semitic phrases are more likely to have come from Jesus than Greek constructions.

Perrin thought that whatever stood in contrast with first-century Judaism was attributable to Jesus: 'Material may be ascribed to Jesus only if it can be shown to be distinctive of him, which usually will mean dissimilar to any tendencies in Judaism before or after him' (1969, p. 71). Perrin stands in a long line of Christians who were certain that Jesus had little in common with the religion of his peers, in contrast to Reimarus, who argued that Jesus had no intention of deviating from Judaism. Critics of Perrin point out how his criterion of dissimilarity inevitably pits Jesus against Judaism and rejects as authentic anything said by Jesus that was consistent with Jewish belief (see Marshall, 1977, p. 202; Borg, 1998, p. 37). Heschel characterizes Perrin's Jesus as a 'non-Jewish and non-Christian Jesus . . . a far cry from Reimarus' contention that closeness to Judaism marks the authenticity of Jesus' sayings' (1998, p. 239). Similarly, she criticizes Jeremias for representing Jesus as standing 'in opposition to the Judaism of his day, not as a representative of its teachings and practices' (p. 233). I return to Heschel's work on Jewish views of Jesus in Chapter 5.

In the 'new quest', the opposite criterion emerges as primary in the work of E. P. Sanders, for whom Jesus was in many respects a typical first-century Jew. If Sanders cannot locate anything in first-century Judaism, he is reluctant to attribute it to Jesus. The other two criteria developed by Perrin (to which I return below) were those of multiple attestation and coherence. Multiple attestation deems a saying more likely to be authentic if it is found in more than one source (say, in Matthew and in Luke). The idea of coherence assumes that Jesus had a characteristic speech style and posits that similar sayings are more likely to be authentic.

## The new and third quests (from 1953 and 1985 respectively)

The 'new quest' differs from the 'no quest' in being more confident that biographically useful material can be identified in the New Testament. It is also generally more confident of at least some continuity between the Jesus of history and the Christ of faith. The 'new quest' is usually dated from a speech given in 1953 by Ernst Käsemann (1906–98), a pupil of Bultmann, on 'The Problem of the Historical Jesus'. Käsemann suggested that while the Gospels are not biographies, careful study could none the less reconstruct enough authentic Jesus material to give us some reliable biographical information. Not to admit this possibility, he said, fails to do justice to the historical nature of at least some of the gospel material. He set out to probe the 'question of the continuity of the Gospel within the discontinuity of the times and within the variation of the kerygma' (Käsemann, 1964, p. 46). Other new-quest writers reject the distinction between biographies, and the genre of gospel, as false; Hunter (1969) believes that the Gospels contain much eyewitness evidence: 'in its essentials the tradition goes back to Jesus himself, and . . . was handed on by trustworthy people' (p. 34). Hunter further states:

Behind the words and deeds of Jesus in the Gospels lies the claim to be the uniquely accredited Representative of 'the lord of heaven and earth'. . . . This unique claim is the very basis and foundation of Christianity; and therefore the study of the Jesus of history is no mere marginal task for New Testament scholarship, but its chief concern . . . the apostles' kerygma without Jesus' 'good news' is only the proclamation of an idea. (p. 134)

Bornkamm (1960), also a protégé of Bultmann, summed up this evaluation of the Gospels as 'real history' in these words:

The gospels bring before us the historical figure of Jesus in the immediacy of his power. What they report about the message, deeds and history of Jesus is marked still today by an authenticity, a freshness and an individuality – unaffected by the Church's Easter faith – which carry us back directly to the earthly figure of Jesus. (p. 24)

'The primitive tradition of Jesus,' he wrote, 'is brim full of history.'

Bornkamm uses expressions such as 'indisputable facts' and 'historically indisputable traits' in his 'rough outline of Jesus' person and history' with which he begins *Jesus of Nazareth* (1960, pp. 53, 55). Allen describes this as 'the first "life of Jesus" to emerge from the German academy since the beginning of World War I' (1998, p. 251). Günther Bornkamm not only had more to say than Bultmann about the details of Jesus' life (though not *that* much more) but also tended to see Jesus as the word made flesh; Bultmann's Jesus was only the *bearer* of the word (see Sanders, 1985, p. 29). J. M. Robinson's *A New Quest of the Historical Jesus* (1959) also gave credibility to the idea that the task of reconstruction was historically feasible. It was Robinson (a Jesus Seminar member) who 'privately circulated' copies of the Nag Hammadi library 'to scholars throughout the world' (Pagels, 1979, p. xix) and edited the English edition (1990). Robinson co-translated Bornkamm's *Jesus*. The 'third quest' runs alongside the 'new quest'. Characteristically, third-quest writers, who include Borg, Crossan, Theissen and Horsley, draw on the social sciences to illuminate their Jesus study.

Tatum distinguishes the new quest's theological concern from the third quest's theological neutrality. Scholars who pursue an apologetic brief, he suggests, are 'new questors', not 'third questors'. See Tatum's footnote on the use of the term 'third quest', coined by Wright (in Tatum, 1999, p. 238 n. 20). In this view, Wright is a 'new questor' since he defends Christian belief. This distinction means that writers such as Sanders and the Jesus Seminar ought not to be included in this 'insider' chapter, where I have placed them, since they do not write as *insiders*. However, many Jesus Seminar members do explicitly address Christian concerns in their individual writing. Sanders describes himself as 'an academic, a professional scholar, and a historian by inclination and education' (1993, p. 76). In his treatment of miracles (1993, pp. 132–68) he remarks that it is a difficult topic to discuss because 'what Christians believe or should believe' easily interferes. Thus, he exercises an 'insider-like' sensitivity towards Christian convictions. A contributor to the volume *Jews and Christians Speak of Jesus* (1994), Sanders also tends to support *some continuity* between what Jesus himself had believed and what the disciples concluded after Easter (see 1985, pp. 231, 328, 334).

## I. Howard Marshall and Norman Thomas Wright: defending the traditional Jesus

Some new questors defend the traditional Jesus and accept the general outline of Jesus' career as reasonably reliable. Here, the work of I. Howard Marshall, Hunter's colleague at Aberdeen, is typical. In his *I Believe in the Historical Jesus* (1977), Marshall defends the traditional Christian view of Jesus:

I believe in the historical Jesus. I believe that historical study confirms that he lived and ministered and taught in a way that is substantially reproduced in the gospels. I believe that this Jesus gave his life as a ransom for sinful mankind, and that he rose from the dead and is the living Lord. (p. 246)

Marshall gives back to Jesus consciousness of his messiahship, sonship and foreknowledge of his own future. He rejects the view that Jesus as Son of God only gained ontological significance 'from the resurrection onwards' and argues that the resurrection served to confirm Jesus' 'existing position and status' (1976, pp. 119–20). Marshall also accepts the historicity of the resurrection and is open to the possibility that Jesus really did perform miracles. While he recognizes that the secular historian may have a problem with writing a life of Jesus in which the supernatural plays a role, as a believer he looks at Jesus through the eyes of faith. To some historians, he says, Jesus is an ordinary man:

and no more. To others, however, the possibility is open that he was more than an ordinary man – but this possibility lies beyond the reach of historical study as such. It is a matter of faith. (*ibid.*, p. 59)

## Convergence and divergence: friendly critics

Wright, another British scholar, says that when he looks at the Jesus of historical reconstruction, he finds that his faith about Jesus is 'supported and filled out' (in Borg and Wright, 1999, p. 26). Marshall and Wright represent recent Jesus scholars who hold on to more rather than to less of the traditional Christian view of Jesus. They believe that Jesus did possess a Messianic consciousness, did die to atone for human sin, and did rise again. Wright, who is currently a Canon at Westminster Abbey, London (and a former Dean of Lichfield Cathedral and Chaplain of an Oxford College), believes that 'serious study of Jesus . . . is best done within the context of a worshipping community' (1992, p. ix; see comment by Witherington, 1995, p. 232). For Wright (1992) the Gospels 'belong to the genre "biography"' (p. 74). They may, though, be best described as 'theological reflective *biographies*' (p. 96). He states quite bluntly:

It will not do to separate the historical from the theological. 'Jesus' is either the flesh-and-blood individual who walked and talked, lived and died, in first century Palestine, or he is merely a creature of our own imagination. (p. 18)

Again, reference here may be made to the work of my Baylor University colleague, Charles Talbert, on Gospel as biography (1977) as well as to the more recent work of Burridge (1992).

Roman Catholic new questor, Edward Schillebeeckx, is a little more cautious. He argues that historical-critical study of Jesus is vital as a 'corrective':

historical-critical investigation can clarify for us how the specific context of earliest Christian belief is 'made up' by the Jesus of history, and have a corrective function with regard to the inadequacy of some later formulae. (1980, p. 33; see also Thompson, 1985, p. 107)

Wright follows the traditional view that Jesus had reflected on 'biblical texts which spoke of the shepherd putting . . . self-giving love into practice as the ultimate outworking of his task', concluding that, 'if God was to come in person to liberate Israel and bring in the kingdom of God, God might do so in and through the person of such an obedient shepherd' (1998, p. xxiv). Wright's Jesus books include *Who Was Jesus?* (1992), *Jesus and the Victory of God* (1996) and *The Original Jesus* (1997).

It is useful to compare Wright with Borg, with whom he shared a mentor at Oxford. Although critical of each other's work, they are also friends; Wright wrote the foreword to the 1998 edition of Borg's *Conflict, Holiness and Politics* and they are co-authors of *The Meaning of Jesus: Two Visions* (1999). Borg's *Meeting Jesus Again for the First Time* (1994) makes his Christian identity quite explicit: he tells of a spiritual journey through pre-critical, critical, agnostic phases (the latter while a seminary student) to a post-critical faith that sees Jesus as the lens through which we glimpse what a Spirit-filled life should look like.

Borg regards Jesus' many titles (Son of God, Messiah, Son of Man, Second Person of the Trinity) as a post-Easter effort to make sense of who Jesus was: ' "Son of God" and "messiah" means to take very seriously what we see in him as a disclosure of God' (in Borg and Wright, 1999, p. 152). For Borg, these titles do not describe an ontological reality. Borg is clearly less comfortable than Wright in applying God-language to Jesus. Borg's 'pointing to God' Jesus is close to some Jewish and Muslim views of Jesus. Seeing 'Jesus as Spirit persons', says Borg, 'shifts the focus of the Christian life from believing in Jesus or believing in God to being in relationship to the same Spirit that Jesus knew' (1994, p. 39). Wright does think that Jesus was the Son of God, in an incarnational sense, but not that Jesus ' "Knew he was God" in the sense that one knows one is tired or happy, male or female. He did not sit back and say to himself, "Well, I never! I'm the second person of the Trinity!" ' (in Borg and Wright, 1999, p. 166). The actual terms may at least in part be the product of Christian reflection, yet they do correspond with Jesus' own understanding of what he 'believed himself called to do and to be' (*ibid.*, p. 166).

Borg does not believe in the resurrection as a physical event but he does believe that the early Christians continued to experience 'Jesus as a living spiritual reality, a figure of the present, not simply a memory of the past' (in Borg and Wright, 1999, p. 135). Describing how Wright's view differs from his, he writes:

My position is that experience of the risen Christ as a continuing presence generated the claim that 'Jesus lives and is Lord' and that the statement, 'God raised Jesus from the dead' and the story of the empty tomb may well have been generated by those experiences. Tom's position is that the fact of the empty tomb and the appearances generated the claim, 'Jesus lives and is Lord'. But we both affirm the claim. This is who Jesus is for us Christians. (*ibid.*, p. 137)

Peter Jennings cited Wright as saying, 'If I didn't believe in the resurrection, I'm in the wrong business' (interview, *Larry King Live*, CNN, 15 June 2000). Wright, though, agrees with Borg (and with Crossan) that Jesus had not predicted the imminent end of the world but instead warned that Israel would be punished unless she mended her ways. Passages predicting that 'this generation will not pass away' before the judgment 'do not refer to the full end. . . . Only to the fall of Jerusalem' (in Borg and Wright, 1999, p. 209). Jesus' message was that if 'Israel did not watch out, she would be swept right away' (Wright, 1992, p. 101). Wright is quite emphatic that what he calls the 'bizarre idea . . . touted around the learned halls of New Testament scholarship all this century' that Jesus expected the end of the world 'should now be given a pauper's funeral' (*ibid.*, p. 100). The idea of the 'Second Coming', he says, is a metaphor for God's final fulfilment of his plan for creation, when the 'presence' of Jesus will become a tangible reality. He understands the Son of Man passages as metaphor; in ancient times, citizens 'went forth' to meet dignitaries. The 'snatched up into clouds' points to the final consummation of God's purposes, when 'the dead will be raised and the living transformed to share his new humanity within a transformed world' (in Borg and Wright, 1999, p. 203).

## Jesus and the Pharisees

Borg's contribution centres on his thesis that the Pharisees, as his mentor at Oxford, George Caird, suggested, 'were not hypocrites . . . not bad people but good people' and represented an interpretation of Torah obedience with which Jesus fundamentally differed. They elevated purity and holiness above all else and wanted to 'separate' from the world. Jesus, who elevated 'compassion', wanted to embrace the world, to reach out in concern to all who experienced material or spiritual poverty. Jesus warned that the Pharisees' quest for holiness was set on a collision course with Rome, which he wanted to avoid. Ongoing conflict with Rome, Jesus warned, would lead to the Temple's destruction and to Jerusalem's encirclement by foreign troops (see Matthew 24:2; Luke 21:20). The Pharisees' goal of purity was narrowly nationalistic; Jesus' compassion was a universal ethic, even if his own goal had been primarily to redeem Israel. Like Reimarus', Borg's Jesus did not intend to found a new religion:

> His sacred scripture remained Jewish and he was loyal to the Torah throughout his life. His thought patterns and symbols remained Jewish. His concern was with Judaism. Did Jesus intend to found a Church? If by this is meant an organization separate from Judaism, the answer is no. The emergence of a Church distinguishable from Judaism was a later development. Rather, his movement was a 'voluntary association' within Judaism, a movement like that of the Pharisees and Essenes. (1998, p. 85)

These different movements competed, but they also had a shared goal: the restoration of Torah obedience. The conflict between Jesus and the Pharisees had obvious political implications; the question of how Israel was to manifest 'faithfulness to YAHWEH . . . was a political as well as a religious one' (*ibid.*, p. 86).

## Richard Horsley

Richard Horsley's *Jesus and the Spiral of Violence* (1993) goes further than Borg in politicizing Jesus' mission. Jesus called on peasants and the poor to act in solidarity against oppression, even though when liberation came it would be brought about by God's intervention, not by human action. Jesus did not engage in armed struggle; 'his calling was to proceed with the social revolution' (p. 324). God would bring about the political revolution. Jesus was a 'Revolutionary, but not a violent political revolutionary. Convinced that God would put an end to the spiral of violence, however violently, Jesus preached and catalysed a social revolution' (p. 326). Jesus' message of the kingdom, which was essentially a 'political symbol' (p. 153), was primarily addressed not to individuals but to the whole nation (p. 208) while his 'healing of bodies as well as of souls' confirms that he 'was concerned with the whole of life, in all its dimensions'. Jesus 'exhorted his followers to maintain egalitarian social relations by not reverting to the traditional hierarchies by which the chain of domination had been maintained' (p. 240). Horsley's Jesus, pitted against the unjust taxes and the collaborating aristocracy of his day, in my view resembles Brandon's, who was 'hostile towards the Romans and those Jews who, for worldly gain, cooperated with them' (Brandon, 1967, p. 327).

Certainly, there are some similarities between Horsley and Brandon; like Brandon, Horsley thinks that the incident in the Temple may have been an attempt at a 'direct takeover of the religio-political-economic center of society' (1993, p. 297). He hesitates to categorically deny that Jesus did not approve of armed struggle – 'it would be difficult to claim that Jesus was a pacifist' (p. 326) – although he also states that there is no evidence that Jesus 'advocated or organized' any 'kind of armed rebellion' (p. 321). Jack Perkins' video, *The Unknown Jesus* (1999), in discussing whether or not Jesus approved of violence, similarly suggests that this cannot be ruled out, in the light of Matthew 10:34, 'I did not come to bring peace but a sword', which contrasts starkly with Matthew 26:52, 'all who draw the sword will die by the sword'. Similarly, in *66 AD: The Last Revolt*, in which Horsley also appears, Allen Callahan of Harvard suggests that Jesus may have entertained revolt. He points out that Jesus moved from safe house to safe house, that some of his disciples were armed and that only his inner circle knew of his whereabouts.

Witherington criticizes Horsley (and Theissen; see below) for paying too much attention to Jesus' social setting and too little to his religious context (1995, p. 146). Horsley's Jesus, like Reimarus', seems to end as a failure: God did not intervene, the kingdom did not come and Jesus does not seem to have intended to leave anything like the Christian Church behind as a legacy. Horsley thinks that the 'spiritual spin' of the Gospels was back-projected in order to obscure the original political message. After interviewing Horsley (during what, interestingly, was Horsley's first visit to Israel/Palestine), Mark Tully found himself asking how Horsley accounted for the origin of Christianity: 'How did the Jesus movement survive? How did the church come about when Jesus himself apparently got it wrong?' (1996, p. 131). Tully describes Horsley's schoolboy-like excitement at seeing 'with his own eyes evidence of the magnificence . . . of the Roman cities which he believed had such an impact on the subject Jews of Jesus' time' (p. 116). In contrast, Brandon had served in Palestine as an army chaplain, where he first formulated the ideas expressed in his book, which he wrote after returning to academia.

### Edward P. Sanders and Gerd Theissen

Sanders, who has studied and taught at prestigious schools on both sides of the Atlantic, is less optimistic than Hunter, Marshall or Wright that a biography of Jesus can be constructed. 'Much about the historical Jesus,' he says, 'will remain a mystery' (1993, p. 280). However, he does believe that 'the work pays off in modest ways' (1993, p. xiii). His writing emphasizes the Jewishness of Jesus and follows Reimarus in positing no real departure from the Judaism of his day. Jesus did have some different opinions, such as on the details of Sabbath observance, but these were within the parameters of contemporary debate (1993, p. 215). This does not mean that Jesus had no argument with his fellow Jews but that his aim was reform and renewal from within, not to establish a new religion. Sanders' Jesus is not critical of Judaism or of Torah obedience as a dead system in need of a successor, but of how some Jews were interpreting the demands of Judaism. I am basing my analysis on Sanders' 1985 book, *Jesus and Judaism*, and on his 1993 *The Historical Figure of Jesus*.

Gerd Theissen, best known for his work on reconstructing the sociology of Jesus' day, also depicts Jesus as the leader of a reform movement within Judaism, and downplays differences between Jesus and first-century Judaism (see Theissen, 1987). He calls the early Jesus movement 'wandering radicals' (1992, p. 33). A professor at Heidelberg, Theissen has been described as 'most likely the last of the truly innovative German scholars working in the Bultmann tradition' (Allen, 1998, p. 273). Max Weber's ideas on 'charisma' also inform Theissen's work (see Weber, 1963). Theissen tries very hard to locate Jesus within the world of Second Temple Judaism. However, his use of ideas from modern social theory may predispose him to find in Jesus what he needs to find, if Weber's theory that all religions begin with charismatic individuals is to be sustained. His Jesus as a wandering charismatic dedicated to peacemaking is similar, in my view, to Borg's and Crossan's Jesuses, and to the Jesus of Jewish scholar Geza Vermes, whose work I discuss in Chapter 5.

Theissen's Jesus preached and practised an inclusive form of Judaism, which had love of God and neighbours at its heart. By relaxing some of the rules, Jesus opened up the possibility that even non-Jews could enter the kingdom (see Witherington, 1995, p. 142). After Jesus' death as a trouble-maker, it was Paul who broke away from Judaism by transforming Jesus' implicit universalism into an explicit one. However, in doing so Paul ended up substituting Gentiles for Jews; Jews who remained Jews 'take over the role of the unredeemed Gentiles' (Theissen, 1992, p. 209). Jesus may not have intended to found a permanent movement, since he expected the end to come soon, but the Church has at least an implicit basis in Jesus' social ethic. Witherington, responding to Theissen, thinks that he is right on the question of Jesus relaxing 'some of the Jewish religious and ritual distinctiveness' but wrong to surmise that Jesus did not intentionally found the Church: 'Jesus did envision the setting up of a community . . . after his death . . . because he believed the coming of the kingdom, not the end of the space-time-continuum, was imminent, and that it created community' (1995, p. 143). The idea of Jesus as a reformer within Judaism is probably the main characteristic of the new quest. I think, for example, that Borg does a good job in locating Jesus' ideas within Jewish thought. Heschel's verdict, though, that Borg's teacher-of-universal-wisdom-Jesus is a Jesus divorced from his Jewish context differs somewhat from mine (1998, p. 234).

## Jesus and Judaism

Sanders' contribution builds on his basic premise that no essential difference existed between Jesus' teaching and the wider Jewish community, including the Pharisees. Anti-Pharisaic Gospel material (such as Matthew 23) reflects the early Church's later desire to distance itself (and therefore Jesus) from rabbinical Judaism, largely the legacy of the Pharisees (see Sanders, 1993, pp. 216–18; Sanders, 1985, pp. 276f.). Theissen (1987) also thinks that scholars have 'a great duty to restore the reputations of the

Pharisees'. Early Christians, for their own reasons, made 'Judaism with its Pharisaic stamp responsible for anything from which [they] wanted to be disassociated' (p. 108). This does not mean that all the material was invented. Rather, an anti-Pharisaic gloss was added to what may have originally been a general condemnation of hypocrisy, or of a rigid legalism. However, the references to Jews 'plotting' against Jesus, which built up to their climax in the Passion, may well be pure invention or, as Sanders calls it, a 'redactional or authorial construction' (Sanders, 1993, p. 218). Material 'indicating that Jesus broke the law . . . [was] retrojected from the situation of the early church into the lifetime of Jesus' (p. 222). In this view, the gospel scene in which Pilate washed his hands reflects the early Church's desire to deflect blame for Jesus' death away from the Romans, whom they wanted to attract, towards the Jews, from whom they were now estranged. The relationship between Jesus and the Pharisees is a major theme in Chapter 5 of this book.

Sanders offers a careful and extensive discussion of Jesus and the law, (1993, pp. 205–36; 1985, pp. 245–69). There is, he concludes, 'no criticism of the law which would allow us to speak of his opposing or rejecting it', which brings him rather close to Reimarus (Sanders, 1985, p. 101). Witherington suggests that Sanders protests too loudly on the issue of Jesus' relaxation of at least some of the ritual laws (1995, p. 143). Sanders does not think that Jesus posed any threat to the Jerusalem Temple either, although he may have advocated its reform and probably believed that this would follow when the kingdom came (1993, p. 261). Reference to its 'destruction', which he takes to be at least based on Jesus' words at Mark 13:2, for example, was part of Jesus' eschatological vision in which the restored Israel would worship in a new and more glorious Temple (see 1985, pp. 74–5). Had the Church placed the prediction on Jesus' lips, 'we would expect it to say that the Temple would be destroyed by fire, not that the stone walls would be completely torn down' (1993, p. 257). Some of Jesus' actions, such as his eating with the wicked, would have annoyed the religious leaders (1993, pp. 232, 235). So too would his claim to autonomous authority, which seemed to bypass the Torah, let alone the priesthood and the trained scholars: '*Jesus was a charismatic and autonomous prophet*; that is, his authority (in his own view and that of his followers) was not mediated by any human organisation, not even by scripture' (p. 238; italics in original). Theissen makes the same point when he places these words into Gamaliel's mouth: 'He acts as though God himself were speaking through him. This contempt for our forms – that's what causes offence' (1987, p. 107).

## Sanders' restorationist eschatology

Where Sanders differs radically from Wright, Borg, Crossan and other recent writers is in his rejection of the 'kingdom as here-and-now' thesis. In fact, he also parts company from Weiss, Schweitzer and Bultmann, in arguing that first-century Judaism was not consumed with apocalyptic ferment. He does, though, think that the key to understanding who Jesus was lies in restorationist eschatology, and his Jesus is first and foremost a prophet of that genre. While this is close to Weiss' view it also resembles Wright's, except that for Wright the end, which started with Jesus' resurrection, *will fully arrive* when God completes his purposes, while Sanders' end *would have taken place* in the first century (see Witherington's comment on the difference between Sanders' restorationist and Wright's reconstitutionist eschatologies; 1995, p. 229). Jesus expected the kingdom to come within his own life. This kingdom would not be quite Weiss' other-worldly kingdom but 'would be on a renewed earth, in a transformed situation' (1985, p. 231). It would probably include Gentiles, as 'a good number of Jews expected this to happen . . . and Jesus was a kind and generous man' (1993, p. 192). In the kingdom, human values will be reversed (*ibid.*, p. 204).

Like Weiss, Sanders says that this kingdom would result only from God's initiative: 'he would create an ideal world. He would restore the twelve tribes of Israel, and peace and justice would prevail. Life would be like a banquet' (1993, p. 184). According to Sanders, while Jesus did not see himself as the Messiah, he did think that he would be God's representative in the kingdom (*ibid.*, p. 248). Sanders is reluctant to ascribe any of the traditional titles to Jesus' self-consciousness, at least in any metaphysical sense. He may have thought of himself as God's son, just as all Jews were children of God, and just as his followers might be 'if they loved their enemies' (*ibid.*, p. 244). Sanders, though, does not think that Jesus used this title (*ibid.*, p. 248). Jesus did use 'Son of Man' but 'it is not possible to come to a firm conclusion about Jesus' use of' this, since it is uncertain whether his reference to the Son of Man 'coming on the clouds of heaven' (Matthew 26:64) referred to himself or to some other figure (*ibid.*, pp. 247–8).

Bornkamm had also argued that Jesus did not call himself 'Son of Man'; Jesus was referring to a figure *distinct* from himself (1960, pp. 228–31). The Son of Man was not, says Sanders, an eschatological figure in first-century Judaism. *The Book of Enoch*, where the Son of Man does feature as a heavenly figure 'who would judge humanity at the end of normal history . . . cannot be proved to be pre-Christian' (1993, p. 246). Sanders thinks that this text may have been edited by Christian revisers (*ibid.*, p. 308). While Sanders is confident that Weiss and Schweitzer were right and the liberals wrong on the end time nature of the kingdom, at least one Jewish scholar disagrees. In his book *Jesus* (1997; original 1968), David Flusser of the Hebrew University, Jerusalem, has no difficulty saying that 'For Jesus and the Rabbis, the kingdom of God is both present and future, but their perspectives are different' (p. 110; and see Chapter 5).

## Miracles

On miracles, Sanders tends towards the view that Jesus' disciples believed he performed miracles, and that the question to be asked is, how did they, and Jesus, understand their significance? (1993, p. 158; 1985, p. 157). He does not associate miracles as a messianic expectation. He does say that Jesus' disciples may have regarded them as preparation for the end times (1993, p. 133; 1985, p. 173). If Jesus' message to John, citing Isaiah 35, is taken at face value, he may have regarded miracles as a sign that the restoration was at hand (1993, pp. 167, 168). He may have regarded miracles as a 'sign' to friends, not to enemies (Strauss considered this option; see 1972, p. 414). Like other new-quest scholars, he is open to the possibility that miracles really did occur:

The need for rational explanation is a modern one . . . some rationalist explanations are far fetched . . . it is plausible to explain exorcism as a psychosomatic cure. . . . Some cannot be explained on the basis of today's scientific knowledge. (1993, p. 159)

On the other hand, Jesus may have possessed some medical know-how (1993, p. 154). Interestingly, while Borg and Crossan have no time for a metaphysically divine Jesus, neither denies the possibility that he could heal; indeed, both identify Jesus' healing as a principal characteristic of his reform movement. Crossan asks, 'Did Jesus heal? I am absolutely certain that he did, and I think that if he didn't we wouldn't remember a word he said' (Perkins, 1999). Even the historically sceptical, existentialist Paul Tillich leaves open the possibility that miracles may be subjectively real for those who experience them: 'miracles are given only to those for whom they are sign-events, to those who receive them in faith,' he wrote; 'Jesus refuses to perform "objective miracles". They are a contradiction in terms' (1953, p. 130; see also 1957, pp. 160–1). Despite Hume's claim as to their improbability, a recent poll shows that '84% of Americans say that they believe that God performs miracles, and 48% claim to have witnessed one' (Woodward, 2000b, p. 57).

## Why did Jesus die?

As noted in my Introduction, many scholars consider this a key question; Jesus' *life* cannot be understood without understanding why he *died*. Numerous books have been written on this subject alone (see Brown, 1994; Crossan, 1995). If conflict with Judaism did not lead to Jesus' death, and if Jesus had not intended to establish a new, distinct religion, Sanders asks, 'Why was he crucified?' Examining Schweitzer, he rejects the idea that Jesus had thought his own death a necessary prelude to God's intervention. He also rejects the possibility that Jesus had any temporal, military or political ambition. There is no evidence that he intended to lead a revolt (unlike Reimarus' Jesus). Had the Romans thought so, they would not have stopped at executing Jesus but would have rounded up his followers too, as they did with those of other trouble-makers (Sanders, 1985, pp. 306, 313, 318). Nor did the disciples, after Jesus' resurrection, expect his return with legions of conquering angels: 'they expected something, but not conquest' (1985, p. 231).

Critics of Borg's, Crossan's and other Jesus Seminar members' Jesuses suggest that their Jesuses caused no one enough offence for anyone to kill him (see Pearson, 1996). I disagree. Their Jesuses pitted themselves against social inequality and injustice, and sooner or later such a policy attracts the displeasure of the powerful and privileged. As Crossan (1994) observes, it was predictable that some 'form of religiopolitical execution' would surely take place (p. 196). In fact, Emperor Domitian (51–96 CE) expelled philosophers and astrologers from Rome simply as a precaution, in case their teachings incited political unrest.

I actually think that Sanders' Jesus does less to deserve death than Crossan's or Borg's Jesuses. Sanders does characterize Jesus' ethic as a reversal of normal values, but he rejects Borg's and Crossan's view that social reform was an essential feature of Jesus' programme. Jesus, he says, may well have had 'views about the social, political, economic conditions of the people, but his mission was to prepare them to receive the coming of the kingdom' (1993, p. 188). Nowhere, he contends, does Jesus urge people to 'get together . . . and *create* the kingdom by reforming social, religious and political institutions' (1993, p. 179). Like Weiss, he emphasizes that Jesus 'thought there was nothing anyone could do to *bring* the kingdom' (*ibid.*). Sanders may be right to say that first-century Jews lacked any concept of the kingdom as a present reality, or as something that human effort could achieve, or at least work towards.

However, a view remarkably close to this is found in the thought of the Jewish philosopher Philo (30 BCE–45 CE), who believed that in order to protect themselves from ignorant anti-Jewish attack (he survived a pogrom in Alexandria) and to help spread peace and rationality throughout the world, Jews must promote knowledge and wisdom. They were to be supplicants before God on behalf of humanity (Johnson, 1987, p. 188). Later, Maimonides (1135–1204), who also saw the Jewish task as one of civilizing and educating humanity, may even have thought that the age of the Messiah would not come 'out of the blue, in a sudden clap of thunder, but as a result of progressive, unmiraculous improvements in human rationality' (Johnson, 1987, p. 190).

Could not Jesus have beaten Philo to the same understanding of the human calling here on earth? I am far from convinced that Jesus' teaching lacks a social ethic. He wants us to do what he did, not just to call him 'Lord' (Luke 6:46). I cannot read Matthew 25:31–46 otherwise. The setting is the Final Judgment but the sentence given out to the sheep and the goats is reward or punishment for actions *in this life*:

I was hungry and you gave me food, I was thirsty and you gave me a drink, I was a stranger and you visited me, I was naked and you clothed me, I was sick and you nursed me, I was in prison and you visited me.

Today, Jesus might say, 'I was oppressed, and you liberated me, marginalized and you empowered me.' Martin of Tours (d. 397), before his conversion, gave his cloak to a beggar. Later, he became convinced that Jesus was that beggar and that when we serve our neighbour's needs, we serve Christ. I think he was absolutely right. Francis of Assisi, Teresa of Calcutta, all said the same. The parable of the Good Samaritan ends with 'Go and do likewise' (Luke 10:37). However, I admire Sanders for resisting the temptation to see in the texts what his own inclinations might very well predispose him to find. In his 1994 chapter, Sanders does note a similarity between Jesus' and Philo's summing up of the law in the language of love.

Sanders' view is that it was not Jesus' social reform programme that caused his death but a misunderstanding resulting from his attitude towards the Temple. Although he presented neither the Romans nor the Jewish religion with any real threat (offended the latter's sensitivities, yes) the high priest may have decided that he was a potential trouble-maker (see 1993, p. 273). John 11:50, 'It is better for one man to die for the people than for the whole nation to perish', is, says Sanders, an 'entirely appropriate statement' (ibid., p. 272). Jesus' arrest followed on from the incident in the Temple, when Jesus turned over the money changers' tables and appears to have predicted its destruction. The charge of blasphemy was a smoke-screen; he was almost certainly executed 'for sedition or treason, as a would be king' (1985, p. 317). The disciples, though, were not eyewitnesses and probably never knew the real reason for his death, or even what the charge had been (ibid., p. 300). Once Jesus realized the inevitability of death, he would have believed that God would somehow 'redeem the situation and vindicate him' so he 'resigned himself to the will of God' (ibid., p. 332; 1993, p. 264). Sanders thinks that Jesus did cry, 'My God, My God . . .' from the cross, perhaps thinking that he had indeed failed, restoring to Jesus' lips words which Strauss had removed (1993, pp. 274–5).

Sanders' Jesus did not regard his death as inevitable or as essential to his mission, nor did he see himself as the suffering servant. Since no conception of a Messiah who would suffer existed within the Jewish thought world of Jesus' day, the early Church must have applied these passages to him. Yet this idea does appear later in Jewish thought. Vermes tells us that after the last Jewish revolt against Rome, some Rabbis speculated that the Messiah might come either in triumph or in humility, depending on the 'virtue or sinfulness of Israel in the last days' (1973, p. 171). Rabbi Joshua ben Levi actually brought Daniel 7:13 and Zechariah 9:9 together, the very verses that Christians apply to Jesus. Similarly, the Talmud speaks of: 'a rather mysterious figure called Messiah son of

Joseph. The passage reads, "they shall look unto me whom they have pierced; and they shall mourn for him as one mourneth for thy only son"' (Suk. 52a, cited in Cohen, 1949, p. 348). Cohen also cites a Talmudic passage that applies Isaiah 53 to the Messiah and other passages suggesting that the Messiah would be 'raised up' (*ibid.*). On one hand, the standard Jewish interpretation of the suffering servant is that it refers to the nation and to the people of Israel, not to a single individual (see Klausner, 1944, p. 140). On the other hand, as with the kingdom as present reality and future event, so with the concept of a suffering Messiah, might Jesus not have seen first what others saw a little later?

Many of the scholars reviewed in this chapter have surmised that Jesus gradually became aware of his role or calling as the suffering Messiah. In this view, Jesus' self-understanding developed, possibly as he reflected on the meaning of scripture. Of course, for many Christians, such a development is unnecessary; Jesus did not need to develop any such understanding but was always aware of his status and calling, from his birth onwards. John 7:15 implies that Jesus' knowledge and wisdom were innate, not acquired: 'How did this man get such learning without having studied?' Incidentally, I think it quite possible that Isaiah 53 refers both to the suffering of God's servant, the people of Israel, and to the suffering of God's servant, Jesus of Nazareth.

## The resurrection

Sanders, who thinks that any treatment of Jesus has to explain how the Church began, does want to establish some continuity between Jesus and early Christianity. This perhaps belies the claim of theological neutrality and justifies his inclusion here, as an insider-scholar. Sanders suggests that although the resurrection was neither predicted by Jesus nor expected by the disciples, both he and they thought that if he did die, God would somehow vindicate his death. He and they expected something to happen. The resurrection may not have been what they expected, but it enabled the disciples to continue to 'see Jesus as occupying first place in the Kingdom', even if its locale shifted 'from this world to the heavenly one' (1985, p. 334; remarkably close to Reimarus). In his 1993 'Epilogue: The Resurrection' (pp. 276–81) Sanders implies that the confusion and differences in the resurrection narratives might result from the disciples' surprise – something *had* happened but not exactly what they had expected. In addition, the actual nature of Jesus' appearances was by no means easy to fathom; Jesus was difficult to recognize, because 'he was not "flesh and blood" but a "spiritual body"' (1993, p. 278). Sanders rejects 'deliberate fraud' on the grounds that 'a calculated deception should have produced greater unanimity' (*ibid.*, pp. 279–80). Reimarus, in my view, failed to consider why the disciples had not done a better job of agreeing their story, like thieves preparing for possible police interrogation.

Sanders concludes that, as far as the disciples were concerned, they 'experienced what they described as the "resurrection": the appearance of a transformed person who had actually died. They believed this, they lived it, and they died for it', although the movement which they created has gone 'far beyond Jesus' message'. Jesus may also have spoken of the resurrection of the dead as a sign of the new age's dawning (1985, p. 237). Sanders thinks that delay in Jesus' return (a return which the disciples obviously expected) led to 'creative and stimulating theological reflection . . . especially in . . . John', just as Strauss and Bultmann had argued. Sanders' view of the resurrection is similar to that of the Jewish scholar Pinchas Lapide, who argues that behind the 'literary additions' of the Easter story, there remains 'a certain "something" . . . which in the apostles' simple manner of expression has been called resurrection' (1983, p. 128). 'In the oldest records,' says Lapide, 'there remains a recognizable historical kernel which cannot simply be demythologized' (*ibid.*, p. 125). Without the resurrection, he says, 'how can it be explained that, against all plausibility, his [Jesus'] adherents did *not* finally scatter, were *not* forgotten, and that the cause of Jesus did *not* reach its infamous end on the Cross?' (p. 69). The 'true miracle', says Lapide, 'is the fact that this Jewish group of Jesus' followers came to faith' (p. 126). Belief in resurrection requires believing 'in-spite-of', as do all beliefs that flow from faith (p. 118). I return to Lapide in Chapter 5.

Where Sanders thinks Christianity went beyond Jesus' message is in distancing itself from its Jewish roots. For Sanders, the Jesus of history and the Jesus of Christian faith are not identical, although Christian belief is a legitimate development and a valid extension, beyond Israel, of what Jesus intended. What did he intend? Sanders replies: 'to love God as a perfectly reliable father, to accept his love and to respond in trust' (1993, p. 194). The disciples believed this and 'were so loyal to him that they changed history' (p. 281). Heschel (1998) praises Sanders' work as 'one of the most significant developments in New Testament scholarship' (p. 233) and regrets that, despite his contribution, 'an important trend in American scholarship continues to de-Judaize Jesus' (p. 234).

## The Jesus Seminar and the no-quest redivivus

I have often referred in this book to the Jesus Seminar. Borg, Crossan and others whose work I have cited are all Fellows. One interesting fact of recent Jesus scholarship is the shift from Germany, with a few British contributors, during the old and no-quest periods, to North America. Borg, Horsley, Crossan and Sanders are all from the Big Apple side of the Atlantic. The Jesus Seminar has taken over from Bultmann as a favourite target for attack by those who defend the traditional Christian view. Tatum dates the 'third quest' from the beginning of the Seminar, which was formed in 1985 at the invitation of Robert Funk to ask, 'What did Jesus really say?', followed by 'What did Jesus really do?' (see Funk *et al.*, 1993, 1998). For scholars who usually work and publish alone (or perhaps in pairs), such a collaborative venture was unusual. While it is open to the criticism that a self-selected group is unrepresentative, that it perhaps attracted like-minded people, I think that the task itself was legitimate and boldly conceived.

In contrast, rather than inviting real scholars to join him in a collaborative project, John P. Meier, a Catholic priest, set out in his *A Marginal Jew: Rethinking the Historical Jesus* (1991) to find common ground between imaginary Catholic, Protestant, Jewish and agnostic scholars locked in the basement of a university library. Only the issues they all agree on are included in his book. This is a very carefully crafted and state-of-the-art study but it would have been really exciting if his exercise had involved live participants. One reason why scholars tend not to work collaboratively, at least in larger numbers, is that less kudos follows from being one of forty or so participants than when you are a solo author or co-editor with perhaps two or three others.

The Seminar's methodology was to establish criteria for judging the authenticity of biblical passages, then to vote on each text as they worked their way through the four canonical gospels and *The Gospel of Thomas*, which the Seminar rate highly enough to merit inclusion in the text of their Scholars Version. This is their own translation of the Gospels, designed to 'produce in the American reader an experience comparable to that of the first readers' by substituting English colloquialisms for Greek and by freeing itself from 'ecclesiastical and religious control' (Funk *et al.*, 1993, pp. ix, xvii). At the first meeting, Robert Funk warned that the Seminar would 'constantly border on blasphemy' and would need to 'forbear the hostility we shall provoke'. He also took pride that many recent developments in Jesus scholarship 'have taken place predominantly, though not exclusively, in America'. Sounding a little like the later Strauss, he complained that the public at large has little knowledge of the findings of critical scholarship because:

The religious establishment has not allowed the intelligence of high scholarship to pass through pastors and priests to a hungry laity, and the radio and TV counterparts of educated clergy have traded in platitudes and pieties and played on the ignorance of the uninformed. (p. 1)

In his *Honest to Jesus* (1996) Funk criticizes 'fundamentalists' for trying to 'turn back the clock to the sixteenth century' (p. 27).

Funk's title clearly owes something to J. A. T. Robinson's *Honest to God* (1963), in which Robinson placed 'the most fundamental categories' of 'theology – of God, of the supernatural, of religion itself – into the melting pot' to find new ways of speaking. He was addressing people inside and outside the Church who were put off less by the Gospels than by 'a particular way of speaking about the world which quite legitimately they find incredible' (pp. 7–8). I return to Robinson towards the end of this chapter. His book allowed a whole generation, including many of my seminary colleagues, to redefine and to retain their faith.

In their 1993 book, the Fellows refer to 'the dictatorial tactics of the Southern Baptist Convention and other fundamentalists' (p. 8). Sharing some of these frustrations I have often remarked how many of my fellow clergy, well trained in biblical criticism and privately aware that at least *some* texts are suspect, operate in what I call denial mode, simply ignoring source, form and redaction criticism in their teaching and preaching. In my own youth I was privileged to be ministered to by some capable and well-educated Baptist pastors but it was not until I began my theology degree that I encountered the view that everything in the Gospels attributed to Jesus' lips may not actually have been spoken by him. Many conservative theological colleges and seminaries still make no reference to this scholarship in their teaching.

## The form critic at work

The result of the Jesus Seminar's work was to accept as authentic 18 per cent of what is attributed to Jesus in red-letter editions of the Bible (a total of ninety sayings). They voted whether to colour verses red, pink, grey or black, that is, authentic or 'Jesus said something very like it', authentic but with some reservations, not authentic but 'ideas contained in it' are close to Jesus', and finally not authentic and an addition by the early Church. The Fellows take it as axiomatic that the burden of proof rests on establishing historicity, rather than on disproving it (Funk *et al.*, 1993, p. 4).

In summary, their criteria are:

*Double attestation* – passages which have double, or multiple, attestation are likely to be authentic.

*Against the bias* – passages which caused some embarrassment to the early Church but which, often in an attempt to explain the story, were preserved (such as the story of John baptizing Jesus). Conversely, passages which serve the interests of the writers too well are suspect, such as fulfilment of prophecies and proofs of Jesus' royal descent. Strauss had also classed all these as mythical; see his detailed discussion of the genealogies in Matthew and Luke (1972, pp. 108–26).

*Dissimilarity* – passages which stand in sharp contrast to the Judaism of his day are thought to be original to Jesus. This, though, may not account for what Jesus shared with Judaism. As I have suggested, the difference between Jesus and Judaism has almost certainly been exaggerated. It does, however, seem to be widely accepted that Jesus' sayings 'cut against the social and religious grain'; they 'characteristically call for a reversal of roles or frustrate ordinary, everyday expectations' (Funk *et al.*, 1993, p. 31). The 'Good Samaritan' is 'red' (see *ibid.*, p. 323), as are 'turn the other cheek', 'go the extra mile' and 'love your enemies' (pp. 143–6).

*Language* – it is widely accepted that Jesus spoke in idiomatic language, that he used humour, exaggeration, metaphor and paradox. He drew on the workaday world for his figures of speech – fishing, farming, cleaning the house. Such passages are likely to be authentic.

The Fellows give many examples of how the life situation of the early Church shaped and changed its Jesus material: a saying such as 'it is as hard for a rich man to enter the kingdom of heaven as it is for a camel to go through the eye of a needle' (Mark 10:25; this is pink) offended wealthier Christians, so 'For mortals this is impossible; for God everything is possible' (with which Mark concludes the saying; this is black) was added (see Funk *et al.*, 1993, pp. 23, 222, 295).

Sometimes, added comment actually missed the original point. Matthew has 'so the last will be the first and the first will be last' (20:16) to sum up the parable of the workers in the vineyard. However, what the parable actually affirms is equality: those who come late will be treated the same as those who came first. It does not suggest a reversal of status. The Jesus Seminar judged the parable itself to be authentic (red). Verse 16 was likely to have been spoken by Jesus: 'those who think they will be first will actually be the last, and those who accept the last position will be moved up to the . . . seems at home on the lips of Jesus' (this scores pink; p. 224). However, it is out of place in Matthew 20, so Matthew has moved it here (p. 225). They call this 'clustering and contexting' (p. 19).

Matthew's gloss to Jesus' teaching on divorce, that 'divorce is permitted if a spouse has already committed adultery' (see Matthew 5:32; 19:9), may also be 'the author's own attempt to make Jesus' views more acceptable for a continuing Christian community' (Sanders, 1993, p. 200; compare the categorical prohibition of divorce at Mark 10:2–12). The Jesus Seminar deem this whole pericope apocryphal. Mark (that is, the early Church) may have added 'The days will come when the groom is taken away, and then they will fast' to justify their practice of fasting. Jesus had not only *not fasted* but had *defended this against criticism* (Mark 2:19; see Funk *et al.*, 1993, p. 30). Sometimes, the simpler account is judged the more authentic, assuming that detail has been added by repetition and story-telling embellishment. An example might be the insertion of 'right ear' at Luke 22:50.

The Jesus Seminar think that passages representing doctrinal correctness are later creations; for example, Peter's reply to Jesus' question 'Who do you say that I am' reflects 'what Christians are supposed to say' (*ibid.*). They reject this whole episode, the crucial turning point in the synoptics' dramatic story-line: 'Jesus rarely initiates dialogue or refers to himself in the first person', thus, 'both the story and the words are the creation of the storyteller in the early Christian movement' (*ibid.*, p. 75). Sanders (1985) also calls this incident, so crucial to Schweitzer's scheme, 'dubious historically' (p. 307). 'Jesus,' say the Fellows, 'did not make claims for himself; the early Christian community allowed its triumphant faith to explode in confessions that were retrospectively attributed to Jesus' (Funk *et al.*, 1993, p. 33). As I have already noted, material linking Jesus with Hebrew prophecy (p. 21), or emphasizing his 'divinity' (if he was God's creative agent, then he could calm storms and walk on water), is generally thought by form critics to have been projected back into the Gospels.

Material positing conflict between Jesus and the Pharisees has also been retrojected (see *ibid.*, and my comments on Sanders above). Tension between Jesus and his own relatives (Mark 3:31–5; Matthew 12:46–50, Luke 8:19–21) reflects the later divide between the Peter–Paul-led Roman Church and the Jerusalem Church, whose leaders were all relatives of Jesus (*ibid.*, p. 53; some traditions say that these bishops were Jesus' own descendants). All but two verses in the whole of John are coloured black and they only scored grey (12:24–5 and 13:20), compared with *Thomas*, which attracted thirty-two pink votes and three red. As noted in Chapter 2, the 'I am' sayings of John are regarded by many scholars to be back-projection, reflecting later Christian dogma. These sayings include John 14:6, 'I am the way, the truth and the life, no one comes to the Father but through me', which Christians have traditionally taken to deny the salvation of Muslims, Hindus and others.

## Redacting the supernatural

The Fellows redact any hint of the supernatural, of Jesus' foreknowledge, from their account. They think that psychosomatic healing might account for some miracles but 'had difficulty in finding stories' they 'believed to be reports of actual cures' (Funk *et al.*, 1998, p. 571). Nor was Jesus the eternal word become incarnate. Rather, he was a mendicant teacher of wisdom (1993, p. 27) who had a special regard for the poor and outcast and taught a Cynic-like doctrine of simplicity. They note similarity between 'Foxes have dens, birds have nests, but the Son of Man has nowhere to lie his head' and Cynic aphorisms (see 1993, pp. 316–17; Luke 9:58). Jesus liked to eat and drink with no thought for tomorrow. He had not expected an imminent 'end'. Instead, Jesus 'conceived of God's rule as all around him but difficult to discern. . . . He had a poetic sense of time in which the present and the future merged' (1993, p. 137).

Passages that support a 'here already' understanding of the kingdom are taken as authentic, the futuristic ones as retrojection (see 1993, pp. 136–7). Their Jesus was not the Messiah. All references to Jesus as Messiah are additions (1993, p. 32). The birth narratives, miracles and resurrection all derive from post-Easter speculation. Jesus was probably born in Nazareth (1998, p. 533). His body 'decayed as do other corpses' (*ibid.*, p. 462). Crossan is even less conventional here, surmising that Jesus' body was dug up by dogs (see 1996, p. 152). Interestingly, this was an early Christian claim about Muhammad; that although he had predicted his resurrection after three days, his body was actually dug up by dogs or pigs (see Bennett, 1998, p. 80).

The Fellows uphold an almost total distinction between the historical Jesus and the Jesus of Christian faith depicted by the Apostles' Creed, who is 'a mythical or heavenly figure, whose connection with the sage from Nazareth is limited to his suffering and death under Pontius Pilate' (Funk *et al.*, 1993, p. 7). The Christian creeds 'smother the historical Jesus'. The mythological Jesus 'was undoubtedly derived from . . . Paul', in whose 'theological schema, Jesus the man played no essential role' (*ibid.*). Here, they sound remarkably similar to such writers as G. A. Wells and A. N. Wilson, whose views I discuss in my next chapter. While the Fellows claim that theology has played no part in their work, ideology has; having attributed major parts of the gospel narratives to Christian dogma, they voted accordingly. Their eschatology influenced how they translated the gospel texts; the 'kingdom of God' becomes 'God's imperial rule', and the 'thy kingdom come' of the Lord's Prayer (which sounds like a future coming) is counted as a 'present'-kingdom saying. This raises the question: Did they allow the texts to speak, or did they impose their scheme on to the texts, as Sanders says Schweitzer did? (1985, p. 329). Pearson (1996) argues that they performed a 'hermeneutical juggling act to remove eschatology from their texts' (6:1), although, as I have demonstrated in this chapter, they are not alone in consigning Schweitzer's eschatology to the dustbin. Wright's emphatic rejection of the idea that Jesus had expected the end of the world has already been noted (1992, p. 100). On the other hand, debate continues around the whole issue of exactly what Jesus and other first-century Jews believed about eschatology, so much so that strong language alone cannot win the argument against all alternatives.

## Luke Timothy Johnson

In his critical response to the Jesus Seminar, Johnson points out how many of the Fellows teach in second-rate colleges: 'the roster of fellows by no means represents the cream of New Testament scholarship in this country . . . most of the participants are in relatively undistinguished positions' (1996, p. 3). I think this is unfair. There are all sorts of reasons why first-rate scholars do not always end up teaching in top-ranked schools: politics, lack of contacts, not being around at the right time, and lots of other factors, are involved in the often risky business of getting an academic job. Nor should it be taken for granted that someone working in a top-rank institution is necessarily a first-rate scholar. Johnson characterizes the Seminar as 'a social mission against . . . the way in which the church is dominated by evangelical and eschatological theology – that is, a theological focus both on the literal truth of the Bible and the literal return of Jesus' (p. 6). This agenda, which is not 'disinterested scholarship', compels them to dismantle the gospel texts. He advocates an approach that allows the scholar to work critically 'within the gospel narratives' by honestly declaring a faith perspective: 'the more recent tendency in scholarship to identify and name the ideological commitments of the interpreter is a positive step' (p. 176). I agree with Johnson that a scholar who declares 'insidership' may choose to work within the texts (an approach I share).

This, of course, also authorizes outsiders who declare their perspective to approach the texts differently from insiders.

Johnson rightly criticizes the Fellows for claiming objectivity and neutrality when in fact they brought *ideology* to bear on their scholarship. On the other hand, they are quite open about what their ideology is: to work free of 'ecclesiastical and religious control' (Funk *et al.*, 1993, p. xviii). Their rejection of a fundamentalist position, too, could hardly be clearer. Johnson concludes by stating:

The Jesus to whom St Francis of Assisi appealed in his call for a poor and giving rather than a powerful and grasping Church was not the Historical Jesus but the Jesus of the Gospels. One must only wonder why this Jesus is not also the 'real Jesus' for those who declare a desire for religious truth, and theological integrity, and honest history. (1996, p. 177)

The community of faith possesses the Gospels and experiences Jesus through faith in him. For this community, there is a *direct correspondence* between inner experience, and the Jesus about whom it reads in the Gospels. Copies of electronic correspondence, *Jesus at 2000: The e.mail Debate*, between Borg, Crossan and Johnson, sponsored by HarperSan Francisco, can be found posted on the internet. I think that in many respects the Seminar's Jesus resembles the Jesus of the 'no quest' rather more than it does either Sanders' or Wright's Jesus.

## Jesus as a Cynic

Reference to Jesus as a Cynic (also found in Crossan, 1991, p. 421) follows a popular trend, as noted by Allen (1998, p. 274). In several lectures, Gerd Theissen surmised that, given the cosmopolitanism of first-century Galilee, convention-flouting, aphorism-spouting, bread-begging Cynics may have been present during Jesus' time. Jesus, who had nowhere to lay his head, sounds like a Cynic. Subsequently, several writers have depicted Jesus as influenced by Cynicism. Burton Mack's Jesus is more a counter-cultural rebel than Borg's and Crossan's peasant leader. In this view, he was a Cynic whose main goal was to break down racial and ethnic barriers, to encourage people to experiment with new lifestyles and to work for the unity of humankind (see 1988 and 1995). Since Jesus was a Cynic, the oldest and most authentic passages of the Gospels are non-Jewish.

Anglican priest Gerald Downing's *Cynics and Christian Origins* (1992) also depicts a Jesus whose lifestyle resembles that of the Cynics. Jesus 'lives simply, he relates to people, he does without a secure home base, he travels light . . . he takes the same examples from the animal world as the Cynics . . . the example of birds which do not store anything' (cited in Tully, 1996, p. 196). Like the Cynics, he accepts no master but God. Others ridicule the idea that Cynics could possibly have influenced Jesus, although it is not in my view necessary to establish direct contact to validate a comparison of similar ideas (see Witherington, 1995, pp. 58–92) for his critique of 'Jesus the itinerant cynic sage').

## Jesus and the sexual revolution

Funk, summing up the results of the Jesus Seminar, says that Christians ought to completely rethink their faith and acknowledge that Jesus was an ordinary man who pointed us to God but who had no divine pretensions (1996, p. 306). He also thinks that if we followed Jesus' example, we would 'Endorse responsible, recreational sex between consenting adults' (p. 314). 'Augustine's notion,' says Funk, 'that the consequences of Adam's sin is transmitted through male sperm is one of the greatest tragedies of theological history' (p. 313). The doctrine of Jesus' virgin birth denies Mary's 'rights as a woman' and should be abandoned, even if it makes Jesus a bastard (which Jefferson had not hesitated to suggest). The majority of Jesus Seminar members also think that Jesus married and enjoyed sexual relations (Funk *et al.*, 1993, p. 221). Phipps, in his 1996 discussion of Jesus and sex, concludes that 'the weight of the evidence is on the side of Jesus having engaged in marital sexuality' (p. 174). He links the Church's negative attitude towards women to the claim that Jesus and Mary were perpetually virginal. He cites Tertullian as an early example of Christian misogyny:

Do you not know that each of you is also an Eve? . . . You are the devil's door, you are the unsealer of that forbidden tree . . . because of the death you brought upon us, even the Son of God had to die. (p. 195)

As radical as a sexually active Jesus sounds, even this idea has some precedence among earlier Christian writers. For example, the proponent of 'muscular Christianity' Charles Kingsley (1819–75) depicted himself as Jesus, and his wife as Mary Magdalene, in two 'drawings done before their marriage in 1844' which illustrated 'his sado-erotic union with his wife' (Haskins, 1994, pp. 358–9). Kingsley's view of Jesus as robust and manly, as well as his passion for social justice, held great appeal for the British at a time when their empire overseas, and industrial achievements at home, offered opportunities aplenty for heroism and adventure. Kingsley had no time for self-denial. He hated asceticism, celibacy and even non-smoking. Kingsley believed himself to be a follower of Jesus. For his part, so did Antony of Egypt (251–356), who pioneered the frugal, flesh-denying lifestyle of the Desert Fathers. In my next chapter, I discuss the view that Jesus actually practised promiscuity.

## Are the Gospels accurate? Some possible responses

The Jesus Seminar's Christ of faith is a later development, drawing on pagan belief in dying and rising redeemers. While the Seminar does not accuse the Church of conscious deceit, it does say that Christology is pure myth. Sanders, who agrees with quite a lot of the Seminar's verdicts on authenticity (such as rejecting the commentaries on the parables, and the birth narratives), does not want to accuse the early Church of fraud. In fact, he says that 'the gospel writers did not wildly invent material' but 'developed and shaped and directed it in ways they wished' (Sanders, 1993, p. 193). However, what may have happened is that the words of Christian 'prophets' were taken to be authentic words of the risen Jesus; thus:

Christians . . . made up things . . . they believed that Jesus had ascended into heaven and that they could address him in prayer. Sometimes he answered . . . the Christians thought it was all the same Lord . . . the spirit that freely communicated with Paul and the other Christians could be thought of as the spirit of the risen Lord, who was in some way or other continuous with the historical Jesus. (*ibid.*, p. 62)

Marshall rejects this theory. He says there is no evidence that such prophets even existed (1977, p. 193) and that, if they had, it is unlikely that their words would have been preserved anonymously: 'in the bible generally prophecies are never anonymous, but are always prescribed to some named person' (p. 194). The Jesus Seminar thinks that the process behind the Gospels' formation may have been like the telling of jokes (Funk *et al.*, 1993, p. 27), which, over time, get embellished. On a somewhat different track, Wright and others have looked at the transmission of oral history. Building on the work of Albert B. Lord (1960), on the accurate transmission of oral stories, Wright has 'been exploring the possibility of applying Lord's theories of oral transmission to the Gospels to determine to what extent they preserve authentic memories' (Allen, 1998, p. 327). Given that the Torah, and other rabbinical literature, were transmitted orally for centuries, the Jews of Jesus' time may well have been faithful and loyal handers-on of oral stories.

## The Gospels as Midrash

Another device for explaining how the gospel writers may have introduced new material into the Jesus story has been suggested by John Shelby Spong, in his *Liberating the Gospels: Reading the Bible through Jewish Eyes* (1996). Some professional academics dismiss his work as popular and sensationalist. Wright, while highly critical of his contribution, calls his arguments 'articulate, well constructed and plausible' and says that they 'reflect . . . what a good many people in some parts of the church think' (1992, pp. 65–6). I therefore include Spong in this chapter. Like Funk, Spong dislikes fundamentalism (see Spong, 1992). Spong, who is an Episcopalian bishop, finds theistic language outmoded. Here, he is not nearly as radical as he sounds. Paul Tillich and J. A. T. Robinson, among others (the latter also an Anglican bishop), advocated the use of a new vocabulary to talk about the 'ground of our being, the god beyond theism'.

Drawing on Tillich, Robinson wrote:

'God' denotes the ultimate depth of all our being, the creative good and meaning of all our existence . . . the transcendent is nothing external or 'out there' but is encountered in, with and under the Thou of all finite relationships as their ultimate depth and ground and meaning. (1963, pp. 47, 114)

For Robinson, Jesus is ' "the man for others", the one in whom Love has completely taken over, the one who is utterly open to, and united with, the Ground of his being' (p. 76). Jesus shows us how to overcome estrangement and to grasp the 'meaning of the kingdom of heaven' (p. 80). For Robinson, Jesus' incarnation and resurrection were not *physical events* but *philosophical truths*.

Spong's *Living in Sin* (1990) advocated that the Church should bless same-sex unions, and argued that while sex in marriage is not always holy, sex outside marriage sometimes tends towards the direction of holiness. The Church, he said, needs to rethink its attitude towards the range of relational lifestyles that people choose today, including young people living together outside of marriage and unmarried older people living together for various economic reasons. Like Funk, he points a finger of accusation at the Church's 'yoking of sex with guilt' (p. 181). Spong also surmises that Jesus may very well have been a married man, and even suggests that Mary may have been raped. His own diocesan home page characterizes his ministry as 'To Comfort the Afflicted and to Afflict the Comfortable' (http://www.dioceseofnewark.org/jsspong/profile.html). His Jesus:

Had a unique capacity to be. His gift was to be whole, free, and giving, which in turn seemed to cause those around him to live more fully and more completely. He seemed to have an infinite capacity to love, to forgive, and to accept others. He appeared to enhance the personhood of every human being who touched his life. He broke every barrier that human beings erected to protect themselves inside their insecure world. Women, Samaritans, gentiles, lepers, those judged to be unclean felt his touch and were called into a new dignity. He had the capacity to live in the present moment, to drink from that moment all of its wonder, to scale its heights and to plumb its depths, to enable that moment to share in eternity. (Spong, 1996, p. 301)

The Gospels represent what Jesus' mainly Jewish followers believed about him, that he was the one in whom prophecy had been fulfilled. The gospel writers, according to Spong, could only write of anything 'new' by filtering this 'through the corporate remembered history of their people, as recorded in the Hebrew scriptures of the past' (p. 37). Thus, the story of Herod seeking to kill the infant Jesus is a retelling of Pharaoh's slaying of the first-born, and Jesus riding into Jerusalem on a donkey is a retelling of what the prophet had predicted at Zechariah 9:9–11. Jesus' baptism is a type of the 'parting of the red sea', except that this time it is the division between heaven and earth that is rent asunder. Stories of past heroes, says Spong, were habitually told and retold of present ones. This Midrashic process, of retelling old stories in new ways, gives us the Gospels. They are 'interpretations of the man, a rendering of insights . . . a wrapping of the symbols of the Jewish sacred past around the one who clearly bore the presence of God and made such a powerful impact on everyone around him' (Doherty, 1999a, p. 11).

Spong acknowledges indebtedness to Michael Goulder but his idea of the role of Midrash here is not so very different from Strauss' description of how gospel incidents were created to endorse Jesus' claims to fulfil Hebrew prophecy (see Goulder's (1974) study *Midrash and Lection in Matthew*). In this book, Goulder (mentioned earlier in this chapter) speaks of habits of mind common to Matthew 'and the Jewish writers of the millennium in which he stands at the middle point' (1974, p. 6). Spong argues, though, that many of the details of the gospel accounts 'in all probability, did not happen' (p. 248). Doherty's review rightly asks, 'How can something have this kind of impact, and yet not survive . . . was the Jewish mind so incapable of engaging present reality that it had to completely bury the real man under artificial creations founded on past concepts' (1999a, p. 12). However, Spong's approach does treat Matthew as a Jewish text and tries to do justice to the Jewish origins of Christianity.

## Did Christmas really happen?

While some of Matthew's references may have been introduced posthumously, I find it difficult to believe that the whole of the nativity stories were the creation of the Midrashic process. Although of all the scholars reviewed in this chapter only Wright comes to anything like the defence of the nativity scenes (see Borg and Wright, 1999, p. 171; Wright, 1992, pp. 72–92, where he discusses Spong), I find their detail arresting. Where did the inn, in which there was no room, come from? Who thought of the manger, and of the stable, as Jesus' birthing place? These were some of the questions that I asked of myself when, in the early 1980s, I stood in Bethlehem's Manger Square on Christmas morning. Spong's problem is that he can never accept a literal reading of the text, only a non-literal one. I return to the Gospels as Midrash in Chapter 5. Horsley (1989) offers an interesting study of the nativity stories, which tries to mediate between their categorical dismissal as myth and the insistence that they are 'historical' by treating them as 'historical legends' (p. 19). They are, he says, 'stories of people's liberation from exploitation and oppression' (p. 161).

The Roman Catholic scholar Raymond E. Brown (1971) has written a 594-page discussion of the nativity stories in which he describes them as primarily vehicles for the evangelist's theology, and 'seeks to discover their value *as theology*' (p. 37; italics added). They are, he says, 'worthy vehicles of the Gospel message . . . namely, that God has made himself present to us in the life of His Messiah who walked on this earth' (p. 8). He does not dismiss them out of hand as fabrication: 'This does not mean that the infancy narratives have no historical value' (p. 7). While the majority of scholars reviewed in this chapter doubt that Jesus was born in Bethlehem, in contrast no Muslim (to my knowledge) doubts that Muhammad was born in Makkah (although some non-Muslims have questioned this). Brown's (1994) volume examines *The Death of the Messiah*.

Many outsiders, however, do reject as myth some of the stories surrounding Muhammad's birth; indeed, they suggest that these were fabricated in imitation of the gospel nativity narrative (see Bennett, 1998, p. 52). Meanwhile, scientists continue to take the 'star of Bethlehem' seriously (the star that guided the three visitors to Jesus in Matthew 2). Two recent books, both published by university presses, suggest that the visitors may indeed have observed some astronomical phenomenon in the night sky *circa* 5 or 6 BCE (see Kidger, 1999; Molnar, 1999). In Egypt, locations identified with Jesus' time there continue to be venerated by Muslims as well as by Christians. I visited some of these sites during a trip to Egypt.

## Jesus and the marginalized of the world

I am conscious that the scholars reviewed in this chapter have been white and male. This reflects the dominance of white, European, male theologians in faculties past and present. Black writers, though, have also written on Jesus. They point out how illustrations in Bibles and Sunday School texts inevitably depict Jesus as a blue-eyed, blond-haired European and that this symbol of a white Jesus is both a symptom and cause of racism. James H. Cone's work on Christ as black (1986) deserves more than a footnote here. With reference especially to Cone in my concluding chapter, I shall ask whether such a view of Jesus can be anything other than what Allen calls 'Avant-Garde Fashion' (1998, Chapter 10), or Schweitzer's creation of a Jesus in our own image. I shall argue that any depiction of Jesus that has some rooting in what can be historically and also theologically affirmed of him is authentic.

In my Conclusion, I incorporate reflections on some feminist Jesus images. Their case is often built on the back of the Nag Hammadi material, which Pagels (1979) says represents 'a powerful alternative to what we know as orthodox Christian tradition' (p. 181). In some of these gospels, Mary Magdalene 'appears to be in charge of the disciples . . . which Peter acknowledges when he . . . urges her to tell them of the Savior's words which she alone, and separately, has been privileged to hear and understand' (Haskins, 1994, p. 38). Haskins argues that it was the increasingly male-dominated and hierarchical Church that excluded Mary's real role 'from the orthodox accounts of [Jesus'] ministry . . . the result of a political decision' (p. 55).

Another reason for the lack of female voices in this chapter was its focus on critical scholarship of the sources. Carried out by professional theologians, this enterprise has been a predominantly male concern. Had I focused on what I call the inner, or spiritual experience of Jesus, many more women would not only have featured, but featured prominently.

Women were allowed to enter religious orders, to engage in contemplative life and in lives of service. A contemplative woman such as Teresa of Ávila (1515–82) saw visions of Jesus the divine bridegroom, and entered the state of 'spiritual marriage'. Through her writing, she shared with others how to discipline the life of the soul. More recently, Mother Teresa of Calcutta found Jesus among the sick and dying, in the face of the poorest of the world's poor. This Jesus of the mystic vision, of inner experience, is often, it seems, a Jesus who inspires love in action. This is the Jesus who sent Schweitzer to Africa, Rauschenbusch to work among the immigrants of New York, Martin Luther King to a police cell in Birmingham, Alabama. This is the Jesus whose voice Francis heard, saying 'leave all' (Matthew 10:7–19) as he repaired the ruined church of St Damiano, who compelled him to form his community of teaching, preaching and serving friars.

## Résumé

Miracles, Jesus' self-consciousness as Messiah and as vicarious redeemer, his resurrection and his relationship with God, were all placed on the agenda of the first, or old, quest of the historical Jesus at the start of this chapter. They continued to feature throughout my survey. Reimarus also put eschatology, and the relationship between Jesus and Judaism, centre stage, and these also featured right through to my discussion of the Jesus Seminar. Of the scholars reviewed, only a few (Hunter, Johnson, Marshall, Wright) accepted the traditional view of Jesus as pre-existent Son of God. The most important issue around which the quest has swirled, and still swirls, in my view, is eschatology. Those who judge that Jesus expected the end, which did not come, have to find some device to explain any relationship that may exist between Jesus and Christian faith.

Did Christians spiritualize Jesus' enterprise in order to rescue something from his life, as Reimarus surmised? Sanders, I think, says something similar, since he does not believe that Jesus taught a here-and-now kingdom, or called anyone to engage in social or economic reform. Jewish scholars, discussed in Chapter 5, complain that Jesus turned his back on 'the kingdom that matters . . . the one we find ourselves in now' (Neusner, 2000, p. 57). This leaves us with a Christianity that, to borrow a term from Crossan, is *sarkophobic*, 'that sensibility that somehow or other wants the real you to be spirit, the real you to be soul, and the other stuff that you temporarily reside in can be . . . expendable, dumpable' (1999, p. 41). Did Jesus even intend to found a permanent movement, or is the Church an accident? Or, did Jesus intend to stimulate an ongoing community of men and women who, yes, develop the inner life of repentance and renewal, who, yes, recognize that the physical is not humankind's ultimate destiny, but who also liberate the oppressed, feed the hungry, visit the sick and care for the dying?

In my view, the biggest divide between Christians today is less about how much of the Bible they accept as reliable, or even how they understand Jesus, than about whether they see the Christian task as almost purely spiritual, or as also religio-political. Reimarus may be thanked for putting politics on the agenda. Is the Christian task only to save souls, individually, one by one, or is it also to transform the world? Can wealth be legitimated in a Christian manner? Rauschenbusch thought it very hard for a rich man to gain access to the kingdom, and claimed to be following Jesus. He also questioned whether Jesus had approved of the private ownership of property (see Rauschenbusch, 1916, pp. 125–30, on property and wealth). Yet other Christians believe that health and wealth are God's blessing, and that poverty is caused by sin. In this understanding, the way to combat poverty is through saving souls. Personally, I am more sympathetic here towards Rauschenbusch, Crossan, Borg and Sobrino than I am towards Sanders.

Others think that the way to fight poverty is by campaigning for a reform of economic systems, and claim that this is what Jesus did and wants them to do. How Christians see Jesus not only determines their understanding of Christian discipleship, it also influences the types of hymns they write and sing. For some, these praise Jesus endlessly as saviour. For others, they encourage followers to work for the poor and oppressed. If your Jesus is egalitarian and anti-hierarchy, it will influence how you organize your Church's life. If your Jesus was a political activist, an advocate of economic and social reform, it will impact on your own political involvement.

I also set out to see how a priori assumptions influenced images of Jesus. What did the scholars from each phase of the quest bring to their task? Old questors brought their philosophical assumptions and tended to see Jesus as a great genius, a moral or spiritual archetype. The no questors brought historical scepticism but also an existentialist vision that allowed them to see Jesus as of unique relevance for every given moment. The new questors brought social, economic and political theory. Some surmise that Crossan's revolutionary Jesus may reflect his childhood experience of growing up in colonial Ireland (see Crossan, 1996, p. 172). If it is our inclinations, or the trends of the times, that produce our images of Jesus then he may very well emerge as a sexual libertarian on the one hand, or as a dreamy, celibate mystic on the other. Inasmuch as the late twentieth century had an anti-authoritarian, anti-establishment, social bias, an anti-hierarchy, egalitarian, pro-feminist Jesus reflects the ethos of the epoch. Many of the recent images also try to liberate Jesus from the Church; while Church membership declines, there is no sign of diminished fascination for Jesus, so perhaps this too matches the colour of the age.

Many of the scholars reviewed accepted little more of the Gospels as authentic than did Reimarus. However, as Christians, quite a few wanted to validate Jesus' spiritual claims, and found ways to do so. Some ended up closer to the traditional Christian view, others further from it. Behind that image, though, lie other possibilities, and silenced alternatives, that may still have value as Christians revisit their understanding of who Jesus was and is. I follow Frances Young's view that early Christological formulations were attempts to 'find the right words', to express profound mysteries, not to prescribe exhaustive or definitive propositions. This, I suggest, gives us licence to continue to test ways of expressing what we believe about Jesus in language that may be more suited to today's culture than that of hypostases, substance or even sonship. We need, says Young, 'not new creeds but a new openness' to elucidate our response to Jesus as Christ (1977, p. 38). Young chaired the Theology Department at Birmingham University when I was a student there.

I believe that the language used of Jesus can be revisited and new and meaningful symbols offered to affirm who Jesus is for the world and for lives today. With reference to how much of the text of the Gospels we judge authentic, whether 18 per cent or 100 per cent, we may choose the former if we think that the early Church projected its theology into the gospel texts, the latter if we think that the disciples, who lived in a culture that was used to oral transmission, revered the memory of Jesus and largely, with some editorial gloss, did justice to that memory. Or, we may choose an approach which recognizes that some passages may not be wholly historically accurate, or even historical at all, yet value them for the message they contain. This approach emerges again in Chapter 6, in my discussion of Hindu views of Jesus.

My next chapter follows Jesus beyond the Christian tradition and examines his encounter with outsiders. I begin with the initial encounter with paganism in the ancient world, then move forward to images of Jesus found in the writing of humanists, secular thinkers and others who offer alternative accounts of who Jesus was. Intriguingly, while these writers consciously distance themselves from a Christian understanding, nor have any wish to be associated with Christianity, similarities exist between their images of Jesus and some insider images discussed in this chapter.

# 4 Outsiders on Jesus

> What can this Gospel of Jesus be?
> What Life & Immortality,
> What was it that he brought to Light
> That Plato & Cicero did not write?
> The Heathen Deities wrote them all,
> These Moral Virtues, great and small.
> (William Blake, 'The Everlasting
> Gospel', in Keynes, 1966, p. 758)

## Introduction

This chapter begins with encounter between Christians and the pagan world. After tracing the complex story of engagement between the Roman world and the Jesus story, I follow Jesus into his European domestication, then to Africa and elsewhere. Next I discuss more recent writers who offer outsider images of Jesus. Some aspects of their approach to Jesus resembles early pagan assessment, considered in the first section of this chapter. A writer's distancing of himself or herself from, or explicit rejection of, conventional Christian beliefs about Jesus, defines outsidership in this chapter. However, these writers very often view their own Jesus image as a legitimate and authentic representation of Jesus, which means they may disclaim the outsider label.

My third section turns to the Jesus-was-a-myth school, which, championed by rationalist and free-thinking writers, began in the nineteenth century. This school draws on early pagan response to Jesus as well as on the work of anthropologist James George Frazer. It finds much of interest, too, in the writings of Sigmund Freud, C. G. Jung and Joseph Campbell. My fourth outsider genre argues that the Church has consistently suppressed the real Jesus story. While not unrelated to the Jesus-was-a-myth literature, this school does accept that there was a man called Jesus but not that he looked anything like the Jesus of Christian faith. The Essenes feature prominently in this material. Finally, before describing how the Branch Davidians, the Church of Jesus Christ of Latter Day Saints and the Unification Church construct their images of Jesus, I discuss D. H.

Lawrence's *The Man Who Died* (1928). Like Muslims on Jesus (see Chapter 5) and many of the writers reviewed in this chapter, the Mormons and the Unificationists both use alternative sources.

## Jesus and non-Jews

In surveying Christian scholarship of Jesus' life, I identified Jesus' relationship with Judaism as problematic. This raises the question whether Jews responding to Jesus were insiders or outsiders. If outsiders, they were the first to formulate a view of Jesus that differed from an insider, Christian view. However, as there is clearly a special relationship between Judaism and Christianity, I do not discuss Jewish views of Jesus in this chapter on outsider images but in my next chapter. In that chapter, I also discuss Muslim views of Jesus, since Islam sees itself, *vis-à-vis* Christianity, as its fulfilment, in the same way that Christianity sees itself *vis-à-vis* Judaism. There is an acknowledged family relationship between these three Abrahamic faiths: Jews, Christians and Muslims all hold Abraham in special esteem.

Jesus had a few encounters with Samaritans and with Romans. These encounters suggest he believed that God's love extended beyond the Jewish people, and that Gentiles would be welcomed into God's kingdom. At Luke 7:9 Jesus spoke of encountering faith in a Roman centurion such as he had never experienced among Jews. As the infant Church expanded, an early dispute was whether or not Gentile converts must be circumcised, and keep the ritual purity laws. At issue was whether Christians were members of a movement within the Jewish tradition, or of a new religion. The majority decided that faith, not obedience to the Torah, saves, and that 'real circumcision is a matter of the heart, spiritual and not literal' (Romans 2:29). I revisit this debate in Chapter 5. The decision to include Gentiles without circumcision encouraged many god-fearers to convert to Christianity. Attracted by Judaism but not by the idea of circumcision, they had stayed on the fringe of the synagogue.

## Paul as Christianity's founder

The Book of Acts tells the story of how Paul, the free-born Roman citizen originally from Tarsus, emerged as the champion of Gentile Christianity. Trained as a Pharisee in Jerusalem, Paul initially persecuted Christians until he had a vision of (or an encounter with) the resurrected Jesus (Acts 9). This transformed him into a fearless exponent of the Gospel. As noted in my last chapter, some scholars depict Paul as leader of the Gentile Church, and suggest that pagan ideas influenced Paul's theology, leading to a transformation of Jesus' original teaching. Paul is depicted as at odds with Peter and the Jewish Church. In Acts, there is evidence of tension between Peter and Paul, but Acts also describes Peter agreeing with the baptism (reception into membership of the Church) of Gentiles without circumcision (see Acts, Chapter 11). He defends this decision again in Acts 15, when the issue of circumcision and Torah obedience was again raised. Tradition also places Peter's and Paul's executions in Rome at about the same time, shortly after the Great Fire of 64 CE, for which Nero blamed Christians (see Clement of Rome, cited by Stevenson, 1963, p. 4). It is actually rather difficult to know for sure what sort of relationship existed between Peter and Paul. Paul appears to have acknowledged the leadership of the senior apostle. His own leadership role may have been more theological; only John can be said to approach Paul's theological capabilities.

If Pauline theology were subtracted from the New Testament, the gap between what it has to say on Jesus and what the creeds say would be considerably greater. Jesus' pre-existence, sonship, role as creator, as the glue that holds the very cosmos together, as the saviour who conquered death, are all strong motifs in Paul. As nineteenth-century scholars reviewed in my last chapter pointed out, Paul's Jesus is a heavenly lord who in some respects bears little resemblance to the humble man who walked about Galilee, telling parables about the Kingdom of God. The Kingdom of God is not a major concern for Paul. Nor does he relate any of Jesus' parables, indeed he rarely cites Jesus directly. Nor does he refer to any of the details of Jesus' birth or death, about which the Gospels have a great deal to say. Unlike Matthew, too, Paul does not always refer to specific Hebrew Bible texts to support his views, even when he speaks of Jesus Christ as having fulfilled scripture, as Paula Fredriksen (1994) points out:

[Christ] 'died for our sins in accordance with the scriptures' (I Cor 15:3), but Paul does not reveal which scriptures support his claim. He would have had difficulty finding anything about a crucified messiah in the Hebrew scriptures. (p. 79)

Some of the accounts of Jesus described in Chapter 3 all but suggested that Paul was the founder of Christianity and that the real Jesus has been obscured by his theological speculation.

Bultmann and the Jesus Seminar, among others, thought that Paul had borrowed many of his ideas from paganism. This accusation, which I discuss below, was actually one of the earliest pagan criticisms of Christianity, although Paul was not specifically singled out for blame. Scholars suggest that while Jewish Christians saw Jesus as a man, born in the usual manner, whom God adopted as Messiah, Paul transformed him into an eternal, virgin-born, pre-existing cosmic lord. The latter emerged as orthodox doctrine. Adoptionism was condemned as heresy. Yet Jewish Christians under James in Jerusalem continued to keep the Torah, and probably worshipped in the Temple. James is said to have regarded his brother as having intended to reform Judaism, not as the founder of a new religion (see Perkins, 1999). Even after their demise, a Christian group known as the Ebionites remained Jewish. They used only Matthew's Gospel and repudiated 'the Apostle Paul' as 'an apostate from the law'. They kept 'those customs, which are enjoined by the Law' and even adored 'Jerusalem as if it were the house of God' (Irenaeus, cited in Stevenson, 1963, p. 97). This is actually the earliest reference to the Ebionites, whose name means 'poor'.

Ignatius (d. 115 CE) railed against those who called themselves Christians while living in Judaism (*ibid.*, p. 46). Stevenson (1963) notes that 'conversion from Christianity to Judaism was not unknown through the whole period of early history' (p. 69). Cerinthus, to whom some credited John's Gospel, had also advocated an adoptionist Christology. He believed that Jesus was:

Not ... born of a virgin, but as ... the son of Joseph and Mary [was born] according to the ordinary course of human generation, while he nevertheless was more righteous, prudent and wise than other men ... after his baptism, Christ descended upon him in the form of a dove from the Supreme Ruler, ... he then proclaimed the Unknown Father. (Irenaeus, cited in Stevenson, 1963, p. 96)

## Paul and the pagan world

Many aspects of Paul's message would not have sounded altogether unfamiliar to Gentile ears, while it would have sounded strange to Jews. His concern, for example, for 'eternal life after death' contrasts sharply with the Hebrew Bible's lack of any developed notion of an afterlife. Similarly, while the object of Jesus' life, according to Paul, was to save humanity *spiritually*, the Hebrew Bible focuses on *life in this world*. Its God intervenes in human history to bless and reward and sometimes punish God's people in the here-and-now. Even the Kingdom of God would be a transformation or restoration of this present world. Indeed, as Renan (1927) says, 'salvation' in the Pauline sense is hardly to be found in Jewish thought. Hebrew thought did not distinguish between 'body' and 'soul ... the ... doctrine which divides man in two parts – body and soul ... was not in the traditions of the Jewish mind' (p. 104).

The idea of someone suffering on behalf of others had some currency among Jews. Klausner (1944) cites Eleazar from 4 Maccabees 6:26–9: 'Make my blood a purification for them and take my life as a ransom for their life' (p. 139). However, the possibility that God might take on human form, and walk on earth, was quite alien. Judaism's uncompromising monotheism, summed up in the 'Hear, O Israel, the Lord your God is One', placed the Trinity beyond comprehension for most Jews. The Jews of Elephanta and the later Kabbalah mystics, however, have spoken of plurality within the Godhead. Unterman (1981) describes the 'unity-in-complexity of the ten *sefirot*, the matrices which have emanated from the Godhead', as 'faces of the divine king, the garments of God, divine names'. Kabbalah, too, is more generous and less sexist with its manifestation of God than Christians; the *sefirot* include 'Father, Mother, Son, Daughter, Husband, Wife' (*ibid.*, p. 101). Philo also incorporated the feminine into his system: Sophia is 'firstborn daughter of G*d', 'the oldest', 'the first fruit' (Fiorenza, 1994, p. 138). This makes the concept of the Trinity less alien to at least some Jews.

For its part, Paul's Gentile audience was used to hearing about dying and rising gods who granted their devotees lives of bliss after death. Bacchus went through an annual death and resurrection cycle. Mithras from Iran, whose birth in a cave was witnessed by a shepherd, like Jesus, was born of a virgin mother. Mithras, like Jesus, died and rose again to save his devotees. His followers drank wine and ate bread during ritual meals in order to claim salvation mediated by Mithras' blood. Mithras was often pictured carrying a lamb on his shoulder. All social and class distinctions were forgotten within the fellowship of believers. The senior priests of his cult, known as 'Fathers', wore ceremonial dress including a *mithra* (mitre) to mark rank, and a ring. Patronized by several emperors, their chief priest in Rome was called *Pater Patrum*. At the sacrament, the priest said, 'Be of good cheer, sacred band . . . your God has risen from the dead. His pains and suffering shall be your salvation.'

Critics think that the notion of Jesus' virgin birth has more to do with the many pagan precedents than with any Jewish belief that the Messiah would be born of a virgin. The word, at Isaiah 7:14, repeated by Matthew at 1:23, often rendered 'virgin' ('and a virgin will conceive'), probably means 'young woman' and has no implication of lack of sexual experience. Horus, son of Osiris, another dying and rising god, also had a virgin mother. Christian depictions of the Virgin Mary and the baby Jesus are said to have been based on ancient Egyptian images of Isis suckling Horus, such as two miniature bronzes found at Saqqar (dated 600 BCE) now on display in the Birmingham Museum and Art Gallery in Britain. Osiris, Isis and Horus are often called the Egyptian Trinity. Many Muslims think that the Christian Trinity comprises Father, Mother and Son.

Frazer tells us that in 'the resurrection of Osiris, the Egyptians saw the pledge of a life everlasting for themselves' (1994, p. 372). Attis, whose conception was also virginal, died from a wound in his side and rose again after three days. His followers celebrated his resurrection, known as the Hilaria or the Festival of Joy, at the spring equinox, which involved 'a sacramental meal and a baptism of blood' (*ibid.*, p. 351). At the Temple at Luxor, Thebes, there is a sequence of scenes depicting the annunciation of Kneph's birth to the god That and his virgin queen. There is even one segment that has three men bearing gifts. The three wise men, or Magi, of Christian tradition is actually a deduction based on the number of gifts listed in Matthew, who does not record how many visitors there were.

Later, many legends developed around the Magi, including their names, Gaspar, Melchior and Balthasar (for a fictional portrait, see Lewis Wallace's *Ben Hur* (1998)). The Christian teaching, too, that between Good Friday and Easter Sunday Jesus had 'descended into hell' would have sounded much more familiar to Gentile than to Jewish ears. Herakles,

Mithras and Aeneas, among others, had made descents into hell. Also familiar to pagan ears would be the notion of a divine son, or king, even an 'only begotten son', being sacrificed. Tammuz (Attis) means 'the son of life' and 'was interpreted by the Semites to mean "the offspring" or "the only son"' (Robertson, 1911, p. 262). Israel's God did not physically walk on earth; the Greek and Egyptian gods and their sons, including Rome's emperors, did.

## Pagan criticism of Christianity

Critics pointed to these similarities between Christian teaching and pagan religion, especially its mystery cults, at a very early stage. We know this from the responses of second- and third-century Christian apologists, who often cite their opponents' views. Of course, criticism of Christian belief and practice does not necessarily represent any particular view of Jesus, who is not always mentioned in this material. However, even when there is no direct reference to Jesus there is a strong implication that the Jesus about whom Christians speak owes more to myth than to history and that this Jesus myth is in all probability a deliberate fraud.

Three criticisms of Christians emerge in this period: first, that they are antisocial, 'haters of the human race'; second, that they undermine the empire's laws, reject its traditions and are seditious; third, that they engage in immoral sexual and possibly even cannibalistic acts. In addition, Christians were charged with having concocted their religion from pre-existing elements. Christianity was also criticized for lacking intellectual rigour and for only attracting people from the lower social orders. Celsus (see below) wrote: 'Their favorite expressions are, "Do not ask questions, just believe" and "Your faith will save you!"' '"The wisdom of this world," they say, "is evil; to be simple is good"' (Hoffmann, 1987, p. 54). Celsus is famous for his description of the preferred audience of Christian teachers:

Wherever one finds a crowd of adolescent boys, or a bunch of slaves, there will the Christian teachers be also . . . let them get hold of children . . . let them find some gullible wives – and you will hear some preposterous statements. You will hear them say . . . that they should not pay attention to their fathers or teachers, but must obey them. They say that their elders and teachers are fools. (*ibid.*, p. 73)

Minucius Felix (*fl.* 200) similarly called Christians 'a gang of discredited and proscribed desperadoes . . . gathered together from the lowest dregs of the population, ignorant men and credulous women . . . a rabble of impious conspirators'. He continued, 'at their nocturnal gatherings and . . . barbarous meals the bond of union is not any sacred rite but crime' (Stevenson, 1963, pp. 190–1).

Lucian (115–200) made fun of a Christian called Peregrinus, who could easily use his cleverness to gain quick promotion within the Church: 'in no time at all he had . . . become their prophet, teacher, head of synagogue and what not all by himself' (cited in Hoffmann, 1987, p. 25). This added fuel to the criticism that Christianity was antisocial, causing the lower classes to rebel against the authority of their betters. From the Christian point of view, Christianity fed these classes with ideas of equality and human dignity. The charge of 'sedition' was based on Christians' refusal to acknowledge the imperial cult and in many instances to serve in the military. Tertullian (160–220) forbade 'his fellow Christians to serve in the army, or in the civil service, or even in schools' (Chadwick, 1967, p. 91). Origen (185–254) defended Christians as loyal to the empire, since even though they did not bear arms they composed for the emperor 'a special army of piety through . . . intercessions to God' (cited in Stevenson, 1963, p. 226).

The antisocial charge was obviously an early criticism. Tacitus' description of Christian persecution after the Great Fire in Rome accused them of hating the human race (cited in Chapter 1). Earlier, this charge had been laid at the door of the synagogue: 'Hecataeus of Abdera, writing before the end of the fourth century BC . . . attacked [the Jews'] . . . abnormal way of life, which he called "an inhospitable and anti-human form of living"' (Johnson, 1987, p. 134). He was referring to the Jews' refusal to join the multiracial, multinational civilization championed by Alexander. On the other hand, many people in the Graeco-Roman world found Judaism's strict moral ethic attractive, and happily worshipped in the synagogue. As long as they did not convert, they did not have to relinquish their traditional religions. Fredriksen (1994) states:

Pagans could judaize without making an exclusive commitment to the religion of Israel. Luke, for example, both in his Gospel and in the book of Acts, mentions such Gentiles who on the one hand assume aspects of Jewish piety but, nonetheless, remain public pagans, worshipping traditional gods. Thus the centurion at Capernaum who 'loves our nation and built us our synagogue' (Luke 7:1–10) . . . would have been understood by Luke's ancient audience to be a practicing pagan, responsible for performing the cult that would have attended his military unit. (p. 82)

Perhaps for this reason, as well as because Judaism represented an age-old national tradition, Rome tolerated its existence. Several emperors issued decrees, which Josephus cited. For example:

Tiberius Claudius Caesar Augustus Germanicus, high priest, tribune of the people, chosen consul the second time, ordains thus: Upon the petition of king Agrippa and king Herod, who are persons very dear to me, that I would grant the same rights and privileges should be preserved to the Jews which are in all the Roman empire, which I have granted to those of Alexandria . . . I think it also very just that no Grecian city should be deprived of such rights and privileges, since they were preserved to them under the great Augustus. It will therefore be fit to permit the Jews, who are in all the world under us, to keep their ancient customs without being hindered so to do. (*Ant.* 19:5:3)

## Christian exclusivism versus Roman inclusivism

What made Christianity problematic was its insistence that worship of Christ demanded the abandonment of all other gods and religious practices, including the repudiation of the emperors' claims to divinity. Obviously, this brought Christians into direct conflict with the Roman state. Had Christians offered Jesus as a saviour alongside other possibilities, as one of the many options available in the supermarket of faiths, Rome would have had no difficulty tolerating Christians just as it tolerated other secret societies and mystery cults. What attracted the fiercest criticism was Christianity's rejection of the 'old ways'. An early Christian view was that paganism was the Devil's work, an attempt to mislead people into error, to prevent the spread of the true faith. This emerges in the work of Justin Martyr, perhaps one of the most distinguished of the Church's early apologists. Martyred with six of his own students at Rome in 165 CE, Justin continued to wear his philosopher's robes after converting to the Christian faith. From a highly educated and privileged background, he was well placed to respond to pagan criticism.

Aware that critics saw Christian belief in Jesus as a virgin-born, dying and rising saviour and of the parallels with paganism outlined above, Justin argued that these were the work of demons. Familiar with prophecies about Jesus, they set out to confuse people through mockery and imitation. Hearing that Jesus would be God's son, they 'put forward many to be sons of Jupiter'. Hearing that Jesus would ascend into heaven, they 'gave out that Bellerophon, a man born of man, himself ascended to heaven'. Hearing that Jesus would 'heal every sickness, and raise the dead, they produced Aesculapius' (1885, p. LIV). Commenting on the similarity between the Christian rite of communion and the Mithraic ritual, Justin wrote that 'wicked devils have imitated' communion 'in the mysteries of Mithras' (*ibid.*, p. LXV). If worshipping false gods makes you a theist, said Justin, then Christians were guilty as charged: 'we confess that we are atheists, so far as gods of this sort are concerned' (p. V). Emperor Domitian had executed several Christians on the charge of atheism (112 CE). Justin also ascribed such Christian heresies as Marcion's to the devil (p. LVIII).

Far from being guilty of the gross immorality of which they were accused, Christians valued chastity above all else, helped the poor and placed spiritual health above worldly gain. Here, Justin cites Jesus' words on not storing up treasures on earth, on praying for enemies and on 'communicating to the needy' (p. XIV). Justin also rejects the charge that Jesus had been a magician: 'What should prevent that he whom we call Christ, being a man born of a man, performed what we call His mighty works by magical art, and by this appeared to be the Son of God?' (p. XXIX). *The Last Temptation of Christ* draws on this ancient charge of magic when it has Pilate accuse Jesus of being a magician. Pilate asks him, 'Can you do a trick for me?' and Jesus replies, 'I am not a magician.' As late as 303–313 CE, in his *Divine Institutions*, Lacantius (240–330 CE) says that the Jews had mistaken Jesus for a magician, who had actually performed his miracles 'not by magical tricks . . . but by heavenly strength and power' (Book 4, Chapter 15). Others, said Lacantius, compared Jesus unfavourably with Apollonius, who they said had been the better magician. Jesus allowed himself to be 'arrested and crucified'; Apollonius 'suddenly disappeared on his trial' (Book 5, Chapter 3). Christians appear to have been embarrassed by similarities between Apollonius and Jesus (see Wheless, 1997b, and my discussion of Morton Smith later in this chapter).

## Sexual licence

Justin more than implies that everything of which the critics charge the Christians, from atheism to sexual promiscuity, actually is but a reflection of their own immoral lives. Given the popularity of the cult of Bacchus, and what we know of court life under such emperors as Tiberius and Caligula, this was not far from the mark. Sexual licence does appear to have been problematic for early Christians. Paul wrote to the Corinthian Church that he had heard reports of 'sexual immorality among you of a kind that does not occur even among pagans' (1 Corinthians 5:1). The passage at Romans 13:13 which produced Augustine's conversion – 'Let us behave decently, as in the daytime, not in orgies and drunkenness' – may also imply sexual misconduct.

Jude complains about 'godless men' who 'change the grace of God into a licence for immorality' and who indulge in 'sexual immorality and perversion' possibly during Christian agape (love) feasts (Jude, verse 7). Fronto (90–168) wrote, 'in the shameless dark, and with unspeakable lust they copulate in random unions' (Hoffmann, 1987, p. 17). Perhaps, as their critics said, they did take the 'love one another' dictum quite literally. There is evidence that some Gnostic Christians were promiscuous: 'and became notorious for their orgies of immorality' (Chadwick, 1967, p. 36). Below, I discuss the contribution of a scholar who believed that Jesus had himself engaged in such activities. For their part, convinced that Jesus was sexually beyond reproach, Christians would later charge Muhammad with sexual indulgence that, they said, disqualified him from comparison with Jesus.

## Celsus (*c.* 180 CE)

Critics did not always say, 'Christians are like this because their Master, who they follow, was', yet it would be difficult to conclude that they held Christianity's central figure in very high regard. The accusation that Jesus had been an ordinary man who used magic to trick people into believing that he was God's son placed deception at the centre of Christianity. Critics implied that Jesus' followers continued this deception by borrowing ideas, and even stories, from the pagan world. What infuriated Celsus was that Christians had the audacity to claim originality for their doctrines, when all they did was replicate others': 'Many of the nations of the world hold similar doctrines to those espoused by the Christians' (Hoffmann, 1987, p. 55). Pointing to numerous parallels of rising gods, Celsus asks, 'Are you ignorant of the multitudes who have invented similar tales to lead simple-minded hearers astray?' (p. 67). Celsus also emphasized indebtedness to Mithraism (p. 95). Talk of forgiveness of sins and of becoming pure abounded among the 'mystery religions', so what was new in Christian teaching? (p. 74).

Celsus thought that almost the entire Jesus story was myth. Celsus' Jesus was conceived by Mary out of wedlock after an encounter with Panthera, a Roman soldier, and was born to an obscure, not royal, family (the genealogies were fabricated; p. 64). 'Clearly,' he wrote, 'the Christians have used the myths of the Danae and the Malanippe . . . in fabricating the story of Jesus' virgin birth' (p. 57). Jesus had learned magic while living in Egypt (p. 57). The flight to Egypt was one of the few parts of the nativity story that Celsus accepted; he rejected the slaying of the infants (p. 58). The charge that Jesus had been a magician, which is also found in Jewish sources, was obviously widespread. As noted above, Justin had responded to this accusation. Jesus, said Celsus and other critics, used magic to deceive and corrupt uneducated Jews, causing them to abandon the traditions of their forebears. This also infuriated Celsus; he was no admirer of the Jews but at least their religion was ancient.

In his *On the True Doctrine*, Celsus depicts a Jew who refutes Christianity as deception and fraud. Actually, Celsus thought that much of the Hebrew Bible had also been concocted to justify the Jews' own revolt against 'their Egyptian cousins' (p. 70). Moses was a brigand who was made to look like a hero. The world was not 'made for man', rather all things were 'proportioned . . . for the good of the universe as a whole' (p. 85). Indeed, elephants may be more faithful to God than people, and Jews and Christians are wrong to elevate the human above the animal and natural worlds (p. 84). The resurrection was based solely on the testimony of a hysterical woman (p. 67). If Jesus had really wanted to convince people that he had conquered death he ought to have appeared to 'the Jews who treated him so badly' (p. 86). Celsus ridicules almost every aspect of Christian belief about Jesus. If he was God, why did he need food? If he was God, why did he die on a cross? Why did one of his own disciples betray him? The Christian God was a shoddy workman; while the real God has no need of 'a new creation', the Christian's God has to rebuild the world 'as if he is an unskilled laborer who is incapable of building something properly first time around' (p. 82). Why does an all-powerful God need to sentence a man to death before he can save people from their sins? (p. 76).

## 'We Romans honor the many'

Celsus finds Christian belief in Jesus as the logos irreconcilable with what the philosophers meant by the logos, which, compared with a Jesus who got 'himself arrested and executed in the most humiliating of circumstances', is 'pure and holy' (p. 64). Compared with those gods who were acknowledged by the proper authorities (by the Roman senate) Jesus falls far short; yet 'Christians brook no comparison between Jesus and the established gods' (p. 72). Christians 'refuse to listen to any talk about God, the father of all, unless it includes some reference to Jesus' (p. 116), while we Romans, says Celsus, 'honor the many' (p. 56). Indeed, asks Celsus, what does it matter what people call God? In Chapter 6, a similar critique emerges in Hindu response to Jesus.

Nor did Celsus think that the Hebrew Bible passages that Christians apply to Jesus could possibly have anticipated 'such a low grade character like this Jesus' (p. 64). Like Reimarus, Celsus called the Gospels works of fiction: 'the writings of the Christians are a lie, and [their] fables have not been well enough constructed to conceal this monstrous fiction' (*ibid.*). Like Reimarus, Celsus thought that this fraud was largely the work of Christians after Jesus, although in fabricating myths and deceiving people they were merely continuing what Jesus had taught them. 'Jesus collected around him ten or eleven unsavory characters . . . and these scurried about making a living . . . through double dealing and other questionable ways', he wrote (p. 59). Note how Celsus does not refer to twelve disciples.

Already, a similarity between Celsus and some of the nineteenth-century insider views described in my last chapter is clear. Like them, he thought it preposterous to think that Jesus had any foreknowledge of what was to happen to him, which was 'an obvious attempt to conceal the humiliating facts' (p. 62). Unlike later critics, Celsus never implied that Jesus had not existed but he does anticipate many of the arguments of the Jesus-was-a-myth school, to which I turn below. Christians, Celsus concluded, are guilty of elevating a mere man, who was not even a good man, to the heights (p. 116). Celsus' text did not survive in its original, intact form but comes to us as part of Origen's response (English translation by Henry Chadwick, 1953). My friend and former colleague, Joseph Hoffmann, reconstructed Celsus minus Origen in his 1987 text, from which I have quoted above.

## The Christianization of paganism or the paganization of Christianity

Christians did find themselves in serious conflict with the pagan world. Their belief in human equality challenged the privileges of the rich and powerful. Their rejection of the emperor's claim to divinity challenged his authority. Their rejection of worldly wealth, and their affirmation of the value of a simple lifestyle, challenged accepted wisdom. Their refusal to serve in the military seemed nothing short of treason. 'The New Testament', says Hoffmann (1989), taught that 'wealth and power are hindrances to salvation . . . ceasing to care about material property contributes to caring about "inexhaustible treasure" – that which cannot be material because it cannot be stolen' (p. 183).

Thus persecution ensued, the earliest under Nero (64 CE). Pliny (112 CE) tells us of Christians tried for treason in Bithynia, although he did not seek them out unless they caused trouble (see Stevenson, 1963, p. 16). Marcus Aurelius instigated persecution of Christians at Lyons (177 CE). By Tertullian's day, Christians could be conveniently blamed for any catastrophe: 'If the Tiber reaches the walls, if the Nile does not rise to the fields, if the sky doesn't move or the earth does . . . the cry is at once, "The Christians to the lion". What, all of them to one lion?' he famously concluded (*ibid.*, p. 169). Tertullian's own plea for toleration was successful, though: Emperor Severus, while forbidding conversion, ceased to execute Christians.

The zenith of anti-Christian activities was probably during the reign of Decius (250 CE), who ordered that all citizens must sacrifice to the state gods and obtain a certificate to confirm this. In 257 CE, Valerian ordered the execution of all Christian clergy who refused to apostatize. Church property was confiscated. Gallienus (270 CE), though, cancelled these orders. In 303 CE, Diocletian began to re-confiscate Church property, to burn Bibles and instituted mass executions of Christians. Then Constantine (d. 337 CE) had his vision on the eve of the Battle of Milvian Bridge against a rival for the imperial throne, in which he was told to 'put the "Chi-Rho" monogram on his shields and standards as a talisman of victory' (Chadwick, 1967, p. 126). The meaning of the 'Chi-Rho', the first two letters of the Greek word CHRIST, says Chadwick, 'was universally understood to be Christian'. Winning the battle, Constantine ascribed his victory to Jesus and converted.

## Constantine's contribution

Constantine may well have confused the Christian God with his own preferred deity, the sun, and his grasp of Christian doctrine may never have been especially clear, yet his conversion changed the course of history. He legalized the Church, gave it rich endowments of land and revenue, and convened councils to decide on a creed for all good Christians. He moved a long way towards totally replacing the old Roman cultus with the new Christian one. Certainly, in reversing the old order of a Church–state divide, he instead wedded the Church to the state as an instrument of imperial solidarity and identity. He built his new, eastern capital, Constantinople, as a Christian city, although he also placed an image of the sun god in its main forum, which bore his own features (Chadwick, 1967, p. 127). Indeed, as persecution gave way to tolerance and tolerance to official religion of the Roman state, the Church, its priests and bishops took on the ceremonial functions of their pagan predecessors, and Christian bishops adopted the dress of civil dignitaries. As already noted, existing religious festivals in the winter and spring became Christmas and Easter.

Constantine's motive in converting is subject to much speculation. He may, of course, have seen what he said he saw and genuinely believed that Christian faith was the best option. He may have looked to an appeasement of the by then quite large Christian minority as a strategy in his own struggle for the imperial throne. Despite persecution, people continued to convert to Christianity. Although Celsus had thought all Christians stupid, their numbers included distinguished and capable thinkers, not least of all Origen, who responded to Celsus' criticism. Even the polemicist Porphyry (230–305 CE) expressed admiration for Origen, 'who had a great reputation, and still holds it, for the writings he left behind' (Stevenson, 1963, p. 222).

## The extent of persecution

Some recent critics suggest that Christians, through whose lenses the history of this period is viewed, have greatly exaggerated the extent of Roman persecution. 'What persecution the Christians did suffer,' says one writer, 'were not as gross as portrayed by propagandists in either number or severity . . . pious Christians began around the ninth century to forge the martyrdom traditions' (Acharya S, 1999, p. 5). In this view, the tolerant pagan world had more or less allowed Christianity to exist alongside all the other mystery cults, only to become itself the victim of Christian intolerance. 'When the "great idea", threats of hell and other sweet talk failed to impress the pagans, the Christian conspirators began turning the screws by establishing laws banning Pagan priests, holidays and "superstitions",' says Acharya S (*ibid.*, p. 8).

Constantine's Edict of Milan (313) legalized Christianity. It was Theodosius I (379–95 CE) who declared Christianity the exclusive religion of the state, and who proscribed not only paganism but also those Christians, such as Arians and Gnostics, whom he judged heretical. This means that most of our information on pagan and Gnostic criticism of orthodox Christianity comes to us from the pens of Christian writers. Between Constantine and Theodosius, paganism enjoyed a resurgence under Julian (332–63 CE). While Julian stopped short of persecution, he reopened pagan centres, downgraded Christianity and wrote works of polemic against the faith. His policy of returning all exiled bishops to their sees was intended to create conflict among rival claimants. To annoy Christians, he even decided to allow the Jews to rebuild the Temple in Jerusalem (abandoned after an earth tremor; see Chadwick, 1967, p. 156).

## Christians before Christ

Even within the New Testament, there is evidence of what Chadwick refers to as a policy of accepting 'the positive value of the best Greek philosophy and of the peace-keeping Roman government, but to be vehemently opposed to the pagan cult and myth' (Chadwick, 1967, p. 153). Paul used his Roman citizenship to claim the right to speak to the people even after his arrest (Acts 21:39), then to be tried in Rome itself (Acts 25:11). At Athens, Paul praised the religious spirit he encountered there: 'I see that in every way you are very religious' (Acts 17:22). He suggested that he could now name for his hearers the unknown God whom some of them were worshipping. This approach to pre-existing beliefs would later be called the *fulfilment approach*. In other words, pre-existing beliefs need not be totally abandoned. Christianity could *subsume* rather than *displace* whatever was deemed wholesome within other religious systems (see my discussion in Chapter 6).

Choice, too, of the term 'logos' in the prologue of John to describe the pre-existing word of God that became flesh in Jesus opened up the possibility of affirming truth spoken by people, Jews and Gentiles, before the birth of Jesus. As Tertullian put it, as 'Artificer of the Universe' the logos about which the philosophers spoke was identical with the logos of John's Gospel, which had 'formed and ordered all' (Stevenson, 1963, p. 171). This device could find truth not only in the teaching of Moses and Elijah but also in that of Socrates, Plato and Aristotle.

Justin Martyr wanted it both ways. As well as condemning pagan parallels with Christianity or with the life of Jesus as the work of the devil he claimed that 'whatever things were rightly said among all teachers, are the property of us Christians', since each speaks well 'in proportion to the share he had of the regenerative word (or reason)' (*Apology* 11, 13). Heraclitus (570–490 BCE), the father of Greek philosophy, had called the logos 'the wisdom that shapes all things' (Freeman, 1996, p. 18). Of course, Philo (see Chapter 1) had also equated the logos with biblical manifestations of God, so its use by Jews was not altogether novel (see Sandmel, 1958, pp. 48–50, on Philo, Paul and the logos).

Many aspects of Cynic and Stoic thought, such as the former's rejection of luxury and the latter's suppression of desires, all found in the 'classic past', resonated too deeply with Jesus' life and words to be rejected out of hand (see Chadwick, 1967, p. 177). There was, it seemed, *continuity* between Jesus' teaching and pagan philosophy, while there was *discontinuity* between Jesus and pagan polytheism. Celsus put this rather more starkly: the Greeks had not merely 'spoken well' but earlier and better than the Christians; 'many of the ideas of the Christians have been expressed better – and earlier – by the Greeks' (Hoffmann, 1987, p. 91).

Justin declared that men such as 'Socrates and Heraclitus' and all who had 'lived with reason were Christians, even though they were thought atheists' (*Apology* 1, 46). Indeed, Jesus was often compared with Socrates. Jesus and Socrates were both charged with breaking conventions, and were executed. Socrates, of course, took the poison himself (see *Apology* 1:5). Having 'rightly perceived how corrupt the old religion was', Socrates had been 'hounded to death' and properly served as 'a model of integrity for

Christian martyrs' (Chadwick, 1967, p. 76). Both attracted disciples. Neither wrote anything himself, although disciples wrote about them. Socrates was renowned for his unattractive physical appearance; as noted, some surmise that Jesus may have been ugly. Like Moses, Socrates could be regarded as a 'type' or forerunner of Jesus.

Justin and others could find 'types' of Jesus as readily in pagan literature as they could in the Bible; passages in Plato, Virgil, some Sibylline oracles, were all taken as pointing to Jesus. Later, it was Virgil who guided Dante (1265–1321), at least in his imagination, through inferno and purgatory as he journeyed towards his beloved. Virtuous non-Christians, such as Moses and Aristotle (384–322 BCE), the Muslim philosophers Avicenna (Ibn Sina, 980–1037 CE) and Averroes (Ibn Rushd, 1126–98 CE) and the Muslim leader, Saladin (1137–93 CE), are encountered in purgatory (see Dante Alighieri, 1984, p. 101).

Ancient Christian writers such as Clement of Alexandria (150–215) could quote from the Greek masters to verify such Christian teachings as the immortality of the soul, 'a doctrine on which Scripture and philosophy were agreed' (Pelikan, 1985, p. 44). Not all Christians were happy with this appropriation of Greek philosophy, though. Tertullian, for example, famously retorted, 'What has philosophy to do with Jerusalem? What has the Academy to do with the Church. . . . Away with attempts to produce a Stoic, Platonic and dialectic Christianity' (Stevenson, 1963, p. 178). Tertullian was not against an informed and reasonable believing but he did think that only faith, gifted by grace, could 'grasp' Christian truth.

In my view, something is akin here to Kierkegaard's idea that since absurdity lies at the heart of Christian teaching, it is necessary to crucify the intellect. Tertullian ended his life among the Montanists, a charismatic group that expected the imminent end of the world, and the return of Jesus, and travelled to the desert with its own prophets and prophetesses. Such spontaneous, non-official, anti-hierarchical, even female leadership was just what the male-dominated Roman Church, as it tried to exert centralized authority, could not tolerate, and Montanism was condemned. Other groups in which women, perhaps following the tradition of Mary Magdalene, exercised power were similarly suppressed.

## A Church above the state

Whether it was paganism that subsumed Christianity or vice versa, by the end days of the Roman Empire, being Christian and a citizen was synonymous. The adoption of familiar feast days, even of some pagan symbols, made former pagans feel at home in the new religion. For example, symbols such as the peacock for immortality, even the good shepherd 'carrying his sheep', were copied from paganism. Of course, the latter does evoke biblical images, but it was also 'a conventional pagan symbol of humanitarian concern' (Chadwick, 1967, p. 278). Some of the earliest visual depictions of Jesus resemble pagan images of Adonis. These may pre-date any real *rapprochement* with paganism, and represent Christian desire to see their master as just as worthy of adoration as the beautiful pagan god. Yet the fact that Adonis was also a dying and rising god suggests that Christians may have seen some similarity between him and Jesus. After the collapse of Rome, it was Christianity that prevented Europe from total anarchy; the eastern Roman Empire continued until its last stronghold, Constantinople, fell to Islam in 1453. As Braudel puts it:

It was not a hesitant or infant Church that was overtaken by the apocalyptic disasters of the barbarian invasions. In that dark fifth century, it had already taken shape like the Empire itself, as the civilization of the ancient world which it had taken over, and which it was to save, in some respects, by saving itself. (1993 p. 335)

Arguably, though, the Christianity that now claimed ultimate temporal and spiritual authority over the medieval world was different from that of the first Jerusalem Church. There, property had been held in common, and the idea that Christians ought to rule the world would have seemed heretical as well as preposterous. Now, the Church was identified with 'the whole of organized society', so that: 'During the whole medieval period there was in Rome a single spiritual and temporal authority exercising powers which in the end exceeded those that had even lain within the grasp of a Roman Emperor' (Southern, 1970, p. 25).

## Christians make peace with the world

Far from condemning worldly wealth and power, the Church embraced it; success in material, even in political and military, terms represented God's blessing. The Jesus of the Church was now the Christ of faith, the risen and exalted King of Kings, and not the humble peasant of Galilee. The Church had now made its peace with the world; it dropped its preference for poverty, just as it dropped total opposition to war. Augustine, whose 'two cities' theology contrasted the perfect city of God that was yet to come with the imperfect here-and-now, said that while war was wrong, it could be tolerated when waged for a just cause. Later, in its encounter with Islam, the Church waged a holy war designed to annihilate the enemy of God. Christian art could now depict the crucified Jew of Nazareth as also *Christus Rex*, Christ the King of Kings.

After several centuries, with Christian churches dotted about the European countryside and village life revolving around its liturgy and life-cycle rituals of baptism, confirmation, marriage, death, few French, Germans or English thought that the Jesus whom they called 'Lord' had been anything other than a European. The tendency of Christian art, as already noted in this book, to depict Jesus as a blond-haired, blue-eyed European, would hardly have encouraged anyone to think of Jesus as a Jew. Even in the Gospels, there is evidence of a desire to depict Rome and Romans in positive hue, while the Jews are painted in dark colours. Pilate is made to offer the Jews a way of releasing Jesus, while the Jews, apart from Jesus' disciples, are depicted as constantly at odds with Jesus.

Of course, some monks and hermits continued to pursue the life of poverty. Some reform movements, too, advocated the rejection of worldly wealth, such as the Waldenses (referred to in Chapter 1) and the Albigenses from the twelfth century. While both of these movements separated from the Catholic Church, Francis of Assisi's order of friars, which also embraced poverty and simplicity, remained within. Christianity spread throughout Europe by adapting earlier stories and symbols, not by destroying them. Thus, pagan feasts were transposed into Christian ones, ancient myths were wrapped around stories of Christian saints, and the Germanic warrior ideal transformed itself into the Christian hero. Anton Wessels' *Europe: Was It Ever Really Christian? The Interaction between Gospel and Culture* (1994) is a readable and engaging account of this process, in which he explores encounter between the new religion, Christianity, and Europe's older cultures and religions.

## To Africa and beyond

When Christianity began to export itself from Europe to the rest of the world, opened up by colonial expansion, it not only went hand-in-hand with western imperialism but also saw itself as part and parcel of European civilization. As Hilaire Belloc (1870–1953) put it, 'The Faith is Europe and Europe is the Faith' (cited by Pelikan, 1985, p. 222). Similar sentiments will be encountered in Chapter 6, voiced by British colonialism. The Europeanizing or civilizing mission to which Europe thought herself called, and the Christianizing task, were one and the same. The Pope thought himself quite entitled to cede the West Coast of Africa and east of the Azores to Portugal, as he did the west of the Atlantic to Spain. Later, this was adjusted to allow Portugal to claim Brazil (bulls of 1454 and 1493; for the latter, see Lunenfeld, 1991, pp. 186–8). The bulls were intended to convey only ecclesiastical jurisdiction in these areas but were 'quickly . . . treated as formal title to the lands . . . despite challenge from . . . the French and English crowns that they did no such thing' (*ibid.*, p. 185).

The Christianity, and the Jesus, that reached the African, Asian and American was intimately bound up with attitudes of European racial and evolutionary superiority, as the pioneering Scottish missionary and explorer, David Livingstone (1813–73), said:

We come among them as members of a superior race . . . we are adherents of a benign holy religion, and may, by consistent effort and wise patience, become the harbingers of peace to a hitherto distracted and downtrodden race. (cited in Davidson, 1986, p. 170)

Europeans equated black with evil, which predisposed them to see black Africans as 'of the Devil'.

For their part, although some Africans mistook Europeans for their reincarnated ancestors, many thought their whiteness a portent of danger (see Davidson, 1986, p. 130). Whiteness had a common association with the dreaded disease of leprosy. Reginald Bosworth Smith (1839–1908), himself a devout Christian but a critic of nineteenth-century Christian work in Africa, put it like this: 'From the lessons he learns every day, the Negro [sic] unconsciously imbibes the conviction that to be a good man, he must be like the white man.' Despite Livingstone's desire to spread peace, when Africans heard the word 'Christian', they thought more readily of gunpowder, of slavery and gin (Smith, 1876, p. 807).

Incidentally, the racial superiority which colonialism and Christianity took with them into non-Western spheres would have been alien to the Greek and Roman world of Jesus' day. True, the Greeks despised barbarians. However, the classical world generally regarded Africa not as the dark continent but as the source of ancient wisdom. Blacks were at ease in Roman society. Augustine and Tertullian were African. Despite Christianity's early *rapprochement*, if not accommodation, with paganism and the possibility of embracing at least some aspects of the new religions they now encountered, missionaries chose to condemn all they saw as diabolical and bad. 'Africans were taught,' says Schreiter (1991), 'that their ancient ways were deficient or even evil and had to be set aside if they hoped to become Christian' (p. vii). Nigerian writer Chinua Achebe accurately translates this missionary message into fiction in his powerful and haunting novel, *Things Fall Apart* (1959):

The white man . . . told them that the true God lived on high . . . evil men and all heathen who in their blindness bowed to wood and stone were thrown into a fire . . . the gods you have named are not gods at all. They are gods of deceit. (pp. 45–6)

Achebe continues: 'the white man had not only brought a religion but also a government. It was said that they had built a place of judgement . . . to protect followers of their religion' (*ibid.*, p. 155). The District Commissioner, who had spent many years bringing 'civilization to different parts of Africa', was planning to write a book on 'The Pacification of the Primitive Tribes of the Lower Niger' (pp. 208–9).

Baptized Christians, too, exported Africans as slaves to work colonial plantations in the Americas. An estimated twenty million lost their lives during the cross-Atlantic 'middle passage'. Millions died *en route* to African ports. Some twelve million slaves made it to the New World. It is a sobering thought that these slavers, Protestants and Catholics, called Jesus 'Lord'. In Africa, Christianity has flourished, although this has often been at the expense of things African. Freed from European ecclesiastical control, some thirty million or more Africans have blended Christianity with native African traditions, producing what Europeans may think syncretistic or heretical. Yet these Europeans forget that the same process once domesticated Christianity within their own ancient cultures.

Members of the Legio regard their founder, Simeon Ondeto, as the black Messiah. Commenting on their numerical success, despite being called 'pagans, guilty of heresy' by the official Roman Catholic Church, their second-in-command, Mama Gaudencia, declared, 'We get the key to heaven from Jesus and not from Rome' (cited in Pettifer and Bradley, 1990, p. 121). This process was to be repeated in India, where Indians too have claimed direct access to Jesus, bypassing missionary and European interpretations. Both Ondeto and Gaudencia claim to have had visions of Jesus and Mary. Allowing polygamy, which the European missionaries condemn, the Legio baptize many whom other churches turn away. Of course, Christianity in Africa pre-dates European missions. In Egypt and Ethiopia there are Oriental Orthodox Churches dating back to the earliest period of Christian history. Similarly, in India, the Syrian or Thomas Christians of Kerala, and smaller communities of Nestorians and Armenians elsewhere, are equally ancient.

For a detailed examination of how African Christians have perceived and perceive Jesus, see Robert J. Schreiter's *Faces of Jesus in Africa* (1991) and Wessels' 'The African Christ' (1990, Chapter IV, Section 2). Africans find images of Jesus as healer, ancestor or as chief more relevant and meaningful than many of his more traditional, indeed biblical, titles. African Independent, or Instituted, Churches include the Church of the Lord Aladora and the Church of Christ on Earth, founded by the prophet Simon Kimbangu. Spirit possession, prophets and prophetesses all feature in the life of these churches. The challenge that African Christians face is to forge a 'style of Christianity' that does not result in cultural bifurcation, says Schreiter, causing Africans to 'reject a cultural heritage and identity to become a Christian' (1991, p. vii).

## Rasta Fari

In the Caribbean and North America, Africans whose old ways and tongues and traditions, even their names, had been blotted out by slavery and cultural dissonance, began to look to Africa with new pride. Marcus Garvey (1867–1914) was an important figure in this 'black is beautiful' 'return to Africa' movement. Garvey tried to reverse the stereotypes: not white is best but black is best, not Europe as the source of all wisdom, but ancient Africa. He wanted a self-confident, self-sufficient black community. He encouraged Black emigration to Africa (Liberia) and called on white colonialists to 'get out of Africa' (Lincoln, 1994, p. 57). Africa, he believed, had a heritage and ancient civilizations of which blacks could be proud. He 'delighted in references to the greatness of black civilizations at a time when white men were only barbarians and savages' (*ibid.*, p. 55). Blacks who simply copied white men were 'sycophants' (*ibid.*, p. 60).

As well as founding the Universal Negro Improvement Society (UNIS), Garvey helped establish the African Orthodox Church. Its first bishop, George Alexander McGuire, a former Episcopalian priest, was consecrated by a patriarch of the Syrian Orthodox Church, one of the oldest Christian bodies (see Lincoln, 1994, p. 58). McGuire preached, 'erase the white men's gods from your hearts . . . forget the white gods', and images of the black Madonna and child soon 'became a standard picture in the home of the faithful and the worship of a Black Christ became the hallmark of the faith' (*ibid.*). Although the media ridiculed the idea of a black Jesus, the Church attracted many members. More recently, black theology has also pictured Jesus as black (see my concluding chapter).

The UNIS created its own order of nobility, with ranks and uniforms. Garvey was provisional president of Africa. In the 1920s, Garvey stated: 'Look to Africa for the coming of a Black king, he shall be the Redeemer' (cited in Barrett, 1997, p. 67). In 1930, Ras Tafari Makannen became Emperor of Ethiopia, with the titles, 'Haile Selassie (Power of the Trinity), Conquering Lion of the Tribe of Judah, Elect of God and King of the Kings of Ethiopia'. Many blacks in the Caribbean recognized him as Garvey's 'Redeemer' and the Rasta Fari were born. They are God's chosen people. Rasta Fari resist systematizing their ideas but a central concept is the 'I and I', which means that God dwells within all Rasta. His Highness, whom Rastas believe is the incarnation of Moses, Elijah and Jesus, is the link that unites all in unity, the head of the family. Jesus had predicted Haile Selassie's coming. Although Haile Selassie died in 1975, his divinity lives on in the hearts of the Rasta people.

Traditional Christianity was too European, too racist, too much a religion of slavery, to attract Garvey and his followers. The singer Bob Marley (1945–81) did much to popularize Rasta through his 'redemption songs': 'emancipate yourself from mental slavery, no one but ourselves can free our minds . . . how long shall they kill our prophets while we stand aside' ('Redemption Song', 1980). He sang of 'one love, one heart' ('One Love', 1977), of world peace and unity: 'international peace, world citizenship, international morality' ('War', 1976). Marley died of cancer. Some admirers have even called him 'a reincarnation of Jesus Christ' and see the cancer that killed him 'as a modern version of the crucifixion' (Chris Salewicz, inset of compact disc, *Natural Mystic*, 1995).

## Black Hebrews

Many African-American negro spirituals found inspiration in the story of the Hebrew people's Egyptian captivity and Babylonian exile, more so than in the Gospels. Exodus emerged as a major theme. Some African Americans, also influenced by Garvey, saw Judaism, not Christianity, as the African's real religion. Had not the ten lost tribes moved into Africa? Had not the Queen of Sheba married Solomon, before returning to Ethiopia with their son Menelik? An ancient Ethiopian epic, *Beta Israel*, tells how 'the glory of Zion passed from Jerusalem and the children of Israel to the new Zion, Aksum, and the new Israel, the Ethiopian people' (Kaplan, 1992, pp. 22–3). Today, the Falasha Jews of Ethiopia (Falasha = moved, exiled) still practise a pre-Talmudic form of Judaism and are recognized as Jews, with the right of return, by the State of Israel. They are believed by some to be descendants of the lost Israelite tribe of Dan. Elsewhere in Africa, other tribes, have practised a form of biblical religion akin to pre-Talmudic Judaism, such as the Lembo in South Africa, who claim Jewish identity and use the Star of David as their symbol.

In Harlem, New York, W. A. Matthew (1892–1973) and his friend Arnold J. Ford, who had worked with Garvey in the UNIS, led a group of African Americans into a movement known as the Black Jews of Harlem. Today, members of this movement prefer to be known as Black Hebrews, or simply as Israelites. Their college, founded in 1925, is now called the Israelite Rabbinical College. Among other black Jewish groups are the Twelve Tribes and the Kingdom of God; the home page of an affiliated synagogue, Beth Elohim, Inc., has links to Rasta sites. Rasta Fari also identify themselves with the ten lost tribes. These Africans reject Jesus and the religion that reveres him. Christianity, they say, has enslaved and oppressed, not liberated or dignified them. Other African Americans, who also reject Jesus as the white man's God, see Islam as their historical, normative religion.

## Black Islam

This movement was pioneered by Elijah Muhammad (1897–1975), formerly Robert Poole, son of a Baptist preacher. Like many African Americans, he renounced the name given to his forebears by white slavers. Many simply use the letter 'X' to denote a lost or stolen identity. While working in Detroit in the 1930s, Elijah met a mysterious man called W. A. Fard, who he believed was Allah, calling him to become Allah's prophet to the black nation. Followers of Elijah Muhammad, who belong to what became known as the Nation of Islam, believe that his prophethood was predicted in the Bible, in such passages as Deuteronomy 18:18 and Malachi 4:2. Christians often cite these passages as predictions of Jesus, while Muslims see them as pointing to Muhammad.

Elijah Muhammad began to teach that the white race was a race of devils created not by God but by a mad, black chemist over 6000 years ago. The black race is superior to the white race. The white race, together with the USA, would be destroyed by a giant spaceship. On the positive side, the movement stressed hard work, self-sufficiency, family values, and did much to combat alcohol and welfare dependency among its members. Fathers especially were encouraged to take their responsibilities seriously. Taking a leaf from the UNIS book, the Nation of Islam developed its own symbolism and ranks and a sense of black pride. Its leader was the 'Most Honorable'. The Fruit of Islam was its security service, or army. The bow-tie, probably because of its upper-class image, became an integral part of the Nation's uniform. White men and white religion, said Elijah Muhammad, only kept the blacks servile and dependent. Christianity was 'the master stratagem for keeping the so-called Negroes enslaved' (Lincoln, 1994, p. 73). Black blood had been shed 'to help keep America for white Americans'.

Only by establishing their own nation could blacks realize their real dignity and full potential. Jesus' 'religion was Islam, and not the Christianity of the Pope of Rome' (Muhammad, cited in Lincoln, 1994, p. 70). Jesus and other prophets had been sent by God to invite white people to embrace Islam, but 'the white race . . . evil by nature' could not 'accept anyone who [was] not white', and so rejected the truth (*ibid.*, p. 75). Black Christian preachers were traitors, merely trying to copy whites. The white man's heaven was the black man's hell.

## Christianity's fatal flaw: racism

Malcolm X (1925–65), for many years Elijah Muhammad's deputy, was a powerful spokesperson for rejection of white religion. He wrote:

Where has Christianity brought this world? It has brought the non-white two-thirds of the human population to rebellion. Two-thirds of the human population today is telling the one-third minority white man, 'Get out!' And the white man is leaving. And as he leaves, we see the non-white peoples returning in a rush to their original religions, which had been labeled 'pagan' by the conquering white man. Only one religion – Islam – had the power to stand and fight white man's Christianity. (X, 1965, p. 486)

Christianity's 'fatal flaw', said X, 'is its failure to combat racism' (*ibid.*, p. 487). The same charge is made against Christianity for its anti-Jewish record in my next chapter. Interestingly, Liberia, created for returned ex-slaves, is today one of the least Christian countries in Africa. After performing the pilgrimage at Makkah, Malcolm X realized that Islam embraced people of all races, and converted to orthodox Islam. He then denounced the doctrines of Elijah Muhammad as 'religious fakery', accusing him of sexual misconduct (*ibid.*, p. 46).

Of course, the title 'prophet' which Elijah Muhammad claimed for himself marked a major departure from orthodox Islam. It had, however, been used by Mirza Ghulam Ahmad (1835–1908), founder of the Ahmadiyyah movement, whose teaching that the Christian world was *ad-dajjal* (the deceiver) or the end-time power that would oppose Allah's purposes may have influenced Elijah Muhammad. There were Ahmadiyyah missions in the USA from the late nineteenth century. Mirza Ahmad claimed to be the *Mahdi*, the figure who will usher in the end time of peace and righteousness, as well as Jesus and Vishnu's last *avatara*, who would all unite to destroy *ad-dajjal*. God had 'repeatedly told' Mirza that he was 'Krishna for the Hindus and the promised Messiah' for Christians and Muslims: 'Spiritually, Krishna and the promised Messiah are one and the same person,' he said (cited in Jones, 1939a, p. 220). I return to

Ahmadiyyah beliefs about Jesus in Chapters 5 and 6. This movement is spurned and even persecuted by mainstream Muslims.

Elijah Muhammad was as apt to cite the Bible as he was the Qur'an to support his ideas. Malcolm X was murdered shortly after denouncing his former hero's teachings. However, after Elijah Muhammad's own death, his seventh son and chosen successor, W. W. D. Muhammad, led the majority of black Muslims into orthodox Islam as the American Muslim Mission. A minority, under Louis Farrakhan, continues as the Nation of Islam, still teaching black-on-white and black-on-Jewish hatred. The us-israel.org website has a number of Farrakhan anti-Jewish statements; for example:

They [the Jews] are the greatest controllers of Black minds, Black intelligence. They write the scripts – the foolish scripts on television that our people portray. They are the movie moguls that feature us in these silly, degrading, degenerate roles. The great recording companies that portray our people in such a filthy and low-rating way, yet they would not allow such a man as Michael Jackson to say one word that they thought would besmirch their reputation, but they put us before the world as clowns and as purveyors of filth. No, I will fight that. ('Meet The Press interview', 18 October 1998; www.us-israel.org/jsource/anti-semitism/Farrakhan. html#Jews)

The claim that Jesus was a Muslim (which surfaces again in my next chapter) makes this response to Jesus in its self-understanding an *insider's response*. Again, my distinction proves problematic.

## White supremacists and the children of Israel

As much as I personally detest any form of racism, whether white-on-black or black-on-white, all that Elijah Muhammad did was to take the language of white supremacists and turn it against its inventors. Much earlier than black-on-white racism, earlier too than the notion of black supremacy, the Knights of the Ku Klux Klan (KKK), or of the Invisible Empire, were preaching that America is for white Christians only. Founded in 1866, the KKK continues to teach that the USA was founded as a white, Christian nation and ought to be ruled by white Christians. Anyone who does not like living under white Christian laws will be 'repatriated' to the lands of their forebears. The KKK uses a flaming cross to show 'that Jesus Christ is the light of the world', while the colour red on their symbol represents Jesus' blood shed 'for the White Aryan Race' (see www.kukluxklan.org). The Klan's first Grand Wizard, former Confederate General Nathan Bedford Forrest (1821–77), resigned because he believed the Klan was too violent in pursuing its anti-black agenda. Only 'pure white Christian people of non-Jewish, non-negro, non-Asian descent' can join. Today, the Klan's aim is to restore America's white Christian heritage.

Behind the ideology of the Ku Klux Klan lies the concept of British Israel, which dates back to the sixteenth century. This movement teaches that the Celtic, Anglo-Saxon, Germanic and kindred peoples are the ten lost tribes of Israel. Adam was the first white man, not the first man. The black races are descended from Cain, whom Eve bore after a sexual encounter with Satan. When Jesus commissioned his disciples to preach to the 'House of Israel', he meant the peoples of Western Europe, which now include North America, Australia, New Zealand and the white population of South Africa. These are the ten lost tribes, who had migrated west, not south into Africa, as others claim. Elaborate maps have been produced, tracing this movement. The Jews are not the legitimate children of Israel but Cananite imposters, and Christianity's implacable enemy. Blacks should live in Africa, whites in the Northern Hemisphere, of which Australasia is an honorary component. Jesus, who died to save white people only, will return to earth to establish his kingdom, the House of David, which he will rule over together with his saints. The British monarchy will be instrumental in this process. When Oliver Cromwell (1599–1658) readmitted Jews to England, he may have thought that 'his victory would establish the New Jerusalem on British soil' (Woodward, 1999, p. 69). Contemporary British Israel groups include the Canadian-based British Israel Church of God (www.british-israel.net). See Barkun's *Religion and the Racist Right* (1997) for more information on this topic.

There are many white supremacist groups in the USA who teach that the white race is the true Israel. Some of these groups believe that Zion, or Israel, will be established in North America. God wants a theocratic government to replace the present system, which corresponds to Babylon (see Revelation, Chapter 18). Some members of these groups refuse to pay taxes or to pass driving tests, since Babylon is godless. Celtic crosses, together with the swastika, feature in their insignia. According to the Christian Identity Movement, the swastika is a biblical symbol. In fact, although now synonymous with fascist racial hatred because of its adoption by Hitler, the swastika is a Jain symbol, representing the four levels of the cosmos.

For these groups, which include the Church of Israel, the Aryan Nation, the National Association for the Advancement of White People, the Church of Jesus Christ Christian, the White Aryan Resistance, the White Separatist Banner and the Yahweh's Chosen, Jesus is saviour of the Aryan race. Jesus was also an Aryan, not a Jew. His kingdom will be an earthbound, white paradise. (See www.melvig.org's 'god's order affirmed in love reference library for reconstituting a national identity for white Christians', whose resources include Luther's 'On the Jews and Their Lies' and other anti-Jewish titles such *as Jewish Ritual Murder* and *The Talmud: Judaism's Holy Book Exposed,* all listed under 'Know Your Enemy'. Examples of Holocaust denial are found under 'Uncommon History'.)

## Ghosts of Mississippi

In Reiner's film, *Ghosts of Mississippi* (1996), white supremacist Beckworth, tried for the murder of black civil rights leader Medger Evers, says: 'God put the Whiteman here to rule the dusky races, the Bible says so . . . it is no crime for a white man to kill a black man.' During his trial, Beckworth sits reading his Bible. The film is based on actual events; indeed, Beckworth's words echo a view voiced early on in Europe's encounter with the Americas, 'that certain peoples are by nature slaves', which 'justified the Spanish oppression of the Indians' (Neill, 1964, p. 171). A church that had only recently decided that women had souls easily doubted whether Indians had either. Perhaps Jesus was only saviour of European souls. Famously, Juan Ginés de Sepúlveda (1490–1573) argued that Indians were natural slaves. While 'talent, magnanimity, temperance, humanity and religion' were the natural qualities of all Spaniards, he saw no trace of humanity in the 'pitiful men' encountered in the Americas, which he never actually visited (Lunenfeld, 1991, p. 219). They devoted themselves 'to all kinds of intemperate acts and abominable lewdness', including 'the eating of human flesh' (*ibid.*). They possessed 'neither science nor even an alphabet' nor preserved 'any monuments of their history' and worshipped 'the Devil as God'. 'Natural law . . . obligated' their acceptance of Spanish rule (*ibid.*, p. 221).

Sepúlveda cited Aristotle, who believed that certain people's physical and mental abilities (excess of the former, scarcity of the latter) mean that they actually benefit from slavery, since it allows them to flex their muscles while their betters, their natural masters, do their thinking for them. Natural slaves resemble animals: 'The difference in the use made of them is small.' Unlike an animal, a slave 'shares in reason to the extent of understanding it . . . but does not have it himself. . . . It is evident, then . . . that some people are naturally free, others naturally slaves, for whom slavery is both just and beneficial' (Aristotle, 1998, p. 9; the translator discusses Aristotle's view of slavery on pp. 259–60). Sepúlveda saw the Spanish as parents: the Indians were as 'inferior to the Spanish as infants to adults and women to men' (Lunenfeld, 1991, p. 218). To his credit, Bartolomé de Las Casas (1474–1566) opposed Sepúlveda's views and his compatriots' treatment of the natives, whom they slew 'like wolves, tigers and lions . . . with strange and new, and divers kinds of cruelty, never before seen, nor heard of, nor read of' (*ibid.*, p. 206; see also pp. 205–11 and 217–27 for extracts from these two writers). 'The reason why the Christians have killed and destroyed such an infinite number of souls,' he wrote, 'is that they have been moved by their wish for gold and their desire to enrich themselves in a very short time' (Las Casas, 1909, p. 36).

Anti-Islamic sentiment also motivated Europe's voyages of discovery, especially to what became known as the 'New World'. Wessels (1990) points out how Columbus may have hoped to find and to forge an alliance with the legendary Christian kingdom of Prester John, which was believed to lie somewhere 'behind' the Islamic world. This would 'enable the Christians to take the Muslims between tongs, as it were' (p. 59). On Shrove Tuesday 2000, Pope John Paul II apologized for the way in which, over two millennia, the Church had deviated from the path of Christ by its treatment of Jews, of people of other faiths, indigenous peoples, immigrants, women and the poor. He regretted how the Church had 'violated the right of ethnic groups and peoples and shown contempt for their cultures and religious traditions'. 'Confessing an "objective collective responsibility for past errors", the Pope called for a church-wide 'purification of memory' (*New York Times*, 13 March 2000). His statement attracted some criticism for speaking in the passive voice about what had 'befallen the Jews' and for failing to explicitly condemn the Holocaust (see Chapter 5).

Although the above Jesus images are included here among *outsider* responses, their proponents regard themselves as *insiders*, and claim that their understanding of who Jesus was is authentic. The idea, too, that the Kingdom of Christ may emerge in North America may date from the first white settlers, who after 'enduring a transatlantic exodus' saw 'their theocratic colony' in Massachusetts 'as a real, if imperfect, model of the New Jerusalem' (Woodward, 1999, p. 72). The Pilgrims, suggests Woodward, saw themselves 'as participants with God in creating a millenarian kingdom of God on earth'. Indeed, they may have believed that 'Christ would return after – not before . . . his American saints had established a millennial society' (*ibid.*). In 1832, says Woodward, 'This optimistic vision was well expressed . . . by revivalist Charles Grandison', who thought that education, fair wages, healthy souls and bodies might all result in the millennium coming 'in this country in three years' (*ibid.*).

Similarity between the agendas of the Nation of Islam and of white supremacist groups has not passed unnoticed by either side. Both advocate separate nations for black and white. Elijah Muhammad is said to have received funds from the KKK following a meeting with its leadership at Atlanta, Georgia, in 1961. In 1967, the founder of the American Nazi Party attended a Nation of Islam (NOI) convention. In 1985, Farrakhan invited Tom Metzger of the White Aryan Resistance to attend a meeting of the NOI. Metzger reported how both groups denounced 'the Jews and the oppressors in Washington. . . . They are', he said, the 'black counterpart to us' (reported in the *Washington Times*, 30 September 1985).

The idea that the USA is a Christian nation is not novel. Welcoming delegates to Chicago's Parliament of World Religions, the liberal Presbyterian John Henry Barrows (1847–1902) stated:

There is a true and noble sense in which America is a Christian nation, since Christianity is recognized by the supreme court. . . . The world calls us Christian, and we call ourselves a Christian people. (cited in Tweed and Prothero, 1999, p. 128)

Barrows' Christian vision, though, like Jefferson's and Wallace's, could embrace those of any faith who affirmed ethical monotheism. He 'sincerely believed', writes Braybrooke (1992), 'that in an evolving Christianity all could be at home' (p. 16). Sessions began with the Lord's Prayer recited in English and concluded with Handel's *Hallelujah Chorus*.

## Humanists and free-thinkers on Jesus

Reimarus, discussed in Chapter 2, and Deistic writers such as Chubb and Jefferson, were among the first Europeans to dare to question the orthodox picture of Jesus. Instead of the divine, miracle-working, incarnate Son of God who died and rose to save humankind from sin, they saw an ordinary man. For Reimarus, Jesus was a failed political rebel. For Jefferson, he was a teacher of eternal wisdom. Reimarus, like Celsus, saw official Christianity as fraud and deception. Many subsequent writers allege that the origin of Christianity and its continued existence represent a deliberate, ongoing conspiracy. I discuss some of these theories below, many of which assert that Jesus never existed, something that neither Reimarus, nor even Celsus, appears to have contemplated. I will suggest, though, that aspects of Celsus', Reimarus' and Strauss' work on Jesus anticipated the arguments of the Jesus-was-a-myth school. First, however, I will discuss two writers, Renan and Smith, for whom Jesus, while a mortal man and not God, was still a good man, and one, William Blake, for whom Jesus was not so much the God-Man as the Man-God.

Celsus' Jesus had been irredeemably bad. These writers see Christianity as a departure from what Jesus had really intended and taught, but regard Jesus himself as a well-intentioned man. As the truth about Jesus becomes known, they argue that Christians ought to abandon Christianity as it is currently practised. Strauss, Funk and others whose ideas I have already discussed offer the same challenge. In many respects, Ernest Renan, a nineteenth-century French humanist, gives us a conventional picture of Jesus, minus his divinity, miracles and resurrection. Yet, in his handling of the material, he did pave new ground. Allen (1998) says that he pioneered what later became a popular twentieth-century image of Jesus, one somewhat different from the Christian norm:

Renan's Jesus was . . . matinee idol: handsome and languorous, with perfect manners and winning ways, whose attractiveness to women added a sexual frisson to the traditional Gospel stories. There is a direct line of descent from Renan's *Life of Jesus* to DeMille's *King of Kings*, for Renan had invented the cinematic Jesus. (p. 187)

Morton Smith uses alternative sources to reinterpret the canonical gospels, and offers a more radical reworking of the Jesus story. There is quite a lot in common between Smith and early pagan criticism. Like Renan, he gives us a sexual Jesus (Renan implicitly, Smith explicitly), which could suggest that early pagan criticism of Christians' sexual morals had hit the mark, and that such Christians were imitating Jesus. On the other hand, a sexual Jesus was also encountered in my discussion of insider images. Once again, the gap between insiders and outsiders seems to narrow. William Blake also advocated a sexual spirituality. His words quoted at the start of this chapter suggest that (as Celsus had claimed) Jesus had taught nothing new. Blake's Jesus differs radically from that of the Christian Church, against which, like Renan, he rebelled.

## Joseph Ernest Renan (1823–92)

Renan started out studying for the Catholic priesthood but resigned to pursue a career within the secular academy. Although he remained open to the devotional and artistic, perhaps even to the spiritual within human experience, he became a humanist. He detested the Catholic religion. His academic work was in the field of oriental studies and he wrote much on religious topics. His 1852 book on Averroes, the Muslim philosopher, made his reputation. He expressed very negative opinions about Islam, as he did about native Arab ability. He interpreted Averroes as largely dependent on Greek thought. Contemporary Islam, for Renan, was anti-rationalist, a hindrance to human progress. In 1860 the emperor sent Renan on an archaeological mission to Palestine. While there he wrote his *Life of Jesus* (1863). He may qualify as the first Jesus scholar to combine fieldwork with textual study. None of the great German writers of this period, from either the right or the left of the theological spectrum, thought that a trip to Palestine might enhance their scholarship.

Allen (1998) comments how, for such scholars, 'the life of the historical Jesus was . . . solely a matter of interpreting texts' (p. 187). Lewis Wallace, while writing *Ben Hur* (1880), spent hours studying maps of Palestine so that he could 'paint it, water, land, and sky in actual colors'. At the time, Wallace was Governor of New Mexico. Later, while serving as US Minister to Turkey, he did visit Palestine and was gratified to find that he felt 'no reason for making a single change in the text' of his novel (Wallace, 1906, p. 937). In Turkey, drawing on the experience of encountering Islam and of visiting many historical venues, Wallace wrote *The Prince of India* (1893), in which his hero, the Wandering Jew, encounters the religions of the world. Increasingly, spending time in the Holy Land was to become *de rigueur* for Bible scholars. Many of the writers discussed in this chapter used 'alternative sources', or an alternative hermeneutic, to construct their Jesus story. Renan used what he called a 'fifth gospel':

I had before my eyes a fifth gospel, torn, but still legible, and henceforward, through the recitals of Matthew and Luke and Mark, in place of an abstract being, whose existence might have been doubted, I saw a living and moving and admirable human figure. (1927, p. 61)

The book was written, says Renan, 'almost entirely near the very places where Jesus was born, and where his character was developed' (p. 61). An admirer of Strauss, he generally made Strauss' evaluation of the text his own. Interestingly, he does criticize Strauss for 'taking up the theological ground too much, the historical too little' (p. 28).

Renan thought John's Gospel overly theological and too late to be useful, except for John's possibly more accurate description of Jesus' final days. He did not think that the non-canonical gospels had any historical value (p. 53). In his 'Introduction' (pp. 15–65) he sketched the generally accepted view of Gospel authorship, and made his own presuppositions clear. Schweitzer (1998b) calls this section 'a literary masterpiece' (p. 182). Renan makes his disbelief in the miraculous quite explicit: 'That the gospels are in part legendary is evident, since they are full of miracles and of the supernatural' (1927, p. 33). Neither miracles nor the supernatural plays any role in Jesus' life as painted by the rationalist Renan. Yet he does not reject material merely because different versions exist: 'The historian ought not to conclude that a fact is false because he possesses several versions of it, or because credulity has mixed with them much that is fabulous' (p. 58).

Renan explains many miraculous aspects of the Gospels as the result of enthusiasm and after-the-fact conjecture. 'Jesus,' he states, 'was born in Nazareth' (p. 31), indicating in a single sentence his rejection of the birth narratives as myth, or after-the-fact invention. He claims to approach the Jesus story as an objective historian. He is, though, open about his own assessment of Jesus: 'Let us place, then, the person of Jesus at the highest summit of human greatness. Let us not be misled by exaggerated doubts in the presence of a legend which keeps us always in the supernatural' (p. 286). Here, he all but anticipates Bultmann. Like Bultmann, he wants to liberate Jesus from the mythological worldview in which the biblical material has incarcerated him. Renan's Jesus is not the creation of his disciples but their superior (*ibid.*). Renan does use the word 'conspiracy', although not as ubiquitously as some of the writers discussed later in this chapter. 'The legends,' he says, 'were . . . the fruit of a great and entirely spontaneous conspiracy' (p. 238). His readership was always intended to be popular as well as academic. He may have seen himself as a redactor, as a broker of scholarship to the masses. Strauss had coveted this function when he wrote his *New Life*: 'I hope,' Strauss wrote in his preface, 'that I have written a book as thoroughly well adapted for Germans as Renan's is for Frenchmen' (cited in Schweitzer, 1998b, p. 193).

## A new gospel

Renan may actually have invented a new genre of Jesus book, what might be called a *neo-gospel*. He tried, he said, to capture 'the very soul of history' rather than its 'material circumstances, which it is impossible to verify' (1927, p. 63). He refers to this enterprise as an 'art' and was always, suggests Allen (1998), 'conscious that he was producing literature as well as scholarship' (p. 189). According to some of his critics, he may have succeeded in the former but dismally failed to produce the latter. Schweitzer gave Renan a whole chapter (Chapter 13), a rare honour in *The Quest*, and expressed some admiration for a book that, despite all its flaws, possessed 'imperishable charm' (1998b, p. 192). It was, though, more fiction than fact, more subjective than objective, and sentiment and romance won out over 'the power of distinguishing truth from artificiality' (p. 182).

Renan, says Schweitzer, like the great French artist that he was, looked 'at the landscape with the eye of a decorative painter seeking a motif for a lyrical composition' (p. 181). Renan claimed to have looked at the Galilean landscape and to have seen Jesus there, in his imagination, as a 'living, moving human figure'. Schweitzer says Renan superimposed his own Jesus onto the landscape. While the skill with which Renan accomplished this gave the book its irresistible charm, it also misled many into thinking that they could really see Jesus:

He offered his readers a Jesus who was alive, whom he, with his artistic imagination, had met under the blue heaven of Galilee . . . Men's attention was arrested, and they thought to see Jesus, because Renan had the skill to make them see blue skies, seas of waving corn, distant mountains, gleaming lilies, in a landscape with the lake of Gennesareth for its centre. (p. 181)

It is easy to cite many beautiful, evocative passages from Renan's *Life* that conjure up vivid pictures of a Jesus against the backdrop of Galilee:

On leaving Tiberias, we find at first steep rocks, like a mountain which seems to roll into the sea. Then the mountains gradually recede, a plain . . . opens up almost at the level of the lake. . . . At the other extremity, we come to . . . a pretty road which Jesus often traversed. (1927, p. 167)

While we cannot know for sure that Jesus had really traversed such a road, this imaginative approach to the material does allow readers to reach beyond dry, academic textual criticism to the personality and experience of the man Jesus. Bultmann places this beyond our reach.

This is the same strategy that some recent writers of what I call *neo-gospels* have used, such as James P. Carse (1997), Donald Spotto (1998) and Reynolds Price (1996). These books all combine scholarship with imaginative reconstruction. Spotto describes his book as 'a series of meditations on the significance of Jesus of Nazareth' (p. xvi). Carse says that, while he took 'no more liberty with the known historical material than the earlier gospels took', he used imagination to 'let the unique and terrible experience of our own century reflect itself in our writing about another' (p. ix). I think that Allen (1998) is too negative when she says that Renan 'tried to make his book academically respectable, peppering it with learned footnotes' (p. 190). In contrast, Allen calls *Ben Hur* 'meticulously researched' (p. 180). She notes how Wallace's novel even gained popularity among many Christians 'who disapproved of fiction' (p. 181).

What Renan was actually doing was pioneering a new genre of Jesus literature. Both Renan from the academy and Wallace from the world of fiction perhaps produced a similar type of text, in which fact and imagination served each other. Renan was beyond doubt a scholar of outstanding ability, a 'supreme . . . figure among the scholars of his time . . . among the scholars of all time' (Holmes, 1927, p. 19). Introducing the 1927 English translation, Holmes calls *The Life* 'a work of profound learning' (p. 19). As a result of the 'whirlwind of rage and calumny' that the book caused, Renan 'lost his professorship in the College of France'. However, it sold so well that he made a fortune (as had Strauss). Unlike Strauss', though, Renan's academic career was by no means over, and under a later, more radical government he returned to the college not merely as professor but as its Dean (1871). Since Schweitzer thought that Jesus could not be made to walk before us, in our own time, he was hardly likely to admit that Renan had succeeded in this task, even if he had. Renan saw his treatment of Jesus as comparable to any other historical study of a significant figure; he did not doubt that Jesus had really lived.

## Renan's Jesus

Renan's Jesus was an extraordinary man who developed a philosophy of love, of the human spirit that rebelled against the legalistic, external religiosity of his day. His increasing hatred of the sacrificial system he saw in the Jerusalem Temple transformed his goals from reforming to destroying Judaism (1927, p. 224). Renan's anti-Jewish rhetoric equals his anti-Arab: 'The Pentateuch has . . . been in the world the first code of religious terrorism' (p. 359); 'He [Jesus] proclaimed the rights of man, not the rights of the Jew' (p. 225; but see p. 390 for some positive comments). Renan did acknowledge similarity between Jesus' stress on the spirit and the teachings and proverbs of such rabbis as Antigonus and Hillel, but says that he added something 'superior' to this 'oral tradition' (p. 126). Jesus did see himself as God's son but 'never dreamt of making himself pass for an incarnation of God' (p. 239). He understood 'sonship' in a metaphorical sense, as a spiritual 'sonship' available to all people. 'He was not sinless' (p. 392).

Jesus despised rituals and external trappings, although he did share common meals with his followers, which later developed into the Mass, or Lord's Supper. He taught no dogmas and would never have envisioned either creed or New Testament: 'it was contrary to the spirit of the new sect to produce sacred books' (p. 279). He did enjoy the close friendship of an inner circle, thus 'the fertile idea of the power of men in association (ecclesia) was doubtless derived from Jesus' (p. 277). The idea of a sacerdotal priesthood, though, was alien to Jesus (p. 271). Above all, he taught about love, about a divine kingdom that would embrace the poor, Samaritans and even pagans. Jesus preferred the countryside to the town: 'True religion does not proceed from the tumult of towns, but from the tranquil serenity of the fields' (p. 306), although he went *annually* to Jerusalem (p. 213).

Renan's Jesus seems confused about his own apocalyptic vision. At times, he thought that his own human action might bring about the kingdom through teaching and influencing people. Later, he accepts the inevitability of death, of becoming 'all powerful by suffering and rejection' (p. 158). Renan hints that Jesus' purely spiritual movement presented no real threat to the authorities, who none the less, 'persuaded that it was essential for humanity not to be disturbed, felt themselves bound to prevent the new spirit from expanding' (p. 328). Jesus' spirituality, though, did not separate the 'soul' from the 'body'. Jesus may or may not have regarded himself as the Messiah. However, he did allow the people to call him this (p. 236). He also gave into the crowd's demand for healing 'miracles'. Renan thought that most of the miracles were legendary, but conceded that Jesus may have exercised a positive influence over at least the *mental health* of certain 'unfortunates' (p. 253). He became, says Renan, 'a thaumaturgist late in life and against his inclination' (p. 254).

### Jesus' sexuality

Above all, Renan's Jesus was a man whose charismatic personality attracted fierce devotion, perhaps especially from women. Although Renan's Jesus never indulged in any sexual relationships, sexuality lurks in the background: 'Three or four devoted Galilean women always accompanied the young master' (p. 175), and 'women, with tearful hearts and disposed through their sins to feelings of humility . . . would passionately attach themselves to him' (pp. 200–1). Allen (1998) suggests that Renan wrote into his script his own experience of being caught between two lovers: his sister Henrietta (to whom *The Life* is dedicated) and his wife Cornélie, who were vying for his attention (p. 191).

Renan's Mary Magdalene, says Allen, informed the

long looks that pass between Jesus and Mary Magdalene in DeMille's *King of Kings* and the scene in Scorsese's *Last Temptation of Christ* in which the Magdalene takes off her clothes in front of Jesus and tries to lure him into her bed. (p. 195)

Later on in the film, Jesus climbs down from the cross and finds sexual and domestic bliss not only with Mary Magdalene but with other women too, with other Marys, for all women are Mary. What Allen calls a 'sexually charged Mary' similarly features in the musical *Jesus Christ, Superstar*, where she sings of her unreciprocated love for Jesus:

I don't know how to love him, I don't see why he moves me. . . . Just one more . . . Don't you think it's funny – I am the one who has always been so calm, so cool, running every show. I never thought I'd come to this. I want him so. I love him so. (Rice, 1970; I first saw the Sydney production in 1973; it was picketed by Christian activists, including members of my own Church)

Like many writers reviewed in this book, Renan has no real explanation for Jesus' death. He died because he annoyed the authorities, and accepted death because he thought that his suffering would bring the kingdom to fruition. Even though this did not happen, Jesus' death 'purchased the most complete immortality' (1927, p. 368).

On the resurrection, Renan surmised that perhaps the body was stolen, or that enthusiasm produced the narratives on which faith in a risen Jesus was later based. Either way, Jesus had left such an impression on a 'few devoted women that during some weeks more it was as if he were living and consoling them' (p. 374). The Church, says Renan, has buried the real Jesus beneath superstition and dogma; yet he can be recovered, and remains 'an inexhaustible principle of moral regeneration for humanity' (p. 388). As noted in Chapter 3, some Marxists have also found significance and meaning in the Jesus story, whose appeal 'cuts across all denominations, worldviews and ideologies' (Machovec, 1976, p. 204).

## Morton Smith (1915–91)

Smith was Professor of History at Columbia University, and held doctorates from Harvard and from the Hebrew University, Jerusalem. He wrote for 'educated men and women in all walks of life' as well as for 'professionals in New Testament studies' (1978, pp. vii–viii). Like Renan's *Life*, his writing is popular as well as scholarly. He offers an alternative explanation of who Jesus was, drawing on external sources, on non-canonical material, as well as on critical study of the Gospels. Sanders, like other scholars reviewed in my earlier chapter, takes Smith's work seriously, referring to 'his unrivalled treasury of learning'. He does not endorse Smith's analyses but sees in his work 'the earnest sweat which comes from the effort to explain history' (1985, p. 7; see also pp. 164–70 for a detailed discussion of Smith's views).

Smith accepts the basic outline of Jesus' life as authentic (1978, p. 5). He regards the antithesis between the 'Christ of faith' and the 'Jesus of history' which the Jesus Seminar takes as read to be 'a gross exaggeration'. Like Sanders, he thinks there must be some continuity between the life of Jesus and what Christians came to believe about him, since 'Whatever else he may or may not have done, he unquestioningly started the process that became Christianity' (*ibid.*). However, says Smith, the Church suppressed evidence that told a different story from that which received official sanction.

This included polemic, some of which has survived and which ought to be revisited. He began by noting similarities between aspects of this polemic and views about Jesus which can be detected in the Gospels, attributed to his critics and enemies; for example, that he was mad, or a magician. In John 18:30, Smith points out that the Jews accuse Jesus 'of being a "doer of evil"', which was, he says, 'a vulgar term for a magician' (1978, p. 33; see also Horbury, 1998b, p. 164, on the same term). Assuming that there is no smoke without fire, he asks whether there is any truth in these alternative explanations. He also uses the 'secret gospel of Mark'. Stranded in the monastery of Mar Saba about twelve miles from

Jerusalem, as a student in the early days of the Second World War, he returned there in 1951 to help the monks catalogue their collection of ancient manuscripts.

Working away in the library, he discovered an eighteenth-century copy of a letter by Clement of Alexandria, in which he found references to a document called 'secret Mark', from which Clement quoted some twenty lines. In this text, after the story of the raising of Lazarus, we read how the resurrected man, wearing only a linen cloth, spent a whole night with Jesus learning the mystery of the Kingdom of God (see Mark 14:51, where a youth wearing 'nothing but a linen cloth' fled from the scene of Jesus' arrest). Was there any link here, Smith surmised, with later anti-Christian charges of promiscuity, cited above? *The Gospel of Thomas* may also suggest that Jesus had a more relaxed attitude towards nudity: 'When you strip without being ashamed, and you take your clothes and put them under your feet like little children . . . you will see the son of the living one and not be afraid' (Thomas 37; see also 21). Some early illustrations show Jesus naked at his baptism. The very existence of 'secret mark' has been debated. An interesting website is dedicated to this discussion (http://www.alf.zfn.uni-bremen,de/~wie/secretmark_home.html).

## Miracles, or magic?

Next, turning to the magical papyri (mainly Egyptian material about ancient magic, magicians and their practices), Smith found more clues that suggested parallels between Jesus' career and that of magicians in the ancient world. Working with these alternative texts, with pagan polemic and with the canonical gospels, Smith proceeded to create a composite picture of Jesus drawn from all these sources. He uses his external material as a sort of cipher to decode the canonical gospels. He wants to penetrate through the apparent story to the real one, which lies buried within the Christianized text. He sees many parallels between Jesus' miracles and the practices of first-century magicians. Like Jesus, they often healed by touch and speech. Smith points out, as I have already shown in this chapter, that this association between Jesus and magic continued in much anti-Christian polemic, and says that 'only as Christianity gradually spread and became better known (and as its lunatic fringe died out) was this picture discredited' (1978, p. 66).

Jesus as magician, says Smith, depends not only on 'outsiders' traditions about him'; rather, 'some of their most important elements were accepted by hundreds of thousands of believing Christians through the first millennium, and more, of Christian history' (p. 64). Did a 'secret society' continue to perpetuate Jesus' real work (p. 67), until that version eventually lost out to the 'branch of the Church that finally triumphed' (p. 2)? Smith compares Jesus' life with that of the magician Apollonius of Tyana (pp. 85–96), whose cult, as noted above, enjoyed imperial patronage. There are interesting similarities between Apollonius' biography and the

Gospels, such as lack of information on their subjects' early lives (see pp. 86 and 96). Renan had given the Life of Apollonius no credit, dismissing it as pure romance (1927, p. 33). Smith regards it as typical of the biographical genre of the period. Apollonius, he says, 'like Jesus, is a figure of indubitable historicity' (1978, p. 85). Here, he is close to writers such as Talbert and Burridge, who also identify the Gospels as belonging to the ancient genre of Graeco-Roman biography.

Citing controversy about 'in whose name' Jesus performed miracles, Smith claims that both Apollonius and Jesus became 'deified' so that they could perform 'miracles' in their own name, not in that of another spirit. Apollonius, though, was the educated son of a 'well-to-do Greek family' (p. 84) while Jesus' origins were somewhat humble. Anti-Christian polemic mirrors, says Smith, polemic against magicians: 'Cannibalism, incest, and sexual promiscuity were reported of magicians. Therefore, the Christians were persecuted as magicians' (p. 66). With Celsus, Smith surmises that Jesus may have learned magic in Egypt, thus accepting part of the Jesus story rejected by many of the insider scholars discussed in this book (p. 150). Jesus, says Smith, was even depicted as a magician in primitive art (pp. 63–4). Within some Christian circles his name was also used in spells (see p. 63). At the ends of their lives, 'Apollonius escaped miraculously from his trial; Jesus, executed, rose miraculously from the dead' (*ibid.*). Yet, as magicians used pharmacology, hypnotism and other devices, actual cures may lie behind at least some of Jesus' miracles (see p. 113). Like Renan, Smith accepts that Jesus really did perform healings. In fact, Smith sees magicians as basically good men.

While Smith agrees with Celsus on several points, including Jesus' illegitimacy, he is closer to Renan in his overall appraisal of Jesus. Strauss had also considered hypnosis as an explanation of Jesus' healings (see Hodgson, 1972, p. xliii). Quite a few writers have worked this theory into their Jesus stories. For example, in his 1894 novel, which depicts Jesus as an Essene, Paul de Régla depicts the miracles as some form of 'suggestion and hypnotism' (Schweitzer, 1998b, p. 325). Similarly, in Pierre Nahor's (1905) novel, *Life of Jesus*, Jesus received indoctrination 'into all kinds of Egyptian, Essene and Indian philosophy', including 'a practical acquaintance with the secrets of hypnotism'. He survived the cross by 'putting himself into a cataleptic trance' (*ibid.*, pp. 325–7; I return to Essenic links below).

Later, says Smith, Christian embarrassment that Jesus had apparently used 'magical or semi-magical elements' to perform his healing may be why Matthew omits 'spitting' from Mark's account (Sanders, 1993, p. 153). Jesus might also have read people's minds, since some sort of telepathy is 'almost necessary for a successful magician' (Morton Smith, 1978, p. 115). Jesus, says Smith, clearly recognized 'belief' as an important factor in his ability to effect cures; a faith-healer's power 'depends to some extent on the patient's belief in him' (p. 14).

## Who was Jesus?

Smith's sources allow him to provide many aspects of the Jesus story with alternative explanations. The Eucharist becomes a rite in which the disciples (the magician's inner circle) identify themselves symbolically with their master, the 'magician identifies himself with a deity, and . . . wine and/or food with the blood and/or body of this deity and of himself' (p. 138). The rite's purpose was to unite all participants in common love; hence 'I give you a new commandment, that you love one another' (p. 123; John 13:34), and other references to unity between Jesus and his disciples. Jesus' promise that whenever his name is invoked he will be present parallels similar promises found in the magical literature (p. 124). Baptism, the scene in *Secret Mark*, and at Mark 14:51, and the transfiguration (see p. 122) all become initiation rites or magical seances, probably involving nudity. Smith's Jesus was a sexual libertine (see p. 67). The secret knowledge, or mystery of the Kingdom of God, or 'The truth which shall set you free' (p. 136) refers to initiation. Love becomes 'sexual promiscuity'.

Jesus' retreat into the wilderness, after receiving a spirit (or being deified at his baptism; p. 96), parallels how a shaman, at the start of his career, withdraws 'into solitude and subjects himself to a strict regime of self-torture' (p. 104). 'Flying through the air and turning stones into bread', too, 'were typical feats of magicians' (p. 105). The friends of a Magus, says Smith, would see him as a 'divine man' (p. 74), while his family probably would not. Thus, the estrangement between Jesus and his family (his denial of Mary at Mark 3:33; see pp. 24–8), and his inability to perform miracles in Nazareth (p. 15), can be explained. His followers became his substitute family: 'If anyone comes to me and does not hate his own father and mother . . . he cannot be my disciple' (Luke 14:26). If Jesus' birth was irregular, says Smith, he would have been 'ridiculed as a child'. In response, he rejected his own family and townsfolk and 'had nothing to do with them through all his later career' (p. 27). Embarrassment over Jesus' parentage may be one reason why the Church later provided a supernatural alternative, or doctored genealogies, 'with lists of ladies in the holy family who were not wholly holy' (p. 28). The Marxist scholar, Maxime Rodinson (1961), similarly drew on parallels between aspects of Muhammad's experience and shamanism to shed light on the former (see p. 56 on the 'opening of the heart' incident). Such comparisons place these phenomena in a universal context, which can then be analysed and discussed scientifically.

## Jesus and Judaism

A Magus would place himself above the law; thus Jesus' antinomian sayings (see Morton Smith, 1978, p. 55). His miracles, too, would give these sayings a special authority (p. 137). Smith agrees with Sanders, though, that Jesus would not have been in conflict with the Pharisees ('Appendix A, 'the Pharisees in the Gospels', pp. 153–7). Indeed, Smith thinks it unlikely that Jesus would have encountered many (p. 157; cited by Sanders, 1985, p. 390 n. 90). Yet like Renan's, Smith's Jesus is otherwise pitted against the Mosaic code and Jewish religious practice. The followers of a Magus would believe that he could survive death; Magi could 'send men alive into the world of the dead and bring them back again' (p. 73). Ascent into heaven was taken as 'the true test of deification' (p. 124). The post-resurrection appearances to the initiates (who usually numbered ten, not twelve, in early polemic; see p. 66) may have 'reflected what they saw at his suggestion' (that is, by hypnosis). Jesus' 'postmortem appearances . . . going through locked doors, empowering his followers to handle serpents . . . breathing into them the holy spirit' are all 'without exception paralleled in magical material' (p. 124).

There is a sense, then, in which Smith's Jesus stage-managed the resurrection, as he does in other accounts (see Thiering, below). However, Smith's Jesus did so within a wider magic tradition, of which he was part, not to cheat or to deceive people. Smith surmises that Jesus' popularity, his ability to attract crowds, somehow led to his incidental implication as a messianic pretender. His crowd-pulling potential frightened the Jewish authorities, who eventually 'had him seized and handed him over to Pilate', who 'had him crucified as a would-be-Messiah' (p. 17). Citing the tradition, alluded to several times in this book, that Jesus had been 'small, ugly and undistinguished' (p. 66), Smith suggests that magic might well account for Jesus' popularity. Neither Renan's nor Smith's Jesus had any political ambition, even though they were eventually executed on a trumped-up political charge (see Renan, 1927, p. 360).

Like Celsus, Reimarus, Strauss, Renan and others, Smith agrees that the incarnate son of God who, after preaching and teaching in Galilee, died and rose again to redeem mankind, is not a 'historical figure, but a mythological one' (1978, p. 3). Yet surprisingly, more so than many of the above, he retains the basic pattern, indeed many of the traditional events, of Jesus' life. Instead of rejecting material, he reinterprets it. As noted above, he accepts the Magi (the higher rank of magicians) as a genuine type of quasi-religious practitioner, who had something real to offer by way of actual cures to those who believed in their ability. 'They were,' he says, 'a powerful, ancient, mysterious, and oriental caste', even though 'scandalous stories circulated about them' (p. 71). Apollonius, for example, gained a reputation as a cultic reformer and became a hero in influential Pythagorean circles (p. 86).

Smith's Jesus does not resemble the Christ of faith. Nor need he, since Smith makes no claim to insidership. In the end, both Renan's and Smith's outsider Jesuses were good men, if overtaken by events beyond their control. Their Jesuses' motives were sincere, not devious (unlike Celsus' Jesus). Renan's Jesus would liberate us from dogma and from ecclesiastical authority. Smith's might lead us to rethink our approach to sexuality, which other writers have already encouraged us to do. William Blake, the eccentric English poet and engraver who lived in poverty and who never knew fame in life, also offers us a Jesus freed from dogma, who flew in the face of convention, and turned norms upside down. Unlike Renan or Smith, whose interests lay in historical research and in questions of textual interpretation, Blake's lay exclusively in the Christ of faith.

## William Blake (1757–1827)

I became a Blake admirer while at Manchester University, first attracted by his engraving, *The Ancient of Days*, displayed in the university's Whitworth Art Gallery. In my final year as an undergraduate, I wrote my special study on Blake. Later, this became one of my earliest published articles (Bennett, 1982). Blake lived in two worlds, the miserable world of an unknown artisan-artist and the world of visions. He believed that the latter world was more real than the former, and that a system of 'correspondences' connected the two. The life of the spirit, of freedom, of imagination, of art, was more real than that of the body. As long as we remain captive to reason, to empirical laws, to constraints, to 'do's' and 'don'ts', we remain cut off from the world of power and energy. 'Energy,' he wrote, 'is eternal delight' (Keynes, 1966, p. 149). In the physical world, Man is the 'correspondent' of the Divine, which is why the 'naked human form divine', beautifully executed, dominates Blake's art: 'Art and Science can not exist but by naked beauty display'd' (*ibid.*, p. 755).

In his system, Jesus is the Man-God, Man as he was before the Fall, Man as he will one day become ('Man' is correct here, since Blake thought that ultimately the female would be subsumed into the male). The Fall is less a historical event than a dimension of human experience. Jesus is pure spirit, unrestrained energy, which is 'the only life' (*ibid.*, p. 149). The Bible contains many errors, such as the false teaching that there is a body and a soul, that God will torment people in eternity, that desires should be restrained, that hell is real. By embracing opposites, progress can be made: 'Without contraries is no progression, Attraction and Repulsion, Reason and Energy, Love and Hate, are necessary to the human condition' (*ibid.*). By rejecting constraints, by embracing hell, through freedom from dogma, from schooling, from all that binds the soul, the life of energy can be achieved. Blake sympathized with revolutions, because they break laws and liberate people. Jesus had known no dogma:

> And the gates of the chapel were shut,
> And 'Thou shalt not' writ over the door,
> So I turned to the Garden of Love,
> That so many sweet flowers bore. (p. 215)

### Conversations with Socrates and Jesus

Intriguingly, Blake's writings touch on many issues or questions raised throughout this book. 'Was Jesus born of a Virgin?' he asks, and continues that if 'He intended to take on sin, / The Mother should an harlot been', which almost sounds as if he had read Celsus. 'Was Jesus Chaste?' he asked (p. 754). Blake appears to have advocated the breaking of sexual taboos: 'Abstinence sows sand all over / The ruddy limbs and flaming hair, / But Desire gratified / Plants fruits of life and beauty there' (p. 178). Priests were wrong to bind 'with briars' our human 'joys and desires' (*ibid.*). In the passage quoted at the start of this chapter, Blake asked whether Jesus had said anything original that the philosophers had not already said. For Blake, Jesus' significance lay not in his sayings but in his life of the spirit that allowed all sins to be forgiven (p. 757). Jesus cursed the rulers, disobeyed his parents, associated with sinners. Blake also expressed concern for the poor and needy: 'The Church is cold but the Ale House is healthy and pleasant and warm,' he wrote in *The Little Vagabond* (p. 216).

Blake had little time for conventional Christianity that preoccupied itself with matters of dogma, not charity. Blake, I believe, can properly be described as a free-thinker. He was also a humanist. In the end, for Blake, the human and the divine are synonymous. We are all divine, all Christ. He once called himself 'Socrates', suggesting that the wisdom that informed Socrates informs all people. Blake had infinite confidence in Man: 'the desire of man is infinite, the possession is infinite and himself infinite' (p. 97). The diarist Henry Crabb Robinson (1775–1867) recorded this conversation:

On my asking 'In what light he [Blake] viewed the great questions of the duty of Jesus', he said, 'He is the only God. But then', he added, 'and so am I, and so are you' . . . 'I was Socrates' [he said], and then, as if correcting himself, 'a sort of brother. I must have had a conversation with him. So I had with Christ . . . we all co-exist with the Divine Body. We are all partakers of Divine Nature.' (cited in Langridge, 1904, pp. 63–4)

Robinson's records of his conversations with Blake contribute significantly to our knowledge of his thought.

## The Jesus-was-a-myth school

I now turn to the genre of writers who argue that there never was a Jesus of Nazareth, that he never existed. They also draw on early pagan critique, and suggest that all that Paul did (he is often credited with Jesus' invention) was to create a composite character from pre-existing pagan beliefs. This reminds me of a scene towards the end of Scorsese's *The Last Temptation*. The married and sexually active Jesus is visiting a market with his son when he hears Paul preaching about the risen and crucified Jesus Christ. He approaches Paul, and points out that he had not died on the cross but is alive and well. Paul's response is, 'Oh, I'm not talking about that Jesus! That is not the Jesus the world needs. My Jesus is much more powerful.' Jesus rebukes Paul for telling lies. Incidentally, the film shows the married Jesus as one of two possible futures. In the end, when he sees the consequences of his disciples' militancy against Rome, he rejects this option and returns to the cross.

There have been some distinguished contributors to the Jesus-was-a-myth school, beginning with Robert Taylor (1784–1844), a British free-thinker, and Bruno Bauer (1809–82), an early admirer of Strauss. Many of these scholars are self-confessed rationalists, or free-thinkers. Several held high office in such organizations as the Rationalist Press Association. Like Blake, a number of these writers, who achieved no mean reputation for their scholarship as well as distinction in their professional careers, were completely self-educated. There is considerable overlap between the contents of these books, so I will not discuss individual titles in any great detail. Instead, I indicate the main arguments of this approach and introduce some of its most important contributors.

### Robert Taylor

The credit for inventing the Jesus-was-a-myth view may go to Robert Taylor. Taylor qualified as a Member of the Royal College of Surgeons in 1807, then graduated in divinity from Cambridge (1813). Ordained as an Anglican cleric, he served several curacies but quickly encountered criticism for preaching Deism, as well as for ministerial incompetence (Gordon, 1932, p. 461). Denied promotion, Taylor set up his own independent congregation. After hiring an old chapel, he and his supporters moved to the former Salters' Hall Chapel in London's Cannon Street, which they purchased following their successful petition to Parliament to allow Deists to 'give evidence on oath' (ibid., p. 462). From his new pulpit, Taylor preached a natural religion based on 'love of Truth, practice of virtue and the influence of Universal benevolence' (Taylor, 1828, p. 1).

Found guilty of blasphemy in 1828, Taylor was imprisoned in Oakham Gaol. During the trial, he had to wear full clerical dress. While in prison, he wrote *Syntagma* (1828) and *The Diegesis* (1829), in which he explained Christianity's origin as a rehash of pre-existing myths. The Free Thought Press republished *The Diegesis* in 1882. Taylor regarded himself as a prisoner of conscience (title-page, 1828). After his release from prison in 1833 he married a wealthy widow and worked as a surgeon in France.

'Every dogma and every ceremony,' he wrote, 'of the Evangelical Mythology' can be found in the legends of the 'gods and goddesses of Greece and Rome, and more especially of the Indian idol, Chrishna' (1828, p. iv). He identified numerous parallels between Jesus and Krishna (and note how he rendered Krishna's name; see *ibid.*, pp. 91–101). He referred to Adonis, Apollo, Krishna, Prometheus, Mercury and others as pre-Christian Jesuses. Christianity, he stated, merely reworked the ideas of 'Heliolatry and Idolatry' (p. 123). Thus, all its doctrines were 'in the world many ages before the period which Christianity assigns as their first promulgation' (*ibid.*, p. 125). If he sounds like Celsus this is no surprise, since he quotes him several times (pp. 113, 121, 127).

Put bluntly, Jesus never existed, and the idea that he did contradicts 'the immutable laws of sound reason' (p. iii). On the other hand, 'Paul of Tarsus . . . is unquestionably a real character' (p. 101). The Gospels are 'forgeries', a term that became popular with the Jesus-was-a-myth school (p. 19). Their authors plagiarized 'pagan documents' and other stories (p. 124). The crucifixion was pure myth (p. 109). Taylor thought that sun-worship lay behind all religions. He drew on Sir William Jones' *Asiatic Researches* (1799–1801) for his material on Krishna. Jones (1746–94), founder of the Asiatic Society of Bengal (1784), proposed the theory that Sanskrit, Greek, Latin, German and Celtic were linguistic cousins.

Since Taylor did not reference his comparison of Christ and Krishna, it is impossible to tell whether his ideas were original, or derived from earlier writers. Jones certainly hinted at a comparison. He referred to 'Chrishna' as 'the incarnate deity, born of a virgin, and miraculously escaping in his infancy from the reigning tyrant' (Jones, 1799–1801, Vol. 7, p. 273). He also noted that Christian missionaries resorted to Justin Martyr's strategy to explain similarities between the two stories: the Devil had counterfeited Christianity. Taylor's writing was polemical, lacking finesse, yet it demonstrates how much material was available for theorists to use, even before Strauss pioneered biblical criticism, or Frazer comparative mythology.

In 1877, when Madame Helena Petrovna Blavatsky (1831–91), co-founder of the Theosophical Society, wrote *Isis Unveiled*, she could take it for granted that the Buddha, Krishna and Jesus stories were all versions of the same legend and that the 'Christian dogmatizers' had 'added the fables of Hercules, Orpheus and Bacchus' (1995, Vol. 2, p. 539). Taylor's idea that sun-worship lay behind the hero myth may also have been pioneering, pre-dating the work of F. Max Müller (1823–1900), for whom Indo-European mythology began as stories about the sun. Salman Rushdie (1999) refers to 'Müller's disciples' attempting to 'prove that Jesus Christ and his disciples were nothing more than fairy-tale versions of the sun and the twelve signs of the zodiac' (p. 41).

## Bruno Bauer

Bauer was a professor at Bonn when he developed his theory that Jesus had never existed. Examining Strauss' *Life of Jesus*, he came to the conclusion that a writer armed with a list of Hebrew prophecies about the Messiah, and with notions drawn from paganism of an eternal logos, did not need a historical Jesus to write the gospel narratives. Rather, everything that is 'said of Him, everything that is known of Him, belongs to the world of imagination' (Schweitzer, 1998b, p. 156). In 1842, Bauer was deprived of his job. He spent the rest of his life writing secular histories.

Bauer dated the 'original gospel', which formed the basis of the four Gospels, as late as Hadrian's reign (117–38). Jesus was a 'Judaeo-Roman' idol concocted from Seneca (4 BCE–65 CE) and Josephus. Schweitzer commented, 'In place of the personality of Jesus', Bauer 'set up a hybrid thing, laboriously compounded out of two personalities of so little substance as those of Seneca and Josephus' (*ibid.*, p. 158). Bauer, said Schweitzer, wanted to free the human soul from history, to free the world 'for a higher religion in which the ego will overcome nature . . . by penetrating it and ennobling it' (*ibid.*, p. 156).

## James George Frazer (1854–1941)

Frazer, the Cambridge anthropologist, who turned to a systematic study of religious myth and symbol in the ancient world, discovered that certain beliefs and practices were widespread across a range of cultures. Interested in its origins, Frazer believed that religion sprang from a primitive desire to manage the environment, to control the sun, the rain and fertility. Basic patterns kept emerging within different mythologies. Frazer even found multiple 'hanged Gods'. This did not necessarily mean contact and borrowing, but suggests that humans develop similar myths in similar situations. Others developed the concept of an ancient 'hero' myth, which was replicated in the stories of Jesus, Mithras, Krishna and the Buddha.

In *The Golden Bough* (originally published in 1890), Frazer gathered together many parallels between Christianity and pagan religion, and the idea of archetypal myths and stories was born. Although a devout Christian, Frazer believed that religion would eventually yield to science. He wrote:

The skeptic . . . will . . . with . . . confidence . . . reduce Jesus of Nazareth to the level of a multitude of other victims of a superstition, and will see in him no more than a moral teacher, whom the unfortunate accident of his execution invested with the crown, not merely of a martyr, but of a god. (1994, p. 676)

While Frazer did not doubt that Jesus had lived, or claim that Christians had invented the Jesus myth, his work became a source book of ideas and data for many who did. In fact, Schweitzer includes Frazer in a list of scholars who 'contested the historical existence of Jesus . . . John M. Robertson, William Benjamin Smith, James George Frazer, Arthur Drews' (1998a, p. 125).

Frazer, as an anthropologist, claimed scientific status for his theories about religion. So did Sigmund Freud (1856–1939), the father of psychoanalyses, who drew on Frazer in his writing about religion. Freud claimed that all mental illness is caused by sexual neuroses, including religion, which for him was a type of malady. The common association of the Fall (Genesis) with sex fitted Freud's thesis. So did the crucifixion of a divine son. This, said Freud, represents restoration for the primordial, archetypal father's murder by his son, consumed with sexual jealousy. Later, the primal father was deified (Freud, 1990, p. 330). Jesus had to die because the crime of slaying the father could only be expiated by the death of the son. Furthermore, 'Atonement with the Father was all the more complete since the sacrifice was accompanied by a total renunciation of the woman on whose account the rebellion against the Father was started' (*ibid.*, p. 216). Later, says Freud, the son replaced the father and 'the ancient totem meal was revived in the form of communion in which the company of brothers consumed the flesh and blood of the son – no longer the father' (p. 217). This page quotes Frazer: 'The Christian communion has absorbed within itself a sacrament which is doubtless far older than Christianity.'

## Carl Gustav Jung and Joseph Campbell

The idea of archetypes standing behind all salvation stories and saviour figures also informed the work of Carl Gustav Jung (1875–1961) and Joseph Campbell (1904–87). Jung was an early colleague of Freud who parted company with him on the sexual origin of all maladies as well as on the idea that religion was a form of psychosis. Jung held the religious, or the sacred, in high esteem, claiming that the spiritual dimension of human experience is as real and important as the physical or the scientific and enables us to access our true, inner selves. For Jung, an archetype lay behind all hero myths and represents a positive primordial awareness of our spiritual origins. Jung also saw his work on religion as *science*, not as philosophical speculation, or as *theory*. Campbell, a graduate of Columbia who taught for many years at Sarah Lawrence College, New York, was influenced by Frazer, Freud and by Jung. His *The Hero with a Thousand Faces* (1949) advanced the theory that a single myth stands behind the stories of Krishna, Buddha, Apollonius of Tyana, Jesus, and other hero stories.

Campbell also studied Sanskrit and assisted Swami Nikhilanda (1895–1973) in his translation work on *The Gospel of Ramakrishna* (1942). More so than Frazer, and like the earlier and pioneering Taylor, he looked eastwards for his data. A friend of filmmaker George Lucas, something of Campbell's belief in the *Power of Myth* (1991) informed the science fiction *Star Wars* series, in which the forces of light and good fight those of darkness and evil, and heroes rise up to lead the righteous. Typically, hero myths feature pre-birth omens, predictions of future greatness, the slaying of infants, mysterious visitors, followed by the subject's display of precocious wisdom. The baby Buddha walks and speaks; in the Qur'an, the infant Jesus speaks. When Muhammad's mother conceived him, a light shone from her, illuminating even the faraway castle at Busra. Lao Tzu, old and wise at birth, was born from a star. Undoubtedly ancient, this hero-myth formula continues to give story-tellers good service, even through such a thoroughly modern genre as science fantasy. In James Cameron's *The Terminator* (1984), a machine-villain (later a machine-guardian) comes from the future to murder the yet unborn saviour's mother. The saviour has the initials 'JC'.

In Larry and Andy Wachowski's *The Matrix* (1999) an oracle prophesies that 'the one' will become humanity's redeemer. 'The one' is sought out by a John the Baptist-type forerunner. He dies and lives again to become a 'new man' possessed of remarkable powers. *The Power of Myth* was Campbell's own television programme, shot at Lucas' ranch between 1985 and 1986. Campbell did not believe in 'the Other' but he did believe in human ability to think thoughts and to dream dreams. All these concepts, primordial myths, archetypes, cosmic duels between good and evil, inform the writing of the Jesus-was-a-myth school. Renan, Smith and Blake were disgusted by many aspects of traditional Christianity, as they were by the Church's historical record, yet they were able to see through Christian dogma to a remarkable personality, to a real Jesus behind the Christians' Jesus. Convinced that religion was bad for people, Taylor, Bauer, and the writers to whom I now turn perhaps feared that, if they admitted anything redeemable about Jesus, some might claim that Christianity could also be redeemed. Their goal, the demise of religion, demanded the death of Jesus.

### John Mackinnon Robertson (1856–1933)

Before entering politics as Member of Parliament for Tyneside between 1906 and 1918, Robertson worked as a journalist and editor. He served briefly in the Cabinet and was made a Privy Councillor, with the title of Right Honourable. A leading member of the Rationalist Press Association and a committed free-thinker, he wrote erudite and scholarly works on modern rationalism and the history of free-thought, as well as becoming 'one of the leading Shakespearean scholars of his time' (Laski, 1949, p. 736). Apart from some early schooling, Robertson was self-educated. He defined free thought as 'a conscious reaction against some phase or phases of conventional or traditional religion . . . a claim to think freely . . . not of disregard for logic, but of special loyalty to it' (Robertson, 1957, p. 5). On Jesus, he wrote *Christianity and Mythology* (1900) and *Pagan Christs* (2nd edn 1911). He drew on Frazer and on early pagan polemicists, including Celsus.

Robertson stresses Christian indebtedness to Mithraism, whose symbols and institutions it assumed (1911, p. 338). He documented similarities between the Krishna, Buddha and Jesus stories, and suggests that none of these men had ever actually existed:

All the leading gods, as we have seen, were in some measure regarded as teachers, and for none of them do we surmise a historic original in the sense of a real teacher and lawgiver. (p. 237)

Robertson implies direct contact between the Jesus and the Vedic traditions (see 1911, pp. 218–20). The possibility of actual contact between India and the Mediterranean world cannot be ruled out. The Aryans appear to have settled in Europe and India and there are too many linguistic as well as mythic similarities to dismiss contact. Iran's Mithra is probably related to the Vedic god Mitra, the day counterpart of the night sky god Varuna. Alexander the Great invaded India. The Emperor Ashoka

(273–232 BCE) sent Buddhist missionaries out far and wide. One of Salman Rushdie's characters in *The Ground beneath Her Feet* (1999) compares 'The abduction of Helen of Troy by Paris' with Sita's by Ravana. He goes on to speak of 'the relationship between Hanuman, the wily monkey god, and the devious Odysseus'; and of 'the parallels between the tragedy of the House of Atreus and that of Rama's clan' (p. 41).

John Adams (1735–1826), second president of the USA, writing in 1817 to its third president Jefferson (1743–1826), claimed that 'Pythagoras passed 20 years in his Travels in India [where] he conversed with the Brahmans and read the Shastras, 5000 years old, written in the language of the sacred Sankritists with the elevated elements of Plato' (cited in Tweed and Prothero, 1999, p. 39). Robertson credits Paul with combining elements of paganism with aspects of messianic Jewish expectations to concoct Christianity (1911, p. 146). He wrote: 'The only conclusion is that the teaching of Jesus of the gospels is wholly a construction of the propagandists of the cult' (*ibid.*, p. 237). Paganism provided all the ingredients: virgin birth, dying and rising, the divine victim, vicarious salvation, drinking of the blood, wonders surrounding the saviour's birth. Robertson thought that Christianity's dogmatism stifled progress, that civilization needed free-thought to flourish. He seemed, though, to warm to Christianity's antinomian expressions. According to one writer, Robertson advocated 'free love' (Historicus, 1972, p. 8, citing McCabe).

## A New Age contributor

One recent proponent of the Jesus-myth theory, Acharya S, who also sees Christianity as an ongoing conspiracy, argues that there was an ancient global civilization in which ideas and hero myths circulated freely (1999, p. 391). Like other writers, Acharya S criticizes the Christian conspirators for using force and deception to perpetuate the Jesus myth, annihilating cultures, destroying books and murdering millions. 'Yet,' she says, 'there are those today who not only support its monstrous edifice, built on the blood and charred bones of tens of millions, as well as the death of learning in the Western world, but, unbelievingly, wish it to be restored to its full "glory"' (p. 11). Acharya S writes from a New Age perspective. She suggests that as the world moves into a new epoch, towards the threat of chaos, it can learn something positive from the unity of ideas that lies behind the Jesus myth. 'By realizing the cultural unity revealed behind the Christ conspiracy,' she suggests, 'humanity can pull together and prevent this fall, to create a better world' (p. 417).

She gives lists of similarities between the stories of Horus, Bacchus, Mithra, Buddha, Krishna, Zoroaster and Jesus (see Chapter 9, 'The Characters', pp. 103–27). Among others, she draws on Frazer, Robertson, Wheless and Campbell as well as on Robert Taylor and another pioneer in this field of comparative Jesus study, Godfrey Higgins (1771–1833). Higgins, who also wrote a book endorsing Muhammad's sincerity (1829), placed Jesus in the context of the Essenes, Pythagoras and astrology. His *Anacalypses: An Attempt to Draw Aside the Veil of the Saitic Isis: Or an Enquiry into the Origins of Language, Nations and Religions* was published posthumously (1836; reprinted 1965). Although dismissed critically, it was valued for the 'thousands of statements' which it served to index, and was therefore placed in the public reading room of the British Museum (*The Athenaeum*, No. 1501, 2 August 1856, p. 953). There are several recent reprints.

## Arthur Drews (1865–1935)

In Germany, Robertson's ideas found an able champion in Arthur Drews, a high school teacher of philosophy at Karlsruhe. He developed a monistic understanding of the relationship between the human and the divine, and saw Christianity as of Gnostic origin. Like Robertson, he denied the historicity of the person of Jesus. Robertson, he wrote, had 'traced the picture of Christ . . . to a mixture of mythological elements in heathenism and Judaism' (1998, p. 8). 'As a purely historical individual', wrote Drews, Jesus 'sinks back to the level of other great historical personalities, and from the religious point of view is exactly as unessential as they' (p. 19). Robertson and Drews gained considerable recognition for scholarship but professional Christian academics dismissed their work as unscientific. Drews observed:

The storm which has been raised against my book in theological circles and in the press, and has even led to mass meetings of protest . . . shows me that I have hit the bull's eye. (p. 23)

Schweitzer, in discussing Drews and the Jesus-was-a-myth school, dismissed this theory out of hand: 'How can men who think seriously come to the conclusion that the ideas of Christianity do not go back to Jesus, but merely represent a transformation of ideas which stirred religious circles in the heathen world?' (1923, p. 23). 'The hypothesis of His existence,' he wrote, 'is a thousand times easier to prove than that of His non-existence.' Drews' reference to every myth he could find strained the imagination (1998a, p. 125).

## George Albert Wells

Wells, author of several Jesus-was-a-myth books, writes how 'others took the view that only trained theologians and not an outsider such as' himself could 'contribute to the discussion' (1975, p. 2). A professor emeritus of German at Birkbeck College, London, and a former president of the Rationalist Press Association, Wells received the Humanist Laureate in 1983 from the Academy of Humanism, the highest honour for a free-thinker. In his writing, he discusses many of the pagan parallels offered by Robertson and Drews and dismisses Josephus' references to Jesus as forgeries. His own preferred explanation of Christianity's origin is as Paul's creation, drawing on Jewish wisdom traditions. 'Paul,' he writes, 'found Jesus portrayed in terms of Wisdom in some already preexisting Christ hymns and assimilated them because they accorded well with his own thinking' (1975, p. 28).

Wells makes much of the fact that Paul seems to have no knowledge of Jesus' life. Like Taylor, he does not seem to doubt that Paul had really existed. Interestingly, one could argue that Paul's existence is less well documented than Jesus'. Also commenting on Paul's apparent lack of interest in the details of Jesus' life, Jewish scholar Samuel Sandmel suggests that Jesus' earthly career was irrelevant for Paul's purposes: 'The death of Jesus meant nothing to Paul; the death of *Christ Jesus* meant a cosmic incident.' Had reference to details of Jesus' earthly life aided Paul's theological project he would have supplied this, says Sandmel (1958, p. 216; on Sandmel, see my next chapter). In 1987, Wells edited a book on Robertson, which suggests that he self-consciously identifies with the earlier *Liberal, Rationalist and Scholar* (from the book's subtitle).

## Joseph Wheless (1868–1950)

Also self-taught, Wheless was a successful lawyer and a very outspoken Jesus-was-a-myth writer. He studied for the bar while articled in his uncle's firm. Wheless served as counsel for several American free-thinking organizations and defended many cases involving issues of atheism. A specialist in South American law, he was also for some time an instructor in military jurisprudence at the University of Arkansas and a major in the Judge Advocate General's Department. For his writing on religious topics, he received the honorary DD from the University of Denver. His writing did not spare any punches. Not only had no one called Jesus ever lived, but Christianity and the Bible are based on deliberate fraud. Christianity's continued existence is a conspiracy. It uses persecution and oppression to perpetuate its myths, to enslave people with its dogmas. His titles include *Is It God's Word?* (1926), *Debunking the Law of Moses* (1929) and *Forgery in Christianity* (1930), and his books are still in print. Many are available on various internet sites, such as http://www.infidel.org and www.freethinkers.org. Wheless set out his 'indictment' in Chapter 1 of *Forgery*: 'The Bible is in its every book, and the strictest legal sense, a huge forgery . . . of the Christian church', and 'That every conceivable falsehood, lie, fraud and imposture has ever been the work of Priests' (p. 10).

## Joseph Martin McCabe (1867–1955)

In England, a similarly robust and hard-hitting exposition of the forgery and fraud theory came from the prolific pen of Joseph McCabe, the only writer reviewed in this section to have had formal theological training. McCabe was a Franciscan monk for twelve years. As a monk, he served as professor of philosophy, then left the priesthood to spend the rest of his life denouncing the Church and defending free thought. In 1897, he wrote *Twelve Years in a Monastery* and *Modern Rationalism*, which earned him his literary reputation. Sir Leslie Stephen (1832–1904), probably the most influential agnostic in Victorian England, befriended him and encouraged him to write. A founder of the Rationalist Press Association, McCabe produced countless titles, tracts, translations and articles. He married in 1899 and wrote *The Key to Love and Sex* in 1929. He was very outspoken against the Church's attitude towards sex.

In *The Story of Religious Controversy* (1930) he described himself as 'a Feminist' (p. 10), joining in the fight for the female franchise. He believed that women in particular had fallen victim to Christian bigotry. His biographer describes him as 'a great humanist' who 'championed many unpopular causes designed to free man from the tyranny of Church, squire and industrial magnate' (Reeves, 1971, p. 662). An advocate of evolutionary thought, he dismissed any necessary link between religion and morality. Popular within humanist and free-thought circles, this view gained a powerful spokesman in Bertrand Russell. The main virtue, said Russell, 'is intelligence', which is 'impeded by any creed, no matter what' (1957, p. 205). Russell also singled out for criticism the Christian attitude towards sex, which he called 'the worse feature of the Christian religion . . . so morbid and unnatural' (*ibid.*, p. 26). Freud from psychology and Russell from philosophy did much to advance the notion that religious belief is a relic of humanity's infancy, not a mark of maturity.

In *The Testament of Christian Civilization* (1946), McCabe chronicled a dismal tale of Christianity's negative influence on human progress. His tracts include such titles as *The Totalitarian Church of Rome* (1942) and *The Tyranny of the Clerical Gestapo* (also 1942). Many of his publications are available on the internet at www.infidel.org, including his *Biographical Dictionary of Ancient, Medieval and Modern Freethinkers* (1920). He accused the Pope of supporting Hitler during the Second World War (see *The Vatican's Last Crime* (1942)). His *Forgery of the Old Testament and Other Essays* was republished by the Free Thought Library in 1993. On one vital issue, he distanced himself from Robertson, whom he criticized:

Robertson who was tireless in research though not very critical when he found something that seemed to suit his theory, supported the negative view with such an impressive apparatus of comparative mythology that even his dullest and most ponderous works on the subject had a large circulation. (1943, p. 11)

McCabe believed that the origin of Christianity was 'more intelligible on the theory that a human teacher of great impressiveness really forms the core of the story' (1909, p. 102). McCabe resigned from the Rationalist Press Association before his death, claiming that it was not radical enough. He was also disgusted by the reactions of some free-thinkers to his rejection of the 'there never was a Jesus' theory. How could this be mandatory for free thought when free thought had no dogmas, he said.

Former Carmelite nun Phylis Graham, in *The Jesus Hoax* (1974), recounts how her not un-McCabe-like disillusionment with Christianity, especially with its ideas of punishment or reward, led her to reject its historical basis. 'One is left,' she wrote, 'with the impression that the character depicted in the gospels, if not entirely mythical, presents such insuperable problems to human interpretation, that it could well be a piecemeal collective portrait rather than a genuine report' (p. 187). Citing McCabe, Celsus and Bertrand Russell among others, she looks forward to the day when 'rational man' will finally free himself from the shackles of religion, from belief in heaven and hell, to explore the universe for himself. Thus, something 'grander' and 'better' than religion will evolve (p. 230). Josephus, she says, is a 'key witness to the non-existence of a historical Jesus' (p. 189).

## A. N. Wilson

Wilson is a self-declared anti-Christian apologist, whose life of Jesus (1992) became a bestseller and received 'the media equivalent of a 21 gun salute' (Wright, 1992, p. vii). In *Against Religion* (1991), Wilson wrote, 'We cannot see any hope of a society in which formal organized religion dies out. But we can stop behaving as if it was worthy of our collective respect' (p. 48). Like McCabe, Wilson detests the Church but upholds the historicity of Jesus. He argues, though, that the Christ of faith is Pauline, with very little if any connection with the real Jesus (see *ibid.*, p. xvi; pp. 17–43 are on Paul). His *Paul: The Mind of the Apostle* was published in 1997. He draws especially on the work of Geza Vermes and Hyam Maccoby (see Chapter 5). Jesus had only wanted to make Jews better Jews (1992, p. 106). His real legacy was kept alive by James (see 1992, p. 248; 1997, pp. 68–9). Wilson rejects the traditional account of Jesus' trial and death, including the institution of the Lord's Supper, which he attributes to Paul (1992, p. 21). 'No real evidence can be found,' he writes, 'for Jesus' arrest or execution' (*ibid.*, p. 227). In fact, we can know very little for sure (p. 270). We may surmise that Jesus was executed, perhaps because the crowds took him to be a revolutionary, or the Messiah, which brought him unfavourably to the notice of the authorities. Jesus' message, though, was unintelligible to the crowds, who soon deserted him (p. 177). Wilson also points out that Jesus liked female company.

Wright (1992) calls Wilson's Jesus a 'pale and distorted version of the real thing' (p. 63). I do not find Wilson's account as engaging or as convincing a humanist portrait as Renan's, which shows how much difference is possible even when initial assumptions are similar. I am, however, less confident than Wright that we have an agreed picture with which to contrast or compare Wilson's Jesus. Given Wright's view that insiders can best address the Jesus material, it is not surprising that he rejects Wilson's claim to historical impartiality. 'This is the myth of objectivity,' says Wright, 'the idea that a "neutral" observer . . . is a mere fly on the wall, perceiving things with almost a God's-eye view' (1992, p. 45). Wilson brings his presuppositions to the task, just as Christians do. Speculation on Paul's role, represented by such writers as Wells and Wilson, has produced many texts, including *From Jesus to Paul*, edited by Richardson and Hurd (1984), *Paul: Follower of Jesus or Founder of Christianity?* by David Wenham (1995) and *The Paul Quest* by Ben Witherington (1998). I refer to some books on Paul by Jewish writers in Chapter 6.

## R. Joseph Hoffmann and other contributors

Hoffmann has been closely associated with the Jesus-was-a-myth theory, although like McCabe and Wilson he upholds Jesus' historicity. He thinks there are many 'possible configurations' of Jesus' life (1986, p. 22). Hoffmann's doctoral work at Oxford was on Marcion (see Hoffmann, 1984). Subsequently, he has done work on Jesus outside the canonical gospels (1987, 1996), on Celsus (1987), from which I quoted earlier in this chapter, and on Porphyry's *Against the Christians* (1994). A 1986 volume on *Jesus in History and Myth*, which Hoffmann co-edited, brought together some of the writers reviewed in this chapter: G. A. Wells, Morton Smith, John Allegro. Hoffmann launched the series that recently republished Strauss' *The Old Faith and the New* and Drews' *The Christ Myth* (1998). With Morton Smith, he edited *What the Bible Really Says* (1989), which gave me some useful background for segments of this book.

Among other Jesus-was-a-myth writers are Earl Doherty (1999b), who maintains a website on *The Jesus Puzzle*, and Michael Martin (1993). Defending Jesus' historicity, Josh McDowell's writing (1989, 1993) is often targeted by the mythicists. Finally, the Jesus-was-a-myth theories of John Allegro (1923–88) and Barbara Thiering, which differ from those already discussed in drawing mainly on Dead Sea Scrolls material. These two writers serve as a bridge to the blood-line and neo-Gnostic material, to which I turn next in this chapter.

## 'Will the *real* Jesus Christ please stand up?' John Allegro and the Dead Sea Scrolls

When I began my theology degree at Manchester in 1974 the university was still recovering from the shock created by the publication of John Allegro's *The Sacred Mushroom and the Cross* (1970). Allegro (himself a Manchester graduate), who taught Near Eastern and Old Testament studies in the university, was a member of the first team of translators to work on the Dead Sea Scrolls, and told the story of their discovery, and investigation, in *The Dead Sea Scrolls* (1956). He later wrote *Discoveries in the Judaean Desert of Jordan* (1968). He is cited several times in Vermes (1997). Baigent and Leigh say that Allegro was the only member of the team who had an established 'academic reputation . . . before working on the scrolls' (1991, p. 29). In his 1956 book, Allegro shows how the scrolls shed useful light on the context in which the New Testament was written. He suggests some similarities between what Jesus taught and the teaching of the Qumran community's Master. In his chapter on 'The Qumran Sect and Jesus' he seems to accept the general outline of the traditional Jesus account as authentic. He writes, 'certain essential features of Jesus' life do seem to stand out clearly' (p. 151), and, 'Jesus is more of a flesh and blood character than the Qumran Teacher could ever be . . . due to the more complete records we possess of Jesus' life and ministry.' Nor had Jesus had any direct contact with Qumran (p. 166), although he would have known of the Essenes.

While Jesus' beliefs were similar to those of Qumran, their impact was much more 'widespread'. Thus, 'it seems reasonable to assume that Jesus was acquainted with them' (p. 161). Allegro also hinted that the Pauline Christianity which reached the Graeco-Roman world parted company from the Judaic roots of original Christianity; thus 'the faith that broke the bounds of Judaism and became a living fount of inspiration for the western world was far removed from Qumran Judaism' (p. 162). On the other hand, long after Qumran had been 'swept away', the 'basic elements' of its 'faith' found, through Christianity, 'a far wider setting and a significance for all mankind' (p. 162). By 1970, his views on the relationship between the Dead Sea Scrolls and the Jesus story had matured; in this bestseller, Jesus emerges as the 'code-name' of a secret society whose worship revolved around a sacred mushroom, the *ammanata muscaria*, a hallucinogenic fungus. Allegro located Christianity's origins 'Within the fertility cults of the Near East' (his subtitle).

In 1979 (the year after I graduated from Manchester) Allegro published his *The Dead Sea Scrolls and the Christian Myth*. I can detect no mention of mushrooms in this text. Here, Jesus is a 'myth' created by a complex process of synthesizing Essene, Gnostic and nascent Christian ideas about redemption. There never was a Jesus of Nazareth, although there might have been an Essene master, possibly called Joshua, who modelled himself on the teacher of righteousness: 'The Christian myth was based upon the Essene Teacher of Righteousness, and given his type-name, Joshua-Jesus' (1984, p. 226). Allegro has it that the early Church deliberately obscured the Essenic origin of its Messiah because this had little appeal for Roman and Greek believers: 'The words of the Nazarene Jesus reflected many of the teachings of the Essene Master, but were adapted to a more universal outlook and social order' (*ibid.*). It was by 'reckoning back from the destruction of the temple' that the later 'myth makers fastened upon the year AD 30 for the crucifixion of their latter day Joshua/Jesus' (*ibid.*). The resulting myth, too, was 'full of compromise and illogicalities' (*ibid.*). Allegro's Jesus never existed, yet by keeping aspects of Qumran's teaching alive his invention has served some good purpose. This radical reinterpretation of the Jesus story, which Allegro offered as serious (if difficult to take seriously) scholarship, serves to highlight just how much room there is for divergence of opinion on who Jesus was; indeed, on whether he even existed at all.

Despite the controversy it provoked, Allegro's theory was not novel. Speculation about Christianity's Essenic origin began with such works as Bahrdt's *Aushührung der Plans und Zwecks Jesus* (1792) and Paul de Régla's *Jesus von Nazareth* (1894). In the 1950s, Jacob Teicher of Cambridge advanced 'the thesis that Jesus was the Teacher of Righteousness and Saint Paul the Wicked Priest' (Vermes, 1997, p. 21). Another version, which also has St Paul playing the wicked priest, 'ignores Jesus, and casts his brother James in the role of the Teacher' (*ibid*.; see also Eisenmann, 1998). Groothuis (1990) has a chapter on 'Was Jesus an Essene?' (pp. 175–94). 'Will the *real* Jesus Christ please stand up?' asks Allegro (1984, p. 190). He may not be so far from the mark. A link, too, between this alternative account and the genre of blood-line and holy grail literature which I discuss below is suggested by the dedication to Allegro's memory, as a man twenty years ahead of his time, of *The Hiram Key: Pharaohs, Freemasons and the Discovery of the Dead Sea Scrolls* by Christopher Knight and Robert Lomas (1997). Allen (1998) is critical of Allegro's earlier scholarly achievements (p. 320). Baigent and Leigh tend to see him as the only objective member of the Dead Sea Scrolls' team, who regarded him as a 'renegade' because he completed, and published on time, 'all the material entrusted to his charge' (1991, p. 51). When Allegro wrote *The Sacred Mushroom*, he not only had a respected academic post but also a bestselling title to his name (the 1956 Penguin book). Rumour on campus had it that he had been turned down for ordination, and subsequently turned against Christianity. However, Baigent and Leigh say that Allegro went 'to Jerusalem as an agnostic' (p. 29). It is, though, to Barbara Thiering's work that blood-line writers usually look for scholarly support.

### Barbara Thiering and the pesher code

Thiering has taught Old Testament, Hebrew and feminist theology at the University of Sydney since 1967. She developed an early interest in the Essenes and the Dead Sea Scrolls, and wrote a number of journal articles on similarities between the initiation rites of the Qumran community and Christian baptism (for example, in the *Journal of New Testament Studies*). She writes, 'A series of articles in academic journals established my speciality in the scrolls' (1992, p. 2). In publications from the early 1980s, she began to link Christian origins with Qumran (see 1981, 1983). She refers to Allegro's theory that 'the Church had stolen all its ideas from Qumran' as 'bizarre', and commented that his claims 'made it difficult for any genuine scholar to investigate closely the questions of Christian connections with the scrolls' (1992, p. 10). Her own credentials as a 'genuine' Dead Sea Scrolls scholar are hardly comparable with Allegro's. Her apparently critical, even dismissive, comment on Allegro is surprising, since she goes on to argue that Christian origins indeed lie within Qumran.

Her theory differs radically from Allegro's in its detail but there is at least one major similarity. Allegro attributed the obvious differences between Christianity, and the religion of Qumran, to the former's need to attract a wider constituency, within which the 'fundamentally anti-imperialist attitude of the Essenes of the teacher's time could hardly be expected to appeal' (1984, p. 226). In other words, a type of 'split' occurred, from which Christianity spread throughout the then known world while Qumran was swept into oblivion. Similarly, Thiering attributes the differences between Qumran and Christianity to a split between the latter and the former: 'There was a split, the Christians reacting strongly against some aspects of Qumran practice, while retaining basic organization and some doctrines' (1992, p. 11).

Thiering's thesis is that the differences between Jesus' teaching and Qumran (which I outlined in Chapter 1) have been 'used to *negate* the similarities'. Thus, in over-reaction to such writers as Allegro, scholars have stressed the 'striking differences' at the expense of the 'striking similarities'. The 'split' resolves the problem for Thiering, as for Allegro. Thus, in his foreword to Thiering's bestselling and controversial, *Jesus the Man* (1992), Leonie Star writes: 'that connections between the Dead Sea Scrolls and the gospels have been either down played or totally rejected by other scholars does nothing to invalidate Thiering's argument' (p. x). Crucial to Thiering's thesis is dating the teacher of righteousness, and the wicked priest, as contemporary with Jesus, which Thiering argued in her 1979 book, *Redating the Teacher of Righteousness* (see also 1992, p. 17).

Thiering believes that there was a man called Jesus, and that the Gospels record the main events of his life, but argues that the story they tell on the surface is a cover for the real story in which he was the wicked priest, whose lax and liberal attitude to the law opposed the teacher of righteousness. Events (virgin birth, miracles, resurrection) as described did not happen literally but 'nor were they myths, traditional legends, as scholars have often held' (1992, p. 4). Rather, 'the surface' contains a 'general religious message' suitable for unsophisticated readers, while 'beneath' lies 'specific historical matter, available only to those with special knowledge' (p. 21). This included the disciples, who possessed the secret code, or key, necessary to interpret the text. There is similarity here with mystic and Gnostic views – texts have layers of meaning accessible to people at different stages of spiritual development. Thiering's key to the real historical content of the Gospels (and of the Book of Acts) is the 'pesher technique' (pesher = interpretation in Hebrew), which, she says, 'is like the solution to a puzzle' (1992, p. 21). She first developed this theory in her 1981 book, *The Gospels and Qumran: A New Hypothesis*. She points out that Philo's 'life work was to go through the . . . Law finding . . . in allegorical form the insights of Greek philosophy' (1992, p. 409).

Her technique involves identifying a type of hidden code. Examples best explain how this works. The feeding of the five thousand, for example, becomes a type of ordination service: loaves = Levites. Jesus allowed twelve non-Levites to distribute 'loaves of the Presence from the sacred table' to the crowd of uninitiated Gentiles, who, by 'eating the loaves, became loaves themselves' (p. 25). In other words, Jesus was extending the privilege of priesthood not only to non-Levites but even to Gentiles. Thiering's Jesus broke Essene conventions in order to widen his own power base. Similarly, the 'turning water into wine' of John 2 refers to Jesus extending the privilege of receiving wine as well as water to community members who had not undergone the second, higher initiation (which was restricted to celibate Essenes). From this point, 'all adult members of Jesus' following, whether married, gentile, women, physically handicapped, racially different, slave or free, could come to the communion rails and receive the bread and wine' (p. 24). Terms such as 'crows', 'the Pharisees', are actually code-names for particular individuals; the 'dove' at Jesus' baptism refers to a person, as do animals in other passages. Stories of Jesus healing people, or of raising people from the dead, are code for people's promotion within the organization. In Thiering's favour, if Jesus was close to the Pharisees, who wanted the priestly rules of ritual purity to apply to all, and if Jesus was actually more radical than they were in his ideas, perhaps he did regard himself as the high priest's equal.

### Inside the text

Writers from Reimarus onwards have regarded these stories as fabrications; for Thiering, such stories as Jesus feeding the five thousand or raising Lazarus from the dead are authentic but their apparent meaning hides their real meaning. She is close here to Smith. His Jesus did much of what the Jesus in the Gospels did but he was really a magician mistaken as a Messiah. Thus, the gospel writers described what really did happen but glossed it with later Christian belief about who Jesus was, much of which had some authentic origin within his actual magician identity. Smith's key, which came from outside the Bible, provides its own 'magical' explanation of Jesus' life. Thiering's key lies, at first sight, embedded in the biblical text. However, from where does her explanation of the events referred to above derive? How does she know that the feeding of the five thousand was not a miracle invented to make Jesus greater than Elijah, or indeed that Jesus did not really feed a crowd? How does she know that it was an illicit ordination ceremony? She knows because she is convinced that Jesus was closely connected with the Essene community, so she interprets Jesus' whole life in terms of Essenic practice, indeed as a struggle for power within the movement. Without reference to Qumran, she cannot uncover her 'hidden' meaning. Her code did not emerge from a close reading of the biblical text as such but from a comparison of the Gospels with Qumran documents – her real 'key' is not so much her 'pesher technique' as her theories about the Qumran community. This, for her, is the real context in which Jesus lived, taught and ended his days. It provides for her what Smith's magical papyri provided for him, a framework, a system of practices and beliefs into which Jesus can be placed.

Thiering retains enough aspects of the 'surface' story to ensure that her alternative account bears some resemblance to the standard one. However, her Jesus was a man, born illegitimately to Mary and Joseph in a cave (known as Bethlehem) within the Qumran complex (see her Appendix II on 'Locations', 1992, pp. 285–331). Joseph sometimes worked as a carpenter while he was living among the village Essenes but his real identity was as 'the David' in waiting. According to Thiering, the Essenes expected that, when God intervened to drive out the Romans, a living descendant of David would rule as Messiah-king. Jesus' birth, and most gospel events, take place in Qumran, including the turning upside-down of the treasury tables (see 1992, p. 235) and his crucifixion (see below). *Jesus the Man* contains a chronology (with specific dates) of events leading up to, and following, Jesus' career; she gives a long and very detailed chronology at Appendix I (pp. 162–284). The book also contains tables and maps – for example, outlining the geography of Qumran, its hierarchy and worldview. These, says Wright (1992), 'give the book an appearance of scholarship' (p. 23).

## Jesus' political aspirations

Jesus, as an illegitimate son, spent his whole life attempting to gain recognition as 'the David' against his rival claimant, James (see Thiering, 1992, p. 65), and attracted sufficient support to his cause to lead a schismatic group of Essenes. For those who opposed him, he was 'the man of a lie' – thus Thiering sees him as 'the wicked priest'. John the Baptist was the teacher of righteousness. Jesus 'was with the Teacher at first but then separated, adopting a less strict view of the law' (1992, p. 19). Jesus engineered support by blurring the distinctions between lay and priestly functions, and by admitting Gentiles into full membership. He also usurped for himself the role of high priest; the Davidic Messiah plays a less important role in the Qumran documents than the priestly Messiah and was 'ranked below all the priests and Levites' (1992, p. 344). Jesus was claiming 'that there was no difference between himself and a man born into the tribe of Levi. According to this view,' says Thiering, 'Jesus could rise as far as being high priest and Pope' (1992, p. 92); the Pope, in Thiering's system, was the highest office in Herod's 'new Israel' (p. 352). Jesus was now 'claiming a status that no heir of David could ever hold' (p. 93). As noted in Chapter 1, there is actually a Muslim tradition that Jesus was of priestly descent. Thiering constructs a complex scenario, in which the Herod family is involved in an uneasy alliance with the Essenes, uneasy because the traditional hierarchy only has a place for David's heirs. The rank of 'Herod' appears to have co-existed among the Essenes, and Thiering makes much of Herod's desire to be seen as leader of all Jews, inside and outside of Israel. She also assumes that some Essenes (including Herod) were influenced by Hillel's 'idea of a New Covenant . . . a covenant of personal choice and initiation' involving baptism and initiation rites. Jesus developed this idea in order to extend his power base (Gentiles, too, could choose to enter the new covenant). He also advocated peaceful co-existence with Rome and appears to have believed that he would become 'king' by divine intervention, which he predicted several times.

Eventually, Jesus' enemies conspired to have him tried for heresy. They succeeded, and he was crucified within the confines of Qumran. However, he recovered and 'was helped to escape from the tomb by friends, and stayed with them until he reached Rome, where he was present in AD 64' (p. 116). Thiering thus changes the location of Jesus' life's events and has him outliving the crucifixion, probably dying 'of old age in Rome' (p. 160). One of the most controversial aspects of Thiering's thesis is actually incidental to her main argument, that Jesus was a political leader, a man, and not the divine son of God, although it tends to support her view of Jesus' humanity. I am referring to her assertion that Jesus married Mary Magdalene (p. 88), whose children he fathered (they eventually settled in southern France). Indeed, he divorced Mary (p. 146) and later remarried (Lydia, p. 148). Jesus continued to lead the movement, frequently meeting with Paul and others in private (see e.g. p. 155). The idea that he had risen was invented by Simon Magus (who figures in the scheme as another would-be leader of the 'new Israel') as a 'means of keeping in membership the great number of Gentiles holding a hellenistic view of the immortality of the soul' (p. 118). Paul's party, who knew the truth, used the 'pesher technique'; thus the 'surface story retained the myth' while the 'real events were told for those "who had ears"' (p. 118). Jesus continued to direct the affairs of his movement, though in secret.

The similarity with Bahrdt here is striking. His Jesus, after surviving the crucifixion due to drugs administered by Luke, supervised the Church from his Essene hideaway. Jesus' 'appearances' were taken to be those of the risen Lord. In the end, Jesus died a natural death. Bahrdt's Jesus was completely stage-managed by the Essenes, by secret helpers who assisted him at every turn. Schweitzer actually thought Bahrdt's book 'too deeply censured' (1998b, p. 39). Allen (1998) calls it 'a hoot' (p. 134). Certainly, it became a source book for many rationalist and alternative explanations of Jesus' life, and pioneered the idea that he died as an old man. Bahrdt was Professor Extraordinary of Philosophy at Leipzig until 1766, when he was 'requested to resign on account of [his] scandalous life' (Schweitzer, 1998b, p. 39).

### The myth survives

After the political aspirations of the movement and the hope for 'a material kingdom . . . went up in flames', it was the myth of the resurrection that enabled the Gospel's transformation into a spiritual message, in which the kingdom became a 'spiritual empire held in the hearts and minds of women and men' (p. 160). This sounds remarkably like Reimarus; for Thiering, as for Reimarus, it has been in the Church's interest to keep the real Jesus story hidden. It is no surprise that Thiering's work is much cited by authors of 'conspiracy theory' literature. Wright (1992) offers some positive points of criticism. For example, Thiering rightly identifies Jesus' pacifist stance, and inclusion of Gentiles, as significant (p. 25). However, continues Wright, 'the scrolls simply weren't written when she says they were' (p. 25), and 'there is nothing in actual pesher works which corresponds in any way to what we find in the gospels' (p. 27). Her pesher technique seems to allow her to make the Gospels say whatever she wants them to say: 'It's like someone trying to solve a Rubik's cube by peeling off the coloured stickers and arranging them neatly together, side by side, without ever wrestling with the cube itself at all' (p. 35).

As described by Finkel (1964), the teacher of righteousness' pesher technique had used existing Bible texts to predict, describe or interpret contemporary events (p. 152). An example of Jesus' use of pesher as described by Finkel is John 6:30–59, where Jesus refers to Moses feeding people who later died (with manna in the wilderness) while those whom he fed with spiritual food would never die (p. 159). Thiering's pesher is rather a code that is written into new scriptures, without which their real meaning remains hidden. The idea that there is a code hidden in the text of the Bible has also proved to be popular, however, not least due to Michael Drosnin's bestselling *The Bible Code* (1997), which sees the Bible as a quarry of futuristic predictions.

Wright (1992) dismisses Thiering's work as 'bizarre', as she does Allegro's, although he does discuss her in some detail (pp. 19–36). What I find interesting is the wide appeal that her ideas have enjoyed: in Australia, they resulted in a television debate (Palm Sunday, 1990) and a book about the debate, *The Dead Sea Scrolls: The Riddle Debate* (1991) by Leonie Star. Thiering herself offers no evaluation of Jesus. She calls him 'the wicked priest' not because he was wicked but because he fits the description of Qumran's anti-hero. In other words, this was what his enemies called him. However, a Jesus who devoted his life to manipulating his way to power hardly fits the Christian image. I cannot help but ask whether there is any link between Thiering's felt need to fly in the face of accepted scholarly opinion, and the lack of female voices in the field of New Testament studies.

## The blood-line literature

This literary genre is mainly the product of investigative journalism. Writers were attracted by rumours of sequestered Dead Sea Scrolls that tell a different Jesus story from that told by the Church. Several titles address this controversy, including Baigent and Leigh (1991), cited above in my discussion of Allegro, whom they frequently quote. Baigent and Leigh argue that the genuine, messianic Jesus movement was the James-led group (see also Eisenmann, 1998; Perkins, 1999). Paul, they say, parted company with James to embark on an enterprise of his own. He 'shunts God aside and establishes for the first time, worship of Jesus –

Jesus as a kind of equivalent of Adonis, of Tammuz, of Attis, or any one of the dying and rising gods who populated the Middle East at the time' (1991, p. 182).

References in the Nag Hammadi collection to a relationship between Jesus and Mary Magdalene also proved irresistible, since if Jesus was married he may well have had children. Baigent *et al.* (1982) write, 'On the basis of the Nag Hammadi scrolls alone the possibility of a bloodline descended directly from Jesus gained considerable plausibility for us' (p. 357). They cite the famous 'kiss' (p. 356). Speculation about Jesus' relationship with the Essenes, not to mention the work of Allegro and Thiering, is all good material for these writers. Examples include *Holy Blood, Holy Grail* (1982) and *The Messianic Legacy* (1986), both by Baigent *et al.*, and *Bloodline of the Holy Grail: The Hidden Lineage of Jesus Revealed* (1996) by Laurence Gardner. While Paul invented the Christ of Christianity, the real Jesus movement continued to pursue his political ambitions. Jesus was 'a priest-king – an aristocrat and . . . claimant to the throne' (Baigent *et al.*, 1982, p. 330). They think it very unlikely that Jesus was poor or uneducated (p. 318).

Gardner cites Thiering as an authority on the Dead Sea Scrolls. Her studies are 'undoubtedly the most thorough to date in this field of research' (1996, p. 133). Baigent *et al.* and Gardner also refer to Morton Smith's work (Baigent *et al.*, 1982, pp. 289–98; Gardner, 1996, pp. 91–2). At times, the scions of Jesus' blood-line have ruled kingdoms, such as the Merovingians of France and the Crusader states. The movement has often operated underground, through secret societies such as the Knights Templar, the Rosicrucians and the Freemasons. Many European royal houses are traced back to Jesus, including the Stuarts (or Stewarts) of Scotland, whose head writes the foreword to Gardner's book. The 'holy grail' of legend is actually the blood-line of Jesus, the *Sangreal*. Baigent *et al.* (1986) cite sources which claim that 'descendants of Jesus' family and possibly of Jesus himself survived to become leaders of various Christian churches' (p. 100). Joseph of Arimathaea probably accompanied Jesus' family first to Marseilles, then possibly to England (see Baigent *et al.*, 1982, p. 332; Gardner, 1996, p. 174).

The Templars were founded in 1118 to protect pilgrims *en route* to Jerusalem. During the Crusades, the order grew very rich and powerful. Gardner says that the Templars found wealth beneath the Temple mound in Jerusalem, which he links with the Dead Sea's copper scroll (1996, p. 328). Myths associate the Templars with magic, even with the worship of Baphomet (Muhammad). They were disbanded in 1312, accused of blasphemy, sodomy and heresy. This link between the blood-line of Jesus and the Crusades adds romance to an already intriguing tale of conspiracy, secrecy and high ambition. References to lost, stolen and suppressed documents abound. Baigent *et al.* (1992) argue that *The Protocols of the Learned Elders of Zion* (Marsden, 1922; and see Chapter 5) were actually based on a real document that set out the *Sangreal*'s plan to achieve its aims (p. 168). The Templars may have sought to reconcile Jews, Christians and Muslims by placing a descendant of Jesus on the throne of Jerusalem. They write, 'for if Jesus were acknowledged as a mortal prophet, as a priest-king and legitimate ruler of the line of David, he might well become acceptable to both Jews and Muslims' (*ibid.*, p. 377).

Baigent *et al.* describe the Templars as enjoying 'sustained and sympathetic contact with Islamic and Jewish culture', becoming 'a clearing house for new ideas, new dimensions of knowledge, new sciences' (*ibid.*, p. 44). They speculate that during the Crusades the Templars discovered something that confirmed the blood-line theory, perhaps Jesus' 'mummified body' or proof that he had married (p. 375). Thereafter, the Templars did not believe in the Jesus-God, but 'in a "higher God"' (p. 58). However, they also state that any such evidence would have been excised by the Roman Church. Anything that contradicted its God-myth, 'all political and dynastic elements, were rigorously excised from Jesus' biography' as 'the secret the church forbade' (pp. 336, 333). Similarly, the nature of Jesus' true relationship with Mary Magdalene was suppressed, especially 'the marriage evidence' (p. 91). Much of this literature complains that Mary's reputation has been tainted by the charge of prostitution, elevating instead her mother-in-law (Gardner, 1996, pp. 153–4). There is an echo here of the film *Stigmata*, as well as of the forgery and conspiracy theories of Wheless, McCabe and others. The blood-line theorists argue that the *Sangreal* continues in active pursuit of its goal, namely the placing of Jesus' descendants in positions of power, and 'plays a role in high level international affairs' (Baigent *et al.*, 1982, p. 79).

## Neo-Gnostic literature

What I call neo-Gnostic literature (and websites) takes the idea of a blood-line seriously, although it is primarily concerned with Jesus as teacher of eternal wisdom, available to all without the trappings or dogmas of traditional Christianity. There is also overlap here with Hindu and Buddhist responses to Jesus, since often the 'wisdom' that dwelt in, or was taught by, Jesus is identified with that which dwelt in, or was taught by, the sages and avatars of India.

A married Jesus is not essential to neo-Gnosticism but serves to suggest that true spirituality can embrace sexuality, as implied by the budding relationship between Paige and Kiernan in *Stigmata*. Incidentally, the stigmata (the appearance of Jesus' wounds on a human body) has more often than not been associated with women, although it began with Francis of Assisi. Some see the recovery of Mary Magdalene's true role, both as Jesus' lover and as an apostle and teacher, as a restoration of the female within God, or as adding a goddess to the Godhead; see the Esoteric Theological Seminary's website, www.Christiangoddess.com. There is also extensive Magdalene material available at www.marymagdalene.org. Mary Starbird gives us titles such as *Woman with the Alabaster Jar: Mary*

*Magdalene and the Holy Grail* (1993) and *The Goddess in the Gospels: Reclaiming the Sacred Feminine* (1998).

An example of a link with India is provided by Peter Longley's website, www.spiritualchallenge.com, and his novel, *Two Thousand Years Later* (1997). Longley points to the divine in each of us. For him, Christ consciousness and Krishna consciousness are identical. Longley identifies himself with the Jesus Seminar and with John Shelby Spong, on whose scholarship he draws in his writing. He also looks to such eastern concepts as *karma*, *yin* and *yang*, and reincarnation. In the novel, present-day counterparts of Jesus and Mary Magdalene are reunited aboard a cruise ship. They dream of their first-century experiences, although some pieces of the puzzle emerge in regression therapy sessions (1997, p. 126). Only Mary and Jesus' son, Ben Joshua, had known his real message. She was silenced as a 'lone, female voice crying spiritual renewal in the wilderness of Rome's male-dominated world', while Ben Joshua 'dies in India and is never able to bring his message to the world' (p. 298). However, while in India he realizes the essential unity between his father's and Indian thought. 'The crucifixion was not part of Jesus' plan' (p. 295), which was to teach people how to live in spiritual harmony 'with the light and sound of God' (p. 296). 'Confused and misguided people' like Peter and Paul carried what passed as the Christian message to the world (p. 298).

Some of this literature depicts Jesus as having spent his hidden years in India or Egypt, where he acquired knowledge of the way of true cosmic consciousness. For example, Levi H. Dowling's *The Aquarian Gospel of Jesus the Christ* (1979) has Jesus spending eighteen years studying and travelling in the East. Dowling (1841–1911) set out his book in a format resembling 'modern translations of the Bible', giving it 'the appearance of a "fifth Gospel"' (Groothuis, 1990, p. 202). He claimed to have received the text from what he called the 'ethers', or the 'Akashic records'. Similarly, Madame Blavatsky, co-founder of the Theosophical Society, received teaching from the masters, or mahatmas, whose secrets she had learned in Tibet. I return to 'Jesus went to India' material in Chapter 6.

*Thomas*' 'turn over a stone, and I am there', from which *Stigmata* develops its message, links with ancient goddess cults, the cycle of the seasons and with the idea that Jesus' real message will reconnect us with the natural world. New Age tells us that the distinction between matter and spirit, upheld by normative Christian thought, must yield to a holistic, integrated worldview, or all will perish in ecological mayhem. The Essenes also feature in New Age Jesus writing. Typically, they are 'viewed as a kind of halfway house between orthodox Judaism and Eastern mysticism' (Groothuis, 1990, p. 135). For example, actress Shirley MacLaine 'waxes exuberant on the Essenes . . . and confidently identifies Jesus as an Essene' (*ibid.*, p. 176; see also MacLaine, 1989, p. 178).

Chris Knight's extensive website invites us to enter into conversation on such diverse topics as 'Wisdom Earth Democracy . . . genetic ethics to the sacred marriage, or to participate in apocalypsia, the feminine unveiling rite of passage of our coming of age'. Through 'Sacred marriage' (*hieros gamous*), he says, 'we find God and Gaia, the Feminine face of deity, in divine union' (www.math.aukland.ac.nz/~King/Preprints/books/genesis). Mary Magdalene is the goddess counterpart of Jesus as the rising and dying God. Former Dominican priest Matthew Fox, an advocate of creation spirituality, sees the cosmic Christ as linking 'heaven and earth, past and future, divinity and humanity, all creation' so that at the profoundest, most mystical level, people of all faiths can unite in 'deep ecumenism' (1988, pp. 30, 228). Fox calls for an abandonment of the quest for 'the historical Jesus' in favour of 'the quest for the Cosmic Christ' (*ibid.*, p. 7).

The twenty-first century, says Fox, needs a 'spiritual vision that prays, celebrates and lives out the reality of the Cosmic Christ, who lives in all God's children, in all the prophets of religions everywhere, in all creatures of the universe' (*ibid.*, p. 21). Dismissed by the Roman Catholic Church, Fox is now an Episcopalian priest in California. While the Church has tended to separate human from planetary fate, this approach reunites the two. Fox says that we are all, potentially, 'Cosmic Christs' (p. 138). 'In our century,' Fox writes, 'the Cosmic Christ has taken form in Gandhi, in Martin Luther King, Jr, in Dorothy Day, and in other prophets of peace and justice' (p. 224). Fox certainly regards himself as an 'insider' on Jesus, as do quite a few New Age and neo-Gnostic writers. However, he anticipates the day when present religious labels will no longer matter.

Typically, says Groothuis (1990), New Age writers regard Jesus as a principle or as a pattern, not as a person, and as one of many of its manifestations: 'The individual, personal, historical Jesus is separated from the universal, impersonal, eternal Christ or Christ consciousness, which he embodied but did not monopolize' (p. 17). Written for an evangelical readership, Groothuis' *Revealing the New Age Jesus: Challenges to Orthodox Views of Christ* treats its subject as worthy of serious investigation. His own view is that when you look at the canonical gospels, you see the real 'Jesus . . . his life, death and resurrection, is what you get – or what you reject' (p. 241). However, his book deals in detail with neo-Gnostic and New Age contributors and represents a useful survey of this material. He is certainly not as harsh as Texe Marrs, for whom New Age is part of *Satan's Designs for World Domination*, the subtitle of his *Mystery Mark of the New Age* (1998).

All these writers look at the Jesus of the Church and find little there to attract them. They look at the Jesus of Gnosticism, or reflect on the possibility that Jesus married, or had political goals, and find much of interest. In many respects, they all see a human Jesus. Yet some aspects of the above Jesus image also featured in my chapter on insider views; for example, in Borg's and Crossan's social reformer Jesus, in Spong's sexually active Jesus, as well as in several references to the sidelining of alternative gospel accounts, or in the triumph of Pauline over primitive Christianity. Speculation that Jesus established an underground dynasty may reflect controversy in the primitive Church about the role that ought to be played by his relatives, just as controversy surrounded Muhammad's blood-line. The relatives involved may not have been Jesus' children but the brothers and sisters of Mark 6:3. A church that wanted to elevate celibacy and Mary as a perpetual virgin would have had difficulty conceding that ecclesiastical authority could be inherited. The issue of Jesus' sexuality has also surfaced quite frequently in this book. It appears to address a genuine human need; the question 'Was Jesus as human as ourselves?' lurks in the background of all this literature. Kazantzakis put it like this:

The dual substance of Christ, the yearning, so human, so superhuman, of man to attain to God, or more exactly, to return to God, and identify himself with him – has always been a deep inscrutable mystery to me. This nostalgia for God, so mysterious and real, has opened in me large wounds and also flowing spirits. (Cited at the start of the film, *The Last Temptation of Christ*)


## Dogma

Kevin Smith's recent film *Dogma* (1999), a huge box-office success, also raises questions about Jesus' attitude towards issues of race and gender. It features a forgotten thirteenth apostle who never made it into the Bible, because he was black, and a female descendant of Jesus and Mary Magdalene who works in an abortion clinic. Jesus, the film implies, was also black. The Roman Catholic Church has classified the film as 'morally offensive'. Smith is himself a devout Catholic. Several of my students who have seen the film said that they found it thought-provoking and engaging. Even blood-line books, albeit more fiction than serious scholarship, discuss a valid aspect of Jesus study: the relationship between religion and politics. If Jesus did have this-worldly ambitions, it is merely faithfulness to his legacy to pursue the same agenda, whether or not any of Jesus' descendants are involved. There is, too, as Baigent *et al.* (1982) point out, 'a desire for a true "leader", not a führer, but a species of wise and benign figure, a priest-king in whom mankind can safely repose its trust' (p. 387). Christians, in Jesus' name, have ruled empires and raised armies. If God's kingdom is to be established here, on earth, perhaps an opting out of the secular into a discrete spiritual realm is to betray what Jesus intended. Of course, some of the views discussed would exclude many from Jesus' kingdom. Here, the vision of the Templars as portrayed by Baigent *et al.* sounds preferable to me to that of the Christian Identity Movement.


## D. H. Lawrence (1885–1930)

Novelists and playwrights have also depicted alternative Jesus scenarios, including several already referred to in this book. Perhaps one of the most audacious of these is Lawrence's *The Man Who Died* (1928), a rather short book of only 103 pages, but beautifully written in an almost poetic style.

The man is not named but his identification with Jesus is strongly suggested by the text: 'Master, it is said that the body was stolen from the garden, and the tomb is empty' (p. 22), and 'I offered them the only corpse of my love. This is my body – take and eat – my corpse' (p. 90). On the pouring of ointment, we read, 'She only wanted to serve – she had been a prostitute', clearly a reference to Mary Magdalene (p. 89). The man still bore 'the death wound through his belly' (p. 87). The woman 'clutched for the man in him who had died and was dead, the man of his youth and his mission, of his chastity' (p. 36). Then, as he finds love and sensual pleasure: 'How could I have been blind to the healing and the bliss in the crocus-like body of a tender woman!' (p. 72).

Desire grows, he becomes one with his lover: 'he knew only the crouching fullness of the woman there, the soft rock of life. . . . "On this rock I build my life" . . . he felt the blaze of his manhood rise up in his loins, magnificent. "I am risen!" . . . "Father" he said, "Why did you hide this from me?"' (pp. 94–5). The woman becomes pregnant with his child (p. 99). Nature and the divine seem to blend together at the novel's end, as he departs from her in a boat:

when the nightingale calls again from your valley-bed, I shall come again, sure as Spring . . . I have sowed the seed of my life and my resurrection, and put my touch forever upon the choice woman of this day, and I carry her perfume in my flesh like essence of roses. (p. 103)

Some may find this portrait of Jesus offensive. Of course, given that the book is fiction, it really does not describe the Jesus who was but a Jesus who may have been. Like *The Last Temptation*, it uses a possible Jesus scenario to explore human desires and yearnings, and the degree to which a Jesus who was tempted in every respect, as we are, may also have faced desire (see Hebrews 4:15).

Some forms of Hindu and Buddhist spirituality have embraced sexuality, including intercourse. Through the act of union, 'the actual or represented union of the tantric practitioners symbolizes the union of Siva and Sakti, of the male and female polarity in the cosmos, and their joy reflects the joy (*ananda*) of that ultimate condition' (Flood, 1996, p. 191). Bede Griffiths (1917–93), a Benedictine theologian who delved deeply into Hindu spirituality, argues that the West has lost 'the intuitive knowledge of the body', which it has replaced with 'rational knowledge of the mind'. Griffiths continued:

D. H. Lawrence was the prophet of this kind of knowledge, when he reminded us that, 'We have lost . . . the great intrinsically developed sensual awareness or sense-awareness and sense-knowledge of the ancients . . . arrived at by instinct . . . not by reason . . . knowledge based not on words but on images.' (Griffiths, 1982, p. 158, citing Lawrence, *Apocalypse*)

There is also some precedence for a nature-embracing spirituality in the life and writing of Francis of Assisi (1181–1226), who preached to birds and addressed the sun and the moon as his brother and sister. For many Christians, Francis' rejection of wealth, his dedication to a life of simplicity and of service, approximates Jesus' life more closely than almost any other attempt to live as he did.

## The Branch Davidians

'Left-handed' approaches to spirituality, however, can lead to excesses, which may have characterized some Gnostic groups, as noted above. Not so far from where I am writing this book, a more recent example of apocalyptic antinomianism came to a tragic end in 1993, when the New Mount Carmel Complex, also known as Apocalypse Ranch, of the Branch Davidians, was burned to the ground. This followed a fifty-day siege by the Federal Bureau of Investigation. The Davidians appear to have armed themselves, ready for the final battle. The Branch Davidians is an offshoot of the Adventist movement, founded by William Miller (1787–1849) in 1831 to prepare people for Jesus' return, which he predicted would occur in 1844. The name Seventh Day Adventist was chosen by the movement in 1860. After 1844 had come and gone, several other dates were predicted but without Jesus' return. The Davidians broke away from their parent body in the 1920s. Their leaders were called 'prophets', or the 'Anti-typical David' whose destiny was to become Jesus' deputy. They regarded their own leadership as a 'theocracy', the restored House of David. Their community aimed at self-sufficiency, with its own flag, currency, school and farm.

In 1986, David Koresh, formerly Vernon Howell (1959–93), became 'prophet'. He called himself the 'Sinful Messiah' and taught that the end was approaching, and that, when Jesus returned, the 'Sinful Messiah' and his faithful disciples would rule paradise earth with Jesus. Koresh believed himself to possess secret knowledge of the Seven Seals of Revelation, the 'acid test for who knows God and who doesn't' (cited in Storr, 1996, p. 14). The USA corresponded to the biblical 'Babylon'. For women, being faithful to Koresh meant having sexual relations with him. As the 'Sinful Messiah', Koresh was *spiritually blind* just as Samson had been *physically blind* (see Judges 16:21). Koresh pointed to odd behaviour by some Hebrew prophets, such as eating defiled food (Ezekiel 3:13) or marrying a harlot (Hosea 1:2), to justify his own 'left-handed' behaviour. Lois Roden, a former leader of the movement, had stressed the femaleness of the Holy Spirit.

In Tantric Hinduism, the unclean is sometimes embraced in order to overcome all duality, between pure and impure, good and bad, matter and spirit, the *atman* within and the *brahman* without. On the other hand, claiming sexual favours appears to be characteristic of authoritarian, charismatic leaders. Anthony Storr (1996), analysing personality traits of such leaders whom he calls gurus (including Koresh), writes, 'Gurus . . . often engage in sexual behaviour which would be condemned in an ordinary person' (p. xvi). Towards the end, Koresh signed himself 'Yahweh Koresh'. Some surviving members of the Branch Davidians believe that Koresh will return.

Perhaps the above represents less an image of Jesus than a proposed end time scenario in which Jesus will have a role. Throughout history, some Christians have expected Jesus to return, and have felt called either to separate from the world in readiness for this event, or to make some sort of specific preparation for Jesus' second coming. Aspects of the Branch Davidians' end time scenario are not uncommon among such groups. For example, in the sixteenth century, convinced that Jesus' return was imminent, a former innkeeper called John of Leiden and his Anabaptist followers took over Münster, where they set up a commune with common ownership, banned money, established polygamy and waited for Jesus (see Woodward, 1999, pp. 70–2). One leader married nine women. They called their city 'New Jerusalem'. John, who was crowned king, wore 'vestments as his royal robes. . . . The world would perish, and only Münster would be saved' (Chadwick, 1964, p. 190). 'The glorious armour of David' would be needed to promote the world rebellion that would prepare for the end. In Amsterdam, supporters ran naked through the streets, crying 'Woe! Woe! The Wrath of God Falls on this city' (*ibid.*, p. 191). Ever the pro-establishment Anglican, Chadwick calls all this 'the catastrophic fringe of lunacy' (*ibid.*).

## Aum Shinrikyo

In Japan, the apocalyptic movement known as Aum Shinrikyo also predicts end time battles and cataclysmic events. In 1995, it was responsible for a poison attack on the Tokyo subway system. Its former leader and founder Asahara Shoko (b. 1955) claimed that he was Christ, not merely his deputy. Like Koresh, he possessed exclusive knowledge of Jesus' teachings. He drew on Buddhist and Hindu sources as well as on Revelation and the prophecies of the French astrologer Nostradamus (1503–66) to construct his end time scenario in which only the faithful would survive. Again, separation from the world and opposition to government characterize the movement, which is now run by Asahara's daughter. In Uganda, in March 2000, some 900 members of Joseph Kibwetere's Movement for the Restoration of the Ten Commandments of God lost their lives, apparently at the hands of their leader. Jesus had told Kibwetere that when he returned in the year 2000 only Kibwetere's followers would be saved. Several thousand donated their property to the Church, and lived communally in expectation of surviving the tribulations of the end. Sex and speaking were forbidden, the latter lest anyone should miss the sound of the bell that would summon them to heaven. Tragically, when 2000 was well underway but Jesus had not returned, some members began to demand a refund, and Kibwetere thought mass murder the better option (see Hammer, 2000).

## Latter Day Saints

Insider, or outsider? This is a difficult question to answer. Even though I have, sometimes arbitrarily, placed people in these categories, I have not found it possible to apply them rigidly. Indeed, to show similarity between some insider and some outsider images of Jesus, I discussed Marxists in my insider chapter, while this chapter refers to the Pilgrims of Massachusetts, who were hardly outsiders. If Jesus is 'a man for all the world', then the entire world has a right to own him and anyone who claims to own Jesus (or to be owned by him) may call themselves an insider. I am none the less including Mormons and Unificationists as outsiders because, while both regard themselves as Christians, their Jesus images differ from the Church's traditional image. In addition, similarities exist between their views of Jesus and some of the Jesus images surveyed in this chapter. Both use alternative sources to tell their Jesus story.

The Mormons, properly the Church of Jesus Christ of Latter Day Saints, were founded by Joseph Smith (1805–44) in New York in 1830. Two ideas already encountered in this chapter feature prominently in his teaching. One, the chosen people are to be found in the New World; two, Jerusalem, or Zion, Christ's kingdom, will be built in America, where Jesus will reappear as well as in Jerusalem. Smith saw his Church as a revival, or restoration, of true Christianity. Historical Christianity, he said, had got everything wrong. He received *The Book of Mormon*, revealed to him by an angel who also provided him with a key, special spectacles, to decipher its language of reformed Egyptian. The book tells of a lost tribe of Israel that came to the American shores thousands of years ago. After his appearance in Palestine, Jesus visited this lost tribe to institute the ordinances (a very Protestant word, used instead of 'sacrament') of baptism, communion and priestly ordination.

Smith thought that Jesus would return within his own lifetime, predicting 1890. He saw his converts as the elect of God, as the chosen people of the New World, heirs of the lost tribe. He excluded blacks, who carried Cain's curse. The Church of Israel, referred to earlier in this chapter, is a breakaway movement from the Latter Day Saints. In 1978, the Saints officially revoked the doctrine of white supremacy. Early Saints practised polygamy, which they believed was divinely ordained. As had the Anabaptists of Münster, they looked into the Hebrew Bible and decided that it permitted polygamy. There may also have been some idea that polygamy was demanded by the end times. All members of the Church hold rank within a complex hierarchy. There is no professional or paid clergy. Mormons believe that Jesus was married and had children, another similarity between the Mormons and many of the views described in this chapter. Jesus' birth had involved normal sexual intercourse between God and Mary, just as God's own birth had once been like that of any other human.

Both God and Jesus are 'exalted men'. The title 'God' can be earned by good works and by progress along the spiritual path. The reward is a planet over which you will eventually rule, just as Jesus rules the earth. The conviction that Zion would be established in the Americas led the Mormons to trek across the land, to Utah, where they built their Temple and Tabernacle, a restored Jerusalem. They also, at least in their early days, regarded the government of the USA as 'illegal', opposed to the 'Kingdom of God'. Again, there is some similarity here with the Christian Identity Movement, indeed with the Branch Davidians. Today, the Mormons are respectable, moral, loyal, law-abiding citizens. A Reorganized Church, which never accepted polygamy, was formed in 1860 and has its headquarters in Independence, Missouri. Stressing 'the establishment of Zionic conditions merging both spiritual and temporal dimensions', it has also traditionally supported pacifism (www.rlds.ord/history.asp).

### The Unificationists

Founded in Korea by Sun Myung Moon in 1954, the Unification Church regards itself as God's agent in bringing about unity between Christian denominations and world faiths. While it understands its own teaching, or Divine Principle, to be the correct version of Christianity, it does not condemn other churches as corrupt or heretical. In fact, despite a lot of negative publicity, the movement can hardly be faulted for its commitment to ecumenism and unity. It has sponsored many inter-religious meetings, several of which I have attended. Its background is fascinating; it draws on elements of Calvinism, especially on its work ethic, on Confucian love of learning, on a Taoist concern for balance and harmony, and on popular Korean shamanism's belief in a spirit world. Its aim is to restore a proper balance to the universe by filling the world with scholarship, with art, with morality, with human co-operation. Thus, its texts talk about the *yin* and the *yang* (female and male principles) which unite in the ordinance of marriage. Humanity enjoys three blessings: the ability to perfect moral character, to have children and to dominate the earth. The realization of all three will bring humanity, God and the cosmos into 'complete harmony'. This will be 'the kingdom of God on earth' (*Outline*, 1980, pp. 30–1).

The word 'restoration' is common to the vocabulary of the Mormons and the Moonies, as Moon's followers are often called. Korea was chosen as the venue for God's servant, Moon, to begin his work because of its own rich religious and cultural heritage. 'God . . . created and guided all the major religions towards the restoration' (*ibid.*, p. 109); thus 'the nation suitably prepared to receive the lord would be a nation bearing the fruits of all major religions' (p. 310). Moon is called the Lord of the Second Advent, or the Messiah. Jesus, who was a perfect man but not God, succeeded in achieving spiritual salvation but not physical salvation, because he died before he could marry and have children. 'Because of the crucifixion, mankind lost the physical body of the savior and thus lost its physical object of faith and could not receive physical salvation', says Moon (p. 248). Jesus is not God: 'if Jesus were God, how could he intercede with himself? . . . how could he be tempted . . . and tortured and driven to the crucifixion by Satan?' (p. 142). Moon's task is to complete the mission left unfinished by Jesus: the parenting of the perfect family. Moon and his wife are the true parents, and select brides and grooms for their disciples, who regard their choice as infallible. His mission must 'simultaneously fulfil the purpose of all . . . religions' (p. 310); thus the movement is self-consciously multiracial.

## Your Jesus is my Jesus' greatest enemy

Marriage and family are central to both of these movements, as is the building of the kingdom here on earth, and the idea of restoring true Christianity. They are reacting against the idea that the celibate, priestly life is the more spiritual option than marriage and family life. Susan Haskins, among others, has shown how the Church elevated virginity at the expense of sexuality, or, as some put it, Mary the Virgin Mother of Jesus over Mary Magdalene, Jesus' lover. Haskins writes, 'According to Gregory [of Nyssa, 330–95] in his terrible indictment of marriage, the treatise *De Virginate*, this first sin [intercourse between Adam and Eve] had contaminated man's spiritual essence, and the wages of his sin has been sexuality and death' (1994, p. 74). However different the images of Jesus reviewed in this chapter are from our personal view, they represent a genuine effort to respond to the question, 'What sort of a man was Jesus?' Our vision of Jesus may be the opposite of others'; as Blake wrote, 'The vision of Christ that thou dost see, / Is my vision's greatest enemy' (Keynes, 1966, p. 748).

As for those who say that Jesus never existed, Christians might reflect on whether or not there is any justification for the hatred of Christianity that informs this judgement. In my next chapter, I turn to the encounter of the Jesus story with Jews and Muslims. Some of the images of Jesus encountered in this chapter resurface in early Jewish views – Jesus was a bastard, a deceiver, a trickster. Other Jews see Jesus as a good man who connected people with God but who never claimed to be God, or even the Messiah. Without exception, Muslims speak well of Jesus, whom the Qur'an reveres as a prophet. However, both Muslims and the Qur'an criticize Christians for claiming that Jesus is God. For Muslims, too, Jesus was not crucified but ascended into heaven. Some Muslims believe that when Jesus returns, he will marry and father children. Alternative sources, too, feature in Jewish and Muslim responses. So does Paul's role, another familiar theme in this book. Since Jews and Muslims have little to criticize in a Jesus who did not claim to be divine, I also allude to some Unitarian views of Jesus.

# 5 Jewish and Muslim Images of Jesus

One of the many puzzles that Jews struggle with in their encounters with Christians is how difficult Christians find it to accept the reality of the Jewishness of Jesus and how, at the same time, they readily acknowledge that Judas Iscariot was a Jew – in fact, the quintessential Jew, because only a bad Jew would betray the Messiah for 30 pieces of silver. Jesus is good: therefore, not really a Jew. Judas is bad, therefore he must be a Jew. (Rabbi Dow Marmur, speaking at Regis College, Toronto, 21 January 1998)

While the figure of Jesus is doctrinally more central to Christianity than to Islam, it is the differing perceptions of his status upon which both faiths ultimately reject each others' message. From the Christian point of view, the popular expression of this rejection often includes the reductionist view of the Prophet Muhammad who is used as a comparison with Jesus and whose mission as a messenger is denied as a result of this comparison. (Siddiqui, 1997, pp. 161–2)

## Jesus was a Jew; and also a Muslim

Jesus was a Jew. This hardly sounds like Christian heresy, yet when Geza Vermes published a book under that title in 1973, many found the idea shocking. Jews were the first to respond to Jesus, and even though they did not all respond to Jesus in the same way as Christians, they were none the less responding to one of their own. In fact, only a minority of Jews became Christians. The majority did not see Jesus as Christians saw him, despite the Christian claim that he had fulfilled their scriptures and was their expected Messiah. While several of the Christian Jesus scholars encountered in Chapter 3 did not think that Jesus was the Messiah, Jewish rejection of Jesus as Messiah remains deeply problematical for many Christians, who cannot understand why Jews continue to be Jewish, not Christian. They cannot grasp that Jesus may not have been the Messiah expected by the Jewish people. Edgar (1940) wrote, 'History has proved that Jesus was not the Messiah whom the Jews were eagerly awaiting. He did not deliver them from the yoke of Rome and the Perfect Age most certainly did not come' (p. 5). Lapide (1983) makes a similar point: 'We

Jews . . . do not know a Savior-King with the kingdom already come. Every morning television and the press confirm with terrible clarity that this world is not yet redeemed' (p. 14). Silver (1977) points out that Jews did not reject either Jesus or Jesus' concept of God. He wrote, 'What they rejected was the Messianism of Jesus, Paul's onslaught on the Law, his gospel of redemption through the atoning death and resurrection of Jesus, and the doctrine of God incarnate in man' (p. 344).

This impasse between Christian insistence that Jesus is the Jews' Messiah and Jewish rejection of Jesus as Messiah emerges as a major theme in the first part of this chapter, in which I discuss Jewish images of Jesus. Jews, who were often blamed for killing Jesus and were regarded as stubborn members of a dead and bankrupt religion for much of Christian history, had little reason to speak of Jesus in glowing or generous terms. In the early period, Jews were more numerous than Christians and from this position of comparative strength could call Jesus a renegade, a deceiver, a bad Jew. Later, suffering persecution from Christians, they tended to simply ignore Jesus. As someone whom their oppressors revered, he was of little interest to them. Still, any images of Jesus that Jews did form were likely to be uncomplimentary. This changed only when emancipation enabled Jews to take their place at the civic table.

Subsequently, as relations between Christians and Jews moved on to a different footing, some Jews thought it worthwhile to invest at least a little energy in rethinking their approach to Jesus the Jew. Part one of this chapter explores the history of Christian–Jewish relations. Recent Jewish discourse on Jesus, which has been called 'the Jewish reclamation of Jesus', can only be understood within the context of this broader narrative. I believe that Christians ought to rethink their Jesus images in the light of what Jews say about him, instead of simply assuming that it is Jews who must change.

Part two of this chapter discusses Muslim images of Jesus. For Muslims, Jesus was a Muslim, a messenger of Allah in the same cycle of prophets and messengers that includes Adam, Noah, Moses, David, among others named in the Qur'an. Muslims revere Jesus as one of their own, even if Christians fail to see their Jesus in the Muslim Jesus. The Qur'an's respect for Jesus ensures that he remains a revered figure, so while Muslims may ridicule, even lampoon, Christians and Christianity, they never speak ill of Jesus. *Vis-à-vis* Jews on Jesus, Christians claim the high ground, regarding their Jesus image as the authentic image, the Jewish image as deficient. *Vis-à-vis* the Muslim image of Jesus, Christians are surprised to discover that it is Muslims who claim the high ground, accusing Christians of misrepresentation, of getting it all wrong. Muslims also elevate the Qur'an over the Bible as the best source of information on Jesus, charging Christians with having corrupted the text of their scriptures. This is a debated issue. Some Muslims accept the text of the Bible as accurate, but argue that Christians misrepresent its meaning.

Either way, like Jews, Muslims do not see Jesus as Christians see him.

Instead, they offer an alternative, different view. Yet, like Christians, they claim a God-given authority for their understanding of Jesus. Can Christians learn anything from the Muslim Jesus? Must Muslims accept the Christian Jesus, and reject their own, in order for them to please the one true God in whom Jews, Christians and Muslims all claim to believe? Can there be two-way traffic between Muslims and Christians on Jesus? As Mona Siddiqui points out in the passage at the start of this chapter, Christians invariably compare Jesus with Muhammad, whom Muslims say came to perfect and to complete God's will for humankind, and find him wanting. Conversations between Muslims and Christians about Jesus often result in dispute about whose claims – Islam's about Muhammad or Christianity's about Jesus – are actually true.

There is so much literature available on Jewish and Muslim images of Jesus, including such excellent survey texts as Hagner (1997) and Leirvik (1999), on Jewish and Muslim Jesus images respectively, that I cannot cover everything in one chapter. On the internet, www.jcrelations.net also has many articles relevant to the focus of Part one of this chapter. However, to achieve a degree of originality, I try to:

(1) look at some of the main issues involved, especially those arising from the story of encounter;
(2) look at the writings of significant Jewish and Muslim contributors;
(3) draw on my own experience of dialogue;
(4) create links, whenever possible, with themes, images and agendas identified earlier in this book. There are, I suggest, several common threads that run through many people's responses to Jesus, be they insiders, outsiders or loyal members of a faith tradition of which Jesus is not the most revered or central figure.

Martin Forward, in commenting on the text of this book, raised the question of the 'plausibility of Muslim views of Jesus (as of any view!)' (2000, p. 1). It is, of course, possible for Christians to dismiss Jewish and Muslim views of Jesus as biased or as based on unhistorical sources. Historically, Muslim and Jewish as well as Hindu and Buddhist views of Jesus may not be plausible. However, this is unlikely to prevent people from holding them, just as Christians continue to hold views about Jesus on which New Testament scholarship casts doubt. Many Christians dismiss Muslim beliefs about *anything*, regarding them as false, just as they dismiss Jewish beliefs as outmoded. In this chapter, I describe Jewish and Muslim images of Jesus less to evaluate them – although I do offer some critical comment – than to show Christians how others view their own seminal personality. These images of Jesus are rooted in people's faith convictions and worldviews. Scholars may regard these as untenable, yet such beliefs often persist, despite critical scrutiny and historical scepticism.

## Part one: Jesus through Jewish eyes

Some of Jesus' Jewish contemporaries believed his message, and followed him. Even if we admit that we cannot say much about the nature of their belief in Jesus, or about what Jesus may have claimed about himself, no one disputes that Jesus had disciples. These included the twelve members of his inner circle, and a larger group of close admirers, in which women such as Mary Magdalene, Martha, and men such as Lazarus, were prominent. Others, however, did not accept his teaching. Some, possibly members of his own family, suggested that he was mad, or that he was possessed by Satan (see Mark 3:21–2). Later, both of these accusations were destined to become popular Christian explanations of Muhammad's conduct. Jesus' association with 'sinners', which presumably compromised his ritual purity, apparently displeased some Jews. The Pharisees especially wanted all Jews to observe the purity rules of the priests. Certainly, Jesus and they seem to argue about the rules of cleanliness (Mark 7:1–23).

Jesus attracted criticism for claiming authority that belonged exclusively to God (Mark 2:7; 11:28) and for his attitude towards the Sabbath (Mark 2:24). He appears to have had some sharp exchanges with the Pharisees (Mark 8:11). I chose references from Mark because, as the earliest gospel, it may present a less doctored account of the relationship between Jesus and contemporary Judaism. It does, though, record that Jesus predicted that the 'elders, chief priests and teachers of the law' would reject and 'kill' him (Mark 8:31). Mark 14:1 then has these people 'looking for some sly way to arrest and to kill Jesus'. This may represent retrojection of material unfavourable to Jews, while Pilate's behaviour in Mark 15 may be retrojection in favour of Rome.

Perhaps, too, as Sanders, Finkel and others suggest, there was dispute between Jesus and the Pharisees but within accepted ground rules of debate. Rabbinical literature is full of debate about the meaning of texts and customs. Very different interpretations live happily alongside each other within rabbinical texts; see how Leibowitz (1980) brings together different voices and invites her readers to join in the debate. Borg's thesis, too, that Jesus and the Pharisees offered competing visions of Judaism, does not necessarily mean that he and they were locked in mortal combat. None the less, Jesus' death may have resulted from this conflict, if the crowd's enthusiasm for Jesus led the Jewish nobility to think that their privileges were at risk.

Although charged with 'blasphemy' when tried before the high priest (Mark 14:64), the charge that was taken before Pilate was political, namely that Jesus called himself 'King of the Jews' (Mark 15:2). Of course, almost all Jews thought that a king who was descended from the House of David would also be a righteous, divinely anointed ruler, which means that the king would be a religious as well as a political leader. However, Jesus would only have been executed by the Romans for political reasons, as a threat to national security. The Gospels try to shift the blame for Jesus' death on to Jewish actors in the drama, on to Judas, the priests, the crowd that shouted, 'Crucify him.'

## Early Jewish–Christian conflict

Acts continues to present a story of conflict between the early Christians and some Jews. Acts 5 depicts the Sadducees initiating persecution. In Acts 7, Stephen is stoned. Acts 8 speaks of a 'great persecution against the Church'. In Acts 22, the Romans, at the instigation of 'some Jews', arrest Paul (who had been a persecutor before his conversion). This reference to 'some Jews' rather than to 'Pharisees' (that is, to a named group of Jews) suggests that Christians now regarded themselves as non-Jewish. On the other hand, the relationship between early Christianity and Judaism remains complex, and was itself a major topic of debate in the Book of Acts.

In my view, even given the differences between Paul and the Jerusalem Church on Torah obedience, Paul was just as convinced as James and Peter that the way of Jesus was the way *for all Jews*. Simply because it also embraced Gentiles does not mean that Paul did not think that Christianity stood in continuity, not discontinuity, with his own Jewish past. That the Gentiles had been 'grafted into' God's covenant did not mean that all Jews were now 'cut off' (Romans 11). In fact, Paul speaks of God's election of the Jews as 'irrevocable' (11:29), although his letters do tend to contrast the Law of Moses as the 'dispensation of death' with the 'Christian 'Gospel' as 'that which brings life' (Sandmel, 1965, p. 6). Fredriksen (1988) put it like this:

Israel's reception of the Gospel would take an eschatological miracle, for which Paul was uniquely responsible. He worked to redeem the Gentiles; Israel, God's beloved, would be redeemed by God himself. (p. 170)

Unfortunately, what passed into the Christian mindset was the notion that the 'old covenant' of *law and works* between God and Moses was now replaced by the new covenant of *faith and grace* through Jesus. Therefore, Jews who remained Jews were damned, beyond the reach of God's love. Yet Jews and Christians still had a lot in common, including the same scripture. Where Jews and Christians parted company was in interpreting this scripture. Matthew, for example, obviously looked at the Hebrew Bible and saw Jesus on almost every page. For him, all sorts of passages pointed at Jesus, even some that no other Jew thought of as messianic. Anxious to depict Jesus as the Jewish Messiah, Christians proof-texted the Hebrew Bible, yet these proof-texters were Jews, and rightly or wrongly they were convinced that Jesus *had* fulfilled these passages.

It is equally clear that many Jews disagreed, and that when they looked at Jesus they did not recognize him as their expected messiah. As Jewish writers point out, this is not surprising:

'Christ crucified' was 'unto Jews a stumbling block, and unto Gentiles foolishness' [1 Corinthians 1:23]. Against this doubly unfavorable view the apostles were forced to fight continually – and first of all to fight with the Jews, for whom the idea of a defeated and hanged ('crucified') Messiah could not fit any of their conceptions of the promise and function of the saving and liberating – and hence victorious Messiah. (Klausner, 1944, p. 263)

On the other hand, the way in which the gospel writers used biblical passages to describe events in the life of Jesus was itself very Jewish.

In his book, *What Is Midrash?* (1987), Jacob Neusner discusses Matthew's Gospel as an example of Midrash. Klausner, too, referring specifically to the content of Jesus' teaching, comments that 'So extraordinary is the similarity' between the Gospels and Tannaitic writing that, 'it might almost seem as though the gospels were composed simply and solely out of matter contained in the *Talmud* and *Midrash*' (1977, p. 185). For example, 'every single clause' of the Lord's Prayer 'is to be found in Jewish prayers and sayings in the *Talmud*' (p. 183).

In his meticulously researched *The Pharisees and the Teacher of Nazareth* (1964), Finkel shows how Jesus' teaching style resembles that of the Rabbis, as well as how both Jesus and the apostles, like the teacher of righteousness, 'unveiled the hidden meaning of Scriptures to describe current events and personalities'. Finkel, as noted previously in this book, calls this 'pesher' (p. 152). Eventually, the interpretive tradition derived from Jesus became the Christian gospels, while that derived from the Rabbis became the Tannaitic writings (Mishnah, Talmud). The documentary *66 AD: The Last Revolt*, which discusses disputes between Peter–James and Paul, traces how the Jesus movement parted company with Judaism. Spong, discussed in Chapter 3, also uses Midrash to explore the Gospels as theological commentaries rather than historical accounts.

## *Mutual animosity: Jewish–Christian competition*

From the perspective of those Jews who did not follow Jesus, if he had thought himself to be the Messiah, he must have been mistaken. Even if Jesus had not claimed to be the Messiah, the early Christians said that he had, and continued to call him Messiah. Horbury (1998b) and others suggest that 1 Thessalonians 2:3, where Paul defends himself from the charge of 'error or impure motive', may be a response to the accusation of 'false prophecy'. In other words, Jesus and Paul misused scripture; see passages such as Deuteronomy 13:1–3: 'If a prophet . . . appears to you and announces . . . a miraculous sign or wonder . . . you must not listen . . . God is testing you', which may have been applied to Jesus (p. 111).

Yet evidence emerges that Christians who kept the Torah, who worshipped in the Temple, and who did not aggressively try to persuade other Jews to join them, were regarded as a harmless sect. These Christians were almost certainly Unitarian, seeing Jesus as God's anointed rather than as

237

God's pre-existent son. Klausner suggests that the Jewish authorities only censured, or 'persecuted', those Christians (at this stage called Nazarenes) who 'failed to do honor to the Temple, which was at that time a *political-religious institution*' (1944, p. 348). This is why James, who was 'punctilious about observing the ritual requirements and honoring the Temple', went untouched. His 'peculiar Messianic ideas' could be tolerated, perhaps like the eccentric teaching of other contemporary Jewish movements.

Only after what Klausner calls a 'new interpretation' of Christianity, one that 'involved a negation of Judaism', had won the day were the Jerusalem Christians compromised. They then 'became transgressors of the law'. Klausner can find no other explanation for James' execution in 62 CE; up until then 'this ritually correct Ebionite' had been left alone (pp. 597–8). Eisenmann (1998) cites traditions that James was allowed to enter the Holy of Holies, which only the high priest could do. He argues that James, in succession to Jesus, was leader of a Zadokite opposition to the Jerusalem, Rome-linked high priesthood. He thinks that the Zadokites, the Nazarenes, Zealots and Essenes may have been part of the same anti-establishment movement.

Once Paul's Christianity had become the dominant tradition, Jews began to perceive sufficient difference between themselves and Christians, indeed between themselves and Jesus, to regard Christians as 'the other'. 'The majority of Palestinian Jews,' says Schiffman (1994), 'did not follow this teacher' and 'after his death the majority of Jews continued not to follow him, and Judaism considered that Christianity was "the other"' (p. 50). Schiffman, Professor of Jewish Studies at New York University, and Fredriksen, Professor of the Appreciation of Scripture at Boston, also cited in this chapter, are two of the scholars featured in the documentary *66 AD: The Last Revolt*. Fredriksen, author of *From Jesus to Christ: The Origin of the New Testament Images of Jesus* (1988) and historical consultant to the PBS series *From Jesus to Christ* (1998), is currently one of only a few women within the top rank of Jesus studies.

For their part, as noted earlier in this book, some Christians continued to think of themselves as Jewish, some still went to the synagogue and may well have continued to do so well into the third, even fourth centuries. This in part explains why the Church Fathers felt they had to denounce Christians who 'lived as Jews', as well as why they said what they did say about Jews and Judaism. If Judaism was not a threat, or a competitor, why did they devote so much time to speaking ill of the Jews? Rubenstein (1972), commenting on Paul's harsh words to his fellow Jews, wrote: 'When Paul wrote that . . . Jews had proven faithless to their God, he was speaking of his own kith and kin in what he regarded as a family dispute. Some things are often said within the family that have a very different meaning when repeated by outsiders' (p. 115). I have heard it suggested that the anti-Jewish words of the Church Fathers, some of which I cite below, may be mitigated when understood in the context of a family feud.

On the one hand, when Christianity began its spread throughout the

Roman world, Judaism hardly represented a threat. More and more non-Jews were targeted for conversion. After their failed rebellion against the Romans, too, the Jews lost their privileged status as a national religion, under which Christianity may actually have sheltered. Now, they were themselves among the persecuted. On the other hand, there is plenty of evidence that Gentiles continued to find the synagogue an attractive religious option, alongside Christian Jews who insisted on worshipping there, much to the disgust of the bishops. Why else did Emperor Severus need to forbid pagans from becoming Jews? (200 CE). It has even been suggested that rigorous competition was involved here, between local churches and synagogues contending for the same congregation. Where will I go this week, church or synagogue?

The proximity to each other of the church and synagogue at Dura-Europos in Syria suggests that such competition may not have been uncommon. The Mithraic shrine is also nearby. Dura-Europos was a rather insignificant Roman station on the Euphrates, abandoned in about 256 CE. Well preserved, it is now an archaeological site of considerable importance. In his debate with the Jewish scholar Trypho, Justin Martyr was asked whether Christians who continued to live as Jews were saved. Yes, he said, but not if they persuade other Gentiles 'to keep the commandments that he does, saying that you will not be saved unless they keep them'. On the salvation of a non-Christian Jew, Justin was blunt: 'they cannot be saved' (Stevenson, 1963, pp. 68–9). Justin seems to have regarded assimilation of Christianity into Judaism to be a real possibility. Fredriksen (1994) comments that 'this gentile habit of judaizing continued even after conversion to Christianity' (p. 82).

Justin wanted to stress Christian separateness, indeed the end of God's covenant with the Jews. This is interesting. He was quite willing to call those pagans who spoke wisely 'Christians even though they were thought pagan', but *non-Christian Jews* were simply *lost*. Justin could pioneer a fulfilment approach towards paganism, yet could only see Judaism as *displaced* by Christianity. Justin is thought to have debated with Trypho while teaching at Ephesus in about 135 CE. His two *Apologies* (see Chapter 4) are later, dating respectively from about 155 CE and 161 CE. The second-century Epistle of Barnabas, which did not make it into the canon of scripture, also feared Christian assimilation to Judaism. The epistle appears to see Christians as 'weak and upstart by comparison with the large, ancient and determinative Jewish body' (Horbury, 1998b, p. 149). The epistle, though, does refer to some Christians who 'admit that the Jews are the people chosen to receive the covenant, and simply claim a share in it (iv 6)' (p. 148).

Much dispute surrounded Christians' reading of the Hebrew Bible, in which they saw so many pointers to Jesus. Origen complained that Jews stuck to a literal translation, missing 'the true sense' (*ibid.*, p. 220). Justin could see Jesus' cross in every reference to a 'tree', in Plato, Homer, Virgil as well as in the Bible. He called the Rabbis 'blind guides' because they never mentioned or expounded 'the great matters of the Law of Moses', meaning passages which Christians see fulfilled in Jesus, and 'when we expound them, they forbid you entirely to listen or to enter into conversation' (1885c, p. cxii). In seven passages, he complains that the Rabbis 'curse' Christians, sometimes in the synagogue (*ibid.*, pp. xvi, xciii, xcv, xcvi, cviii, cxxiii, cxxxiii). This may be a reference to the twelfth benediction against heretics, *Minim*, which in some later formula actually named 'Jeshua bar Pandera' (in the *Halakhoth Gedoloth*, an eighth-century Babylonian work; see Horbury, 1998b, p. 95). Here, Jesus is identified as the son of the Roman soldier whom Celsus had named.

## Jewish anti-Christian polemic

Reference to Jesus as 'son of Pandera' also appears in an earlier rabbinical work, the *Tosephta* (second century) where two passages forbid Jews to accept healing or teaching from him. The charge that Jesus used magic or sorcery to deceive Jews was clearly an early accusation, to which Justin responded in his *Dialogue* (1885c, p. lxix), as he had against the same charge from pagans in his *Apology*. A possible reference in the *Babylonian Talmud* to Jesus, too, seems to accuse him of having studied magic or witchcraft in Egypt, although this is also the passage that places him 130 years too early. It reads, 'Jesus fled to Alexandria in Egypt . . . practiced magic and led Israel astray' (*Sanhedrin*, 107b; Epstein, 1935, Vol. 2, p. 736).

Several Talmud passages refer to someone called Balaam, which may be 'an alias for Jesus'; for example, 'At first he was a prophet, but he became a soothsayer.' Balaam's mother 'played the harlot with carpenters' (*ibid.*, p. 726). 'Balaam the Lame was 30 years old when Phineas the Robber killed him' may be read as a reference to Pilate (alias Phineas) executing Jesus. Balaam was 'subjected to four deaths, stoning, burning, decapitation and strangulation'. The text debates how old Balaam was at the time: 'Bloody and deceitful men shall not live out their days; it follows that he was thirty-three or thirty-four.' If Balaam is Jesus, then we also have here the charge of sexual licence: 'He practiced enchantment by means of his membrum . . . committed bestiality with his ass' (*ibid.*, p. 717).

Acceptance of a link between Jesus and Egypt becomes commonplace in rabbinical writing: 'they knew from other legends and reports' that Jesus had gone 'to Egypt, learned in Egypt the magical arts by which he performed his miracles' (Lauterbach, 1977, p. 55). Jesus is described as 'an enticer who led Israel astray . . . a sorcerer' who 'held false doctrines and followed the practice of magic' (Epstein, 1935; *Sanhedrin*, 107b). Elsewhere, we read that no one is to take pity, or attempt to excuse, a *Mesith* (enticer) (*Sanhedrin*, 29a; Epstein, 1935, Vol. 1, p. 178). Stoning is usually given as Jesus' form of execution, since had Jesus been found guilty of blasphemy, 'the penalty would have been stoning, not crucifixion'

(Schonfield, 1965, p. 148). Jews are often puzzled by the Christian charge that they killed Jesus, pointing out that they could not possibly have been responsible for his crucifixion, which was a political and a Roman penalty. Schonfield (1965) describes 'the calumny that the Jewish people were responsible for the death of Jesus' as an 'antisemitic fraud perpetuated by the Church when it became paganised' (p. 149).

Many passages suggest that although Jesus claimed to use the divine name, the Jews knew that he used magic. Some Rabbis take 'Woe unto him who maketh himself alive by the name of God' to be a 'covert allusion to Jesus' (*Sanhedrin*, 106a; Epstein, 1935, Vol. 2, p. 722). This magic might include the letters of the divine name. The *Tosephta Shabba*:

> says cryptically [that Jesus] learned the means by which he could perform miracles only in this manner which might . . . echo or have given rise to the later legend that Jesus learned in this manner the letters of the holy name by which he performed his tricks or miracles. (Lauterbach, 1977, p. 55)

Jesus is commonly seen as a renegade Jew; excommunicated from the community, he steals Jews away, just as Celsus had claimed. Horbury says that rabbinic sources see Jesus 'as *inter alia* the leader away of whole communities' (1998b, p. 103). Another Talmud passage says, 'on the eve of Passover they hanged Yeshu [Jesus]. . . . He is going forth to be stoned because he has practiced sorcery and enticed Israel to apostasy . . . was he not a *Mesith* (enticer).' Here, Jesus is said to have had five disciples and to be somehow 'connected with the government (or royalty)' (*Sanhedrin*, 43a; Epstein, 1935, Vol. 1, pp. 281–2).

The charge of 'brigandage', found, for example, in Lactantius, may have reflected Jewish polemic: 'Christ . . . put to flight by the Jews, collected a band of nine hundred men [and] committed robberies' (1885, Book 5, Chapter 3). False prophet, magician, brigand, deceiver, appear to characterize early Jewish views of Jesus, who may also have been a demon-possessed trickster (see various gospel passages, such as Matthew 9:34), which later emerged as a common Christian explanation of Muhammad's utterances. Incidentally, many early Christian references to Muhammad contain no details about his career, nor date him correctly. Similarity with Christian views of Muhammad is striking; Muhammad is called a deceiver, a false prophet, and a magician. He is often credited with luring people into Islam by a clever combination of sexual licence and magic. In one famous legend, Muhammad was depicted as a renegade cardinal who set up a rival religion after failing in his bid for the papacy. This made Islam a Christian heresy, against which Jewish scholar Abraham Geiger (see below) reacted, seeing Islam instead as a Jewish progeny.

### Christian anti-Jewish polemic

It is difficult to know who threw the first stone. There was certainly no shortage of Jewish anti-Christian polemic, but neither was there a lack of

Christian polemic against Judaism, some of which I have already cited. Justin, despite his negative view of Judaism, at least wrote in a reasoned and apologetic style. Not so others, whose attitude towards Judaism seemed to harden as it became clear that Jews intended to persist in what Christians believed was a dead, redundant, bypassed religion. Sandmel (1965) writes:

It is the Christian grievance that it was the gentiles who responded affirmatively to the Christian propositions, and that the Jews, who might reasonably have been even more prone to respond, did not do so, and instead obdurately rejected, and malevolently tried to refute, the Christian propositions, thereby making the Christian task more arduous. (p. 7)

The Church Fathers expressed their antipathy, even hatred, of the Jews in blunt, direct, sometimes violent language. The severity of their pronouncements increases as we move into the period of Christianity's ascendancy, when imperial decrees against non-Christians and against Christian heretics supported their views. The charge, though, that the Jews were Christ killers emerged before the Roman establishment of Christianity. In 248 Cyprian (d. 258) wrote: 'That by this alone the Jews can receive pardon of their sins, if they wash away the blood of Christ slain, in His baptism, and, passing over into His Church, obey His precepts' (1885, 1:24). Clement of Rome (c.88–97) blamed Jews for the Neronian persecution. Nero appears to have had some sympathy towards Judaism. The following citations, transcribed from the opening scenes of Feurstein's documentary *Shadow on the Cross* (1990), show how entrenched rejection of Judaism was by the end of the second century:

St Basil (330–79): 'The synagogue of the Jews was formally a court but after the sin against Christ their habitation was made desolate.'

St John Chrysostom (347–407): 'Do not be surprised if I have called the Jews wretched, for though they have received many good things from God they spurn them and violently cast them away' (*Adversus Judaeos* 11:1, available at www.fordham.edu/halsall/source/Chrysostom-Jews6.html).

St Jerome (342–420): 'The godlessness of the Jews and the pagan is on a par, but the Jews practise a deceit which is more dangerous; in their synagogues stands an invisible altar of deceit on which they sacrifice not sheep or calves but the souls of men.'

## The teaching of contempt

By the pontificate of Gregory (540–604), the charge that the Jews had murdered Jesus was firmly linked with the idea that Jews were servants of Satan: 'The Jews are murderers of the Lord, rebels and detesters of God, they resist grace and repudiate the faith of their fathers. Companions of the devil, darkeners of the mind, enemies of all that is beautiful' (Feurstein,

1990). Now, Jews are associated with ugliness, with darkness, with the diabolical. Later, the idea emerged that God had allowed Jews to persist as a punishment, as a sign or witness to Christians of what befalls a people who spurn their own God. In 1235, the Bishop of Lincoln declared that Jews were condemned to wander the earth, bearing the mark and the curse of Cain. Wallace, in *The Prince of India* (1893), refers to a legend that Jesus cursed a Jew who struck him while walking the *Via Dolorosa* (The Way of the Cross). As a result, the Jew became an immortal wanderer: 'At the end of every one hundred years, the undying man falls into a trance, during which his body returns to the age it was when the curse was pronounced' (Vol. 2, p. 549). In the novel, the Wandering Jew encounters and explores the various faiths of the world, a device Wallace uses to suggest something of his own vision of 'Unity in God . . . the evolution of peace and goodwill amongst men' (Vol. 1, p. 287; see also p. 60).

In both the Catholic West and the Orthodox East, disabilities, persecution, polemic, pogroms, expulsions, were all characteristic of the official Christian attitude towards Jews. Forcible conversions, the confiscation and burning of Talmuds, accusation that Jews desecrated the 'host' (communion wafer) to again kill Jesus were rampant. Jewish children would be taken away from their parents to be raised by Christians. In the West, after 528 CE, no Jew could testify against a Christian. In 628–9 CE, Emperor Heraclius in the East renewed the code that forbade Jews from entering Jerusalem. Jews were enslaved or declared to be the king's property, for him to dispose of as he wished. Most professions and the universities were closed to Jews, apart from banking, so they often became the main source of royal revenue. When a ransom was charged in 1194 for the release of King Richard I of England, Jews had to pay three times the amount paid by Christians.

Perhaps for his own vested interest, Richard was actually quite well disposed towards the Jews of England, protecting them on several occasions. From the Fourth Lateran Council onwards (1215), Jews were required to wear a yellow badge, so that no one could mistake their identity. Hitler resurrected the yellow badge, an arm band with the Star of David, and many other restrictions and disabilities throughout his Third Reich. At various times other dress codes were also imposed, such as the wearing of a horned hat (*pileum cornutum*). Christian art suggests that people really did believe that Jews had horns and tails. Restrictions also limited the Jews' freedom to travel as well as place of abode. Soon, the 'blood libel' was added to the list of anti-Jewish calumnies. Each Passover, it was alleged, Jews ritually slaughtered a young Christian boy so that they could use his blood in their Passover bread. This accusation began in England in 1144.

Pictures show demonic-looking Jews wearing yellow badges, sacrificing beautiful, blond-haired, blue-eyed boys (see *The Martyrdom of Simon of Trent*, painted by Gandolfino d'Astri in the late fifteenth century). About twenty saints were eventually canonized as victims of this ritual slaughter.

In art, the Church was made to rise triumphant above the synagogue; see the images *Ecclesia* and *Synagoga* (*c*.1230) at the south entrance of Strasbourg Cathedral. Any misfortune, from bad water to the plague, was blamed on the Jews, just as Tertullian complained that Christians had once been scapegoated for every calamity. It was Jules Isaac (1877–1963), a French Jew whose family was killed by the Nazis, and a friend of Pope John XXIII, who first described the Church's teaching about Jews as a 'teaching of contempt'.

## Jews charged with concealing the truth

Many Christians remained convinced that the Jews knew the truth about Jesus. They claimed that even the Talmud testified to him as redeemer in secret language, yet the Jews stubbornly refused to admit this (see Johnson, 1987, p. 206). From 1231, the Inquisition often tried to get Jews to confess to their secret knowledge of Jesus. At Barcelona in 1263, Rabbi Moses ben Naleman, or the great Nahmonides, among the ablest of all Jewish scholars, was summoned to a public disputation with a former Jew, Pablo Christiani, 'who tried to prove Christianity's efficacy from the *Talmud*' (Voll, 2000, p. 7). Nahmonides argued that only indoctrination from birth could convince anyone that God had been born in a woman's womb. Anyway, he said, belief in the Messiah was not obligatory for Jews (mentioned in Chapter 1). Nor did he see in Jesus the promised Messiah, since Christ had not brought peace but bloodshed (see Johnson, 1987, p. 219).

Talmuds were periodically destroyed or censored; the translator Isidore Epstein (1894–1962) refers to passages that exist in 'uncensored editions' (1935, Vol. 2, p. 735). Not surprisingly, quid pro quo, some Jewish literature circulating from as early as the sixth century disparaged the Jesus story in no uncertain terms. The *Toledot Jeshu* was, says Sandmel, 'quite unedifying'. He calls its contents 'lamentable' but rightly points out that all it did was 'counterpart . . . Christian disparagement of Judaism' (1965, p. 12). In this work, Jesus was illegitimately born to Mary after Pandera (Celsus' Roman soldier) had seduced her. Her own husband then disowned her. Jesus was expelled from the community at an early age for being rude to his teachers (an echo of the *Infancy Gospel of Thomas*?). He then stole the 'ineffable Name' from the Temple and used it to perform magic, and to pretend to be the virgin-born Messiah. Jesus and Judas became embroiled in a contest over the 'Name'. Jesus lost, was captured by the Temple authorities for his crimes and sentenced to death by stoning. Once dead, he was 'hung on a cabbage stalk, since no other tree consented to bear his body' (Hagner, 1997, p. 49). Later, his body was thrown into a ditch before being tied to a horse's tail and dragged about.

There are two points of interest here. First, Christians were to come up with all sorts of stories about the fate of Muhammad's body after his death, which suggests a similar motive, that is, to discredit and to ridicule. Second, by this time the image of Jesus on the cross was venerated by Christians, whose own legends of the true cross contrast sharply with this version. Justin had reprimanded Jews for failing to see the cross predicted in scripture. In Christian legend, the cross on which Jesus hung was identified with the tree from the Garden of Eden. Thus, the tree that had once witnessed humanity's fall later witnessed humanity's salvation.

Remnants of the cross were believed to have been found by Constantine's mother, Empress Helena, near a temple dedicated to Venus. Neo-Gnostics pick up this link with the feminine, and point to such pictures as *Christ on the Tree of Life* (the cross is a tree) by Hendrix Goltzius (1610) to support their synthesis of Jesus, nature, fertility, the female and age-old wisdom. In this picture, a verdant new garden sprouts around the tree. The enigma of the cross is perhaps second only to the question of the Messiah in Jewish–Christian relations. Sandmel (1965) asks, 'How could Christians regard Jesus as divine in the light of his crucifixion, and at the same time blame Jews, mere men, for the death of a divine being?' Further, how could they extend the blame to Jews born 'centuries later and thousands of miles away' (p. 7)?

## Emancipation: Jews look again at Jesus

The litany of repressive Christian acts towards Jews makes sobering and lengthy reading (see Voll, 2000). Martin Luther (1483–1546), in some of his early writing such as 'That Jesus Was Born a Jew' (1523), advocated kinder treatment, in the hope and belief that Jews would convert. If we 'really want to help' Jews, he wrote, 'we must be guided in our dealings with them not by papal law but by the law of Christian love' (1962, Vol. 45, p. 229). Later (1543), when this had not happened, he changed his tune in no uncertain terms:

[the Jews] have failed to learn any lesson from the terrible distress that has been theirs for over fourteen hundred years. (1971, p. 138)

They were never able to tolerate a prophet, and always persecuted God's word. (p. 163)

Wherever they have synagogues, nothing is found but a den of devils in which sheer self-glory, conceit, lies, blasphemy . . . are practices. (p. 172)

We are at fault in not slaying them. Rather, we allow them to live freely in our midst, blaspheming, lying and defaming. (p. 267)

What should we do with this rejected and condemned people . . . First, to set fire to their synagogues or schools and to bury and cover with dirt whatever will not burn, so that no man will ever again see a stone or a cinder of them. This is to be done in honor of our Lord and of Christendom, so that God may see that we are Christian. (p. 268)

If I had power . . . I would deal severely with their lying mouths. (p. 289)

These quotations are from 'On the Jews and Their Lies', reprinted in Nazi Germany. At the Nuremberg trials, Julius Streicher, Hitler's propagandist, claimed that, were he alive, Luther ought to have been a co-defendant.

Luther used the term 'Pharisee' as a synonym for formal, legalistic, hypocritical religion. Roman Catholics, Reformed Christians, anyone with whom Luther disagreed, were 'Pharisees' (see Heschel, 1998, p. 79). On the other hand, Oliver Cromwell (1599–1658), as I noted in Chapter 4, allowed Jews to return to England (expelled by Edward I), believing that this would hasten the return of Jesus; Deuteronomy 28:64 and Daniel 12:7 suggested this could not happen until the scattering of the Jews was complete, 'from the one end of the earth even unto the other'; thus the attempt by some Christians as well as Jews to identify and locate the missing tribes (Johnson, 1987, p. 276). The rise of rationalism, together with disgust at the oppression and cleavage caused by the religious wars of the seventeenth century, when Protestants and Catholics vied with each other to impose their faith on the masses, led to a new desire for toleration and freedom. Post-revolutionary France granted Jews full rights in 1791. Holland followed in 1796.

Germany, where emancipation had some powerful Christian opponents, took longer. Paulus (see Chapter 3) argued that since Jews regarded themselves as a nation within a nation, they could not be assimilated into German society. 'Although one of the most distinguished liberal theologians of his era,' says Heschel, 'Paulus brought anti-Judaism to the heart of his theology and made his reputation as a noted theological scholar the legitimation for his political pamphlets opposing Jewish emancipation' (1998, p. 72). Anton Theodor Hartmann, in a series of articles in the *Leipziger Literaturzeitung* (1833–4), claimed that the Jews viewed Christianity as a form of idolatry and therefore could not be admitted into a Christian country (Heschel, 1998, p. 69).

In the 1820s, German cities were still expelling Jews. Emancipation finally came in 1869, but this did not quell opposition. In 1881, Bismarck received a petition with 250,000 signatories, demanding severe anti-Jewish measures. The petition read, 'fidelity and reverence with respect to anything great and noble are alien to them . . . the race is inferior and depraved' (Voll, 2000, p. 12). Riots and attacks on Jews and Jewish property followed in its wake. The idea of an international Jewish conspiracy began to surface, against which the German Anti-Semitic Alliance was formed in 1886. Later, this gave rise to *The Protocols of the Learned Elders of Zion*, a document purporting to be an outline of how the Jews planned to gain world domination (Marsden, 1922). In 1894, a Jewish officer Alfred Dreyfus (1859–1935) serving on the general staff of the French Army was accused of treason, based on evidence that was later proved to be false. However, he was found guilty and imprisoned.

Adolf Hitler (1889–1945), Germany's Führer (supreme leader) from

1934, became obsessed with the idea that the Jews were conspiring to weaken and eventually destroy Germany: 'the Jew today is the great agitator for the destruction of Germany. Wherever in the world we read of attacks against Germany, Jews are their fabricators.' Their eventual aim was 'world conquest' (Hitler, 1969, p. 568). Marriage with both Jews and blacks represented a mortal 'danger for the existence of the white race in Europe', and resulted in the 'bastardizing [of] the European continent at its core . . . through infection with lower humanity' (*ibid.*, p. 569).

During the Second World War, Hitler's final solution to the 'Jewish problem' was the total annihilation of all Jews, and almost six million were murdered in Nazi Germany's death camps. The word 'anti-Semitic' was first used by Wilhelm Marr, in 1879, 'to designate the contemporary campaigns against Jews throughout Europe' (*A Very Light Sleeper*, 1994, p. 23). In England, Sir Robert Peel (1788–1850) declared: 'For the Jews I see no place of justice . . . they are voluntary strangers here.' Karl Marx (1818–83) opined, 'What is the worldly cult of the Jew? Huckstering. What is his worldly good? Money.' Even the liberal Voltaire called Jews 'the maddest of the lot. The Kaffirs, the Hottentots . . . are much more reasonable and more honest people than . . . the Jews' (*ibid.*, p. 18). Some Jews began to believe that only by replacing the 'Jew as a victim' stereotype with a more confident, active, heroic self-image (what we would now call the 'action hero') could Jews hope to survive. This meshed well with dreams of returning to Israel, of a free state for all Jews, beyond the reach of persecution and pogroms. The more aggressive, even militaristic language of Zionism was problematic for some Jews, since the Talmud tends towards a pacifist stance (see Wiesel (1978) on 'The Jew and War', pp. 198–217).

## The progressive and the Zionist movements

Two contrasting developments began within the Jewish world as a result of emancipation: the progressive and the Zionist movements. Progressive Judaism stood for assimilation, for the minimizing of difference between the synagogue and liberal Protestantism. The first progressive temple opened in Seesen, Westphalia, in 1810. In contrast, Zionism, or the back to Israel movement, wanted a separate Jewish state. Its proponents feared that assimilation offered false hope. Wiesel writes that assimilation denuded Jewish identity: 'Instead of strengthening our identity, we emptied it of substance.' 'Instead of revolutionizing our own history,' he continued, 'we set out to change that of others' (1978, p. 132).

In England, Zionism enjoyed unexpected support from high places. Prime Minister Disraeli (1804–81), who was Jewish by birth, wrote two novels in which his chief characters worked for and achieved the return of Jerusalem to the Jews. His heroes were Messiah-type figures. Disraeli thought that Britain was somehow destined to play a decisive part in the ultimate fulfilment of God's purpose. Disraeli is described in the *Protocols* as a 'dumped', or 'baptized', Jew (see Marsden, 1922). At one point, Britain offered the Jews part of Kenya, but Palestine was already attracting Jewish migrants. By 1914, 80,000 or so Jews had 'returned'. The founder of political Zionism, Theodore Herzl (1869–1904), had attended Dreyfus' trial, which convinced him that Jews would never be fully trusted, despite the granting of civic rights (see Uris' fictionalized account in *Exodus* (1958), pp. 219–24).

In 1897, after the first meeting of the World Zionist Organization, Herzl said that he had 'founded the Jewish state' (cited in Cornwell, 1980, p. 270). Later, Britain manoeuvred herself to gain control of Palestine as a mandated territory (1918–47) after Turkey's defeat in the First World War. During the war, Britain, as ever playing a double game, had pledged Palestine both to the Jews and the Arabs, hence the term 'the twice promised land'. She then made little effort to do anything other than keep the mandate for herself. In November 1947, after the Second World War, the newly established United Nations voted to allow the formation of the State of Israel, where Jews could live in dignity and freedom if not at peace with their Arab neighbours.

The progressive movement in Germany, later exported to Britain and the USA (and further afield), began to use the vernacular in worship, along with the organ, hymns and choirs. Shortening the weekly Torah reading, it adopted a form-critical approach to the text of the Bible. It regarded the Bible as the record of human experience of God, not as a complete text revealed to Moses at Sinai. Its understanding of revelation resembles Lessing's, described in Chapter 3. Progressive Rabbis began to wear the dress of reformed clergy; during the Second World War the first female Rabbi was ordained. Men and women started to sit together, and rules of purity, of diet and other *mitzvot* were relaxed, or rather reinterpreted for today. Tradition, that is, the oral law (Talmud), became less important for progressive Jews. It may even be an 'obstacle to the religious belief of the enlightened man of the modern era' (Hagner, 1997, p. 58). To denote that the restoration of the priesthood and the sacrificial system is no longer desired, the word 'temple' is often used instead of 'synagogue'. In Germany, due to the popularity of the progressive movement, Jewish assimilation seemed to be an outstanding success. Herzl would have said 'I told you so' in the light of what subsequently took place.

I use the term 'progressive' to embrace several modern Jewish movements, such as reform, liberal and progressive. To stress their traditionalism, synagogues outside the progressive movement began to call themselves 'Orthodox'. In the United States, progressive Jews and Conservatives (a half-way house between Orthodox and progressives) form the majority. Two progressive Jews, Abraham Geiger in Germany and Claude Joseph Goldsmid Montefiore in England, pioneered the Jewish reclamation of Jesus. I discuss their contribution below, then move on to those of several more recent Jewish writers on Jesus, including Joseph Klausner, Samuel Sandmel, David Flusser, and my friend and colleague, Marc Ellis.

My aim is to draw out common responses, as well as each scholar's distinctive contribution. For these Jews, as for Christians, writing about Jesus is a risky enterprise.

Sandmel (1965) wrote that for some of his Jewish friends, 'it has seemed impossible for one and the same person to combine in himself an unswerving loyalty to Judaism and a willingness seriously to inquire into Christianity' (p. 13). Or, as Hyman Gerson Enelow (1877–1934) put it, 'consideration of Jesus on the part of a Jewish scholar is regarded as a sign of weakness, if not disloyalty, as a leaning in the wrong direction' (1920, p. 1). If the Jesus image offered looks at all attractive, the writer may be charged with having colluded with the enemy. I have sensed this reaction from fellow Christians to my effort to deal sympathetically with the person of Muhammad. As far as some Christians are concerned, by depicting him as a good man, whose example I can follow in some areas of my life, I am guilty of getting into bed with the Devil!

### Reclaiming Jesus: some Jewish pioneers

Before I turn to Geiger and Montefiore, I will refer briefly to a few extraordinary Jews who, despite suffering at the hands of Christians, spoke well of Jesus during what I think of as the penal period of Jewish history. Catholics in England call their long period of civic disenfranchisement 'penal times'. Maimonides (1135–1204) more than hinted that while the Jews' calling was to fill the world with knowledge and reason, Christianity's was to bring Gentiles to a love of God. The Jews' 'mission', says Wiesel (1978), 'was never to make the world Jewish but, rather, to make it more human' (p. 16).

Rabbi Menachen Ham-Meir (1249–1316) suggested that Christians were not idolaters but followers of Jesus' high ethical teaching. Rabbi Jacob Emden (1679–1776) said that Jesus had never wanted to convert Jews, or to annul the Torah (Matthew 7:17f.), only to teach Gentiles the Noachide code. Jews see the 'commands' given at Genesis 9 as binding on Gentiles; they do not have to keep the Torah, which is peculiarly a Jewish responsibility. The proposal I find most exciting of all was made by Abraham Farissol (1451–1525), who dared to suggest that, while Jesus was not the Messiah of the Jews, he was the Messiah of the Gentiles (Maimonides may also have had this distinction in mind; see Hagner, 1997, p. 51).

Finally, Moses Mendelssohn (1729–86), often called the father of progressive Judaism, argued that a good, rational case could be made for Christianity, provided that belief in Jesus' divinity was dropped and Jesus' moral example formed the basis of Christian action. Mendelssohn, who advocated Jewish assimilation, wanted non-doctrinal religion and the complete separation of church and state. He was a friend and co-campaigner of G. E. Lessing, who, in addition to editing Reimarus, was a renowned literary critic and playwright. Lessing wrote *Nathan der Weise* (1779), whose hero, an enlightened and very generous Jew, was a champion of rationalism. Actually, Nathan was Mendelssohn. Lessing argued for religious toleration. Some ground, then, already existed on which progressive Jewish Jesus scholars could build.

## Geiger 'writes back' on Jesus

Abraham Geiger (1810–74), a pioneer reform Rabbi in Germany, gained his doctorate in 1834 from Marburg for a thesis on the origins of Islam. He saw more Jewish than Christian material in the Qur'an, which he believed drew from Talmudic and Midrashic sources. He argued against the view that Islam had developed within 'the world of Christian heretical movements in Arabia' (Heschel, 1998, p. 51). Geiger applied source and form criticism to the Qur'an in a way that no Muslim would affirm but which compared with how contemporary Christian scholars were approaching the text of the Bible. In published form, Geiger's thesis attracted critical acclaim, and his academic respectability was established. His lifelong ambition of working in the mainstream academy, however, was never fulfilled. Although one of the first German Jews to pass through the university system, because of the Church's control over both divinity faculties and the theological press, employment as an academic theologian, and publishing in theological journals, was impossible for him. He had to write either in oriental studies journals or in periodicals which he published himself with other Jewish intellectuals.

Heschel analyses and discusses Geiger's work on Jesus as an example of postcolonial discourse. As emancipation approached, German Jews were able to revisit Second Temple Judaism. While this was *part of their own history*, in the main its story had been told *only by Christian writers*, whose accounts redounded negatively on the Jewish religion. A sharp contrast between Christianity and Judaism suggested that Jews could not be properly assimilated into German society but were somehow at odds with its core values. On the other hand, if the contrast between Judaism and Christianity could be reduced, stressing continuity rather than discontinuity, Judaism itself emerges as 'the most important religious force in the West, and for that reason alone Jews ought to be granted a social and political emancipation' (Heschel, 1998, p. 16).

Geiger's project was to establish that Judaism was the parent of Islam and Christianity, and as such was the real universal religion. Obviously, this put the dominant Protestant view that Jesus has pitted himself over and against Judaism, and the age-long caricature of Judaism as legalistic, narrow, nationalistic and obscurantist, right in Geiger's firing line. Other Jewish scholars were also trying to minimize the differences between Judaism and Christianity. Geiger's goal, though, was even more ambitious. Unlike these Jews, he did not want to affirm the Christianity of nineteenth-century Germany but Jesus' religion, which, he argued, was actually much closer to reform Judaism than to German Christianity. Heschel says that, as 'the first Jew to be so thoroughly versed in New Testament scholarship, and to be armed with an array of rabbinic textual evidence unknown to his Christian counterparts', Geiger not only refuted 'Christian claims, but enters the Christian story' (p. 22).

As a qualified and ordained Rabbi who was also trained in Christian scholarship, Geiger stood simultaneously on the *same* and on *different* ground as his Christian counterparts. Jews outside the progressive movement tended to see these efforts towards some sort of reconciliation with Christianity as a betrayal of Judaism's distinctiveness, even of its purity. Despite the evils of persecution and of restrictions on Jewish participation in the public sphere, the ghetto had actually preserved Jewish *national* as well as *religious* identity: 'To the reformers, the Jew was a European who practiced the Jewish religion' (Hagner, 1997, p. 58). Jews could be loyal German, French or English citizens. Others saw this as a betrayal of Jewish nationhood, which Zionism aimed to preserve.

## Jesus as a Pharisee

Geiger's Jesus was a loyal but reforming Jew, whose teaching was very much in the Pharisaic tradition of Hillel (first century BCE), who stressed the spirit and not the letter of the law. Hillel was 'a man of living, continuous development . . . a restorer or reformer of Judaism' (Geiger, 1911, pp. 103–4). Such sayings as 'the Sabbath was made for man, not man for the Sabbath' were typically Pharisaic, not diametrically opposed to the Pharisees (Mark 2:27–8). It would have been with the Sadducees, whose stress was on purity rather than holiness, that Jesus differed. A passage such as 'first cleanse the inside of the cup, and then the outside will be clean also' (Matthew 23:26) directed against Pharisees makes more sense as a critique of Sadducean concern for ritual purity. Sadducees, not Pharisees, would have been 'whitewashed tombs'.

Of course, the Pharisees did stress ritual purity but for them, as for Jesus, external piety had to be accompanied by ethical conduct. Geiger suggested that since the early Church found itself in competition with a rabbinical Judaism that evolved from Second Temple Pharisaism, it simply read this conflict into the Gospels. After 70 CE, the Sadducees, wed both to the Temple and to the Romans, ceased to exist as a group. They simply lost any relevance. On the other hand, the Pharisees, in laying down the Mishnah and the Talmud, became increasingly obscurantist; concerned with 'fencing in the law', exactly as Jesus accused them, 'they tie up heavy loads and put them on men's shoulders'. Further, the Pharisees would not have had anything to do with Jesus' arrest, since the Sadducees, not they, were politically dominant.

After the death of Jesus, says Geiger, it was actually from the Sadducees that the apostles borrowed many of their ideas about Jesus as the high priest, about the atonement and about sacrifice. He attributes the Letter to the Hebrews to Sadducean influence. Geiger argues that as they had nowhere else to go, many Sadducees became Christian. However, 'despite their newfound adherence to Jesus', they 'persisted in rejecting Pharisaism, and the continued conflicts between the two tendencies became a major factor in shaping early Christianity' (Heschel, 1998, p. 166).

Oddly, Geiger built some controversial ideas about aspects of the difference between Sadducees and Pharisees into his scheme, which I think works perfectly well without them. He tended to see the Samaritans and the Karaites as the Sadducees' forerunners and successors. The Samaritans, descendants of the tribes of Ephraim and Manasseh, developed their own form of Judaism independent of Jerusalem and of the Levitical priesthood. Until the Hasmoneans destroyed it in 129 BCE, their Temple stood on Mount Gerizim (see Chapter 1). The Karaites were an eighth-century sect which denied the rabbinical tradition, recognizing only the Bible.

Identification of Jesus with Pharisaism has become an increasingly acceptable view. Flusser (1997), for example, also tends to see Jesus as 'closest to the School of Hillel who' had 'preached love' (p. 92). Finkel (1964) depicts Jesus as adopting 'the Pharisaical stand' on 'controversial issues concerning religious principle' (p. 130). He also thinks that any criticism of the Pharisees would have been directed only at some, 'the zealous Pharisees, the disciples of Shammai's academy', since 'Hillel's school . . . was close in spirit to that of the teacher of Nazareth' (p. 134; see pp. 136–43 for an extended discussion). However, when Geiger first suggested this it would have sounded outrageous, given the equation of Pharisee with 'hypocrite' that was so deeply engrained in the European psyche.

### Jesus and Hillel: the start of a trend

Basically, Geiger's Jesus 'was a Pharisee who walked in the way of Hillel' (Geiger, 1911, p. 117). Geiger also saw similarity between Jesus and 'Hillel's opponent, Shammai' (Heschel, 1998, p. 150; see also Flusser, 1997, p. 76). Shammai advocated a stricter approach to the law, as Jesus does when he overrules Moses on the issue of divorce (Mark 10:11). Jesus and the Pharisees 'read the Bible in the light of the times, whereas the Sadducees stuck to the letter of the Bible and wanted to force the times to be in accord with it' (Heschel, 1998, p. 83). Geiger's Jesus 'did not utter a new thought' (Geiger, 1911, p. 117). Jesus probably did think that he was the Messiah, as this was actually a common belief, perhaps especially among the Galileans.

Geiger describes Jesus as 'a Jew . . . with Galilean coloring – a man who shared the hopes of his times and believed that these hopes were fulfilled in him' (*ibid.*). The Galileans, he said, bred an especially apocalyptic and revolutionary form of Judaism. Geiger thought there some resemblance between Jesus and Honi the Circle Drawer, who tried to bridge divisions and was stoned for his efforts. Geiger even suggested that the prayer, 'Lord, forgive them', attributed to Jesus on the cross, may also have been

Honi's dying words. Geiger's comparison of Jesus with Hillel, with Honi and other Second Temple teachers or prophets began a trend that continues to this day in Jewish writing on Jesus.

## Rabbinical sources?

To help to reconstruct the issues and debates that characterized Second Temple Judaism, Geiger turned to rabbinical sources. This challenged Christian reliance on the Gospels (plus Josephus), even if it proved controversial. Scholars still debate whether the Talmud has any contribution to make to the study of Christian origins; is it too late as a written source? Does it reflect so many later debates that any material relevant to Jesus' time has been buried or even distorted? Similarly, rabbinical accounts of the life and personality of such teachers as Hillel, which indeed has much in common with the gospel portrait of Jesus, may equally represent after-the-fact doctoring, either to deliberately make Hillel at least Jesus' equal, or, as Finkel (1964) suggests, because this was common practice:

For the masses, Moses represented the redeemer par-excellence, Samuel and Ezra the teachers par-excellence and Elijah the prophet par-excellence. In the period before and after the Destruction [of the Temple] a portrayal of the activities of the teachers assumed unconsciously the image of the heroic prophets of the past . . . [thus] the miraculous acts of the Jewish masters were described along the lines of the stories related of Moses, Elijah and Elisha. (pp. 95–6)

In other words, the way in which Matthew took Bible passages and wove them into his account of Jesus' life was not a radical departure from rabbinical practice but typically Jewish.

## Geiger on Paul

Geiger blamed Paul for Christianity's break with Judaism, which transformed Jesus into a Messiah in whom belief or faith was necessary for salvation. Paul's fatal error was his insistence that Jesus was *himself* the object of faith. Paul's abandonment of 'Jewish religious observance . . . opened the way to the corruption of pure Jewish monotheism with pagan ideas' (Heschel, 1998, p. 151). While many of Christianity's ideas remained Jewish in origin, compromises were made in a bid for popularity and success: 'if the gods were but human beings, it was easy to understand making gods out of human beings' (Geiger, 1911, p. 136). Thus, *Jesus the man* became *Christ the God*.

Geiger also argued that Christian ideas began to creep into Jewish thought. Here, he especially singled out the idea that *blood sacrifice* was necessary for the atonement of sin, which is central to the Letter to the Hebrews. He found the notion of 'original sin' as objectionable as he found the concept that God had a son. He argued that the sacrifices in the

Temple had never been intended as the means by which salvation would be gained but only to invite repentance and a change of heart. Talmudic references that appear to accept such ideas as vicarious atonement were the result of Christian influence (see Epstein, 1935, *Rosh Hashanah* 16a and *Shabbat* 146a). Writing about the reform prayer-book, Geiger said, 'Passages which only remotely remind us of ancient human sacrifice, regarded as an abomination by the Judaism of all periods, must be totally removed from the prayerbook' (1968, pp. 166–7). As it evolved, Christianity's outlook was more universal than rabbinical Judaism's, yet

Christianity won not through the unique greatness of Jesus, not through its own specific truth, it won through the eternal truths borrowed from Judaism, which it – and this is its only accomplishment – knew to free from their nationalistic and dogmatic bounds. (Geiger, 1875, p. 182)

## Reform Judaism as Jesus' real heirs

Far from progressive Judaism being a clone of contemporary Protestant Christianity, or a betrayer of authentic Judaism, it was the closest of all to the reform movement of which Jesus, Hillel and others had been leaders. Christians in nineteenth-century Germany who wanted to follow Jesus' religion rather than the religion of Jesus ought to join the Reform Synagogue, just as should any Jew who wanted to practise Second Temple Judaism. Geiger's writing was as much a defence of progressive Judaism against the Orthodox criticism that progressive Jews might just as well become Christian as it was an effort to redefine Judaism's relationship with Christianity. In fact, in the 1870s some Christians did convert, attracting vehement protest from Christian leaders and theologians. Geiger defended this. It was, he said, in the spirit of Lessing, and wholly consistent with the supposed civil and spiritual equality of Judaism. Thus, 'conversion . . . to Judaism was not a backward step, from Jesus to Moses, as it was being portrayed by Christian leaders, but a return to the original faith' (Heschel, 1998, p. 45).

Heschel's book, a well-deserved tribute to Geiger, also makes sobering reading. She describes Christianity's anti-Jewish bias as a fatal flaw. Christians applauded Geiger's writing on Islam. They took his work on Jesus seriously, cited him and reviewed him, but rejected his theories, almost always continuing to stress *discontinuity* between Jesus and Judaism. Renan's *Life of Jesus* and Geiger's *Das Judentum und Seine Geschichte* (*Judaism and Its History*, translated 1911) appeared the same year. The contrast between their Jesuses' relationship with Judaism was stark. Geiger described Renan's Jesus as a 'visionary hypocrite' and called Renan's and Strauss' work 'a retrogressive step' (Heschel, 1998, p. 155). Germany, too, was far from ready to see Jesus as a loyal first-century Jew. Many Germans were convinced that Jesus' Jewishness was almost accidental. Scholars debated 'Jesus' racial heritage, and the suitability of a Jewish-derived religion . . . for the German volk' (p. 12).

## An Aryan or a Jewish Jesus?

In 1899, Houston Stewart Chamberlain (1855–1927) published his *Foundations of the Nineteenth Century* (English translation, 1910) in which he strongly suggested that Jesus had been an Aryan. 'In religion and education' Jesus 'was a Jew' but 'in the narrow and real sense of the word "Jew" – most probably not', he claimed (Vol. 1, p. 202). The son of British Admiral William Chamberlain, Houston Chamberlain was educated in France and Switzerland before settling in Germany, where he made his name as a Wagnerian scholar.

In this bestselling book, Chamberlain argued that many residents of Galilee or the 'district of the heathen' were regarded as foreigners by the Jews. In fact, he says, people of 'purely Aryan blood' had been 'transplanted there' (p. 205). 'The probability,' he continued, 'that Christ was no Jew, that he had not a drop of genuinely Jewish blood in his veins, is so great that it is almost equivalent to a certainty' (pp. 211–12). Such ideas as 'sin, redemption, rebirth, grace' were 'ancient Aryan ideas . . . unknown to Jews' (p. 237).

Under Hitler, the Deutsche Christen presented Jesus as an Aryan who had opposed everything Jewish, as should Germans: 'the reconciliation of Christianity with Nazism . . . required nothing less than the eradication of everything Jewish . . . to create a *judenrein* [Jew-free] Christianity for a *judenrein* Germany' (Heschel, 1998, p. 12). The idea that Jesus had not been a Jew may date from Marcion, who thought that Jesus was directly from God, while the Jews worshipped a demiurge; 'the Jews belong to the devil', said Marcion (cited by Rosenzweig, 1977, p. 413). The white supremacist movement's Jesus is also an Aryan Jesus, as noted in my last chapter.

## A deafening silence

During the Second World War, Pope Pius XII remained silent, maintaining diplomatic relations with Germany. He left a letter from his predecessor, Pope Pius XI, which explicitly condemned Hitler's policy, unpublished. A statement by Pope John Paul II on Shrove Tuesday 2000 confessed 'sins against the children of Israel'. However, his reference to the Holocaust as 'the result of the pagan ideology of Nazism' raised objections from commentators, who point out that the Holocaust's perpetrators were in the main baptized Christians, Catholic and Protestant. 'The Nazis,' says Leo (2000), 'may have drawn their direct inspiration from a post-Christian version of purely racial anti-Semitism . . . but Christianity clearly prepared the way and lit the fuse' (p. 14). 'Among the SS,' observed Wiesel, 'a large proportion were believers who remained faithful to their

Christian ties to the end', even going 'to confession between massacres' (1978, p. 13).

Even the Confessing Church, which opposed Nazi idolatry and dictatorship, led by such men as Karl Barth (1886–1968) and Martin Niemöller (1892–1984), failed to oppose Hitler's Jewish policy. Niemöller was sent to a concentration camp. Later, he regretted that:

They came for the communists, and I did not speak up because I wasn't a communist; They came for the socialists, and I did not speak up because I was not a socialist; They came for the union leaders, and I did not speak up because I wasn't a union leader; They came for the Jews, and I didn't speak up because I wasn't a Jew. Then they came for me, and there was no one left to speak up for me. (Many versions of this are attributed to Niemöller, usually dated 1945)

The terrible truth, says Wiesel, is that people, the whole civilized world, 'knew – and kept silent. People knew – and did nothing' (1978, p. 224). Hauntingly, he asks, 'Where was man in all this, and Culture, how did it reach this nadir?' (*ibid.*, p. 12). In fact, a few did speak out. Paul Tillich, cited in Chapter 3, unequivocally condemned the death camps. Some, called the 'righteous Gentiles', did help the Jews; in Nazi-occupied Denmark and Holland, for example, whole communities of Jews were protected or spirited to safety. Leon Uris' *Exodus* (1958), a bestselling novel, chronicles these and other events surrounding the rebirth of Israel.

### After Geiger: Montefiore

Identification of Jesus as a Pharisee, the idea that he never departed from Judaism, that he pointed people towards God but did not claim to be God, comparison with Hillel and with Honi the Circle Drawer, all found in Geiger, surface repeatedly in later Jewish writing on Jesus. So does the question of continuity and discontinuity between Paul's Jesus and the historical Jesus, and the idea that Galilee was especially prone to apocalyptic or Zealous leanings. All this suggests that his scholarship was pioneering and trend-setting, as well as of enduring value. Claude Joseph Goldsmid Montefiore (1858–1938), who graduated from Oxford and from the Hochschule für Wissenschaft des Judentums, Berlin, became President of Southampton University College (1915–34), and so achieved what Geiger had always coveted: a post in the mainstream academy.

Montefiore also served a term as President of the World Union for Progressive Judaism and helped to establish the Liberal Jewish Synagogue in London (1926). He became, says Hagner (1997), 'the outstanding Jewish scholar on Jesus' (p. 28). An Anglophile, Montefiore opposed Zionism. Since Christianity was the established religion of England, he was predisposed towards a sympathetic treatment of its seminal personality, Jesus. More so than Geiger, he was prepared to entertain original elements in Jesus' teaching, which he said represented a distinct understanding of the Mosaic law. Eventually, it was this that led to Jesus' death.

Jesus elevated the law of love above all else, so that ceremonial and external aspects of obedience became secondary to morality and ethics. The Rabbis, though, 'detested hypocrisy no less hotly than Jesus did' (Montefiore, 1970, p. 322).

Montefiore hesitates to say that Jesus had intended to extend 'love' to the non-Jew: 'it is going too far to say that Jesus deliberately and consciously "freed the conception of neighbour from its Jewish limitations"' (Montefiore, 1970, p. 345). Yet Jesus' real significance, said Montefiore, does lie in his universalizing of Jewish ideas. Montefiore's Jesus was a prophet of the apocalypse but his understanding of the kingdom was as at least partially already present. Nor had Jesus anticipated a purely spiritual and therefore un-Jewish kingdom. Here, Montefiore is closer to such Christian scholars as Dodd, Crossan, Borg and Wright than to Weiss, Schweitzer or Sanders. While the latter insisted that anything like a 'realized eschatology' was alien to Jewish thought, Montefiore is not the only Jewish scholar who suggests that, as a Jew influenced by Jewish thought, Jesus may have pioneered this concept.

In other words, the kingdom as in some sense a present reality was a notion that preceded not anteceded the crucifixion. Flusser (1997) writes, 'Jesus . . . is the only Jew of ancient times known to us who not only preached that people were on the threshold of the end of time, but that the new age of salvation had already begun' (p. 110). More so than Sanders, who cannot allow Jesus an original thought, these Jewish scholars can. However, 'Jesus . . . wanted to remain in the Jewish faith', and drew on the 'long preparatory work of contemporaneous Jewish faith' in his teaching (*ibid.*, p. 13).

## The question of Jesus' authority

Montefiore suggests that Jesus may well have thought of himself as possessing a greater authority, even more power, 'than any prophet before him' (1910, p. 120). Yet this did not mean that he claimed to be God, or demanded that people worship or believe in him, except 'so far as to recognize that he was the prophet and messenger of God' (1923, p. 225). Again and again, Jews who comment on Jesus insist that no Jew would have invited people to place their trust in him; rather, Jesus would have pointed people towards God. This is very close to Borg's and Crossan's understanding, which is one reason why I disagree with Heschel's (1998) verdict that 'there is nothing particularly Jewish in Crossan's portrayal of Jesus as a Mediterranean peasant' (p. 234). She dislikes the implication she sees in Borg and Crossan that Judaism represented 'hierarchy and oppression', and Jesus 'equality and freedom' (p. 234).

The way in which Jesus, in the Gospels, seems to override the Mosaic law by saying, 'you have heard' but 'I say' (Matthew 5:38), has proved problematic for many Jewish writers. Vermes (see below) tends to think that Jesus' healings and exorcisms would have afforded him peculiar authority. Jewish scholar Solomon Schechter sought a linguistic solution. Is what we have in the Gospels a bad rendering of an Aramaic expression into Greek? Did Jesus actually say something more like 'one might hear so and so . . . but there is a teaching to say that the words must not be taken in such a sense' (cited by Hagner, 1997, p. 99)? Or, was Jesus offering alternative interpretations, namely others interpret the text this way but here is my interpretation? Finkel (1964) refers to 'ye have heard' and 'but I say unto you' as 'rabbinical formulas' which set up a contrast between negative and positive teachings (p. 166).

## Geza Vermes

Comparison of Jesus with Honi the Circle Drawer and other northern, charismatic, healing prophets, especially Hanina ben Dosa, pioneered by Geiger, has more recently been popularized by Geza Vermes, the renowned Dead Sea Scrolls scholar. After his family (Hungarian Jews) became Roman Catholics during his youth, Vermes entered Seminary and eventually became a member of the Order of Notre-Dame de Sion. Co-founded by Theodore Ratisbonne, an Alsatian Jew converted to Catholicism, and his brother Alphonse, 'who claimed to have a vision of the Virgin Mary in Rome in 1842' (Vermes, 1999, p. 55), this order originally aimed at evangelizing Jews. Sandmel (1965) comments on how Christians consistently fail 'to understand the Jewish instinct about apostates that they still today ordinarily entrust to former Jews the task of converting Jews' (p. 9). Vermes himself saw his mission as helping to lead a 'new crusade against the age-old Christian anti-Judaism in the Catholic Church' (1999, p. 62).

In 1950, having gained his doctorate from the College St Albert, Belgium, Vermes was assigned to the Dead Sea Scrolls team. Stationed next in Paris, he fell in love, got married, and left the Catholic Church. He moved to England, where he became a UK citizen, and taught at Newcastle, then at Oxford as Reader (later Professor) of Jewish Studies. By the late 1960s he had left 'Christianity, with its fundamental tenets of the Trinity, the divinity of Jesus, and was becoming increasingly aware of his Jewish identity. On 7 October 1970 he became a member of the London Liberal Synagogue. Later, he also joined the advisory board of Leo Baeck College, the UK's progressive Jewish rabbinical Seminary. In 1973, he published *Jesus the Jew*. The following year, he delivered the Claude Goldsmid Montefiore Memorial Lecture on the same topic. Martin Forward interprets Vermes' work on Jesus as a polemically motivated attempt to justify his 'own pilgrimage from Judaism to RCism and back to Judaism again' (2000, p. 2).

Vermes subtitled his book *A Historian's Reading of the Gospels*, indicating that his aim was neutral, objective scholarship. However, his overriding concern was to understand Jesus as a Galilean Jew, as a man firmly rooted in a specific context. He attributes the Christ of faith to post-crucifixion Christian dogmas, a view shared by almost all Jewish writers. Hyam

Maccoby (1995), for example, does not think that either Jesus' divinity or the doctrine of the Trinity can be traced to Jesus. Rather, 'this change was initiated by Saint Paul, who should therefore be regarded as the founder of the central trend of Christianity' (p. 17). Vermes' Jesus is a charismatic, northern prophet who stood in a long line of healers and teachers stretching back to the great biblical characters of Elijah and Elisha, as well as the more recent Honi the Circle Drawer. Vermes does not seem to doubt that Jesus really did heal.

Like other northern teachers and reformers, or *Hasids*, Jesus had little interest in the Temple. He also claimed an authority that came straight from God, as did they. His consuming passion was to know and do God's will. He possessed penetrating insight into the inner, spiritual meaning of the law, which was, above all, designed to bring humanity into a relationship with God. His sense of intimacy with God may have led him to use the term 'God's son', but only in the sense that the Bible speaks of Israel as God's son. Any notion of a divine or miraculous birth belongs to the realm of psychology, not history (Vermes, 1973, p. 222).

## Praise for the Mennonites

Flusser (1997) offers a similar assessment, although unlike Vermes he thinks that Jesus 'eventually embraced the conviction that he would be revealed as the Messiah' (p. 176). Jesus did not 'demand that others accept his own high aspirations', or 'speak about belief in himself' but 'solely of belief in God' (*ibid.*). 'Jesus himself,' says Flusser, 'was far from enjoying the cult of his personality during his lifetime' (*ibid.*). These convictions were added by the early Church, which 'began making internal revisions to' the gospel materials (*ibid.*, p. 177). Similarly, Schonfield (1965) writes: 'Jesus had not even uttered the sacred Name of God. . . . Early Nazarean teaching knew nothing of trinitarianism' (pp. 148–9).

Describing them as a 'small group' for whom the original teaching of Jesus has remained vital, David Flusser dedicated his *Jesus* (1997) to the Mennonites (p. 177). The Mennonites are deeply committed to peace, justice, social welfare and development but 'recognize no common doctrine, so that some of them are practically Unitarian in their views' (Cross and Livingstone, 1983, p. 903). Flusser taught Second Temple Judaism and Early Christianity at the Hebrew University, Jerusalem, and drew on almost fifty years of research in writing his Jesus book. Vermes, who first met Flusser during work on the Dead Sea Scrolls, says that he used to converse with the Jesuits in what he called 'his favorite language, medieval Latin' and continued, 'but I can add that New Testament Greek came a close second' (1997, p. 87).

Like all the writers reviewed in this chapter, Flusser takes the gospel stories that surround Jesus' birth and death to be the product of the disciples' faith. He writes, 'It would seem . . . that both the tradition that Jesus was born in Bethlehem, and the proof of his davidic ancestry, rose because many believed that the Messiah would be of David's line' (1997, p. 26). 'Jesus,' says Flusser, 'was a Galilean Jew who was probably born in Nazareth' (*ibid.*, p. 27). Flusser also discusses similarities between Jesus' teaching and the Essenes', suggesting at least indirect influence, perhaps especially on his Sermon on the Mount (p. 97). He seems reluctant to speak of Jesus after the crucifixion, but he does refer to the belief in a pre-existent Jesus and in the resurrection as 'a meta-historical drama' (p. 176). The birth of Gentile Christianity, he says, led to the unraveling of 'Christianity's formal ties with Judaism' (*ibid.*).

## Marc Ellis

My colleague Marc Ellis, University Professor of American and Jewish Studies at Baylor, warms rather more than Heschel does to Crossan's Jesus. As well as referring very positively to Crossan in his writings, Ellis has mentioned his appreciation of Crossan several times in conversations between us about my work on Jesus. Ellis' own work has been controversial because of his unremitting support for the Palestinians. The Jews, at great cost, gained Israel-Palestine (Ellis always uses this designation), yet in displacing and persecuting the Palestinians, they are in danger of reversing their role from victim to victimizer. He asks, 'are . . . the Palestinians . . . a stand-in for the defeat we longed to deliver to those who had oppressed us for over a thousand years?' (1994, p. 9). Ellis reads the covenant between God and Israel as primarily concerned with *freedom and liberation*.

Ellis often uses the term 'partial practice' to describe those who fail to live up to the fullest potential and highest demands of their own ethical convictions. Christians are guilty of partial practice when they trample on the very people for whom Jesus voiced especial concern. Jews are guilty of partial practice when they replace God's sovereignty with their own power. Jesus, says Ellis, criticized partial practice wherever he saw this, including within the Judaism of some of his contemporaries. This does not mean that all Jews were hierarchical and oppressive. 'Jesus' sense of the kingdom', as 'Crossan interprets it', included 'nobodies and undesirables', which challenged the sensibilities of those who set up boundaries between pure and impure, between themselves and others (*ibid.*, p. 102). Unfortunately, Christians resurrected all the boundaries that Jesus had crossed, and did so in his name. The very hierarchy he hated within the Jewish establishment has been replicated within Christianity (*ibid.*, p. 126).

## Jesus 'belongs outside the Church that claims him'

Ellis stresses that Jesus and his disciples did what they thought had to be done, offering an unbrokered relationship with God that bypassed mechanisms set up to protect the power and privilege of the establishment. This was not anti-Jewish, as Heschel seems to suggest, but a way of 'being faithful within their history as they saw it' (*ibid.*). He accepts that anti-

Jewish content was later written into the Gospels, making it 'difficult to maintain Crossan's Jesus within the canonical gospels' (*ibid.*, p. 124). Ellis does not think that Jesus claimed to be the Messiah, nor does he think that Jesus was the Messiah whom some Jews were expecting. However, he does see Jesus as a figure about which Jews and Christians can converse. Provocatively, he suggests that, in building its empire, Christianity has forfeited ownership of Jesus: 'perhaps it is the fear that he belongs outside the Church that claims him that redoubles the attempt to hold him fast within its normative tradition' (*ibid.*, p. 126).

Ellis argues that Jesus did not intend to place himself between people and God. Indeed, following Crossan, Ellis argues that Jesus was opposed to any barrier, such as rules of ritual purity, social etiquette or a rigid application of the Mosaic code, that erected boundaries around God. Geiger, Montefiore, Ellis, in various ways, stress commonality between Jesus and Judaism. This opens up the possibility of shared praxis between Christians and Jews, to confront the empires that separate humanity and God. Other Jewish writers stress that original Christianity was closer to Judaism, whereas the Christianity that triumphed contained too many pagan notions, representing a negation of Judaism.

### Joseph Klausner (1874–1960)

This term 'a negation of Judaism' was much used by Joseph Klausner, who focused a great deal on Paul's contribution. After doctoral work at Heidelberg on Jewish eschatology, he taught at the Hebrew University, Jerusalem. His *Jesus of Nazareth* (1925) and *From Jesus to Paul* (1944) were written in modern Hebrew. He argues that Paul combined Judaism with Hellenism. Paul replaced the physical, this-worldly kingdom envisioned by Jesus with a spiritual, non-geographical kingdom that was more akin to the thought of Hellenism. More recently, Fredriksen writes: 'Paul radically redefines the concept of redemption, as he does the concepts of Kingdom and Christ: through the originally political vocabulary of liberation, he praises a reality that is *utterly spiritual*' (1988, p. 173; italics added).

Jesus, says Klausner, elevated ethics above ritual (see 1944, p. 257), had thought himself the Messiah, and expected to judge the twelve tribes of Israel, to whom he had exclusively preached. He was a Pharisaic Rabbi but was concerned much more with *haggada* than with *halacha*, which Sandmel describes thus: '*haggada* is the edifying aspect of rabbinical literature, *halacha* the legal' (1965, p. 115 n. 27). Jesus was a Jew, and remained a Jew 'until his last breath' (Klausner, 1977, p. 164). He certainly did not say anything like ' "This is my body" . . . "this is my blood" . . . and of course he did not say that his blood was "unto the remission of sin" ' (p. 512). Unlike Flusser, Klausner thought that Jesus did encourage veneration; unlike Vermes, he was reluctant to concede to Jesus the title 'prophet', since 'he lacked political perception' (Sandmel, 1965, p. 92).

It was after the unplanned and totally unexpected shock of their Messiah's shameful death by crucifixion that Jesus' disciples 'began – of course not immediately, but after a short time – to apply Isaiah 53 . . . to the Messiah who had been abused and unjustly put to death' (Klausner, 1977, p. 267). Klausner does not accuse the disciples of insincerity, or fraud, yet here he does sound similar to Reimarus. Even so, despite this eccentric form of Messianism, which added to the belief that the 'Messiah was *still* to come, the belief that he had *already* come', the early Nazarenes remained within Judaism (*ibid.*, p. 281). Sharing possessions, stressing ethical conduct, they formed a sectarian group not dissimilar to the Essenes, with whom Klausner compares them (p. 278). They held, says Klausner, that 'Jesus was only a man born of Joseph and Mary' (p. 279). '*Everything else*,' he stresses, '*is Jewish*' (translator's italics).

Paul, a Hellenic Jew, wanted Judaism to be above all of universal, not merely of Jewish, nationalistic, significance (see *ibid.*, pp. 444–5). He knew that Gentile hearts were crying out for a saviour, even eager for one 'from the East' (p. 448). Pagan ideas 'hovered in the air in the Hellenized cities in which Paul lived and preached', and he breathed these in (p. 485). These Greeks were hardly expecting a crucified and risen Messiah, any more than the Jews were, but this is exactly what Paul offered them:

Paul came to those yearning for salvation and preached an attenuated Judaism, from which had been taken the sharp edge of the Torah and the difficulty in the observance of the ceremonial laws; and in place of a dying and rising *god*, such as was common in the various pagan religions of that time, he added to this attenuated Judaism a dying and rising *Messiah*. (*ibid.*, p. 449)

Under Hellenic influence, the once 'flesh-and-blood' Jesus is increasingly spiritualized, just as the distinction between Jesus and God becomes blurred.

Luke, the Greek physician who travelled with Paul, added the virgin birth (*ibid.*, p. 485). Paul's concept of 'being in Christ' was borrowed from the mystery cults: ' "To be in God" is not an ancient or an authentic Jewish idea; "to be in the Messiah" is even less so' (p. 492). Paul did not intend to lead Jews out of Judaism. This, though, was the result of his synthesis, which he always saw as a 'new and improved kind of Judaism, like Essenism' (p. 453). On the other hand, through Paul, alongside 'strange and natural superstitions', the Gentiles also 'accepted . . . the Jewish Bible' as their faith's 'foundation and basis'. Klausner thus concludes: 'in this sense – and only in this sense – was Paul also what Maimonides so beautifully called Jesus: *A preparer of the way for the King-Messiah*' (p. 610).

If the Essenes influenced Jesus, he may have borrowed his preference for celibacy from them, if indeed he was celibate, which as I have shown is a much debated issue. Klausner points to such similarities between Jesus and the Essenes as baptism and a shared meal (p. 278). Sandmel comments that some Christians take Klausner to 'represent not only the Jewish mind but also the epitome of rabbinic learning, apparently unaware of how severely rabbinists have taken him to task' (1965, p. 93). Like other Jews who write about Jesus, Klausner has been accused of 'truckling to Christians'. Sandmel, though, praises his 'undoubted Jewish loyalties' (*ibid.*).

## Jesus and the Essenes: Hugh Schonfield's theory

In constructing his Jesus story, Schonfield draws on the Essenes, from whom Jesus 'imbibed a good many . . . notions' (1965, p. 63). In addition to a translation of the New Testament (1955), Schonfield has written books on Paul (1947), on the Dead Sea Scrolls (1957), and a provocative and bestselling title, *The Passover Plot* (1965). In this book, Schonfield reverses Klausner's judgement that it was the disciples and not Jesus who thought up the 'suffering servant' idea. He takes this to have been an available interpretation of Isaiah 53 during Jesus' time, contrary to Vermes' opinion that this only arose after 125 CE.

Jesus, says Schonfield, like the teacher of righteousness, used scripture to map out his career. Consciousness of his messiahship permeated Jesus' self-awareness, says Schonfield. Passionately believing in his mission, he spared no effort to make the kingdom become a living, earthly reality. Convinced that his own suffering would precipitate the kingdom's birth, he plotted and planned the events of Passover. Jesus, though, had no intention of dying. Yes, he believed that he would have to suffer, but the possibility of dying never entered his head. Rather, he planned to survive the crucifixion (1965, p. 162). The 'cloth saturated with vinegar' given him on the cross was really a drug, administered by a secret, prearranged helper (p. 167).

Aspects of Schonfield's theory remind me of Paulus, even of Bahrdt. A Jesus who expected to *suffer* but not to *die* may bypass the psychological problem posed by Schweitzer's death-wishing Jesus. Unfortunately, Jesus had not expected the spear wound in his side (p. 172). He was only able to regain consciousness briefly, surprising his disciples, who later became convinced that their Lord had risen from the dead. Resurrection, together with eagerness to magnify their Lord, later resulted in the disciples turning *Jesus the man* into *Christ the God*, especially under the influence of pagan ideas. Thus, Christianity's 'development as a new religion was conditioned by its non-Jewish environment . . . it became transformed by the assimilation of alien ideas and modes of thought' (p. 205).

Schonfield, like Geiger, fully identifies with Jesus' religion, but not with the religion of Jesus. A Jesus who is not an object of worship, he says, still represents an important role model for all who believe in acting to achieve what Jesus himself desired: world peace. If we would but work for this as single-mindedly and as relentlessly as Jesus did, 'the victory for which Jesus . . . schemed and strove will be won. . . . There will be peace throughout the earth' (p. 187). Schonfield reacts strongly against the charge that the Jews killed Jesus. He does concede that some Jews were implicated in Jesus' crucifixion but thinks that the masses would not have favoured this.

Indeed, they may have reacted 'to the deed if it leaked out' (p. 153). Schonfield (1947) actually identifies himself as a believer in Jesus as Messiah but continues, 'I am not a Christian . . . if that is to be applied only to those who have subscribed to the dogmas of the Church . . . I confess the Unity of God, not a Unity in Trinity' (p. viii). It was Paul's enthusiasm to include Gentiles that transformed the kingdom from an earthly to a heavenly one, no doubt influenced by 'the pagan mysteries with their conception of individual salvation by identification with a god in his death and resurrection' (1965, p. 203).

### Rubenstein on my brother Paul

Marc Ellis' teacher, Richard Rubenstein, among other Jews, has written somewhat more appreciatively of Paul. In *My Brother Paul* (1972), Rubenstein sees some similarity between his own often tense relationship with 'establishment Judaism' and Paul's (pp. 6–7). He uses Freudian theory to offer an alternative explanation of Paul's thought on Jesus, whom he represents as wrestling with the question, How can people enjoy a relationship with God? Paul attributed alienation between God and humanity not to sexual rivalry but to the human 'quest for a godlike omnipotence' (p. 162). Rubenstein 'can not share Paul's answer', which was to 'see Christ as the ultimate solution to the problems of mankind' (p. 20) but he does 'strongly empathize with him' (p. 22). Paul's thought, he suggests, far from simply bringing Hellenic ideas into Judaism, made explicit what was repressed in Judaism.

The strongest motif in Paul, says Rubenstein, is Jesus as the second Adam, who made restoration for the mistakes of the first Adam so that ultimately all things 'can return to their originating Matrix' (p. 171). Linking humanity's past and future with the metaphor of the Garden of Eden, he says, was not alien to rabbinical myth (p. 146). Jews often saw the human condition as one of exile, which makes Paul's 'metaphors of exile and return, Source and Ground' very Jewish (p. 171). Paul, he says, saw Jesus less as 'son' than as the 'elder brother' who leads us back to God, who was almost as much a victim of human disobedience as we are (see p. 35; Romans 8:29). The alienation of God from God's self, or God from God's *Shekhinah*, is 'dealt with explicitly within the Jewish mystical tradition' (p. 167).

For Paul, suggests Rubenstein, the restoration will annihilate any 'subject–object dichotomy between' the human and the divine (p. 170). Everything will return to the 'sacred womb', which is itself a dormant feminine motif in Pauline thought. In summing up Paul's thought, Rubenstein appears to draw on process theology, in which God is regarded as evolving towards an inherent yet still-to-be-realized perfection. He writes, 'As "all in all", God will become the absolute perfection of what Christ the man-God anticipates and acts to bring about' (p. 172). In the end, distinctions between the human and the divine, source and ground disappear, making obsolete debate about the exact nature of the relationship between Jesus Christ and God. The relationship between Christ and God is potentially identical with that between humanity and God, except that, as elder brother, Christ precedes while we follow. Sandmel (1958) and Schonfield (1947) have also written sympathetic Paul studies.

Sandmel calls Paul 'a religious genius' (1958, p. 1) and sees many similarities with Philo, who he says has never been called 'unJewish' for viewing God and God's relationship with the logos in metaphysical terms (*ibid.*, p. 69; see also pp. 48–50, 70, 210). Paul, says Sandmel, did not regard the law as fixed; revelation and scripture were 'a continuous matter'. Therefore, he did not see himself departing 'from scripture, but from the Law encased in it, for the revelation contained in scripture had not come to an end' (pp. 59–60). Schonfield admires Paul for so earnestly wanting to 'unite the world under the beneficent rule of the Messiah' (1947, p. xi). He thought Paul's idea that the law could be 'abrogated in the Messianic age' current among some Jewish groups (p. 183). Buber (1951) (see below) is less convinced that Paul can be regarded as a Jewish thinker: 'I . . . can connect the Pauline doctrine of faith . . . only with a peripheral Judaism, which was actually "Hellenistic"' (p. 14). Buber says that the notion of faith in Christ originated with Paul, doing 'precisely what Jesus . . . did not do' (p. 96).

### Samuel Sandmel: towards a two-covenant theology

Implicit in the writing of some Jewish scholars is the idea that Christianity *is valid for Gentiles* while Judaism remains *the path of obedience for Jews*. This idea seems to me to have informed the writing of Sandmel's *We Jews and Jesus* (1965), which aimed to 'arrive at a calm and balanced understanding of where Jews can reasonably stand with respect to Jesus' (p. vi). Sandmel (1911–79), Provost at the Hebrew Union College, Cincinnati, after graduating in the Old Testament from Duke University, turned to New Testament studies. His mastery of Christian scholarship shines through *We Jews and Jesus*, as does his knowledge of what Jews have said about Jesus. He admits to finding it difficult to read the Gospels without wanting to refute them (p. 128).

Like Klausner, Sandmel argues that Jews who accepted Jesus as Messiah 'made an initial significant alteration in the Messianic pattern', one that transformed the Messiah's 'specific and temporal characteristics' into 'something . . . more superhuman' (p. 33). It also split the Messiah's 'coming' into two, opening up the possibility that in the meantime he enjoyed a very unique relationship with God. Christian speculation resulted in the absolute identification of Jesus with God, something that Jews refused and still refuse to accept: 'Jews, except for those Greek Jews who took the dead-end road of Philo, have always been immutably unitarians' (p. 44).

Yet even Christian Unitarianism may go beyond what Jews can affirm of Jesus: 'Unitarians and . . . "unitarians" within Protestant denominations . . . supposedly' view Jesus as 'a man and no more than a man' but insist on seeing him as 'the supreme man of all history' (p. 77). Jews, says Sandmel, do not see 'any special working of the divine' in Jesus' life or in his death (p. 76). He finds Paul's view of Jesus, and his antithesis between 'faith' and 'works', irreconcilable with 'the main lines of Jewish traditions' (p. 132). Christianity's breach with Judaism resulted in hostility towards its parent, which Sandmel also thinks has been written into the gospel record.

This explains the illogical accusation that Jews killed Jesus: 'the Gospels show me no pervasive basis on which Jews as Jews' would have willed Jesus' death (p. 140). Yet Christians have consistently blamed Jews for Jesus' murder; thus church bells have accompanied pogrom after pogrom against the Jewish people, perhaps suggesting that it is Jews' stubbornness in accepting Jesus that makes Christians 'regard us as Christ-killers' (p. 141). Sandmel concedes that some Jews may have been implicated in Jesus' death, but to blame Jews is as absurd as blaming Americans for assassinating Presidents Lincoln and Kennedy (p. 141).

Christians, Sandmel points out, have always found it impossible to understand *why Jews refuse to see Jesus as they do*, sometimes responding 'with hostility and even with scorn' to the Christian Jesus (p. 7). I was reminded of this when Marc Ellis recently addressed some of my students. They questioned him about why Jews do not accept Jesus as the Messiah, when the Bible clearly describes him as such. Jesus, they insisted, fulfils all messianic expectations. They were obviously puzzled when Marc replied that, while some Jews agree with this view, for him and for the vast majority of Jews, Jesus simply does not qualify as the Messiah.

The love and forgiveness that Christians teach sound false and hollow to Jewish ears: 'The anti-Jewish motif in Christianity,' Sandmel wrote, 'appears to me to be greater in scope and deeper in intensity than the comparable motifs in Judaism which I find abhorrent', that is, 'hatred of Gentiles' (p. 141). Christianity, he suggests, cheapens itself 'by harboring hatred for anyone'. However, he speaks positively of post-Second World War developments, and looks forward to Vatican Two's forthcoming repudiation that 'what happened to Christ in His Passion cannot be attributed to the whole Jewish people' (p. 149). Sandmel says that he can co-operate with Christians on issues of common concern: 'the welfare of man, the urgency of ethical and moral standards, the crying need for the uplift of man's spiritual life' (p. 150). Sandmel calls himself an admirer of the purposes and achievements of the social gospel movement, yet he remains a Jew, 'inextricably bound up with . . . Judaism'. He would like Christians to feel for Christianity what he does for Judaism. Christians should not try to convert Jews.

Here, strong support comes from some Christians, who believe that the Jewish religion remains the valid path for Jews; Jesus may indeed not be the Jewish Messiah but the Gentiles'. Bishop Hugh Montefiore wrote:

For Jews as a whole, without a massive change of heart on the part of all Christendom, it is impossible to expect them in this life to respond explicitly to the gospel of Jesus Christ. A few individuals like myself may be called to do this, as pointers towards the destiny of the whole. The Jews are not to be judged for remaining Jews; and indeed their experience of suffering down the ages brings them very close to the central mystery of our faith, the passion, death and resurrection of Christ. (1983, p. 12)

Few Jews have found anything beautiful or meaningful in the cross. Wiesel, a Holocaust survivor and recipient of the 1986 Nobel Prize for Peace, even suggested that the suffering and pain of Jesus' death about which Christians have so much to say pale into insignificance beside Jewish suffering:

You speak of Christ. Christians' love of him. The passion of Christ, the agony of Christ, the death of Christ. In your religion, that is all you speak of. Well, I want you to know that ten years ago . . . I knew Jewish children every one of whom suffered a thousand times more, six million times more, than Christ on the Cross. And we don't speak about them. Can you understand that, Sir. We don't speak about them. (1978, p. 22)

For Wiesel, the more penetrating question is not 'Where was God?' but 'Where was humanity?' However, in one haunting passage in his novel, *Night*, he uses language reminiscent of Jesus' crucifixion to describe the execution of three inmates, one a child, suggesting that God was present in their suffering. He wrote:

Behind me, I heard the . . . man asking:
'Where is God now?'
And I heard a voice within me answer him:
'Where is He now? Here He is – He is hanging here on this gallows. . . .'
That night the soup tasted of corpses. (1982, p. 62)

The 'two-covenant' view has been championed by the Commission on the Church and the Jewish People of the World Council of Churches, on which I served in the 1990s. Its *Sigtuna Statement* (1988) says:

We rejoice in the continuing existence and vocation of the Jewish people, despite attempts to eradicate them, as a sign of God's love and faithfulness to them. This fact does not call into question the uniqueness of Christ and the truth of the Christian faith. We see not one covenant displacing another, but two communities of faith, each called into existence by God, each holding to its respective gifts from God, and each accountable to God. (p. 10)

## Martin Buber: Jesus my great brother

Buber (1878–1965) was perhaps one of the most famous advocates of the validity of Christianity for Christians, of Judaism for Jews. Born in Vienna, he taught philosophy at Heidelberg until removed from his post during the Third Reich, after which he migrated to Israel and taught at the Hebrew

University. In his writing, he acknowledged 'fundamental instruction' from Bultmann and speaks of 'treasuring' in his heart a meeting he had with Schweitzer (1951, pp. 13–14). Buber's writing became enormously popular among Christian scholars, influencing Tillich, whom some Jews also read with respect. Buber and Tillich are both examples of academics who wrote for a global community, as much for those outside as for those inside their own faith tradition. Both thought that theology had to address a world agenda, or as Tillich put it, questions of ultimate concern.

Buber was above all interested in relationships and dialogue. He formulated the concept of the 'I–Thou' relationship as the ideal, one in which the subject–object dichotomy of the 'I–It' relationship yields to equality and mutuality. Buber saw Christianity's emphasis on individual faith and Judaism's on the obedience of a people as suited to their peculiar vocations under God. These two types of faith, he wrote, 'are by nature different, each in conformity with its human basis, and they will indeed remain different, until mankind is gathered in from the exiles of the "religions" into the Kingship of God' (p. 174).

Each, though, can learn a lesson from the other: Jews may benefit from individual religious renewal, Christianity by 'striving for the . . . rebirth of nations' (*ibid.*). 'Even from my youth I have found in Jesus my great brother . . . I am,' he wrote, 'more than ever certain that a great place belongs to him in Israel's history of faith and that this place cannot be described in any of the usual categories' (p. 13). Buber recognized, too, that Christianity and Judaism are not exclusive: 'Each of the two has extended its roots into the other camp . . . the "Jewish" into the Christian, but the "Christian' also into the Jewish" (p. 11). Although a committed Zionist, Buber worked to improve understanding between Jews and Arabs, attempting to practise his ideal of dialogue.

Buber was enormously attracted to the *hasidic* tradition, which started in the eighteenth century under a charismatic leader, Israel ben Eliezer (1700–60), known as Baal Shem Tov. Like Jesus, the Tov healed. Also like Jesus, he had no formal rabbinical training. Like Jesus, he offered his followers 'an alternative authority structure to the intellectually based one accepted by the . . . Rabbis' (Unterman, 1981, p. 107). Purity of heart, said the Tov, is better than study. The *hasidics* stress ecstasy and joy in their relationship with God, whose presence they recognize in the world of nature as well as in personal experience. Their leaders, known as *tzaddik* (great souls), are seen as 'points of contact between the human and divine worlds', and there is 'a very thin line between . . . adulation of the *tzaddik* and his powers and the belief that he is a semi-divine being' (*ibid.*, p. 110). In the modern *hasidic* tradition, the *tzaddik*, or the *Rebbe*, fulfils a mediating role between God and his followers which may not be altogether different from Jesus' role within Christianity. There is thus some similarity between Jesus and more recent *hasidics*, as well as between Jesus and an ancient *hasidic* such as Honi.

## Judaism: Christianity's conscience

For many Jews, Jesus remains an insignificant figure, irrelevant to their lives and to their understanding of the world, while for others he is of considerable interest. The most popular view among Jews who find a place for Jesus in their worldview is probably as a first-century reformer. In this view, Jesus had wanted to connect people with God. His teachings, though corrupted by subsequent developments, have a role to play in spreading 'ethical monotheism over all the world' (Klausner, 1944, p. 610).

Franz Rosenzweig (1886–1929), friend and colleague of Buber, suggested in his *The Star of Redemption* (1916) that Christianity needs Judaism to 'convert the inner pagan within each Christian' (Goldman, 1999, p. 1). In a Germany where Houston Chamberlain's Aryan Jesus was already popular, this was a bold proposal. Rosenzweig argued that, without its Jewish side, Christianity was on a slippery slope towards idolatry. Christianity had transmuted 'Judaism's God into an earthly being with whom heathens might identify' (*ibid.*, p. 2). Christians hate Jews 'precisely because they depend on them' (*ibid.*, p. 1).

As Goldman (1999) shows, there is an interesting and disturbing overlap here with traditional Christian dogma that 'the Jewish people must be protected as "witnesses"' (*ibid.*). Or, as Neusner points out, 'Judaism survived in the Christian world not only because Jews chose to remain Jewish, but also because Christianity chose to permit it to survive' (cited by Goldman, *ibid.*). Yet, above all, it has been Jewish tenacity and pride that have enabled Judaism's survival, the conviction that even if it seems as if God may have forgotten the Jews, they must not forget God. Wiesel's grandfather replied to his son's questions, 'And God?', 'Will he simply stand by while we suffer?', with, 'You are Jewish, your task is to remain Jewish. The rest is up to God' (Wiesel, 1978, p. 81).

## A Jew on the resurrection of Jesus

The publication of *The Resurrection of Jesus* (1979) by the German Orthodox Jew, Pinchas Lapide, has been described as 'an event without precedent in the long history of Jewish–Christian relations'. Like Rosenzweig, Lapide argues in favour of Christianity's need of Jewish witness. Not surprisingly, says Carl Braaten in his introduction to the English translation, Lapide's book made 'the "Religion" section of *Time* magazine (May 7, 1979)' (Braaten, 1983, p. 7). Indeed, discussion of the resurrection has hardly featured in this chapter, especially when compared with its prominence in earlier chapters. Lapide rejects the idea, suggested by Reimarus and others, that the resurrection was purely a fiction invented by the disciples. Rather, he believes that the resurrection of Jesus *really happened*. As an event, it retains certain ambiguities, but its effect on the disciples was unambiguous (Lapide, 1983, p. 144).

Lapide criticizes some Christian theologians for being 'ashamed of the facticity of the resurrection' (*ibid.*, p. 130), which he says 'belongs to the category of the truly real' (p. 92). Theologians 'frequently use strange paraphases (*sic*)', he says, 'for the resurrection', citing Bultmann, among others (p. 128). Christianity, he suggests, can no more be understood without the resurrection than Judaism can without Sinai (p. 92). In his chapter 'The Must of the Resurrection' (pp. 85–93) he describes the resurrection as a categorical necessity and as a 'must' rooted in Jewish conviction:

This categorical *must* was not the illusory wishful thinking of a deceptive flight from the world which conjures up for itself a mirage, but it was based on the Jewish insight that the God who is willing to love and to suffer with human beings cannot be a cruel despotic God like the idols of the Greeks and Romans. (p. 89)

Lapide also parallels the resurrection with the creation of the State of Israel. 'The same abyss,' he suggests, 'yawns between cross and resurrection as between the mass Golgotha of the Hitler years and the national resurrection in the year 1948' (p. 149). 'Auschwitz,' he says, 'without the successive new foundation of Israel could have meant the end of the Jewish people', just as 'Without the resurrection . . . after Golgotha, there would not have been any Christianity' (*ibid.*). The 'cause of Jesus,' he continues, 'is basically the cause of Israel'. The themes of suffering, the faith experience of God, the survival after martyrdom, are all profoundly Jewish. The details of the resurrection stories, though, result from 'the pious fraud of later generations' (p. 128).

Lapide's discussion of Jesus' resurrection is set in the context of Jewish belief (see especially pp. 44–65, 'Resurrection in Judaism'). Like other Jewish writers discussed in this book, he stresses continuity between Jesus and Judaism. While, for Jews, the resurrection does not prove Jesus' messiahship, through the Church it has carried 'faith in the one' into the Gentile world (p. 153). As cited in Chapter 3, too, it is Lapide's own Jewish faith that compels him to take Jesus' resurrection seriously: 'as a faithful Jew, I cannot explain a . . . development which . . . carried the eternal message of Israel into the world' without reference to the activity of God (p. 142). As an atheist, he might have accepted that 'self-deceit' could 'establish a faith that conquers half the world' (p. 141). Like Maimonides, he sees Jesus as 'a paver of the way for the Messiah of Israel', not as the Messiah. Jews and Christians can 'remain together until Easter Monday and even conceive of the resurrection in Jewish terms', but 'Jews cannot accept . . . the messiahship of Jesus, the belief that he is the "eschatological watershed"'.

Yet, like Rosenzweig and Buber, Lapide sees Christianity and Judaism as 'two roads that lead to the Father' (Braaten, 1983, p. 20). While Jews will continue to pray *for* the Messiah, Christians 'will continue to pray *to* the Messiah' (p. 21). Christians need Jews to remind them that the kingdom has *not yet fully come*, even if the King is already here (p. 13). Sin, suffering, war, are testimony enough that 'the world is not yet redeemed'

(p. 14). Despite their differences, Judaism and Christianity have a 'common origin and a common messianic goal'. Jews ought to engage in dialogue with Christianity as a 'faith fellowship desired by God which concerns' them ' "for God's sake" ', even if they 'do not see in it a way which' they themselves 'can or must go' (p. 153). Jesus can be honoured by Jews as 'a sign of hope along the way, renewing faith in the future fulfillment of the promises of God' (p. 20). This includes their post-Holocaust experience of resurrection symbolized by the creation of the State of Israel. Like Ellis, Lapide suggests that, post-Holocaust, there is a new urgency to place Jewish–Christian relations on a firmer footing. Such a dialogue should not involve merely 'polite contact at the edges' or 'the removal of the tensions of the past' but 'should seek contact from center to center' (p. 153). This concludes my discussion of Jewish images of Jesus.

## Part two: Muslims on Jesus, prophet of Islam

In contrast with Jewish images of Jesus, there is a certain cohesiveness about Islamic responses, due to what might be called an official or normative Jesus view that has no equivalent in Judaism. Muslims who want to formulate a response to Jesus can turn to their most authoritative and sacred text, the Qur'an. (Some Muslims object to the idea that the Qur'an is a text.) Of course, as noted earlier, this wrongfoots Christians, who prefer the canonical gospels over other sources. Jesus, too, belongs emphatically within the Muslim worldview, whereas within the Jewish worldview his status is much more problematic, peripheral, even irrelevant. Parrinder (1995) usefully discusses all Qur'anic references to Jesus, including passages that refer to him by one of his titles, such as Son of Mary or Messiah.

The Qur'an affirms that God always sends prophets, or messengers, to humankind in order to remind humanity of God's unity, sovereign power and will. In the Garden of Eden at the start of time, Adam sinned but was later forgiven by God (Q2:35–7). Muslims, like Jews, do not believe that humanity is inherently evil, or that everyone inherits sin as a result of the Fall. Muslims do believe that the ideal relationship between God and humanity was disturbed by the Fall, and speak of human propensity towards forgetfulness, or sin. However, God constantly reminds us of God's will, of the distinction between permitted and prohibited conduct. This Jewish and Muslim understanding of sin is closer to the eastern Church's view of sin as a barrier between people and God than it is to western Christianity's concept of the utter depravity and lostness of humanity.

### Prophecy in Islam

All prophets and messengers receive, in essence, the same revelation, or word, from God. Jesus is revered as a prophet in the same cycle or sequence of prophets that began with Adam and culminated with Muhammad. The difference between Muhammad, the final prophet, and previous prophets can be said to be a difference in *degree*, not *kind*. They were prophets for particular communities of people at specific periods of time, while Muhammad is the universal prophet. His message is for all people and until the end of time, that is, from his own life, 570–632 CE until the Day of Judgment. On the one hand, the Qur'an teaches that all prophets are of equal status, although there is a distinction between prophet (*nabi*) and messenger (*rasul*); thus, 'To some of these messengers we gave pre-eminence.' The passage then refers to 'Jesus' as one 'raised in rank' (Q2:254).

On the other hand, the example of Muhammad is clearly elevated above that of all other prophets. Anyone who wants to obey God's will can do no better than to imitate Muhammad, the perfect man. Later, belief developed that a pre-existing 'light' (*nur*) rested on Muhammad, or was incarnate within him. In popular Muslim piety, too, he assumes a semi-divine status: Muslims pray for visions of him, for healing, for him to intercede with God on their behalf. The idea of the light of Muhammad evolved from Q5:15: 'There has come to you from Allah a new light. And a splendid Book.' Q24:35, too, describes Allah as 'the Light of the heavens and the earth'.

### Jesus: a word and a spirit

Yet the Qur'an also singles out Jesus as having peculiar significance. His virgin birth is upheld: 'Jesus in God's eyes is in the same position as Adam' (Q3:52), which means that like Adam he had no human father. He is referred to as a 'word' and as a 'spirit' from God (Q4:171). Muhammad stated that all prophets are 'paternal brothers, having one religion' (Bukhari, 1986, Book LV, Chapter 43, *hadith* 651). All prophets receive a word from God but Q4:171 almost suggests that Jesus was the very manifestation of that word. One Muslim scholar, my former teacher Hasan Askari, calls Jesus 'the Word from God' and the 'Symbol par excellence of the relationship between God and man' (1972, pp. 482, 484). I remember Dr Askari giving a series of talks on the Gospels, in which he linked Mark 4:36f. (the calming of the storm) with God's word bringing order out of chaos in Genesis and with the logos of John's prologue. Several Qur'anic verses also refer to God aiding Jesus by 'the Holy Spirit' (see Q2:81). Elsewhere, he is called a 'sign' and a 'parable' for the children of Israel (see Q19:21; 43:57).

Parrinder points out that Jesus has more titles than 'any other figure of the past' (1995, p. 16). Eleven passages call Jesus the Messiah, although the meaning of this term is never explained. Messiah appears to have been used as a surname. Earlier, I argued that 'Christ' really became Jesus' surname within Christianity, after its Jewish roots were left behind. Later, upwards of fifty different interpretations emerged in Muslim discourse.

Usually, *Al-masih* is understood as a title of honour, similar to *al-Siddiq*, the 'truthful', a surname of Abu Bakr, the first caliph (Parrinder, 1995, p. 31). Muhammad himself referred to Jesus as 'nearest of all people to the Son of Mary', since no other prophet stood between Jesus and himself (Bukhari, 1986). Many Qur'anic verses, however, rebuke Christians for exaggerating Jesus' importance, for claiming that he was God's son, or one of three gods (see Q4:171). Christians are wrong to associate a partner with God; that is, to worship others besides God (Q3:64). Jesus, says the Qur'an, is 'but a messenger' (Q4:171). Speaking from the cradle, Jesus calls himself 'a prophet' (Q19:33).

## The Qur'an on the cross

Most problematic for Christians is a verse which appears to deny that Jesus was crucified but was instead taken to be with Allah (Q4:157–8). This verse says that something resembling a crucifixion occurred, which leaves open the possibility that *a substitute died in Jesus' place*. Many Muslims believe that Judas was that substitute. Other verses have Jesus predicting from infancy that God would raise him up, although Christians might read this as a reference to the resurrection (see Q19:33). Muslims do not have any difficulty believing that Jesus survived the crucifixion, or that he showed himself to his disciples before God raised him up to heaven (see Chapter 6 of Hussein's novel, *City of Wrong* (1994)).

Cragg describes 'the prevailing' Muslim view as 'that at some point, undetermined, in the course of the final events of Christ's arrest, trial and sentence, a substitute person replaced Him while Jesus himself was . . . raised or raptured into Heaven'. From there, he 'returned . . . in personal appearances' before his disciples (1994, p. 12). Hussein's novel actually treats the crucifixion as a real event from its perpetrators' perspective. They *believed* they were killing Jesus, who is called 'The Wise Man' in the book. In fact, says Hussein, they were crucifying their own conscience. In the crucifixion, 'Evil . . . overwhelmed the good' (p. 214). For Hussein, the crucifixion is a metaphor for what can happen when wrong choices are made: 'In the events of Good Friday all the factors in evil and sin were present,' he wrote. 'Every day of life its tragedy is repeated,' he continued (p. 218).

Muslims, like Jews, reject the idea that a blood sacrifice was necessary for the forgiveness of sins: 'The doctrine,' says Ulfat Aziz Us-Samad, 'is not only a denial of the mercy of God but also of His justice. To demand the price of blood in order to forgive sins is to show a complete lack of mercy, and to punish a man who is not guilty for the sins of others, whether the former is willing or not, is the height of injustice' (1979, pp. 49–50). It may be said that Muslims bypass crucifixion and resurrection, going straight to the ascension. Both the idea that Jesus only seemed to die and that of a substitution were encountered earlier in our discussion of Gnostic texts.

For Muslims, as for these Gnostic writers, neither Jesus' message nor his significance depends upon his death. Rather, as Cragg (1994) comments, 'The Gospel they [Jesus' disciples] were . . . to preach was a moral law only and not glad tidings of a vicarious, redemptive encounter with sin and death' (p. 12). Muslims no more than Jews see any need for a saviour figure; obedience of the law or of Islam's *fard* (mandatory) duties can fulfil righteousness. The Qur'an's account of Jesus' childhood miracle of creating birds from clay (3:49) is also reminiscent of Gnostic texts. The same verse refers to Jesus healing lepers and restoring sight to the blind. Christians have long attributed these passages to Muhammad's supposed familiarity with earlier, 'heretical' sources.

None the less, quite a few aspects of the Qur'an's Jesus story, such as the annunciation, his 'ascension', virgin birth, his healing powers, correspond with the traditional Christian view. Indeed, while many insider scholars considered elsewhere in this book attribute all these to the faith, or to the enthusiasm, of the disciples, they remain cardinal convictions for most Muslims. This has not passed unnoticed by Muslims, as Seyyed Hossein Nasr comments: 'It's a very strange situation, where Muslims are defending the miraculous birth of Jesus against Western deniers' (cited by Woodward, 2000a, p. 56).

Nasr compares the theological necessity of Jesus' virgin birth in Christianity with that of Muhammad's unletteredness in Islam. 'One could not with any logic reject the unletteredness of the Prophet and in the same breath defend the virginity of Mary', says Nasr, since 'both symbolize a profound aspect of this mystery of revelation', each ensuring that the divine word remains uncontaminated from human waywardness (1994, p. 44). Ironically, perhaps, many Christians reject both Mary's virginity and the idea that Muhammad received every word of the Qur'an from God. I return to Nasr, an Iranian Muslim who teaches at George Washington University, later in this chapter.

As we see below, many Muslims also anticipate Jesus' return, while the so-called second coming may well qualify as the most disputed of all Christian dogmas. On the other hand, as the Qur'an appears to deny that Muhammad performed miracles (see Q2:23), Christians often cite this as proving the falsehood of Muhammad's claims. It has been suggested that the miracles and the stories surrounding Muhammad's birth found in the *sira* (biographies of Muhammad) were written into the account in imitation of the Gospels. Ibn Ishaq (the oldest life of Muhammad) begins with a genealogy, and with the words, 'This is the book of the biography of the apostle of God' (Guillaume, 1955, p. 3), which sounds remarkably like 'The beginning of the gospel about Jesus Christ' (Mark 1:1).

## Jesus as a true Muslim

Jesus' mission, in the Qur'anic account, was to 'confirm that which was before him' and to point people towards the worship of God: 'Allah is my

Lord and your Lord, so worship Him' (Q3:51). He preached about the oneness of God (see Q3:5) and denounced those who associated a partner with God: 'They do blaspheme who say, "Allah is Christ, the Son of Mary." But the Christ said, "O Children of Israel, worship Allah, my Lord." Whoever joins other gods with Allah shall be forbidden from the Garden' (Q5:73). Q5:116 has Jesus explicitly denying that he had ever asked anyone to worship either himself or Mary (often taken by Muslims to be part of the Trinity). This all pictures Jesus as a true Muslim.

Qur'anic verses also cite Jesus predicting Muhammad's coming, for example, at Q61:6: 'I am Allah's messenger, confirming The Law which was revealed before me and giving glad tidings of a Messenger whose name shall be Ahmad' (Ahmad and Muhammad are variants of the same word, meaning 'blessed'). At John 14:16, Jesus promises that his disciples will receive the gift of the 'Paraclete' (often rendered Comforter). In Arabic, this was traditionally translated as 'Ahmad', thus becoming a prediction of Muhammad. Ibn Ishaq wrote, 'Among the other things which have reached me about what Jesus the Son of Mary said in the Gospel' was that 'Muhammad is the paraclete' (Guillaume, 1955, pp. 103–4). Ulfat Aziz Us-Samad in her popular *Islam and Christianity* (1979) identifies Muhammad as the promised 'Spirit of Truth': 'Five centuries after' Jesus, 'the Spirit of Truth appeared in the person of the Prophet Muhammad to convey the whole truth to mankind'. She then cites Q5:3: 'This day I have perfected your religion for you and completed my favour unto you.' Jesus, she says, admitted that he had not brought the 'final or complete divine message' (p. 77).

### The charge of tahrif

As Christians have accused Jews of knowing but concealing the truth about Jesus, so Muslims accuse Christians of knowing but concealing the truth about Muhammad. There are quite a few Qur'anic passages that appear to charge Jews and Christians with corrupting, concealing or somehow obscuring biblical predictions about Muhammad (see Q2:140; 2:146; 3:71). This is known as *tahrif* (corruption of scripture), although, as noted earlier, there is debate about whether the actual text of the Bible has been tampered with, or whether the charge is of textual misinterpretation. Others point out that these verses refer to 'some' Christians, implying that not all are guilty of concealment. Farid Esack (1997) sees Muhammad's calling *vis-à-vis* the people of the book (Christians, Jews and other scripture-possessing communities) as challenging them to live up to the demands of their books, to refrain from distorting their message but not to become Muslim.

Esack cites as an example the Christians from Najran, who declined the invitation to become Muslim but towards whom Muhammad continued to exercise respect and friendship (1997, p. 174). Traditionally, Islam has not required Christians to convert, although certain civil disabilities have applied. Several Qur'anic verses endorse the salvation of believing Christians, or at least tolerate religious diversity, stating that God will reward both Muslims and Christians for their respective deeds (Q2:139; see also Q2:62; 6:108; 42:14). These verses, says Esack, place religious pluralism within God's will and plan (p. 159). For most Muslims, reading earlier scriptures is pointless, since the Qur'an is the book in which there is no doubt (Q2:2).

There is an obvious stylistic difference between the Qur'an and the canonical gospels. In the former, only God's words appear while the latter record what Matthew or Luke wrote, what people said to Jesus as well as Jesus' own words. Some Muslims argue that the real *injil* (the gospel that God revealed to Jesus) was lost. 'The original Gospel of Jesus,' says one popular Muslim publication, 'is nowhere to be found' (Bawany, 1977, p. 176). What the New Testament preserved seems to Muslims more like *hadith* (the sayings and doings of Muhammad) than scripture.

Many Muslims think that the Gospels reflect later Church dogma, not Jesus' authentic teaching; Bawany (1977) calls the four canonical gospels 'merely pious productions comparable to Dean Farrar's *Life of Christ*' (p. 171). On the other hand, M. Kamel Hussein, writing in 1972, suggested that Muslims might accept the four Gospels, which contain portions of the original *injil*, as inspired but not as revealed. Popular South African Muslim propagandist Ahmed Deedat has written numerous tracts on how the Bible predicts Muhammad. He also debates with Christian scholars, challenging them to prove the Christian as opposed to the Islamic version of Jesus' identity. Josh McDowell, who defends the traditional Christian Jesus image in his writing, has participated in several debates. Deedat's tracts are widely available on the internet. For example, 'Christ in Islam', 'Muhammad in the Bible' and 'Was Jesus Crucified?' (a debate with McDowell) are all posted at www.ais.org/~maftab/Christ.html, which also has a lot of Jesus-related material. Christian response to Muslim polemic is found at www.answering-islam.org.

## The Gospel of Barnabas

As noted earlier in this book, many Muslims identify *The Gospel of Barnabas* as the real gospel, although stylistically this also resembles *hadith* rather than the Qur'an, whose Jesus story it mirrors. While some *Barnabas* passages parallel the canonical gospels, its overall message is critical of Christianity's traditional picture of Jesus. Muslims often claim that *Barnabas'* 222 chapters (200 pages in printed format) represent the only surviving gospel written by *an actual companion of Jesus*. Many state that *Barnabas* enjoyed canonical status until the Council of Nicaea (see Rahim, 1977, pp. 39–41; and see www.barnabas.net). In *Barnabas*, Jesus constantly complains that people call him Son of God, and venerate him. The *hadith* cite Muhammad saying, 'Do not exaggerate in praising me as the Christians praised the Son of Mary, for I am only a Slave' (Bukhari, 1986, *hadith* 654).

The Jesus of *Barnabas* prohibits the consumption of pork, commands circumcision and predicts Muhammad's coming. Judas takes on Jesus' likeness and dies in his place. Jesus says, 'I am not the Messiah. . . . I am a voice that crieth through all Judaea, and crieth: "Prepare ye the way for the messenger of the Lord," even as it is written in Esaias' (Chapter 43). *Barnabas* also gives a very detailed description of heaven and hell (chapters 135–7), which Leirvik describes as 'close to medieval parallels, as in Dante' (1999, p. 129). Jesus' birth was painless, as was the Buddha's. A passage in Chapter 12 (Jesus' first sermon) 'even reflects the Muslim legend of Muhammad's pre-existence', while the notion of the eternal *nur Muhammadi* is expressly referred to in one of the Arabic glosses to the Italian text (*ibid.*, p. 130).

## Jesus and eschatology

Turning to the *hadith* (sayings) of Muhammad, a significant eschatological role emerges for Jesus. Muhammad himself speaks of several encounters with Jesus, either through dreams or during a mystical experience such as his night journey and ascension. This event, dated about 620 CE, involved Muhammad journeying from Makkah to Jerusalem, then upwards through the seven heavens. Meeting with Moses, with Jesus and other prophets, Muhammad 'acted as their Imam in prayer' (Guillaume, 1955, p. 182). This signifies that Muhammad is first among equals. Traditions state that even if Jesus were asked to lead the prayers, he would defer to Muhammad, saying, 'No, you have some put over others as an honor from God' (Robson, 1994, p. 1159).

Several descriptions of Jesus are given in the *hadith*, sometimes in order to distinguish him from the figure of *ad-Dajjal*, the enemy of righteousness: 'I saw a man of brown complexion and lank hair walking between two men, and water was dropping from his head. I asked, "Who is this?" The people said, "He is the son of Mary." Then I looked behind and I saw a red-complexioned, fat, curly-haired man, blind in the right eye . . . I asked, "Who is this?" They replied, "He is ad-Dajjal"' (Bukhari, 1986, Book LVI, Chapter 43, *hadith* 650). Other *hadith* describe Jesus as 'red faced' and of medium height (*ibid.*, *hadith* 647). Jesus, Muhammad said, will return, judge humanity 'by the Law of the Qur'an and not by the Gospel', 'break the cross' and establish prayers (see *ibid.*, *hadith* 657 and 658). He will also abolish the *jizya* (tax levied on non-Muslims such as Jews and Christians).

Mirza Ghulam Ahmad, in *Jesus in India*, gives a detailed description of Muslim end time beliefs, which he himself revised quite radically. Ahmad's version of Islam is regarded as heretical, as noted in Chapter 4. However, I am quoting him at length here since what follows does reflect much popular Muslim belief about Jesus' eschatological role:

And, just as I have stated, these people, i.e. the Ahl-i-Hadith etc. from among the Muslims, are enthusiastic about their belief that a short time before the coming down of the Messiah there will appear an Imam from the Bani Fatima whose name will be Muhammad, the Mahdi. He it is who will be Khalifa and King of the time, and as he will belong to the Koraish, his real object will be to kill all non-Muslims except those who readily recite the Kalima. Jesus (on whom be peace) will come down in order to help him in his work; and although Jesus himself (on whom be peace) will be a Mahdi – nay, a greater Mahdi – yet, because it is essential that the Khalifa of the time should be a Koraish, Jesus (on whom be peace) will not be the Khalifa of the time; the Khalifa of the time will be that same Muhammad, the Mahdi. Muslims say that these two together will fill the earth with the blood of man, and they will shed more blood than has ever been shed before in the history of the world. No sooner will they appear than they will start this bloody campaign; they will neither preach nor plead, nor show any sign. And they also say that although Jesus (on whom be peace) will be like an adviser or a lieutenant of Imam Muhammad, the Mahdi, and although the reins of power will be in the hands of the Mahdi only, Jesus (on whom be peace) will instigate Hazrat Imam Muhammad, the Mahdi, to massacre the whole world and will advise him to adopt extreme measures, i.e. he will make amends for the humane teaching which he had given to the world before, namely, 'not to resist evil', and, being struck on one cheek, 'to turn the other cheek also.' (Ahmad, 1989, 'Introduction')

The Qur'an itself implies that Jesus will have a role on Judgment Day: 'On the day of resurrection he will be a witness regarding them' (Q4:159). Here, his role seems to be confined to the Children of Israel, while Muslim legends ascribe to him the task of destroying Ad-Dajjal. Muhammad, however, will be 'pre-eminent among the descendants of Adam on the Day of Resurrection' (Robson, 1994, p. 1230). *Hadith* also predict that Jesus will eventually die (about forty years after descending) a normal death, after marrying and having children, 'to be buried next to Muhammad' (*ibid.*, p. 1160). The idea that Jesus will marry and father children suggests that he has not fulfilled all his human obligations. Muslims regard marriage as *fard* (compulsory). Again, we have a married Jesus. In Chapter 4 on outsiders, I referred to the Unificationist belief that Jesus failed to complete his physical mission because the cross intervened before he was able to marry.

Other Muslim traditions have Jesus living on after the crucifixion for another 125 years before God took him into heaven (see Leirvik, 1999, p. 127). Muslim eschatology often involves Jerusalem. Traditions (known as *al-fada'il*) speak of Jerusalem as the venue of the final conflict between Jesus and Ad-Dajjal. Muslims will seek sanctuary in the Rock. A second *hijrah* will occur as God's 'best and most faithful creatures' gather there on the eve of the Day of Resurrection (Talhami, 1993, p. 23). A work known as the *Kitab qusus al Anbiya* by Ibn Ibrahaim Ath-Tha'labi (d. 1036) gathered together many Muslim stories and legends about Jesus and presented them in the form of a biography (that is, a connected account) of Jesus' life. S. W. Zwemer (1867–1952) describes this material as 'fabulous' (1920, p. 258), but usefully translated quite a lot into English. Al-Ghazali (d. 1111), the leading theologian and Sufi scholar, reproduced much legendary material and sayings in his writing. At Jesus' birth, idols fell flat on their faces (*ibid.*, p. 261).

Interestingly, these sayings contain information on what Jesus may have thought in some areas neglected in the Gospels. I stated in Chapter 1 that we do not know what Jesus thought about animals. In fact, we do, from Muslim sources, where Jesus once rebuked people for complaining about the stench from a dead dog, and even told a pig to 'go in peace' (*ibid.*, pp. 267–8). Al-Ghazali comments that it was as if Jesus 'wanted to rebuke them for abusing the dog and to warn them not to mention anything of what God has created save at its best'. This tradition was rendered into poetic form by Jalal ud Din Rumi (1207–73) (see *ibid.*, p. 268). Jesus' healing, indifference towards material possessions, his other-worldliness, are stressed throughout these sayings. Indeed, some Muslims find Jesus too other-worldly, an issue which resurfaces at the end of this chapter.

One typical tradition says, 'It is related that one day Jesus was pillowing his head on a stone; and the devil passed by and said, "O Jesus, now you have shown your love for the world!" Then Jesus picked up the stone, threw it at him and said, "Take it and the world"' (p. 262). Another has Jesus describing this world as a 'bridge to the next': 'Pass over it,' said Jesus, 'But build not your dwelling there.' Jeremias describes this verse inscribed on a gateway of the beautiful mosque at Akbar's Fatipur Sikri, outside Agra, as 'the most impressive of all the sayings of Jesus which have been preserved within the Mohammedan world' (1957, p. 99). Al-Ghazali's works also cite some canonical sayings, such as 'whosoever strikes you on the right cheek, turn to him the left also', and 'whosoever desireth you to go with him a mile go with him twain' (Zwemer, 1920, pp. 276–7).

### Jesus in Sufi thought

Sufi Muslims stress Jesus' spiritual significance, perhaps suggesting that he achieved his spiritual goals, while Muhammad represents the best example of temporal accomplishment. There is something akin here to the Unifica-tionist view that Jesus did not complete his physical mission. Sufis share with most Muslims the idea that, at the end, Jesus will marry and father children. Sufis developed an image of Jesus as 'a model of virtue, of modesty and of 'spiritual poverty', a homeless traveller and a true Sufi (Schimmel, 1999, p. 207). Sufi writers, including Al-Ghazali,

set forth the poverty, humility and homelessness of Jesus. . . . 'Consider Jesus Christ, for it is related of him that he owned nothing save one garment of wool which he wore for twenty years and that he took nothing with him on all his wanderings save a cruse and a rosary and a comb. One day he saw a man drinking from a stream with his hands, so he cast away the cruse.' (Zwemer, 1920, p. 269)

Later, Jesus also abandoned the comb when he realized that he could use his fingers instead. In Muslim tradition, Jesus is bearded. As the Gospels do not describe Jesus, we cannot know for sure whether he was bearded or clean-shaven except that the former is much more likely, since Jewish men did not shave (he is bearded in the cover illustration of this book). Above, I cited Muhammad's descriptions of Jesus' physical appearance.

The idea that Jesus was a traveller became popular among Muslims. Sufis are all *saliqun*, that is, travellers along the spiritual *tariqah* (path) away from self-centredness towards a passing away (*fana*) of selfhood into union (*baqa*) with the divine. Non-Sufi Islam stresses *firaq* (distinction) between God and humanity; Sufi Islam and, to a lesser degree, Shi'a Islam, blur the divine–human distinction, initially with Muhammad, then with those who follow him or who inherit his spiritual essence. While Sunnis believe that, after Muhammad's death, no single individual has a privileged or unique ability to lead the community, Shi'a believe that Muhammad's descendants possess a special authority (*ilham* = inspiration). Sufis believe that their sheiks, or masters, receive what Nasr describes as the 'Muhammadan sanctity' (*wilayah muhammadiyah*). This is 'ever present . . . and the means by which the spiritual energy of the tradition is continuously renewed' (1994, p. 87).

Sufi and Sufi-influenced Muslims are more likely to accept that Jesus enjoyed a special relationship with God, even if this was not unique to him but enjoyed by other prophets as well. Nasr says that every prophet is to be considered 'an aspect of the Universal Logos, which in its perspective is identified with the "Reality of Muhammad" (*al-haqiqat al-muhammadiyah*)' (p. 88). Ibn 'Arabi (d. 1240), whose Sufi thought elevated love (*mahabbah*) over knowledge (*ma'rifah*), gave Jesus the title 'the seal of sanctity', and called him his greatest teacher. Muhammad was the 'seal of prophecy', the guide to legal and exoteric religion. Jesus was the spiritual guide.

Ibn 'Arabi emphasized the divine power that dwelt in Jesus which enabled him to raise the dead and to 'bring forth birds from clay' (Ibn 'Arabi, 1980, p. 174). Jesus shared something of God's creating ability, symbolized by his 'breath'; 'thus one might call him the Spirit of God, which is to say that life is manifest into whomsoever he blows' (*ibid.*, p. 178). 'Whoever wishes to know the divine Breath,' he wrote, 'then let him first know the Cosmos, for "Who knows himself, knows his Lord", Who is manifest in him' (*ibid.*, p. 181). Jesus' humility, said Ibn 'Arabi, came from his mother, Mary, while his 'powers of revival . . . came from the blowing of Gabriel in human form' (*ibid.*, p. 177).

Jalal al-Din Rumi (d. 1273), founder of the Mevlevi order of Sufis and another great exponent of love mysticism, also made frequent mention of Jesus in his writing. 'Logic,' says Rumi, is 'from Satan,' love is 'from Adam' (Nicholson, 1995, p. 165). Where love is, says Rumi, 'naught stands up to come between' God and God's lovers; 'feel with me, be one with me', cries love (*ibid.*, p. 30). He equated Jesus with 'love' and stressed love's selfless, other-centred nature as 'first of all a healing love of others' (Leirvik, 1999, p. 92). Like Ibn 'Arabi, Rumi associated Jesus' breath with his ability to restore and to give life. James Roy King says:

Rumi carries the meaning of Jesus well beyond what we would normally identify as Islamic norms, well beyond what might be required of a prophet, identifying him as one of a very rare body of individuals qualitatively different from normal human beings and endowed with a special capacity to renew and transform human lives, to render them whole and complete, but without ever going beyond the Islamic insistence that there is no God but God. (1990, p. 89)

Jesus enjoyed complete at-oneness with God, the goal of the Sufi path. However, as Al-Ghazali pointed out, Christians who call Jesus God make the same mistake as Sufis when they claim identification with God; both fail to distinguish God's presence from the vehicle in which God's presence dwells. There is, he wrote, a 'difference between saying, "The wine is the wine glass" and saying, "It is as if it were the wine glass"' (cited by Zaehner, 1994, p. 165). Ultimately, then, it is possible for all people to achieve the status enjoyed by Jesus: 'everyone of us has a Jesus within him, but until the pangs manifest in us our Jesus is not born' (cited in Leirvik, 1999, pp. 94, 89). For Sufis, as for New Agers and many Hindus, Jesus is, as Leirvik puts it, not only a 'role model', but a 'cosmic principle' (p. 89). As a 'Perfect Man', with Muhammad and all the saints, Jesus achieved what all people have the *potential* to achieve: complete at-oneness with God.

Rumi wrote, 'The Faithful are many, but their Faith is one; their bodies are numerous, but their soul is one' (Nicholson, 1995, p. 51). The 'Universal Spirit', he says, became 'Noah and went into the ark', became 'Abraham and appeared in the midst of the fire', became 'Jesus and ascended into heaven and glorified God' (*ibid.*, p. 142). In this sense, Jesus can be called a 'theophany': 'he is that Perfect Spirit which is a theophany (*mazhar*) of the All-Comprehensive Name, Allah' (Nurbakhsh, 1982, p. 26). This is why, in much Sufi writing, Jesus is shown as manifesting the very qualities of God. Sufis also speak of Jesus as possessing special knowledge of the name of God. Rumi, says Leirvik, 'associates Jesus' miraculous powers with his intimate knowledge of the Name' (1999, p. 93).

## Jesus in Muslim dreams

Many Muslims believe that our dreams and the real world in which we live are intimately related. Muhammad said quite a lot about dreams in the *hadith*; for example, he attributed good dreams to God, bad dreams to Satan (see Bukhari, 1986, 87:3, *hadith* 113, 114, 115). As Muhammad saw Jesus in dreams, so do Muslims. Schimmel cites traditions which claim that when a Muslim sees Jesus in a dream he or she 'becomes a blessed person full of goodness and destined to travel' (1999). Schimmel writes of a Thai lady, an agnostic, seeing Jesus in a dream 'at the end of 1996 . . . who told her, "I am a Muslim", whereupon she embraced Islam' (*ibid.*, p. 211). Ibn 'Arabi, says Schimmel, also 'often saw Jesus in dreams and visions for he felt extremely close to him' (p. 208).

## Jesus died in India

The tradition that Jesus was a traveller was picked up by Mirza Ghulam Ahmad (referred to in Chapter 4), who believed that, after the events of Passover week, Jesus travelled to India, where the ten lost tribes had settled and had also embraced Buddhism. This is the third time that the ten lost tribes have surfaced in this book. Jesus' sojourn in India, according to Ahmad, accounts for similarities between Christianity and Buddhism (see my next chapter). Ahmad took the verse at Qur'an 3:45 which says that the Son of Mary would be held in honour 'in this world' to predict that Jesus would travel to reach the ten lost tribes, and preach to them the true message of Islam. Jesus died in Kashmir, and was buried there. His spirit then ascended into heaven.

Ahmad's *Jesus in India* appeared in 1899 (reprinted 1989; online version available). A website, www.tombofjesus.com, has much material related to Ahmad's theories, including a list of Kashmir tribal and caste names and their biblical equivalents. He drew on the earlier work of members of a London-based society, the Identification Society, dedicated to tracing the lost tribes, such as George Moore's *The Lost Tribes and the Saxons . . . with New Views on Buddhism . . . and Translations of the Rock-Records* (1861).

Moore (1803–88) cited travellers in Afghanistan and Kashmir who testified to many tribes' belief that they were of Israelite descent. One of the Rock-Records is the Throne of Solomon Monument in Srinagar, on which these words are inscribed: 'The mason of this pillar is Bhisti Zargar, Year 54, Khaja Rukun son of Mirjan erected this pillar. During the period, Yuzu Asaph declared his ministry. He was Yusu, the Prophet of the Children of Israel' (as cited at tombofjesus.com). I return to 'Jesus in India' in my next chapter.

Ahmad (as noted in Chapter 4) claimed that he was the Messiah, armed not with a sword but with persuasion. He wrote, 'I have publicly announced, having been informed by God through revelation, that the real and Promised Messiah who is also the Mahdi . . . is myself, who is, moreover, not provided with any sword or gun' (Ahmad, 1989, p. 19). He believed that Muhammad had only permitted warfare in self-defence, rejecting the idea that *jihad* to propagate Islam condoned arbitrary aggression (M. M. Taha also rejects *jihad*; see 1987, pp. 132–7).

The authorities of Egypt's Al-Azhar University have given some support to the claim that Jesus died after surviving the cross, and might therefore have died in India. In 1942 they ruled that, 'according to the Qur'an, Jesus died and was taken in soul and body to God, thus being rescued from his enemies'. There is no indication in the Qur'an, the *fatwa* (legal opinion) continued, 'that Jesus is now alive in heaven, and the *hadith* materials concerning his return are not secured by sufficient *isnad*' to be binding on Muslims (Leirvik, 1999, pp. 43–4). An *isnad* is a chain of transmitters, each one tracing back to an original narrator who must be a companion or relative of Muhammad. On the other hand, many Muslims take the whole of Bukhari's collection to be sound; the traditions concerning Jesus' return and end time role are from Bukhari.

### Jesus, Paul and Unitarian theology

Muhammad 'Ata-ur Rahim's *Jesus, Prophet of Islam* (1977), a very popular text, especially in his native Pakistan, and in England, where he researched much of the book, is an accessible compendium of Muslim ideas about Jesus. Two chapters list relevant Qur'anic and *hadith* verses (9 and 10). He takes the *Gospel of Barnabas* to be the most reliable account of Jesus' life. He sees the Christian doctrines of atonement, redemption, Trinity and of Jesus' divinity as *corruptions of Jesus' original message*. He calls Christianity a 'metaphysical fiction . . . a fantasy' (pp. 3, 5). Jesus established neither the priestly hierarchy nor the Church. Rahim is not unusual among Muslim writers in blaming what passes for Christianity on Paul. Barnabas (see Acts 13:1–2) and not Paul 'endeavored to hold to the pure teachings of Jesus' (p. 51).

Rahim cites traditions that Barnabas was educated by Gamaliel, and that Jesus was 'brought up by the Essenes' (p. 52). In fact, Jesus 'took care not to deviate from the teaching of the Essenes' (p. 33). For him, the key to Christianity's corruption lies in a breach between Paul and Barnabas, which he treats in a similar way to others' treatment of debate between James–Peter and Paul. Paul 'knew he was lying' but believed that 'the ends justify the means' (p. 71; he cites 1 Corinthians 6:12).

Eager to attract Greeks and Romans, Paul produced a mixture of Jewish 'unitarianism and pagan philosophy'. In the process, 'Jesus was deified and the words of Plato were put in his sacred mouth' (p. 72). The result was a 'synthetic religion . . . mathematically absurd, historically false yet psychologically impressive' (*ibid.*). Genuine Christianity was 'de-railed by the powerful Paul explosion' (p. 5). He quotes Schonfield: 'The Pauline heresy became the foundation of Christian orthodoxy and the legitimate church was disowned as heretical' (p. 72).

Rahim writes that as there are as 'many versions of Christianity as there are Christians', the Church has no right to act as the guardian of Jesus' message (p. 203). According to Rahim and other Muslim writers, original Christianity was Unitarian. He praises the contributions of such men as Arius, Servetus, Sozini (or Socinus), Biddle, Lindsey, Priestley and others whose doctrines represented authentic Christianity over and against the official but corrupt Paul-inspired teaching. A gap grew, he says, 'between what Jesus had taught and what those in authority desired' (p. 13). Areas loyal to Arius, he suggests, found it easy to embrace Islam, 'Because they had held to the doctrine of the One-God and the pure teaching of Jesus' and therefore saw Islam as 'the truth' (p. 13). He also cites Tolland (pp. 74–5).

Similarly, Bawany (1977) sees early Christianity and Unitarianism as identical: 'Due to Paul, Jesus acquired a dual personality and became both God and Man' (p. 187). A whole section extols Unitarianism, even suggesting that it can

act as a bridge between the Islamic and the Christian world, leading to a better understanding between the two so they can put up a united front to counteract the forces of anti-God movement that are out to destroy all the religions of the world. (p. 193)

Paul's role, the idea that Christianity became corrupt – even wilfully corrupt – suppressing embarrassing truths (the real *injil*), Essenic influence, are all familiar themes. My copy of *Islam: The First and Final Religion* advertises John Hick's *The Myth of God Incarnate* on its back page, and obviously approves its argument. It quotes thus from Hick's preface: 'that Jesus was . . . "a man approved by God" and that later conception of him as God Incarnate . . . is a mythological or poetic way of expressing his significance for us' (Hick, 1978, p. ix).

In March 1888, a letter was published in the newspaper of the English Unitarians, *The Inquirer*, by Mahommed Auzum Saheb, who 'stated that the advanced Christian Theism of the English Unitarians would find a hearty acceptance among a large class of educated Mahommedans' (Taylor, 1999 p. 134). Anglican cleric Isaac Taylor (1829–1901) in his *Leaves from an Egyptian Notebook* (1999) responded that 'the time may come when Mahommedans, who do not differ greatly from English Unitarians in their interpretation of the New Testament, may be designated, if they desire, by the name of Unitarian Christians' (p. 135). In *Concerning Jesus* (1975), an anthology of Unitarian essays, Wigmore-Beddoes comments that, while English Unitarians 'adopt a stance that . . . many within its ranks regard as broader than Christianity', its origins 'lie deep within Christianity' (p. 6).

## A Unitarian on Jesus

Confidence in Unitarianism's ability to mediate between Islam and orthodox Christianity is probably misplaced, although a Unitarian understanding of Jesus obviously has strong appeal for Muslims. Abraham M. Rihbany (1870–1945), a Syrian migrant to the United States, offered a particularly fascinating Unitarian view of Jesus. Given his Middle East origin, and the above Muslim commendations of Unitarianism, it seemed appropriate to include his contribution in this chapter. Rihbany graduated from Ohio

Wesleyan University in 1895 and was ordained a Unitarian minister in 1900. His books include *The Syrian Christ* (1916) and *The Five Interpretations of Jesus* (1940).

Rihbany called *The Syrian Christ* an 'inside view of the Bible' (1940, p. 5); it presents a charming account of Jesus' life and teaching. 'You cannot study the life of a people,' said Rihbany, 'successfully from the outside' (*ibid.*, p. 7). 'Born not far from where the Master was born, and brought up under almost identical conditions' but sojourning in the West, he found himself reading the Bible as if it were 'a letter from home' (*ibid.*, p. 5). Throughout the book, Rihbany used his 'insidership' to explain the idiom, symbol and metaphor of the gospel texts. The book is not a critical examination of the sources but an exploration of the Jesus story against the background of Near Eastern culture and history into which Rihbany weaves many personal anecdotes and stories. On miracles, he comments that the Oriental tends to demand proof that they did not occur, rather than proof that they did (*ibid.*, p. 21). 'For the purpose of this work,' Rihbany wrote, 'every Scriptural passage which reflects a phase of Eastern thought and life is "genuine"' (*ibid.*, p. 408).

Well aware of Western caricatures of the Oriental, Rihbany sometimes seems to play up to his readership: 'I have no doubt that the Oriental suffers more from the universal affliction of untruthfulness than does the Anglo-Saxon, and that he needs . . . to have more respect of facts' (*ibid.*, p. 108). On the other hand, what Westerners deem as fanciful is actually cultural: 'Poetry, not prosaic accuracy', is the Oriental's 'dominant feature of speech' (*ibid.*, p. 108). The Jesus portrayed by Rihbany is a wise and gentle teacher, who taught faith in God. Jesus, he said, was God's son 'by anointing' (*ibid.*, p. 406). The early Church, he wrote, was interested in worship not theology and 'had it been left to itself, it is certain that the Christianity of Palestine never would have built up such a massive structure of doctrine as the Athanasian creed' (*ibid.*, p. 405). The bondage of the letter needs to give way to the freedom of the spirit (*ibid.*, p. 409).

*The Five Interpretations of Jesus* were originally pulpit discourses. Here, Rihbany blamed Paul for the paganization of Christianity: 'Paul was influenced by the doctrines of the Graeco-Roman cults of Adonis, Attis, Osiris, Isis and Mithra' with their 'idea of the god who dies and returns to life' (1940, p. 66). Jesus, he wrote, 'is our supreme spiritual guide, the first among many brethren', and 'our reverence for him is also reverence for what is noblest in ourselves' (*ibid.*, p. 116). Recently, a *Newsweek* correspondent from Ohio, describing his background as 'Christian . . . via a liberal Unitarian church', stated that, alongside his 'appreciation of Jesus as a great spiritual master', he 'easily accepted that the Buddha, the Prophet Muhammad and other religious leaders . . . also came to guide humanity' (Smith, 2000, p. 17).

## Kamal Salibi: Jesus was an Arab

Kamal Salibi, a Jordanian Christian, directs the Royal Institute for Inter-Faith Studies, Amman, Jordan, and edits its *Bulletin*. His writing presents a view of Jesus that resembles the Jesus of the Qur'an rather than that of Christian dogma, which is why I have included this 'insider' image in this chapter. In *The Bible Came from Arabia* (1985) he argued that Asir, near Yemen, not Palestine, was the location of the Promised Land, based partly on the similarity of local to biblical place names. This locates Abraham, for example, nearer Makkah, where, according to the Qur'an, he visited Ishmael and rededicated the Ka'bah to the worship of the one true God.

In *Who Was Jesus? A Conspiracy in Jerusalem* (1998) Salibi argues that what was recorded as Jesus' life in the Gospels is an amalgam of material about a Jewish would-be Messiah, Joshua Ben Nagara, stories about a much earlier Arabian prophet called Issa, and heretical ideas about Issa which were current in Arabia. The original Issa was a prophet who called people to worship Allah, and no one else. Later, some people began (incorrectly) to revere Issa as God's son. Salibi argues that Paul, aware that information on Jesus was available in Arabia, created this synthesis when he visited Arabia following his conversion. Galatians 1:17 tells us that Paul went 'immediately to Arabia', only visiting Jerusalem after three years. Salibi suggests that Paul knew Arabia was the better venue for reliable information on Jesus. Then,

by a highly sophisticated use of this lore, he succeeded in transforming the primitive heresy of the Nazarene Way into a great faith, whose central figure Jesus Christ, was identified as Jeshu Bar Nagara – the leader of the Nazarene apostles who had died on the cross and . . . had risen from the dead in the manner mythologically attributed to the god Jesus. (p. 157)

Paul may have 'secured local gospels' during his visit to Arabia (p. 189).

Joshua Ben Nagara, says Salibi, was a political activist, not the divine, dying and rising saviour who emerges in Paul's teaching, or in the four canonical gospels. While Salibi parts company with Muslims in arguing that the Jesus of the Gospels and the Issa of the Qur'an are different, his Jesus image closely resembles the Muslim Jesus. This is one of the most radical reworkings of the Jesus story encountered in this book. Like Thiering's, it involves an alternative geography, in this instance a dramatic shift from Palestine to Arabia.

Interestingly, Patricia Crone and Michael Cook (1977) reverse this, shifting Islam's venue from Makkah to Jerusalem, arguing also for a later date for Muhammad than the traditional 570–632 CE. Muhammad, they argue, was probably from north-west Arabia, and died after the Muslim conquest of Palestine when the standard life of Muhammad was invented and back-projected to authenticate Arab expansion. They also argue that Muhammad was of relatively little importance, that he was a tool in the hands of others.

## Islam and Christianity: a way forward?

Christian and Muslim images of Jesus appear to be irreconcilable, as do their doctrines about Jesus. Christians see Jesus as God's son, who died to redeem humankind from sin. Muslims state that Jesus was not God's son and see no need for an atoning death. Christians look to the Gospels to authenticate their ideas about Jesus, while Muslims see these texts as unreliable, even corrupt. How, then, can Christian–Muslim relations make any progress? For some Christians, the only desirable progress is for Muslims to convert to Christianity. Muslims, as noted, have not tradition-ally denied the ultimate salvation of Christians, although Christians are gladly received into Islam if they choose to convert. Arguing that we are all naturally 'Muslim', the term 'revert' is often preferred. Yet Christianity does, for Muslims, fall short on several points.

The association of Jesus with God within the Trinity is very close to the sin of *shirk* (belief in God and God's partners). Christians, too, tend to separate the political from the spiritual and focus on life after death more than life in this world. Muslims, like many of the Jewish scholars cited above, think that Christians are overly concerned with eternity, to the neglect of justice and social welfare in this world. Jesus may indeed be the seal of sanctity, but his example remains deficient without Muhammad's *sunnah*, the practical example of his life, to complement it. Many Muslims find Muhammad's example more comprehensive, more relevant to the daily agenda of living, than Jesus'.

Faced with a choice between Jesus and Muhammad, Muslims do not hesitate to choose Muhammad. Lacking rules or laws taught by Jesus, says Rahim, Christians have had to deduce these, but 'extracting moral principles from the gospels . . . is not the same as acting in a certain manner because it is known that Jesus acted that way' (1977, p. 200). We have 'no record of how Jesus walked, ate, sat, how he stood', yet as I have stated elsewhere, all this information is available about Muhammad. Christians cannot imitate Jesus, he says, because 'there is hardly any account of his code of behavior' (*ibid.*, p. 195). Ulfat Aziz Us-Samad (1979) similarly finds Jesus' life lacking in several areas: 'he never married, so he could not become an ideal husband and father.' Jesus 'did not rise to power', and so never became 'a model of a benevolent just ruler and judge' (p. 26). Jesus 'did not get the chance to put into practice many of his precepts', she continues. His 'life and character', she says, 'are shrouded in mystery'.

By contrast, Muhammad offers us 'the perfect example in all walks of life'. He gives us the 'picture of an ideally happy and pious married life and of a wise, just and benevolent ruler working for the material and moral amelioration of his people' (*ibid.*). In short, it is 'Islam, and not Christian-ity' that 'gives complete guidance for all aspects of life, individual as well as social, national as well as international' (p. 77). S. H. Nasr speaks of Christianity's lack of a 'Divine Law, a *shari'ah* in the strict sense of the term'. The problem for Nasr is that Christianity, including its teachings about Jesus, is *too* spiritual. Political life is too divorced from the spiritual (1994, p. 69). Judaism, says Nasr, represents the law and the religion of this world, Christianity the religion of the heart and of the next world, while Islam established the perfect balance between law and spirit, body and soul. He describes Jesus (he uses the title 'Christ') as representing 'the esoteric aspect of the Abrahamic tradition, the internal dimension of the primordial religion, which is a spiritual way rather than a law' (*ibid.*, p. 34). Judaism, he says, is based on fear of God, while Christianity stresses love of God and Islam knowledge of God (p. 35). Similarly, the Talmudic scholar Jacob Neusner thinks that Jesus was in error to preach about a *heavenly kingdom*, which he considers inherently un-Jewish: 'The Torah teaches that the kingdom that matters is not in heaven, but the one we find ourselves in now; sustaining life, sanctifying life, in the here and now of home and family.' He calls Jesus' repudiation of family 'a wrong turn'; 'Jesus,' he says, 'took a wrong turn in abandoning the Torah' (2000, p. 57).

Like other writers cited in this book, Nasr singles out Christianity's attitude towards sex for censure: 'while being seen as a sacrament in Islam', Christianity sees it as 'tainted with sin' (cited by Griffiths, 1990, p. 130). Incidentally, in both Islam and Judaism, it is considered obligatory for husbands to sexually pleasure their wives. Not to do so is a ground for divorce. The Sudanese reformer Mahmoud Mohamed Taha (1909–85) similarly stated that 'Jesus came with excessive spirituality, in contrast to the excessive materialism of the Jews' (1987, pp. 120–1). Islam, however, 'represents an equilibrium between the two extremes of the lack and excess'; that is, of spirituality and of materialism (p. 121).

Incidentally, Taha did not regard Islam as practised or recorded in the classical texts (law books) as perfect, but called for a radical rethinking of Islam's rules: 'progress in it [Islam],' he said, 'is eternal' (*ibid.*, p. 147). He distinguished between Islam's first and second messages. The first message, legalistic prescriptions, was necessary given the circumstances in which Muhammad lived. It took 'account of human weaknesses and limited capacities' but in doing so represented a *descent*, not an *ascent* (p. 145). 'Many aspects of the present Islamic *shari'a* are not the original principles . . . of Islam' but 'reflect a descent in accordance with the circumstances of the time' (p. 137).

The second message (which is really its primary message) is eternal. Islam's attitude towards war, polygamy, separation of the sexes, rights of minorities, and much more, can be revisited in order to achieve the ideal society. *Shari'a* is not found in the existing texts but lies ahead, as Muslims 'elevate legislation by evolving and basing it on the original Qur'anic verses' (p. 161). He calls this *'tatwir al-tashri'* or 'evolution of the law' (p. 167). 'Vitality, development and renewal', he says, are central to Islam's second message (p. 168). Taha argues in favour of democratic structures: 'The good society is based on three equalities; economic equality, today known as socialism . . . political equality or democracy . . .

sharing in political decisions . . . and social equality' (p. 153). Human 'dignity', says Taha, derives from our ability to learn and develop (p. 159). The 'good society' would also permit 'different life-styles and manners' provided they are beneficial and not harmful (*ibid.*). The Sudanese government, on a charge of sedition, executed Taha, a pacifist, in 1985.

## Jesus and Muhammad

For their part, Christians may find Islam too this-worldly, and sometimes point to the part that both Jesus and Muhammad have played, and still play, in Islamic devotion as evidence that compensation is required against Islam's bias towards the legal or material. In addition, if we admit that our practice of our traditions falls short of their ideal, perhaps we can accept the need for reminders to call us back to a truer obedience, as Esack argues. In this instance, Jesus' role as the seal of sanctity may be to remind Muslims that ultimately it is the heart that God will judge; as the seal of prophecy, Muhammad's role may be to remind Christians that the life of the kingdom begins with social justice in this world. Isaac Taylor, visiting Egypt in 1888, wrote of the prospect for reform of both Christianity and Islam. He met with Muslim scholars who hoped that both Christians and Muslims would return to the original creeds of Jesus and Muhammad. An Islam, they said, that followed more closely the 'spirit of the Koran' would also have more in common with Christianity (Taylor, 1999, pp. 138, 126).

Comparison of Jesus with Muhammad can be criticized: Jesus is God's word for Christians; Muhammad, for most Muslims, is not the word but the word's messenger. Arguably, then, a like-with-like comparison would compare Jesus with the Qur'an. Christians believe that Jesus is God's final, complete, perfect revelation; Muslims describe the Qur'an in exactly the same terms. However, the relationship between Muhammad and the Qur'an (the message) is so close that a Jesus–Muhammad comparison is to all intents and purposes the same as a Jesus–Qur'an comparison. Unless read through the lens of Muhammad's life, much of the Qur'an remains opaque. Nasr, cited above, actually identifies Muhammad with the universal logos. Further, the reverence and esteem in which many Muslims hold Muhammad closely resemble the esteem with which Jesus is regarded within Christianity.

Can Christians have any regard for Muhammad? Some Christians look at Muhammad and see nothing noble or of value. Others see a pragmatic concern for justice, social welfare and equality, for a balancing of spirituality and worldly involvement, that by no means opposes Jesus' ethic. Indeed, it may even supplement it, adding some detail to Jesus' minimalist 'love your neighbour'. I am thinking here of Muslim conventions on the treatment of employees as well as on wealth redistribution, for example. Islam's emphasis on community may offset a Christianity that has often focused almost exclusively on individual salvation, perhaps contributing to what Taha called Western civilization's inability to reconcile the needs of the individual with the needs of the community, that is, the need of the individual for absolute individual freedom and the need of the community for total social justice. (1987, p. 53)

Christians themselves add detail to Jesus' ethic; many of us look to the lives of the saints because they provide us with solid, tangible examples of a Christlike life.

Jesus, for Christians, represents salvific finality but this does not mean that God no longer guides or inspires us. The spirit of God, which blows where it will (John 3:8), continues to do God's work, sometimes outside, sometimes within, the Christian community, sometimes through unusual people, at times in unexpected places. That same spirit, said Jesus, may teach us additional truths: 'I have yet many things to say to you but you cannot bear them yet. However, when the Holy Spirit comes, he will guide you into all truth' (John 16:12f.). I think it is possible to recognize Christlikeness, even if the individual concerned did not, or does not, hold to a Christian understanding of Christ. Gandhi, for example, respected, even venerated Jesus, but was not a Christian. I am suggesting not that Muhammad's *sunnah* can have the same value for Christians as Jesus' ethic, but that recognition of its value does not necessarily conflict with a primary loyalty to Jesus.

For Christians, Jesus will always be the *criterion of truth*. For Muslims, the Qur'an (and the *sunnah* of its messenger) is and will remain the criterion (Q2:185). Yet these primary loyalties do not exclude other loyalties. In the end, God may prefer Muslims, Christians and Jews to act justly than to argue about unity, Trinity or the reliability or interpretation of scriptures. Perhaps the Christian Jesus, as both Jews and Muslims suggest, is too other-worldly. Perhaps, in order to rediscover the real Jesus, Christians need to listen to what Jews and Muslims say about him.

Love of Jesus, love of God, may best be expressed in acts of loving kindness towards others, summed up in the Unitarian dictum that Rihbany cites: 'In the freedom of the truth and in the spirit of Jesus, we unite for the worship of God and the service of man.' Here, says Rihbany, 'there is no dogma and no creed, but a voluntary resolve to follow the Master in worship and service' (1940, p. 116). Or, as the Qur'an enjoins both Christians and Muslims: 'If Allah had so willed, he could have made you [Jews, Christians, Muslims] one community but his plan is to test you in what he has revealed, so as in a race strive in all virtues' (5:48). Christians might consider applying Gamaliel's advice, cited in Acts, to Islam: if of God, it will flourish, if of men, it will fail (5:38–9). 'He who is not against us,' said Jesus, 'is for us' (Mark 9:40), and as he also said, 'By their fruits shall you know them' (Matthew 7:16).

Perhaps a Jesus who calls people to do as he did, to believe in the goodness of God rather than to worship him, as Jews and Muslims see him, is closer to the Jesus who stands behind the Gospels. I realize that some Christians will find my suggestion that Muhammad may complement

Jesus quite preposterous. Others will reject my view that Jews do not need to call Jesus 'Messiah' in order to please God. To a large degree, Europe asserted its self-identity over and against Jews and Muslims. Jews, a minority within Europe, were accused of deicide, and were persecuted. Regarded as a fifth column, they were the 'other', or the 'enemy', within. Muslims were the enemy without. Europe was civilized, its religion God-given; therefore Muslims were barbaric, Islam diabolical. National epics in Spain and France celebrated their hero's victory over the Moors.

When the Muslim Turks threatened Vienna (1529, 1683) it seemed that Europe's cultural heart was about to be amputated. Muslims, traditionally, were seen as aggressors. Even though Europeans initiated the Crusades, they were a response to Islam's capture of previously Christian territory. Biblical passages depicting false prophets and anti-Christs (Matthew 24:24) seemed tailor-made for Muhammad. Traditionally, this has shaped Christian thought on Islam. A mass of Christian writing ridicules and repudiates Muhammad; a modest amount sees him as a sincere servant and seeker of God. I have referred to some Christian images of Muhammad in this chapter, as they tend to mirror early Jewish views of Jesus. For a more detailed discussion, see my *In Search of Muhammad* (1998). Ulfat Aziz Us-Samad (1979) writes, 'while Muslims . . . love and respect Jesus as they love and respect the Prophet Muhammad, the Christians not only reject Muhammad, but are never tired of speaking of him in the most disparaging manner possible' (p. 11).

I now turn to the Jesus of India and of the East, to Hindu and Buddhist images of him, asking what lessons Christians may learn from these perceptions of Jesus. Some familiar themes emerge yet again, including Essenic links and travels beyond Palestine. Also, like Jews and Muslims, Hindus and Buddhists see no value in Jesus' sacrificial death. In fact, unlike Jews and Muslims, Hindus and Buddhists show relatively little interest in the historical Jesus. Rather, their interest lies in Jesus' religious experience, in his awareness of at-oneness with the 'absolute', which they believe is a universal possibility, available to all people.

# 6 Hindu and Buddhist Images of Jesus

> It is one and the same Avatara that, having plunged into the ocean of life, rises up in one place and is known as Krishna, and diving again rises in another place and is known as Christ. (Sri Ramakrishna, Saying No. 52; Müller, 1900, p. 109)

> As a Buddhist, my attitude towards Jesus Christ is that he was either a fully enlightened being, or a bodhisattva of a very high spiritual realization. (The 14th Dalai Lama, 2000, p. 56)

## Indian religion and culture

Judaism, Christianity and Islam acknowledge common roots. To some degree, they share the same story. In places and at various times, Jews, Christians and Muslims have enjoyed intellectual, social as well as commercial exchanges, notably in Spain during the Moorish period but also in Egypt and Turkey. From its own historical beginnings until the present day, Christianity has had relations with Jews. *Vis-à-vis* Islam, Christian contact with Muslims began during Muhammad's own lifetime. Encounter, however, of Christians with Hindus and Buddhists has been less extensive, at least historically. Hinduism and Buddhism spring from the same soil, the soil of India. They belong to a distinct family of religions from the three Abrahamic faiths. In the Republic of India, Buddhists are subject to 'Hindu Law', which applies to any citizen who is 'a Hindu . . . Jain, Buddhist or Sikh' and who is not a 'Muslim, Christian, Parsi or Jew' (Hindu Succession Act, cited in Staffner, 1987, p. 98).

I might have called this chapter 'Indian Images of Jesus', since it is difficult to totally separate Buddhist from Hindu encounters with Jesus, or indeed the Indian encounter from that of any specific, distinct religious tradition. In practice, if not according to classical theory, it is impossible to maintain a rigid boundary around the religious traditions of India. They mix and mingle. Of course, Buddhism spread to influence some three-quarters of humanity, and so encountered cultures over a wide geographical area. The two principal Buddhist writers whose views of Jesus I discuss, the Dalai Lama and Thich Nhat Hanh, are from Tibet and Vietnam respectively.

In the subcontinent (present-day India, Bangladesh, Bhutan, Sikkim, Pakistan, Nepal and Sri Lanka) the spiritual is part and parcel of culture, of tradition, of life itself. Much has been written about the appropriateness of applying such terms as 'religion' and 'world religion' to the traditions of India, as well as the degree to which Buddhism and Hinduism are Western abstractions (see W. C. Smith, 1978, 1981; King, 1999). A 'religion', says King, had to be homogeneous, and 'compatible with the universalistic and proselytizing elements of Christian theology' (p. 67), so constructions were created to meet this requirement. Theoretically theologically neutral, religious studies often imposes assumptions about what a religion should look like drawn from Christianity's self-description. Indian languages, too, lack a word meaning 'religion'. *Dharma* is used but actually means the inherent nature of every object.

The very word 'Hinduism' is a term dating from the nineteenth century. It was first used in English, not in any Indian language, making its debut in the *Oxford English Dictionary* in 1829. Perhaps my teacher at Manchester University was right when she began our first lecture on Hinduism by saying that the most important lesson we needed to learn was 'that there is no such thing!' That was in 1974 when I was a freshman religion major. Since then, I have encountered many attempts at defining 'Hinduism'. Perhaps the best is: Hinduism is 'all things to all men' (1946, p. 75). Here, I am citing India's first Prime Minister, Jawaharlal Nehru (1889–1964). While he thinks it misleading to 'refer to Indian culture as Hindu culture' he yet concedes that 'Americans who call all Indians Hindus are not far wrong' (p. 76). He also points out that Hindus may hold views that seem to contradict each other but that they 'live and let live'.

Weightman (1997) suggests that acceptance as a Hindu by another Hindu is itself an affirmation that Hinduism 'is one single tradition' (p. 262). Westerners sometimes write as if they invented India and its religions, which is exactly what Edward Said charges in his writing. While it would, he says, be 'wrong to conclude that the Orient was *essentially* an idea, or a creation with no corresponding reality' (1978, p. 5), he goes on to suggest that Westerners believed that only they could *codify* and *define* the East:

The Orient is thus *Orientalized*, a process that not only marks the Orient as the province of the Orientalist [Western scholar of the East] but also forces the uninitiated Western reader to accept Orientalist codifications . . . as the *true* Orient. Truth, in short, becomes a function of learned judgement, not of the material itself, which in time seems to owe even its existence to the Orientalist. (*ibid.*, p. 67)

In *Midnight's Children*, one of Salman Rushdie's characters expresses his annoyance that, while studying medicine in Europe, he had

learned that India – like radium – had been 'discovered' by the Europeans; even Oskar [best German friend] was filled with admiration for Vasco de Gama, and this was what finally separated Aadam Aziz from his friends, this belief of theirs that he was somehow the invention of their ancestors. (1981, p. 11)

None the less, Hinduism as commonly taught in university courses may not have existed until Annie Besant (1847–1933), the English theosophist and President of the Indian National Congress, developed her *sanatana dharma* (eternal truth) curriculum for the Hindu Central College, which she founded in 1898 (see Besant, 1899). Although the materials she used, such as the four classes, four stages of life, four aims, four ages, were taken from ancient sources, this particular presentation of them as a *coherent system* may have been original to her. Similarly, theosophist Colonel Henry Steele Olcott (1832–1907) published *The Buddhist Catechism* in 1881 in an attempt to express the basic tenets which he believed 'all Buddhists in the world should be able to subscribe to'. He also invented what became known as the Buddhist flag, now used by the World Fellowship of Buddhists (Gombrich, 1988, p. 186). Gombrich suggests that this type of world Buddhism was a conscious response to Christian mission, guided by the Theosophical Society.

In this chapter, I begin with descriptions of the Hindu and Buddhist worldviews, then explore their encounter with the Jesus story. Despite the very serious problems associated with the terms 'Hinduism' and 'Buddhism', I use them both in this chapter. My descriptions are quite detailed; no response to Jesus can be analysed in isolation from what people *bring* to their Jesus encounter, as I have argued throughout this book. Inevitably, this story mingles with Western colonialism and with Western response to things Eastern. It also mingles with the story of Christian mission. Like all stories, too, the version told depends on the teller. Indians have their own narrative of encounter. I identify general trends in Hindu–Buddhist response to Jesus and discuss the contributions of some significant thinkers.

Indian Christians also struggle with their Jesus images, as they struggle with the relationship between Christianity and their Indian heritage, so I include the Jesus images of some Indian Christians. There has been two-way traffic from the start of West–East encounter. Some Indians found a ready place for Jesus in their worldviews, some Westerners found Indian thought very attractive, including the Boston Transcendentalists and the founders of the Theosophical Society. Finally, alternative sources and theories surface yet again, as, intriguingly, do the Essenes. Paul, however, hardly features in this chapter, nor does textual analysis, at least not in much detail.

## Hinduism: worldview

### *The* Vedas

Hinduism's origins lie in the ancient Vedic scriptures (*Veda* = knowledge). Originally, these were oral traditions brought into India by the invading Aryans around 1500 BCE. The lighter-skinned invaders pushed the darker-skinned Dravidians south, although there is evidence that they absorbed much of the pre-existing culture. The gods, it is said, eternally breathe out the *Vedas*. They are *Sruti* (revealed). The New International Version of the Bible uses 'God-breathed' at the much-cited 2 Timothy 3:16. The *Vedas* contain stories of the gods and demons, of the mysterious *rishis* (neither men nor gods, the *rishis* are above both), numerous sacrificial formulas and magical incantations for the priests, and creation narratives. Throughout, *dharma* (righteousness, correct order) is pitted against *adharma* (chaos, unrighteousness). *Dharma* (who is also a god) refers both to the sacrificial and other rituals of the priests and to moral conduct that is appropriate for every individual's gender, class and stage in life. The four classes of Indian society (in descending order, the Brahmans, or priests, followed by the Ksatriyas, or warriors, the vaisya, or merchants, and sudras, or serfs) emerge from the sacrificed body of a primordial, cosmic *purusha* (man) in one *Rig Vedic* hymn (10:90; Embree, 1988, p. 18). Some Indian scholars reject the 'Aryan invasion' as a product of European 'colonization' of Indian history.

*Rig Veda* 10:129 implies that since 'the gods are on this side' even they do not really know how the world began. However, an unknown, unnamed One lies behind all that is: 'That One breathed without wind through its independent power. There was nothing other than it' (Embree, 1988, p. 21). Creation, though, is understood as an aspect of, rather than as distinct from, this unfathomable One. The sacrifices and rituals of the Brahmans maintain order in the Vedic system. Originally, *brahman* appears to have denoted the prayers or the power behind the prayers of the priests. Eventually, it was adopted to designate the priests themselves. *Soma* (an intoxicating substance; also a god) and *agni* (the sacred flame; also a god) were vital to the sacrificial system.

The idea of appeasing the gods is not absent from the *Vedas* but the real purpose of the sacrifices was to maintain cosmic balance. In the *Brahmanas* (priests' manuals) that were written to accompany the *Vedas*, *Vac* (speech) is associated with creation and also with the priests' rituals. *Vac* (which is feminine) is also said to have created the *Vedas*. It is interesting to note parallels here with the role played by the spoken word in the Genesis narrative, as well as in John's prologue: 'the Word was with God. Through the Word everything was made.' In the Bengali Bible, *Vac* (*baca*) is used for *logos*.

## The Upanishads

In the ninth or eighth centuries, the *Upanishads*, philosophical commentary on the inner meaning of the *Vedas*, were 'revealed'. The term 'Vedantic', meaning 'end of the *Vedas*', is applied to Upanishadic thought. Sometimes, the *Upanishads* seem to scoff at those who place their faith in sacrifices: 'Regarding sacrifice and merit as most important, the deluded ones do not know of any other higher spiritual good' (*Munkara Upanishad*, 1.2.1, 2, 7–13; Embree, 1988, p. 31). Instead of a physical, an inner, spiritual sacrifice is enjoined: 'sacrifice in knowledge is better than sacrifice with material objects' (*Gita*, 4:33; Miller, 1986, p. 53).

Now, the object of religious observance is not just the maintenance of cosmic order, but escape from the endless cycle of existence. Multiple existences, multiple births, deaths and rebirths, multiple acts of creation, *sat* (truth, or essence) all feature in the *Upanishads*. *Sat* (truth, essence), or *Brahman*, is the All-in-All, or the Universal Soul, from which the many emanate: 'Being thought to itself: "May I be many; may I procreate"' (*Chandogya Upanishad*, 6; Embree, 1988, p. 37). Although the word *srshti* is translated as 'create' (see Bengali Bible, Genesis 1:1 and verse 27) it means the 'projection of that which already exists'.

*Brahman* is also ultimate bliss (*ananda*). Only *Brahman* is uncontingent. The many gods, Vedic and post-Vedic, are usually said to be various manifestations of the attributes or qualities of the single, and ultimately transcendent, reality. For some, that reality is non-personal, without attributes (*nirguna*), but at a lower level manifests its attributes in the form of a personal god, *Isvara*. *Isvara*, unlike *Brahman*, is turned towards the world: '*Brahman* is so immutable and unmanifest,' wrote Panikkar (1981), 'that *Isvara* has to take over its functions in relation to the universe and to souls' (p. 153). Within all sentient beings, the *atman* (self) is actually a manifestation of *Brahman*. It is uncreated and eternal.

*Ananda* follows when people realize their oneness with *Brahman*, which is the condition of *samadhi* (absorption) and its fruit is *moksa* (liberation from rebirth). Meanwhile, our *karma* (action), good or bad, determines our status, punishment and reward in future existences. While Brahmanism did not leave non-Brahmans very much to do religiously, except to behave ethically, Vedanta opened up the possibility of philosophical speculation (*sankhya*) and of yogic practice for almost anyone, except that the *shudras* were forbidden from reading the sacred texts.

### Shankara (788–820 CE) and Ramanuja (1017–1137)

In the development of Vedantic thought, two of the greatest contributors were Shankara and Ramanuja. Shankara taught that plurality is an illusion (*maya*) and that *moksa* results from the realization (*cit*; awareness) of absolute identification of *atman* and *Brahman*. *Brahman* is beyond space and time. When the knowledge that 'everything is indeed the *absolute*' (*sarvam khalu ilam brahman*) is achieved by deep meditation and mental discipline (*yoga*), the *atman* is freed of ignorance (*avidya*) and is forever liberated from *samsara*. Shankara thought that worship of *Isvara* (or of an *Isvara*, since different people choose different gods to honour) represented a low level of religious practice, unsuitable for people of an advanced spiritual status.

Ramanuja disagreed. For him, *Brahman* is both the self-without and the self-within, the essence of the universe and a personal deity. Plurality is real, not *maya*; the many *really exist* but *only exist fully* when aware of absolute dependence on *Brahman*. The realized self participates in God's being, yet is not to be confused with the entireness of God. For Ramanuja, it is God's dominant quality of love that enables us to gain true knowledge of our relationship with God. Thus, God remains the only self-illuminated reality; we can only enter a true relationship with God with the aid of God's grace (*prasada*). Individuality (*ahamkara*), for Shankara, must perish; for Ramanuja, it continues, but *in communion* with *all other selves*. The primary concern of Vedanta is right *jnana* (knowledge), although right action remains a necessary corollary. Knowledge does not play such an important role in orthodox Christianity, where it is neither *what we know* nor *what we do* but *faith* that saves. Of course, knowledge is central to Gnostic thought. There are, though, some gospel passages (see Chapter 1) where Jesus speaks of conveying knowledge of God.

### *The* Puranas

Finally, around about 300 BCE, the great epics known as the *Puranas*, which include the *Ramayana* and the *Mahabharata*, were 'remembered' (*smriti*). For accessible, prose paraphrases of these two texts, see Narayan (1972 and 1978), which I use with my own students. Donald A. Mackenzie (1994) also has substantial extracts, and lots of information on the Vedic literature, but his text does reflect negative assumptions, some of which I cite below. The famous *Bhagavad Gita*, probably the most widely read Hindu religious text in and outside India, is part of the *Mahabharata*. There are many excellent English renderings. I chose Barbara Stoler Miller's highly acclaimed Bantam Classic (1986) because it offers a clear and concise translation; some are rather verbose. I cite *Gita* chapter and verse as well as by Miller's pagination.

Technically, the *Gita* is a Puranic text but it is quintessentially philosophical and Vedantic in outlook. The epics have human, or rather superhuman, narrators, Valmiki and Vyasa. Vyasa is also said to have arranged the *Vedas*. My own interest in things Indian began when I met some Krishna devotees in Sydney, Australia, where I was working as a civil servant. I bought a copy of the *Gita*. At about that time, a friend introduced me to Buddhism and I quickly became fascinated with it, especially its Tibetan form. I bought my copy of Edward Conze's *Buddhist Scriptures* (1959) on 7 July 1972. That was two years before I started my undergraduate degree in religion.

By the time the *Puranas* were written, the Vedic deities, such as Varuna (sky), Mitra (sun), Indra (war) and Yama (death) had been superseded in popularity by a pantheon of three, Brahma, Vishnu and Shiva, each with a female counterpart, Saraswati, Lakshmi and Parvati. The gods' principal functions are, respectively, creator, preserver and destroyer; their consorts are associated with education (speech), prosperity and the arts (creativity). In some stories, Lakshmi and Saraswati are both wives of Vishnu: 'in this relationship, Saraswati ... represents spiritual ... goals and values, whereas Lakshmi represents . . . wealth, power and fertility' (Kinsley, 1988, p. 58). The *Gita* refers to the 'feminine powers' of 'fame, fortune, speech, memory, intelligence, resolve' and 'patience' (10:34; Miller, 1986, p. 94), no mean list of qualities which Hindus associate more with the female than with the male cosmic principle.

The three gods are often referred to as the Hindu Trinity; like the three persons of the Christian Trinity, they are regarded as different aspects of a single, ultimate reality. While their consorts are represented as dutiful, obedient wives they also complement the power of their mates, so much so that a *deva* without his *Sakti* (consort, literally strength) becomes impotent. Kinsley (1988) describes *Sakti* as 'the active dimension of the godhead' (p. 137). In some accounts, creation itself results from the union of the cosmic male (*purusha*) and female (*prakriti*) principles, themselves originally singular.

For devotees of each of the three, for whom they function as *Isvara*, their qualities merge, so much so that some competition for pre-eminence among them is evident in the *Puranas*. For example, in the *Mahabharata*, which is a Vaishnavite text, Shiva declares himself to be 'Shiva in the form of Vishnu and Vishnu in the form of Shiva' (Mackenzie, 1994, p. 147). As the preserver, Vishnu manifests himself in human form whenever *dharma* is threatened, to save humankind (*Gita* 4:7; Miller, 1986, p. 50). Vishnu (as *Isvara*) is especially concerned with human welfare. In the *Gita*, Krishna, Vishnu's *avatara* (manifestation or descent, that is, as a human), declares himself to be the All-in-All: 'I am the universal father, mother, granter of all, grandfather, object of knowledge, purifier, holy syllable Om' (*Gita* 9:17; Miller, 1986, p. 85). He also identifies himself as 'Shiva among the howling storm gods' and as 'Vyasa among sages' (10:37; p. 94). Krishna exists in 'all things', his 'unmanifest form' pervades the 'whole universe' (9:4; p. 83). Krishna creates and destroys everything (11:32; p. 103). Evidence of rivalry between devotees of the old order Indra and the new order Vishnu is found in the story of Indra, who, jealous of people venerating Krishna, sent a rain storm against them. Krishna promptly picked up a mountain and used it as an umbrella to shelter his followers.

While Brahma tends to take a back seat in popular devotion, Shiva, like Vishnu, takes on all three functions: for his devotees he creates, preserves and destroys. Shiva is both the great ascetic and the god of sexual prowess. Parvati is a loving, obedient and very erotic wife and the enemy of ignorance, the slayer of demons (in her *Sakti* or Kali manifestations). In his *Purana*, all the other gods address Shiva as 'Shankara' (giver of peace), saying: 'God of Gods, great god, ocean of mercy, lord, you move within all creatures . . . you know everything' (*Shiva Purana*; O'Flaherty, 1976, p. 163). As we shall see, the *bhakti* tradition (devotion to an *Isvara*) that emerged from the *Puranas* cared little for class or even for gender distinctions. Anyone at all, whether educated or uneducated, could pray and sing to a personal saviour; Krishna says, 'If they rely on me . . . women, commoners, men of low rank, even men born in the womb of evil, reach the highest way' (*Gita* 9:32; Miller, 1986, p. 87).

## Krishna and Christ

As noted in Chapter 4, a writer as early as Sir William Jones, who was Supreme Court Judge in Calcutta, hinted at parallels between the Krishna and Christ, or Jesus, stories (for an excellent Christ–Krishna discussion, see Ovey M. Mohammed, 1993). The full Krishna narrative is thought to be a combination of three stories: that of the child Krishna, or of Gopal, that of the adult Krishna and that of the Krishna of the *Gita*. The first is associated with a tradition of child veneration that is often compared with 'devotion to the infant Jesus' (Mohammed, 1993, p. 10). The Gopal stories are found in the *Bhagavata Purana* (ninth century CE). I have sat watching Hindu women washing and dressing Gopal's image in Krishna temples. The adult Krishna is one of the heroes of the *Mahabharata*, a type of 'tribal hero' (*ibid.*, p. 9).

Tradition says that Krishna was born while his parents, Devaki and Vasudeva, were chained up in prison because Devaki's brother, King Kansa, had been warned that one of her children would succeed in defeating him. To ensure that she had no children, he imprisoned both her and her husband. Children were born anyway, so he slaughtered them. The parallel with Herod is self-evident. One son, Balarama, was saved by Vishnu's intervention. After Krishna's birth (which was itself a miracle, and marked by a star), the prison gates opened, chains fell off, and Vasudeva was able to take Krishna across the Jumna River, which parted before him, to safety in the village of Gokula. Here, we are reminded of Joseph and Mary's flight to Egypt.

Krishna then lived as the adopted son of Nanda and Yashoda. Miracles were associated with Krishna from the moment of his birth and some of his village pranks may bring to mind the Jesus of the Gnostic texts. He would steal girls' clothes as they bathed in the river, and he defeated monsters, and was certainly on the side of the good against the wicked. He was kind to all, regardless of rank. As he grew older, he became renowned for his flute-playing and dancing, as well as for his military prowess. Girls would steal away from their husbands' beds to be with Krishna. As he danced, he would multiply his body so that each woman felt that she was dancing with him. Sometimes, they did not only dance. Krishna's own relationship with Radha, his companion, was ambiguous. Were they married? Some Bengali interpreters praise illicit love: 'illicit love is freely given, makes no legal claims, and as such is selfless' (Kinsley, 1988, p. 89). It is such selfless love for which all true devotees of *Bhagavan*, the Lord, must aim. Krishna was above all a 'thief of hearts', and sometimes stole people away from their licit spouses. Gods do call us to leave our biological families for their sake; Jesus did too: 'Anyone who loves his father or mother more than me is not worthy of me' (Matthew 10:37).

Tradition says that Krishna married 16,100 princesses and fathered countless sons. After defeating King Kansa he did not assume power, to which he had a valid claim, but instead went to the aid of the Pandavas in their struggle against the evil Karauvas. During the eighteen-day battle, the *Mahabharata*'s central event, he revealed his true nature to Arjuna, who said in awe as he gazed at Krishna-Vishnu: 'You alone fill the space between heaven and earth and all the directions, seeing this awesome form of yours, Great Soul, the three worlds tremble' (*Gita* 11:20; Miller, 1986, p. 100). The *Gita* does not despise *jnana*, or yogic discipline, or *karma* (action). True understanding of one's relationship with the Absolute, though, is as much a gift as an intellectual achievement: 'At the end of many births, the man of knowledge finds refuge in me; he is the rare great spirit who sees, "Krishna is all that is"' (17:19; p. 73). 'What I deem to be knowledge,' says Krishna, 'is knowledge of the field and its knower' (13:2; p. 115). Action, too, must be performed without *any attachment to its fruits* (see below). The object is to 'abide', or to 'be', in Krishna: 'men devoted to me are in me, and I am within them' (9:29; p. 87). This sounds like the Johannine Jesus: 'Remain in me, and I will remain in you' (15:4). Further, just as Jesus expects his disciples to 'bear fruit' (verse 5), so does Krishna: 'dedicate yourself to action, performing actions for my sake' (*Gita* 12:10; Miller, 1986, p. 112).

Law, too, is superseded by grace; compare *Gita* 18:66 with John 1:17. Just as Jesus makes the unseen God known (John 1:18), so does Krishna: 'By devotion alone can I, as I really am, be known and seen' (*Gita* 11:53; Miller, 1986, p. 108). When devotees see Krishna, they see the All-in-All (11:16); whoever sees Jesus sees God (John 14:7). True knowledge is from Krishna (*Gita*, 7:2; Miller, 1986, p. 72); Jesus makes known what he has learned from the Father (John 15:15). Having attended, even spoken, at Krishna worship, I can vouch for the depth of devotion that worshippers display, as I can for their love of Krishna and for the fervour of their belief that through him they enjoy at-oneness with God. In summer 1999, my wife and I were invited to take part in a *kirton* in a Krishna temple in Bangladesh by one of her distant Hindu relatives. I spoke and Rekha sang. I was introduced as researching for a 'book on Krishna'. Perhaps I was. Below, I quote a Christian saying of Gandhi that he felt no 'religious concern' for him, seeing him as manifestly a 'man of God'. My opinion is purely subjective, but I find it difficult to say that Krishna devotees must substitute Christ for Krishna before they can know God. Krishna honours all sincere worship, even when offered to other gods (see citations later in this chapter).

After the Pandavas' victory, Krishna ruled his own ideal city of Dvarak. One day, after relaxing his own rule prohibiting the drinking of alcohol during a festival, disaster followed. Even Krishna failed to stop the mayhem and murder that destroyed the city. Saddened, he sought solitude in the forest, where, mistaken for a gazelle, he was mortally wounded by an arrow. Dying, he returned to heaven. Some proponents of the 'Jesus and

Krishna are really the same' theory claim that Krishna died by crucifixion (see Acharya S, 1999, p. 76). The Krishna story clearly has erotic elements that are lacking in the Jesus story, although some would supply this. Eroticism results at least in part from India's more relaxed attitude towards sensuality, even to the extent that the sensual and the spiritual are not always polarized as opposites. On the other hand, these elements have long been interpreted allegorically, as a metaphor of the devotion of the true worshipper for his or her *Isvara*. While the historical basis for Krishna's existence is not strong, scholars believe that a deified king or hero could lie behind the narrative. Flood (1996) points out that 'the historicity of Krishna is important for the tradition' itself, although I cite below Hindu writers for whom the historicity of a text is less important than the 'truth' it contains. None the less, a visit to http://krishna.avatar.org will show that devotees date Krishna's birth as 19 July 3228 BCE; the site has a time-line of Krishna's life and much material of interest, including illustrations.

## Buddhism: worldview

Each in their own way, the *Upanishads* and the *Puranas* rebelled against Brahmanism's stranglehold on religion. Brahmanism did not offer much by way of spiritual development or participation to non-Brahmans, although it did demand ethical conduct. Duties and responsibilities, debts and obligations were meticulously laid down according to one's class, stage in life and gender. The *Upanishads*, for their part, invited intellectual enquiry and yogic practice designed to achieve awareness of at-oneness with the ultimate (the state of *samadhi*). Even non-Brahmans could think. However, the lowest class was forbidden from studying Sanskrit and therefore from reading the sacred texts. For them, the *bhakti* tradition had enormous appeal; anybody at all can worship and serve a personal Lord. Buddhism also rejected the *Upanishads*' epistemology and expressed discontent with Brahmanism.

Like those of Jesus, the Buddha's dates are uncertain. He was possibly born in 566 BCE in the town of Lumbini (in modern Nepal) to a powerful chief or ruler of the Sakya tribe. The Sakyas were Ksatriyas and appear to have thought themselves equal to if not better than Brahmans. They may well have had little interest in the sacrificial system. The Buddha is actually a title (meaning enlightened being). The man who became the Buddha was born as Siddhattha Gotama (in the Pali language). Many legends surround his birth. His mother, Maya, is said to have conceived him when a white elephant touched her side. A tree bent to lend her support when the Buddha was born. The child could walk and speak at birth. A miraculous shower of water bathed him. Lotus blossoms sprouted under his feet.

The seer Asita predicted that Siddhattha would become either a great world leader or a great world teacher. His father, eager to see the first and not the second fulfilled, did his best to protect Siddhattha from the realities of life. He built splendid palaces and gardens for him and peopled them with young, beautiful, healthy men and women. Siddhattha married and had a son. Yet when he was about 29 years old he found himself asking what life in the world was really like, and insisted on visiting the city which all thought it was his destiny to rule. His father did his best to stage-manage the excursion by removing all blemishes from Siddhattha's route. Unfortunately, the prince deviated from the planned itinerary (or the gods intervened) and he saw for the first time evidence of human misery: an old man, a diseased man and a corpse. When his charioteer assured him that all this could even happen to him, the prince was filled with despair.

## The great renunciation

Then, seeing an emaciated yet happy-looking mendicant holy man, Siddhattha began to wonder whether this lifestyle might not offer some possibility of solving the meaning of human suffering. He resolved to become a world renouncer. Swapping his princely apparel for a beggar's clothes, he left behind his life of ease to travel and search for spiritual truth. For six years he practised asceticism, breathing control and meditation, becoming the leader of a small band of forest dwellers. One day, almost comatose from hunger, he suddenly realized that such extreme self-denial was as unproductive as his earlier excesses. He started to eat. Disgusted, his followers abandoned him. Resolving not to move from where he sat, under a Bodhi tree at what is now called Bodh Gaya, he went into a deep meditation. This was the moment for which his previous 549 lives had prepared him, since he first met the Buddha of the previous age and vowed to become a Buddha himself. The demons knew that the hour of his enlightenment was near, and tried to tempt him:

> But he who is the Prince
> of darkness, Mara – knowing this was Buddha,
> Who should deliver men, and now the hour
> When he should find the Truth and save the worlds
> Gave unto all his evil powers command.
> Wherefore there trooped from every deepest pit
> The fiends who war with wisdom and the Light.
>
> (Arnold, 1879, p. 147)

His enlightenment was inevitable. He resisted temptation and achieved his 'awakening'. Once 'awake', Siddhattha's first thought was to continue his life of seclusion. Then Brahma appeared to him, and persuaded him to teach. Indeed, he became generous with his teaching. Out of compassion for all creatures, he began to preach at Varanasi, where his former companions became the very first to respond, and joined his infant community (*sangha*) of celibate renunciates. In fact, they became 'stream enterers', whose own enlightenment was also inevitable.

Of course, the above is an idealized version of the Buddha's life, but it does follow traditional, if late, accounts (see Conze, 1959, pp. 35–66, for a translation of the *Buddhacarita*, 'the first, and in many respects the finest, full length biography', which dates from the first century CE). The canonical writings (fixed within three generations of the Buddha's death) do not recount the Buddha's life 'from birth to death', making these sources much later, by comparison, than the Jesus sources. The scriptures do contain a lot of biographical references however (see Carrithers, 1983, pp. 5–7). While the Buddha's existence as a historical person has been doubted (as have those of Confucius and Lao Tsu), many would agree with Carrithers that 'at least the basic outline of his life must be true' (p. 3).

## *The* dharma

This sermon set in motion 'the wheel of life', or the *dharma* (the Buddha's teaching). The Buddha taught a middle path between excess and extreme denial. Believing that people are at different stages of spiritual development, he sometimes gave different people different advice. The Dalai Lama says that it would be harmful to try to 'impose certain religious beliefs onto a person whose inclination is clearly opposed to it'. There is, he says, 'great diversity in human dispositions' (1996, p. 97). He also comments that teachings which 'may even seem to contradict each other' prevent Buddhists from 'falling into dogmatism' (p. 72). The doctrine of skilful means encouraged hearers to test and adapt the Buddha's message. Do not believe what I say because I say it, he taught; rather, believe whatever works for you. Different religions may even be appropriate for people at different stages. He gave precepts or guidelines rather than rules or commands.

The Buddha saw himself as a physician, diagnosing the human condition, prescribing the medicine (*dharma*), with the *sangha* as the nurse. The full-time mendicants, who are celibate, can only eat one noon meal of what others freely give them. After some persuasion, the Buddha did allow women to join the *sangha*, although they were considered junior to all (even the youngest) male monks. *Dana* (giving) is an act of great merit; helping others is an expression of selflessness. He often used lists, such as the four noble truths: all is suffering (*dukkha*), suffering is caused by desire, desire can be overcome, the answer is the eight-fold path. This path includes wisdom (right understanding, right resolve), ethics (right speech, action, livelihood – including non-violence) and meditation (right effort, mindfulness and meditation).

In short, the way to escape from the cycle of *samsara* is to overcome all desires and attachments. The Buddha taught that everything is impermanent; there is no eternal *atman*, no *Brahman*. Attachment to a false sense of self-worth, to possessions, to power, to bodily pleasures, traps us in *samsara*. Existence is a temporary condition, a combination of matter, feeling, imagination, will and consciousness. When one has 'awakened', or realized complete detachment, rebirth ceases. You leave *samsara* and enter *nibhana* (the Sanskrit *nirvana* is more commonly used in the West). The Buddha never defined this, suggesting that it is as impossible to say what happens after all desire has been extinguished as it is to say where a blown-out flame has gone.

*Nibhana* is often translated as 'cessation'. Some substitute 'bliss'. *Nibhana* is understood to be outside *samsara*. Gods, whose existence the Buddha accepted, are powerful celestial beings but are unable to help humanity towards enlightenment except by encouragement, as they encouraged Siddhattha. They can, though, grant *worldly favours*. After the Buddha died (possibly in 486 BCE) he was regarded as being no longer available to offer any help to anybody still in *samsara*. Only his *dharma* remains. What is now called Theravada (school of the elders) Buddhism, which flourished in Sri Lanka, Burma and Thailand, is often described as a self-help system.

## Mahayana

Between 100 BCE and 100 CE another school, or tendency, emerged, calling itself Mahayana, or the Great Vehicle, and claiming that Theravada was only suitable for people at a preliminary stage of spiritual development. Mahayana introduced three key concepts. First, the goal of becoming a Bodhisattva (*Bodhi* = understanding; *sat* = truth). An *arhat* is someone who has achieved enlightenment, so after death they will enter *nibhana*. As fully enlightened beings, *arhats* are just like the Buddha. The only difference is that while the Buddha was the first in this age to complete the quest, *arhats* follow his *dharma*. The Bodhisattva is an enlightened being who vows to delay final entry into *nibhana* until all sentient beings have achieved enlightenment. This, say Mahayana Buddhists, is the more compassionate, less selfish, goal.

Second, the doctrine of merit transfer. Mahayana teaches that as the Bodhisattvas have an abundance of merit they can give it away, thus aiding others along the path towards enlightenment. Most Bodhisattvas are viewed as heavenly or celestial beings but especially in Tibetan (Vajrayana) Buddhism; some choose to re-enter human existence as teachers, or Lamas. The present Dalai Lama is the fourteenth incarnation of the Bodhisattva of Compassion. Theravada teaches that enlightenment is very difficult to achieve outside the *sangha*; Mahayana blurs the distinction between lay and ordained. Traditionally, Theravada had less interest in social or domestic life, positing the celibate life as the ideal. The goal lies beyond, not in, this world. Merit transfer makes it possible to attain *nibhana* much more quickly, too. Mahayana has been called the *express train*.

Third, Mahayana teaches the doctrine of the three bodies of the Buddha: the historical Buddha, the cosmic Buddha (located in paradise) and the truth body, or the Buddha as eternal truth or ultimate reality. The pure land Buddha will reward your love and devotion with birth in his realm, from where *nibhana* is easily obtainable. Zen stresses the inner Buddha, the Buddha nature within. In popular Theravada as well as in all forms of Mahayana, the Buddha is looked upon as a semi-divine being, or as one Buddhist has written: 'No teacher was as godless as the Buddha yet none so Godlike' (Goddard, 1970, p. 20). Depictions of the Buddha attempt to portray not what Shakyamuni (one of the Buddha's many titles) may have looked like, but his qualities of compassion, wisdom and right-mindfulness.

Indeed, Buddha images often reflect their artist's own ethnicity and features. Popularly, there are said to have been twenty-five Buddhas, one for each age. Whenever truth is forgotten, a Buddha comes. The Buddha of the next age will be Maitraya, whom many Buddhists expect soon, just as many Christians think that Jesus' second coming is imminent. Hindus also believe that Vishnu's next *avatara*, Kalki, will soon come, as the present age of darkness nears its end. Buddhism has tended to adapt easily to different cultural contexts, accepting many pre-existing beliefs, if not directly contrary to the *dharma*. Local heroes, teachers and deities are incorporated as Bodhisattvas. It is not uncommon for people in China to regard themselves as a Buddhist-Confucianist-Taoist, or in Japan as a Shinto-Buddhist. This reminds me of how Christianity once accommodated the stories of pre-Christian heroes, especially Celtic and Germanic, by adopting them as saints (see Chapter 4).

### Jainism

Another reform movement, contemporary with Buddhism, deserves brief mention, Jainism. Mahavira (540–468 BCE), whom Jains honour as a world conqueror, agreed with the Buddha (of whose teaching he may or may not have been aware) that there is no *Brahman* but asserted the reality of the self (or *jiva*). Indeed, he taught that the self is eternal and self-sufficient. The goal of humankind is rebirth as a world soul, achieved by complete detachment from matter (*ajiva*). *Ahimsa* (non-violence), reverence for all life forms and extreme asceticism characterize the Jain ideal. One group of Jains goes about naked.

### Jesus comes to India

Here, my subject is encounter between India and the Jesus image as imported from the West rather than with the claim, which I discuss below, that Jesus visited India. According to tradition, the apostle Thomas landed in Kerala in 52 CE to preach Jesus' message to Indians, and died as a martyr near Madras in 72 CE. *The Acts of Thomas* tell how King Gundaphorus commanded Thomas, a carpenter, to build a palace for him. When Thomas offered him a spiritual palace instead, the king imprisoned him for his impertinence. Then Jesus saved him, the king accepted Christ and the work of evangelizing India was off to a propitious start. Thomas is said to have won a hundred Brahmans to faith in Christ. Some supporters of the 'Jesus was in India' theory cite *The Acts of Thomas* to support their claims. In the text, there are passages in which Jesus appears to be present. For example, verse 11: the king 'saw the Lord Jesus bearing the likeness of Judas Thomas and speaking with the bride' (James, 1924a). The problem with this reading is that in the Gnostic tradition, of which this text is a part, much was made of *bearing the likeness*, or of being a twin, of Jesus (see Chapter 1).

The Syrian or Thomist Christians of Kerala are certainly an ancient community. Some elements of the Thomas story may well be true: 'a voyage by St Thomas to South India would have been perfectly possible' (Neill, 1964, p. 51). Unfortunately, we do not have any accounts by Indians of the response to the Jesus story from this early period. Syrian Christianity was not aggressively confrontational, or very creed-centred. Rihbany (1916) commented:

As is well known to church historians, the Syrian Christians . . . have had very little to do with the development of the 'creeds of Christendom' . . . They have been worshippers rather than theologians, believers rather than systematic thinkers. (pp. 404–5)

The Christian community eventually formed some 20 per cent of the population of Kerala, and appears to have meshed in alongside other communities as a religious option amidst other options. Claiming descent from the one hundred Brahmans converted by Thomas, they are regarded as a high-caste community (for a contemporary novel set among the Syrian Christians of Kerala, see Arundhati Roy's Booker Prize-winning *The God of Small Things* (1997)). A walk down Cochin's streets readily shows how integrated Christianity is in the tapestry of life. It is as easy to buy Christian as Hindu artefacts, often from the same market stall. Roy says that Christianity 'seeped into Kerala like tea from a teabag' (p. 33). In some areas, Christians perhaps adapted too comfortably to the Hindu context, adopting many attitudes related to caste divisions. One of Roy's characters remembers how, in her childhood, untouchables had to walk backwards so that no Brahman or Syrian Christian would even 'accidentally defile themselves by . . . stepping into' their footprints (p. 71). Thomist Christians may well have thought Hinduism false or idolatrous, but they do not appear to have gone around destroying *murtis* (images) or preaching vile threats of hell-fire. Later, Western missionaries did just this, denouncing Hindu practices as pernicious. On Elephanta Island off Mumbai, the Portuguese broke the legs off the ancient rock carvings of Brahma, Vishnu and Shiva.

### Early East–West encounter

Some information on Hinduism and Buddhism travelled West. Buddhist missionaries may have reached Alexandria by the first century or even earlier. Pythagoras is said to have had extensive knowledge of Hindu texts, as noted in Chapter 4. The possibility of Buddhist influence on John's Gospel was referred to in Chapter 1. Clement of Alexandria (d. 215) appears to have had a reasonably detailed knowledge of Hindu and Buddhist groups. He wrote:

The Indian gymnosophists are also in the number, and the other barbarian philosophers. And of these there are two classes, some of them called Sarmanae, and others Brahmins. And those of the Sarmanae who are called Hylobii neither inhabit cities, nor have roofs over them, but are clothed in the bark of trees, feed on nuts, and drink water in their hands. Like those called Encratites in the present day, they know not marriage nor begetting of children.

Some, too, of the Indians obey the precepts of Buddha; whom, on account of his extraordinary sanctity, they have raised to divine honours. (1885, 1:15)

Clement's comment on the Buddha as 'raised to divine honours' is interesting, since it invites comparison with some of the heretical Christian views that Clement rejected. Origen, Clement's student, is famous for teaching 'cycles of existence':

Those rational beings who sinned . . . are purified [then] rise again to the state in which they formerly were. . . . Then a second time or a third time or many more times they are enveloped in different bodies for punishment . . . it is probable that different worlds have existed and will exist. (cited in Stevenson, 1963, pp. 216–17)

Had Origen heard of *karma*? Thich Nhat Hanh notes that Origen's idea was 'close to reincarnation' (1995, p. 132). It was Mani (d. 272), founder of the Manichees, whose evil–good dualism attracted Augustine for some time, who may have first explicitly compared Jesus and the Buddha:

Wisdom and deeds have always from time to time been brought to mankind by messengers. So in one age they have been brought by the messenger called Buddha to India, by Zaradusht to Persia, in another by Jesus to the West. (*ibid.*, p. 281)

## Medieval encounter

Trade between the Middle East and India, by overseas spice route and by dhow across the sea, ensured some cultural as well as commercial exchange. *The Arabian Nights* may have had Buddhist origins. As Smith (1981) points out, the medieval Christian legend of Barlaam and Josaphat is in fact the story of the Buddha's great renunciation (p. 20). Early encounter between Christian and Buddhist monks appears to have resulted in cordial relations. Despite their different doctrines, they seem to have mutually recognized each other's lives as authentically monastic, perhaps from as early as the thirteenth and fourteenth centuries when Franciscans reached China.

## Robert de Nobili (1577–1656)

When Robert de Nobili, a Jesuit, reached Madurai (now in Tamil Nadu), he was dismayed to find that Christians were all looked upon as *feringhis* (foreigners), and as having lost their Indian identity. He allowed converts to wear Hindu dress, including 'the Brahman cord, the *Kudumi* (tuft of hair) and sandalwood ashes on their foreheads, which by Europeans were regarded as marks of the Hindu religion' (Staffner, 1987, p. xi). Nobili did not see Christianity and Hinduism as 'mutually exclusive'. However, he experienced difficulty ministering on the one hand to Christian converts, who unlike the Syrians of Kerala were classed as outcastes, while on the other developing dialogue with Brahmans. Caste remains problematic in the Indian Church. In many areas, different caste groups converted to different denominational missions, thus perpetuating divisions between communities. In Delhi, I photographed a rally outside the Catholic cathedral protesting against caste-based discrimination within the Church (organized by the All India Christian Association on 9 December 1990). I have heard Brahman Christians complaining of prejudice in areas controlled by lower castes, as well as non-Brahmans complaining about their treatment by Brahmans.

Nobili pioneered the use of traditional Indian concepts to elucidate Jesus' significance. He referred to Jesus as the *sarguru* (true Guru; also God's designation in the Sikh tradition). Jesus opened up the way to *moksa*. He described the Lord's Prayer as a *mantra* (sacred formula). He even used *guruparamparai* to explain apostolic succession. In the Vaishnavite tradition especially, all gurus (teachers) stand in an initiatory chain stretching back to Vishnu himself. Nobili showed the depth of his understanding of Indic thought by equating sin with ignorance. In Christianity, lostness is the fruit of sin; for Hindus and Buddhists it is ignorance (and desire) that keeps people trapped in *samsara*. The *Gita* says, 'Know dark inertia born of ignorance, as the delusion of every embodied self; it binds one with negligence, indolence and sleep' (14:8; p. 122).

Nobili was not the only early missionary to 'go native'. Unfortunately, this was later discouraged, especially as the missionary and the civilizing tasks were increasingly equated. Robert Delavignette, a former governor-general of French colonial territories, in his *Christianity and Colonialism* (1964), remarks that 'whether one likes it or not the missionary's mode of life was – and sometimes still is – colonial in style' (p. 66). In Bangladesh, I was entitled to a missionary concession on first-class steamer fares, a relic from the days when the colonial authorities did not want a poor missionary letting the side down by travelling second or third class. Etiquette demanded that Indians, however Westernized, did not 'enter a compartment reserved for Europeans' (Allen, 1975, p. 231, citing *The Indian Gentleman's Guide to Etiquette*). For a European to trespass into an Indian apartment was equally unacceptable.

*Francis Xavier (1505–52)*

Francis Xavier, who pioneered Christian missions in Japan after working in India, befriended a Buddhist abbot. I was once in old Goa on Francis' feast day. The Mass was attended by large numbers of Hindus as well as by Christians. This suggests that his legacy is respected within the majority religious community, as well as by his own. Led by Xavier, many Jesuits came to believe that while the Gospel must 'transform and refine and recreate' the cultures it encountered, Christians 'need not necessarily reject as worthless everything that has come before' (Neill, 1964, p. 156). In fact, says Neill, it is likely that the converts whom Xavier left behind in Japan 'imagined themselves to have *accepted a new and superior kind of Buddhism*' (*ibid.*; italics added). In China, the Jesuits even used Chinese in the Mass and tolerated 'old . . . habits and customs' such as reverence for Confucius and for ancestors (*ibid.*, p. 190). This changed. Later missionaries rejected the use of the vernacular and reverence for ancestors as pagan and incompatible with true Christian faith.

Sadly, as in Africa, the dominant approach was that Indian or Chinese or Japanese culture and habits had to be replaced by European, Christian ones as the tasks of civilizing and of Christianizing were commonly conflated. Achebe shows how this trend, of initial openness later yielding to intolerance, also occurred in the African context. He depicts a Mr Brown, the first missionary to reach the village where his novel was set, as avoiding unnecessary conflict with traditional ways. Then Mr Smith arrived; 'a different kind of man', he 'openly condemned Mr Brown's policy of compromise and accommodation. He saw things as black and white and black was evil' (1959, p. 184).

## Colonial encounter

Africans and American Indians were easily dismissed as primitive, despite the actual sophistication of their cultures, especially their leadership structures and eco-friendly lifestyles. Not everyone could so quickly pass this judgement on India, China or Japan, although no few did. Could Europeans maintain their sense of cultural and religious superiority when they encountered cultures and religions as ancient and as advanced as their own? Some Europeans were inclined to look on Indians as partners, as equals, and greatly valued what they knew of Indian culture. Warren Hastings (1732–1818), for example, wrote the preface to the first English translation of the *Gita*, by Charles Wilkins (1785), and supported Indian institutions and learning. In 1829, Horace Hayman Wilson (1786–1860) opened up the Asiatic Society of Bengal to Indian members. Others valued India's *past* but saw little of interest in her *present*, which they represented as a decadent, decayed culture.

F. Max Müller (1823–1900), who coined the term 'comparative religion', translated the *Vedas* and many Hindu and Buddhist texts into

English yet thought he could learn *nothing important* from living Hindus or Buddhists. He never visited India. Scriptures, he said, gave access to the pure essence of any religion, to the 'lowest, more ancient stratum of religious thought' (1873, p. 157). What comes after is corrupt and impure. He encouraged the work of Hindu reformers (see below), writing *Sri Ramakrishna: His Life and Sayings* (1900), and was quite enthusiastic about the Theosophical Society. He hoped that theosophy's co-founder, Colonel Henry Olcott, would free Buddhism 'from its later excrescences, and bring it back to its earliest, simplest and purest form as taught by the Buddha and his immediate disciples' (cited in Gombrich, 1971, p. 54).

Müller did believe that Europe could benefit from Eastern spirituality. The Transcendentalists, such as Ralph Waldo Emerson (1803–82) and Henry David Thoreau (1817–62), theosophists and others were critical of Western materialism and rationality, seeing the East as more spiritually wholesome. Arthur Schopenhauer (1788–1860), who influenced Müller, did not think there was any *ultimate* spirit, only that engendered by art, music and poetry, which alone can deliver us from *dukkha*, but he looked eastward to Hindu and to Buddhist thought with deep interest and respect. Thoreau, in *A Week on the Concord and Merrimack Rivers* (1849), recommended that anyone interested in scripture should read 'the Bhagvat-Geeta . . . it deserves to be read with reverence even by Yankees' (1985, p. 115). Turning to the Buddha, he commented that 'I trust that some may be as near and dear to the Buddha, or Christ . . . who are without the pale of their churches. It is necessary,' he continued,

not to be a Christian to appreciate the beauty and significance of the life of Christ. I know that some will have hard thoughts of me, when they hear their Christ named beside my Buddha yet I am . . . willing that they should love their Christ more than my Buddha, for the love is the main thing and I like him too. (*ibid.*, p. 55)

Indeed, write Tweed and Prothero, Thoreau 'lavished such praise on the *Bhagavad Gita* and "my Buddha" that it scandalized many Christian readers' (1999, p. 95).

Boston Unitarians (among whom Emerson ministered for some time), too, looked eastwards. James Freeman Clarke (1818–88), the first man to regularly lecture on world religion at an American college (Harvard Divinity School), whose *Ten Great Religions* (1871) became a bestseller, suggested that Hinduism was a religion of the spirit, stressing other-worldliness over this-worldliness. Later, he speculated how similarities between Christianity, Hinduism and Buddhism may have occurred. Did they have common roots? Or, as he preferred to think, had they developed 'striking resemblances . . . because human nature was the same everywhere' (Jackson, 1994, p. 12)? Clarke was Minister of the Unitarian Church of the Disciples, Boston, for almost fifty years. Touring India in 1883, Philip Brooks of Boston's Holy Trinity Church commented that he felt obliged to visit Bodh Gaya, since 'a large part of Boston prefers to consider itself Buddhist rather than Christian' (cited in Jackson, 1994, p. 12).

Translations of the *Gita* and Sir Edwin Arnold's poem *The Light of Asia* (1879) did much to popularize the idea that the East was *spiritually fertile ground*. Arnold's very sympathetic, romantic treatment of the Buddha is reminiscent in places of the lives of the Christian saints, especially St Francis (1181–1226). Francis left his life of ease to become a mendicant preacher. Arnold's description of the Buddha's temptation (quoted above) brings Jesus to mind (see the comparison in Borg, 1997, pp. 93–109). One scene has the Buddha mourning over a dead swan, killed by his cousin: 'But the swan lives; my cousin hath but killed the god-like speed which throbbed in this white wing' (Arnold, 1879, p. 22). This reminds me of the bird episode in some Gnostic texts. Perceptively, Arnold (1832–1904) wrote that he had 'put my poem into a Buddhist's mouth, because, to appreciate the spirit of Asiatic thought, they should be regarded from the Oriental point of view' (*ibid.*, p. 5), which makes his poem an early attempt at virtual insidership.

## Missionary attitudes

In India, though, missionaries and civil servants tended more and more to endorse Müller's idea that contemporary India was corrupt, a civilization in decay. Novelist Vikram Chandra cleverly reflects this attitude in his novel, *red earth and pouring rain* (1995), in which a missionary goes around muttering (as heard by an Indian youth) 'di-gra-did, si–vil-iz-a-shun, prau-gres, di-cay' (p. 228). When an image of Shiva was unearthed, the British officer decided that his clerical friend would

Take the horrifying demonic effigy, with its serpent necklace and tiger-cloth and cavorting pose and . . . travel with it throughout England, from village to village, exhibiting the depths of degradation that characterises the so-called theology of the Hindoos, that collection of libertinism, oppression, superstition and folly that masquerades as religion. (p. 198)

Perhaps surprisingly, the Unitarian Joseph Priestley did not share some of his colleagues' enthusiasm for Indian religion; he represented it as superstition, irrational and absurd: 'The absurdity of the *Hindu* system is as apparent as the superior wisdom of that of *Moses* . . . *Hebrews* . . . had a religion perfectly rational, that of the Hindus was absurd in the extreme' (1972a, p. 306). Governor-General Charles Cornwallis (1738–1805) could declare that 'every native of India, I verily believe, is corrupt' (Spear, 1965, p. 95).

Until 1813, missionaries were not officially allowed within British-controlled territory. East India Company policy was not to interfere overmuch with local customs lest trade be adversely affected. Company Director Charles Grant (1746–1823), an evangelical Christian, whose *Observations on the State of Society among the Asiatic Subjects of Great Britain*

(1792) depicted Indian society as depraved and immoral, successfully introduced the 'pious clause' into the 1813 Charter. Missionaries were then admitted into company territory. Grant also founded the company's training college, and designed its curriculum to produce 'men who would be not just capable civil servants but also bearers of a moral and religious tradition from a superior to an inferior society' (Embree, 1962, p. 201).

## Macaulay's minute men

Thomas Babington Macaulay (1800–59) was entrusted with the job of determining British education policy in India. In his infamous minute of 1835, he reversed earlier support for Indian learning and declared that funds would only be spent on promoting Western science and literature through the medium of the English language, since 'a single shelf of a good European library was worth the whole native literature of India and Arabia' and 'the English language stands pre-eminent even among the languages of the West' (cited in Cracknell, 1986, p. 22). Macauley could neither write nor speak an Indian language. I can, and I reject his evaluation of India's literary heritage. This policy aimed to form a class of people who were Indian in blood and colour but English in taste, dress, opinion and morals, whose job was then to raise all Indians to the same standards. Many Christian educators whole-heartedly endorsed Macaulay's views. William Miller (1838–1923), Principal of the prestigious Madras Christian College, and a Vice-Chancellor of Madras University (1901–7), stated, 'Very largely, especially when contrasted with the tendencies in Hinduism, European thought is Christian thought.' Western knowledge would serve as the 'congenial medium' through which the gospel message would be conveyed (cited by Thomas, 1997, p. 156). Miller served a term as Moderator of the General Assembly of the Free Church of Scotland (1896). 'Macaulay's minute men', however, were never quite the breed the British hoped for. Instead, as novelist Salman Rushdie put it:

Thus, a class of Macaulay's minutemen would hate the best of India. Vasco was wrong. We were not, had never been, that class. The best, and the worst, were in us, and fought in us, as we fought the land at large. In some of us the worse triumphed; but still we could say – and say truthfully – that we had loved the best. (1996, p. 376)

The problem was that what Indians read, and appreciated, in English literature about fairness, liberty, care for the underdog, were not what they experienced in British India. Nehru (1946) cites the Bengali Noble Prize-winning poet Rabindranath Tagore (1861–1941):

Born [with] . . . an intuitive bias for literature, I naturally set the English on the throne of my heart. Thus passed the first chapters of my life. Then came the parting of the ways, accompanied with a painful feeling of disillusion, when I began increasingly to discover how easily those who accepted the highest truths of civilization disowned them with impunity whenever questions of national self-interest were involved. (p. 322)

Tagore, known in Bengali as the *Bisa Kabi*, or universal poet, wanted union of East and West, nature and spirit. He did not think that all India's ills stemmed from colonialism, valuing international co-operation (see Nehru, 1946, p. 340). However, he resigned his knighthood in 1919, following the Amritsar massacre. Nehru, who describes Tagore as an 'internationalist par excellence', says that he did more than 'any other Indian . . . to bring into harmony the ideals of the east and the west' (*ibid.*, p. 340). He founded Visva Bharati University to revive Indian educational methods. I shall refer to Tagore again in the course of this chapter.

### To support Hinduism as treason to humanity

Macaulay depicted Indians as 'idolaters, blindly attached to the doctrines and rites which, considered merely with reference to the temporal interests of mankind, are in the highest degree pernicious'. To offer Hinduism any support was to 'commit high treason against humanity and civilization' (cited in Shourie, 1994, p. 64). Macaulay's attitude soon characterized Westerners' in India. Consequently, what R. C. Majumdar refers to as an 'overwhelming sense of racial superiority' made 'even some eminent Eng-lishman, including Governors-General and British Cabinet Ministers, look upon Indians *as little better than animals or primitive savages*' (1951, p. xxv; italics added). Sir Charles Trevelyan (1807–87), a senior civil servant in India, whose *Hinduism and Christianity Contrasted* appeared in 1882, wrote:

Hinduism is the only remaining great system of idolatry; and of all the religions which mankind have invented for themselves, it has gone furthest in deifying human vice and holding out its impersonations as objects of imitation and worship. (cited in Shourie, 1994, p. 84)

Since only Christian nations 'progress towards perfection', it followed that part of the civilizing task was also to spread Christianity.

English education gave the leaders of the independence movement the tools they needed to pursue their agenda, yet it was largely destructive of Indian institutions. John Nicol Farquhar (1861–1929), a missionary in India between 1891 and 1923, wrote of how Hindus regarded 'missionary propaganda as an unjustifiable attack on the national spirit and genius'. Citing Har Dayal, he pointed out that missionaries were perceived as enemies of 'whatever bears the name Hindu, as destroyers of . . . that marvel of moral, intellectual, and civic achievement which is known as Hindu culture'. 'The missionary,' the citation continued, 'is the most dreadful adversary you have to meet . . . the greatest enemy of *dharma* and Hindu national life in the present age' (1913, pp. 33–4). He believed Hindus objected to Christianity not because it was 'untrue, but as being

313

destructive and denationalizing' (*ibid.*). For the last six years of his life, Farquhar was Professor of Comparative Religion at Manchester.

Anglican missionary William St Clair Tisdall (1859–1928), who enjoyed a considerable reputation as an expert on world religions, could only ever depict Buddhism as a 'selfish religion'. He spoke of practices so vile that missionaries were constrained by decency from depicting the religions as they really were (1901, p. 128; for Tisdall, see Bennett, 1992, Chapter 6). Baptist missionary John Drew Bate (1836–1923), who also received some recognition for his writing on Islam, wrote:

Hinduism, Buddhism, Mohammedanism and all the other systems which frighten 'Little Faith' are dying, not of old age (for the gospel is as old as Adam, and therefore older than any) but of inanition. (1884, p. 7; for Bate, see Bennett, 1992, Chapter 7)

Thich Nhat Hanh (1995) cites Alexander de Rhodes, 'one of the most active missionaries' in seventeenth-century Vietnam:

Just as when a cursed, barren tree is cut down, the branches that are still on it will also fall, when the sinister and deceitful Sakya [Buddha] is defeated, the idolatrous fabrications that proceed from him will also be destroyed. (p. 5)

Gandhi, while speaking of early respect for Jainism, Islam and Zoroastrianism, said that 'Christianity was at the time an exception'. 'Missionaries,' he complained, 'used to stand in the corner near the high schools and hold forth, pouring abuse on Hindus and their gods. I could not endure this' (Gandhi, 1982, p. 46). Donald Mackenzie's *India: Myths and Legends* (1994), in many respects a useful compendium, reflects some typical European criticism of Buddhism as an *anti-social philosophy*. He calls Buddha 'the great psychologist' but describes his doctrines as 'intensely pessimistic', 'cold and gloomy'. He is 'the enemy of society'. 'His solution for all problems was Death . . . he was the apostle of benevolent Nihilism and Idealistic Agnosticism' (p. 130). Even eminent philosophers found fault with the Buddha's teaching. In Hegel's scheme, for example, Buddhism represented 'an early stage in religious development' that had been 'totally abandoned by history, because it denied the spiritual' (Tillich, 1963, p. 56).

## Hindu and Buddhist responses: general themes

Surprisingly, while few if any Indians shared the West's assessment of their religions, many warmed to the Jesus story as they heard missionaries tell it or as they read the Gospels for themselves. However, much to the missionaries' surprise, what emerged was a view or views of Jesus that differed in many respects from their own. Once they had presented the Jesus story, they could no longer control it. As Sugirtharajah says, the Hindus neither accepted Jesus on 'conventional Christian terms nor' perceived him 'through traditional biblical categories'. Rather, they incorporated 'Jesus into the Hindu framework' (1997, p. 154). Indeed, as Indian Christians including Sugirtharajah have done, they drew on their Indian heritage and religious concepts to 'elucidate their experience of Jesus' (*ibid.*, p. 155). I begin by identifying three general trends, then discuss some significant Hindu and Buddhist thinkers on Jesus.

## Indians like Jesus, not Christianity

First, Indians have little difficulty accepting Jesus as a divine teacher, either as an *avatara* manifesting god on earth, or as an example of a man who realized what we all have the potential to realize: our inner divine natures. The *Gita* says: 'I exist in all creatures, so the disciplined man devoted to me grasps the oneness of life; wherever he is, he is in me' (6:31; Miller, 1986, p. 67). Characteristically, Indians accept Jesus on their own terms, while rejecting Christianity. In other words, they take what they like from what Christians say of Jesus and leave the rest. Swami Abhedananda (1866–1939), in *Why a Hindu Accepts Christ and Rejects Christianity* (1901), distinguished between what he called the 'Churchianity', or pseudo-religion found in churches, and the 'true Christianity taught by Jesus', which had 'no dogma, no creed, no system and no theology' (p. 1). Jesus' religion was of the heart, the Church's was organized dogmatism.

What Abhedananda and others could not accept was the denationalization that was demanded of converts, alongside acceptance of Jesus as saviour. Keshub Chunder Sen (1838–84) had the utmost respect for Jesus, whom he called 'My Christ, my sweet Christ, the brightest jewel of my heart, the necklace of my soul' (Staffner, 1987, p. 7). However, he protested 'against the denationalization which is so general among native converts to Christianity'. With their new religion, they embraced European dress, diet and modes and abandoned 'the manners and customs of their forefathers' (*ibid.*, p. 11). I can testify from numerous visits to the Subcontinent how Christians today are still perceived as pro-Western, perhaps as even more loyal to Western than to national interests.

## Jesus Christ, one among many gods

Second, like the early pagans, Indians reject the claim that Jesus is the only *avatara*, or the only man who has achieved the state of at-oneness with the divine. *Avataras* are 'descents of the divine'. They are god, yet also human, which is why Krishna could die from an arrow wound. Rama 'displayed the tribulations and limitations of the human frame', says Narayan, and it was 'necessary from time to time to remind him of his divinity' (Narayan, 1972, p. 164). Indeed, in the *Ramayana*, Rama slowly develops consciousness of his own true identity, as Jesus seems to do in the Gospels. Vaishnavites believe that the Buddha was an *avatara* of Vishnu, whose task it was to fight against all those who rejected the authority of the *Vedas*. Of course, this is the opposite of what Buddhists believe. Gurus (teachers)

315

also manifest god to their devotees. Indians easily accept that Jesus is God to *his disciples*. However, they equally believe that Vishnu and Shiva are also God to *their followers*. Like Celsus, Indians 'honour the many'. Strauss also thought it mean of God to limit divinity to a single individual.

Of course, Hindus find it easier to use god-language of Jesus than do Buddhists, although the distinction in Mahayana between a Buddha or a Bodhisattva and a divine being is somewhat blurred. The Dalai Lama prefers to relate to 'Buddha as a historical figure and personality' but points out that for many Buddhists he also has 'a timeless, infinite dimension', the *'dhamakaya*, or Truth Body' (1996, p. 61). Generally, Buddhists have little difficulty accepting Jesus as a Buddha, as long as he remains one among many enlightened beings (see the Dalai Lama's comment at the start of this chapter). I return to this apparent impasse between Christian theism and Buddhism's non-theism later in this chapter.

### Lack of interest in historicity

Third, although some Indians do refer to what Jesus said and did, to the source documents, they play less of a role here than in previous chapters. Characteristically, Hindus and Buddhists focus on Jesus' *experience of the divine* or on his *grasp of religious truth*, which is eternal. Inasmuch as Jesus personified this truth, he is looked upon as a figure of history. However, as with New Agers on Jesus, the cosmic Lord takes priority over the Jesus of history. Swami Aseshananda, in an article entitled 'The Hindu View of Christ', stated that: 'To the Hindu, the historicity of Christ is not of much concern: for they always care more for the principle than for the person-ality' (cited by Andrews, 1939, p. 259). Gandhi, who did not personally doubt Jesus' historicity, similarly remarked: 'I may say that I have never been interested in a historical Jesus. I should not care if . . . Jesus never lived.' For Gandhi, the 'events of Jesus' life' are not 'historical but ever-recurring eternal events in the moral life of every individual or corporate self engaged in sacrificial love' (Gandhi, 1940, p. 35). While Western scholars ask of a text, 'Is it historically true, or reliable?', Indians ask, 'Does it contain truth?' Swami Vivekananda (1863–1902) expressed unin-terest in whether the details of Jesus' life as set out in the Gospels were true, asking instead, 'Is there something behind it, something we want to imitate?' (Vivekananda, 1963, Vol. V, p. 146). He commented that half the details of the lives of religions' founders were 'not now seriously believed' and that the 'other half is seriously doubted'. Like Tillich, he did not think that *faith* depended on historical events (I return to the Swami below). Tillich believed that faith requires courage as well as risk-taking, thus historical certainty can never translate into genuine faith.

## Hindu experience of Jesus

Given their primary interest in experience, in Jesus' inner awareness of *atman* as *Brahman* and their comparative lack of interest in the details of Jesus' life, I ought more properly to speak of *Hindu encounter with the Christ*. Hindus typically use the title 'Christ' in their writing. For them, Christ is a cosmic title, or principle, an inherent inner potentiality, not the end-time Messiah. Characteristically, as already noted, Hindus elucidate Jesus', or rather Christ's, significance from within the Hindu worldview, drawing on Hindu concepts rather than analysis of the gospel record, or of Second Temple Judaism.

### Sri Ramakrishna (1836–86)

One of the most influential Hindu gurus to emerge in the nineteenth century was Sri Ramakrishna, whose disciple, Swami Vivekananda, founded the Ramakrishna Mission. He describes how, while meditating on an image of Mary and Child, he experienced *samadhi* (at-oneness) with Jesus as *Isvara*. Earlier, he had experienced *samadhi* with Kali (he was a priest at a Kali temple), Ram, Radha, Krishna and with other deities. Swami Nikhilanda (1895–1973), translator of *The Gospel of Ramakrishna*, wrote:

Thus he experienced the truth that Christianity too was a path leading to God-consciousness. Till the last moment of his life, he believed that Christ was an incarnation of God. But Christ for him was not the only incarnation; there were others – Buddha, for instance, and Krishna. (1942, p. 34)

Ramakrishna believed that *Brahman* is singular and unknowable in its totality but that at the level of *Isvara* it manifests itself differently for different people. Or, people simply call *Isvara* by different names but all name the same reality.

Ramakrishna used the metaphor of different words for water. In India, water is called *pani* and *jal*. Both words, he says, designate the same object: 'the substance is one under different names, and everyone is seeking the same substance' (*ibid.*, p. 35). Different *ishtams* (paths) lead to the same goal, a relationship with *isvara*. In the *Gita*, Krishna declared: 'When devoted men sacrifice to other deities with faith, they sacrifice to me . . . however aberrant the rite' (9:22; Miller, 1986, p. 86). At 7:21 he says that he 'grants unwavering faith to any devoted man who wants to worship any form' (p. 73). Ramakrishna was convinced, based on his own experience, that one person's religious experience is as valid as anyone else's. What he objected to was not individuals choosing to call *Isvara* exclusively by one name but the denial that others could choose a different name. Incidentally, his own interest in Jesus was inspired by a Hindu devotee to Jesus as *Isvara*, Jadu Mallick, who 'read the Bible to him' (Thomas, 1991, p. 113).

Faithful to the *Gita*'s inclusivism, Swami Prabhupada (1896–1977), founder of the International Society for Krishna Consciousness (ISCON), held that it was immaterial whether someone followed Krishna, Buddha or Jesus: 'follow Krishna, follow Christ, follow Buddha,' he said, 'but don't just talk' (Goswamy, 1980, Vol. 2, p. 128). Jesus, said ISCON's founder, 'was a *sakty-avesa-avatara*, an empowered incarnation of God' who 'sacrificed everything for God' (*ibid.*, Vol. 1, p. 77). However, after replying to the question 'What do you think of Jesus Christ?' that Jesus was 'the Son of God', he added that the questioner was also 'a son of God' (Vol. 2, p. 15). On another occasion, Swami Prabhupada advised Christian clergymen to co-operate with his movement. In Roy's *The God of Small Things*, the Jesuit missionary, Father Mulligan, actually converts to Vaishnavism (1997, pp. 281–2). After setting out to study 'Hindu scriptures in order to be able to denounce them intelligently' (p. 23), he ends up swapping his priest's dress for a saffron robe.

### Ramakrishna's Jesus

Who was Jesus for Ramakrishna? Ramakrishna's Jesus was, on the one hand, an *avatara*, a manifestation of the divine in human form, like Krishna. Like Krishna, his task had been to 'protect the good' and to establish 'the law of righteousness', to rescue humanity from evil (*Gita*, 4:8; Miller, 1986, p. 50). Jesus, like Krishna, brought true knowledge of the human condition (18:63; p. 157), gifted people with faith (7:21; p. 73) and granted refuge to all, of whatever class or gender, who responded to his call (9:29, 9:32; p. 87; 18:66; p. 152). For Ramakrishna, Jesus and Krishna had fulfilled the same task. Yet, on the other hand, while their pre-existence is explicit in the *Gita* and in the prologue of John's Gospel respectively, what really signified for Ramakrishna was not that they were gods before birth but that both were true *Advaitin* (those who attain union with the Absolute). For Ramakrishna, it was Jesus' *experience* that rendered him the Christ, not his *ontological status*, not that he would have denied that Jesus was also ontologically God. Shortly before he died, the master founded the Ramakrishna Math, a monastic organization for spiritual training.

### Swami Vivekananda

The Swami was the first Hindu teacher of note to visit the USA. In 1893 he attended the Chicago Parliament of World Religions, then stayed on for a few years to establish the Vedanta Society (1895). The same year, returning to India, he set up the Ramakrishna Mission, which works alongside the Math to engage in humanitarian endeavours. It has been said that Vivekananda was the first to articulate a Hindu message for all the world. Abhedananda headed the New York centre from 1897 until 1921, where Nikhilanda was Director from 1931 to 1973. Both gave distinguished leadership. Vivekananda agreed with Müller, the Boston Transcendentalists and with the theosophists that India was a rich storehouse of spiritual insight and wisdom. Indeed, he believed that India had nothing much to learn from Christianity, although it could benefit from Western technology and science. India as a nation suffered when she lost touch with other nations. Vivekananda admired the social welfare, medical and educational programmes of the missionaries, making this integral to the work of his own organization.

### Vedanta based on eternal principles not historical contingency

Vivekananda's Hinduism was rational and scientific, based, he said, on eternal principles. Indeed, this was Vedanta's strength; it was 'not only spiritual but rational and in harmony with scientific investigations of external nature' (Nehru, 1946, p. 337). Both science and Vedanta, wrote the Swami, 'posit a self-evolving Cause' (1963, Vol. VII, p. 50). Vedanta was not locked away in the past but ever-evolving: 'When, O Lord,' he prayed, 'shall our land be free of this eternal dwelling on the past' (Nehru, 1946, p. 341). Other religions stood on the backs of founders whose historicity was at worst dubious, at best subject to critical examination and doubt. In contrast, Vedanta alone 'is not based on persons but on principles' (Vivekananda, 1963, Vol. III, p. 249). The God of Vedanta, he said, 'is principle, not person. You and I are all Personal Gods' (Vol. VII, p. 134). This qualified it to be the 'end', the 'fulfilment of all *sadhanas* and religions' (Thomas, 1991, p. 121; *sadhana* = Hindu path). However, he did not envision a displacement of other religions by Vedanta but mutual enrichment and co-operation:

The Christian is not to become a Hindu or a Buddhist, nor a Hindu or a Buddhist to become a Christian. But each must assimilate the spirit of the others and yet perceive his individuality and growth according to his own law of growth. (*ibid.*, p. 120)

Vivekananda spoke of two-way traffic between religions: 'unity will come by the fusion of all existing religions into one grand philosophy' (Vol. IV, p. 376).

Of course, his organization did attract adherents, and I think that, at the highest level, Vivekananda regarded all true believers as Vedantists, even if they did not call themselves Hindu. This reminds me of Karl Rahner's concept of 'anonymous Christians'. In other words, we may call God Allah, the Tao, Krishna or Christ, but when we see God we will finally know that God is the Christ and that Christ is God. Like Ramakrishna, Vivekananda did not believe it matters whether the ultimate is named Christ or Krishna, but he did think Vedantic thought was right to assert that any name we use for God, at the level of *Isvara*, is limited and provisional. When we reach the highest level of awareness, we will know that God as *brahman* is above and beyond all labels. To the Hindu, he said, 'man is not traveling from error to truth, but from truth to truth, from lower to higher truth' (1999, p. 132).

He thought that spiritual truth could best be elucidated and interpreted within the Vedantic framework. Only this, he believed, 'could be the future religion of thinking humanity' (Nehru, 1946, p. 337). For some, the final religion would have a distinctly Christian colour; for Vivekananda, its colour would be Vedantic. The organizers of Chicago 1893 anticipated a universal religion. This would combine the best of all religions, yet for many participants it would in fact be a type of evolved, fully developed Christianity. In my view, Vivekananda thought that the universal religion would be more Hindu than Christian, implied in his (8 April 1900) San Francisco lecture, 'Is Vedanta the Religion of the Future?' (1963, Vol. VIII, pp. 122–41). The theosophists, despite teaching that the same truth underlies all religion, almost certainly shared this conviction.

## Vivekananda's Jesus

In 1900, Vivekananda gave a lecture on 'Christ, the Messenger' in Los Angeles, California (1963, Vol. IV, pp. 138–53). He approached Jesus through Vedanta. Although uninterested in issues of historical criticism, he did cite Bible texts when they fitted his understanding of Jesus. For example, John 14:10, 'I am in the Father and the Father is in me', means that reality is within. In fact, a glance through his eight-volume *Works* reveals numerous allusions to the gospel stories. How, then, did he understand Jesus? He saw Jesus as a fully awakened Yogi, who knew at-oneness with the ultimate and who then turned in sacrifice and service towards the world, which for Vivekananda was the true mark of sainthood. He called such a saint a *jibanmukta*, one who has realized liberation while still living, who then helps to liberate others. Jesus was an 'unfettered, unbound spirit, who showed others, saint or sinner, rich or poor that they embodied the "same undying spirit as himself"' (Vol. IV, pp. 145–6). The true saint has 'faith in all and love for all' because he or she knows that they *are all* and 'one with all'.

Against the view that Hinduism lacked a social ethic to motivate his mission's humanitarian programme, Vivekananda argued that *karma-yoga* included selfless service, not to attract a reward but to express complete detachment, union in love with all people. The *Gita* encourages action for others while avoiding any regard for its fruit: 'Be intent on action, not on the fruit of action, avoid attraction to the fruits' (1:47; Miller, 1986, p. 36; see also *Gita* 12:11; compare Matthew 6:2–4). Jesus had also taught 'renunciation. . . . That there is only one ideal in morality: unselfishness. Be selfless' (Vivekananda, 1963, p. 150). True religion for Vivekananda was active, not passive, or, as he put it, not found in dogmas or books but in 'being and becoming' (Vol. III, p. 257). His mission, in my view, has represented Christlike love in action to millions of needy people through-out the world, just as Vivekananda himself worked tirelessly, selflessly, to practise what he preached. Nehru wrote: 'so Vivekananda thundered from Cape Comorin on the southern tip of India to the Himalayas, and he wore himself out in the process, dying in 1902 when he was thirty-nine years of age' (1946, p. 339).

Jesus' divinity was not an issue for Vivekananda. He wrote that only 'the Christ who has not forgotten his divinity . . . can help us' (Vol. VII, p. 4). He rejected what he called the Unitarian Christ as nothing more than 'a moral man'. Yet he constantly stresses that to worship Jesus is also to worship Mankind: 'Man is the greatest being that ever can be. The highest worship there is, is to worship men as Krishna, Buddha and Christ' (Vol. VII, p. 76). What Jesus knew, or experienced, can be known or experienced by us all: 'Jesus had our nature; he became the Christ: so can we and so must we. Christ and Buddha were the names of a state to be attained. Jesus and Gautama were the persons to manifest this' (Vol. VII, p. 29). The potential for Christhood and Buddhahood is present in every person: 'We are the light that illumines all the Bibles and Christs and Buddhas that ever were' (Vol. VII, p. 89).

In the *Gita*, Krishna says that he is 'deep in the heart of everyone, memory, knowledge and reasoning come from me. I am the object to be known through all sacred love, and I am its knower, the creator of its final truth' (15:15; Miller, 1986, p. 130). In John's Gospel, Christ is the light that enlightens all people (John 1:9), as he is 'the way, the truth and the life' (John 14:6). Most Christians think that Jesus is absent in people's lives, or hearts, until he is invited in, or explicitly named. Karl Rahner (1904–84) suggested that Christ may already be present, awaiting that day when his name will finally be named (see Philippians 2:31). Below, I discuss the view that Christ is already present in Hinduism, where he is waiting to be named.

Jesus' death and resurrection held no meaning for Vivekananda. Vedanta does not require a blood sacrifice, or atonement, for estrangement to be overcome. Ignorance keeps us trapped in *samsara* but the potential to overcome ignorance is inherent within each of us. There is, though, scope for taking on others' burdens. Krishna describes himself as 'the sacrifice that links salvation in this world to the next' (Mohammed, 1993, p. 16; *Gita* 9:16). *Avatars* take on others' *karma*, as Jesus does human burdens (Matthew 11:28). Some point to Krishna's death from an arrow wound to suggest that it carried atoning value. However, it is reading into the story to suppose that Vaishnavism needed a unique, critical, sacrificial act for human salvation. Rather, Krishna died when his task was complete, to show that death comes when our *karma*, good or bad, is ready.

Vivekananda thought it blasphemous to 'think that if Jesus had never been born humanity would not have been saved' (J. Russell Chandran, cited in Thomas, 1991, p. 132). Indeed, since *Brahman* cannot suffer, Vivekananda endorsed a Docetic view of the crucifixion: 'Christ was God incarnate; they could not kill him. That which was crucified was only a semblance, a mirage' (Thomas, 1991, p. 127). He may well have been quoting from the Qur'an or from a Gnostic text. Incidentally, for

Vivekananda, Jesus was second in nobility next to Buddha, who was 'the greatest the world had ever seen but,' he continued, 'the teachings of Krishna as taught by the *Gita* are the grandest the world has ever known.' The 'first and highest manifestation', though, was 'Mother', or Kali, the feminine power of the godhead (Vol. VII, p. 22). Ramakrishna believed that Kali had manisfested herself through his wife, whom he worshipped.

## Jesus as an Oriental

Vivekananda on Jesus as a Yogi resulted in some artistic portrayals of Jesus sitting in the lotus position, looking rather Oriental. Indeed, Vivekananda thought Jesus' actual teaching and lifestyle more Oriental than Occidental. He wrote: 'With all your attempts to paint him with blue eyes and yellow hair, the Nazarene was still an Oriental.' He reminds me of Rihbany when he goes on to say that all gospel similes, symbols and scenes 'speak to you of the Orient' (Vol. IV, p. 142). This theme was taken up by another Swami who taught Vedanta in the USA, Swami Paramananda, founder of the Ananda Ashram in California, which attracted several Hollywood stars. In *Christ and Oriental Ideals* (3rd edn 1923) he presented the Oriental approach to religion as non-doctrinal, more a matter of *being* and of *becoming* than of *belief* and *believing*.

Being spiritual involves harmonizing our thoughts, words and actions, not merely loving our neighbour but realizing that we *are* our neighbour. The Swami repeated the teaching that the 'truth' manifests through many human teachers, not exclusively through one, and that all who follow their guru sincerely would attain the goal. Christ, he said, was an Oriental, and therefore no stranger to the soil of India. Like all Orientals, he had not made proselytizing a priority but living the life of 'holiness and loving service to others' (1999, p. 88). Paramananda took it for granted, too, that Buddhism influenced the Essenes and that they in turn 'had a great influence on Jesus' (*ibid.*).

## Mohandas Karamchand Gandhi (1869–1948)

In Gandhi, East meets West and merges to form a creative synthesis. Gandhi increasingly emphasized his Hindu and Indian identity, yet for him the former especially was open to insight and truth wherever this was found. Christian, Jain and Buddhist thought moulded Gandhi's philosophical and religious ideas. Indeed, several Western writers mediated his appreciation of Indian thought; he first read the *Gita* in Sir Edwin Arnold's translation, since he 'did not know Sanskrit well enough to read' it 'without help'. He judged Arnold's *Gita*, *The Song Celestial*, an 'excellent translation' (Gandhi, 1980, p. 9), and admitted to theosophist friends that he had not as yet read 'the divine poem' (Gandhi, 1982, p. 76). Gandhi was then a law student in London.

At about that time, he also discovered Arnold's *The Light of Asia*, which he 'read with even greater interest than' he had the *Gita* (*ibid.*, p. 77), and Madame Blavatsky's *Key to Theosophy*, which stimulated him to 'read books on Hinduism' and 'disabused [him] of the notion fostered by the missionaries that Hinduism was rife with superstition' (*ibid.*). He likewise read Besant, whom Nehru describes as 'a powerful influence in adding to the confidence of the Hindu middle classes in their spiritual and national heritage' (1946, p. 341). In London, Gandhi went to hear some of the most highly acclaimed Christian preachers.

### Renunciation: the highest form of religion

Later, in South Africa, Gandhi discovered Tolstoy's *The Kingdom of God Is Within You* (1894), calling his second community Tolstoy Farm. Gandhi made Tolstoy's interpretation of the Sermon on the Mount his own. In the Sermon, said Tolstoy (1828–1910), Jesus invites us to suppress all anger and to live at peace with all; to sexual chastity; to refrain from taking oaths; not to resist evil by force or to serve as police or judges; to love our enemies without reservation. As love increases, God's kingdom on earth gets built: 'The sole meaning of life is to serve humanity by contributing to the establishment of the kingdom of God' (1984, p. 368).

Through his influence on Martin Luther King and others, Gandhi has, in his turn, given back to the West (see Jeffrey Paine's *Father India: Westerners under the Spell of an Ancient Culture* on Gandhi (1988, pp. 227–68)). 'Gandhi,' says Paine, 'spoke to Europeans and Americans in ways that resonated for them, as intimately and strangely as their own dreams' (p. 232). When Gandhi turned to the *Gita* and to the *Light of Asia*, he saw all Tolstoy's principles in these texts. In his mind, he reconciled the teachings of the *Gita*, *Light of Asia* and the Sermon, becoming convinced that 'renunciation was the highest form of religion' (1982, p. 78).

In order to interpret the *Gita* as non-violent, which Gandhi took as central to the messages of the Sermon and of the Buddha, he allegorized the battle between the Pandavas and the wicked Kauravas. Allegory is commonly used in interpreting Hindu texts. Gandhi calls the *Mahabharata* not history but *dharma-grantha* (a book of values, or discourse on truth: my translation) (*ibid.*, p. 15). Krishna's admonishment of Arjuna to fight was not an endorsement of violence; rather, he was rightly encouraging Arjuna to fulfil his duty with detachment, confident that *karma*, not himself, was responsible for the fruit of his action. He must be 'impartial to friend or foe . . . free from attachment' (12:18; Miller, 1986, p. 113). Indeed, Krishna demands that his devotees 'rejoice in the welfare of all creatures' (12:4; p. 111) and says that 'nonviolence, equanimity, contentment, penance, charity, glory, disgrace' all 'arise from' him (10:5; p. 89). While Gandhi loved the *Gita*, he said that it was from the Sermon that he first began to form his ideas on 'the rightness and value of passive resistance'. If he were 'deprived of the *Gita* and forgot all its contents', he continued, 'but had a copy of the Sermon, I should derive the same joy from it as I do from the *Gita*' (1941, p. 26).

Gandhi's early, negative attitude towards Christianity was somewhat alleviated by his later friendship with several Christians who shared his ideals, especially British missionary Charles Freer Andrews (1871–1940) and American missionary E. Stanley Jones (1884–1973). Andrews, who was also a close friend of Tagore, resigned from the Anglican ministry in 1914, convinced that being a Christian involved (as it did for Gandhi) 'not the expression of an outward creed but the living of an inward life' accompanied by service and social activism. Between 1914 and 1936, when he resumed his Anglican orders, he was a freelance writer and lobbyist, working for Indians in South Africa, Fiji as well as India. He died in Calcutta. Jones, whose *Christ of the Indian Road* (1925) became a bestseller, did much to popularize development of an authentically Indian Christianity through his ashram movement. During the Second World War, the British excluded him from India because of his support for the independence movement. Twice nominated for the Nobel Peace Prize, he used contacts with Japanese Christians to try to mediate between President Roosevelt and Emperor Hirohito to prevent Japanese–American hostilities, before war broke out. He turned down promotion to a bishop.

## Riches to rags

The work Gandhi made his own was the struggle for Indian independence, which he pursued with all his energy. This included boycotting British, in favour of homespun Indian, products. He preferred traditional Indian to Western technology, and practised what he preached at his ashram. 'Ideally,' he said, 'I would rule out all machinery' (Thomas, 1991, p. 224). This is where Tagore and Nehru parted company from him. Gandhi's own simple lifestyle may have owed something to Jesus' example. Incidentally, Gandhi's father, chief minister to a Hindu Rajah, had always thought that Gandhi would succeed him. Gandhi's, like the Buddha's, is a riches to rags story. In the ashram, all were equal and all had to take a turn doing every task.

Like Schweitzer, Gandhi appears to have placed great demands on those close to him. Paine writes that 'Gandhi's sons could have told an ashram visitor about the dark side, the iron oppressiveness of ashram life, that went under the name of idealism' (1988, p. 233). In the ashram food could not be enjoyed, nor close friendships forged. Gandhi himself practised celibacy, though he remained married. Francis of Assisi's followers also found it difficult to emulate his example, modifying the Rule Francis wrote for the community. Richard Attenborough's film *Gandhi* (1982) faithfully reproduced a scene in which Gandhi's wife found his idealism difficult to accept. Incidentally, the film does justice to Gandhi's achievements but is incorrect in picturing him as *single-handedly* winning independence. As portrayed, neither Nehru's nor Jinnah's character does justice to their legacies (see Rushdie, 1991, pp. 102–6, on 'Attenborough's Gandhi').

### Gandhi's Jesus

As already noted, Gandhi had little interest in the Jesus who may have lived, although more so than Vivekananda he valued Jesus' teaching. Gandhi's *Experiments with Truth* (from the title of his autobiography) led him to conclude that God is truth, and that truth is universal and all-pervading. Perhaps theosophical influence can be discerned here. More-over, 'Truth is *Ahimsa*' and a 'perfect vision of Truth can only follow a complete realization of *Ahimsa*' (1982, p. 453). In several passages, Gandhi says that he did not envision God as a 'person', but as an 'idea', or as 'law'. All who realize the truth (*satya*) will practise *ahimsa*, which for Gandhi meant utter unselfishness, and *swadeshi* (service to one's neigh-bours). This results in the *satyagrahi*, the lover and fighter for truth. Gandhi saw himself as a man of action and indeed tried to live and to practise what he preached, which for him was always more important than correct dogma. This is why Tagore dubbed him the *mahatma*, or Great Soul.

When Gandhi looked at Jesus, he saw the personification of *satyagrahi*, a 'beautiful example . . . of the perfect man' (1940, p. 30). He was greatly moved by images of Jesus 'wearing only a loin cloth, such as poor men in the villages of India wear', comments Wessels (1990, p. 137). However, he did not understand the cross as a once and for all, one and only act of atonement but as an invitation to do *today* what Jesus did *yesterday*: 'Living Christ means a Living Cross, without it life is a living death' (1940, p. 21). He did not think Jesus unique: 'if Jesus was like God, or God Himself, then all men were like God and could be God Himself' (*ibid.*, p. 19). Clearly, Jesus' significance lies in the principle he practised, or in the insights he taught, not in his ontological relation with God. Gandhi's *The Message of Jesus Christ* was published in 1940; his book on *Christian Missions: Their Place in India* appeared the following year.

### Gandhi on Christian missions

Gandhi said that if Christ is indeed a 'principle', then 'India has accepted its protecting power' (1941, p. 35). Like Vivekananda, Gandhi valued the humanitarian endeavours of the Christian missions but thought these were compromised by their hidden agenda of evangelism. Some missionaries saw their medical and educational activities as pure, unconditional love-in-action, but many saw them as tools to aid the winning of souls. Gandhi advised missionaries to abandon their efforts to convert people, which turned them into cultural misfits, and to concentrate on philanthropy:

Christian missions will render true service to India if they can persuade themselves to confine their activities to humanitarian service without the ulterior motive of converting India or at least the unsophisticated villagers to Christianity. (1941, p. 78)

Being Christian, said Gandhi, is not a matter of *dogma* but of *doing*:

It is not he who says, Lord, Lord, that is a true Christian, but he that doeth the will of the Lord, that is a true Christian. And cannot he who has not heard the name of Christ Jesus do the will of the Lord? (1941, p. 159)

Thich Nhat Hanh (1995) similarly criticizes the missionaries for offering the Vietnamese help in 'refugee camps in Thailand and Hong Kong' while also urging 'us to give up our roots' (p. 197).

Like Vivekananda, Gandhi was scandalized by the Christians' claim that only Christians were saved. This view condemned 'a large part of humanity'. Gandhi did not oppose conversion *per se* but thought cultural, religious and national identities were so tightly linked that it often stranded people, leaving them in a sort of betwixt and between zone. Conversion, said Gandhi, as had Keshub Chunder Sen, denationalized people. However, Gandhi is cited as saying that if he ever had power and could legislate, he would 'certainly stop all proselytizing' (cited in Harper, 2000, p. 327). In independent India, there have been several attempts to criminalize conversion. It was on this issue that Gandhi parted company from Bishop V. S. Azariah (1874–1945), the first Indian Anglican prelate, calling him his 'enemy number one' (1941, p. 7). For his part, Azariah not only denied that Indian Christians were any less Indian or loyal than anyone else but he also did much to counter their denationalized image. He drew on indigenous forms in developing new 'liturgy, music, drama . . . and Christian expression' in his diocese (Harper, 2000, p. 261). At Dornakal, he built a splendid Cathedral combining Hindu, Christian and Islamic architecture in 'a wholly unique synthesis' (p. 262).

Personally, I find it difficult to think of Gandhi (with all his flaws) without seeing Jesus reflected in his life. Albert Einstein's remarks on Gandhi, marking his seventieth birthday, might equally have been said of Jesus: 'Generations to come. It may be, will scarce believe that such a one as this ever in flesh and blood walked this earth.' E. Stanley Jones said of Gandhi that he had taught him 'more of the Spirit of Christ than perhaps any other man in East or West', even though Gandhi had 'fought a system in the framework of which' Jones himself stood (Jones, 1948, p. 11). A. G. Hogg (1875–1956), Scottish missionary and Principal of Madras Christian College, stated in 1938 that he held Gandhi to be 'clearly a man of God' (1939, p. 106). He could muster no 'religious concern' for him. India achieved independence on 15 August 1947, although the Muslim majority areas in the north-west and north-east became a separate nation, Pakistan (in 1972, after a civil war, the East seceded as Bangladesh). In India, Gandhi attempted to prevent anti-Muslim violence. Some Hindus accused

him of betraying Hinduism. On 30 January 1948 he was assassinated by a
Hindu activist. Nehru said, 'The light has gone out of our lives . . . the
Father of the Nation is no more' (cited in Cornwell, 1980, p. 495).

## Jesus: his religion was a hoax

Most of the Hindu writers reviewed so far, while critical of some aspects
of the Christian enterprise in India, were by no means totally opposed to
Indian Christianity. Some Hindus, however, have a much more negative
perception. For example, Ram Sita Goel (1997) dismisses Christianity as
an agent of Western imperialism (p. 1). 'The mischief created by Christian
missionaries,' he says, 'has to be known in order to be believed.' Even
'Mother Teresa is part of this gang,' he continues, 'presenting India as a
. . . diseased and corrupt country . . . and collecting fabulous sums for the
missionary machine' (p. 2). Arun Shourie (1994) sees the funding of
Christian majorities in the north-east, where separatist movements are
active, as a deliberate attempt to destabilize India, to perpetuate the old
policy of divide and rule (pp. 205–7; see his critique of Mother Teresa on
pp. 8–9). Vivekananda, Gandhi, Tagore, all represent a universal or global
Hindu worldview, as advocates of what is known as *Hindutva* (a Hindu-
India) and offer a more narrowly nationalistic version.

### Dayananda Sarasvati (1824–83)

When Dayananda Sarasvati read the Gospels, he saw them as silly and
absurd. In contrast, he said, the *Vedas* are scientific and rational. Indeed,
they are inerrant. Regarding Christianity as an arm of colonial oppression,
he rejected Christianity, the Bible, the Christian God and Jesus in favour
of India's own religious heritage. Sometimes called the Luther of Hindu
reform, like Luther's, his language was often very blunt, if not vulgar. Of
course, several missionaries were quite vulgar when speaking about Hindu
beliefs. 'Had Christ possessed even a little knowledge,' Sarasvati wrote,
'why would he have talked such nonsense' (Sarasvati, 1990, p. 200).
'Christ,' he continued, 'can be of no count among the learned and wise of
the present day' (*ibid.*, p. 201). The Most High has no need of any
mediator, thus 'To say that no man cometh to the Father but by me can
never be true' (*ibid.*). Rather, it was 'a hoax'. He ridiculed the Lord's
Supper: 'no enlightened man would ever call the food of his disciples his
flesh nor their drink his blood' (*ibid.*).

Sarasvati had been a priest in a Kali temple. One day, seeing a rat
crawling over the goddess' image, he became disillusioned and began to
question many contemporary Hindu practices, including veneration of
places and images. Looking to the *Vedas*, he could find there no mention
of image worship or indeed of manifestations of God, so rejected these as
later corruption. He founded the Arya Samaj in 1875, which revered the
*Vedas* as 'absolutely free from error'. Later Hindu scriptures (except the

*Laws of Manu* and the *Dharma Shastras*, which are all ethical) were also rejected. The Arya Samaj set out to re-convert Muslims, Sikhs and Christians. Vedic learning, Aryan culture, are taught in its *gurukulas* (schools). While its insistence that the *Vedas* and modern science are completely compatible is similar to Vivekananda's view, the Arya Samaj does not tolerate any form of religious pluralism within or outside Hinduism.

The Arya Samaj has had many spin-offs, including the BJP, the political party that won power in May 1996. While Sarasvati rejected the *Ramayana*, others have increasingly turned to this text as the most authentic presentation of the ideal Hindu-Indian man-woman. Devotees of Ram (Vishnu's incarnation) believe he was a historical figure, born in Ayodhia, and that a mosque was later built at his birthplace. In December 1992, they stormed and destroyed the mosque. 'Every Indian,' many supporters cry, 'is a child of Ram.' This means that any Indian who does not regard Ram as his or her *Isvara* is not a genuine Indian. In one of his novels, Rushdie critiques this exclusivist as opposed to a more pluralist version of Hinduism:

Point one, in a religion with a thousand and one gods they suddenly decide that only one chap matters. Then what about Calcutta, for example where they do not go in for Ram? And Shiva temples are no longer suitable places of worship? Point two: Hinduism has many holy books, not one, but suddenly it is all Ramayana, Ramayana. Then where is the Gita? Where are the Puranas. . . . Point three: for Hindus there is no requirement for a collective act of worship, but without that how are these types going to collect their beloved mobs? So suddenly there is this invention of mass puja. (1996, p. 338)

The communal act of worship that characterizes many of these reform movements (both national and global) owes more than a little to Christian practice. Sarasvati's unitary view of Hinduism owes as much to Christian influence as does Vivekananda's and Gandhi's global version. Neither response was what the missionaries had hoped for.

### Rajah Ram Mohun Roy (1774–1833)

When Vivekananda criticized the Unitarian view of Jesus as 'merely a moral man' he was actually responding to the writings of Roy, often called the father of modern India. Roy was a Brahman who entered the employ of the British and reached the highest rank that an Indian could attain. For this, he was given the title 'rajah'. Earlier, he had studied Arabic and Persian. Influenced by Sufi thought, he developed a dislike of image veneration, a dislike that Sarasvati would later share, although his religious outlook differed markedly from Roy's. He also studied at Varanasi, learning Sanskrit. Along the way, he added some Hebrew and Greek, as religion increasingly dominated his time and interest. Still in his early forties, he left the Civil Service to become a full-time writer and activist. His interest in religious ideas and literature as well as his linguistic skills led him to collaborate with the Baptist missionaries at Serampore in their work of Bible translation.

The missionaries, especially William Carey (1761–1834), Joshua Marshman (1768–1837) and William Ward (1769–1823), were outspoken in their criticism of Hindu polytheism, idolatry and of the practice known as *sati* (widow self-immolation). Ward wrote several books on Hinduism which had little positive to say about their subject matter. One writer commented: 'Mr Ward can only see the hateful and the devilish, of what good it may be the counterfeit, what Divine truth may be concealed in it, or may be needed to supplant it, he had not the courage to enquire' (Maurice, 1846, p. xxii). The missionaries commonly represented Hinduism as polytheistic. At a village level, worshippers may well have believed that each deity existed as an independent power. Actually, the senior Baptist, Carey, was the more positive of the three in his approach to Indian culture, translating the *Ramayana*, which he believed had great literary merit, against the advice of colleagues, who thought he was wasting his time.

Not surprisingly, Roy was sensitive to his colleagues' criticism of his religion. Turning to the *Upanishads*, which he believed contained ageless wisdom, he saw there only a single, utterly transcendent, unmanifest God, whose essence is ineffable. He could find no justification for image worship (the missionaries called this idol worship), nor for *avataras*, nor of course for *sati*. Müller, as noted above, heartily endorsed this view. He translated Ramakrishna's *Sayings* (1900) and some of Keshub Chunder Sen's writings (1976). Like Sarasvati later, Roy rejected all these as a corruption of authentic, original Hinduism. He developed a theology that has much in common with the Deists: God can be known by exercising reason; anything irrational, superstitious, including supernatural happenings, must be rejected. God could also be experienced, or known, within the world of nature. Roy believed, as would Vivekananda, Gandhi and Tagore, that truth, which is universal, can be realized through all true monotheistic religions.

## Roy and the Baptists

As Roy's affirmation of monotheism and his support for the missionaries' social reform programme became known, they thought they were about to recruit a very distinguished convert. In fact, instead of converting, Roy turned back to his own tradition, and found within it answers to all their criticisms. What he developed has been described as Hindu theism, or as Protestant Hindu theism. It could even be called Deistic. In rejecting the Hindu *avataras*, Roy also rejected the notion that Jesus had been the incarnate son of God. His ineffable, unmanifest God was singular, not a Trinity. Marshman entered debate with him on all these issues, which was published by the Mission Press. Working with William Yates (1792–1845) and William Adam on translating the prologue of John, Roy found himself agreeing with Adam, against Yates, on the choice of 'all things were made through him' instead of 'by him'. For Roy, 'by him' made Jesus an independent entity; 'through' represented him as an agent, subordinate to God.

The following day, complaining of Arian tendencies, Yates resigned from the panel. Shortly after, Adam himself announced that he had become a Unitarian. William Ward expressed the Baptist response: 'he lived in a country which Satan had made his own to a degree that allowed as a final blow a missionary to be converted to heathenism.' Or, Roy has converted 'a Missionary! O Lord. How we have fallen' (cited in Potts, 1967, p. 214). Adam founded a Unitarian mission in Calcutta, with which Roy was also associated. Adam, though, who later served a Unitarian congregation in Boston, always 'regarded himself as a Christian', while Roy never ceased to be a Hindu (*ibid.*, p. 239). In 1828, Roy founded the Brahmo Samaj to promote his ideas. Its worship, with readings and hymns, may have begun a trend towards the more congregational-style worship of several reform movements. Keshub Chunder Sen (see above) was an early leader of the Samaj, which he later left to set up his Church of the New Dispensation. Sen anticipated a universal religion that would adapt differently within different cultural contexts. In India, it would wear Hindu dress. Sen saw Jesus as a supreme example of the fully self-realized man; to worship Jesus was to worship humanity.

## Roy's Jesus

Who was Jesus for Ram Mohun Roy? Roy set out his ideas on Jesus in his 1820 book *The Precepts of Jesus* (American edn 1828). Like Jefferson, he was interested in Jesus the teacher of moral truth, not in Jesus the Son of God. Like Jefferson, he extracted the miraculous from his text. Indeed, this statement from his preface sounds very much like Jefferson:

I feel persuaded that by separating from the other matters contained in the New Testament, the moral principles found in this book, these will be more likely to produce the desirable effect by improving the hearts and minds of men in different persuasions and degrees of understanding. (1828, p. xviii)

When he used such terms as 'redeemer' or 'mediator' he made it clear that he did not in any way affirm Jesus' divinity (*ibid.*, p. 213). He could accept Jesus as 'first born of all creation', not as identical with the Creator (Thomas, 1991, p. 20).

Roy found more of interest in the synoptics than in John, unlike other Hindu writers, for whom the 'I and the Father are one' of John has great appeal. Roy thought Jesus' ethical teaching absolutely sublime. 'Unity of will, not identity of being', says Thomas, characterized Roy's understanding of Jesus in his relationship with God (*ibid.*, p. 19). Roy always maintained close links with Unitarians. Visiting England – probably the first Brahman to do so – he died while a guest of Unitarians in Bristol, where he was buried in the Unitarian cemetery. Leadership of the Brahmo Samaj passed into the hands of Debendranath Tagore (1817–1905), whose son, Rabindranath, shows the influence of Roy's nature theology in his poetry and teaching. Incidentally, the universal poet also had a deep reverence for Jesus, who for him was above all the Son of Man, who seeks out 'the last, the least and the lost' (Sugirtharajah, 1993, p. 3). In his Hibbert Lectures, *The Religion of Man*, Tagore spoke of his belief in both the humanity of god and the divinity of humanity (Tagore, 1931, p. 15). All 'true knowledge, love and service' emanate from the 'Super Soul which permeates all things', he said (*ibid.*, p. 22). This reminds me of Blake's view of Jesus.

## Jesus as miracle worker and Hindu response

Apart from Roy's subtraction of the supernatural from his Jesus response, the question of miracles, so prominent in insider discussion, has hardly arisen in this chapter. This may well be because Indian literature is itself full of miraculous happenings, as are the stories of God's *avataras*. Yogis, too, at the highest stages of progress, perform such feats as hovering, becoming invisible, lying on burning coals, which makes Jesus' walking on water or appearing to his disciples after the crucifixion sound quite acceptable. Modern gurus, too, perform acts of healing. Satya Sai Baba, for example, who is venerated by millions of followers as the embodiment of all aspects of the godhead, regularly heals people. I have known well-qualified Hindu physicians who swear by Sai Baba's ability to heal. Some devotees believe that Sai Baba is Jesus Christ.

## Some Christian responses to the Hindu Jesus

Keshub Chunder Sen is often cited as an example of a Hindu Christian. It was, apart from theological considerations, the denationalized image of Indian Christians that kept him from formally associating with the Church. For their part, some Indian Christians continue to regard themselves as also authentically Hindu. Brahmabandhab Upadhyana (1861–1907) left the Brahmo Samaj for the Roman Catholic Church but said that he was by birth a Hindu and that he would remain Hindu until he died. He wrote: 'We are Hindus so far as our physical and mental constitution is concerned, but in regard to our immortal souls we are Catholic' (cited by Staffner, 1987, p. 32).

One of my Ph.D. students, Laju Balani, formerly also my graduate assistant, was told to abandon all Hindu symbols and practices when he first became a Christian. Although he had taken the sacred thread, to mark his membership of the twice-born classes, his attachment to Hinduism had been fairly nominal. Therefore, he did not feel that he was really losing very much of any significance or meaning. Later, he read the writings of Thomas Merton (see 1973), Bede Griffiths (see 1982) and other Western theologians whose respect for and interest in Eastern spirituality caused him to re-examine his former tradition in a new light. Griffiths, a Benedictine monk, studied with Panikkar (see below) and adopted the lifestyle of a Hindu renunciate. He succeeded to the leadership of the ashram at Shantivanam, founded by Jules Monchanin (1895–1957) and Henry Le Saux (1910–73). Their aim was 'nothing less than the assumption into the Church of the age-old Indian *sanyyasa* [life of total renunciation] itself' (cited by O'Connor, 1998). Laju also read Raimundo Panikkar and M. M. Thomas, and other Indian Christians (see below) who did not believe that a Hindu has to totally repudiate Hinduism in order to be a faithful Christian. Now, he can happily wear a cross and the OM symbol side by side, to indicate that he does not see a dichotomy between his Hindu and his Christian identity.

## The fulfilment approach

However, is the OM symbol wearable because the cross has Christianized it, or because it has inherent, independent value of its own? This is the question that Christian theologians have asked since the pioneer days of Nobili and Xavier. Is acknowledgement of Jesus' superiority necessary in order for anything Hindu to possess spiritual worth? Or, is Jesus Christ present but unnamed within Hinduism, which therefore already possesses its own value and worth? J. N. Farquhar, although critical of his colleagues' total negativity towards Hinduism, endorsed the first view. In his *The Crown of Hinduism* (1913) he wrote:

To Him [Christ] all that is great and good is dear, the noble art of India, the power and spirituality of its best literature, the beauty and simplicity of Hindu village life . . . Christ passes everything through His refiner's fire, in order that the dross, which Hindus know so well, may pass away. . . . He is not the Destroyer but the Restorer of the national heritage, and all the gleams of light that make Hindu faith and worship so fascinating to the student will find in Him their explanation and consummation. It is one of the chief aims of this volume to show that Christianity is the crown of Hinduism. (pp. 52–3)

Without this crown, Hinduism remains incomplete, more a seeking than a finding of truth. Christ must be supplied – from outside.

## The unnamed presence approach

Raimundo Panikkar, in *The Unknown Christ of Hinduism* (1981), argues the opposite. He believes that Christ is *present* but *anonymous* within the ancient Hindu texts. The Christian task is not to supply Jesus from *outside* but to uncover where he is *already present*. Panikkar cites Acts 14:16–17: 'In the ages that are past He let all the people follow their own ways, and yet He did not leave Himself without witnesses.' He points to the relationship between the ineffable *Brahman* and the personal, revealing *Isvara* as a parallel between the relationship between God the Father and Jesus Christ. The former are both knowable only to the degree that the latter disclose their nature. Others point out that in Christian thought, Jesus is only ever called *wholly God*, not the *whole of God* (*totus Deus, non totum Dei*; see Pieris, 1993, p. 58).

Panikkar suggests that *Isvara*'s function within Hinduism is equivalent to Christ's in Christianity. Therefore, Christians can recognize that *Isvara* is Christ: 'that from which this World comes forth and to which it returns and by which it is sustained, that is Isvara, the Christ' (1981, p. 162). The Holy Spirit can be equated with *ananda*, that links *Isvara* and devotee in their sense of at-oneness with the ultimate. Thus, 'All that exists . . . is nothing but God, Father, Son and Spirit. All that exists is nothing but Brahman as *sat*, *cit* and *ananda*, as being, consciousness and bliss' (pp. 161–2). It is possible that Christian investigation of Hindu texts is guided by the Holy Spirit, who takes what is Jesus' and makes this known: 'All that belongs to the Father is mine. That is why I said the Spirit will take from what is mine and make it known to you' (John 16:15). Jesus clearly stated, too, that he had not shared all knowledge during his life on earth: 'I have much more to tell you,' he said. A Catholic priest, Panikkar has taught at Harvard, University of California at Santa Barbara as well as at the Hindu University, Varanasi. His father was a Hindu, his mother a Christian.

## A named Christ

In this chapter, I owe much to M. M. Thomas' *The Acknowledged Christ of the Indian Renaissance* (1991), which he wrote as a companion volume to Panikkar's. While Panikkar looked at Hindu scripture, where he says that Christ is *implicitly present*, Madathliparampil Mammen Thomas (1916–1996), a member of the Mar Thoma Church (a reformed branch of the Syrian Church), looked at how Hindus within the modern period have explicitly acknowledged Christ. He shows, as I have in this chapter, that they did so from within their own systems, not from within a Christian framework. I had the pleasure of meeting Thomas shortly before he died. The paper he gave at my former college (Thomas, 1997) is published in a volume in which I also have a chapter. Towards the end of his distinguished career, Thomas was Governor of the majority Christian State of Nagaland.

## Christ as guru

Indian theologian Thomas Thangaraj offers an important contribution in *The Crucified Guru: An Experiment in Cross-Cultural Christology* (1994). Thangaraj looks at the role of the guru in the Shaivite tradition of Tamil Nadu. His object is not to argue, as had Nobili, that Jesus is the only true guru but to explicate Jesus' significance by locating him in the context of the guru–disciple relationship. This is not merely a *metaphor* but a *method* for applying insight from one culture within another, to see 'what Jesus the Christ might look like when one uses the concept of guru' (p. 33).

Thangaraj shows how, for their devotees, gurus manifest, or function as, God. This function does not depend on the metaphysical nature of the guru's relationship with God but on the believers' experience of God as mediated by the guru. The guru 'works in the heart of the believer' (p. 58). Thangaraj prefers the guru analogy to the *avatara* analogy, since while the latter inevitably invites metaphysical questions, the former does not. He writes, 'the guru's humanity is never doubted or denied; yet at the same time the guru functions as god to the disciple . . . what the guru does for the disciple is far more important than what or who the guru is' (p. 56).

Applied to Jesus as the Christ, this is a perfect analogy; Jesus functions *as God* for those who recognize him as the Christ. Through Jesus, his disciples enjoy a relationship with God. Paul Tillich similarly argued that Jesus is only the Christ in the context of the Church: 'without the reception of Jesus as the Christ by the Church, he would not have become the Christ, because he would not have brought the New Being to anyone' and 'the appearance of the Christ in an individual person presupposes the community out of which he came and the community which he creates' (1957, pp. 135–6).

## Buddhist responses

An early Buddhist response to Jesus appeared in Sri Lanka in a tract published in 1835 which said 'that Christ had been incarnated on earth after an existence in heaven (just like a Buddha), was virtuous and benevolent, and taught the truth *in so far as he understood it*' (Gombrich, 1988, p. 179; italics added). Many Buddhists would agree with this view. Some, such as the Dalai Lama, are prepared to go further and suggest that Jesus was either a Bodhisattva or even a Buddha, and was therefore a fully awakened or realized being (see quotation at the beginning of this chapter and 1996, p. 83). Thich Nhat Hanh calls Jesus a 'great teacher', one of his 'spiritual ancestors', and says that he has 'statues of Buddhas . . . and also an image of Jesus' in his hermitage (1995, pp. 99–100). For Buddhists, though, Jesus is only one of many Buddhas; also, when compared with Shakyamuni, he may not be the most important Buddha either. This is why Hanh took Pope John Paul II to task on the issue of Jesus' uniqueness, rejecting the 'notion behind' the Pope's view 'that Christianity provides the only way to salvation and all other traditions are of no use' (p. 193).

Julian Pettifer's documentary series, *Missionaries* (1990), although one-sided, offers some good coverage of Christian attitudes towards the religious Other, which I use in my teaching. The section on African independent churches, for example, is worth watching, as is the episode 'Stony Ground', which begins in Pakistan, moves into Thailand and then to Japan. Thailand is an officially Buddhist country. Pettifer comments that the first Protestant missionaries arrived there in 1831, and left after eighteen years without having made a single convert. On the one hand, says Pettifer, Thais 'never shied away from making full use of the excellent [humanitarian] services the missionaries saw fit to provide'. On the other hand, 'they rarely considered this a reason to convert'.

Interviewee Sulak Sivaraksa, himself educated in a prestigious Christian school, added:

anything which is helpful, we took . . . in fact, we would have taken more from the missionaries if they had not been too exclusive. We would even have worshipped Christ, as we worship Vishnu and Shiva, provided we also worship Buddha and of course the Buddha is the more superior, whether you like it or not.

In the book, Sivaraksa complains about:

evangelical literature that describes Thailand as 'the territory of Satan'; that declares '99 percent of Thais are in bondage to demons'; that condemns Buddhism as 'idolatry' and a 'religion of hopeless escapism'; and which insists that 'without Christianity, there is no relationship with God'. (Pettifer and Bradley, 1990b, p. 187)

Unlike the older anti-Buddhist sentiments cited above, which date from a past century, these reflect contemporary attitudes.

## The God issue

His Holiness the Dalai Lama points to a difference between Buddhist and Christian understanding when he notes that while a Buddha has passed through many stages of spiritual perfection, Christians believe that Jesus was God from birth, therefore 'the process of stages does not apply' (1996, p. 118). The main reason why the Sri Lankan Buddhist thought that Jesus had only 'taught the truth in so far as he understood it' was because Christianity teaches the existence of a personal, creator God who saves people, which has no place in Buddhism. This is probably the main issue on the agenda of Buddhist–Christian dialogue, equivalent perhaps to the Messiah and Son of God issues in Jewish–Christian and Muslim–Christian dialogue. It is easier for Buddhists to deal with the person of Jesus than with God the Father. In Theravada Buddhism, the Buddha is technically dead, unable to help anybody who is still in *samsara*. Yet Theravadins still take 'refuge' in the Buddha, and at a popular level many believe that his force (*Budubulaya*) still exists, and will exist until the end of this age (see Gombrich, 1971, p. 142).

The Buddha, too, founded the community through which the *dharma* continues to be mediated, just as Jesus Christ founded the Church that continues to preach the Gospel by which salvation is experienced. No Church, no salvation, no kingdom of heaven: no *sangha*, no *dharma*, no *nibhana*. Thich Nhat Hanh wrote, 'The Buddha relies on us for the dharma to continue to develop as a living organism – not a stale dharma, but a real *Dharmakaya*, a real "body of teaching"' (1995, p. 39; *Dharma-kaya* = the eternal or truth body of the Buddha). For Mahayana, the idea that Christ is a cosmic power or principle as well as a man who once lived is easy to accept, since the doctrine of the three bodies of the Buddha affirms this of the Buddha.

Thich Nhat Hanh wrote: 'According to Mahayana . . . the Buddha is still alive, continuing to give Dharma talks. . . . The enduring Buddha has become the living Buddha, the Buddha of faith. This is very much like the Christ of faith' (1995, p. 51). The 'best way,' he continued, 'that a Buddhist can keep the teachings of the Buddha alive' is to live by them. Similarly, Jesus needs Christians 'for his energy to continue in this world' (p. 73). Tillich would agree. In his 1963 book (based on his Bampton Lectures), *Christianity and the Encounter with the World Religions*, Tillich identified the Christian notion of God's kingdom with the Buddhist notion of *nibhana*: 'both represent the *telos* of everything' (p. 64; *telos* = end, goal). A visit to Japan and friendship with Buddhists in the USA convinced Tillich, towards the end of his life, that a Christian theology which failed to engage with other belief systems missed 'a world historical moment', and remained provincial (1964, p. 6).

Tillich also thought it would be a 'tremendous step forward if Christianity were to accept' dialogue instead of conversion (1963, p. 95). When pursued vigorously, he believed, dialogue could be 'extremely fruitful and, if continuous, even of historical consequence' (*ibid.*, p. 62). For Tillich, a statement only qualified as theological if it dealt with 'being and non-being', which Buddhist discourse certainly does. Whatever 'determines our being or non-being' represents, he said, our 'ultimate concern', and anything that addresses this deserves serious analysis (1953, p. 17). The term 'ultimate concern' is deliberately ambiguous, suggesting both *object* and *subject*, that is, our ultimate concern with truth, salvation, being or non-being, and truth itself, the goal of salvation, the dawning of the kingdom, entry into *nibhana*.

I have long found process thought or theology attractive. This postulates that God is not a fully realized being but unfolding potentiality. God's potentiality, rather than God's present actuality, is infinite. However, the unfolding of more and more divine potential is contingent on the cosmos also progressing, on our shouldering a share of responsibility for our own self-development. A humanity that meets the 'ground of its being' half-way may be more Buddhistic than one that does nothing at all to help itself. Nor do I believe that we are all born sinful, though I do accept that the world conditions us towards sinfulness. However, we do not have to conform to the world. We can assert values that challenge its conventions, just as did Jesus and the Buddha and Gandhi. Pelagius (late fourth to early fifth century CE) has always been my favourite heretic. He taught that men and women are able to take the first and critical step towards salvation, independently of God's grace. Tagore (1931) spoke of 'The God in Men' depending 'upon men's service and men's love for his own love's fulfilment' (p. 70). Process theology also resonates with some Islamic thought, especially with Muhammad Iqbal's understanding of God. When humanity fulfils its true role as God's co-worker, says Iqbal, God may even take a rest from being God (for Iqbal, see Bennett, 1997).

## The fourteenth Dalai Lama and Thich Nhat Hanh

Both the Dalai Lama (DL) and Thich Nhat Hanh (TNH) see interesting parallels between the teachings of the Buddha and Jesus. Both taught the importance of community (TNH, p. 65; DL, p. 76); both taught a simple lifestyle and sent their disciples out with similar instructions (DL, p. 96); both taught compassion (DL, p. 68; TNH, p. 81). Both taught oneness of body and mind, that is, that convictions must translate into deeds (TNH, p. 95; DL, p. 58). Both teachers personified their teaching (DL, p. 58; TNH, p. 69); both taught that the goal could be realized immediately, in this life (TNH, pp. 38, 138, 179). The idea that both the Buddha and Jesus personified their teaching is significant: Jesus not only *taught* the word, he *was* the word; similarly, 'The words of the Buddha are called the *dharma*, so the Buddha is the manifestation of this.' In fact, 'the Buddha describes himself as "born of the Dharma"' (DL, p. 76). The idea that the 'Kingdom of God' is within sounds like the notion of the Buddha nature within each of us.

The Dalai Lama's *The Good Heart: A Buddhist Perspective on the Teaching of Jesus* (1996) was based on his contribution at the 1994 John Maine Seminar held at Middlesex University, London. Here, he looks deeply at the *intent* of Jesus, at what lay in his heart. Of course, we have encountered elsewhere the view that this is opaque. None the less, when the Dalai Lama looks at Jesus he sees *ideals* and *practices* (which, he says, are inseparable) that, if followed, can result in 'the creation of . . . good human beings, who are spiritually mature and ethically sound', which is just what he sees in the Buddha (p. 82).

Thich Nhat Hanh, in *Living Buddha, Living Christ* (1995), like the Dalai Lama, argues for a necessary relationship between faith and praxis, for becoming and for being what you believe, which he sees in both Jesus' and the Buddha's teaching. He writes: 'True understanding comes from true practice. Understanding and love are values that transcend all dogma' (p. 198). He thinks it wise not to try to express the ultimate, lest we spend too much time talking about it instead of experiencing it (p. 140). Thich Nhat Hanh says that 'salvation' in Buddhism results from 'understanding' (p. 84).

The Dalai Lama points out that for many Buddhists, the goal of the spiritual path is achieved by developing 'a sense of personal responsibility', rather than by relying 'on a transcendent being' (p. 80). Of course, this does not preclude the help towards *nibhana* that a Bodhisattva can offer. Even then, *nibhana* is ultimately achieved, not given. Even the pure land is a temporary haven: 'a kind of University where you practice with a teacher for a while' (TNH, p. 128). One of Pettifer's interviewees in Thailand pointed out that Buddhists find the Christian heaven and hell *superficial*. While in Christianity these are singular and permanent, in Buddhism they are plural and temporary, places where *karma* continues to accrue. It is perhaps Christianity's idea of vicarious salvation, rather than the notion of a God as such, that Buddhists find objectionable. Both Buddhist writers find the concept of God as 'ground of being' more attractive than the more traditional idea of a person (TNH, p. 154; DL, p. 73).

Thich Nhat Hanh twice refers to Paul Tillich, for whom 'God' was a 'figure of speech'. Tillich 'said that God is the ground of being . . . He also said that God is the ultimate reality', which for Hanh means *nibhana*. Thus, he says, 'I do not think there is much difference between Christians and Buddhists' (p. 154; see also p. 140). Again, we encounter a writer for whom dogma takes a back seat to praxis – liberational praxis, too. Incidentally, the terms 'liberation', 'awakening' and 'salvation' are not exact equivalents within Hinduism, Buddhism and Christianity. However, I am using them interchangeably, because despite significant differences they do all designate the end or the goal of the religious quest within each tradition. In the Bengali Bible, *mukti* is used for salvation, *muktidata* (the liberator) for saviour.

Both these eminent Buddhist writers speak about how encounter with Christians changed their perceptions of Christianity. Both pay tribute to Thomas Merton (DL, p. 39; TNH, p. 4), among others. Martin Luther King nominated Hanh for the Nobel Peace Prize, which the Dalai Lama received in 1989. King was the recipient in 1964. Both writers have done much to represent Buddhism in the West, as both are tireless campaigners for their own peoples and for justice and peace worldwide. Both live in exile, the Dalai Lama in India, Hanh in France. The experience of exile is not always negative; exiles and émigrés who straddle cultures can, to cite Said, 'try to mediate between them' (Said, 1993, p. xxiii). Rushdie says that 'we are all, black and brown and white, leaking into each other' in today's world of mass movement, migration, of 'unexpected combinations of human beings, cultures, ideas, politics, movies, songs' (1991, p. 394). He suggests that from 'the migrant condition' a 'metaphor for all humanity' might be derived.

Both Buddhists cite the Sermon on the Mount with obvious respect (TNH, p. 75; DL, pp. 53f.). Hanh's version of *socially engaged Buddhism* has been criticized as adding a this-worldly dimension to Buddhism that was not part of the Buddha's original message. Gombrich (1988) says that the Buddha, who taught a 'pure soteriology', was not a social reformer, a view which he realizes puts him 'at odds with many modern interpreters of Buddhism' (p. 30). He argues that the social welfare programmes of some modern Buddhist organizations were an imitation of Christian missionary endeavours (see 1988, Chapter 7). If he is right, then *vis-à-vis* both the Hindu and the Buddhist worlds, Christlike love-in-action may have attracted more disciples than has Christian dogma. On the other hand,

E. P. Sanders (see Chapter 3) rejects the idea that Jesus had intended to bring about social change, making Christian social action a post-Jesus development. Gombrich is Oxford's Boden Professor of Sanskrit. I attended some of his lectures during my time in Oxford (he represented the university when I was interviewed for my last job). For two excellent essays by Christians on Buddha and Jesus, see Aloysius Pieris and Seeichi Yagi in Sugirtharajah's *Asian Faces of Jesus* (1993). Pieris is a Sri Lankan Jesuit, Yagi a Japanese theologian. Sugirtharajah, whom I have also cited in this chapter, a Sri Lankan, currently teaches at the Selly Oak College, University of Birmingham. We served together on several committees.

## Krishna, the Buddha and Jesus

Comparison of these three figures has surfaced several times in this book. Some of those whose Jesus theories I have discussed believe that similarity between these three results from the fact that *all are legendary*, based on an ancient hero-saviour myth. In this view, there is no historical basis for the myth, nor is its origin explainable with reference to anything non-human. I would identify Taylor, Robertson, Acharya S and Campbell, all reviewed in Chapter 4, with this approach. Campbell did believe that the hero myth expresses something positive about the human ability to dream, to think, to explore life's meaning and purpose, to push beyond physical limitations towards the infinite.

Sometimes, it is difficult to classify a writer's view; for example, Madame Blavatsky headed her comparison of Krishna, Buddha and Jesus 'The Legends of Three Saviours' and clearly believed that aspects of these stories had a common source (1995, pp. 537–9). On the other hand, she believed that the same fundamental truth underlies all religions. Convinced that Jesus was a Bodhisattva, Kersten (1986) is able to deduce that the three wise men were actually Buddhist monks searching for the next incarnation (p. 90). Other writers who compare Krishna, Buddha and Christ argue for cultural and philosophical traffic between India and the Near East; for example, Arthur Lillie in *Buddhism in Christendom: Or, Jesus the Essene* (1887) and *India in Primitive Christianity* (1909).

Lillie identifies the Essenes as mediators, strongly hinting that they owed their existence to Buddhist missionaries, that Jesus was an Essene and that Christianity draws on Buddhism almost as much as on Judaism: 'the Essenes are pronounced of the same faith as the Gymnosophists of India' (1909, p. 173). He compares the lifestyle, practices and even the architecture of the Essene community with Buddhist monks; for example, Essenes, like Buddhist monks, could 'return to civil life; if they find that they lacked a genuine vocation' (*ibid.*, p. 166). In a chapter entitled 'More Coincidences', Lillie parallels sayings of the Buddha and of Jesus as well as incidents from their lives (*ibid.*, pp. 200–18). For example, he cites Matthew 13:45, the parable about the single pearl bought by the merchant with all his worldly wealth, and compares this with a Buddhist story in which a merchant loses a pearl and 'tries to drain the sea dry' in order to recover it (*ibid.*, p. 212). He also compares Jesus' 'not that which goeth into the mouth defileth him' with the Buddha's 'The passions of the receiver of . . . alms choke, as it were, the growth of merits' (*ibid.*, p. 204) and many other passages.

Marcus Borg's *Jesus and Buddha: The Parallel Sayings* (1997) gives many more examples than Lillie. Jesus said, 'Blessed are you who are poor, for yours is the kingdom of heaven'; the Buddha said, 'Let us live most happily, possessing nothing; let us feed on joy' (pp. 56–7). Jesus said, 'Let anyone among you who is without sin be the first to throw a stone'; the Buddha said, 'Do not look at the faults of others, or what others have done or not done' (pp. 38–9). However, like Clarke, Borg attributes corres-pondence to 'the similarity of their wisdom' (p. xvi); both teachers 'had formative enlightenment experiences' (p. xv). If John's Gospel was influ-enced by Indian traditions, this readily explains its attractiveness to Hin-dus, who cite John more often than the synoptics.

James W. Deardorff, who describes himself as an independent New Testament scholar, a former Lutheran (he is now a Unitarian-Universal-ist), in *Jesus in India: A Re-examination of Jesus' Asian Traditions in the Light of Evidence Supporting Re-incarnation* (1994), thinks that what Jesus actually taught, reincarnation, was later misrepresented as resurrection. Deardorff is a Professor Emeritus of Atmosphere Science at Oregon State University.

Elaine Pagels, who wrote the introduction to Thich Nhat Hanh's *Living Buddha, Living Christ* does not categorically assert Buddhist influence on Christian thought (as I noted in Chapter 1), *but nor does she rule this out.* She identifies some correspondence between Gnostic thought and Hanh's:

I wondered: Does Thich Nhat Hanh know the Gospel of Thomas . . . or did he choose the term 'Living Christ' – a term more characteristic of gnostic texts than of the New Testament – by a kind of spiritual intuition? (1995, p. xxvii)

Some writers who subscribe to the cultural debt theory claim that 'Christ' was the Greek equivalent of Krishna, or rather of their preferred rendering, Chrishna. The similarity of these two words has attracted a great deal of speculation. Krishna, though, means 'black', and *christos* means 'anointed'.

Many of the Hindu writers discussed in this chapter would explain similarities between the Krishna, Buddha and Jesus narratives as the result of their realizing, or manifesting, the same awareness of truth. Some think that all three were *born* with a full awareness of this 'truth', for others, they *acquired* it. Yet what about the more supernatural aspects of the stories, such as predictions of greatness, visits by wise men (Krishna also had a visit), guiding stars (which feature in both the Jesus and Krishna stories), murdering kings (Krishna and Jesus), miraculous escapes (Krishna and Buddha)? All three, at some point, revealed their true status. Krishna did so to Arjuna, Jesus did so to Peter, James and John at the transfiguration, while at the Buddha's awakening the 'earth swayed like a woman drunk with wine . . . mighty drums of thunder resounded through the air' (Conze,

1959, p. 51). Krishna told Arjuna that only he had seen him in his glorious form, which is rarely revealed (*Gita* 11:47; Miller, 1986, p. 107); Jesus told the disciples to keep the transfiguration a secret.

Is this evidence that all the stories have a common source? Perhaps, or perhaps these incidents express the conviction that the closest disciples of any teacher indeed see what others cannot see. Personally, I think that all three stories have been embellished, so certain common features may result from their universal association with spiritual greatness. Some similarities could result from the simple fact that similar incidents really did happen. Indeed, some of these, such as temptation (all three were tempted: Jesus in the desert, Buddha at his enlightenment, while Krishna could have assumed power after defeating the wicked king Kansa), may well be experienced by anyone who chooses the path of renunciation, not of wealth and power. Similar spiritual or lifestyle choices may well result in comparable experiences. Perhaps, too, the same hand guided all three. Jesus, though, was certainly less ascetic than the Buddha, enjoying a good party!

## Did Jesus visit India?

The Christ–Krishna–Buddha topic is actually inexhaustible. A lot of internet material could be referenced here; see, for example, Kersey Graves, 'Three Hundred and Forty-six Analogies Between Christ and Chrishna', Chapter 32 of his *The World's Sixteen Crucified Saviors* at www.infidels.org/library/historical/kerseygraves/16 (original, 1875). Infidels.org issues a health warning: 'the scholarship of Kersey Graves has been questioned by numerous freethinkers.' Some writers seem to be preoccupied with finding numerous examples of crucified saviours to undermine the Christian view that Jesus' death was uniquely redeeming. Godfrey Higgins, referred to in Chapter 4, pointed to veneration of the cross in pre-Christian Mexico, and to other uses of cross imagery (see Higgins, 1965). Many of those who compare the three are also convinced that Jesus spent time in India.

Some, such as Levi Dowling, think that Jesus lived in India during the 'hidden years'. Others, such as Prophet, Deardorff (see also 1998), the Sufi scholar, Fida Hassnain (1994), former Director of Archives and Archaeology for the State of Kashmir, Kersten (1986), Gruber and Kersten (1995), as well as Mirza Ghulam Ahmad, all believe that Jesus returned to India after surviving the crucifixion, and died there. Mary went with him. Deardorff and Kersten both cite *The Acts of Thomas*, as do other writers, as proof. I have already indicated that there is emphasis in the Thomas literature on *bearing Jesus' likeness*, thus passages in which Jesus appears cannot be taken literally.

Kersten (1986) gives a time-line (pp. 218–19) indicating Jesus' movements in India both during the hidden years and after he had survived the crucifixion. He places him with Thomas at King Gundaphorus' court before 50 CE (two years before Thomas is believed to have reached India). Jesus was 'interned in Srinagar' after 80 CE. Kersten refers to Paul, who was alone responsible for what we should more properly call Paulism, not Christianity (p. 28). Lillie also devoted a chapter (1909, Chapter xiv) to 'Paulism'. Paul, he says, invented the theories of 'redemption', 'expiation', 'original sin', as well as reintroducing the notion of forgiveness 'by the shedding of blood, which the Essenes and the Therapeuts were struggling hard to banish' (1909, p. 226). This is similar to theories encountered elsewhere in this book. Gruber and Kersten (1995) draw out parallels between the infancy narratives of Jesus and the Buddha; Asita is Simeon (Luke 2:25–35; see 1995, pp. 79–88). They also cite Lillie: 'It seems to me that the biographies of Jesus and the Buddha throw constant light the one on the other' (p. 81; Lillie, 1997, p. 181).

Kersten (1986) argues that both Jesus and the Essenes were Buddhist, which is why Jesus was sent to India to study with the most enlightened teachers. He finds an explanation for the disciples' discussion in Matthew 16 about who Jesus was: was he Elijah, or Jeremiah? They knew, says Kersten, 'that he was an Incarnation, but were unsure who Jesus could have been in his previous' existence (p. 114). His book is somewhat erratic. It moves from the Turin Shroud to the ten lost tribes, to Notovitch's footsteps, which the author followed, to a rather bizarre theory that Kashmir is the promised land. He says that Moses, who is the Indian lawgiver Manu, was buried and Solomon's Temple built there (see pp. 53 and 62–4). He never explains how the Second Temple ended up in Palestine. The Throne of Solomon monument in Srinagar is widely cited in this literature. It is, in my view, not beyond the realms of possibility that exiled Jews built a temple there, as they did in Elephanta. Kersten refers to Salibi to support his theory, despite the fact that Salibi locates Palestine near present-day Yemen, not in India (pp. 62–3).

Prophet's book (1984) reproduces Nicolas Notovich's 'The unknown life of Jesus Christ' (pp. 89–190), with his version of 'The life of Saint Issa' (pp. 191–221). In 1877 to 1878, the Russian journalist and minor aristocrat travelled in the Himalayas, spending time in the secluded Himis Monastery in Ladack. There, he claims to have heard a translation of an ancient Tibetan scroll telling of one Issa who arrived in India at about age 13, from his native Palestine. Issa is described as a 'divine child' who 'spoke from his earliest years of the one and indivisible god' (Prophet, 1984, p. 196). Issa engaged in learned discourse with the Brahmans and Jains. The Brahmans, he said, will become the Sudras. Returning to Palestine, Issa taught the people for three years, then fell foul of the religious leaders. Under the authority of Pilate, Issa was crucified, but 'the soul of this just man left his body to become absorbed in the Divinity' (*ibid.*, p. 220). In 1922, Swami Abhedananda (see above, p. 315) followed in Notovitch's footsteps. He also published a version of the life of Issa, originally in Bengali. Prophet reproduces an English translation (pp. 232–7). Prophet has beautiful illustrations of the Himis Monastery and its splendid surroundings. It is intriguing that the Qur'anic Issa is used for Jesus. She also maps Jesus' journey to India.

These writers cite numerous travel accounts which allude to traditions that Jesus had lived in Kashmir. Quite a few Muslim sources are also cited, which appear to locate one Yuz Asaf in India after his supposed crucifixion. For example, the *Ikmal-ud-Din*, whose author Al-Sa'id-us-Sadiq died in 962 CE, says, 'He traveled in it far and wide . . . until death overtook him, and he left his mortal body' (this work was translated by Müller into German in 1882; my quotation is from the tombofJesus.com). Even more intriguing is an extract from a Puranic text, the *Bahavishyat Maha Purana*, which possibly dates from 115 CE. Kersten and the tombofjesus.com both reproduce the Sanskrit original (Kersten, 1986, p. 196). This text places 'the Messiah' (*isa masih*) in Kashmir, where he died at the age of 120, which means that 'it was written while, according to the theory, Jesus would still have been alive' (from tombofjesus).

The tombofJesus website has abundant material, including quotations from all the popular sources. A lot of material is linked with the ten lost tribes, following Ahmad's conviction that Jesus went to India to preach to the lost sheep of the House of Israel. Here, the evidence is actually rather impressive. As well as small communities of practising Jews whose antecedents appear to be Israelite (such as the Bene Israel of Bombay, many of whom now live in Israel), there are larger communities of Afghans and Pathans who, though Muslim, are proud of their Israelite ancestry. In Manipur, some two million people assert that they are the lost tribe of Manashe (see Jacobovichi, 1999, and the Jews of India website at haruth.com/AsianIndian.html).

Of course, for Indians, India is a Holy Land, even *the* Holy Land. Perhaps this is why it is not too hard for some Indians, and non-Indians, to believe that a truly religious man would have made the difficult journey to India to study with the masters. On the other hand, apart from Muslim Indians, the 'Jesus went to India' theory is mainly supported by Western writers. Abhedananda's contribution, though, cannot be overlooked, given his stature and reputation. What need does this theory meet? Perhaps the felt need to assert that all great religious leaders not only teach the same truth but stand firmly in a single historical tradition, drawing on identical insights and texts, literally walking in the footsteps of their spiritual forebears.

Is it possible that Jesus went to India? Many insider scholars doubt that Jesus ever left Palestine, since the flight to Egypt is widely attributed to the disciples' imagination. Others transport Jesus to England, some think he visited the Americas. Since the Gospels are silent, and the status of alternative sources can be debated, in my view nobody can prove that he did go, or indeed that he did not go, to India or anywhere else. In my view, the statement that Jesus went to India is a faith conviction, expressing a *theological* rather than a *historical* claim, although proponents of the theory offer it as the latter, not the former. If one is convinced that Jesus did go to India, or is inclined to think that he did, one may find the evidence compelling, and declare 'case proven'. If one is less inclined to place Jesus in India, or thinks the whole idea incredible, the evidence is unlikely to change one's mind. What can be said with confidence is that Christ is in India, in the lives of Christians and of others for whom he has meaning and significance.

Can Christians learn anything from Hindu and Buddhist images of Jesus? One lesson might be that Christians are too concerned about the naming of the name, that perhaps the name or label 'Christian' does not always have to be explicit. Stanley Samartha, an Indian Christian who has devoted his life to studying the challenge of religious pluralism, suggests that what matters is Christian rootedness in Christ. 'A one way proclamation of the name of Jesus without any sensitivity to other faiths,' he says, 'alienates Christians from their neighbors', becoming 'an obstacle to co-operation with them' (1991, p. 152). The Christian task 'is not to make other people Christian but to invite people to enter the kingdom of God' (*ibid.*, p. 153). In India, he says, there are 'many people . . . whose lives are transformed by Christ, who . . . show the marks of love and self-sacrifice . . . who are not baptized members of the institutional church' (*ibid.*).

In my concluding chapter, I discuss the status of many alternative approaches to the question, 'Who was Jesus?' Was he God, a good man, or a Buddhist? Did the same eternal principle inspire him that inspired other great spiritual leaders? Was he black or white, a Jew or an Aryan? Was he a social activist? Was he uninterested in social issues? Was he born a human who then acquired divinity? Was he a feminist? I shall argue that although some of these statements appear to deal with the *Jesus of history*, they are all also theological, affirming something about the *Christ of faith*. Not all assertions, I suggest, have any historical basis, which may or not make them less tenable theologically. On the one hand, I support anyone's right to see Jesus, or the Christ, as they wish to, even if their understanding differs from mine. On the other hand, some understandings of Jesus sit very uncomfortably with what can be reasonably affirmed of the Jesus of history. These, I think, can be critiqued. If a spirit does flow from Jesus' time into our own, as Schweitzer suggested, then that Spirit ought to inform our Christ images as well as our Jesus images.

# 7 Conclusion

# A Liberated and a Liberating Jesus: 'The Reconciliation of All Things'

> We think that today the understanding or lack of understanding of Jesus' message does not depend on the religious denomination. The frontier cuts across all denominations, world-views and ideologies. Jesus did not, however, as we have emphasized throughout this book, propound an ideology. But he was concerned with man, with his future and his present, his victories and failures, his love and pain, his despair and unconquerable hope. (Machovec, 1976, p. 204)

Throughout my search for Jesus, reviewing insider and outsider images of him, I encountered the idea that any attempt to domesticate Jesus is doomed to failure. The claim that more books have been written on Jesus than on any other person may be true; at least, there are many more Jesus books than I have managed to read in researching this one. Almost daily, someone mentions another Jesus book which I 'must read', or another programme, or mini-series, is screened on television. Perhaps the first lesson any Jesus searcher learns is that as soon as you think you have 'tied Jesus down', the ground shifts from under your feet. Tully (1996), answering his own question 'Why *Lives* [of Jesus], plural?', comments that, 'The result of . . . scholarly activity has been to produce differing schools of interpretation, with their advocates arguing fiercely that they alone hold the key to understanding Jesus. They are the *Lives of Jesus*' (p. x).

Several thinkers whose Jesus images I discussed in this book share Machovec's opinion that Jesus is not the exclusive possession of the Christian Church. From a humanist perspective, Renan suggested that Christian dogma and superstition obscure the Jesus of history. 'Jesus,' he wrote, 'cannot belong solely to those who call themselves his disciples. He is the common honor of all who share a common humanity' (1927, p. 65). Henry David Thoreau wrote, 'It is necessary not to be a Christian to appreciate the beauty and significance of the life of Christ' (1985, p. 55). From a Hindu perspective, Swami Abhedananda distinguished between Churchianity, a religion of dogma, and true Christianity, which knows no dogma. Many Jewish scholars see a clear distinction between the religion of Jesus and Jesus' religion. Marc Ellis writes of how every 'deal that Jesus and his disciples broke' has been 'resurrected, and in his name' (1994, p. 102). He does not think that Christians can claim an exclusive copyright on Jesus, suggesting it is 'perhaps the fear that' Jesus 'belongs outside the Church that claims him' that results in Christians trying to keep him within their 'normative tradition'. Pelikan (1985) described Jesus as 'an issue not only for Christians . . . but for all humanity' (p. 232). Muslim writer Rahim says that since there are so many versions of the Jesus story, Christians have no right to assume guardianship of Jesus' message (1977, p. 203).

I also kept encountering the view, among no few insiders as well as among outsiders, that even if Jesus is not God's son, or unique, he is still 'an inexhaustible principle of moral regeneration for humanity', again citing Renan (p. 388). Many, such as Schweitzer, Borg, Crossan, Ellis, Gandhi, Thich Nhat Hanh, have no place for a sacrificial, atoning death or for a Jesus whose nature is any different from yours or mine, yet all see meaning and significance in Jesus' life, if not always in his death. Nor does Jesus' resurrection play a necessary role in many of these Jesus responses. Paul Tillich thought history, including accounts of the resurrection, too contingent, too accidental, too uncertain to be the basis of faith. For Tillich, it is experience of new being flowing through the community from Jesus that supports and nourishes our faith. For him, too, faith always involves an element of risk.

## Being and becoming

Faith, for Tillich, is not a *set of beliefs*, but a courageous act *of being and of becoming*, of substituting dependence on the finite with openness towards the infinite, which is of ultimate concern. The notion that the most authentic life is one of 'being and becoming' resonates with much Hindu thought. Swamis Vivekananda and Abhedananda also used this expression. Vivekananda did not find true religion in dogmas or in books but in 'being and becoming' (1963, Vol. III, p. 257). Schweitzer more or less abandoned the quest for a historical reconstruction of Jesus' life yet spoke of a spirit flowing from him to us, calling us to loving action, perhaps even to a life of self-sacrifice, in our time. Bultmann, too, did not think we could say much about the details of Jesus' life, or about his inner thoughts and self-understanding, but he did think that Jesus summons us to abandon faith in ourselves for faith in God. Free yourselves from this world, he said, open yourselves up to God's future. Abandon security, abandon certainty: 'faith in this sense is the abandonment of one's own security and the readiness to find security only in the unseen beyond, in God' (1958a, p. 41).

Some responses reviewed might hardly qualify as images of Jesus, since they rejected Jesus as the creation of a myth, of conspirators pursuing their own agendas of personal power, or of white-over-black domination. The Jesus against whom the Jews of Harlem and the Nation of Islam reacted was a white Jesus, so domesticated within European and North American majority culture that he had become an oppressor, a denier of the black person's full humanity. For some, Jesus and Christianity were so linked that hatred of Christianity resulted in their rejecting any view of Jesus. In the Jesus-was-a-myth literature, we do not find a *bad Jesus* (like Celsus' Jesus), or a *Jesus who takes sides* (an Aryan Jesus) but a *Jesus who never existed*. Yet for me, personally, I did not find the Jesus-never-existed theory as disturbing as I did images that tried to do exactly what those cited above declare we cannot do; that is, to lay an exclusive claim to him.

Yet, asking what is it that so alienated and offended people that they rejected Jesus' existence, or Christianity in favour of Islam and Judaism, I find myself admitting that it was often Europe's recruitment of Jesus for her own purposes that caused this offence. The Aryan Jesus, the Jesus of the white supremacists, is only an extreme version of the Jesus that Europeans have too often preached around the world. When the 'believe in Jesus' invitation has had 'and become European' on the other side of the card, Africans and native Americans and Asians have found this offensive. I noted the denationalized image of Indian Christians.

For some, Christianity's attitude towards the feminine and towards women also caused and continues to cause offence. I return to feminism later in this chapter. Some reacted so strongly against the dogmas and policies of the Church, which they saw as repressive of the human spirit and of human freedom, that they jettisoned Jesus along with Christianity. Others chose to abandon Christian dogma but to keep Jesus. Others, such as Thiering, Smith, Baigent, Kersten, also retain Jesus but offer a picture of him that departs radically from the traditional Christian picture. It is interesting that alternative sources and theories of interpretation loom large in writing of this genre. Perhaps the official canon of scripture does not tell the whole story. Perhaps something can be learned from other texts, perhaps not about the historical Jesus but certainly about some understandings of the Christ of faith.

## Jesus as all things to all people

I was intrigued by the fact that quite a number of those discussed in this book found that their interest in Jesus compelled them to take other people's understanding of truth and perception and experience of the ultimate very seriously as well. Schweitzer, Tillich, Borg, for example, have written about another religious tradition or traditions. If culture and language are God's gift, then any attempt to understand Jesus within the givenness of a cultural milieu is an authentic exercise. Only when Jesus is Chinese for the Chinese, Indian for the Indians, will he be regarded as truly *for* these contexts. F. D. Maurice, writing in 1846, was insightful when he suggested that missionaries were wrong to convey the impression that they wanted to convert people to 'their modes and habits of speech' (p. 239). A Jesus, he said, who is not 'of man', or 'by man', but 'for man', everywhere, must not be the pet possession of Englishmen, Frenchmen or Spaniards.

The Bible suggests that God is Lord of all the nations; Psalm 82:8, 'To thee belong all the nations.' Psalm 86:5 tells us that 'the nations' will praise God, who rules and guides all peoples. Israel is described as a 'light to the nations' (Isaiah 49:6). Isaiah also tells us that many people will converge on Jerusalem: 'Many peoples will come and say, "let us go up to the mountain of the Lord"' (2:3). These and countless other verses suggest that *cultural plurality* is part of God's plan, that he respects and values the 'wealth' of the nations: 'The nations will walk by' the light of the New Jerusalem, 'and bring their splendour into it' (Revelation 21:24). The 'glory and honour of the nations' will be gathered in. As Cracknell (1986) says, 'This is no negative judgement upon the cultural traditions and religious achievements among the peoples . . . the nations will still be recognizable entities, smitten indeed but being healed' (p. 52). Babel (Genesis 11) may read like a curse, speaking about a confusion of language and a scattering of peoples. However, what the biblical record affirms is that God created the nations, and God will redeem them. The plan from the word go was to bless all families of the world. A Jesus, then, who is *saviour of the world* cannot be the exclusive possession of any single people. Several Qur'an passages also speak of the existence of the many nations as standing within God's purposes (see 7:168; 49:13).

## Jesus and 'one and only' claims

Ramakrishna, Vivekandanda, Gandhi and our two Buddhist writers all revered or revere Jesus but thought Christians wrong to make 'one and only' claims about him. I am inclined to agree with Stanley Samartha that naming the name is not always necessary, indeed the question may well be not do we name or recognize Jesus but does he name and recognize us. I sometimes preach that we do not 'own' Jesus, though he may 'own' us. I was reminded of this recently while reading Uris' *Exodus*, in which one of the characters is told by his father that the question was not whether he recognized the Messiah but whether the Messiah, when he came, would recognize him (1958, p. 205). Perhaps Jesus-like life, or deeds, counts for more than calling him Lord, as Gandhi pointed out. Cracknell (1986) believes that the 'splendour', 'wealth' and 'honour' of the nations includes their religious insights and traditions and that God is savingly at work within the many nations.

If this is so, what claims, if any, can Christians make about Jesus? Personally, I believe that Jesus' life represents a paradigm, a model of the life hidden in God. Through Jesus, God shows us how God wants us to live in relationship with God's self. This does not mean that God has not disclosed the same truth or way elsewhere, indeed I believe that God has done so. Similarly, while I regard God's disclosure of God's self through Christ as definitive, this does not mean that no other definitive revelations exist elsewhere. What it does mean is that any truth that is of God or from God will match the revelation of God that has come to us in Jesus. Lewis

Bevan Jones (1880–1960), the pioneer Baptist participant in Christian–Muslim relations, wrote:

The self-revelation of God, then, in Jesus Christ, is in every way adequate to human need. It is more, it is distinctive – there can be no uncertainty about the quality of the life revealed; and it is decisive and final – we need not wait for more, because revelation can go no further. Having said that, however, we need not and indeed cannot claim that God is, in Jesus, exhaustively revealed. It has been truly said, 'In Christ, God is known as He actually is, yet in Him, even so, there remains regions unknown, which faith can never exhaust . . .'. Let it not seem strange to confess that our faith holds fast to contradictories – God is known, and yet not known. After all, in the revelation of Himself in Jesus we stand face to face with profound mysteries. (1939a, p. 76)

Jones served with the Baptist Missionary Society in India, where he was born, from 1907 to 1941 (see Bennett, 1993).

Discussion of Jesus' uniqueness sometimes involves asking whether he actually said anything new. Some argue that everything Jesus said had already been stated by pagan philosophers or by Jewish sages (see chapters 4 and 5). Perhaps this is true. Why, then, does Jesus remain the subject of so much interest two thousand years after his own lifetime? Perhaps what can be claimed is this: unique or not, Jesus spoke and acted so boldly that what he said and did continues to influence people's thoughts, words and acts today.

Must all people accept Jesus' death as the unique saving act that mediates God's gift of grace? In my search, I encountered people for whom Jesus' death holds great meaning and some for whom, while a noble and courageous act of refusing to bow to tyranny, it has no salvific meaning. Some attribute the whole notion of a need for a blood offering, of a sinless substitution for human failing, to pagan influence. Among the Jesus responses discussed, some see the Christ of Christian faith as almost wholly the product of a pagan-influenced Church. As I read different theories, including critiques of traditional Christian beliefs and ideas, I tried to take every contribution seriously, asking how my own convictions stand up in the light of each particular critique. Paul's role looms large throughout this book. Is there discontinuity or continuity between the Jew of Nazareth and the Jew of Tarsus' teaching about the Jew of Nazareth? Did Paul paganize Christianity?

## A paganized Christ?

Personally, I think some pagan notions did impact on the formulation of Christian thought. However, this was inevitable, as early Christians drew on their culture and worldview to interpret and explicate the meaning of Jesus' life. Christians were convinced that Jesus' death also had meaning. The idea that Jesus' death represented a substitution for human sin was readily available at the time. This helped them to make sense of Jesus' death. They lived in a world where sacrifices were commonplace. This plays no role in my world today. However, what the primitive Church did, what Paul did in his writing, was to reflect on what had happened in Jesus, and to express this 'truth', this 'experience', in available language, terms and metaphors.

Paul especially was eager to share with Gentiles what he had experienced. He therefore began the business of translating Hebrew ideas into Greek. He was indeed concerned with faith in Jesus Christ, through whom he enjoyed new being (a life of fellowship with God), rather than with the details of Jesus' public ministry. Others were more competent to write the Gospels than Paul; his task was theoretical construction. Yet I do not feel bound by Paul's articulation of who Jesus was, though I honour it as the work of a profound and inspired theological pioneer.

For me, Jesus' death is a meaningful symbol of his willingness to resist the powers of oppression, but I am not convinced that my salvation derives from the cross. Nor am I convinced that God planned the crucifixion. Rather, Jesus' whole life, for me, was an act of redemption. Through Jesus' life, God savingly engaged with the human condition, sanctifying humanity, renewing life, setting forth the paradigm of the life that is lived in fellowship with God, in tune with God's will. Of course, Jesus did die a cruel and undeserved death, which means that in a sense *he died in my place*. This is why Christians continue to speak of Jesus' death as saving them.

If God was intimately involved in Jesus' life, he could not have been unmoved by Jesus' death. This is why, at an emotional level, 'Jesus died for me' language remains deeply meaningful: 'Died He for me, who caused His pain? For me, who Him to death pursued? Amazing love! How can it be, That Thou, my God, shouldst die for me' (Charles Wesley, 'And Can it Be', *Baptist Hymn Book*, 1962, No. 426). However, what I am suggesting is that Jesus' *life* was as significant as his *death*. Orthodox Christians affirm that in Christ the divine became human so that the human 'might participate in the divine' (2 Peter 1:4). Tagore, from a Hindu perspective, also spoke of the humanity of God and of the divinity of humanity.

## Is Jesus God?

Was Jesus God, as Paul believed? Or was Paul wrong, as Muslims and Jews argue, to present Jesus as mediating God rather than as merely pointing to God, like a prophet? Interestingly, Hindus and some Buddhists have no difficulty accepting that Jesus mediates the ultimate or that he is the ultimate, unlike Jews and Muslims. Hindus and Buddhists, though, like the early pagans, reject the claim that Jesus is the only manifestation of the ultimate or the sole mediator between the ultimate and humanity. My view that Jesus is paradigmatic, a definitive expression of God's will to humanity and a link between humanity and God, leaves open, as suggested above, the possibility that the same paradigm has been expressed elsewhere. Whatever names these other expressions are known by, to adapt the *Gita*, are merely alternative names for Jesus. This is why Panikkar can find Jesus in the *Upanishads*.

However, I think that the question of mediation between God and humanity may be fruitfully discussed at inter-faith meetings, especially by those whose traditions support and by those whose traditions reject the need for a go-between. When Christians speak of Jesus as God, or as mediating God, they are saying that Jesus was so close to God, so consumed with God-consciousness, that he was or became *one with God*. Traditionally, language of ontology was used to describe this. Yet existential language may be just as adequate, which attests to what is subjectively held to be true but which cannot be scientifically proven, or empirically investigated. On the other hand, science cannot disprove this either. Christians believe, experience, feel, too, that their own relationship with God is intimately linked with Jesus, which is why they find it difficult to separate God from Jesus as the definitive pointer to, or mediator between, themselves and God.

Muslims have sometimes come very close to speaking of Muhammad in similar terms, although they criticize Christians for turning Jesus the prophet into Christ the God. Yet when Muslims reflect on Muhammad's indispensability within Islam, might they not gain an appreciation of what Christians really mean when they speak about Jesus as their link with God? Muhammad remains the best interpreter of the Qur'an; the *shahada* (declaration of faith) links Muhammad with God so intimately that it is difficult for many Muslims to think of God without also thinking of God's messenger. The God language that Christians use of Jesus expresses faith in him as the one who links humanity and God. This is as much a statement about our ongoing, cumulative experience of God through Christ in our lives today, as it is about the historical Jesus of Nazareth. It testifies to our existential, subjective experience.

Lewis Bevan Jones stressed the 'why' not the 'what' of Christian belief in his dealings with Muslims. Jones was convinced that by speaking of the experience behind their dogmas, Christians could best help Muslims (and, I would add, Jews) to better understand why they have formulated these dogmas about Jesus. We should not, he says, 'needlessly obtrude' the Name (God, or Son of God) on to Jesus, 'as though it were the foundation, not the fruit, of faith in Christ'. 'We ourselves,' he continued, 'first find out what Christ is to us, and how He stands to God, and them we find this "Name above every Name" . . . but the chief thing is not the Name, but the experience of His redemptive work in our hearts' (1939a, p. 80). 'Other nations and peoples of other religions,' he boldly stated, 'have a real contribution to make in the fulfillment of God's purposes for the world through Jesus Christ' (*ibid.*).

## Jesus as a miracle worker

Many of the writers discussed redacted the supernatural from the Gospels. Ram Mohun Roy from India, Thomas Jefferson from the USA, produced images of Jesus as a moral man who worked no miracles. Paulus, Strauss, the Jesus Seminar, among others, object to a Jesus who performed miracles and who rose from the dead. Again, the existentialists provide me with a faith-sustaining response. Bultmann clearly doubted that anything like a physical resurrection happened but said that Jesus rose in the preaching of the Church, in the *kerygma*. On the other hand, Pinchas Lapide, an Orthodox Jew, chided Bultmann for rejecting the historicity of the resurrection, which he upholds.

Tillich suggested that, whether miracles did or did not happen, *people believed that they did*. Others, such as Crossan, say that healings took place. Later, people described these as miracles. The worldview of that time did not 'draw boundary lines between credible and incredible where medical science today would draw them' (Sanders, 1993, p. 136). People experienced something, and used available language to describe this. I think people also experienced Jesus' presence in their lives after Easter. For them, this experience was real, real because it changed their lives. Exactly *what* they experienced, like the exact nature of Jesus' relationship with God, lies beyond scientific enquiry. It is the stuff of faith.

As I encountered the different Jesus responses discussed in the preceding chapters, I tried to identify what genuine human needs were being met by various Jesus images. Sometimes, I struggled harder than at other times! However, I wanted to take all images seriously, even when – perhaps especially when – they challenged my own image. The challenge that pagan ideas have obscured the real Jesus, that we who are Christian exaggerate Jesus' importance, referred to above, merits careful consideration. What about the view that we can say nothing for certain about Jesus? If this is true, then a racist Jesus image, or an image that women find offensive, might be no less authentic than any other Jesus image. However, I am convinced that a bare set of facts can be asserted, with reasonable confidence, about the historical Jesus.

On the one hand, I am sceptical that anyone can properly adjudicate between images of Jesus. On the other hand, I think a modicum of resemblance between a Jesus image and what can be said with some confidence about the Jesus of the Gospels ought to be expected. None the less, in offering even the following minimalist image of Jesus, I am aware that there is nothing like a consensus on what the first-century Jew called Jesus was really like. It may be argued, as Forward points out, that primitive Christian thought on Jesus, 'however convoluted', was 'a development of what was there from the beginning, not a series of culturally appropriate innovations' (2000, p. 2). However, we read neither the Jesus sources nor early Christian theology as first-century people. Nothing can guarantee the accuracy of our reconstruction, or ensure that we see in the texts what their authors wanted us to see. We read as twenty-first-century readers.

I am aware that my Jesus portrait is just as much the product of cultural and of ideological conditioning as anyone else's. In other words, I cannot insist that it represents a more authentic response, only one that seems to be meaningful at this moment in time. Perhaps all Jesus images are time-limited. I can only claim that I have tried to bracket out preconceptions, to resist the temptation to see what I want to see. On the other hand, it would be disingenuous to claim that I do not find my own Jesus image attractive or compelling, or I would surely abandon it in favour of a different image. In the end, Jesus remains significant for me personally because he calls me to meaningful action in the world. However, as I have gleaned my minimalist Jesus image from what the most sceptical scholars concede as historically probable of Jesus, I dare to suggest that it may prove to be more rather than less durable in the long term. Of course, only time will tell whether this hope represents anything other than wishful thinking or self-conceit.

## A historically sustainable, minimalist Jesus image

Jesus opposed all forms of oppression. Jesus opposed the elitism of his day. Jesus affirmed the value, worth and dignity of all people. Jesus turned many social norms upside-down. He had little regard for wealth, for power, for privilege. He was above all for the ʿamme ha-arets, the common people. Sanders calls Jesus' inclusion of sinners in the kingdom a 'distinctive note' of Jesus' teaching (1985, p. 174). Any follower of Jesus who has wealth, power or a position of privilege stands on shaky ground. This includes Christian agencies that exercise power over subordinates' lives. I think that Jesus was always open and honest with people; he spoke his concerns to their faces, not behind their backs. Any Christian individual or agency that fails to treat people similarly fails Jesus.

Jesus, I believe, was 'liberated' from social conventions, from conforming to the expectations of the world, from what it expected him to do. Any Christian agency that merely apes the world needs to look carefully at its bona fides. Close to home, for example, the vast sums of money spent on sport by a Christian institution invites the question, is this pro-liberational, is this promoting Jesus' agenda, or our own image and respectability in the eyes of a human constituency? Jesus the 'liberated' cannot be boxed in, or tied down. Jesus the 'liberated' wants to liberate all captives, all the oppressed, all who are enslaved. Any image of Jesus that limits his love to some or denies it to others is a false image.

The above checklist can, I believe, be used to test the legitimacy of any Jesus image. This picture of Jesus, I suggest, shines through the texts of the four Gospels, despite over-enthusiastic, or pre-scientific, language or their theological colouring. In the end, though, since the texts we possess are open to a multiplicity of interpretations, I must concede everyone's freedom to construct their own Jesus image. At the same time, I claim a right to offer a critique of any Jesus image, based on my reading of Jesus' life. As I read the Jesus images surveyed in my six chapters, I was surprised by how much I learned.

Often, the predetermined agendas that people bring to their study of Jesus actually help to illuminate particular aspects of the narrative, or of how that narrative has traditionally been understood. Those who looked for pagan influence found it, *and found it everywhere*. Largely, this was because they expected to find it. However, it would be wrong to dismiss everything they have to say. Those convinced that Jesus had enjoyed sexual relations *discovered that he had*. Here, the apocryphal sources cited are subject to various interpretations, yet Christians could do worse than to re-examine some of their teachings about human sexuality.

## Jesus and the feminine

When I turned to the writing of some feminist scholars, I was rewarded with new insights. I, like others, failed to see what they saw because I was not looking for it. In a lengthy discussion of the 'Kingdom of God', so crucial to Jesus' teaching, Sanders (1985, Chapters 2–7, and 1993, Chapters 11–13) never points out that the Greek word '*basileia*' can be feminine. Nor had I known this until I read Elizabeth Schüssler Fiorenza's work (see especially 1992, 1994, 1998). Throughout, she uses *basileia* instead of translating the word into English, because its usual renderings evoke *masculine* images: kingly power, kingdom (see 1998, pp. 114–16). I even checked my Greek lexicon and was surprised to learn that *basileia* can indeed be feminine and that it can also carry the meaning of *queenly rule*. Fiorenza says that the 'imperial' language of male domination traditionally used by Christians reinforces 'kyriarchal' images; kyriarchal = 'elite male, relations of ruling' (1992, p. 8). In Jewish counter-cultural usage, *basileia* had, she says, an inclusive, even democratic aspect that 'spells wellbeing and freedom for all in the global village' (1994, p. 89). She sometimes renders *basileia* as 'commonweal'.

Why had my own teachers, Sanders and countless others, failed to mention anything about the gender permutations of this crucial term? In all probability, because they had no reason to think this significant. However, if one is a woman looking at the Gospels for signs of the feminine, one may well notice that this crucial concept is feminine. Fiorenza is interested in reading the texts to see how 'patriarchal discourse constructs the reader, and how gender, race and class affect the way we read' (1992, p. 35). It seems to me that in its rendering of *basileia*, Christian tradition missed a rare historic moment to use inclusive language, instead of perpetuating the notion of God as a king, as a male, who rules over a kingdom that is for men first, women second. 'As long as the church and theology insist upon masculine language,' says Fiorenza, 'patriarchal images and kyriocentric discourses about the heavenly

Queen Mary as well as the kyriarchal Father-Son they will continue to inculcate the subordination and secondary status of women' (1994, p. 177). Language, the 'power of naming', she argues, *does matter* (see *ibid.*, p. 10).

The more I reflected on Jesus' use of *basileia*, the more I found myself thinking that indeed the values of Jesus' kingdom, love, compassion, sacrifice, service, going the extra mile, embracing the vulnerable and the ostracized, are more feminine than masculine. I am indebted to Fiorenza for pointing this out. She also notes, as have others, that women played a prominent part in the Jesus movement; certainly several were part of an extended intimate circle that included the twelve, but there were other women and men. The empty tomb was 'named and proclaimed by women' (1994, p. 119). Women, she says, were instrumental in 'founding, sustaining and shaping the primitive 'house-*ekklesia*' (1998, p. 118). Fiorenza goes so far as to suggest that the Jesus movement was 'a emancipatory movement of wo/men' (1994, p. 88).

Note that her terminology is *deliberately inclusive*: she uses the term 'wo/men' to embrace 'oppressed and marginalized men' as well as 'all women' (1994, p. 191). Indeed, she says that within the Jesus movement, all people – men, women, high born, low born – were regarded as equal. It is odd that the Church and Christian institutions elevate some people above others. 'The Living One', she says, goes ahead of G⋆d's people, enabling them to 'continue the tradition and vision of Sophia's messengers by announcing the good news of G⋆d's new "world order" of justice and well-being for every wo/man without exception. The Living One is present,' she continues, 'wherever the disciples of the *basileia* practice the inclusive discipleship of equals, making it a present reality among the poor, hungry, abused, and alienated wo/men' (1994, p. 188).

The 'Sophia G⋆d of Jesus loves all humanity irrespective of ethnic and social links and shows concern for the liberation and empowerment of the underprivileged', says Fiorenza (1994, p. 157). Jesus, for Fiorenza, 'is Wisdom herself', and 'reveals Wisdom to all those to whom he wants to reveal himself' (1994, pp. 143–4; see Matthew 11:25). Moreover, this same Sophia is present 'among all peoples, cultures and religions. . . . S/he accompanies us in our struggles against injustice and for liberation' (1998, p. 180). Fiorenza makes more of the notion that Jesus was a bringer of *sophia* (wisdom), also feminine, than do many other writers, apart from neo-Gnostics.

The mother-*sophia* language of the Gnostics, together with women's leadership roles in some Gnostic circles, fell victim to official Christian censure. Elaine Pagels, one of the most distinguished scholars of the Gnostic tradition, on whose work I have drawn considerably, may well have chosen this field because of its feminist possibilities. Fiorenza's work may be of the neo-Gnostic genre, or is this where men put it in order to marginalize her from the mainstream of Jesus study? As Krister Stendahl Professor at Harvard Divinity School, though, her work is not easily sidelined. She certainly views her work as a contribution to biblical interpretation *per se*.

Following in the footsteps of the man whose name her Chair honours, himself an architect of the Sigtuna Statement, Fiorenza is an active participant in Jewish–Christian dialogue, and draws on this in her work (see 1994, p. 69). She points out that feminist theologians, in proclaiming 'Jesus the feminist', have been accused of anti-Jewish bias, inasmuch as they represent Jesus as 'an exception to the patriarchal rule' (*ibid.*, p. 82). Her argument, though, is that Jesus stood in a long tradition of female-male inclusiveness, and the Jesus movement was 'part of the various *basileia* holiness movements that in the first century sought the "liberation" of Israel from imperial exploitation' (p. 90). The women who followed Jesus, too, 'were *Jewish women*. They were *not Christian* in our sense of the word' (p. 89).

Fiorenza uses 'G*d' because it indicates the inadequacy of our language, and perhaps avoids the male imagery that the word 'God' often conjures up (see 1994, p. 191). She calls for new and imaginative ways of thinking about the divine, pointing out that neither 'G*d' nor 'G*ddess suffices', since 'Divinity is always greater and always more than human language can express' (1994, p. 180). 'The Divine,' she says, 'must be renamed again and again in the experience of women' (1998, p. 180). On the other hand, she does not think that the G*dness of G*d is put at risk by use of feminine language, which presents no threat today, although Paul and others may have perceived it as threatening in the first century (p. 178). Rather, G*d is 'endangered' when idols of domination are put in G*d's place (1994, p. 178).

Women, she says, were involved in the early Church in articulating *sophia*-language of Jesus, although men were at some point also happy with this way of speaking about Jesus (*ibid.*, p. 149). This language, too, is embedded in the earliest 'Q' traditions, yet was jettisoned in favour of an 'exclusive understanding of revelation' (p. 144) when male language of Jesus as 'cosmic lord/master and sovereign' became dominant. Fiorenza borrows G*d from Orthodox Jews, who never pronounce YHWH, the Divine Name (1994, p. 191). They often substitute *Adonai* (Lord) in its place.

Paul, suggests Fiorenza, saw himself as 'father of the community' with a special authority of interpretation (p. 150). I think she is right to suggest that the increasingly male-dominated early Church chose masculine, imperial language to serve its own purposes of power and control rather than the more female-friendly sophia language, which it could have used. Here, Marxist analysis may lurk below the surface. Theologians who unashamedly offer their writing as of political consequence are also likely to see in the text, or in traditional readings of the text, what others fail to see. That our usual reading of the Gospels may serve the interests of some people, while subjugating or alienating others, has been brought home to me by reading the work of Marxist, feminist, black and political theologians. Like many other Jesus scholars, Fiorenza urges action:

A critical feminist discourse on Jesus and Mary will be able to bring about the transformation of patriarchal church and kyriarchal society for the liberation of all only if it does not limit itself to intellectual theological speculations . . . Instead it must engage in an uncompromising liberationist praxis that consciously seeks to transcend its kyriarchal predicaments, locations and limitations. (1994, p. 180)

As I worked on this chapter, the Southern Baptist Convention voted that women cannot be pastors. On television, several representatives stated that it is not for the Church to alter what the Bible says. Of course, the verse cited is usually 1 Corinthians 14:33–4, a Pauline verse. However, I also heard some say, 'Jesus was a man', 'God sent his Son to die for us', and 'Jesus has made men, not women, leaders of his Church'. 'Men, not women, represent Jesus, who was a man.' Catholics also say that as Jesus was a man, only a man can represent him at the consecration of the bread and wine. In fact, Jesus did not mention anything about a priest representing him, or ever say that women must remain silent (see Fiorenza, 1994, p. 74). Nor do I think that Paul, of all people, thought he was prescribing eternal law when he wrote those words.

Paul knew that he had been freed from law by the grace and truth he had encountered in Jesus Christ. 'Christ,' he wrote, 'redeemed us from the curse of the law', and continued, 'There is neither Jew nor Greek, slave nor free, male nor female, for you are all one in Christ Jesus' (Galatians 3: 13, 28). As Fiorenza points out, women in the Corinthian Church, who 'were leaders and . . . prophets', recognized 'the Resurrected One as identical not only with the Spirit of G*d but also with Divine Sophia' (p. 149; see 1 Corinthians 2:7). This raises the question whether Paul said what he said to assert his own hermeneutic, though I think he was sincerely trying to restore order and harmony to a divided community.

That Jesus appointed twelve men as disciples within the historical context of first-century Palestine was not surprising. It does not mean that women cannot occupy positions of leadership in his movement. His inclusion of women within his wider circle of intimates was groundbreaking, revolutionary and *liberating*. Fiorenza suggests that 'Jesus can only be known in and through the witness of his disciples, women and men. Jesus and his movement are intertwined and cannot be separated' (1994, p. 52), a point also made by Tillich. It seems to me that the thrust of Jesus' actions and attitude *vis-à-vis* women favours women in ministry, not their exclusion. Only when women are included will we have a chance to hear the whole voice of Jesus' body. The Holy Spirit, too, will lead us into all truth. A Jesus image that disenfranchises women, that denies them their full equality with men, fails my litmus test. Its Jesus is neither 'liberated' nor a 'liberator' but the privileged possession of men and an oppressor of women.

Jesus manifested eternal *sophia*, which is feminine, as well as the word of God, which is masculine. In a sense, he was male and female. The *yin* and the *yang*, in Chinese thought, permeate all existence – likewise, God could be androgynous. Here, Christians might usefully reflect on some Hindu imaging of the divine. My understanding of the incarnation is that what 'incarnated' itself in Jesus (leaving aside discussion of the mechanism involved) was humanity, wo/manhood. Accidentally, Jesus was a man – he had to be either a man or a woman. However, I regard his male gender as his accidental nature and suggest that his substantial nature embraced both genders.

This reflects Catholic belief that at the point of consecration, while the *accident* of the bread and wine remains food and drink, its *substance* becomes Jesus' body and blood. Further, if Jesus' substance was male and female, or humanity, it does not follow that only a man can represent him. Men and women can both equally represent his substantial nature, even if their accidental natures do not match the one Jesus adopted in first-century Palestine. We are certainly not limited, as Fiorenza points out, to the language chosen by past generations to describe a G*d who is ultimately ineffable. Insistence on the maleness of Jesus leaves open the question, 'Can a Male Savior Save Women?' (asked by Rosemary Radford Ruether; see Fiorenza, 1994, p. 46).

Traditional Christology is 'rhetorical', not 'scientific', open to renegotiation 'for every-body and every wo/man in the global village' (1994, p. 96). A view encountered several times in this book is that Jesus had neither taught any dogmas nor propounded 'an ideology' (Machovec, 1976, p. 204). Fiorenza is quite open about her own agenda, which is to reconstruct a Jesus image that speaks to, for and from *women's experience*. Since all Jesus images are interpretations, the question is not so much, 'Who was Jesus?' but, 'Who is he for wo/men today?' Her task is not the articulation of a systematic ontological account of Christology proper but rather 'to test out the implications and elaborate the power of christological discourse either for legitimating or for changing kyriarchal relations of domination' (1994, p. 61).

Although Fiorenza says quite a lot about the quest for the historical Jesus, she does not seek to validate her work *vis-à-vis* 'the methodological procedures of biblical studies' (*ibid.*, p. 62). Her 'criteria of validation' are 'embedded in the potential of texts' to render a reading that will 'transform kyriocentric mind-sets and structures of domination' (*ibid.*). While I may properly have dealt with her work in my insider chapter, it seems that her reader-response approach to the gospel texts places her in a different genre of writers from most, though not all, of those whose work I discussed in Chapter 3. I did make reference to liberation theology, with which she identifies, citing its founding father, Gustavo Gutiérrez (1994, p. 60). The vital question, she says, is not 'what kind of G*d exists but rather . . . what *kind* of G*d Christians proclaim in a world of oppression' (*ibid.*).

## Was Jesus an Essene, or a Buddhist?

Finally, what about Jesus the Essene, Jesus the Buddhist, and a black Jesus? On the Essene question, I find it interesting that the Gospels are silent. There are no references to Essenes. Might this be because Jesus knew that he had much in common with them, or was even sympathetic towards them? Certainly, he shared their antipathy towards the Temple establishment. Since most gospel references to specific groups of Jews are in the context of debate with them, exclusion of the Essenes could indicate that Jesus did not dispute their ideas.

Some of those surveyed see the Essenes as a bridge between the Buddhist and the Jewish worlds. Did Jesus know anything about Buddhism? As an Indiaphile, I actually find this notion quite attractive. However, I am inclined to ascribe similarity and parallels between Jesus and other religious systems to a common source, to God at work among the nations, rather than to physical contact. If there is a single paradigm, of which Jesus is a definitive expression, we should not be surprised when we read a Hindu text and find that it speaks to us of Him. Lewis Bevan Jones put it like this: 'How . . . are we to account for the innumerable fragments of truth to be found in other religions except on the ground that God's Spirit is quietly at work in the hearts and minds of men?' (1939a, p. 254).

Bowden (1988) asks, 'What is the relationship between the historical Jesus of Nazareth and representations of him as having been of another culture, colour or race?' (p. 101). The risen, living Christ Jesus, it seems to me, is free to inculturate into any culture, for all cultures will bring their honour and wealth and splendour into the eternal city. However, the Aryan Jesus is intended to *exclude* non-Aryans from that city. The Aryan, white, European Jesus is the exclusive possession of whites, an oppressor of non-whites. This Jesus is neither a liberated nor a liberating Jesus, and fails my test. If the white, racist Jesus fails my test, must a black Jesus also fail?

I do not think that all representations of Jesus as having something in common with a given culture other than the Jewish are automatically suspect, even from a historical point of view. For example, representation of him as Asian, as an Oriental, rightly asserts that as a man of the Middle East, Jesus knew many customs, habits and mores that are similar to those of Oriental lands (Rihbany, Vivekananda, Abhedananda). He may well have been at home in Kashmir, had he travelled there, just as Egypt would have felt familiar. What fails my test is the contention that Orientals exclusively possess Jesus, that only they can interpret him, or really appreciate who he is and what he taught. This denies non-Orientals access to new being, which God wants to gift to us all.

Similarly, the claim that Jesus can relate to white Europeans – as he did to Romans in the Gospels – is legitimate, provided this claim does not turn into an exclusion of others. All such claims are partly theological, speaking of the Christ of faith who crosses cultures and national and racial boundaries. This Christ becomes, as Paul aspired to be, all things to all people, a Jew for Jews, a white person for white people, a black person for black people, an Indian for Indians. Such a Christ affirms the 'splendour', 'wealth' and 'honour' of the nations, just as does God who created them.

## A black Jesus?

Does Jesus' skin colour matter? One response is to say that at a theological level Jesus as the eternal Christ can be represented as of any and indeed as of all races, colours, genders. On a historical note, it is less easy to make out a case for Jesus having been other than a single colour – whatever that was. Of course, it is quite possible for some people to pass off as dark or light, depending on the circumstances. I worked for three months on a Moshav out in the sun of the Jordan valley, and I was not exactly white when I finished. Since Jesus was a Mediterranean Jew who spent a great deal of time in the open air, his skin colour was in all probability black, not white. Cone (1986) writes, 'It seems to me that the *literal* color of Jesus is irrelevant. . . . But as it happens, *Jesus was not white in any sense of the word*' (p. 123). The question, then, of Jesus' skin colour may seem to be irrelevant. However, for many black people, the colour of Jesus' skin is a real issue. An article posted on the website of the Baptist Center for Ethics by Robert M. Parkham, headed 'Jesus Color is More than Skin', cites one delegate at a Baptist World Alliance conference on the colour issue:

An African delegate . . . said that the white world is the creator of racism. For those with such a perspective, a white Jesus reinforces the existing white power that harms people of color. Thus, one way to reverse white power is to strip Jesus of his whiteness. Making Jesus a person of color gives nonwhites power.

Parkham continues, 'The color of Jesus skin does matter, if it causes others to stumble' (Baptist Center for Ethics, www.baptist4ethics.com/ht_race.htm). There is a clear parallel between the problem of Jesus' colour for many people of colour and the problem of Jesus' maleness for many women. To adapt Fiorenza's words, these may be the most 'central issues in Christology' today (1994, p. 34).

In his poignant and powerful book, *A Black Theology of Liberation* (2nd edn 1986), James H. Cone, Charles A. Briggs Distinguished Professor at Union Theological Seminary, New York, argues in favour of a black understanding of God and of Jesus. He writes, 'The blackness of God, and everything implied by it in a racist society, is the heart of the black theology doctrine of God' (p. 63). God, says Cone, is for the oppressed, for the poor, over and against the oppressors and the wealthy (see p. 120). The oppressed, he says, are black.

However, just as for Fiorenza 'wo/men' includes marginalized men, so Cone's 'black' includes all who identify with the black experience: 'everyone in this country [the USA] knows' that 'blacks are those who say they are black'. How, then, 'can white persons become black?', he asks. The answer, he says, is the same as that to the question, 'What must I do to be saved? . . . blackness and salvation', he continues, 'are synonymous' and both are 'the work of God' (p. 66). Cone's God is also, ultimately, 'Wholly Other' but as the God of the oppressed, it is as 'black' that God reveals God's self. Thus, 'to receive God's revelation is to become black with God by joining God in the work of liberation' (p. 67).

'Liberation,' he says, 'represents the very essence of divine activity' (p. 64). Blackness for Cone is both a physiological and an ontological reality; whites can be ontologically black. Indeed, Cone says that until whites 'hate their whiteness', because it symbolizes oppression, and ask, '"How can we become black" . . . there will be no peace in America' (p. vii). The oppressors' God, the white God, is a God of slavery and 'must be destroyed along with the oppressors' (p. 58). It is an 'idol created by racists'. The old-time religion that stressed moral purity but accepted oppression without complaint must be abandoned as bankrupt: 'religion unrelated to black liberation is irrelevant' (p. 59). Such a religion is a tool of oppression, as a Marxist would claim. However, authentic Christianity is always and everywhere liberational. Ultimately, the oppressors are liberated when they identify themselves with the oppressed. Where is the Kingdom of God today? It is 'the liberation struggle in the black community. It is where people are suffering and dying for want of human dignity' (p. 125).

Only the oppressed, only those who are self-consciously 'black', have realized full humanity, 'because only they have encountered both the depravity of human behavior from oppressors and the healing powers revealed in the Oppressed One' (p. 87). Repeatedly, Cone says that only a God, a Christ, who is unequivocally for the liberation of black people can hold any meaning for the black community. Only such a Christ can have anything to say to and for the black experience. Thus, 'the very existence of black theology is dependent on its ability to relate itself to the human situation unique to oppressed persons generally and blacks particularly' (p. 36). Black Christology is rooted deeply in black experience. Similarly, says Fiorenza, 'G*d-language, discourses about Jesus Christ', if they are to have any meaning for women, 'must remain embedded in feminist liberation movements and practices of transformation' (1994, p. 189).

Cone's Christ is, above all, 'The Oppressed One whose earthly existence was bound up with the oppressed of the land' (p. 113). Like God, Christ is black: 'taking our clue from the historical Jesus who is pictured in the New Testament as the Oppressed One, what else, except blackness, could adequately tell us the meaning of his presence today?' If Christ has taken 'upon himself the suffering of his people', says Cone, 'he must be black' (p. 122). 'Christ,' he continues, 'must be black so that blacks can know that their liberation is his liberation' (p. 120). How could God or Christ be white, when whites have enslaved and oppressed and exploited non-whites and Jews throughout the ages? For many women, how could God be male, when a male-imaged God's self-proclaimed servants have subjugated women over the centuries?

Blacks' affirmation of the blackness of Christ expresses rejection of white concepts as well as of whites' insistence that they know what is in the blacks' best interest: 'Only blacks can speak about God in relationship to their own liberation' (p. 63). On the other hand, Cone is sceptical that whites realize the true 'nature of their own enslavement . . . because if they really knew, they would liberate themselves by joining the revolution of the black community'. Indeed, 'they would destroy themselves and be born again as beautiful black persons' (p. 103). Black theology, the blacking of God and of Jesus, however, affirms the dignity, freedom and self-determination of black people. Cone writes, 'Preaching the gospel is nothing but proclaiming to blacks that they do not have to submit to ghetto-existence. Our new existence has been bought and paid for; we are now redeemed, set free' (p. 131).

Does Cone's black Jesus pass my test? Yes, a Jesus who liberates the oppressed, who is 'for the poor against the rich, for the weak against the strong' (p. 120), is my type of Jesus. Cone, too, invites all who follow 'the black Christ' Jesus to co-operate in the kingdom-building task of fighting oppression: 'To participate in God's salvation is to co-operate with the black Christ as he liberates his people from bondage. Salvation . . . has primarily to do with earthly justice and the injustice inflicted on those who are helpless and poor' (p. 128). Here is an inclusive Jesus image around which Gandhi, Machovec, Thich Nhat Hanh, Ellis, Esack, Crossan and countless other Hindus, Buddhists, Marxists, Jews, Muslims and Christians can unite and make common cause.

## The reconciliation of all in Christ: beyond liberation

Have I found Jesus? In one sense, as a professing Christian, I could claim to have 'found' him before I started my quest. However, I prefer to say that Jesus found me, at least I believe he did. What I can say, with some confidence, is that there is more to Jesus than I can ever imagine. As Pelikan puts it, 'his person and his message are, in the phrase of Augustine, a "beauty ever ancient, ever new" and now he belongs to the world' (1985, p. 233). Perhaps, too, I have some idea where to look for the liberated and liberating Jesus. Wherever human kindness, generosity, goodness lurks, there is Jesus. Jesus summons us, I believe, to *make the world more humane*, which, as it happens, is a very Jewish goal. The Jews' 'mission', says, Wiesel (1978), 'was never to make the world Jewish but, rather, to make it more human' (p. 16). This also resonates with Confucianism. Master Kung's goal was a humane, benevolent, generous society. Asked about humaneness, Master Kung replied, 'Love your fellow man' (Lao, 1979, p. 116; *Analects*, 12:22).

Elie Wiesel's haunting words 'where was humanity at Auschwitz' echo in my ears as I write these concluding words. Like Matthew Fox, I believe that as people – women, men, black, white – of whatever faith affirm their common humanity, the 'in' and the 'out' of their 'sideship' *vis-à-vis* Jesus will cease to matter. Indeed, I have struggled to maintain this distinction throughout this book, although it has had, I believe, some use as an analytical tool. In the end, what Jesus invites us to enter is a relationship of *koinonia* (fellowship) with each other, with the ultimate, with the cosmos (see Isaiah 65), with himself. Liberation that does not also lead to reconciliation is a shallow and partial victory. God commanded the Hebrews to exercise especial concern for the *gerim* (strangers), since they had been strangers in Egypt (see Deuteronomy 10:19; also Matthew 25:35). For them to oppress others as they had once been oppressed would be to negate the Exodus. This, as Ellis points out, has implications for how Israel treats the Palestinian people today.

Such liberation is only a reversal of oppressed–oppressor roles, in which the oppressed become the oppressors, the victimized become the victimizers, black become white, women become men. Reconciliation of all with all, a very Hindu goal, must be the end for which we work, hope and pray. This is also a very Chinese goal. Chinese thought, above everything else, wants unity, harmony, order, balance, at-oneness with the Tao, the singular reality that permeates and produces duality (the *yin* and the *yang*) and plurality:

The Tao gives birth to the One, One gives birth to Two, Two gives birth to Three, Three gives birth to all things. All things have their backs to the female, and stand facing the male. When male and female combine, all things achieve harmony. (Mitchell, 1988, p. 42)

Paul wrote, 'For God was pleased to have God's fullness (*pleroma*) dwell in Christ Jesus and through Christ *to reconcile all things* to God's self, whether things on earth or things in heaven, making peace (*eirene*) through the blood of Christ' (Colossians 1:19–20). Of course, the blood language here would not be my first choice, yet I share Paul's hope, Paul's dream and his *certainty*. Paul is perhaps much maligned in this book, yet his faith in Jesus was universal, not narrow or exclusive. Some of those discussed in this book who were highly critical of conventional Christianity, such as John Allegro, saw Christianity's universal concern as a positive development. For Montefiore, Jesus' real achievement was the *universalizing* of Jewish ideas. Even Klausner, who thought that Paul's version of Christianity negated Judaism, commended his desire to reach out to the Gentile world.

## Where is Jesus?

Where is Jesus? Wherever reconciliation – dare I say resurrection – succeeds the cross, the often passion-filled struggle for human liberation. 'For creation itself,' Paul confidently predicted, 'will be liberated from its bondage . . . and brought into the glorious freedom of the children of God'

(Romans 8:21). As Gandhi, a Christlike non-Christian, said, 'God did not bear the Cross only nineteen hundred years ago, but He bears it today, and He dies and is resurrected from day to day. . . . Do not then preach the God of history but show Him as He lives today *through you*' (1940, p. 21; italics added). 'By their action,' said Jesus, 'shall you know them' (Matthew 7:20). Perhaps our inability to definitively find Jesus leaves us open to the prompting of his spirit, leading us on towards unexpected, unfulfilled possibilities of inclusiveness, of reconciliation, of peace and well-being *for all people*.

# References

**Books**

Abhedananda, Swami (1901) *Why a Hindu Accepts Christ and Rejects Christianity*, New York, The Vedanta Society.

Abhedananda, Swami (1984) 'Jesus Christ, the leader of men: as described in the manuscript of the Himis retreat', pp. 232–7, in *The Lost Years of Jesus* by Elizabeth C. Prophet, Livingston, MT, Summit University Press.

Achebe, Chinua (1959) *Things Fall Apart*, New York, Anchor Books.

Adams, Dickinson W. (1983) *Jefferson's Extracts from the Gospels*, Princeton, NJ, Princeton University Press.

Ahmad, Mirza Ghulam (1989) *Jesus in India*, Islamabad, International Publications. www.geocities.com/Athens/Delphi/1340/jesus_in_india.htm. First published 1899.

Ali, Yusuf 'Abdullah (1989) *The Meaning of the Holy Qur'an: New Edition*, Beltsville, MD, Amana Publications.

Allegro, John M. (1956) *The Dead Sea Scrolls*, Harmondsworth, Penguin.

Allegro, John M. (1968) *Discoveries in the Judaean Desert of Jordan*, Vol. V, Oxford, Clarendon Press.

Allegro, John M. (1970) *The Sacred Mushroom and the Cross: A Study of the Nature and Origins of Christianity within the Fertility Cults of the Near East*, London, Hodder & Stoughton.

Allegro, John M. (1984) *The Dead Sea Scrolls and the Christian Myth*, Buffalo, NY, Prometheus. First published 1979.

Allen, Charles (1975) *Plain Tales from the Raj*, London, Futura.

Allen, Charlotte (1998) *The Human Christ: The Search for the Historical Jesus*, New York, The Free Press.

Andrews, Charles Freer (1939) 'The Hindu view of Christ', *International Review of Missions* 28, pp. 259–64.

Annet, Peter (1995) *A Collection of the Tracts of a Certain Free Enquirer*, edited by John Vladimir Price, London, Routledge; Tokyo, Thoemmes.

Aristotle (1998) *Politics*, translated by C. D. C. Reeve, Indianapolis, Hacket Publishing.

Arnold, Sir Edwin (1879) *The Light of Asia, or The Great Renunciation*, Chicago, Momewood Publishing.

Arnold, Sir Edwin (trans.) (1934) *The Song Celestial, or, Bhagavad-Gita*, Philadelphia, David McKay. First published 1885.

Askari, Hasan (1972) 'The dialogical relationship between Christianity and Islam', *Journal of Ecumenical Studies*, pp. 477–88.

Augustine, St (1991) *Confessions*, translated by Henry Chadwick, Oxford, Oxford University Press.

*A Very Light Sleeper: The Persistence and the Dangers of Antisemitism* (1994) London, The Runnymede Trust.

Bahrdt, Karl Friedrich (1784–92) *Aushührung der Plans und Zwecks Jesus*, 11 vols, Berlin, August Mylius.

Baigent, Michael and Leigh, Richard (1991) *The Dead Sea Scrolls Deception*, New York, Summit Books.

Baigent, Michael, Leigh, Richard and Lincoln, Henry (1982) *Holy Blood, Holy Grail*, New York, Delacorte Press.

Baigent, Michael, Leigh, Richard and Lincoln, Henry (1986) *The Messianic Legacy*, New York, Dell.

*Baptist Hymn Book, The* (1962) London, Psalms and Hymns Trust.

Barkun, Michael (1997) *Religion and the Racist Right: The Origins of the Christian Identity Movement*, Chapel Hill and London, University of North Carolina Press.

*Barnabas, Gospel of* (2000). www.barnabas.net.

Barrett, Leonard E. (1997) *The Rastafarians*, Boston, Beacon Press.

Barth, Karl (1936–77) *Church Dogmatics*, translated by G. T. Thomson *et al.*, 13 vols, Edinburgh, T. & T. Clark.

Barth, Karl (1967) *Call for God: New Sermons from Basel Prison*, translated by A. T. Mackay, London, SCM Press.

Bate, John Drew (1884) 'Report', *92nd Report of the Baptist Missionary Society*, London, BMS, p. 7.

Baur, Ferdinand Christian (1878) *Church History of the First Three Centuries*, Vol. 1, edited by Allan Menzies, London, Williams and Norgate. First published in German 1853.

Baur, Ferdinand Christian (1879) *Church History of the First Three Centuries*, Vol. 2, edited by Allan Menzies, London, Williams and Norgate. First published in German 1853.

Bawany, E. A. (1977) *Islam: The First and Final Religion*, Karachi, Begum Aisha Bawany Waqf.

Baxter, Margaret (1988) *The Formation of the Scriptures*, London, SPCK.

Belo, Fernando (1981) *A Materialist Reading of the Gospel of Mark*, translated by Matthew J. O'Connell, Maryknoll, NY, Orbis.

*Bengali Bible, The* [*Pabrita Baibel*] (1979) Dhaka, Bangladesh Bible Society.

Bennett, Clinton (1982) 'William Blake, 1757–1827: a pilgrimage of discovery', *Faith and Freedom: A Journal of Progressive Religion* 35:105, pp. 122–8.

Bennett, Clinton (1992) *Victorian Images of Islam*, London, Grey Seal.

Bennett, Clinton (1993) 'The legacy of Lewis Bevan Jones', *International Bulletin of Missionary Research* 17:3, pp. 126–9.

Bennett, Clinton (1996a) *In Search of the Sacred: Anthropology and the Study of Religions*, London, Cassell.

Bennett, Clinton (1996b) 'The legacy of Karl Gottlieb Pfander', *International Bulletin of Missionary Research* 20:2, pp. 76–81.

Bennett, Clinton (1997) 'Islam and Muhammad Iqbal', pp. 127–43, in *Modern Spiritualities: An Inquiry* edited by Laurence Brown, Bernard C. Farr and R. Joseph Hoffmann, Amherst, NY, Prometheus.

Bennett, Clinton (1998) *In Search of Muhammad*, London, Cassell.

Besant, Annie (1899) *Dharma: Three Lectures*, Madras, Theosophical Society.

Bhabha, Homi K. (1994) *The Location of Culture*, London and New York, Routledge.

Blavatsky, Helena Petrovna (1896) *The Key to Theosophy*, New York, Theosophical Publishing, 2nd edn.

Blavatsky, Helena Petrovna (1995) *Isis Unveiled*, Pasadena, CA, The Theosophical University Press. First published 1877.

Borg, Marcus J. (1994) *Meeting Jesus Again for the First Time: The Historical Jesus and the Heart of Contemporary Faith*, San Francisco, HarperSanFrancisco.

Borg, Marcus J. (1997) *Jesus and Buddha: The Parallel Sayings*, Berkeley, CA, Ulysses Press.

Borg, Marcus J. (1998) *Conflict, Holiness and Politics in the Teachings of Jesus*, Harrisburg, PA, Trinity Press, 2nd edn.

Borg, Marcus J. and Wright, Norman T. (1999) *The Meaning of Jesus: Two Visions*, San Francisco, HarperSanFrancisco.

Borg, Marcus J., Crossan, John D. and Johnson, Luke T. (2000) *Jesus at 2000: The e.mail Debate*. www.xtalk.org/j2000/debate.html.

Bornkamm, Günther (1960) *Jesus of Nazareth*, translated by Irene and Fraser McLuskey with James M. Robinson, London, Hodder & Stoughton.

Bowden, John Stephen (1988) *Jesus: The Unanswered Questions*, London, SCM Press.

Braaten, Carl E. (1983) 'Introduction', pp. 7–29, in *The Resurrection of Jesus* by Pinchas Lapide, Minneapolis, Augsburg Publishing House.

Brandon, Samuel George F. (1967) *Jesus and the Zealots: A Study of Political Factors in Primitive Christianity*, Manchester, Manchester University Press.

Braudel, Fernand (1993) *A History of Civilization*, Harmondsworth, Penguin.

Braybrooke, Marcus (1992) *Pilgrimage of Hope: One Hundred Years of Global Interfaith Dialogue*, London, SCM Press.

Bright, John (1972) *A History of Israel*, London, SCM, revised edn.

Brown, Raymond E. (1971) *The Birth of the Messiah: A Commentary on the Infancy Narratives in Matthew and Luke*, Garden City, NY, Doubleday.

Brown, Raymond E. (1994) *The Death of the Messiah: From Gethsemane to the Grave: A Commentary on the Passion Narrative in the Four Gospels*, New York, Doubleday.

Buber, Martin (1951) *Two Types of Faith*, translated by Norman P. Goldhawk, London, Routledge & Kegan Paul.

Bukhari, Imam (1986) *Sahih al Bukhari*, 9 vols, translated by Mohammed Muhsin Khan, Lahore, Kazi Publications, 6th edn.

Bultmann, Rudolf (1952) *Theology of the New Testament*, translated by Kendrick Grobel, London, SCM Press.

Bultmann, Rudolf (1958a) *Jesus and the Word*, translated by Louise Pettibone Smith and Ermine Huntress Lantero, London, Collins. First published in German 1934.

Bultmann, Rudolf (1958b) *Jesus Christ and Mythology*, New York, Scribner.

Bultmann, Rudolf (1969) *Faith and Understanding*, edited and with an Introduction by Robert Funk, translated by Louise Pettibone Smith, London, SCM Press.

Bultmann, Rudolf (1971) 'Foreword', pp. xi–xii, in *Jesus' Proclamation of the Kingdom of God* by J. Weiss, London, SCM Press.

Bundy, Walter E. (1922) *The Psychic Health of Jesus*, New York, Macmillan.

Burridge, Richard A. (1992) *What Are the Gospels? A Comparison with Graeco-Roman Biography*, Cambridge, Cambridge University Press.

Camara, Helder (1974) 'Violence – the only way?', pp. 139–44, in *A Reader in Political Theology* edited by Alistair Key, London, SCM Press.

Campbell, Joseph (1949) *The Hero with a Thousand Faces*, Princeton, NJ, Princeton University Press.

Campbell, Joseph (1991) *Power of Myth: Joseph Campbell with Bill Moyers*, New York, Anchor Books/Doubleday.

Carrithers, Michael (1983) *The Buddha*, Oxford, Oxford University Press.

Carse, James P. (1997) *The Gospel of the Beloved Disciple*, San Francisco, HarperSanFrancisco.

Case, Shirley J. (1927) *Jesus: A New Biography*, Chicago, University of Chicago Press.

Chadwick, Henry (ed. and trans.) (1953) *Origen, Contra Celsus*, Cambridge, Cambridge University Press.

Chadwick, Henry (1967) *The Early Church*, Harmondsworth, Penguin.

Chadwick, Owen (1964) *The Reformation*, Harmondsworth, Penguin.

Chamberlain, Houston S. (1910) *Foundations of the Nineteenth Century*, 2 vols, translated by John Lees, New York, John Lane & Co. First published in German 1899.

Chandra, Vikram (1995) *red earth and pouring rain*, Boston, Little, Brown and Co.

Chubb, Thomas (1738) *The Gospel of Jesus Christ Asserted*, London, printed for Tho. Cox.

Clarke, James Freeman (1871) *Ten Great Religions: An Essay in Comparative Theology*, Boston, J. R. Osgood & Co.

Clement of Alexandria (1885) *Stromata*, Anti-Nicene Fathers, translated by Ernest Wallis, Vol. 2, Grand Rapids, Calvin College Christian Classics Ethereal Library. www.ccel.org/fathers2/ANF-02/anf02-57.htm.

Cohen, A. (1949) *Everyman's Talmud*, New York, Schocken Books.

Cone, James H. (1986) *A Black Theology of Liberation*, Maryknoll, NY, Orbis, 2nd edn.

Conze, Edward (1959) *Buddhist Scriptures*, Harmondsworth, Penguin.

Cornwell, R. D. (1980) *World History in the Twentieth Century*, London, Longman.

Cracknell, Kenneth (1986) *Towards A New Relationship: Christians and People of Other Faiths*, London, Epworth Press.

Cragg, Kenneth (1994) 'Introduction', pp. 11–30, to *City of Wrong: A Friday in Jerusalem* by M. Kamal Hussein, Oxford, Oneworld.

Crone, Patricia (1987) *Meccan Trade and the Rise of Islam*, Princeton, NJ, Princeton University Press.

Crone, Patricia and Cook, Michael (1977) *Hagarism: The Making of the Islamic World*, Cambridge, Cambridge University Press.

Cross, F. L. and Livingstone, E. A. (eds) (1983) *The Oxford Dictionary of the Christian Church*, Oxford, Oxford University Press.

Crossan, John D. (1991) *The Historical Jesus: The Life of a Mediterranean Jewish Peasant*, San Francisco, HarperCollins.

Crossan, John D. (1994) *Jesus: A Revolutionary Biography*, San Francisco, HarperSanFrancisco.

Crossan, John D. (1995) *Who Killed Jesus?*, San Francisco, HarperSanFrancisco.

Crossan, John D. (1996) *Who Is Jesus? Answers to Your Questions about the Historical Jesus*, New York, HarperPaperbacks.

Crossan, John D. (1999) 'The meaning of Jesus', *Books and Culture: A Christian Review*, March/April, pp. 40–2.

Cunliffe-Jones, Herbert (1970) *Christian Theology Since 1600*, London, Gerald Duckworth.

Cyprian (1885) *Three Books of Testimonies against the Jews*, translated by Ernest Wallis, Anti-Nicene Fathers, Vol. 5, Grand Rapids, Calvin College Christian Classics Ethereal Library. www.ccel.org/fathers2/ANF-05/anf05-122.htm.

Dalai Lama, His Holiness the 14th (1996) *The Good Heart: A Buddhist Perspective on the Teaching of Jesus*, edited by Robert Kiely, Boston, Wisdom Publications.

Dalai Lama, His Holiness the 14th (2000) 'The karma of the Gospel', *Newsweek*, 27 March, p. 56.

Dante Alighieri (1984) *The Divine Comedy* Vol. 1: *Inferno*, translated by Mark Musa, Harmondsworth, Penguin.

Davidson, Basil (1986) *The Story of Africa*, London, BBC Books.

Deardorff, James W. (1994) *Jesus in India: A Re-examination of Jesus' Asian Traditions in the Light of Evidence Supporting Re-incarnation*, San Francisco, International Scholars Publications.

Deardorff, James W. (1998) *Survival of the Crucifixion: Traditions of Jesus within Islam, Buddhism, Hinduism and Paganism.* www.proaxis,com/~deardorj/legends.htm.

Delavignette, Robert (1964) *Christianity and Colonialism*, London, Burns & Oates.

Derrett, J. Duncan (1999) 'An Indian metaphor in St John's Gospel', *Journal of the Royal Asiatic Society*, 3rd series, 9:2, pp. 271–86.

Doherty, Earl (1999a) 'Review of John Shelby Spong's *Liberating the Gospels*'. www.magi.com/~oblio/Jesus/spongrev.htm.

Doherty, Earl (1999b) *The Jesus Puzzle: Did Christianity Begin with a Mythical Christ? Challenging the Existence of an Historical Jesus*, Ottawa, Canadian Humanist Publications.

Donahue, John R. (1994) 'From crucified Messiah to risen Christ: The trial of Jesus revisited', pp. 93–121, 135, in *Jews and Christians Speak of Jesus* edited by Arthur E. Zannoni, Minneapolis, Fortress Press.

Dowling, Levi H. (1979) *The Aquarian Gospel of Jesus the Christ*, Marina Del Rey, CA, Devors & Co. First published 1911.

Downing, Gerald F. (1992) *Cynics and Christian Origins*, Edinburgh, T. & T. Clark.

Drews, Arthur (1998) *The Christ Myth*, translated by C. Delisle Burns, Amherst, NY, Prometheus.

Drosnin, Michael (1997) *The Bible Code*, New York, Simon and Schuster.

Duchesne-Guillemin, Jacques (1973) *Religion of Ancient Iran*, Bombay, Tata Press.

Edgar, L. I. A. (1940) *A Jewish View of Jesus*, London, The Liberal Jewish Synagogue.

Eisenmann, Robert (1998) *James, Brother of Jesus: The Key to Unlocking the Secret of Early Christianity and the Dead Sea Scrolls*, Harmondsworth, Penguin.

Ellis, Marc H. (1994) *Ending Auschwitz: The Future of Jewish and Christian Life*, Louisville, KT, Westminster/John Knox Press.

Embree, Ainslee T. (1962) *Charles Grant and British Rule in India*, London, Allen & Unwin.

Embree, Ainslee T. (ed.) (1988) *Sources of Indian Tradition*, Vol. 1, New York, Columbia University Press, 2nd edn.

Enelow, Hyman G. (1920) *A Jewish View of Jesus*, New York, Macmillan.

Epstein, Isidore (ed. and trans.) (1935) *The Babylonian Talmud: Translated into English with Notes*, 18 vols, London, Soncino Press.

Esack, Farid (1997) *Qur'an, Liberation and Pluralism: An Islamic Perspective of Interreligious Solidarity against Oppression*, Oxford, Oneworld.

Evans, Craig A. (1997) 'Images of Christ in the canonical and apocryphal gospels', pp. 34–72, in *Images of Christ: Ancient and Modern* edited by Stanley E. Porter *et al.*, Sheffield, Sheffield Academic Press.

Farquhar, John N. (1913) *The Crown of Hinduism*, London, Humphrey Milford/ Oxford University Press.

Farrar, Frederick W. (1996) *The Life of Christ*, London, Cassell.

Finkel, Asher (1964) *The Pharisees and the Teacher of Nazareth*, Leiden, E. J. Brill.

Fiorenza, Elizabeth S. (1992) *But She Said: Feminist Practices of Biblical Interpretation*, Boston, Beacon Press.

Fiorenza, Elizabeth S. (1994) *Jesus: Miriam's Child, Sophia's Prophet: Critical Issues in Feminist Christology*, New York, Continuum Publishing Group.

Fiorenza, Elizabeth S. (1998) *Sharing Her Word: Feminist Interpretations in Context*, Boston, Beacon Press.

Flood, Gavin (1996) *Introduction to Hinduism*, Cambridge, Cambridge University Press.

Flusser, David (1997) *Jesus*, Jerusalem, The Magnes Press, The Hebrew University. First published 1968.

Fortna, Robert T. (1970) *The Gospel of Signs: A Reconstruction of the Narrative Source Underlying the Fourth Gospel*, Cambridge, Cambridge University Press.

Forward, Martin (2000) 'Report on MS of *In Search of Jesus* by Clinton Bennett', for Continuum International Publishing Group, July.

Fox, Matthew (1988) *The Coming of the Cosmic Christ: The Healing of Mother Earth and the Birth of a Global Renaissance*, San Francisco, Harper & Row.

Frazer, James G. (1994) *The Golden Bough: A New Abridgement*, edited by Robert Fraser, London and New York, Oxford University Press. First published 1890.

Fredriksen, Paula (1988) *From Jesus to Christ: The Origin of the New Testament Images of Jesus*, New Haven, CT, Yale University Press.

Fredriksen, Paula (1994) 'From Jesus to Christ: the contribution of the Apostle Paul', pp. 77–91, in *Jews and Christians Speak of Jesus* edited by Arthur E. Zannoni, Minneapolis, Fortress Press.

Freeman, Laurence (1996) 'Introduction', pp. 1–32, in *The Good Heart* by the 14th Dalai Lama, Boston, Wisdom Publications.

Freud, Sigmund (1990) *The Origin of Religion*, translated by James Strachey, Harmondsworth, Penguin.

Funk, Robert W. (1985) 'The issue of Jesus'. www.westarinstitute.org/ Jesus_Seminar/Remarks/remarks.html.

Funk, Robert W. (1996) *Honest to Jesus: Jesus for a New Millennium*, San Francisco, HarperSanFrancisco.

Funk, Robert W. and the Jesus Seminar (1998) *The Acts of Jesus: The Search for the Authentic Acts of Jesus*, San Francisco, SanFranciscoHarper.

Funk, Robert W., Hoover, Ray W. and the Jesus Seminar (1993) *The Five Gospels: The Search for the Authentic Words of Jesus*, New York, Macmillan.

Gandhi, Mohandas K. (1940) *The Message of Jesus Christ*, Bombay, Bharitiya Vidya Bhavan.

Gandhi, Mohandas K. (1941) *Christian Missions: Their Place in India*, Ahmedabad, Navajivan Press.

Gandhi, Mohandas K. (1980) *The Bhagvadgita*, New Delhi, Orient Paperbacks.

Gandhi, Mohandas K. (1982) *An Autobiography, or the Story of My Experiments with Truth*, Harmondsworth, Penguin.

Gardner, Laurence (1996) *Bloodline of the Holy Grail: The Hidden Lineage of Jesus Revealed*, Shaftesbury, Dorset, Element Books.

Geiger, Abraham (1875) 'Celsus', *Jüdische Zeitschrift für Wissenschaft und Leben* 10, p. 182.

Geiger, Abraham (1911) *Judaism and Its History*, translated by Charles Newburgh, New York, The Bloch Publishing Co. First published in German 1863.

Geiger, Abraham (1968) 'Denkschrift', pp. 166–7, in *Prayerbook Reform in Europe* by Jacob Petuchowski, New York, World Union for Progressive Judaism. First published in German 1865.

Gellner, David (1996) 'Review of Clinton Bennett's *In Search of the Sacred*', *Discernment: An Ecumenical Journal of Inter-religious Encounter*, NS 3:2, pp. 46–7.

George, Timothy (1997) 'Evangelicals and Catholics together: a new initiative', *Christianity Today* 41:14, 8 December, p. 34.

Glassé, Cyril (ed.) (1991) *The Concise Encyclopaedia of Islam*, London, Stacey International.

Goddard, Dwight (1970) *A Buddhist Bible*, Boston, Beacon Press.

Goel, Ram Sita (1997) 'Defining religion: Ram Sita Goel answers the questions raised in the Antaios' Appeal number on Hindutva', New Delhi, *Observer*, 22 February; at www.voi.org.

Goldberg, David J. and Raynor, John D. (1989) *The Jewish People: Their History and Their Religion*, Harmondsworth, Penguin.

Goldman, David P. (1999) *Has Franz Rosenzweig's Time Come?* www.jcrelations.net/articl1/goldman1.htm.

Gombrich, Richard (1971) *Precept and Practice: Traditional Buddhism in the Rural Highlands of Ceylon*, Oxford, Oxford University Press.

Gombrich, Richard (1988) *Theravada Buddhism: A Social History from Ancient Banares to Modern Colombo*, London, Routledge.

Gordon, Alexander (1932) 'Robert Taylor', pp. 461–3, in *Dictionary of National Biography*, Vol. XIX, London, Oxford University Press.

Goswamy, S. D. (1980) *Sraila Prabhupada – Lailaamtra: A Biography of His Divine Grace A. C. Bhaktivedanta Swami Prabhupaada*, Los Angeles, Bhakitvedanta Book Trust.

Goulder, Michael (1974) *Midrash and Lection in Matthew: The Speaker's Lectures in Biblical Studies, 1969–71*, London, SPCK.

Goulder, Michael (1995) *St Paul versus St Peter: A Tale of Two Missions*, Louisville, KT, Westminster/John Knox Press.

Graham, David J. (1997) 'Christ imagery in recent film: a saviour from celluloid?', pp. 306–14, in *Images of Christ: Ancient and Modern* edited by Stanley E. Porter, Michael A. Hayes and David Tombs, Sheffield, Sheffield Academic Press.

Graham, Phylis (1974) *The Jesus Hoax*, London, Frewin.

Granberg-Michaelson, Wesley (2000) 'Letter to the Editor on "Visions of Jesus"', *Newsweek*, 17 April, p. 17.

Grant, Charles (1792) *Observations on the State of Society among the Asiatic Subjects of Great Britain*, London, Parliamentary Papers.

Graves, Kersey (1971) *The World's Sixteen Crucified Saviors, Or, Christianity Before Christ*, The Truth Seeker Company; New Hyde Park, NY, University Books. First published 1875.

Grey, James M. (1910) 'The inspiration of the Bible: definition, extent and proof', *The Fundamentals*, 3, pp. 7–41.

Griffiths, Bede (1982) *The Marriage of East and West*, London, HarperCollins.

Griffiths, Paul J. (ed.) (1990) *Christianity through Non-Christian Eyes*, Maryknoll, NY, Orbis.

Groothuis, Douglas R. (1990) *Revealing the New Age Jesus: Challenges to Orthodox Views of Christ*, Downers Grove, IL, Inter-Varsity Press.

Gruber, Elmar R. and Kersten, Holger (1995) *The Original Jesus: The Buddhist Sources of Christianity*, Shaftesbury, Dorset, Element Books.

Guillaume, Alfred (ed. and trans.) (1955) *The Life of Muhammad: A Translation of Ibn Ishaq's Sirat Rasul Allah*, London, Oxford University Press.

Gutiérrez, Gustavo (1973) *A Theology of Liberation: History, Politics and Salvation*, translated by Caridad Inda and John Eagleson, Maryknoll, NY, Orbis.

*Η Καινη Διαθηκη* (1954) London, The British and Foreign Bible Society, 2nd edn.

Hagner, Donald A. (1997) *The Jewish Reclamation of Jesus: An Analysis and Critique of the Modern Jewish Study of Jesus*, Eugene, OR, Wipf and Stock Publishers.

Haight, Gordon S. (1968) *George Eliot: A Biography*, Oxford, Oxford University Press.

Hammer, Joshua (2000) 'An apocalyptic mystery', *Newsweek*, 3 April, pp. 46–7.

Handel, George F. (1987) *Messiah: Vocal Score*, London, Edition Peters.

Hanh, Thich Nhat (1995) *Living Buddha, Living Christ*, New York, Riverhead Books.

Harper, Susan B. (2000) *In the Shadow of the Mahatma: V. S. Azariah and the Travails of Christianity in British India*, Grand Rapids, MI, and London, Wm B. Eerdmana and Curzon Press.

Haskins, Susan (1994) *Mary Magdalene*, London, HarperCollins.

Hassnain, Fida (1994) *A Search for the Historical Jesus: From Apocryphal, Buddhist, Hindu and Sanskrit Sources*, Bath, Gateway Books.

Hayward, Isabel C. (1989) *Speaking of Christ: A Lesbian Feminist Voice*, Boston, Beacon Press.

Hegel, G. W. F. (1948) 'The spirit of Christianity and its fate', pp. 182–301, in *Early Theological Writings*, translated by T. M. Knox, Chicago, University of Chicago Press.

Henrix, Holland Lee (1998) 'A plurality of Jesuses'. www.pbs.org/wgbh/pages/frontline/shows/religion/jesus/reallyknow.html.

Heschel, Susannah (1998) *Abraham Geiger and the Jewish Jesus*, Chicago, University of Chicago Press.

Hick, John (ed.) (1977) *The Myth of God Incarnate*, London, SCM Press.

Hiers, Richard H. and Holland, David L. (1971) 'Introduction', pp. 1–54, in *Jesus' Proclamation of the Kingdom of God* by Johannes Weiss, London, SCM Press.

Higgins, Godfrey (1829) *Apology for the Life of Mohamed*, London, Rowland, Harper.

Higgins, Godfrey (1965) *Anacalypses: An Attempt to Draw Aside the Veil of Saitic Isis: Or an Enquiry into the Origins of Language, Nations and Religions*, New Hyde Park, NY, University Books. First published 1836.

Historicus (1972) *Did Jesus Ever Exist, or is Christianity Founded upon a Myth?* United Secularists of America. www.infidels.org/library/historicus/historicus/jesus.html.

Hitler, Adolf (1969) *Mein Kampf*, translated by Ralph Manheim, London, Hutchinson.

Hodgson, Peter C. (1972) 'Introduction', pp. x–l, in *The Life of Jesus Critically Examined* by D. F. Strauss, Philadelphia, Fortress Press.

Hoffmann, R. Joseph (1984) *Marcion, on the Restoration of Christianity*, Chicago, Scholars Press.

Hoffmann, R. Joseph (1986) 'Introduction: Jesus in research', pp. 11–22, in *Jesus in History and Myth* edited by R. Joseph Hoffmann and Gerald A. Larue, Buffalo, NY, Prometheus.

Hoffmann, R. Joseph (ed. and trans.) (1987) *Celsus on the True Doctrine: A Discourse against the Christians*, New York, Oxford University Press.

Hoffmann, R. Joseph (1989) 'Wealth', pp. 171–86, in *What the Bible Really Says* edited by Joseph R. Hoffmann and Morton Smith, Buffalo, NY, Prometheus.

Hoffmann, R. Joseph (1994) *Porphyry's Against the Christians*, Amherst, NY, Prometheus.

Hoffmann, R. Joseph (1996) *The Secret Gospels: A Harmony of Apocryphal Jesus Traditions*, Buffalo, NY, Prometheus.

Hoffmann, R. Joseph and Larue, Gerald A. (1986) *Jesus in History and Myth*, Buffalo, NY, Prometheus.

Hoffmann, R. Joseph and Smith, Morton (eds) (1989) *What the Bible Really Says*, Buffalo, NY, Prometheus.

Hogg, Alfred G. (1939) 'The Christian attitude to non-Christian faiths', pp. 102–25, in *The Authority of the Faith* (Tambaram Series), New York, International Missionary Council.

Holmes, John H. (1927) 'Introduction', pp. 15–23, in *The Life of Jesus* by Ernest Renan, New York, The Modern Library.

Horbury, William (1998a) *Jewish Messianism and the Cult of Christ*, London, SCM Press.

Horbury, William (1998b) *Jews and Christians in Contact and Dialogue*, Edinburgh, T. & T. Clark.

Horsley, Richard A. (1989) *The Liberation of Christmas: The Infancy Narratives in Social Context*, New York, Crossroads.

Horsley, Richard A. (1993) *Jesus and the Spiral of Violence: Popular Jewish Resistance in Roman Palestine*, Minneapolis, Fortress Press.

Hume, David (1963) *Hume on Religion*, edited by Richard Wollheim, Cleveland and New York, Meridian.

Hunter, Archibald M. (1969) *Bible and Gospel*, London, SCM Press.

Hunter, Archibald M. (1972) *Introducing the New Testament*, London, SCM Press, 3rd edn.

Hussein, M. Kamal (1994) *City of Wrong: A Friday in Jerusalem*, translated by Kenneth Cragg, Oxford, Oneworld.

Ibn 'Arabi, Abu Bakr Muhammad Muhyi-d-Din (1980) *The Bezels of Wisdom*, translated by R. W. J. Austin, New York, The Paulist Press.

Isenberg, Wesley W. (1990) *The Gospel of Philip*, The Gnostic Society Library, Los Angeles. www.gnosis.org/naghamm/gop.html.

Jackson, Carl T. (1994) *Vedanta for the West: The Ramakrishna Movement in the United States*, Bloomington and Indianapolis, Indiana University Press.

James, M. R. (1924a) *The Acts of Thomas*, The Gnostic Society Library, Los Angeles. http://www.gnosis.org/library/actthom.htm.

James, M. R. (1924b) *The Infancy Gospel of Thomas*, The Gnostic Society Library, Los Angeles. http://www.gnosis.org/~gnosis/library/inftoma.htm.

Jefferson, Thomas (1975) *Thomas Jefferson's Life of Jesus: Bicentennial Edition*, Springfield, IL, Templegate Publishers.

Jeremias, Joachim (1957) *Unknown Sayings of Jesus*, translated by Reginald H. Fuller, London, SCM Press.

Johnson, Luke T. (1996) *The Real Jesus: The Misguided Quest for the Historical Jesus and the Truth of the Traditional Gospel*, San Francisco, HarperSanFrancisco.

Johnson, Paul (1987) *A History of the Jews*, London, Weidenfeld & Nicolson.

Jones, Eli S. (1925) *The Christ of the Indian Road*, Cincinnati, OH, The Abingdon Press.

Jones, Eli S. (1948) *Mahatma Gandhi: An Interpretation*, London, Hodder & Stoughton.

Jones, Lewis B. (1939a) *Christianity Explained to Muslims*, Calcutta, YMCA Press.

Jones, Lewis B. (1939b) *The People of the Mosque*, Calcutta, YMCA Press, 2nd edn.

Jones, Sir William (1799–1801) *Asiatic Researches*, London, G. G. and J. Robinson.

Josephus, Flavius (1987) *The Works of Flavius Josephus*, translated by William Whiston. wesley.nnu.edu/josephus.

Justin Martyr (1885a) *The First Apology of Justin*, Anti-Nicene Fathers, translated by Ernest Wallis, Vol. 1, Grand Rapids, MI, Calvin College Christian Classics Ethereal Library. www.ccel.org/fathers2/ANF-01/TOC.htm.

Justin Martyr (1885b) *The Second Apology of Justin*, Anti-Nicene Fathers, translated by Ernest Wallis, Vol. 1, Grand Rapids, MI, Calvin College Christian Classics Ethereal Library. www.ccel.org/fathers2/ANF-01/anf01–47.htm.

Justin Matryr (1885c) *Dialogue of Justin, Philosopher and Martyr, with Trypho, a Jew*, Anti-Nicene Fathers, translated by Ernest Wallis, Grand Rapids, Calvin College Christian Classics Ethereal Library. www.ccel.org/fathers2/ANF-01/anf01–48.htm.

Kant, Immanuel (1960) *Religion within the Limits of Reason Alone*, translated by Theodore M. Greene and Hoyt H. Hudson, New York, Harper. First published in German 1793.

Kaplan, Steven (1992) *The Beta Israel (Falasha) in Ethiopia from Earliest Times to the Twentieth Century*, New York, New York University Press.

Käsemann, Ernst (1964) *Essays on New Testament Themes*, Philadelphia, Fortress Press. First published in German in 1954.

Kazantzakis, Nikos (1961) *The Last Temptation of Christ*, translated by P. A. Dien, Oxford, Bruno Cassirer.

Kee, Howard Clark and Young, Franklin W. (1960) *The Living World of the New Testament*, London, Darton, Longman and Todd.

Kersten, Holger (1986) *Jesus Lived in India*, Shaftesbury, Dorset, Element Books.

Keynes, Geoffrey (ed.) (1966) *Blake: Complete Writings*, Oxford, Oxford University Press.

Kidger, Mark (1999) *The Star of Bethlehem: An Astronomer's View*, Princeton, NJ, Princeton University Press.

King, James R. (1990) 'Jesus and Joseph in Rumi's Mathnawi', *The Muslim World* LXXX:2, pp. 81–95.

King, Richard (1999) *Orientalism and Religion: Postcolonial Theory, India and the Mystic East*, London, Routledge.

Kimball, Glen (1997) *Hidden Stories of the Childhood of Jesus*, Houston, BF Publishing.

Kinsley, David (1988) *Hindu Goddesses: Visions of the Divine Feminine in the Hindu Religious Tradition*, Berkeley, University of California Press.

Klausner, Joseph (1925) *Jesus of Nazareth: His Life, Times and Teaching*, New York, Macmillan.

Klausner, Joseph (1944) *From Jesus to Paul*, London, George Allen & Unwin.

Klausner, Joseph (1977) 'The teaching of Jesus', pp. 157–93, in *Jewish Expressions of Jesus: An Anthology* edited by Trude Weiss-Rosmarin, New York, Ktav Publishing.

Knight, Christopher and Lomas, Robert (1997) *The Hiram Key: Pharaohs, Freemasons and the Discovery of the Dead Sea Scrolls*, Shaftesbury, Dorset, Element Books.

Knight, Christopher and Lomas, Robert (1998) *The Second Messiah: The Turin Shroud and the Great Secret of Freemasonry*, Shaftesbury, Dorset, Element Books.

Lactantius, Caecilius Firmianus (1885) *The Divine Institutes*, Anti-Nicene Fathers, Vol. 7, translated by William Fletcher, Grand Rapids, MI, Calvin College Christian Classics Ethereal Library. www.ccel.org/fathers2/ANF-07/.

Lahaye, Tim and Jenkins, Jerry (1999) *The Assassins (Left Behind)*, Wheaton, IL, Tyndale House.

Langridge, Irene (1904) *William Blake*, London, George Bell.

Lao, D. C. (ed.) (1979) *Confucius: The Analects*, Harmondsworth, Penguin.

Lapide, Pinchas (1983) *The Resurrection of Jesus*, translated by Wilhelm C. Linss, Minneapolis, Augsburg Publishing House. First published 1979.

Las Casas, Bartolomé de (1909) *Very Brief Account of the Destruction of the Indies*, translated by F. A. MacNutt, Cleveland, Arthur H. Clark Co.

Laski, Harold J. (1949) 'John Mackinnon Robertson', pp. 736–8, in *Dictionary of National Biography, 1931–1940*, Oxford, Oxford University Press.

Lauterbach, Jacob Z. (1977) 'Jesus in the Talmud', pp. 1–98, in *Jewish Expressions of Jesus: An Anthology*, edited by Trude Weiss-Rosmarin, New York, Ktav Publishing.

Lawrence, David H. (1928) *The Man Who Died*, New York, James Laughlin, The New Classics.

Layton, Bentley (1987) *The Gnostic Gospels: A New Translation*, London, SCM.

Leibowitz, Hahama (1980) *Studies in the Pentateuch*, 5 vols, Jerusalem, World Zionist Organization.

Leirvik, Oddbjørn (1999) *Images of Jesus Christ in Islam*, Uppsala, Swedish Institute of Missionary Research.

Lessing, Gotthold E. (1779) *Nathan der Weise*, Berlin, C. F. Voss.

Lessing, Gotthold E. (1956) *Lessing's Theological Writings: Selections in Translation*, with introductory essay by Henry Chadwick, London, Adam and Charles Black.

Leo, John (2000) 'A penitent Pope', *US News & World Report*, 27 March, p. 14.

Lewis, Clive S. (1947) *Miracles*, London, Fount.

Lillie, Arthur (1909) *India in Primitive Christianity*, London, Kegan Paul, Trench, Trübner & Co.

Lillie, Arthur (1997) *Buddhism in Christendom: Or, Jesus the Essene*, New Delhi, Unity Book Service. First published 1887.

Lincoln, C. Eric (1994) *The Black Muslims in America*, Grand Rapids, MI, William B. Eerdmans Publishing Co, 3rd edn.

Lindsey, Hal and Carlson, C. C. (1970) *The Late Great Planet Earth*, Grand Rapids, MI, Zondervan.

Lockhart, Douglas (1997) *Jesus the Heretic: Freedom and Bondage in a Religious World*, Shaftesbury, Dorset, Element Books.

Longley, Peter (1997) *Two Thousand Years Later*, Minnetonka, MN, Hovenden Press.

Lord, Albert (1960) *The Singer of Tales*, New York, Atheneum Press.

Lunenfeld, Marvin (1991) *1492: Discovery, Invasion, Encounter. Sources and Interpretation*, Lexington, MA, D. C. Heath and Co.

Luther, Martin (1957) '95 Theses', pp. 17–23, in *Luther's Works*, Vol. 31, translated by C. M. Jacobs and revised by Harold J. Grimm, Philadelphia, PA, Mohlenberg Press. First published in German 1517.

Luther, Martin (1962) 'That Jesus was born a Jew', pp. 199–229, in *Luther's Works*, Vol. 45, edited and translated by Walther Brandt, Philadelphia, Mohlenberg Press. First published in German 1523.

Luther, Martin (1971), 'On the Jews and their lies', pp. 137–306, in *Luther's Works*, Vol. 47, translated by Martin H. Bertram and edited by Franklin Sherman, Philadelphia, Mohlenberg Press. First published in German 1543.

McCabe, Joseph (1897) *Twelve Years in a Monastery*, London, Watts & Co.

McCabe, Joseph (1909) *Modern Rationalism: A Sketch of the Progress of the Rationalist Spirit in the 19th Century*, London, Watts & Co. First published 1897.

McCabe, Joseph (1920) *A Biographical Dictionary of Ancient, Medieval and Modern Freethinkers*, London, Watts & Co.

McCabe, Joseph (1929) *The Key to Love and Sex*, Girad, KS, Haldeman-Julius.

McCabe, Joseph (1930) *The Story of Religious Controversy*, Boston, Stratford Publishing.

McCabe, Joseph (1942a), *The Vatican's Last Crime*, London, The Black Internationalist, No. 1.

McCabe, Joseph (1942b) *The Totalitarian Church of Rome*, London, The Black Internationalist, No. 11.

McCabe, Joseph (1942c) *The Tyranny of the Clerical Gestapo: Catholics and the Most Priest Ridden of All People*, London, The Black Internationalist, No. 12.

McCabe, Joseph (1943) *How Christianity Grew out of Paganism*, Little Blue Book 1775, Girard, KS, Haldeman-Julius.

McCabe, Joseph (1946) *The Testament of Christian Civilization*, London, Watt & Co.

McCabe, Joseph (1993) *The Forgery of the Old Testament and Other Essays*, Buffalo, NY, Prometheus, Free Thought Library.

McCutcheon, Russell (1999) *The Insider/Outsider Problem in the Study of Religion*, London, Cassell.

McDowell, Josh (1989) *Christianity, Hoax or History?*, Wheaton, IL, Tyndale House.

McDowell, Josh (1993) *Evidence That Demands a Verdict: Historical Evidence of the Christian Faith*, Nashville, TN, Thomas Nelson.

Mackenzie, Donald A. (1994) *India: Myths and Legends*, London, Senate/Studio Editions.

McKnight, Gerald (1964) *Verdict on Schweitzer*, London, Frederick Miller.

MacLaine, Shirley (1989) *Going Within*, New York, Bantam Press.

McNally, Terrence (1998) *Corpus Christi: A Play*, New York, Grove/Atlanta.

Maccoby, Hyam (1995) *Jewish Views of Jesus*, London, Middlesex University Centre for Inter-Faith Dialogue.

Machovec, Milan (1976) *A Marxist Looks at Jesus*, London, Darton, Longman and Todd.

Mack, Burton L. (1988) *A Myth of Innocence: Mark and Christian Origins*, Philadelphia, Fortress Press.

Mack, Burton L. (1993) *The Lost Gospel: The Book of Q and Christian Origins*, San Francisco, HarperSanFrancisco.

Mack, Burton L. (1995) *Who Wrote the New Testament: The Making of the Christian Myth*, San Francisco, HarperCollins.

Majumdar, Romesh Chandra (1951) *History and Culture of the Indian Peoples*, Vol. 9, Bombay, Bharatya Vidya Bhavan.

Marley, Robert N. (1984) *Legend*, compact disc, London, Island Records.

Marley, Robert N. (1995) *Natural Mystic*, compact disc, London, Island Records.

Marmur, Dow (1998) *Jesus and the Jews – Today*, Lecture given at Holy Blossom Temple, Toronto, Canada, 21 January. www.jcrelations.com/articl1/marmur1.htm.

Marrs, Texe (1998) *Mystery Mark of the New Age: Satan's Designs for World Domination*, Westchester, IL, Crossway Books.

Marsden, Victor E. (trans.) (1922) *The Protocols of the Learned Elders of Zion*, London, Britons Publishing.

Marshall, George and Poling, David (2000) *Schweitzer: A Biography*, Balitmore, Johns Hopkins University Press. First published 1971.

Marshall, Ian H. (1976) *The Origins of New Testament Christology*, Downers Grove, IL, Inter-Varsity Press.

Marshall, Ian H. (1977) *I Believe in the Historical Jesus*, Grand Rapids, MI, Eerdmans Publishing Co.

Martin, Michael (1993) *The Case against Christianity*, Philadelphia, Temple University Press, 2nd edn.

Mathews, Shailer (1897) *The Social Teachings of Jesus: An Essay in Christology*, New York, Macmillan.

Maurice, Frederick D. (1846) *The Religions of the World*, London, Macmillan.

Meier, John P. (1991) *A Marginal Jew: Rethinking the Historical Jesus: The Roots of the Problem and the Person*, New York, Doubleday.

Merton, Thomas (1973) *The Asian Journal of Thomas Merton*, edited by Naomi Burton, Patrick Hart and James Laughlin, New York, New Directions.

Miller, Barbara Stoler (1986) *The Bhagavad-Gita*, New York, Bantam Books.

Miller, Joel (1999) 'Letter to the Editor on "The way the world ends"', *Newsweek*, 22 November, p. 20.

Mitchell, Stephen (1988) *Tao Te Ching: A New English Version*, San Francisco, HarperPerennial.

Mohammed, Ovey M. (1993) 'Jesus and Krishna', pp. 9–24, in *Asian Faces of Jesus* edited by R. S. Sugirtharajah, London, SCM Press.

Molnar, Michael R. (1999) *The Star of Bethlehem: The Legacy of the Magi*, New Brunswick, NJ, Rutgers University Press.

Montefiore, Claude J. G. (1910) *The Religious Teaching of Jesus*, London, Macmillan.

Montefiore, Claude J. G. (1923) *The Old Testament and After*, London, Macmillan.

Montefiore, Claude J. G. (1970) *Rabbinical Literature and Gospel Teaching*, London, Macmillan.

Montefiore, Hugh (1983) *The Church and the Jews: A Lent Lecture*, Birmingham, The Additional Curates Society.

Moore, George (1861) *The Lost Tribes and the Saxons . . . with New Views on Buddhism . . . and Translations of the Rock-Records*, London, Longman and Roberts.

Morgan, Robert (1989) 'Rudolf Bultmann', pp. 109–33, in *The Modern Theologians* edited by David Ford, Oxford, Blackwell.

Muir, Sir William (1894) *The Life of Mahomet*, London, Smith, Elder & Co, 3rd edn.

Müller, F. Max (1873) *Introduction to the Science of Religion*, London, Longmans & Co.

Müller, F. Max (1892) *Anthropological Religion*, London, Longmans & Co.

Müller, F. Max (1900) *Sri Ramakrishna, His Life and Sayings*, London, Longmans, Green & Co.

Müller, F. Max (1976) *Keshub Chunder Sen*, edited by Nanda Mookerjee, Calcutta, S. Gupta.

Musser, Donald W. and Price, Joseph L. (eds) (1992) *A New Handbook of Christian Theology*, Cambridge, The Lutterworth Press.

Nahor, Pierre (1905) *Life of Jesus*, Berlin, W. Bloch.

Narayan, R. K. (1972) *The Ramayan: A Shortened Modern Prose Version of the Indian Epic*, Harmondsworth, Penguin.

Narayan, R. K. (1978) *The Mahabharata: A Shortened Modern Prose Version of the Great Indian Epic*, London, Heinemann.

Nasr, Seyyed H. (1994) *Ideas and Realities of Islam*, London, The Aquarian Press.

Nehru, Jawaharlal (1946) *The Discovery of India*, Calcutta, The Signet Press.

Neill, Stephen (1964) *A History of Christian Missions*, Harmondsworth, Penguin.

Neusner, Jacob (1987) *What Is Midrash?* Philadelphia, Fortress Press.

Neusner, Jacob (2000) 'A Rabbi argues with Jesus', *Newsweek*, 27 March, p. 57.

*New International Version of the Holy Bible* (1973) London, Hodder & Stoughton.

Nicholson, Reynold E. (1995) *Rumi: Poet and Mystic*, Oxford, Oneworld Press.

Niebuhr, H. Richard (1951) *Christ and Culture*, New York, Harper & Row.

Niebuhr, Reinhold (1943) *The Nature and Destiny of Man: A Christian Interpretation*, 2 vols, New York, C. Scribner & Sons.

Nikhilanda, Swami (1942) *The Gospel of Ramakrishna*, New York, Ramakrishna-Vivekananda Center.

Notovitch, Nicolas (1984) 'The unknown life of Jesus Christ', pp. 89–190, in *The Lost Years of Jesus* by Elizabeth Clare Prophet, Livingston, MT, Summit University Press. First published 1894.

Nurbakhsh, Javad (1982) *Jesus in the Eyes of the Sufis*, London, Khaniqahi-Nimatullahi Publications.

O'Connor, Daniel (1998) 'Monchanin, Jules (Para-Arubi-Ananda)', p. 467, in *Biographical Dictionary of Christian Missions* edited by Gerald H. Anderson, New York, Simon & Schuster.

O'Flaherty, Wendy D. (1976) *Hindu Myths*, Harmondsworth, Penguin.

Olcott, Henry S. (1881) *The Buddhist Catechism*, Madras, Theosophical Society.

Orr, James (1910) 'The virgin birth of Christ', *The Fundamentals*, 1, pp. 1–28.

*Outline of the Divine Principle (Level 4)* (1980) New York, Holy Spirit Association for the Unification of World Christianity.

*Oxford English Dictionary, The* (1929) London, Oxford University Press.

Pagels, Elaine (1979) *The Gnostic Gospels*, New York, Vintage Books.

Pagels, Elaine (1995) 'Introduction', pp. xix–xxvii, in *Living Buddha, Living Christ* by Thich Nhat Hanh, New York, Riverhead Books.

Pagels, Elaine (1999) 'The meaning of Jesus', *Books and Culture: A Christian Review*, March/April, p. 40.

Paine, Jeffrey (1988) *Father India: Westerners under the Spell of an Ancient Culture*, New York, HarperPerennial.

Panikkar, Raimundo (1981) *The Unknown Christ of Hinduism: Towards an Ecumenical Christophany*, Bangalore, Asian Trading Corporation, revised edn.

Paramananda, Swami (1923) *Christ and Oriental Ideals*, Boston, Vedanta Centre, 3rd edn.

Parrinder, Edward G. (1995) *Jesus in the Qur'an*, Oxford, Oneworld Press.

Parrinder, Edward G. (1996) *Sex in the World's Religions*, Oxford, Oneworld Press. First published 1980.

Patterson, Stephen and Meyer, Marvin (1994) *The Gospel of Thomas*, The Gnostic Library, Los Angeles. www.gnosis.org/naghamm/gosthom.htm.

Pearson, Birger E. (1996) 'The Gospel according to the Jesus Seminar', Santa Barbara, Claremont Graduate School, CA, Occasional Paper 35. www.ucsb.edu/fscf/library/pearson/seminar/home.html.

Pelikan, Jaroslav (1985) *Jesus through the Centuries: His Place in the History of Culture*, New York, Harper & Row.

Pelikan, Jaroslav (1997) *The Illustrated Jesus through the Centuries*, New Haven, CT, Yale University Press.

Perrin, Norman (1969) *What Is Redaction Criticism?*, Philadelphia, Fortress Press.

Pettifer, Julian and Bradley, Richard (1990) *Missionaries*, London, BBC Books.

Phipps, William E. (1970) *Was Jesus Married? The Distortion of Sexuality in the Christian Tradition*, New York, Harper & Row.

Phipps, William E. (1996) *The Sexuality of Jesus*, Cleveland, The Pilgrim Press.

Picknett, Lyn and Prince, Clive (1997) *The Templar Revelation: Secret Guardians of the True Identity of Christ*, London, Doubleday/Transworld Books.

Pieris, Aloysius (1993) 'The Buddha and the Christ', pp. 46–59, in *Asian Faces of Jesus*, edited by R. S. Sugirtharajah, London, SCM Press.

Porter, Stanley E., Hayes, Michael A. and Tombs, David (eds) (1997) *Images of Christ: Ancient and Modern*, Sheffield, Sheffield Academic Press.

Potts, E. Daniel (1967) *English Baptists in India, 1793–1827*, Cambridge, Cambridge University Press.

Price, John V. (1995) 'Introduction', pp. v–x, in *A Collection of the Tracts of a Certain Free Enquirer* by Peter Annet, London, Routledge; Tokyo, Thoemmes.

Price, Reynolds (1996) *The Three Gospels*, New York, Scribner.

Priestley, Joseph (1972a) 'A comparison of the Institutes of Moses with those of the Hindoos and other ancient nations', pp. 129–319, in *The Theological and Miscellaneous Works of Joseph Priestley*, Vol. 17, New York, Kraus Reprint Co. First published 1799.

Priestley, Joseph (1972b) 'Socrates and Jesus compared', pp. 400–39, in *The Theological and Miscellaneous Works of Joseph Priestley*, Vol. 7, New York, Kraus Reprint Co. First published 1803.

Priestley, Joseph (1972c) *The Theological and Miscellaneous Works of Joseph Priestley*, 25 vols, New York, Kraus Reprint Co.

Prophet, Elizabeth C. (1984) *The Lost Years of Jesus*, Livingston, MT, Summit University Press.

Pulford, Cedric (1999) 'Muslim group issues fatwa on author of gay play about Christ'. www.Christianityonline.com/ct/current/9B11/9B11d.html, Christianity Today, Inc.

Rahim, 'Ata-ur (1977) *Jesus, Prophet of Islam*, Wood Dalling Hall, Norfolk, Diwan Press.

Rauschenbusch, Walter (1916) *The Social Principles of Jesus*, New York, Grosset and Dunlap with the Women's Press.

Reeves, Joseph (1971) 'Joseph McCabe', pp. 661–2, in *Dictionary of National Biography* 1951–1960, London, Oxford University Press.

Régla, Paul de (1894) *Jesus von Nazareth*, Leipzig, A. Just.

Renan, Ernest (1852) *Averroès et l'averroïsme, essai historique*, Paris, Calmann-Levy.

Renan, Ernest (1927) *The Life of Jesus*, introduction by John Haynes Holmes, New York, The Modern Library. First published 1863.

*Revised Standard Version of the Holy Bible* (1971) London and New York, Oxford University Press, 2nd edn.

Richardson, Peter and Hurd, John C. (1984) *From Jesus to Paul*, Waterloo, Ontario, Wilfrid Laurier University Press.

Rihbany, Abraham M. (1916) *The Syrian Christ*, Boston, Houghton Mifflin Co.

Rihbany, Abraham M. (1940) *The Five Interpretations of Jesus*, Boston, Houghton Mifflin Co.

Ritschl, Albrecht (1902) *The Positive Development of the Doctrine*, translated by H. R. Mackintosh and A. B. Macauley, Edinburgh, T. & T. Clark.

Rivkin, Ellis (1986) 'Josephus on Jesus', pp. 103–18, in *Jesus in History and Myth* edited by R. Joseph Hoffmann and Gerald A. Larue, Buffalo, NY, Prometheus.

Robertson, John M. (1900) *Christianity and Mythology*, London, Rationalist Press Association/Watts & Co.

Robertson, John M. (1911) *Pagan Christs: Studies in Comparative Hierology*, London, Watts & Co, 2nd edn.

Robertson, John M. (1957) *A Short History of Freethought, Ancient and Modern*, New York, Russell and Russell.

Robinson, James M. (1959) *A New Quest of the Historical Jesus*, London, SCM.

Robinson, John A. T. (1963) *Honest to God*, London, SCM Press.

Robinson, John A. T. (1976) *Redacting the New Testament*, London, SCM Press.

Robinson, John M. (1990) *The Nag Hammadi Library in English*, San Francisco, Harper & Row.

Robson, James (1994) *Mishkat-al-Masabih*, 2 vols, Lahore, Ashraf Publishers.

Rodinson, Maxime (1961) *Mohammed*, Harmondsworth, Penguin.

Rosenzweig, Franz (1977) 'Judaism despite Christianity', pp. 410–21, in *Jewish Expressions of Jesus: An Anthology* edited by Trude Weiss-Rosmarin, New York, Ktav Publishing.

Rosenzweig, Franz (1985) *The Star of Redemption*, translated by William W. Hallo, London, University of Notre Dame Press. First published in German 1916.

Roy, Arundhati (1997) *The God of Small Things*, New York, Random House.

Roy, Rajah Ram Mohun (1828) *The Precepts of Jesus, The Guide to Peace and Happiness, Extracted from the Books of the New Testament, Ascribed to the Four Evangelists*, Boston, Christian Register Office.

Rubenstein, Richard L. (1972) *My Brother Paul*, New York, Harper & Row.

Rushdie, Salman (1981) *Midnight's Children*, London, Vintage.

Rushdie, Salman (1991) *Imaginary Homeland: Essays and Criticism 1981–1991*, London, Granta and Penguin.

Rushdie, Salman (1996) *The Moor's Last Sigh*, London, Vintage.

Rushdie, Salman (1999) *The Ground beneath Her Feet*, London, Vintage.

Russell, Bertrand (1957) *Why I Am Not a Christian, and Other Essays on Religion and Related Subjects*, New York, Simon and Schuster.

S, Acharya (1999) *The Christ Conspiracy: The Greatest Story Ever Told*, Kempton, IL, Adventures Unlimited Press.

Said, Edward (1978) *Orientalism*, Harmondsworth, Penguin.

Said, Edward (1993) *Culture and Imperialism*, New York, Vintage Books.

Saldarini, Anthony J. (1994) 'Pluralism of practice and belief in first century Judaism', pp. 13–34, in *Jews and Christians Speak of Jesus* edited by Arthur E. Zannoni, Minneapolis, Fortress Press.

Salibi, Kamal (1985) *The Bible Came from Arabia*, London, J. Cape.

Salibi, Kamal (1998) *Who Was Jesus? A Conspiracy in Jerusalem*, London, I. B. Tauris.

Samartha, Stanley J. (1991) *One Christ – Many Religions: Towards a Revised Christology*, Maryknoll, NY, Orbis.

Sanders, Edward P. (1985) *Jesus and Judaism*, Philadelphia, Fortress Press.

Sanders, Edward P. (1993) *The Historical Figure of Jesus*, Harmondsworth, Penguin.

Sanders, Edward P. (1994) 'Jesus and the first table of the Jewish law', pp. 55–73, in *Jews and Christians Speak of Jesus* edited by Arthur E. Zannoni, Minneapolis, Fortress Press.

Sandmel, Samuel (1958) *The Genius of Paul: A Study in History*, New York, Farrar, Strauss and Cudahy.

Sandmel, Samuel (1965) *We Jews and Jesus*, New York, Oxford University Press.

Sanneh, Lamin (1996) 'The Gospel, language and culture: the theological method in cultural analyses', *International Review of Mission* LXXXV:332/333, pp. 47–64.

Sarasvati, Dayananda (1990) 'The light of truth', pp. 198–203, in *Christianity through Non-Christian Eyes* edited by Paul J. Griffiths, Maryknoll, NY, Orbis.

Schaff, Philip (ed.) (1991) *A Select Library of Nicene and Post Nicene Fathers of the Christian Church*, Grand Rapids, MI, Eerdmans Publishing. First published 1888.

Schiffman, Laurence H. (1994) 'The Jewishness of Jesus: commandments concerning interpersonal relations', pp. 37–53, in *Jews and Christians Speak of Jesus* edited by Arthur E. Zannoni, Minneapolis, Fortress Press.

Schillebeeckx, Edward (1979) *Jesus: An Experiment in Christology*, translated by Herbert Hoskins, New York, Seabury Press.

Schillebeeckx, Edward (1980) *Interim Report on the Books Jesus and Christ*, London, SCM Press.

Schimmel, Annemarie (1999) 'Dreams of Jesus in the Islamic tradition', *Bulletin of the Royal Institute for Inter-Faith Studies*, Jordan, 1:1, pp. 207–12.

Schleiermacher, Friedrich E. D. (1928) *The Christian Faith*, translated by H. R. Mackintosh and J. S. Stewart, Edinburgh, T. & T. Clarke.

Schleiermacher, Friedrich (1958) *Religion: Speeches to Its Cultured Despisers*, translated by John Oman, New York, Harper Torchbooks.

Schleiermacher, Friedrich (1975) *The Life of Jesus*, edited by Jack C. Verheyden, Philadelphia, Fortress Press.

Schoeps, Hans Joachim (1977) 'The Messiahship of Jesus', pp. 194–200, in *Jewish Expressions of Jesus: An Anthology* edited by Trude Weiss-Rosmarin, New York, Ktav Publishing.

Schonfield, Hugh J. (1947) *The Jew of Tarsus: An Unorthodox Portrait of Paul*, London, Macdonald & Co.

Schonfield, Hugh J. (1955) *The Authentic New Testament*, London, Dennis Dobson.

Schonfield, Hugh J. (1957) *Secrets of the Dead Sea Scrolls: Studies towards Their Solution*, New York, A. S. Barnes and Co.

Schonfield, Hugh J. (1965) *The Passover Plot: New Light on the History of Jesus*, New York, Bernard Geis and Random House.

Schreiter, Robert (1991) *Faces of Jesus in Africa*, Maryknoll, NY, Orbis.

Schweitzer, Albert (1914) *The Mystery of the Kingdom of God: The Secret of Jesus' Messiahship and the Passion*, New York, Dodd and Mead. First published in German 1901.

Schweitzer, Albert (1923) *Christianity and the Religions of the World*, translated by Johanna Powells, New York, George H. Doran & Co.

Schweitzer, Albert (1936) *Indian Thought and Its Development*, London, Hodder & Stoughton.

Schweitzer, Albert (1948) *The Psychiatric Study of Jesus: Exposition and Criticism*, Boston, Beacon Press.

Schweitzer, Albert (1956) *On the Edge of the Primeval Forest*, New York, Macmillan.

Schweitzer, Albert (1966) *The Kingdom of God and Primitive Christianity*, New York, Seabury Press.

Schweitzer, Albert (1998a) *Out of My Life and Thought*, translated by Antje Bultmann Lemke, Baltimore, Johns Hopkins University Press.

Schweitzer, Albert (1998b) *The Quest of the Historical Jesus: A Critical Study of Its Progress from Reimarus to Wrede*, translated by W. Montgomery, London, A. & C. Black; reprinted with a new introduction by Delbert R. Hillers, Baltimore, Johns Hopkins University Press. First published in German 1910.

Seaver, George (1947) *Schweitzer: The Man and His Mind*, New York, Harper.

Segal, Allan F. (1994) 'Outlining the question: from Christ to God', pp. 125–35, in *Jews and Christians Speak of Jesus* edited by Arthur E. Zannoni, Minneapolis, Fortress Press.

Sheler, Jeffrey L. (2000) 'Hell hath no fury', *US News and World Report*, 31 January, pp. 45–50.

Shourie, Arun (1994) *Missionaries in India: Continuities, Changes, Dilemmas*, New Delhi, ASA Publications.

Siddiqui, Mona (1997) 'Images of Christ in Islam: scripture and sentiment', pp. 159–22, in *Images of Christ: Ancient and Modern* edited by Stanley E. Porter, Michael A. Hayes and David Tombs, Sheffield, Sheffield Academic Press.

Silver, Abba H. (1977) 'On rejecting treasures', pp. 344–67, in *Jewish Expressions of Jesus: An Anthology* edited by Trude Weiss-Rosmarin, New York, Ktav Publishing.

Smith, Joseph (trans.) (1830) *The Book of Mormon: Another Testament of Jesus Christ* ://scriptures/lds.org/bm/contents.

Smith, Morton (1978) *Jesus the Magician*, San Francisco, Harper & Row.

Smith, Reginald B. (1876) *Mohammed and Mohammedanism*, London, Smith, Elder.

Smith, Steve (2000) 'Letter to the Editor on "Visions of Jesus"', *Newsweek*, 17 April, p. 17.

Smith, Wilfred C. (1978) *The Meaning and End of Religion: A Revolutionary Approach to the Great Religious Traditions*, foreword by John Hick, London, SPCK.

Smith, Wilfred C. (1981) *Towards a World Theology*, Philadelphia, Westminster Press.

Sobrino, Jon (1987) *Jesus in Latin America*, translated by Robert B. Barr, Maryknoll, NY, Orbis.

Sobrino, Jon (1993) *Jesus the Liberator*, translated by Paul Burns and Francis McDonagh, Maryknoll, NY, Orbis.

Southern, Richard W. (1970) *Western Society and the Church in the Middle Ages*, Harmondsworth, Penguin.

Spear, Percival (1965) *A History of India*, Harmondsworth, Penguin.

Spong, John S. (1990) *Living in Sin: A Bishop Rethinks Human Sexuality*, Nashville, TS, Abingdon Press.

Spong, John S. (1992) *Rescuing the Bible from Fundamentalism: A Bishop Rethinks the Meaning of Scripture*, San Francisco, HarperSanFrancisco.

Spong, John S. (1996) *Liberating the Gospels: Reading the Bible through Jewish Eyes*, San Francisco, HarperSanFrancisco.

Spotto, Donald (1998) *The Hidden Jesus: A New Life*, New York, St Martin's Press.

Staffner, Hans (1987) *Jesus Christ and the Hindu Community: Is a Synthesis of Hinduism and Christianity Possible?* Anand, Gujerat Sahitya Prakash.

Star, Leonie (1991) *The Dead Sea Scrolls: The Riddle Debate*, Sydney, ABC Enterprises.

Star, Leonie (1992) 'Foreword', pp. ix–xi, in *Jesus the Man* by Barbara Thiering, London, Doubleday Transworld.

Starbird, Mary (1998) *The Goddess in the Gospels: Reclaiming the Sacred Feminine*, Sante Fe, NM, Bear & Co.

Starbird, Mary with Sweeney, Terrence (1993) *Woman with the Alabaster Jar: Mary Magdalene and the Holy Grail*, Santa Fe, NM, Bear & Co.

Stephen, Sir Leslie (1887) 'Thomas Chubb', pp. 296–8, *Dictionary of National Biography*, Vol. IV, London, Smith, Elder.

Stephen, Sir Leslie (1938) 'John Toland', pp. 918–22, *Dictionary of National Biography*, Vol. XIX, Oxford, Oxford University Press.

Stevenson, J. (1963) *A New Eusebius: Documents Illustrative of the History of the Church to AD 337*, London, SPCK.

Storr, Anthony (1996) *Feet of Clay: A Study of Gurus*, London, HarperCollins.

Strauss, Friedrich (1879) *A New Life of Jesus for the German People*, London, Williams and Norgate. First published in German 1868.

Strauss, Friedrich (1970) 'Herman Samuel Reimarus and his Apology for the Rational Worship of God', pp. 44–57, in *Reimarus: Fragments* edited by Charles Talbert, Philadelphia, Fortress Press. First published in German 1862.

Strauss, Friedrich (1972) *The Life of Jesus Critically Examined*, edited by Peter C. Hodgson and translated by George Eliot, Philadelphia, Fortress Press. First published 1836.

Strauss, Friedrich (1977) *The Christ of Faith and the Jesus of History: A Critique of Schleiermacher*, edited by Leander E. Keck, Philadelphia, Fortress Press. First published in German 1865.

Strauss, Friedrich (1997) *The Old Faith and the New*, introduced by G. A. Wells, Amherst, NY, Prometheus. First published in German 1872.

Sugirtharajah, R. S. (ed.) (1993) *Asian Faces of Jesus*, London, SCM Press.

Sugirtharajah, R. S. (1997) 'The Magi from Bengal and their Jesus: Indian construals of Christ during colonial times', pp. 144–58, in *Images of Christ: Ancient and Modern* edited by Stanley E. Porter, Michael A. Hayes and David Tombs, Sheffield, Sheffield Academic Press.

Tacitus, Cornelius (1996) *The Annals*, edited by R. H. Martin and A. J. Woodman, Cambridge, Cambridge University Press.

Tagore, Rabindranath (1931) *The Religion of Man*, London, Macmillan.

Taha, Mahmoud M. (1987) *The Second Message of Islam*, translated by Abdullah Ahmed An-Na'im, Syracuse, NY, Syracuse University Press.

Talbert, Charles (1970) 'Introduction', pp. 1–42, in *Reimarus: Fragments*, Philadelphia, Fortress Press.

Talbert, Charles (1977) *What Is a Gospel? The Genre of the Canonical Gospels*, Philadelphia, Fortress Press.

Talhami, Ghada (1993) 'The history of Jerusalem: a Muslim perspective', pp. 21–31, in *The Spiritual Significance of Jerusalem for Jews, Christians and Muslims*, edited by Hans Ucko, Geneva, World Council of Churches.

Tatum, W. Barnes (1997) *Jesus at the Movies: A Guide to the First Hundred Years*, Santa Rosa, CA, Polebridge Press, 2nd edn. First published 1982.

Tatum, W. Barnes (1999) *In Quest of Jesus*, Nashville, TS, Abingdon Press, 2nd edn. First published 1982.

Taylor, Edward (1983) *Harmony of the Gospels*, Delmar, NY, Scholars' Facsimiles and Reprints.

Taylor, Isaac (1888) *Leaves from an Egyptian Notebook*, London, Kegan Paul, Trench & Co.

Taylor, Robert (1828) *Syntagma of the Evidences of the Christian Religion. Being a Vindication of the Manifesto of the Christian Evidence Society Against the Assaults of the Christian Instruction Society*, London, R. Carlile.

Taylor, Robert (1882) *The Diegesis; Being a Discovery of the Origin, Evidence and Early History of Christianity, Never Yet Before or Elsewhere so Fully and Faithfully Set Forth*, London, R. Carlile; The Free Thought Press. First published 1829.

Thangaraj, M. Thomas (1994) *The Crucified Guru: An Experiment in Cross-Cultural Christology*, Nashville, TS, Abingdon Press.

Theissen, Gerd (1987) *The Shadow of the Galilean: The Quest of the Historical Jesus in Narrative Form*, translated by John Bowden, London, SCM Press.

Theissen, Gerd (1992) *Social Reality and the Early Christians*, translated by Margaret Kohl, Minneapolis, Fortress Press.

Thiering, Barbara (1979) *Redating the Teacher of Righteousness*, Sydney, Theological Explorations.

Thiering, Barbara (1981) *The Gospels and Qumran: A New Hypothesis*, Sydney, Theological Explorations.

Thiering, Barbara (1983) *Qumran and the Origins of the Christian Church*, Sydney, Theological Explorations.

Thiering, Barbara (1992) *Jesus the Man: New Interpretation from the Dead Sea Scrolls*, London, Doubleday/Transworld.

Thomas, M. M. (1991) *The Acknowledged Christ of the Indian Renaissance*, Madras, CLS, 3rd edn.

Thomas, M. M. (1997) 'The Gospel, secular culture and cultural diversity', pp. 155–67, in *Modern Spiritualities: An Inquiry* edited by Laurence Brown, Bernard C. Farr and R. Joseph Hoffmann, Amherst, NY, Prometheus.

Thompson, John O. (1997) 'Jesus as moving image: the question of movement', pp. 290–394, in *Images of Christ: Ancient and Modern* edited by Stanley E. Porter, Michael A. Hayes and David Tombs, Sheffield, Sheffield Academic Press.

Thompson, William M. (1985) *The Jesus Debate: A Survey and Synthesis*, New York, Paulist Press.

Thoreau, Henry D. (1985) *A Week on the Concord and Merrimack Rivers*, New York, Library Classics of the United States. First published 1849.

Tillich, Paul (1953) *Systematic Theology: Reason and Revelation, Being and God*, Vol. 1, Chicago, Chicago University Press.

Tillich, Paul (1957) *Systematic Theology: Existence and the Christ*, Vol. 2, Chicago, Chicago University Press.

Tillich, Paul (1963) *Christianity and the Encounter with the World Religions*, New York, Columbia University Press.

Tillich, Paul (1964) *Systematic Theology: Life and the Spirit*, Vol.3, Chicago, Chicago University Press.

Tillich, Paul (1998) *Against the Third Reich*, edited by Ronald H. Stone and Matthew Lon Weaver, Louisville, KT, Westminster John Knox Press.

Tisdall, William St Clair (1901) *India, Its History, Darkness and Dawn*, London, Student Volunteer Movement.

Toland, John (1995) *Christianity Not Mysterious*, London, Routledge; Tokyo, Thoemmes. First published 1696.

Tolstoy, Leo (1984) *The Kingdom of God Is Within You*, Lincoln, University of Nebraska Press. First published 1894.

Tweed, Thomas A. and Prothero, Stephen (eds) (1999) *Asian Religions in America: A Documentary History*, New York and Oxford, Oxford University Press.

Tully, Mark (1996) *God, Jew, Rebel, The Hidden Jesus: An Investigation into the Lives of Jesus* (broadcast and book), London, BBC Books and Penguin.

Unterman, Alan (1981) *Jews: Their Religious Beliefs and Practices*, London, Routledge.

Uris, Leon (1958) *Exodus*, New York, Doubleday.

Us-Samad, Ulfat Aziz (1979) *Islam and Christianity*, Lahore, Kazi Publications.

Verheyden, Jack C. (1975) 'Introduction', pp. xi–lxii, in *The Life of Jesus* by Friedrich Schleiermacher, Philadelphia, Fortress Press.

Vermes, Geza (1973) *Jesus the Jew: A Historian's Reading of the Gospels*, London, SCM Press.

Vermes, Geza (1983) *Jesus and the World of Judaism*, London, SCM Press.

Vermes, Geza (1997) *The Complete Dead Sea Scrolls in English*, Harmondsworth, Penguin.

Vermes, Geza (1999) *Providential Accidents: An Autobiography*, Lanham, MD, Rowman and Littlefield Publishers.

Vermes, Geza and Goodman, Martin D. (1989) *The Essenes According to the Classical Sources*, Sheffield, Sheffield Academic Press.

Vivekananda, Swami (1963–6) *Complete Works*, 8 vols, Calcutta, Advaita Ashrama.

Vivekananda, Swami (1999) 'Hinduism', pp. 131–3, in Thomas A. Tweed and Stephen Prothero (eds), *Asian Religions in America: A Documentary History*, New York, Oxford University Press.

Voll, Fritz B. (2000) *A Short Review of a Troubled History*. www.jcrelations.net/res/incidents.htm.

Wallace, Lewis (1893) *The Prince of India: Why Constantinople Fell*, 2 vols, New York, Harper & Brothers.

Wallace, Lewis (1906) *Lewis Wallace: An Autobiography*, New York, Harper & Brothers.

Wallace, Lewis (1998) *Ben Hur: A Tale of the Christ*, edited by David Mayer, Oxford, Oxford University Press. First published 1880.

Ware, Timothy (1993) *The Orthodox Church*, Harmondsworth, Penguin. First published 1963.

Weber, Max (1963) *The Sociology of Religion*, Boston, Beacon Press.

Weightman, Simon (1997) 'Hinduism', pp. 261–309, in *A New Handbook of Living Religions*, edited by John R. Hinnells, Harmondsworth, Penguin.

Weiss, Johannes (1971) *Jesus' Proclamation of the Kingdom of God*, translated by Richard Hyde Hiers and David Larrimore Holland, Philadelphia, Fortress Press. First published in German 1892.

Weiss-Rosmarin, Trude (ed.) (1977) *Jewish Expressions of Jesus: An Anthology*, New York, Ktav Publishing.

Wells, G. A. (1975) *Did Jesus Exist?* London, Elek Books.

Wells, G. A. (ed.) (1987) *J. M. Robertson (1856–1933): Liberal, Rationalist and Scholar – An Assessment*, London, Permberton.

Wells, G. A. (ed.) (1997) Introduction, in *The Old Faith and the New* by D. F. Strauss, Amherst, NY, Prometheus.

Wenham, David (1995) *Paul: Follower of Jesus or Founder of Christianity?*, Grand Rapids, MI, William B. Eerdmans Publishing.

Wessels, Anton (1990) *Images of Jesus: How Jesus Is Perceived and Portrayed in Non-European Cultures*, Grand Rapids, MI, William B. Eerdmans Publishing.

Wessels, Anton (1994) *Europe: Was It Ever Really Christian? The Interaction between Gospel and Culture*, London, SCM Press.

Whealey, Alison (1995) 'Josephus on Jesus: Evidence from the First Millennium', *Theologische Zeitschrift* 51, pp. 285–304.

Whealey, Alison (1998) *Josephus on Jesus: Historical Criticism and the Testimonium Flavianum Controversy from Late Antiquity to Modern Times*, unpublished Ph.D. thesis, University of California at Berkeley.

Wheless, Joseph (1926) *Is It God's Word? An Exposition of the Fables and Mythology of the Bible*, New York, Wheless Publishers.

Wheless, Joseph (1997a) *Debunking the Law of Moses*, Moscow, Idaho, Psychiana; Kila, MT, Kessinger Publishing. First published 1929.

Wheless, Joseph (1997b) *Forgery in Christianity: A Documented Record of the Foundations of the Christian Religion*, New York, A. A. Knopf; Kila, MT, Kessinger Publishing. First published 1930.

Wiebe, Phillip H. (1997) *Visions of Jesus: Direct Encounters from the New Testament to Today*, Oxford, Oxford University Press.

Wiesel, Elie (1978) *A Jew Today*, New York, Vintage Books.

Wiesel, Elie (1982) *Night*, New York, Bantam Books.

Wigmore-Beddoes, Dennis G. (1975) *Concerning Jesus: A Symposium*, London, The Lindsey Press.

Wilkins, Sir Charles (1959) *The Bhagavat-Geeta, 1785*, Gainesville, FL, Scholars' Facsimiles & Reprints. First published 1785.

Wilson, A. N. (1991) *Against Religion*, London, Chatto & Windus.

Wilson, A. N. (1992) *Jesus*, London, Sinclair-Stevenson.

Wilson, A. N. (1997) *Paul: The Mind of the Apostle*, London, Sinclair-Stevenson.

Wilson, Ian (1985) *Jesus: The Evidence*, London, Pan Books.

Witherington, Ben III (1995) *The Jesus Quest: The Third Search for the Jew of Nazareth*, Downers Grove, IL, Inter-Varsity Press.

Witherington, Ben III (1998) *The Paul Quest: The Renewed Quest for the Jew of Tarsus*, Downers Grove, IL, Inter-Varsity Press.

Woodward, Kenneth L. (1999) 'The way the world ends', *Newsweek*, 1 November, pp. 67–74.

Woodward, Kenneth L. (2000a) 'The other Jesus', *Newsweek*, 27 March, pp. 50–60.

Woodward, Kenneth L. (2000b) 'What miracles mean', *Newsweek*, 1 May, pp. 54–60.

World Council of Churches (1988) *Report of the Consultation on the Church and the Jewish People, Sigtuna, Sweden, 30 Oct–4 Nov*, Geneva, WCC.

Wrede, William (1971) *The Messianic Secret*, translated by J. C. G. Greig, Cambridge, J. Clark. First published 1901.

Wright, Norman T. (1992) *Who Was Jesus?*, London, SPCK.

Wright, Norman T, (1996) *Jesus and the Victory of God*, Minneapolis, Fortress Press.

Wright, Norman T, (1997) *The Original Jesus*, Grand Rapids, MI, B. Eerdmans Publishing.

Wright, Norman T. (1998) 'Foreword', pp. ix–xxiv, in *Conflict, Holiness and Politics in the Teachings of Jesus* by Marcus Borg, Harrisburg, PA, Trinity Press.

X, Malcolm (1965) *The Autobiography of Malcolm X*, with the assistance of Alex Haley, Harmondsworth, Penguin.

Yagi, Seeichi (1993) 'Christ and Buddha', pp. 25–45, in *Asian Faces of Jesus*, edited by R. S. Sugirtharajah, London, SCM Press.

Young, Frances (1977) 'A cloud of witnesses', pp. 13–47, in *The Myth of God Incarnate*, edited by John Hick, London, SCM Press.

Young, Robert (1939) *Analytical Concordance to the Holy Bible*, Guildford and London, The Lutterworth Press, 8th edn.

Zaehner, R. C. (1994) *Hindu and Christian Mysticism*, Oxford, Oneworld Publishing.

Zwemer, Samuel W. (1920) *A Moslem Seeker after God*, New York, Fleming H. Revell.

## Films and television broadcasts

A & E Network (2000) *66 AD: The Last Revolt*, documentary and video, A & E Network, New York.

Attenborough, Richard (director) (1982) *Gandhi*, motion picture, Columbia Pictures with Goldcrest Films, USA.

Cameron, James (director) (1984) *The Terminator*, motion picture, Carolco Picture, Inc., USA.

Cran, William (director) (1998) *From Jesus to Christ*, television series/video, Public Broadcasting Service Series, USA.

DeMille, Cecil B. (director) (1927) *The King of Kings*, motion picture, H. B. Warner, USA.

Feurstein, Malcolm (director) (1990) *Shadow on the Cross*, television broadcast, Channel 4, London.

Jacobovichi, Simcha (director/writer) (1999) *The Quest for the Lost Tribes*, documentary, Canadian Broadcasting Company, A & E Network and Alliance Communication.

Jennings, Peter (2000) *The Search for Jesus*, television broadcast on 26 June, ABC Network, USA, London, SCM.

Minoli, Lorenzo (director) (2000) *Jesus*, television series, CBS TV, USA.

Perkins, Jack (presenter) (1999) *The Unknown Jesus*, biography.com, A & E Network.

Pettifer, Julian (presenter/producer) (1990) *Missionaries*, television series, BBC, London.

Reiner, Rob (director) (1996) *Ghosts of Mississippi*, motion picture, written by Lewis Celick, Castle Rock/Columbia, USA.

Rice, Tim (1970) *Jesus Christ, Superstar*, motion picture, music by Andrew Lloyd Webber, sound recording, New York, Decca.

Scorsese, Martin (director) (1988) *The Last Temptation of Christ*, video version, Home Vision.

Smith, Kevin (director/writer) (1999) *Dogma*, motion picture, Lions Gate, USA.

Wachowski, Larry and Andy (directors/writers) (1999) *The Matrix*, motion picture, Warner Bros, USA.

Wainwright, Rupert (director) (1999) *Stigmata*, script by Tom Lazarus and Rick Rumage, motion picture, MGM, USA.

# Name and Subject Index

# Citation Index